A HISTORY OF THE
CANADIAN ECONOMY

A HISTORY OF THE CANADIAN ECONOMY

THIRD EDITION

KENNETH NORRIE
UNIVERSITY OF ALBERTA

DOUGLAS OWRAM
UNIVERSITY OF ALBERTA

J.C. HERBERT EMERY
UNIVERSITY OF CALGARY

THOMSON

NELSON

Australia   Canada   Mexico   Singapore   Spain   United Kingdom   United States

THOMSON

NELSON

A History of the Canadian Economy,
Third Edition

By Kenneth Norrie, Douglas Owram,
and J.C. Herbert Emery

Editorial Director and Publisher:
Evelyn Veitch

Acquisitions Editors:
Brad Lambertus
Anthony Rezek

Marketing Manager:
Bram Sepers

Developmental Editor:
Eliza Marciniak

Managing Production Editor:
Susan Calvert

Copy Editor/Proofreader:
Erin Moore

Production Coordinator:
Helen Jager Locsin

Creative Director:
Angela Cluer

Interior Design:
Sonya V. Thursby,
Opus House Incorporated

Cover Design:
Erich Falkenberg

Cover Image:
The Canadian Rockies and The
Triangle Tour Canadian National
Railways brochure
Cover design by Franklin Carmichael
Gift of Mrs. Mary Mastin
McMichael Canadian Art
Collection Archives

Compositor:
Carol Magee

Printer:
Transcontinental Printing, Inc.

**National Library of Canada
Cataloguing in Publication Data**

Norrie, K.H. (Kenneth Harold),
1946-
   A history of the Canadian
economy

3rd ed.
Includes index.
ISBN 0-7747-3766-2

1. Canada—Economic conditions.
I. Owram, Douglas, 1947–
II. Emery, John Charles Herbert,
1965– II. Title.

HC113. N67 2002   330. 971
C2001-904031-8

Preface

WHEN THE publisher suggested a third edition of this book, we welcomed the idea. We now have the views of our most unforgiving critics, our own students, and all those who completed the response card included with the second edition, as to which parts of the book worked (most of them, fortunately) and which did not. We have also benefited from published reviews and from the comments of a set of anonymous readers. The result, we hope, is a revised volume that manages to incorporate the best of these suggestions for change, yet retains the best features of the original work.

The extent of the revision varies. The basic structure of the book remains as it was, although there is some slight rearrangement of chapters within sections. Some chapters have been rewritten completely, some have been altered significantly, some have been altered marginally, and a very few have escaped with only light editing. The most significant change comes in the addition of Herb Emery as an author on this edition. Herb's insights and considerable rethinking of some of the approaches have had a tremendous impact and brought a fresh perspective to this third edition.

Acknowledgements

As usual, we have incurred a number of debts in preparing this edition. Our deepest gratitude is to the students and instructors who used the book and who took the time to pass along their comments and suggestions for change. We would like to thank Eliza Marciniak for her firm but patient handling of three overcommitted authors. Finally, we acknowledge the efforts of Susan Calvert and copy editor Erin Moore in putting this book into its finished format.

Statistics Canada information is used with the permission of the Minister of Industry, as Minister responsible for Statistics Canada. Information on the availability of the wide range of data from Statistics Canada can be obtained from Statistics Canada's Regional offices, it's World Wide Web site at http://www.statcan.ca, and it's toll-free access number 1-800-263-1136.

Contents

viii

Introduction

FROM ALL the individual reasons that people read an overview of Canadian economic history, two general perspectives are discernible. Interestingly, the perspectives are at least loosely affiliated with the two disciplines involved. The first emphasizes the past. Readers with this perspective want to know why events unfolded as they did, and what life was like in times and circumstances removed from their own. How did the Native population live before European contact? Why were France and Britain the main colonial powers in this land? Why did Canadians resist the entreaties of their counterparts in the American colonies to join the revolution? Did living standards rise as Canadian farmers gained preferential access to the United Kingdom market in the first half of the nineteenth century, or fall when they lost it at mid-century? Why did Confederation come when it did, in the form it did? What was the impact of the wheat boom? Are the origins of the Great Depression more directly traceable to external or to domestic factors? To what extent did the economic dislocation of World War II change the economic fortunes of women?

For other readers, knowledge of the past is sought as a key to understanding the present and to forming some impressions of the future. This perspective creates its own set of questions. Why is Canada among the richest and most economically advanced nations in the world today? What connections are there between this fact and the observations that it is a relatively small nation, that it depends disproportionately on natural-resource production, and that it is among the most trade-dependent economies in the industrial world? Is the economy more cyclically stable today than in the past? How did Canada come to be as regionally diverse as it obviously is? Has economic opportunity become more equal over time, whether viewed across regions, across groups, or among individuals?

In both general perspectives, interest extends beyond mere description to explanation, and even to evaluation. Readers want to know not just what happened, but also why events turned out as they did. They want, as well, to be able to assess the developments. Did Canadians do as well as they might have, given their endowments and the international environment they faced? Specifically, did they make the best use of economic opportunities, given what as a society they were trying to achieve? Were the benefits and costs of economic change shared fairly?

There is a rich tradition of economic-history writing in Canada. Formal study of the subject dates from shortly before World War I, when new academic creatures known as social scientists or political economists began to appear in Canadian universities. Adam Shortt at Queen's (appointed in 1888), James Mavor at the University of Toronto (appointed in 1892), and Stephen Leacock at McGill (appointed in 1903) were among the first generation of Canadian economists. Each saw economic history as a means of comprehending economic development in a nation such as Canada. The tradition they established has influenced Canadian economic writing for many decades.

In spite of their rather small and humble presence at the end of the nineteenth century, economic historians were soon an important part of the academic community. Canada was undergoing rapid urbanization and industrialization, and explanations of what was happening were increasingly in demand. Indeed, it is possible to talk about the initiation of a "golden age" in Canadian economic history, beginning about the time of World War I. In a multi-volume series entitled *Canada and Its Provinces*, published in 1914, economic history was very much present, notably in essays by Shortt and his younger colleague O.D. Skelton. From that point until World War II, Canadian economic history was central to both of the disciplines from which it was derived. The economics profession was dominated by such figures as H.A. Innis of Toronto and W.A. Mackintosh of Queen's. Both were historical in their approaches to researching and analyzing problems. History, which previously had been oriented toward constitutional issues, increasingly fell under the spell of the exciting themes developed by the economists. Thus, Donald Creighton, Arthur Lower, J.B. Brebner, and others wrote books that drew upon the themes developed by the political economists.

For much of the first half of the century, then, economic history was considered as crucial to an understanding of Canada. Books such as Harold Innis's *History of the Canadian Pacific Railway* (1923) and Donald Creighton's *Commercial Empire of the St. Lawrence* (1937) were central both to history and to economics. Later, sociologists, such as Carl Dawson of McGill and S.D. Clark of Toronto, carried the historical tradition into their disciplines. Syntheses and college texts in economic history also abounded, including such works as Mary Quayle Innis's *An Economic History of Canada* (1935) and A.W. Currie's *Canadian Economic Development* (1942). Perhaps the most impressive example of this sort of work, and certainly the most massive, came in the late 1930s. The Royal Commission on Dominion–Provincial Relations (the Rowell–Sirois Commission), which was appointed in 1937 and reported in 1940, continued the tradition with masterful historical studies. Works developed for this commission, such as Donald Creighton's *British North America at Confederation* and W.A. Mackintosh's *Economic Background to Dominion–Provincial Relations*, remain important references to the present day.

The core of this historical tradition lay in what may justly be regarded as Canada's major contribution to economic theory during these years. The staples thesis, pioneered in Canada by W.A. Mackintosh in his 1923 article "Economic Factors in Canadian History"[1] and by H.A. Innis in *The Fur Trade in Canada: An Introduction to Canadian Economic History*, published in 1930, drew upon and further developed an idea expounded by American economic historian G.S. Callender. The thesis, as developed in Canada, argued that the stages in colonial development depended on the exploitation of a succession of key primary-resource products, referred to as staples. The characteristics of the staples—the nature of the demand for them in export markets, the technology of their production, their linkages to other sectors, and the economic and social infrastructures needed to support them—set the pattern of economic and political developments of the colony.[2] Canada, from the period of the fur trade of New France through that of the vast wheat exports and new resource products in the early twentieth century, seemed an especially good example of the staples thesis at work in history.

The staples theory was reinforced by Canada's strength in another discipline, historical geography. Innis was familiar with the geopolitical theories of such leading geographers as Marion Newbigin and saw them as particularly relevant to a nation like Canada, with such a vast land mass.[3] Mackintosh made his contribution to the massive series on prairie settlement in a work that combined geography and economics, *Prairie Settlement: The Geographical Setting* (1934). The course of rivers, the extent of agricultural and timber land, the forbidding Canadian Shield, the inhospitable Arctic, and especially distance and climate were obvious elements in Canadian history and fit in with the emphasis on resources inherent in the staples theory. The land and its resources thus dominated the attempt by social scientists to understand Canadian development in the first half of the twentieth century.

The nature of the staples thesis and its strengths and weaknesses show up clearly in one of the latest and best of the staples-tradition textbooks. W.T. Easterbrook and H.G.J. Aitken's *Canadian Economic History*, first published in 1956, used the themes developed over the previous 30 years to analyze Canadian development in the staples tradition. The fish of the Grand Banks, the fur trade of New France, the timber trade of the Canadas and New Brunswick, and the wheat trades of central Canada and then the West provided the series of staples that allowed Canada to develop. Canals and railways followed in their wake, as governments assisted in economic development. Finally, the authors were acutely sensitive to how dependent Canada was on the international situation.

Excellent though Easterbrook and Aitken's work was for its time, by today's standards it has at least three limitations. First, and most obviously, the book is 40 years out of date. We now have better data for the historical period and, thanks to the efforts of countless scholars in several disciplines, we know much more about the course of economic and social development. Many of the generalizations they were forced to make have since been abandoned, or at least modified.

The other two limitations are more fundamental. Easterbrook and Aitken's text loses much of its momentum as it moves beyond the agricultural economy of the pre–World War I era and tries to come to grips with modern industrial Canada. The authors abandon historical evolution and settle, instead, on a series of theme chapters, looking at some of the key sectors of the twentieth century. This approach was necessary, in part because the transformation was still quite recent at the time they wrote and in part because the organizing principle of the work, staples, had less and less relevance as the story of Canadian development moved toward the present.

The third limitation is related to the second. Critics of the staples school have commented on the way important sectors, or even whole regions, disappear from history once they no longer fit within the staples argument. Thus, the Maritimes are important during the great days of cod fishery, but are not easily comprehended (and, thus, not dealt with to any degree) once attention has turned to new staples. Central Canadian agriculture is crucial during the pre-Confederation era, but, as net exports disappear shortly thereafter, the sector shrinks from sight. Likewise for the timber trade: it virtually disappears from the narrative with the abolition of preferential British duties in the mid-nineteenth century, reappearing again after 1900 as a new staple, pulp and paper.

In sum, traditional Canadian economic-history writing appeals because it is eclectic. Economic developments are described in considerable detail, and political and social factors are woven in as a necessary part of the narrative. That very breadth is, at the same time, the main limitation of the approach. Connections between events are not always drawn explicitly, correlation is sometimes taken to imply causality, and qualitative conclusions are often given when quantitative ones are called for. Nor do accounts often move beyond description and explanation to evaluation. Events are set out in detail, but there is little attempt to assess them by comparing what was with what might have been.

Even as Easterbrook and Aitken wrote, different approaches were beginning to dominate economics in Canada as elsewhere. New specialties had emerged in the graduate schools, and a new emphasis on theory and quantification had severed economics from its political-economy roots. It was not long before economic historians, seeking to keep pace with modern techniques, abandoned the historical approach in favour of model-building, quantification, and hypothesis-testing. The "new economic history" quickly came to dominate the discipline in the United States, and, inevitably, soon spread to Canada.

The literature of the new economic history overcame some of the limitations of the traditional approaches. The work is rigorous. Models describe interrelations (or at least the author's perception of them) precisely, causality is sought explicitly, quantitative answers are prized, and counterfactual exercises are standard fare. Yet, this rigour sometimes comes at the expense of simplification and narrowness. Too often, a historical experience becomes just another data set with which to test conjectures in economic theory. Elegance and cleverness are sometimes sought as ends in themselves. The stress on quantification can mean that topics are taken up as much because data exist as because they are inherently interesting or important.

The new economic history in Canada eventually produced its own textbooks. They updated our knowledge of recent research and introduced the findings of the new economic-history research to a more general audience. In the process, however, they moved from a chronological to a thematic approach. As the first of the new texts—that by William L. Marr and Donald G. Paterson, *Canada: An Economic History* (1980)—states, "Such an ordering of historical material permits a clearer identification of the forces of economic change." Richard Pomfret's volume *The Economic Development of Canada* (1981) largely, but not completely, abandons the chronological approach as well.

As economists were embracing the new economic history, historians were developing in a different direction. After World War II, they rejected what Toronto historian Frank Underhill termed the "bloodless ballet" of economic history in favour of politics and biography. Then, with the ideological and regional debates of the 1960s, they turned to new approaches. These new approaches had two characteristics. First, historians embraced what J.M.S. Careless termed "limited identities."[4] This approach argued that Canada was so divided by region, culture, language, and religion that there was no overarching national identity, but a series of regional and local attachments. Second, the reformism of the 1960s turned history away from the previous emphasis on politics toward an emphasis on "history from the bottom up."

Both changes had their implications for economic history. First, the acceptance of limited identities complemented the increasingly specialized studies appearing in the new economic history. Second, the rise of social history forever changed the study of the Canadian economy. Any economic history written now must take into account not just the writings formally classed as economic history, but also those studies of work, the workplace, and relationships found under the broad rubric of social history.

These observations explain the premises that underlie this book. A fuller understanding of Canadian economic development demands a synthesis of several areas of scholarship: traditional economic-history writings, the new economic history, and modern social history. The account must recognize the force of limited identities, while refusing to despair about the possibility of telling a "Canadian" story. For we believe strongly that there must be a "story" of Canadian economic development. The story must be guided by economic theory, not subverted by it. It must stop at times to ask "why" or "what if," but not so obtrusively as to make it read like an economic-policy handbook. It must relate how Canadians live today to how they lived yesterday, which means that it must continue through to the present. Most importantly perhaps, it must always remember that history involves real lives, in a real social setting, and engaging in daily activities.

Once the approach was decided and the length of the book set, the structure fell naturally into a two-tiered system. The first tier comprises six sections that were seen by us to define major stages in Canadian economic development. Within each era, however, various subdivisions quickly became apparent. Depending on the literature and the issues, the precise deci-sion as to the nature of the division varied. In the colonial era, the most appropriate divisions were usually based on political–constitutional entities (e.g., New France). After Confederation, however, that changed. Subdivisions of time tended to dominate. Whatever the specific deci-sion as to the nature of the new delineation, these subdivisions became the main chapters within the parts. At the outset of each part, however, there is an introductory section that draws together the major connections within the period and, in particular, emphasizes the international context upon which Canada's small open economy is so dependent.

History as a Guide to the Economic Future of Canada

For much of the last 30 years Canada has been viewed as having one of the highest stan-dards of living in the world due in large part to the high incomes generated by her economy. Canada's economic prosperity has contributed to the protection and enhancement of Canadian culture and to the development of an extensive welfare state that provides health care and basic income protection for all Canadians. While many take Canada's economic position for granted, there are perceptions that Canada's high standard of living is at risk and based on a comparison with American incomes, that we should be doing better. How can we assure continued economic prosperity in Canada? Is free trade with other nations the answer? Or would a high-tariff, protectionist Canada be better for Canadians? Are the inter-ests of Canadians best served by a strong central government in Ottawa setting "one size fits all" policies, or should regions or provinces be the appropriate level for policy-making?

In seeking answers to these questions, we should first ask some basic questions. First, has Canada always been a "rich" country? Second, if not, when did Canada emerge as a wealthy nation? Third, why did Canada become a high-income country? Fourth, have all provinces and regions shared equally in Canada's economic prosperity? These questions reveal that an understanding of the state of, and the prospects for, the Canadian economy are rooted in the history of the Canadian economy. Over time, Canada has had eras of regional autonomy in policy-making, and of highly centralized policy-making. Canada has also pursued free trade with the United States several times over her history in between periods of highly protectionist trade policies, such as the National Policy Tariffs of 1879. From this perspective, the current policy debates about how to secure a prosperous future for Canadians are older than Canada itself.

Increasingly, several provinces are questioning whether the best interests of their pop-ulations are within the institutional status quo of Canada, bringing into question the future of Canada as a nation. Canada has always been a collection of provinces diverse in the wealth of natural resources, population size, and culture. Regions have ceded powers to the federal government with the expectation that regional interests would be served by national strategies. From the outset, central Canadians have shown the greatest enthu-siasm for Confederation. Ontario developed Canada's most diversified economy with a prosperous agricultural sector and a high-paying manufacturing sector. In addition, Ontario's interests came to dominate the concerns of federal fiscal and monetary policy-makers.[5] In contrast, Atlantic Canadians have claimed that Confederation failed to deliver prosperity and may have even worsened their economic conditions. Similarly, the prairie provinces remain dependent on agriculture and exports of other natural resources and remain vulnerable to the volatility of world commodity prices.

Canadians are asserting regional interests over national interests. Perhaps most notably, many Quebeçois feel that economic and social independence from the rest of Canada is the best strategy for the survival of French language culture and prosperity for Quebec. Albertans for largely economic reasons have led demands for political reform in Canada through a return to decentralized economic powers as laid out under the terms of Confederation in the 1867 British North America Act.[6] Courchene and Telmer argue that Ontario's interest in seeing a strong central government has diminished. For much of Canada's history, the federal government operated on the premise that what was good for Ontario was good for Canada. This changed through the 1980s in part due to the sovereigntist assertions of Quebec and the economic rise of the West that deflected the federal government's attentions away from Ontario. Ontario's economic development has positioned the province to pursue a destiny independent of the rest of Canada.

Independent of the internal pressures on the future of Canada, globalization poses another important challenge for the future of Canada. As technological changes in communication and transportation make the distance between markets increasingly irrelevant, nation-states themselves become increasingly irrelevant. As John Helliwell states, with globalization, national borders cease to matter leaving little scope for meaningful policies at the national level. Regional interests within Canada will cease to be aligned with national interests, and instead will reflect the linkages and synergies within geographic regions.[7] Helliwell points out that although borders are becoming less important, they are still a surprisingly important influence on trade flows and the capacity for the federal government to pursue national policy goals. Thus, Canadians need to resolve whether the integration of Canada's economy into a global economy is a development to be embraced and encouraged, or a development to be resisted if not avoided at all costs. Once again, history may provide some understanding of the tradeoffs between these strategies. Canada of the nineteenth century was integrated into a global trading system and had to confront the spectre of U.S. annexation. In many respects, the current national strategies of economic development that are considered irrelevant because of globalization were a response to the pressures of an earlier era of continental integration and globalization. Jeffrey Williamson argues that the strong pressures and labour market effects of globalization in the nineteenth century triggered a policy backlash around the Atlantic economy. Immigration restrictions and tariffs, combined with the two world wars, triggered and era of deglobalization from 1914 to 1970.[8]

This book is an exploration of the themes described above. Prior to embarking on that task, it is useful to describe tools and concepts that economists use to study those themes. At the same time, it will be become clear that despite the usefulness of economics for organizing the story of a nation's history, it is an incomplete story. Canada's institutions that include her cultures, structure of governance, and legal system are historical constructs that have set Canada's path of development. Thus, an understanding of economic performance requires historical inquiry.

STANDARD OF LIVING

Standard of living is a term that describes the conditions under which people live in a society. For economists, measures of income are commonly used to measure standard of living with the logic being that more income provides the means to acquire more of what one desires, be it food, shelter, material goods, or security. There are many other possible dimensions to standard of living. For example, leisure time, good health, economic and political empowerment, pride in one's craft, and living in a safe environment all contribute to quality of life.

For an economy as a whole, *gross domestic product* (GDP) provides a measure of total income. *Real GDP* is the inflation-adjusted dollar value of final goods and services produced and traded in markets in a given economy in a given time period. Final goods and services, as the name implies, are products that require no further processing before use by domestic residents and prior to export. Measuring output in this way has two advantages. First, it avoids problems of double-counting. Second, goods and services are only useful to individuals in their final forms, so GDP provides a rough measure of aggregate well-being.[9] Per person, or *per capita GDP* provides the standard economic measure of the standard of living in an economy. The higher the per capita GDP, all else equal, the better off are a nation's residents.

While annual GNP/GDP numbers are available for many countries from the nineteenth century on, the numbers should be considered "best guesses" about the size of the market economy in a given year. Simon Kuznets developed a uniform set of national accounts for the United States in the 1930s that are the prototype for GDP numbers for measuring the size of economies around the world today. Thus, post-Depression GNP/GDP numbers are in most cases derived prospectively; new data are collected each month, quarter, or year, for the purpose of constructing national income. Even with prospective data collection, GNP is not free of problems when it comes to objectively measuring the size of the market economy. Economists have long struggled with what should, and should not, be included in the income accounting; the difficulty of measuring the size of the service sector in an economy and the extent to which hidden or underground economies exist (for example, the illicit drug trade, or cash transactions for the purposes of avoiding taxation), some portion of market transactions is systematically not counted.

Historical GNP/GDP estimates present a different set of challenges. First, they are often based on incomplete records that were collected for purposes other than constructing income estimates for an economy. How these data are combined to provide a single measure of income requires some, often heroic, assumptions about the relative importance of different economic activities, and even about the importance of activity that should be included but for which there is no data. For these reasons and others, there are often several GNP series available for a given economy. In some cases, more recent GNP estimates are revisions of earlier estimates, and in other cases, the series are original estimates. For this reason, the challenge is often to find the "best" GNP numbers and this is typically based upon a consensus amongst economists as to which construction of GNP they feel is most reasonable. The choice of which income estimates to analyze is not a small issue. Early versions of income accounts for England showed rapid, if not spectacular, growth of national income after 1780, giving rise to the application of the term "Industrial Revolution" as a description of nineteenth-century England's economic development. Revised estimates of English GNP after 1780 suggest that economic development was more gradual and steady than spectacular, and quantitatively, not a revolution after all.[10] For Canada, the most commonly used historical GNP estimates are the work of Malcolm Urquhart. It is easy to appreciate the complexity of deriving income estimates when one recognizes that Urquhart's book that describes the creation of the GNP estimates for 1870 to 1926 is almost 700 pages long.[11]

Finally, even with the choice of the "best" historical GNP/GDP estimates, comparisons with current GNP/GDP numbers can also be difficult. For example, comparison of American GNP numbers for the pre-1914 and post-1947 eras suggested that the American economy was much more stable after World War II than it had been prior. Christina Romer demonstrates that the post-war stabilization is probably a figment of the data that results from the methods used to construct the historical data exaggerating cyclical fluctuations in income for the pre-1914 era.[12]

Per capita GDP has its limitations as a measure of standard of living. Simon Kuznets, the architect of national income accounting, warned that the welfare of a nation can scarcely be inferred from a measure of national income.[13] First, as noted above, focusing on income measures alone excludes many dimensions of human existence that many consider to be important determinants of well-being. Second, per capita GNP/GDP ignores issues of how income is distributed amongst the population. Third, expenditures for cleaning up environmental disasters, for alarm systems and police services in response to crime, and for mending people and repairing cars involved in accidents are all examples of things that we would consider negative influences on standard of living, but which increase GDP. Thus, per capita GDP numbers may indicate that well-being in a risky and crime-ridden economy is higher than in a safe and crime-free economy.[14]

Perhaps one of the more important limitations of GDP as a measure of economic performance and standard of living is that GDP values only those goods and services exchanged in the marketplace. Non-market output such as work in the home is not included in aggregate GDP. For the purposes of understanding economic development this is an important omission. In pre-industrial economies, like Canada in its early history or less developed economies today, much of the output produced is through home production. Over time, particularly with rising female labour force participation, work previously done in the home (not for pay) is contracted out to third parties. For example, paid housekeepers and restaurant meals replace the work of women in the home. This will give the appearance of large changes in aggregate economic activity when in fact only the identity of who is doing the work has changed. Nancy Folbre and Barnet Wagman revised real product numbers for the United States for 1800 to 1860 to account for home production.[15] Their estimates for 1800–1860 and 1870–1930 suggest that non-market household production for family members was factored into output and growth statistics only after being transferred to the market economy. Thus, the inclusion of non-market household services in estimates of aggregate output substantially alters the measured trajectory of economic growth over this period.

There are alternatives to per capita GDP measures of standard of living, such as the Human Development Index (HDI) introduced by the United Nations in 1990.[16] N.F.R. Crafts suggests that the HDI is intended as a "better and more comprehensive measure of socio-economic welfare than GDP."[17] The roots of the HDI are attributed to Nobel Laureate Amartya Sen's work that interprets economic underdevelopment as the lack of basic capabilities rather than just the lack of income, and its notion that changes in well-being are a result of expanding people's choices. The HDI has three components: longevity, knowledge, and income. In the HDI, income is assumed to have the largest contribution to well-being at low levels of income. Beyond a threshold level, income is assumed to provide a sharply diminishing contribution to material well-being. Typically, longevity is measured as life expectancy at birth and knowledge is measured as a weighted average of adult literacy and years of schooling.

Crafts shows that in 1870, based on real GDP per person (expressed in terms of common currency and purchasing power), countries with the highest standards of living were Australia ($3,801), the United Kingdom ($3,263), the Netherlands and Belgium (both $2,640), and the United States ($2,457). Canada, with roughly half of the per capita income of the U.K. ($1,620), ranked 12th out of 15 advanced nations in Europe and North America. By 1913, Australia was the highest-income country ($5,505); the U.S. had risen to second-highest ($5,307); New Zealand to third-highest ($5,178); and the U.K. had fallen to the fourth-highest income ($5,032). Canada had the fifth-highest standard of living at $4,213 per person. By 1950, Canada, with $7,047, had the sixth-highest per capita GDP in the world and had surpassed the per person income in the U.K. ($6,847). The United States had the highest income, at $9,573 per person. By 1973, only the U.S. ($16,607) and Switzerland ($17,953) had higher GDPs per person than Canada ($13,644). In 1992, Canada's per capita income was $16,371, second only to that for the United States ($17,986).

Crafts' HDI numbers for 1870 to 1992 do not change our perceptions of relative standards of living for advanced nations across time or countries. If anything, the HDI numbers reveal that GDP-based measures of standards of living understate the rate of improvement in living standards since 1870. HDI measures of standards of living reveal that in earlier times, the high-income countries in 1870 had lower standards of living than most of today's Third World countries because residents of the high-income countries of 1870 had lower life expectancy than residents of poor countries today. This suggests that it is better to be poor today than rich in the past! Crafts finds that since 1870, increased life expectancy and leisure time have been the main reasons for increases in standards of living. Similarly, Richard Easterlin argues that improvements in standards of living are more broad based than even the HDI suggests. Easterlin concludes that "Most people today are better fed, clothed, and housed than their predecessors two centuries ago. They are healthier, live longer, and are better educated. Women's lives are less centered on reproduction, and political democracy has gained a foothold.... Although the picture is not one of universal progress, it is the greatest advance in the condition of the world's population ever achieved in such a brief span of time."[18]

With these numbers we can now answer the questions we posed earlier. Was Canada always a "high income" country? As we will show later in the book, and based on evidence discussed above, Canada did not rank among the countries with the highest standards of living until after 1900. Where Canada stands out compared with most of the advanced nations in Europe is her strong growth after World War I through to 1992. Most notably, from 1973 to 1989, real per capita GDP in Canada converged towards U.S. per capita income levels. Since 1989, Canadian per capita GDP has lost ground to U.S. per capita GDP.

It is interesting to note that even though the *level* of Canadian per capita GDP in 2000 indicates that Canadians have a higher standard of living than at any time in the history of Canada, slow or no *growth* in the *level* of per capita income since the late 1980s is often interpreted as a worsening of living standards, or at least, as economic under-performance. Thus, in evaluating their own standard of living, Canadians seem to care not only about the level of income but also the rate of increase of income, and particularly the rate of increase in income compared with other countries.

MODELING GDP AND GROWTH

Economists have two notions of economic growth. *Extensive economic growth* refers to increases in the output of goods and services over time. For some purposes, it is useful to look at year-to-year changes in aggregate output. For economic history purposes, however, it is best to think of extensive economic growth as sustained increases in aggregate output, or GDP. *Intensive economic growth* refers to increases in per capita GDP over time. From a policy-maker's perspective, intensive growth would seem to be the ultimate target. At the same time, policies that promote a nation's territorial expansion and that promote extensive growth may or may not also promote intensive growth. In other cases, policies that encourage immigration may result in positive extensive growth but negative intensive growth. Even though average incomes decline, some members of the population will have higher incomes because of the immigration and would likely support the policy.

While it is straightforward to measure rates of growth after the fact, it is much more difficult to explain why growth occurred in the first place. Why did people choose to move
to Canada and not somewhere else? Why did investors choose to put their capital in
Canada? The answers to these questions must be that the Canadian economy represented
the best use of what they had to offer in that period of time. Immigrants felt that they
could earn a better living with their skills in Canada than anywhere else, including their
countries of origin. Investors estimated that they could earn a higher rate of return in
Canada than elsewhere. Entrepreneurs saw the profit possibilities in introducing new
technologies and new forms of business organization.

It is certainly the case that, as we shall see throughout this text, increases in the international value of Canada's rich natural resource endowment account for part of the story
that we tell. But there is more to the story than just natural resources. We shall observe
periods of economic growth associated with the development of manufacturing, with the
growth of service industries, with the provision of public infrastructure, and, most importantly, with the incessant efforts by individual Canadians to improve their quality of life.

In the following pages we introduce three approaches for understanding economic
growth. First, we examine the staples thesis that describes economic growth and diversification arising from exports of natural resources (primary products). Second, we describe
the neo-classical growth theory, which is the dominant paradigm for growth studies in
economics. Finally, we introduce themes from the new institutional economics that
emphasize the importance of institutions and culture in determining economic performance. We do not address any of the "stage theories" of economic growth such as that developed by Walter Rostow.[19] Stage theories appeal because they allow for stories of growth
that agree with the "observed facts" in some cases. At the same time, stage theories do not
provide much in the way of guidance as to the timing of "take-off" in growth or for explanations of why some economies fail to develop. We do not examine Marxist models of economic growth here. Several themes from Marxist analyses, such as the use of contracts and
debt as instruments of social control and exploitation, are found in the new institutional
economics.

The Staples Thesis

Staples are commodities that have a high natural resource content produced for export.
The staples thesis describes Canadian economic development as driven by several episodes
of natural resource exploitation, where exports of primary products are the leading sectors
of the economy and set the pace for economic growth.[20] While some of the staples
episodes overlap in time and across regions, Canada's growth has been episodic and
regional in nature, such as the reliance on cod exports that gave way to exports of the fur
trade based in Quebec and timber from New Brunswick, Quebec, and Ontario. By the
nineteenth century wheat exports from Ontario and ultimately the Canadian prairies
became a major source of wealth.

For the staples thesis to apply, the economy must be highly specialized in the production of one or at most a few natural resources for export. There is some debate over the
period of time for which the staples thesis is useful for describing *Canadian* economic
growth. Kenneth Buckley contends that the staples thesis is not a practical explanation for
Canadian economic growth after 1820 since other non-staple sources of national economic
growth and change (such as industrialization) are impossible to ignore.[21] Despite Buckley's
view, the staples thesis figures prominently in explanations for the pace of Canadian economic development after Confederation through to World War I with the rise of the

western wheat economy. Also, while the staples thesis may fail to apply to Canada after some critical date, it may still be a useful framework for describing regional economic growth within Canada, as the economies of many regions, or provinces, of Canada remain highly dependent on the export of natural resources (to other regions or countries). For example, oil may not be a staple episode for Canada, but it may for Alberta.

Where an economy is highly specialized in staples production, the staples thesis posits that a country or region with an endowment of natural resources will grow in response to autonomous increases in foreign demand for natural resources. The exporting country or region thus faces a price set in the world market. As you will see in later chapters, the autonomous increases in demand for primary products has often arisen from, for example, Britain imposing tariffs and trade restrictions, or the American Civil War. In other cases, growing world demand combined with declining existing supplies of the product in demand increases the price of the primary product enough to stimulate Canadian production. If foreign demand for the natural resource exports increases the world price of the exports, then the economy grows and diversifies through economic linkages.

The pace of economic growth, and economic diversification, depends upon the strength of economic *linkages*, or spreading effects, arising from staple production. *Backwards linkages* to staple exploitation are inputs to the production of staples (for example, labour, machines, implements, and transportation infrastructure). *Forward linkages* are activities where the staple is processed or manufactured into other products prior to export (for example, wheat may be milled into flour, timber may be finished into lumber). *Lateral linkages* are non-staple economic activities that are stimulated by the staple production (for example, a railway that ships grain to the world market is also available to manufacturers to ship products to market). *Final demand linkages*, or consumer goods, are the stimuli for domestic manufacturing to produce consumer products in demand by workers employed in staple production, or by population drawn to the economy by staple production.

An expectation of the staples thesis is that the growth effects of the export activity will depend on the intrinsic features of the natural resource endowment. For example, the fur trade resulted in limited attraction of labour and capital to Canada in the 1700s and 1800s since its input requirements were small. The fur trade involved a small number of agents of the Hudson's Bay or North West companies trading with the indigenous populations. In contrast, wheat farming required a great deal of labour and capital not only for farming but also for construction of railways and port facilities to get the wheat to market. Growth due to staples exploitation will also be a function of technical progress in relation to staples production. Where cod fishing has employed the same technology of lines, hooks, and boats for much of the last 300 years, wheat farming has moved from labour intensive production to mechanized production. Technical progress in transportation that reduced the unit costs of transporting the staple to market increased the feasible region of cultivation in agriculture. Thus, one could expect to earn a profit on lands more distant from the market.

The staples thesis provides a convenient after-the-fact description of why growth occurred when it did. At the same time, the staples thesis is not formally developed in a way so as to be proved right or wrong hence it cannot be a "staples theory."[22] This helps to explain some of the important limitations of the staples thesis as a complete explanation of economic development. The staples thesis provides little guidance for understanding why an endowment of a given natural resource will, in one case, result in high incomes and economic diversification; and in another, a poor and non-diversified economy—a situation often referred to as a "staples trap." For example, wheat exports in the 1870s resulted in Ontario developing a wealthy and diversified economy, while wheat exports from the Canadian prairies after 1896 resulted in a prairie economy specialized in wheat production with very little manufacturing.

To overcome the predictive indeterminacy of the staples thesis, John McCallum proposes a "modified staples thesis." Exploitation of natural resources always generates wealth and linkage benefits. Staples episodes are distinguished by who captures the linkages and wealth. Who captures the linkages depends on a complex interaction of the laws or rules that govern trade, government policies, and institutions. For example, McCallum argues that wheat exports expanded and diversified the Ontario economy, since Ontario farmers had competitive outlets for transporting wheat to market either through Montreal or New York City. By overcoming the market power of Montreal merchants that was based on control of the St. Lawrence shipping route, Ontario farmers and merchants captured the linkage benefits of the wheat trade. The retention of the linkages from the grain trade meant that Ontario developed internal sources of capital, a financial sector, and an entrepreneurial class that in turn encouraged the development of high, value-added, capital-intensive manufacturing in Ontario. In contrast, government railway policy after 1870 ensured that western grain growers shipped their wheat to market through Canadian ports and high tariffs ensured that westerners purchased manufactured goods from Ontario and Quebec. Thus tariffs and railway policy resulted in central Canada capturing the linkages of the grain trade in the later episode. Canada may have diversified around wheat exports, but the prairie provinces did not. Manitoba, Saskatchewan, and Alberta remained reliant on external (to the province) sources of capital, and are often seen as having failed to develop an entrepreneurial class. From this perspective, Confederation and Sir John A. Macdonald's national policy were instruments for the economic development of central Canada, not Canada as a whole.

McCallum highlights another predictor of linkage appropriation that he refers to as "initial endowments" at the start of a staple episode. "Initial endowments" are a region's prior accumulation of population, financial capital, productive capacity, entrepreneurial class, and political power. All else equal, linkages from a new staple episode will tend to flow to the region with greater initial endowments. McCallum suggests that greater political power, more abundant capital, advantages of larger local markets, and possibly more advanced technology confer cost advantages on the better endowed regions. Thus, as an emerging economy (periphery region) endowed with staples is linked to a larger established economy (core region), the peripheral region will likely remain specialized in staple production while the core region gains wealth and expands its manufacturing sector. While it is possible that the emerging region accumulates political and economic endowments from its share of the linkages, it may catch up to and surpass the established region, McCallum concludes that "while regional differences in aggregate income and population are not bound to widen over time ... other things being equal, this is likely to occur."[23]

The staples thesis cannot provide much understanding of economic prospects and performances of economies without endowments of staples/natural resources, or for regions that are not endowed with the staple that currently dominates production. For example, in describing Canadian economic development around wheat exports, a staples story does not really tell us much about what was happening in Prince Edward Island. Finally, in a seminal critique of the wheat boom staples story of Canadian economic development by Chambers and Gordon, the authors argue that under the assumptions that labour and capital movements into Canada are extremely responsive to economic opportunities (supplies of labour and capital are perfectly elastic), staples episodes such as a wheat boom can generate extensive growth but not intensive growth. Intensive growth is ultimately driven by improved efficiency in manufacturing or other non-staple sectors.[24]

While themes of the staples thesis are found throughout much of this book, the staples thesis by itself does not provide enough structure for a satisfactory exploration of Canada's long-term economic development. For that reason we now turn to the neo-classical (Solow) growth framework that is the foundation of contemporary studies of the economics of growth.

Neo-Classical Growth

Accounting for national or regional income and income growth after the fact is a relatively straightforward process in principle, if not necessarily so in practice. Economic agents (such as firms, governments, and co-operatives) produce goods and services (GDP) by combining the services of capital (K), labour (L), and land/resources (T) in fashions prescribed by prevailing engineering technology.

Economists distinguish between two basic determinants of *extensive growth*. First, there are changes in GDP that result from changes in the quantity of inputs employed (K, L, T) using a given technology. An economy will grow if the supplies of labour services, capital service, and/or land increase. For an economy to experience *intensive growth*, it must be the case that supplies of K and/or T grow faster than the supply of L. Thus, "capital deepening" that refers to investment increasing K/L, or resource booms that increase T/L, are engines of intensive growth.

Second, extensive growth results from an increase in the efficiency with which each "bundle" of capital, labour services, and land/resources is used. That is, even if there is no change in the amount of inputs employed, an economy will grow if production efficiency improves. Extensive growth that arises from increases in efficiency will always result in intensive growth as well. In practice, this source of growth is measured as a residual and is interpreted as a measure of *total factor productivity* (TFP)—that portion of growth that cannot be attributed to observed increases in capital and labour inputs.

Using this broad distinction, the sources of growth can be further resolved. The supply of labour to an economy increases in a number of ways: natural increase (births minus deaths), migration, and increases in the labour force participation rate (employed plus unemployed divided by population) within the existing population. Where information permits, it is useful to express labour inputs in homogeneous (efficiency) units rather than absolute terms. The process involves distinguishing among workers according to age, education, experience, and any other characteristics that are thought to be correlated with labour productivity.[25]

Natural increase has been an important source of population growth, hence for increasing labour (L), for Canada throughout her history. Like the U.S. and industrialized nations in Europe, Canada experienced a demographic transition through the nineteenth century. In Canada, the total fertility rate fell from 6.83 births per woman in 1871 to 3.54 in 1921, and to 1.76 in 1978.[26] The only interruption in this decline in fertility occurred between 1946 and 1965, the baby-boom period, when the total fertility rate increased to a peak of 3.9 births per woman in 1956. Like fertility, mortality rates also declined in Canada from the early nineteenth century. Life expectancy at birth increased from 40 years for males and females in 1831 to 61 years in 1931. In 1992 life expectancy from birth for both sexes was 78 years.[27]

Canada's population has also been augmented, and diminished, through migration. From 1861 to 1901 the numbers of people emigrating from Canada exceeded the numbers arriving as immigrants. Recent estimates from Marvin McInnis suggest that the emigrants were largely Canadian-born rather than recent arrivals treating Canada as a point of entry to the United States.[28] The net out-migration from Canada reflected that the Canadian economy was growing slower than the U.S. economy, which was industrializing and offering workers high incomes. In addition, good agricultural land was available in the U.S. west at a time when much of the farmland in Ontario was occupied. Where the Canadians chose to move to within the U.S. differed by region, or province, of origin in Canada. Emigrants from Atlantic Canada moved disproportionately to Boston.[29] French Canadian families migrated to the mill towns of Massachusetts and elsewhere in New England.[30] Ontarians, by and large, moved to Michigan, New York state, and the U.S. west.

With the development of the Canadian wheat economy and western settlement after 1896, this situation reversed and immigration became an important boost to the labour force. Immigration as a percentage of current population peaked at 5.5 percent in the wheat boom period, 1896 to 1914.[31] Immigration flows remained at historically high levels until the Depression of the 1930s when immigration to Canada virtually ceased for 10 years. Since World War II, the number of immigrants to Canada has remained at or below one percent of current population.

Prior to 1962, Canada's immigration policy had a racial, or country of origin, basis (Canada preferred immigrants of British origin and beyond that had clear preferences over the racial origins of immigrants) but beyond that, immigrant "quality" was not an important factor. In the early twentieth century Canada had preferred immigrants who would pursue agricultural livelihoods on the Canadian western plains. Despite this preference, immigrants to Canada before 1914 moved into all sectors and regions in Canada. Canada had more success directing immigrants to Canada's west in the 1920s. By the 1960s, Canada abandoned the racial basis for immigration to one that selected immigrants on the basis of the economic needs of the Canadian economy. The education or skills of immigrants replaced nationality as the basis for admitting immigrants.[32]

Finally, with birth rates falling and smaller immigration flows, an important source of increase in Canada's labour force since 1960 has been the rising participation of women, particularly married women, in the labour force. In 1920, 18 percent of women, and only 3 percent of married women, participated in the labour force. As late as 1960, the participation rates were 28 percent for all women and 19 percent for married women. By 1975, 41 percent of women and 38 percent of married women participated in the labour force, and by 1999 the participation rates for all women and married women were over 60 percent.[33] Other increases in labour supply have come through increased investments in the education and training of Canadian workers. By the beginning of World War II, there were roughly three times as many students in secondary schools than there had been at the turn of the century, and by the 1960s, two-thirds of 14–17 year olds were in school.[34] Participation in university education also increased over the century. In 1920, only 1.5 percent of Canadians aged 15 to 24 were enrolled in university, by 1960, 4.3 percent of Canadians 15 to 24 were enrolled in university and by 1986, the enrollment rate was 11.4 percent.[35]

The stock of capital (K) consists of the stock of machinery, equipment, residential and non-residential structures, and public infrastructure (such as roads, bridges, or harbours) in the economy at any moment. The stock of capital is augmented over time through a process known as investment. Private-sector investment requires access to savings, which can be retained earnings, domestic savings, or foreign loans. Governments finance their investment spending through borrowing as well, but also through taxation. Thus, for a given set of expected returns (private or public) to investment, the amount of investment (and thus the size of the capital stock) in any period will depend on the supply of savings and amount of tax room open to governments.

Ian Mclean has estimated the sources of savings for Canada from 1870 to 1985. Until 1910, half of the investment in Canada was financed with domestic savings and half from foreign sources of capital. After World War I, the Canadian savings rate doubled from that for the pre-war period and the reliance on "foreign savings" played a smaller role. Over time, Canadian views changed towards the desirability of foreign capital. When foreign savings are invested in Canada, the share of national income that accrues to the foreign owners of capital leaves the Canadian economy. In the nineteenth century, the attraction of foreign capital was still considered desirable, since it did generate higher incomes for labour and land, even if foreign capital's share of income was exported. After World War II, foreign savings as a source of capital were not considered as desirable. Besides the drain to potential income in Canada, foreign capital was thought to result in a less efficient Canadian economy, since foreign owners of capital were often operating small-scale branch plants in Canada, and because foreign capital discouraged the development of entrepreneurial talent. John McCallum highlights this feature when he characterizes Quebec's manufacturing sector as foreign capital taking advantage of a low-productivity, low-wage labour force, whereas Ontario financed capital through Ontario savings, and businessmen invested in local infrastructure and encouraged the development of high-productivity, high-wage manufacturing.[36]

Offering reasons for growth not explained by measured increases in inputs (residual growth), known as total factor productivity, is more difficult. One source of such growth is technical change. New technologies can often increase the amount of output of a good or service obtainable from a given set of inputs. For example, the replacement of hand-saws with chainsaws in logging meant that a given logger could fell more trees in a workday. Another source of growth is from changes in the way production and exchange are organized. These changes can be at the level of the individual production unit (the firm, mine, factory, or office), as when new management techniques are intro-duced or where a change in communication technology allows for simultaneous opera-tions at different locations. Another source of TFP growth is "learning by doing," where labour efficiency improves with the experience of the labour force. TFP changes can also occur at the aggregate level, as when public infrastructure is added or commercial laws are updated.

TFP estimates may also reflect measurement error. While labour services (L) are ideally measured in terms of efficiency units of labour, often L is proxied by numbers of workers or even population size. If the average level of education of the labour force rises, but L is measured as the number of workers in the economy, then TFP will increase since the improved quality of the labour input will not be captured in the measure of labour serv-ices. For example, David Landes suggests that the invention of eyeglasses in the 1300s more than doubled the working life of skilled craftsmen such as scribes, toolmakers, and metal workers. By extending the working life of skilled craftsmen, eyeglasses had two dis-tinct effects that could affect measured TFP. First, they provided an increase in the number of workers, and second, they increased the average experience of the workers available. Depending on how L is measured, the effect of eyeglasses on the size of L may show up as an increase in TFP.[37] Similarly, quality improvements in machines may not be captured in measures of K. Suppose that we value the stock of machines at work in an economy at the market price for the machine. We may find that after accounting for inflation but not improvements in the quality of the machines, the real cost of a computer in 1980 is the same as the cost of a computer today. Given the relative powers of a computer made today versus one made in 1980, it is clear that the quality adjusted price of computing has fallen enormously in 20 years. If we ignore the quality improvements in the capital inputs, the quality improvements will be accounted for in the measured TFP.

While an economy's output can grow through the accumulation of inputs and/or through technical progress, the long-term prospects for an economy depend critically on how the economy grows. In 1994 Paul Krugman wrote an article predicting that the extremely high growth rates of several of the Asian economies in the 1980s (growth rates in Japan, Korea, Hong Kong, Thailand, and Singapore were in some cases three times higher than U.S. growth rates) were not sustainable.[38] Krugman's view was based on the observation that almost all of the growth in those economies was driven by input accumulation, increases in K and L. The high growth rates reflected massive mobilization resources. Labour force participation rates increased dramatically as did the investment in the education of the workforce. Savings rates in the economies were extremely high due to authoritarian governments sacrificing short-term consumer interests for the sake of longer-term growth. All the while, these economies showed no growth in TFP. Krugman argues that the growth slowdown, if not the economic collapse, of the Asian economies in the 1990s was predictable given how the economies were growing. You can only double a participation rate in the labour force so many times, and once all workers have a high school education, it may not make sense for everyone to obtain a PhD. Similarly, as high savings rates reflect a deferral of consumption from today to the future, aging populations may not be willing to save at such high rates. The high growth rates of the Asian economies reflected one time gains in growth that were not sustainable.

In contrast, Krugman highlights Robert Solow's estimate that 80 percent of the long-term rise in U.S. per capita income was the result of growth in TFP.[39] Increased investment in capital only explains the remaining 20 percent. Thus Americans grew richer because they were smarter and producing more and more with given amounts of inputs. In contrast, Asian economies were working harder, not smarter. While input accumulation will ultimately be subject to diminishing returns, TFP growth has no such bounds.

An important problem with Krugman's arguments for the Asian economies is that the absence of TFP growth at a point in time does not mean that TFP growth will not occur in the future. Abramovitz and David show that for the second half of the nineteenth century, U. S. growth rates are almost entirely explained by rates of input accumulation.[40] TFP growth became important for the U.S. only after 1913 and until 1973 when U.S. growth rates slowed. We do not know why American TFP growth started after World War I, nor why it stalled after 1973. Thus, we cannot conclude that an absence of TFP growth in the Asian economies in the 1980s and 1990s means that it will not occur at some time in the future. Further, Abramovitz and David show that size of the "Solow residual," which Krugman bases his views on, does not lend itself to more detailed treatments of production technology and improvements in the quality of inputs themselves. In their assessment, the majority of long-term economic growth in the U.S. has been the result of input accumulation.

While TFP growth is a desirable way for an economy to grow, it is a troubling explanation for growth. In the neo-classical growth model, the state of production technology is an exogenous feature of the model. Thus, most explanations that invoke technical progress as the reason for strong growth seek to correlate the timing of increasing growth rates with the introduction of new or improved products or processes for producing goods and services.

It is somewhat easier to identify "significant" inventions and innovations after the fact than it is to predict what technical changes may be significant in future. One need look no further than the hype and high expectations for computer technology, and the Internet, for stimulating economic growth. Despite the rapid expansion and improvement of computer technology in the 1980s, growth rates in the U. S. remained modest and hardly revolutionary, which led economics Nobel laureate Robert Solow to remark in 1987 that "we can see the computer age everywhere but in the productivity statistics."[41]

Many economists have spent the better part of a decade trying to explain the computer productivity paradox and have put forward explanations for it such as productivity has increased, but we cannot measure it appropriately; we are still in the pre-take-off phase of growth with this technology; and computers have increased productivity a lot, but the rapid depreciation of the computer capital stock offsets the gains. Robert Gordon argues that relative to the great inventions that powered economic growth from 1913 to 1972, computers and the Internet are limited in terms of what they can add to productivity. As Gordon notes, "Internet surfing may be fun and even informational, but it represents a far smaller increment in the standard of living than achieved by the extension of day into night achieved by electric light, the revolution in factory efficiency achieved by the electric motor, the flexibility and freedom achieved by the automobile, the saving of time and shrinking of the globe achieved by the airplane, the new materials achieved by the chemical industry, the first sense of live two-way communication achieved by the telephone, the arrival of live news and entertainment into the family parlor achieved by the radio and then television, and the enormous improvements in life expectancy, health, and comfort achieved by urban sanitation and indoor plumbing."[42]

Despite Gordon's pronouncement that computers and the Internet should not be expected to have a large impact on productivity in comparison to historic episodes of technical change, Paul David argues that electrification was just as uninspiring as an engine of growth from 1900 to 1914 and at the time, appeared to be just as disappointing as the current information age has been for stimulating TFP growth. The fact that electrification did become important for powering economic growth leads David to conclude that we should not be surprised to see computers having an important impact in the future.[43]

Economists do not have a model to explain why, or even when, technology changes. Economists, and many others, believe that technical progress is a function of investment in research and development (R&D). The model economists have in mind is that if you put enough resources towards an objective, something will happen. Thus, to encourage TFP growth governments can offer subsidies or establish patent laws to create an incentive for R&D investment. History also shows that the arrival of inventions or innovations is correlated with periods of material shortages. Nathan Rosenberg argues that England's Industrial Revolution began when techniques were successfully developed for overcoming resource constraints that limited the industrial output of an earlier age. In particular, England in the sixteenth and seventeenth centuries was heavily dependent on wood as a source of fuel, as a building material, and as raw material for industry. Timber in England was scarce enough by the seventeenth century that British industrial expansion was significantly curtailed. Thus, solving the chemical problems associated with the use of coal allowed for mineral fuels to replace wood as a fuel and iron to replace wood as a building material and bypass the more significant limits to industrial expansion.[44] So, for those who fear slow growth due to a shortage of resources in the future, the only comfort a neoclassical economist can provide is to point out that technological changes in response to resource shortages have solved these problems before, and that we must believe that some innovation "to be named later" will solve the problems of the future.

Institutions

Despite the success of neo-classical growth theory for providing insight into economic performance and development, it has not succeeded as a complete explanation for growth processes. A complication arises from the equilibrium implications of the logic of the neo-classical growth model given above. If labour and capital move to where they perceive their best opportunities to be, then in equilibrium, labour and capital will not move between locations once the returns to changing addresses (net of the costs of migration) are equal across locations. Suppose that we observe two economies in 1850. In economy A, there is an abundance of labour relative to the capital stock. In economy B, there is a scarcity of labour relative to the capital stock. Labour in economy A faces a low wage since by diminishing marginal products the productivity of labour is low. In contrast, labour in economy B with plenty of machines per worker will be characterized by high labour productivity and high wages. Analogously, capital should earn a higher rate of return in economy A. If labour and capital are mobile, some workers in economy A will migrate to economy B while capital moves from B to A. These factor movements continue until there is no further advantage for a worker or a unit of capital to change address. Thus, in a world where goods and/or inputs are mobile between countries, the neo-classical growth model described above predicts that incomes across countries should converge. Another prediction is that poor economies should grow faster than rich economies.

Incomes across countries and regions over the last 130 years have not converged in ways that can be easily reconciled with the predictions of the neo-classical growth framework. European countries, their offshoots and Japan comprise the set of high per capita income countries known as the developed countries. Since 1870, these countries have grown rapidly and at similar rates, and the incomes of the poorer countries within this group have grown sufficiently fast to converge towards the higher income countries. The countries not part of this group are referred to as the developing, or less developed, or non-industrialized countries and have had slower growth rates than the developed countries. As a consequence, the income levels between these groups of countries have diverged from 1870 to 1990 by a factor of almost 5.[45] How large is the size of the gap? David Landes points out that today the difference in income per head between the richest industrial nation and the poorest non-industrial country, Mozambique, is 400 to 1. Over 250 years ago, the gap between richest and poorest was probably at most 5 to 1.[46]

Even within the group of developed countries, there are two notable growth experiences that would seem to be at odds with neo-classical convergence predictions. The U.S. emerged as the richest country in the world in the late nineteenth century and remained rich because it also maintained the highest growth rates. The U.K. fell from its nineteenth century position of economic leadership. Nicholas Crafts notes that while convergence predictions of the neo-classical growth model can provide a reason why Britain's lead would have been "whittled down" over time, it cannot address why Britain became the leader in the nineteenth century in the first place, nor why it actually fell behind.[47] Similarly, within Canada where capital, labour, and goods appear to be freely mobile across provinces, we have not observed convergence in incomes across provinces. Ontario has always been a wealthy province and the Atlantic provinces have always been relatively poor. The failure of the convergence prediction suggests that some other feature of economies must be important.

Mancur Olson, Jr. suggests that there are only two possible types of explanations for dramatic and persistent differences in per capita incomes across countries that should be taken seriously.[48] First, poor countries are poor because they are short of resources such as land, modern technology, energy, etc.; that is, poor countries are poor, but they are producing at their potential. The second possibility is that political boundaries mark the borders of public policies and institutions that are not only different, but in some cases better and in some cases worse. Countries with bad policies and institutions do not produce to their potential and remain poor. Institutions and policies structure the incentives for individual decision making. These incentives depend on economic policies chosen in each period, and over the long run, institutional property rights, political structures, constitutional provisions, culture, and the extent of special interest lobbies and cartels. Olson, Jr. feels that the weight of evidence suggests that differences in institutions are the only plausible explanations. Along similar lines, Paul David and Gavin Wright argue that the legal and institutional adaptations resulted in the U.S. exploiting its natural resource potentials to a greater extent than other countries. Thus, the U.S. was not rich because its natural resource abundance was geologically pre-ordained, but because institutions made its resource abundance a socially constructed condition.[49]

Olson, Jr. characterizes the plight of low-income societies as one where the societies cannot realize many of the largest gains from trade and specialization. They do not have institutions that enforce contracts impartially so they lose most of the gains from capital transactions that require third party enforcement. They do not have institutions that make property rights secure over the long run, so capital intensive production is unlikely to occur in those societies. Misguided economic policies and public and private predation are further handicaps to production and trade.

In the Canadian context, there are many examples of institutions, institutional change, and policies influencing the economic performance of Canada and regions within Canada. In the nineteenth century, reciprocity, Confederation, and Sir John A. Macdonald's national policy are prominent examples. In more recent times, uncertainty over Quebec's future in Canada has likely discouraged investment in that province and possibly even Canada. For the west, the federal government's policies of high tariffs on manufactured goods, creation of monopoly railways, and more recently, the National Energy Program have all been viewed as policies that have limited the potential of the west. One of the more intriguing examples of the possible importance of culture and institutions for the Canadian economy is John Helliwell's finding that in 1996 the typical Canadian province traded 12 times as much with another Canadian province as with a U.S. state of similar size and distance despite the existence of the Canada–U.S. Free Trade Agreement since 1988.[50]

Institutions do not only affect incomes at the aggregate level. Within any society there are identifiable groups according to race, sex, language, immigrant versus native born, and religion to name a few. As Canada has emerged as one of the richest nations in the world, not all members of Canadian society have shared equally in the gains. Historically, the incomes of French speaking Canadians have been lower than incomes of English-speaking Canadians; Catholics have had lower incomes than Protestants.[51] Even today, on average women's earnings are two-thirds of average male earnings and there are substantial differences in earnings between white and visible minority workers in Canada.[52] Discrimination is an economic and cultural institution. The extent to which it may exist, or have existed, in Canadian society may be vital for explaining Canadian economic development.

Unlike standard economic analyses in which time and history have no important role, history is vital to understanding the economies today from the perspective of the new-institutional economics. Societies by and large inherit their institutional structures. This may reflect an economy's colonial legacy, where its current institutions are evolved from those imposed by its "discovering," or (perhaps more accurately) "conquering," nation. Douglass North highlights the differences in economic performance today between nations descended from the institutions of Britain (like the U.S. or Canada) and those of nations descended from Spanish institutions (like much of Latin America).[53] Because they are social and political creations, institutions can be slow to change. While the existing institutions may confer benefits to one segment of society, that does not mean that they are socially efficient. Changing the institutions may result from an extended period of small changes to the pliable margins of institutions, or it may occur abruptly after long periods of the status quo such as with revolutions. Institutional change may be bloody and costly such as with the American secession from Britain in the 1770s or with the abolition of slavery in the U.S. and the Civil War in the 1860s. Institutional change may also occur peacefully such as with Britain granting the Canadian colonies responsible government and Dominion status in the mid-nineteenth century. Preservation, or expression, of property rights can also entail conflict and costs as Canadians discovered with the Red River "resistance" led by Louis Riel in 1870. Following the transfer of Rupert's Land from the Hudson Bay Company to the Government of Canada, the Métis people living in the west of Canada had legitimate concerns that Canadians would not acknowledge Métis land claims, nor respect their French language and Catholic religion if the west was transformed into an English-speaking Protestant region.

While neo-classical economic models will direct us to discussing when and why capital and labour came to Canada, and the impacts of technical change on the standard of living and development of the Canadian economy, institutional factors are probably more important for our understanding of Canada's past and possible future. We will be interested in the extent to which different policy or institutional regimes inhibited or enhanced Canada reaching its potential as an economy. Given that institutions and policies may be limiting economic performance, we are interested in seeing whether the chosen institutions and policies had Canada on a desirable path of development. Indeed, it was this question that was essentially the focus of the MacDonald Commission appointed in 1982 to investigate and report on "the long term economic potential, prospects and challenges facing the Canadian federation and its respective regions, as well as the implications that such prospects and challenges have for Canada's economic and governmental institutions, and for the management of Canada's economic affairs." Most notably, the 1982 inquiry was asked to recommend "the appropriate national goals and policies for economic development" and "the appropriate institutional and constitutional arrangements to promote the liberty and well-being of individual Canadians and the maintenance of a strong competitive economy."[54]

NOTES

1. *Canadian Historical Review* 4 (March 1923): 12–25.
2. The classic exposition of the staples thesis in an economic-development context is M.H. Watkins, "A Staple Theory of Economic Growth," *Canadian Journal of Economics and Political Science* 29 (1963): 141–158. See also H.G.J. Aitken, "Myth and Measurement: The Innis Tradition in Economic History," *Journal of Canadian Studies* 12 (1977): 96–107. Both articles are reprinted in M.H. Watkins and H.M. Grant, eds., *Canadian Economic History: Classic and Contemporary Approaches* (Ottawa: Carleton University Press, 1993).
3. On Harold Innis see Carl Berger, *The Writing of Canadian History: Aspects of English Canadian Historical Writing Since 1900*, 2nd ed. (Toronto: University of Toronto Press, 1986).
4. J.M.S. Careless, "'Limited Identities' in Canada," *Canadian Historical Review* 50 (March 1969): 1–10.
5. Thomas J. Courchene and Colin R. Telmer, *From Heartland to North American Region State: The Social, Fiscal & Federal Evolution of Ontario* (Toronto: University of Toronto Press, 1997).
6. Ted Morton, Stephen Harper, Tom Flanagan, Rainer Knopff, Andrew Crooks, and Ken Boessenkool, "The Alberta Agenda/Programme Pour L'Alberta," *Policy Options* 22 (03) (April 2001): 16–19.
7. John F. Helliwell, "Globalization: Myths, Facts and Consequences,"C.D. Howe Institute Benefactors Lecture, 2000.
8. Jeffrey G. Williamson, "Globalization, Labor Markets and Policy Backlash in the Past," *Journal of Economic Perspectives* 12(4) (1998): 51–72.
9. We cite both gross domestic product (GDP) and gross national product (GNP) in the text, depending on the data source. Formally, GDP is the total value of all final output produced, and hence income generated, within a country, while GNP is the total value of all income received by residents of a country. The two measures differ because Canadians earn income from economic production abroad, while foreigners earn income from economic production within Canada. Formally, GNP equals GDP plus investment income received from non-residents minus investment income paid to non-residents. The two values are virtually identical (GNP was equal to 97. 7 percent of GDP in 1947 and 96. 6 percent in 1993), so we assume that there is no confusion in using them interchangeably.
10. Eric Jones, "A Know-All's Guide to the Industrial Revolution," Chaper 2 in *Growth Recurring* (University of Michigan Press, 2000).
11. M.C. Urquhart, *Gross National Product, Canada, 1870–1926: The Derivation of the Estimates* (Kingston & Montreal: McGill-Queen's University Press, 1993).
12. Christina D. Romer, "Is the Stabilization of the Postwar Economy a Figment of the Data?" *American Economic Review* 76(3) (1986): 314–334.
13. Clifford Cobb, Ted Halstead, and Johnathan Rowe, "If the GDP Is Up, Why Is America Down?" *The Atlantic Monthly* 276 (4) (October 1995).
14. Ibid.
15. Nancy Folbre and Barnet Wagman, "Counting Housework: New Estimates of Real Product in the United States, 1800–1860," *Journal of Economic History* 53(2) (June 1993): 275–288. Nancy Folbre and Barnet Wagman, "Household Services and Economic Growth in the United States, 1870–1930," *Feminist Economics* 2(1)(Spring 1996): 43–66
16. Another alternative is the genuine progress indicator (GPI). Where GDP arbitrarily places no value on social and environmental costs when GDP is interpreted as measuring standard of living, the GPI includes GDP and more than 20 aspects of the economy that GDP ignores such as the household economy, the volunteer economy, crime, resource depletion, degradation of habitat, and loss of leisure. Where GDP numbers suggest that life has steadily improved for Americans since 1950, the GPI presents a different picture. Standard of living as measured by the GPI improved from 1950 to 1970 but has declined 45 percent since 1970. Cobb, Halstead, and Rowe conclude that the GPI shows that much of what we now call growth or GDP is really just fixing blunders and social decay from the past, borrowing resources from the future, and shifting functions from the household and community into the market economy (Clifford Cobb, Ted

Halstead, and Johnathan Rowe, "If the GDP Is Up, Why Is America Down?"). While the GPI is broader based than GDP, the GPI suffers from being a "dog's breakfast" of factors included. Where GDP is narrowly defined, it is theoretically motivated in terms of what will be included and how the item will be weighted in terms of importance. What gets included in the GPI and how it is weighted reflects the subjective judgment of the person calculating the GPI. If you want to show social decay with a GPI, just add more negative entries than positive and give them more weight in the aggregation. In challenging such a measure, one is challenging the beliefs and criteria of the measure's calculator rather than an objective picture of the world.

17. N.F.R. Crafts, "The Human Development Index and Changes in Standards of Living: Some Historical Comparisons," *European Review of Economic History*, 1 (1997): 299–322.

18. Richard A. Easterlin, "The Worldwide Standard of Living Since 1800," *Journal of Economic Perspectives* 14 (1) (2000): 7–26. Quote from page 7.

19. W.W. Rostow, *The Process of Economic Growth* (New York: W.W. Norton & Company, 1962).

20. M.H. Watkins, "A Staple Theory of Economic Growth," *Canadian Journal of Economics and Political Science* 29 (1963): 141–158. Reprinted in M.H. Watkins and H.M. Grant, eds. *Canadian Economic History: Classic and Contemporary Approaches* (Ottawa: Carleton University Press, 1993).

21. K.A.H. Buckley, "The Role of Staple Industries in Canada's Economic Development," *Journal of Economic History* 18 (1958): 439–450.

22. H.G.J. Aitken, "Myth and Measurement: The Innis Tradition in Economic History," *Journal of Canadian Studies* 12 (5) (1977): 96–107. Reprinted in M.H. Watkins and H.M. Grant, eds. *Canadian Economic History:Classic and Contemporary Approaches* (Ottawa: Carleton University Press, 1993).

23. John McCallum, "Agriculture and Economic Development in Quebec and Ontario Until 1870," in Gordon Laxer, ed. , *Perspectives on Canadian Economic Development: Class, Staples, Gender and Elites* (Toronto: Oxford University Press, 1991) 16. See also, John McCallum, *Unequal Beginnings: Agriculture and Economic Development in Quebec and Ontario until 1870,* (Toronto: University of Toronto Press, 1980). For a more formal discussion of under what conditions these predictions may or may not occur, see Paul Krugman, "Space: The Final Frontier," *Journal of Economic Perspectives* 12(2) (1998): 161–174.

24. E.J. Chambers and D.F. Gordon, "Primary Products and Economic Growth: An Empirical Measurement," *Journal of Political Economy* 74 (1966): 315–332.

25. For example, suppose that a carpenter who has worked for 10 years can build 10 shelves in one hour, whereas a carpenter starting work for the first time can only produce 1 shelf in one hour. If we measure L by the number of carpenters, each carpenter counts for 1 unit of L for a total of 2 units of L. These carpenters differ in efficiency/productivity. We could count them as efficiency units of L where the experienced carpenter is worth 10 units of L and the new carpenter is equivalent to one efficiency unit of L. So the homogeneous, efficiency unit measure of L would have L equal to 11 in this example.

26. The total fertility rate measures the number of children a woman would bear if she experienced the prevailing age-specific fertility over her lifetime. Compared to the Crude Birth Rate, the number of births divided by the female population, the TFR accounts for the age-sex composition of the population. Roderic Beaujot and Kevin McQuillan, *Growth and Dualism: The Demographic Development of Canadian Society* (Toronto: Gage Publishing, 1982).

27. Beaujot and McQuillan. Statistics Canada, Catalogue no. 82F0075XCB.

28. Marvin McInnis, "The Anglo-Canadian Hemorrhage: The Great Immigration from Canada, 1861–1901." Paper presented to the annual meeting of the Canadian Historical Association, Laval University, Quebec, May 27, 2001.

29. Gary Burrill, *Away: Maritimers in Massachusetts, Ontario, and Alberta* (Kingston and Montreal: McGill-Queen's University Press, 1992).

30. Bruno Ramirez, *On the Move: French-Canadian and Italian Migrants in the North Atlantic Economy* (Toronto: McClelland and Stewart, 1991).

31. Alan G. Green and David A. Green, "The Economic Goals of Canada's Immigration Policy," *Canadian Public Policy* XXV (4) (1999): 425–452.

32. Ibid.

33. Series D431-448 in the *Historical Statistics of Canada,* Second Edition. The Labour Force Survey, Statistics Canada, Catalogue no. 71F0004-XCB.

34. Doug Owram, *Born at the Right Time: A History of the Baby-Boom Generation* (Toronto: University of Toronto Press, 1996).

35. Table 11-3 in Christopher J. Bruce, *Economics of Employment and Earnings* (Scarborough: Nelson Canada, 1990).

36. John McCallum, *Unequal Beginnings: Agriculture and Economic Development in Quebec and Ontario until 1870* (Toronto: University of Toronto Press, 1980).

37. David S. Landes, *The Wealth and Poverty of Nations: Why Some Are So Rich and Some So Poor* (New York: W. W. Norton & Company, 1998).

38. Paul Krugman, "The Myth of Asia's Miracle," *Foreign Affairs* (November/December 1994), 62–78. Reprinted in Paul Krugman, *Pop Internationalism* (Cambridge: MIT Press, 1996).

39. Robert M. Solow, "Technical Change and the Aggregate Production Function,"*Review of Economics and Statistics* 39, 312–320.

40. Moses Abramovitz and Paul A. David, "Reinterpreting Economic Growth: Parables and Realities," *American Economic Review* 63(2) (May 1973): 428–439.

41. Cited on page 49, Robert J. Gordon, "Does the 'New Economy' Measure Up to the Great Inventions of the Past," *Journal of Economic Perspectives* 14(4) (2000): 49–74.

42. Ibid., 72.

43. Paul A. David, "The Dynamo and the Computer: An Historical Perspective on the Modern Productivity Paradox," *The American Economic Review* 80(2) (1990): 355–361.

44. Nathan Rosenberg, "Innovative Responses to Materials Shortages," *The American Economic Review* 63(2) (1973): 111–118.

45. Lant Pritchett, "Divergence, Big Time," *Journal of Economic Perspectives* 11(3) (1997): 3–17.

46. David S. Landes, *The Wealth and Poverty of Nations: Why Some Are So Rich and Some So Poor* (New York: W.W. Norton & Company, 1998), page *xx*.

47. Nicholas Crafts, "Forging Ahead and Falling Behind: The Rise and Relative Decline of the First Industrial Nation," *Journal of Economic Perspectives* 12 (2) (1998): 193–210.

48. Mancur Olson, Jr. , "Distinguished Lecture on Economics in Government: Big Bills Left on the Sidewalk: Why Some Nations Are Rich, and Others Poor," *Journal of Economic Perspectives* 10(2) (1996): 3–24.

49. Paul A. David and Gavin Wright, "Increasing Returns and the Genesis of American Resource Abundance," *Industrial and Corporate Change* 6(2) (1997): 203–245.

50. John F. Helliwell, "Globalization: Myths, Facts and Consequences,"*C. D. Howe Institute Benefactors Lecture, 2000, 3.

51. John Porter, *The Vertical Mosaic: An Analysis of Social Class and Power in Canada* (Toronto: University of Toronto Press, 1965).

52. Krishna Pendakur and Ravi Pendakur, "The Colour of Money: Earnings Differentials among Ethnic Groups in Canada," *Canadian Journal of Economics* 31(3) (1998): 518–548.

53. Douglass North, *Institutions, Institutional Change and Economic Performance* (New York: Cambridge University Press, 1996).

54. Royal Commission on the Economic Union and Development Prospects for Canada, *Report,* vol. 3, S61–65. See Chapter 22.

Part One

The Era of Imperial Rivalry: Beginnings to 1763

Louis Hébert sowing seed, an illustration by the Abbé A.C. Hébert, Montreal, 1918. In 1623, Louis Hébert, a Quebec apothecary, was granted the first seigneury in New France. National Library of Canada C-016952.

2 | **FOR CENTURIES,** two separate economies and societies had evolved on the two sides of the Atlantic Ocean. Though there was intermittent contact, such as the Viking landing at Newfoundland around A.D. 1000, the reality was that neither the small-scale hunting, trapping, and trading economies of the North American Native population nor the impoverished European feudal system had either the means or the will to take the necessary steps to bridge the ocean. Over time, that situation changed, however. European commerce advanced, and European technology, borrowing from the Middle East and Asia as well as relying on indigenous innovation, increasingly developed and improved the means for trade and travel. Europeans ventured farther and farther beyond their traditional frontiers. Eventually, Columbus linked the two sides of the Atlantic in his famed 1492 voyage.

For the next few centuries, until 1763, England and France jockeyed for control of the northern regions of this "new" world. This era of imperial rivalry divides into two distinct sub-periods. In the beginning, there was regular contact and trade between the two worlds but only a transient European population in North America, consisting of migratory fishermen, fur traders, explorers, and missionaries. Then, in 1607, the Virginia Company began a settlement at Jamestown, and one year later Champlain founded Quebec. The period of uninterrupted European settlement in North America began.

The European presence spread quickly over the next century. As the eighteenth century began, France had clear claim to what are now the Maritime provinces of Prince Edward Island, Nova Scotia, and New Brunswick. French fishermen were active off Newfoundland, but here there was no clear jurisdiction. Inland, France's empire extended, by means of alliances with various Native tribes, from its early bases along the St. Lawrence River, through the Great Lakes, and into the heart of the continent. Explorers, fur traders, and missionaries had gone north of the Great Lakes into the Canadian Shield, and south along the Ohio and Mississippi river systems, reaching the Gulf of Mexico by 1682.

The major British colonial thrust in North America occurred on what is now the eastern seaboard of the United States. The economic future of the settlement at Jamestown was assured when the first tobacco plants were introduced in 1613. Religious dissidents landed at Plymouth in 1619, and stayed despite years of isolation and hardship. Boston was founded in 1629 by the Puritans, followed by further settlements in Rhode Island, New Haven, and along the Connecticut River valley. Colonists survived, and ultimately prospered, by developing an economy based on lumber, fish, whale oil, potash, meat, butter, cheese, shipping, and shipbuilding. Dutch settlements in Manhattan and along the Hudson River, established in the years after 1612, were surrendered in 1674, adding to the area of British influence. Maryland and areas farther south, settlements based largely on the cultivation of tobacco, were occupied from the 1630s on. By 1670, halfway through the colonial period, there were about 100 000 residents in the area stretching from southern Maine to North Carolina.

The American colonies grew rapidly after 1670. The established areas of New England continued to develop, but their progress was slow compared with that of more recent settlements in Connecticut and Rhode Island, and especially compared with that of the middle and southern colonies. The rich farmlands of New York, New Jersey, and Pennsylvania, with their seemingly limitless bounty of fruits and grains and potential for the raising of livestock, attracted thousands of immigrants. Philadelphia, and then New

York, grew to rival and then surpass Boston as centres of shipping and commerce. Rice and indigo were added to tobacco as important staple crops of the south. The colonies' population had increased nearly sixfold, from 470 000 in 1720 to 2.7 million by 1780.

England was also active in the areas of North America that were to become Canada. The activities of the West Country fishermen drew attention to Newfoundland, which England claimed jointly with France. Throughout the seventeenth century, the fur trade drew the British farther and farther inland from their base on Hudson Bay. A royal charter in 1670 granted to the Hudson's Bay Company the sole right to trade and commerce on "all those seas, straits, bays, rivers, lakes, creeks and sounds ... that lie within the entrance to Hudson's Straits, together with all the lands, countries and territories upon the coasts and confines of the seas, straits, bays, lakes, rivers, creeks and sounds aforesaid," although this area remained in dispute with France.

France relinquished part of its claim to North America in 1713 under the terms of the Treaty of Utrecht and withdrew from all but the tiny islands of St. Pierre and Miquelon by the Treaty of Paris in 1763. By this act, the era of imperial rivalries in North America ended.

The development of the New World in the first three centuries after its "discovery" in 1492 can be viewed as a product of the complex interaction between external forces, in the form of British and French colonial objectives, and North America's endowments— its geography, resources, and indigenous population. Here as elsewhere around the globe, colonies were held for economic, military, and religious reasons. For that part of the "new" world that was to become Canada, the most important imperial link by far was economic. Briefly, the northern part of North America contained resources — fish and fur — that were sufficiently valuable to induce private economic agents in Europe to organize to exploit them, and to cause their governments sometimes to support, and always to regulate, these ventures. Canada's early economic history is, in large measure, the story of the European exploitation of these resources.

Part One of the text traces out this early development. Chapter One sets the stage. It looks at the developments that brought about a permanent European presence in North America after 1492. Chapter Two shows how the production of cod fish for European markets led to the eventual settlement of what is today Atlantic Canada. Chapter Three outlines how the exploitation of the second great staple, fur, led to the establishment of what is today the province of Quebec and to a European presence in much of North America.

Chapter One

The Background to Colonization

THE ORIGINS OF CANADA as a nation state are part of the expansion of the European population around the globe and the colonization of North America by Europeans after A.D. 1400. Why is a focus on European territorial expansion appropriate for the start of Canada's story? Primarily because, as Jared Diamond points out, "it was not the case that 51 percent of the Americas, Australia, and Africa was conquered by Europeans, while 49 percent of Europe was conquered by Native Americans, Aboriginal Australians, or Africans. The whole modern world has been shaped by lopsided outcomes" (page 25).[1] On the surface the explanation for the lopsided outcomes is obvious. Europeans developed guns, germs, and steel, but other factors, such as writing and maritime technology, also conferred political and economic powers to the Europeans ahead of other peoples. The big question that Diamond addresses is why the Europeans developed these advantages and how they became wealthy. His answer lies in the origin of Europe's wealth and power from its generous endowment of wild plant and animal species available for domestication that other continents did not share. These advantages led to the production of food surpluses to feed non-food-producing citizens, to boost their population thereby increasing their military strength and potential to invent and innovate. In other words, the determinants of the modern fates of continental populations were set as early as 11 000 B.C. What remains to be explained is why it took until A.D. 1400 for the European expansion to begin in earnest.

Prerequisites to European Expansion

The timing of Europe's outward expansion to the rest of the globe coincided with the emergence of European nation states in the fifteenth century. In A.D. 1400 Europe's territory was comprised of fiefdoms (independent land parcels) controlled by feudal lords, other European monarchs, or in some cases, the offspring of a ruling monarch. Through the 1400s the monarchies of England, France, Spain, and other "nations" of Europe embarked on campaigns of war to consolidate their territorial powers. The establishment of permanent and professional armies as well as the rise of new military technologies such as the crossbow, gunpowder, and cannons favoured the creation of larger scale administration of nation states. This process encouraged expansion out of Europe in two ways. First, Douglass North notes that, the emerging nation states in Europe faced a critical problem — the need to acquire the necessary resources to finance the costs of warfare, to enforce the expanding margins of the state.[2] The riches and natural resources of the New World financed the war on the continent. Second, Leonard Dudley argues that, by the middle of the sixteenth century, the states of Europe had reached an uneasy equilibrium.[3] Once the monarchical states had consolidated their power over their own nobility, they sought to expand outward. Despite frequent military clashes over disputed territories, the areas that the consolidated monarchies controlled in Europe ceased to grow. In the areas of Africa, Asia, and the Americas that had not mastered gunpowder technology, European expansion was much easier, less costly, and the pay-off in resources was potentially enormous.

Europeans were engaged in some long-distance commerce already in the fourteenth century. Coastal shipping plied its way along the Baltic and Atlantic seaboards, carrying goods from port to port. In the Mediterranean, an important trade existed between the ports of Italy and Spain and those of the Middle East and the North African coast. Most valuable and difficult of all was the trade between Europe and Asia, which developed during the thirteenth century.

Nevertheless, the characteristics of medieval European trade were localism, small volume, and an absence of financial services. There were various reasons for this state of affairs. First, since specie was limited in supply and no adequate credit system yet existed, trade was limited to what could be sustained through the relatively inefficient barter system. Equally important was the miserable state of transportation, especially over land. Roads were bad, axle and wheel designs were inefficient, and good horses were scarce. Europe's fragmented political state exacerbated these transportation problems, and tolls, tariffs, and the lack of personal safety further hindered the hauling of goods over long distances. For these reasons, therefore, most trade operated in a series of regional and local markets rather than in continental, much less intercontinental, ones.

The prerequisites for successful European expansion beyond these traditional frontiers (including, ultimately, to North America) were many, but three stand out. First, there had to be a commercial system that allowed private interests to respond to profit opportunities at great distances from home. Second, for profit opportunities that involved long-distance trade, there had to be the technology to journey to the new lands and return safely. Third, since private commercial ventures in far-off lands were rarely profitable without some state subsidy or regulation, there had to be some reason for European governments to become involved in colonial ventures.

THE EUROPEAN COMMERCIAL REVOLUTION

The nature of trade began to change in the fifteenth century. Most historians talk of a commercial revolution encompassing the years from 1450 to 1750. Its cumulative effect was dramatic, for it was as a part of this revolution that transatlantic trade was begun, colonies established, and the assertion of European commercial hegemony in much of the world accomplished.

The various forces that created the commercial revolution are complex. A growing market for goods provided a stimulus to expanding trade. In the Middle Ages, only the very top rungs of society would have been affected by long-distance trade. The vast majority of people depended on products grown or manufactured in the local community. Through the fifteenth and sixteenth centuries, standards of living improved and more and more people were able to purchase goods that were available only outside of the local economy. Traders responded to these potential profits by looking farther afield for new markets and new sources.

The king of the emerging system was the merchant-entrepreneur, who profited not by manufacturing but by buying, transporting, and selling goods. As these merchants undertook longer-distance commitments, they increasingly needed institutions to provide market information, handle credit, transfer funds, trade in foreign currencies, and assist in funding large-scale ventures. As well, since long-distance trade was generally much riskier, they needed to find ways to reduce their exposure. Gradually, institutions evolved to meet these needs. Credit arrangements in domestic and foreign currencies evolved beyond the simple bills exchange of medieval times, and discounting became common. Partnerships and joint stock companies provided means to accumulate savings and spread risk. Insurance, particularly marine insurance, became available. Banking houses began to develop. Many eventually had regional offices and could provide the credit arrangements, financial transfers, and other financial services for a dynamic merchant sector.

Within this expanding commercial system, there was no doubt which trade was the richest, and often the riskiest. It was also at the longest distance, for it was with Asia. The Asian trade was also directly related to the European expansion to the Americas, for it was the lure of profits from Asia that drew Europe beyond its own boundaries and gave it reason to go, albeit unintentionally, to North America.

The Asian trade of the fifteenth and sixteenth centuries was very one-sided in terms of merchandise. The great Asian civilizations such as China wanted little from Europe, except perhaps some muskets and ammunition. In contrast, Europe wanted several things from Asia — jewellery, calico, jade, silks, and spices for the luxury market. Most significant of these items were the spices. In the centuries before refrigeration, spice was essential, not just to enhance the flavour of foods but to disguise the smell and taste of decay. Of all the spices, pepper was the most important. Estimates indicate that between 2 million and 3 million pounds (900–1350 t) of pepper annually were being shipped to Europe by the end of the fifteenth century.[4] Its crucial role in food preparation made pepper more than a luxury good and gave it some of the aspects of a mass-consumption item. Certainly, it was the most important and most widely demanded of all goods imported into Europe before 1500.

The Asian trade was fraught with difficulties. Between the Asian sources and the European market lay the powerful Islamic regions. Europe could not penetrate these regions militarily, and thus had to depend on Islamic self-interest and good will to allow the trade to continue. Except in time of war, it was usually profitable for Muslims to allow the European trade to continue through the region. Pepper caravans regularly made their way from the Persian Gulf overland to Tripoli, or from the Red Sea to Cairo and Alexandria.[5] However, these routes were not without problems. Dependence on the Muslims was unfortunate from the European point of view, given the long-standing religious and military animosity between the two groups. Disruptions such as war or disease in the Middle East could interrupt trade for considerable periods of time. When trade was not interrupted, there was a natural tendency for the Islamic nations to use their strategic position to extract certain tolls and tariffs from the traders. Finally, as was the case elsewhere, trade by land was much less efficient than that by sea, making travel on the Asian routes long and expensive.

One further objection made by much of Europe to the structure of the Asian trade had nothing to do with Muslim or Asian circumstances and everything to do with European economic rivalry. The Asian trade was dominated, from the thirteenth century onward, by a few Italian city-states. Pisa, Genoa, and, above all, Venice had become major centres of European commerce because they dominated the routes to the East. There was, as a result, a growing desire by merchants from other parts of Europe to break the dominance of the Italian city-states and to reap greater rewards from the growing Asian trade. The desire to find a safer and cheaper route to Asia, together with the incentive to circumvent the Venetians, would lead Europeans to major new overseas ventures, including those that resulted in their discovery of the Americas (see Map 1.1).

Map 1.1 The Beginnings of European Expansion

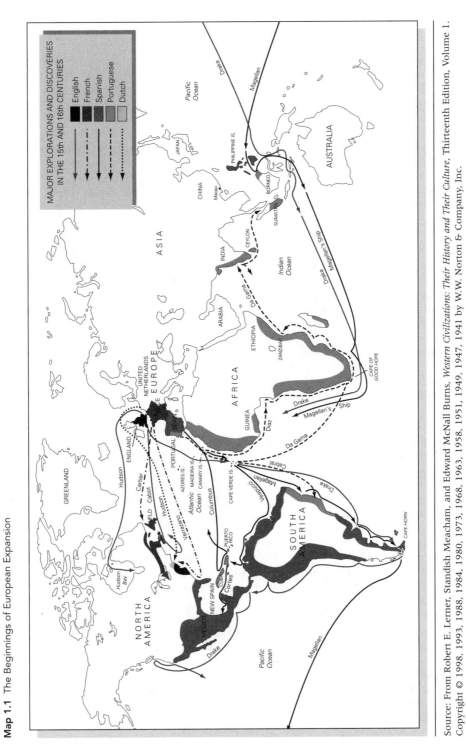

Source: From Robert E. Lerner, Standish Meacham, and Edward McNall Burns, *Western Civilizations: Their History and Their Culture*, Thirteenth Edition, Volume 1. Copyright © 1998, 1993, 1988, 1984, 1980, 1973, 1968, 1963, 1958, 1951, 1949, 1947, 1941 by W.W. Norton & Company, Inc.

Improvements in Technology

Even as the European economy expanded and the Asian trade gave it reason to look outward, considerable improvements in vessel design and navigation techniques were achieved that made the voyages possible. The state of navigation at the time was such that, until the fifteenth century, sailors had no means, once out of sight of land, of determining where they were. All shipping took place along routes close to land. Voyages across open seas and out of sight of land were undertaken, but these were kept as brief as possible and were limited to routes between known points. Certainly, the absence of navigational aids discouraged those who wanted to head off into the unknown for long distances.

By the mid-fifteenth century it was possible for a trained captain to determine latitude (the ship's position along a north–south axis). Longitude (position on an east–west axis) would remain impossible to know with accuracy for another three centuries, but the principle of "dead reckoning," when combined with the new ability to know latitude, gave sailors at least a reasonable idea of where they were at any given time. This development, in turn, led to improvements in chart-making. By the end of the fifteenth century, captains and crew routinely headed off into the open ocean. The medieval sailor's "horror of the open sea," as one historian has described it, had dissipated.[6]

Improvements in navigation were paralleled by changes in ship design. For a long time, European technology, as was the case for European society generally, had been backward in comparison with the technologies of the great Islamic and Asian civilizations. By the fifteenth century, however, the Europeans were gaining ground, both by borrowing from other civilizations and by developing innovations of their own. Overlapping planking on the hull was increasingly replaced by carvel (smooth) planking that had several advantages: it was easier to clean of barnacles, held up better under the stress of heavy seas, and allowed for greater cargo space without loss of stability.

A second area of change was the move from the single- to the triple-masted ship. Most important was the combination of sails hoisted on these masts. The first two masts used a combination of square sails. The third mast used a lateen or triangular sail. This type of sail had been adopted from those in use on Islamic ships in the Mediterranean and probably had its origins in India. The combination of a triangular mizzenmast sail and square sails on the other masts provided a level of power, manoeuvrability, and stability that neither the triangular nor the square sails alone could have done. In particular, the mizzenmast permitted the ship to tack with much greater efficiency against the wind.[7]

Improvements were also made in the sails themselves — flax or cotton rather than wool was used, making sails lighter, especially when wet — and in rigging. These innovations and others increased efficiency, allowing a reduction in crew size, with all the implications that such a reduction had for the cost of provisions and wages. Changing relationships between keel length and beam produced greater cargo space, further improving the cost-efficiency of shipping.

These technological improvements did two crucial things. First, they made the transatlantic voyage less likely to be a suicidal act. By the early sixteenth century, even small ships were routinely making the voyage across the Atlantic on a seasonal basis; a round trip was possible (though far from assured) within about six weeks. Second, the improvements made the trip more efficient and thus less costly. The cost of transporting whatever might be found in the New World steadily decreased as ship design improved. The North Atlantic, which had for so long hemmed Europe in, was about to become a major commercial highway.

COLONIALISM

Some of these long-distance ventures were highly profitable, and economic self-interest was sufficient to see them underway. Others, including those in North America, were more marginal, and private economic agents needed the support of governments if they were to succeed. Thus the third prerequisite for expansion to North America was the interest by European governments (Britain and France, for our purposes) in claiming, and then retaining, overseas territories.

European governments pursued overseas colonies for many reasons, but the main interest was economic, and the guiding doctrine was a set of policies that later writers were to label "mercantilist." Mercantilism was never a conscious strategy of any government, and the set of measures attributed to it varied greatly from country to country. As one text explains, "mercantilism is the name given to that group of ideas and practices particularly characteristic of the period 1500 to 1800 by which the national state acting in the economic sphere sought by methods of control to secure its own unity and power."[8] Many aspects of mercantilism had little to do with colonies, but some did, and it is these aspects that we briefly discuss here.

A basic tenet of mercantilism was bullionism — the accumulation of precious metals. Such metals were valuable for purchasing arms, ships, and soldiers. If gold and silver could not be obtained directly, as the Spanish did from their South American colonies, they had to come indirectly, through a favourable balance of trade, which allowed them to accumulate gold. This goal was achievable through the promotion of agricultural and industrial self-sufficiency and the restriction of trade and commerce to vessels from their nation. Colonies contributed to a positive payments balance by providing raw materials not available in the home country, by absorbing its processed products, and by acting as training grounds for its navy and merchant marine. In all these instances, the colonies reduced the need to pay out specie to competing powers.

Mercantilism probably reached its highest state in France, Europe's most powerful nation, through much of the colonial era. French mercantilism reached its full development in the age of Intendant Jean Colbert (1661–83), chief minister of Louis XIV. There had been earlier efforts to regulate national economic life, particularly after 1600, but these had been "sporadic, uncoordinated and ill-enforced."[9] Under Louis XIII, Cardinal Richelieu had built up the French navy, encouraged and regulated industry and agriculture, and established commercial companies, including some in New France and the West Indies. Colbert, with the support of a powerful monarchy, worked these beginnings into a centralized, well-rounded mercantilist system. Colonies were of particular importance in this scheme, and Colbert strove to make the French possessions valuable sources of raw materials and destinations for French manufactured goods. In the New World, he succeeded in diverting the trade of the French West Indies from the Dutch, but neither he nor his successors were able to link this area economically with New France.

British mercantilism was less structured than that of France, but equally influential. The main goals were the classic mercantilist ones: support of the merchant marine at the expense of foreign competition and promotion of self-sufficiency in resources and manufactured products. Key to the support of domestic shipping were the Navigation Acts, implemented first in 1651 and revised several times thereafter. Under the initial formulation, goods produced in Asia, Africa, and America could be imported into England only in British or colonial vessels. European exporters could use British ships or those of their own country, although, after 1661, goods brought in this way faced higher duties. Foreigners were barred completely from the British coastal trade. Amendments in 1661 added the provision that all goods imported from or exported to British colonies must be transported in British or colonial ships. The Staples Act of 1663 stipulated that no European goods could be imported into the colonies unless they were put on board in Great Britain. A provision ten years later placed duties on trade among the colonies, with the aim of making Great Britain the entrepôt (central warehouse) of all colonial commerce.

The goal of self-sufficiency took various forms. Domestic agriculture and industry were to be developed as much as possible to lessen reliance on imports and to promote sales abroad. Grain exports earned bounties in years of low prices, while imports faced sliding-scale tariffs (i.e., the duty increased as the foreign price fell). Manufacturers benefited from high tariffs and outright prohibitions on the import of some products. Colonies were to serve as markets for manufactured products; this meant that no goods were to be imported from other nations, nor were the colonies to develop industrial expertise of their own. When manufacturing did develop anyway, measures were enacted to discourage it. New England woollens, hats, and iron received special legislative attention.

A related tenet was that Britain's empire should, as much as possible, be able to draw its needed raw materials from within its own territories. The 1661 amendments noted above included a clause that enumerated articles— sugar, tobacco, cotton, indigo, ginger, and dye woods — not to be exported from an English colony save to England or another colony. The list of enumerated articles was extended over time to include naval stores, rice and molasses, copper ore and furs, hides, potash, lumber, and pig and bar iron. This provision cut both ways for colonies: it could mean preferential access to the lucrative British market, but it could also deny access to trade that was otherwise profitable.

Early European Expansion

The Portuguese were the first to break out of Europe's traditional commercial frontiers. Throughout the fifteenth century they extended their trade and knowledge southward, along the coast of Africa. By 1488 they had rounded the Cape of Good Hope and landed in eastern Africa. They had discovered the way into the Indian Ocean, and thereby opened up the possibility of direct sea contact with rich Asian lands. Within a few more years, that contact was established. The economic implications of this development were enormous. The first shipments of Asian goods via Portugal arrived in northern Europe in 1501.[10] The monopoly of the Italian city-states had been broken and, though it would take time, power was beginning to shift northwestward from the Mediterranean basin. Portugal, for its part, was about to reap the rewards of its seafaring adventures with an overseas empire.

In the meantime, the lure of Asia led to a voyage that is much better known to most North Americans. For Christopher Columbus, the logical route to Asia was not around the Cape of Good Hope, but due westward, where, with a little luck, clear sailing would take one directly to Asia. In the 1480s, he petitioned the King of Portugal to fund such a trip. Portugal was not interested, but its neighbour, Spain, was convinced, and in 1492 Columbus proceeded westward toward Asia. As was true for the Portuguese in Africa, economic opportunity provided a motive force, both for the explorers and for those who backed them.

Columbus did not find Asia, of course, but he did find a region that was quickly recognized to be important in its own right. After a few exploratory voyages, the Spanish discovered the vast wealth of the Aztec and Inca civilizations. This wealth provided the impetus for return visits, as military expeditions invaded these American civilizations and plundered their large holdings of gold and silver. Soon after, Spanish colonies were founded and transatlantic commerce was developed to service them. By the 1520s, both Spain and Portugal had converted the central Atlantic into a regularly travelled shipping lane. Gold and silver, plundered from the Native peoples of Central and South America, headed eastward. Soldiers, and then slaves for the growing plantation system, headed west.

The record of Spanish and Portuguese development of the New World is beyond the scope of this book. It is important, however, to note the influence that this chain of discoveries and plunders had on the North Atlantic region. The rapid influx of gold and silver into Europe increased the supply of money on the continent. The result was a steady, though moderate, inflation. Prices doubled between 1550 and 1600, for example. There has been some debate as to whether this inflation undermined or assisted the European economy, but on balance the belief seems to be that the influx of new money was helpful to the ongoing commercial revolution. The specie from America allowed Europe to continue to finance the imbalance in the Asian trade; provided additional money supplies, which spurred economic activity; and, perhaps most important, made it easier to fund later voyages.

The long-term impact of the inflow of American gold was uneven, however. Portugal and Spain experienced a century or more of tremendous power, prestige, and wealth from their American exploits. For the most part, however, these nations did not hold on to the specie from overseas. Few linkages were developed within their economies, and many of the items they sought had to be bought abroad. Much of the bullion from the New World, for example, stayed in Spain only long enough to be readdressed and sent on to China or other Asian destinations. Much also went northward, along the western coast of Europe, to rising trading nations such as England and the Netherlands. Wars further depleted gold and silver reserves.

The movement of Iberian gold and silver paralleled what was happening in the European economy as a whole. Power was slipping northward. The Mediterranean had begun a decline that, by the end of the seventeenth century, would see it reduced from the most economically powerful part of Europe to a relatively poor region. Spain (which absorbed Portugal in 1580) found its fortunes in decline by the late sixteenth century, in spite of its vast overseas empire.

The emergent centres of economic power were in the north. Paris, Amsterdam, and London would dominate the next centuries. So far as the future North Atlantic trade is concerned, two things stand out. First, wealth was accumulating rapidly among the merchants of the major northern commercial centres. Such wealth would make speculative ventures more likely, including the extremely high-risk ones across the Atlantic. Second, these emergent nations were major sea powers. In each, a maritime tradition and access to numerous ships and experienced sailors made transatlantic commerce a natural step. When these nations did venture across the Atlantic, such advantages would make them important presences in the Americas.

Spain's presence there forced these nations to act. "The Spanish King vexeth all the Princes of Europe," complained Sir Walter Raleigh, "and is become in a fewe years from a poore King of Castile the greatest monark of this part of the worlde."[11] Other nations, including England and France, sent expeditions, hoping to emulate Columbus by discovering new lands somewhere to the north of existing Spanish possessions. The lands were discovered, but when the Europeans found there was no quick plunder they returned their attention to Spanish lands to the south, raiding Spanish commerce across the sea lanes. In a way, this dramatic saga of piracy, warfare, and adventure was an economic stage in the development of the New World. It gave other nations reason to go back to the New World — to plunder the Spanish, who had plundered the Indians. In the process, such people as Sir Francis Drake expanded the British knowledge of seamanship, in general, and of the Atlantic world, in particular.

Spain and Portugal initiated much of Europe's expansion to the New World. They ended up as relatively poor and weak nations; England wound up wealthy and powerful. David Landes argues that the divergent outcomes of these colonizers of the New World highlight one of the great themes of economic history and theory. Clearly, the transfer of wealth from the New World to the Old had uneven effects. Spain and Portugal grew rich only to save and spend, while England grew rich to save and invest. Thus Spain and Portugal were little richer in the end than at the beginning, while England used its fortune to create even more wealth. Landes points out that all models of growth have capital as the "chief nourisher of economic development." Spain and Portugal, thanks to their empires, had great access to capital from the gold and silver they plundered from the New World. But the new wealth was available to invest or spend and Spain, without an eye to the future, chose to spend on luxury and war. Thus Spain's wealth went to pay for soldiers, horses, and ships, and to purchase weapons and provisions from their oft-times enemies, England, Holland, and Finland. By relying on trade with other nations to acquire the goods it needed, Spain lost the opportunity to develop its own manufacturing sector.

Douglass North describes Spain's polity (form of government) as a large centralized bureaucracy that was structured to further the Spanish crown's interest in creating the most powerful empire since Rome. With ongoing military conflicts, by the time that the inflow of gold and silver from the New World ended in the mid-seventeenth century, the Spanish crown was deep in debt. The country entered into a long and steady economic decline. Douglass North uses the tale of Spain to illustrate the path-dependent nature of economic development. The Spanish crown and bureaucracy were aware of the decay and decline of their country, but its institutions left the crown and bureaucracy impotent to alter the depopulation of the countryside, the stagnation of industry, and the collapse of the trading system with the New World. As Spain entered into a period of fiscal crisis, the crown responded by raising internal taxes and confiscating wealth, thus affecting the security of property rights.

In contrast to Spain that had the balance of power early on, England and the other nations of northern Europe rose to prominence because their empires were *not* endowed with Spain's gold and silver. Their New World empires were built upon renewable harvests and continuing industry rather than on depletable minerals. The perpetual potential of wealth from renewable resources encouraged the investment to be pumped back into those types of activities. With its wealth from the New World, England's mercantilist institutions favoured the development of domestic manufacturing and retained wealth in the home economy. England also benefited from the triumph of its Parliament as the beginning of representative government. As the Parliament gained political power, it was able to reduce the rent-seeking behaviour of the monarch. This in turn increased the security of property rights and led to a more effective, impartial judicial system.

The contrasting stories of Spain and England's empires are relevant to understand the economic conditions of many nations today. Nations that were properties of the Spanish empire inherited Spain's institutions and consequently have had economic outcomes very similar to that of Spain. Possessions of the British Empire, notably Canada and the United States, inherited British legal and political institutions that are characterized by "a federal political system, checks and balances, and a basic structure of property rights that have encouraged the long-term contracting essential to the creation of capital markets and economic growth."[12]

ABORIGINAL SOCIETIES

Once Europeans began to plant settlements in Canada, incidental contact with the Native peoples of North America would become much more direct. Economic interaction between the newcomers and the original settlers of North America became the fundamental fact that shaped the economy and society of early colonial settlement. Initially, the Native population, knowledgeable in its own habitat and aware of its own economic interests, dominated these relationships. Over time, however, the superior technology and greater numbers of the Europeans would transform the economy of North America. It is, thus, worthwhile to look at the nature of the Native economy that was about to receive the Europeans, as it is to look at the economy that was being received.

Some preliminary points must be made before any description of the economy of the North American Native population is undertaken. First, it is extremely difficult to discuss any single "Native economy" before contact. There were several Native economies, varying from the harsh hunting and fishing economy of the Inuit to the agriculturally based economy of the Huron. Second, the term "before contact" presents problems. Contact occurred over an extended period. The impact of the Europeans on the Micmac of Nova Scotia or the Iroquois of the St. Lawrence came two centuries before European contact with the Blackfoot of the interior plains. Further, the absence of written records makes it all the more difficult to come to any full comprehension of the precontact Native economy, even if the other problems could be resolved.

A final problem is pointed out by recent anthropological studies that demonstrate how the Native peoples were affected by Europe long before they had any direct contact with Europeans. Trade goods filtered inland through intermediary tribes and altered the technology of a society that had never seen a European. For example, archaeological digs in southern Ontario have dated many European items in the region from the late sixteenth century, decades before European settlement began. For all these reasons, Bruce Trigger's concept of "proto-history" is an extremely useful one. This term refers to the period during which European influence altered the economy, technology, or society of a Native group, even though no European had been in the region.[13] These qualifications made, it is still possible to give a general description of the economic structure of Native society on the eve of European contact. Of immediate interest are the people east of Lake Huron, with whom the Europeans would first come into contact.

In general terms, the Native peoples of eastern Canada can be divided into two groups. The first group, which populated the woodlands of Northern Ontario, northern and central Quebec, and much of the Maritimes, included such tribes as the Ottawa, Algonquins, and Micmac. They were hunter-gatherers whose food supplies came from the game of the vast forests and from fishing. This reliance made them nomadic, as they followed game resources and adapted to the demands of the seasons. It also meant that they usually lived in fairly small bands or in individual family units. Any large concentration of the tribe would have quickly outstripped the game resources of an area.

A more complex economy had been developed in the millennium before European arrival by the Iroquois and Hurons of southern Ontario and upstate New York. Corn, beans, and squash had been introduced by tribes to the south, beginning around A.D. 500. By the time John Cabot reached Newfoundland, these people had become primarily agricultural. This agricultural base affected their social and tribal structures. Larger groups could, and did, live together in villages of up to 1000 people. Hunting occurred but, since it was secondary to agriculture, it placed less strain on the game resources. This meant that a given area of land was able to support a larger number of people than was the case in a society totally dependent on hunting. The population of Huronia (roughly between Lake Simcoe and Georgian Bay) is estimated to have been about 10 000 at the end of the sixteenth century. South of the Great Lakes, the Iroquois confederacy is estimated to have had a population of 10 000 at the time of contact (see Map 1.2).

Until recently, it has been common to assume that economic rivalry among the Native peoples and the genocidal warfare observed during the first phase of European settlement were by-products of that European presence. European trade goods, the argument went, created new rivalries, based on economic competition, in traditional warfare. Wars thus escalated from minor skirmishes to all-out assaults. Now, though there is still debate, two things seem apparent. First, since there was considerable trade between tribes, trade rivalries existed long before European contact. Copper from the Lake Superior region had been

Map 1.2 Huronia and Iroquois Territories, Sixteenth Century

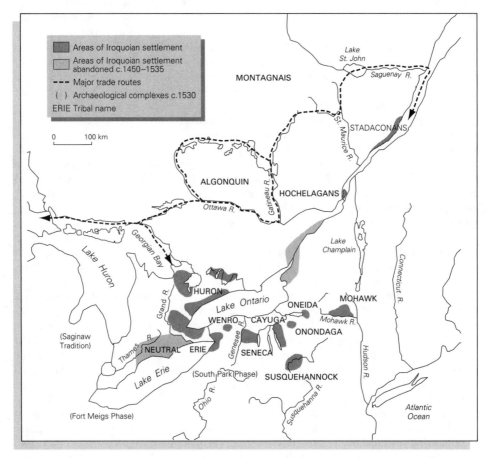

Source: Based on Bruce Trigger, *Natives and Newcomers: Canada's "Heroic Age" Reconsidered* (Montreal and Kingston: McGill–Queen's University Press, 1985), p. 150. © McGill-Queen's University Press.

traded into the lower Great Lakes area for centuries, for example. Likewise, seashells from the east coast of the United States had found their way inland. The filtering of European goods only added to this trade. Second, evidence suggests that economic rivalries had led to extremely destructive wars before the initial contact with Europeans occurred.

When the European goods appeared on the scene, therefore, neither the concept of trade nor that of economic rivalry — including warfare — was strange to the Native population. What was strange and difficult to comprehend was European technological society. Beads and metal initially had associations with magic and were used by Native peoples in a religious rather than utilitarian manner. Such religious overtones meant that, at first, Native peoples would accept in trade almost anything from the Europeans who dabbled in furs along the coasts. As goods filtered inland, traded by the Micmac or other tribes along the coast, they were accepted in the same way.

Sometime about 1580, this pattern began to change. It appears that, after this date, many more European goods penetrated inland. Further, Native traders had by now passed beyond their initial willingness to accept anything and were looking for more practical goods. At the same time, Europeans along the coasts seem to have been doing more and more fur trading. The invasion of European goods into Canada, if not yet of Europeans, was well under way. Indications are that a whole sector of the Native economy now revolved around the acquisition and disposal of European goods. Regular trade routes existed, and tribes jockeyed for a better position to take advantage of this new economic role. Wars and large-scale population movements resulted, and European diseases may have ravaged the Native peoples of the East Coast as early as the late sixteenth century, before European settlement had begun.

On the eve of colonization, therefore, certain key facts stand out about the Native economy. First, although that economy remained primarily dependent on hunting and agriculture, commerce, including commerce in European goods, was an important feature. Second, the impact of European goods had already significantly altered the economies of both the coast and the interior. Anthropologist Bruce Trigger has concluded that, by the end of the sixteenth century, "Tadoussac [at the confluence of the Saguenay and the St. Lawrence rivers] was clearly the most important fur trading centre in North America. It stood at the head of a large number of Native trade routes leading into the interior of North America."[14] Finally, a population shift of considerable importance had taken place sometime during the proto-historic period. When Jacques Cartier sailed up the St. Lawrence in 1535, he found the region occupied by Iroquoian tribes. Between that time and Samuel de Champlain's arrival in 1608, those tribes disappeared from the area. Whether this displacement was the result of the rivalry for European goods or of other events is unknown. It did mean that, when the Europeans came to settle, they had available to them a largely empty stretch of land along the St. Lawrence.

At the beginning of the seventeenth century, the third stage in the expansion of Europe to Canada was about to begin, with the establishment of a permanent settlement at Quebec.

Conclusion

Colonization in North America was preceded by three important events. The first was the development in Europe of a commercial system that could support long-distance trading ventures. The second was the development of the improved technologies necessary to expand to new areas. The third was the decisions by the British and French governments to expend the resources needed to claim, and then retain, colonies in North America, and thereby to provide the support and subsidy that private economic agents required.

With these prerequisites met, the next requirement was some product or products that would make transatlantic commerce worthwhile. The vast supplies of cod ensured that the major nations of Europe remained active in the North Atlantic, even if North America was at first little more than a drydock facility. The fur resources of the interior were less immediately valuable, but served the same purpose. The value of these resources meant that, from the very outset, nations would contend for dominance in the region. Spain and Portugal had yielded to the North Atlantic nations of France and Britain. Now, early in the seventeenth century, these two nations were about to plant themselves in North America. On the North American side, a number of Native peoples, already affected by European goods and attuned to trading possibilities, would see their trade routes, their warfare, and their way of life affected by the arrival of the Europeans.

NOTES

1. Jared Diamond, *Guns, Germs, and Steel: The Fates of Human Societies* (New York: W.W. Norton, 1999).
2. Douglass North, *Institutions, Institutional Change and Economic Performance* (New York: Cambridge University Press, 1990).
3. Leonard Dudley, *The Word and the Sword: How Techniques of Information and Violence Have Shaped Our World* (Cambridge: Basil Blackwell, 1991).
4. Kristoff Glamann, "European Trade 1500–1740," in Carlo M. Cipolla, ed., *The Sixteenth and Seventeenth Centuries: The Fontana Economic History of Europe* (Glasgow: Fontana, 1974), 477.
5. Glamann, "European Trade," 476.
6. J.H. Parry, *The Establishment of European Hegemony, 1415–1715* (New York: Harper and Row, 1961), 18.
7. The best description of the changes in ship technology is in Morison, *The European Discovery of America*, 112–27.
8. S.B. Clough and C.W. Cole, *Economic History of Europe* (Boston: D.C. Heath, 1966), 197.
9. Clough and Cole, *Economic History of Europe*, 215.
10. Glamann, "European Trade," 479.
11. Cited in Davies, *The North Atlantic World*, 22.
12. David Landes, The *Wealth and Poverty of Nations: Why Some Are So Rich and Some So Poor* (New York: W.W. Norton, 1998).
13. Bruce Trigger, *Natives and Newcomers: Canada's "Heroic Age" Reconsidered* (Montreal and Kingston: McGill–Queen's University Press, 1985), 116. Much of the following discussion on the protohistoric period is derived from Trigger's excellent study.
14. Trigger, *Natives and Newcomers*, 141.

FURTHER READING

Davies, K.G. *The North Atlantic World in the Seventeenth Century.* Minneapolis: University of Minnesota Press, 1974.
Dickason, Olive P. *Canada's First Nations: A History of Founding Peoples from Earliest Times.* Toronto: McClelland & Stewart, 1992.
Glamann, Kristoff. "European Trade 1500–1750." In Carlo M. Cipolla, ed., *The Sixteenth and Seventeenth Centuries: The Fontana Economic History of Europe.* Glasgow: Fontana, 1974.
North, D.C., and R.P. Thomas. *The Rise of the Western World: A New Economic History.* Cambridge: Cambridge University Press, 1973.
Trigger, Bruce. *Natives and Newcomers: Canada's "Heroic Age" Reconsidered.* Montreal and Kingston: McGill–Queen's University Press, 1985.

Chapter Two

The Atlantic Colonies

THE CENTRAL THEME in the economic history of Atlantic Canada for the period before 1763 is the evolution of the area from its status as a landmass supporting an international fishery to that of a set of colonies capable of supporting permanent populations. For two centuries after John Cabot's voyage in 1497, only the rich fishing areas along the shores and on the continental shelf were of any economic consequence to the European powers. The landmasses served merely as places to stop temporarily to dry fish and repair boats and fishing gear. The region was still basically a fishery in 1713, when control over most of the area shifted from France to Britain. There were at most a few thousand year-round European residents of Newfoundland at this time, and a slightly larger group of Acadian subsistence farmers scattered along the shores of the Bay of Fundy.

European settlements that can in any real sense be called established did not appear until well into the eighteenth century. Economic and political considerations figure prominently in the establishment of both Newfoundland and the Maritimes, but they do so in quite different ways. In Newfoundland's case, the economics of the fishing industry dictated a transition from a migratory to a residentiary trade, and with this shift came the impetus for the permanent European settlement of the island. Powerful interests in Britain opposed this development and, for a considerable time, were able to influence policy accordingly. Economic reality gradually won out, however, and the mid-eighteenth century marks the transition of the island from fishery to colony.

The same transition in the fisheries occurred in the Maritimes, and here too it contributed to the establishment of permanent European settlement. But more important in explaining the European settlement and economic development of this region were attempts by the British government after 1745 to defend its interests in North America against the French. Soldiers were sent to Nova Scotia, followed by merchants, land developers, and other commercial interests intent on establishing a British presence. Like that of Newfoundland, the European phase of Maritime economic history really does not begin before the mid-eighteenth century. Unlike that of the island, however, European settlement of the Maritimes proceeded because of British imperial policy and not in spite of it.

The Cod Fisheries

The economic history of Atlantic Canada to 1763 is tied inextricably to the cod fishery. Thus it is useful to begin with an overview of resources and techniques and international rivalries in this important sector before moving on to the separate experiences of Newfoundland and the Maritimes.

RESOURCES AND TECHNIQUES

18

Cod breed and survive best in the particular ocean temperatures and currents of the continental shelf and the series of banks that stretches from Cape Cod on the south to Cape Race on the north. The largest of these banks, and certainly the one most familiar to Canadians, is the Grand Banks off the southeast corner of Newfoundland (see Map 2.1). The cod spend the winter months offshore. In the spring, after spawning, they begin to feed. Some of these fish make contact with the caplin that move toward the bays and coastal areas to spawn, and follow them to shore. The dates of arrival of the cod vary, from the first week of June in the areas closest to the banks to mid-July along the Labrador coast. In the fall, the fish return to the deeper waters of the banks to begin the cycle anew.

The habits of the cod supported the development of two distinct and independent fisheries. One practice was to fish for the cod in the open oceans of the continental shelf. This activity was known as the offshore or bank fishery. Fishermen left their European ports in

Map 2.1 Fishing and Fish, Seventeenth-Century Newfoundland

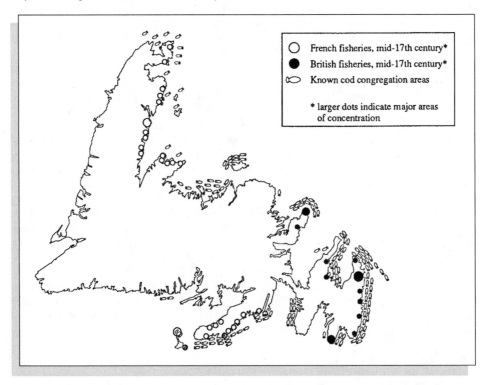

○ French fisheries, mid-17th century*
● British fisheries, mid-17th century*
☾☉ Known cod congregation areas

* larger dots indicate major areas of concentration

Source: Based on Grant Head, *Eighteenth Century Newfoundland* (Toronto: McClelland & Stewart, 1976), pp. 7, 12, and 24. Used with permission of the author.

late January or February. Making the cold Atlantic crossing, they would arrive on the banks in late winter, fish through May, and return home with the catch. With luck and proper management, it was possible to make a second voyage, leaving Europe in May or June and returning with the catch before winter storms made the area too dangerous.

The cod caught offshore were preserved for the long voyage to market by using a technique known as the wet- or green-cure preservation method. The fishing ships would carry huge quantities of salt with them on their voyage from Europe. As the fish were caught, they were gutted, heavily salted, and, after three days, resalted. Thus preserved, they could last long periods of time in reasonable condition. The ship could deliver a load that was, by the standards of the day, reasonably edible and thus find a market in certain parts of Europe.

The other possibility was to fish for cod in its summer habitat along the coastal areas, either directly from the ship or, more commonly, from smaller boats operating from the shore. If salt were available, the catch could be cured in the same manner as for the bank fishery. Alternatively, the fish could be lightly salted and then laid out in the sun to dry. This dry-cure technique, as it became known, required far less salt, which made it attractive to nations such as England where access to cheap salt was a problem. As well, the product offered greater food value than the green-cure method of preservation and thus fetched a better price in European markets. Finally, the end product could be stored almost indefinitely and thus could withstand the long ocean voyages into the hotter climates of southern Europe and the Caribbean.

One difference between the bank and in-shore fisheries was to have important consequences for the subsequent economic history of the Atlantic region. Barring storms or other problems, the bank fishery, with its green-cure preservation technique, functioned independently of land. As a result, it led to little or no exploration or development of the region. In contrast, the in-shore fishery required continuous contact with the land, especially when the fish were preserved using the dry-cure technique. This contact, transient at first, ultimately formed the nucleus of the permanent European settlement that was to develop.

INTERNATIONAL RIVALRIES

John Cabot arrived back in Bristol from Newfoundland in August 1497. Fishermen accompanied him on his return trip the next year, and by 1502 there were reports of loads of Newfoundland cod arriving in England. Obviously, the techniques and technology for the Atlantic trade were already in place. Indeed, there has been speculation that Bristol fishermen may have been aware of the Newfoundland fisheries before Cabot's voyage.[1] True or not, there is no doubt that by the early 1500s the nations of Europe were moving to take advantage of this new resource.

Even though Cabot discovered the fishing grounds on behalf of the king of England, the French and the Portuguese were the first to exploit this new resource extensively. Both nations had plentiful supplies of salt, which facilitated the curing process. In addition, each had a large domestic market for fish due to a large Roman Catholic population and a relatively underdeveloped agricultural sector. The Portuguese fished primarily along the shores of the Avalon Peninsula in Newfoundland. They were a constant presence in the Newfoundland fishery until near the end of the century when, by then part of Spain, they were displaced by the English. Thereafter, the Iberian Peninsula became a major market for the produce of the English and French fishing fleets.

The French fishery was based in western seaports such as La Rochelle, Rouen, St. Malo, Nantes, LeHavre, and other areas of Normandy and Brittany, where a long tradition of Atlantic fishing existed. Their market initially was France, the centre of that market being Paris; as one of the largest cities in Europe, Paris had a tremendous demand for cheap, protein-rich food. By the end of the sixteenth century, the French were also competing for markets in Spain and Portugal.

The French operated from the beginning on the east coast of the Avalon Peninsula alongside the fishing fleets of the other nations, although over time they tended to spread out further to the north, south, and east than did their rivals. Cartier's voyages in the 1530s opened up new areas along the shores of the Gulf of St. Lawrence. They caught the fish in-shore, salted them heavily, and transported them back to Europe. Somewhat later, but certainly by the middle of the sixteenth century, the French were also established in the bank fishery. Their easy access to abundant supplies of salt permitted them to exploit this resource, and domestic taste considerations gave them the incentive to do so.

In the longer term, however, the English were well situated to take advantage of the North American fishery. The West Country fishermen and merchants who dominated the

"A Fishing Station," by Gerard van Edema (c. 1652–c. 1700). The painting shows a harbour in Placentia Bay, Newfoundland, about 1690. Such a station would provide British and French fishermen with a temporary haven where they could dry fish or repair boats and fishing gear. Permanent settlements were not established until the eighteenth century.

North Atlantic trade were closer to the region than were their French and Spanish counterparts. They had the experience and equipment for the Atlantic fishery, as their regular voyages to Icelandic waters showed. Until the latter half of the sixteenth century, however, most British fishermen were content to fish in the vicinity of Iceland rather than face the competitive and often dangerous rivalries in the waters around Newfoundland.

By the latter part of the century, this situation changed. The Royal Navy's presence and power were growing ever stronger, especially with the defeat of the Spanish Armada in 1588. Further, the Danish government began to enforce stricter rules concerning Icelandic waters. Finally, though statistics are far from complete, growing imports into Britain of Newfoundland fish from France may indicate the inadequacy of existing British fishing practices in meeting domestic demand, much less in taking advantage of market opportunities opening up in Spain and Portugal.

Whatever the reasons, by 1600 the fishermen operating out of Dartmouth and other southern and western ports were well established in the Newfoundland fishery. Because they lacked adequate supplies of salt, they had to rely on the dry-cure technique, which meant that they had to have guaranteed access to harbours, shorelines, and timber supplies. The best combination of these necessities by far was found on the Avalon Peninsula, and this is where the English migratory fishery became centred. The dry-cure technique may have been a necessary part of the English presence in the Newfoundland fishery, but, by producing a product that could withstand long voyages to warmer climates, it also gave them access to markets in Spain and Portugal.

The French were pushed out of much of the Avalon Peninsula by this strong English presence. After 1600, they were concentrated along the southern coast of Newfoundland, including the islands of St. Pierre and Miquelon, and along the northeastern coast. Their presence in the south was anchored by a small garrison established at Placentia in 1662. As well, they were represented off the shores of Nova Scotia and in the Gulf of St. Lawrence. This relatively clear division of territory notwithstanding, French–English rivalry in the Atlantic fisheries is a constant theme well into the next century.

Newfoundland

Newfoundland's economic history after 1600 is the story of how this European migratory in-shore fishery ultimately gave way to a residentiary industry, and how, in the process, the island was transformed from a fishery to a colony.

THE MIGRATORY FISHERY OF THE WEST OF ENGLAND

The English migratory fishery was centred in the southwest region of that country, in more than 40 ports located between Bristol and Southampton. The season began each year in January or February, when ship owners sent agents to the surrounding villages, seeking crews for the summer voyages. The next step was to arrange for the necessary provisions, such as naval stores, fishing gear, construction materials, salt, food, and drink. Then, in March through May, supplies and crew were loaded onto ships of all sizes, but generally ranging between 40 and 100 tons (35–90 tonnes), headed for Newfoundland. There was considerable incentive to depart as early in the season as possible because the custom was that the first ship to arrive in a harbour could lay claim to the best fishing rooms, and the captain of that vessel would be the governing authority in that harbour for the season.

Once landed, the crew would set up stations on shore and the fishing ship (actually more of a passenger ship) would be unrigged and moored for the season. Crews of three to five would then go out into the coastal waters early each morning in small fishing boats, returning to shore in the evening. After being unloaded on specially constructed stages (wharves), the fish were gutted, beheaded, and split. Then they were lightly salted and stacked in piles for up to ten days. In a few especially favourable areas, the fish would then be laid out directly on a gravel beach to dry in the sun. More often, however, they were dried on wooden open-frame constructions known as flakes. Once the fish were well dried, they were again put into piles, the salt was sweated out, and the piles covered and left until it was time to load them onto ships bound for market.

The crews fished, as weather permitted, through to September. The cod having largely returned to their winter habitat, and the winter storms approaching, the fishing ships would be brought out of their summer moorings and readied for the return voyage to Europe, laden with the summer's catch. Most often, the ships would travel in convoy back across the Atlantic, although some captains preferred to sail alone to avoid the glut and resulting low prices that inevitably arose when a group of ships arrived in a port simultaneously.

Some of the vessels returned directly to the West Country ports. Here the catch was purchased by other merchants for distribution inland, by outfitters of merchant ships, by representatives of the army and navy, or by foreign buyers. Other ships were involved in a triangular trade pattern. Newfoundland cod went to Spain, Portugal, and Italy, where it was exchanged for specie or salt, wine, and other such produce, which were then brought back to England.

As the number of ships involved in the Newfoundland fishery mounted, a system of finance evolved that would remain more or less constant over the next century. While the details of the arrangements are incredibly complex, the broad outlines can be understood quite easily. Also, they apply, with some minor variations, to both the French and the English fisheries.[2]

The arrangements dealt with two features of the trade: high costs and huge risks. Three types of costs were involved in the migratory fishery: the capital cost of the ship, the cost of the provisions, and remuneration for the ship's master and crew. The risks were many. Ships could be lost in storms, captured by pirates, or seized during one of the many wars of the period. Marine insurance was available at the time, but for various reasons few shipowners purchased it. In Newfoundland, the catch might be poor, or the dry-cure of poor quality. Finally, there was no way of knowing what fish prices might be in the fall, when the catch finally made it to market.

Few individuals could afford to bear these costs or risks alone. Thus a share system developed, whereby profits from the voyage were divided among a number of parties. The first split was a three-way one. Typically, one-third of any profits went to the shipowner; one-third went to the provisioner; and one-third went to the ship's master and crew. Beyond this basic division, any number of further subdivisions was possible. Most often, the ship was owned by several individuals, each of whom likely had small shares in several ships. One-sixth, one-eighth, and one-sixteenth shares were common in both the French and the English fisheries. Less often, the cost of provisioning the ship was shared. Occasionally, one individual was both owner and provisioner, and thus was entitled to two-thirds of any profits.

Often, the ships involved were owned by individuals in London or elsewhere who had nothing directly to do with the fishery. These individuals would charter their ships to merchants either on a lump-sum basis or according to tonnage or the time the ship was out of port. The merchant would then arrange for provisions and crew, and the profits net of charter fees would be shared accordingly.

The one-third share allocated to the master and crew was further divided in any number of ways, according to duties and responsibilities. The master received the largest share, and those in key positions, such as the second mate or carpenter, typically received fixed bonuses. Over time, the share system proved less and less attractive to captains and sailors, and a combination of shares and wages gradually emerged.

In many instances, those who were involved in the voyage did not themselves have the funds to invest. There was thus a secondary aspect to financing, involving the lending of money to those with shares in voyages. Normally, the loan was uninsured, and the lender was entitled to nothing should the ship sink or be captured. The loans were high-risk, and interest rates were commensurate. Those rates varied, depending on the lender, the time, and the ship, but 25 percent rates seem to have been common and figures showing a 40 percent rate have been discovered.

The richness of the Newfoundland fishery soon attracted new forms of participation in the industry. The fishing-ship crews could catch more in a season than their ships could transport to market. Thus, beginning in the early years of the seventeenth century, British merchants, often based in London, began sending vessels (called "sack ships") to Newfoundland to purchase the surplus catch. From Newfoundland they sailed back to England or on to markets in Portugal and Spain, and then back to England. They duplicated the activities of the West Country merchants, in effect, except that they did not fish themselves.

Yet another source of supply was that of the byeboat keepers, who were well established in the Newfoundland fishery by the mid-seventeenth century. Byeboat keepers were merchants who were unable or unwilling to buy shares in the fishing ships operating in Newfoundland. Instead, they would hire workers, known as servants, and transport them as passengers on the fishing ships leaving for Newfoundland each spring. Once in Newfoundland, the servants would fish from shore using boats owned by the byeboat keepers in a similar manner to the crews of the fishing ships. The byeboat keeper sold the catch to the sack ships. In the fall, the servants and the owner would return to England as passengers on the fishing ships, although increasingly over time many either remained on the island or carried on to New England. The fact that the ships from the West Country travelled to Newfoundland in ballast gave the captains an incentive to offer cheap passage to this group of fishermen.

Between 1675 and 1681, as a result of these endeavours, an average of 4033 men arrived in Newfoundland each year on English fishing ships.[3] The largest group was centred in the St. John's area, which each summer received nearly 40 percent of the migrants. The next-largest concentration was in the southern Avalon area, which accounted for another 25 percent, followed by Conception Bay, Trinity Bay, and Bonavista Bay, with between 10 percent and 15 percent each. The number of migrants fluctuated wildly from year to year; the numbers for 1675–1681 marked a period of "extreme contraction." In 1644, for example, an estimated 270 ships with 20 000 men arrived in Newfoundland. All the English sites were centred on the giant schools of cod in the area, as Map 2.1 indicates.

THE BEGINNINGS OF PERMANENT EUROPEAN SETTLEMENT

The English migratory fishery was a seasonal activity. Ships came to Newfoundland in the spring, the crew fished and cured the product during the summer months, and then both ship and crew returned to England in the fall. There was no activity in the fishery during the winter and, given the harsh environment, little else to support year-round occupation of the island.

Yet a permanent European population did ultimately arise out of the migratory fishery. Unlike Jamestown or Quebec, there is no fixed year from which one can date continuous European settlement in Newfoundland; the process was much less formal. Gradually, some of those involved in the migratory fishery remained in Newfoundland over the winter. At first, those staying behind were mostly servants, with instructions to lay claim to the best harbours and fishing stations and to prepare for the next year's activity. There was an added incentive in that boat owners did not have to pay passage back to England for these individuals. Eventually, the boat owners, particularly the byeboat keepers, began to stay over the winter as well.

Not all of the permanent population grew out of the migratory fishery, however. There were attempts to establish colonies in Newfoundland just as there were in other parts of North America. The first proposal was made in 1578, although nothing came of the idea. Sir Humphrey Gilbert claimed the island for England in 1583 but made no real effort to establish settlers there. The first formal colonization effort was at Cupids on Conception Bay in 1610, by John Guy on behalf of the Bristol and London Company. This effort at colonization eventually failed, as did several other attempts in the ensuing decades. In all, there were seven serious colonization efforts between 1610 and 1661, the longest of which lasted fifteen years and the shortest (initiated by a Welsh poet!) only two years. While the formal colonization efforts failed, some remnants of the populations remained, adding to those in the migratory fishery who were wintering over.

The permanent non-Native population grew very slowly in this initial period. By the end of the seventeenth century, 200 years after Cabot's initial voyage, about 1200 individuals might have been considered permanent residents. The summer population at this time was about 8000.[4] Even more revealing of how little permanent settlement had advanced at this time, there were virtually no European women or children in the population. Gordon Handcock reports that the total female population in 1677 consisted of "94 wives, 130 daughters, and 13 women servants, comprising only 12 percent of the inhabitant population, a proportion that was not altered until well into the next century, even as population levels moved upwards."[5]

There has been considerable debate about why the resident population grew so slowly in these first centuries. One long-held view is that the West Country merchants were largely responsible because of their success in influencing imperial policy. Certainly this group opposed settlement, and they wielded considerable political power in the British Parliament. Their opposition to settlement stemmed partly from concern that residents would compete for the best fishing rooms and timber supplies, and partly because they believed, correctly as it turned out, that residents would demand a resident government to replace the rule of the fishing captains.

In fact, however, British imperial policy was split on the issue of permanent settlement. The migratory fishery was viewed as an excellent training ground for the British navy, a fact that argued against allowing a residentiary industry to develop. The main point in favour of allowing settlement was that a permanent population would better establish England's territorial claims in Newfoundland against encroachments by the French. The compromise that Parliament adopted was to allow colonization attempts to proceed on the condition that traditional fishing rights and practices not be interfered with in any way.

As long as this non-interference condition was adhered to, the West Country merchants seem to have paid little attention to the colonization efforts. Only when they perceived that their access was being compromised did they complain to Parliament and seek redress.

After one such confrontation, they succeeded in having a measure passed, the Western Charter of 1634, which reaffirmed the traditional rights and privileges of the migratory fishery. Conflict between residentiary fishermen and West Country merchants grew in the 1660s, in the midst of some very depressed years in the industry. A series of measures aimed at discouraging permanent settlement followed, culminating in an order-in-council in 1675 that ordered all inhabitants of Newfoundland either to return to England or continue on to other British colonies in North America. This injunction was withdrawn two years later, partly because it was unenforceable and partly out of fear of French encroachment.

In 1699, Parliament passed the Newfoundland Act, which, while it reaffirmed the traditional rights of the migratory fishery, did at least recognize and make legitimate the presence of permanent settlement. As Keith Matthews writes, by this act the British government conceded that permanent settlement in Newfoundland was both inevitable and desirable, but it was anxious that the settlement not grow so large as to interfere unduly with the migratory fishery.[6] Problems of local governance continued, however, and finally in 1729 an order-in-council was issued establishing the naval convoy commander as governor and setting up a system of resident magistrates.

If not the actions of the West Country merchants, what does explain the slow growth of permanent European settlement? Increasingly, attention has turned to the island's isolation and the inhospitable conditions on the island. The winters were long and harsh. With little agricultural potential, virtually all food had to be imported. Further, there was limited economic potential beyond the fishery. Thus it is easy to see why those engaged in the fishery opted to return to England in the fall or to carry on to the more hospitable climate and diversified economy of New England.

DEVELOPMENT IN THE EIGHTEENTH CENTURY[7]

The English fishery in Newfoundland remained relatively stable for the half century centring on the year 1700. Average output remained roughly constant, although the year-to-year totals fluctuated wildly. The geographical distribution of the fishery was roughly similar as well. The resident population[8] in 1730 was around 3500, up from about 1200 in the 1670s, was almost entirely made up of people from the southwest of England, and was still overwhelmingly male. There was some shift in the proportion of year-round to summer population. Residents now amounted to about 30 percent of the summer population, compared with less than 15 percent in the 1670s. Like production totals, however, these are averages; annual population totals fluctuated substantially.

Beginning in the 1730s and continuing until the American Revolution, the Newfoundland economy underwent a number of significant changes. Most notably, the fishery expanded significantly after nearly a half century of relative stability. Figure 2.1 shows that total output rose from slightly over 300 000 quintals in 1730 to more than 400 000 quintals in 1750 and to nearly 700 000 quintals by 1770. Part of this increase in output was the result of additional production from existing areas, and part of it was due to an expansion of the inshore fishery to the north, south, and west. Some of the territorial expansion involved taking over fishing areas from the French, who, by the Treaty of Utrecht in 1713, were excluded from all but the shore between Cape Bonavista west to the northern point, and from there south to Point Riche.

Accompanying this expansion in the scale of activity was a slow but steady conversion of the fishery from a migratory to a residentiary activity. Figure 2.1 also shows the proportion of the total catch accounted for by fishing ships, byeboat keepers, and inhabitants

Figure 2.1 British Cod Production, Total and Percentage by Sector, 1710–1830

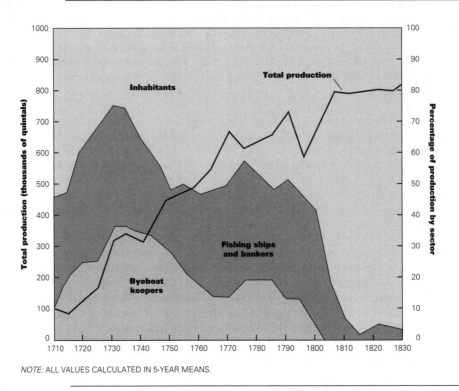

NOTE: ALL VALUES CALCULATED IN 5-YEAR MEANS.

Source: Adapted from W. Gordon Handcock, *Soe longe as there comes noe women: Origins of English Settlement in Newfoundland* (St. John's: Breakwater Books, 1989), p. 76.

for the period 1710–1830. In 1730, residents accounted for slightly more than 20 percent of the total catch. By 1750 this figure had risen to 50 percent, where it remained for another 40 years before rising quickly to over 90 percent. (This later period is discussed in Chapter Four.) The extent of the growth in the residentiary fishery is demonstrated by the fact that the share of output accounted for by the byeboat keepers declined more or less continuously after 1730, even though the number of men engaged in the activity rose from about 2000 in 1730 to a peak of 7000 in 1775.

The fishing ships retained their share of output until 1790, but within these totals there were some interesting changes. The fishing ships were withdrawing from the inshore fishery after nearly more than a century of continuous activity. Increasingly after 1700, they turned their attention instead to the offshore or banks fishery. The English banks fishery was a hybrid operation. The ships would land in Newfoundland as before and lay claim to fishing rooms. Then they would venture out onto the banks for up to several weeks. The catch would be salted on board, and then washed and dry-cured on shore before being shipped to its European markets.

By 1774, Newfoundland's permanent population stood at 12 000, which brought it to about 50 percent of the number of summer residents, compared with 30 percent in 1730.

Much of this new permanent population came from a new source, Ireland. There were very few Irish on the island before 1730, whereas by 1760 they made up nearly half of the wintering population. Initially, they were hired on as crew on the fishing ships or as servants to the byeboat keepers. Of those that stayed, most were labourers, although some were tradespeople and a few even became byeboat operators.

As a result of these developments, the Newfoundland economy was more complex in the 1760s than it had been at the beginning of the century, although by international standards it was still highly specialized. There were three distinct but highly interdependent occupational groups: merchants, boatkeepers, and servants or labourers. Most often, the merchants were individuals who previously had been involved in the migratory fishing ship trade. They established stores in each community, imported provisions of all kinds, and made them available on a credit basis to the boat owners. The boat owners, migratory and resident, employed the labourers and worked the inshore fishery. They paid for their provisions by turning over the catch to the merchant, who would then arrange for its sale abroad. The merchants also often supplied goods on credit to the labourers against their summer wages. These various accounts might be kept in pounds sterling, but very little cash was ever employed. Newfoundland remained largely a barter economy for a very long time.

Until the beginning of the eighteenth century, nearly all the supplies for the migratory fishery and for the residents originated in England. Ireland developed as another source of supply, particularly as the West Country ships began calling at ports in that country on their way to Newfoundland. The more important development, however, was the growing presence of New England traders. Ships from Boston, New York, and Philadelphia would arrive in Newfoundland laden with foodstuffs, lumber, staves, naval stores, rum, and molasses, and exchange them for fish or bills of exchange on England. Generally, they could supply these products more cheaply than could England, so their share of the trade continued to grow. At the time of the American Revolution, Newfoundland was vitally dependent on American supplies.

The defeat of France in the Seven Years' War at midcentury had relatively little impact on Newfoundland. The residentiary fishery prospered during the war, as it had whenever conflicts in Europe interrupted the migratory trade. Article 5 of the Treaty of Paris in 1763 reaffirmed the shore provisions agreed to in 1713, while article 6 granted France control over the islands of St. Pierre and Miquelon. The French remained as competitors in the fishing industry, as they have until this day, but Newfoundland was now indisputably part of the British colonial and mercantile system.

The Maritimes

Besides the fishermen of Newfoundland, the only other permanent European presence in Atlantic Canada in 1713 was that of the Acadians in what is now Nova Scotia and New Brunswick. Descendants of early French attempts to establish a colony at Port Royal in the early seventeenth century, the Acadians had gradually spread northward along the Bay of Fundy, crossing over to the valley of the Petitcodiac by the turn of the eighteenth century. From a handful of households in 1650, population grew to an estimated 5000 in 1713 through immigration from France and through a very high natural rate of increase.

The Acadians were mainly farmers, building dikes to keep the sea from the rich marshland soil. Wheat, rye, peas, and livestock were the principal outputs. Any surplus production went, illicitly, to New England in exchange for British manufactured goods. Fishing and hunting were other economic activities.

The Treaty of Utrecht in 1713 brought a major political change to Nova Scotia, and a minor economic one. France ceded control over most of this area to Britain, but retained Cape Breton and Prince Edward Island (then Île St-Jean) and promptly constructed a large fort at Louisbourg on Cape Breton to defend its remaining interests in North America. The area that is modern-day New Brunswick remained under dispute.

The transfer of Nova Scotia to the British in 1713 had little immediate effect on the region. A dry fishery developed at Canso, by New Englanders at first and then by sack ships from Britain. The port was too close to French territory to grow much, however, and by the 1740s it was in decline. There were a couple of halfhearted attempts to settle western Nova Scotia in order to produce pine masts for the British navy, but they came to nothing. Some settlement came from the south, as New Englanders moved north along the coast of Maine and into the valley of the Kennebeck, but this migration was still quite limited.

The British gained control over the Acadians in 1713. An initial offer was made to move them to areas of French control, but, thereafter, British authorities felt they were less of a security threat, isolated as they were along the Bay of Fundy, and they were largely ignored. Immigration to Acadia from France ceased after 1713, but fertility was sufficiently high that the population increased nonetheless. From around 5000 souls in 1712, the number of Acadians grew to 10 000 by 1750 and to 13 000 by 1755.

Unlike those of Newfoundland, the fortunes of the Maritimes changed markedly with the European wars at midcentury. The reasons were political more than economic. British neglect of Acadia ended in 1745, when the War of the Austrian Succession spilled over to North America. Nova Scotia had to be secured for New England as a barrier against the French. Three thousand settlers were established at the newly founded port of Halifax in 1749 to provide a military and administrative presence, and this figure rose to 5000 the following year. Fifteen hundred German and Swiss settlers were brought to Halifax, settling eventually in Lunenburg in 1753.

With the war, the Acadians scattered along the Bay of Fundy were once again considered a military threat because of their refusal to swear allegiance to the British crown and the supplies they managed to send to the fort at Louisbourg. There was an economic interest in their lands as well. The movement of New Englanders northward after 1713 had generated pressure to expel the Acadian farmers from the rich marshlands. British authorities finally succumbed to the demands, and in 1755 the settlers were forcibly expelled from their lands and scattered among the American colonies, from where many went to Quebec or France.

The immediate impact of the Seven Years' War (1756–63) on Nova Scotia was the influx of some 7000 New Englanders into the region. Some were fishermen who had long worked in the area and were simply moving closer to their sources of supply. Others were farmers, occupying, among other areas, land taken from the Acadians. Still others were merchants and traders, coming very quickly to dominate the economic life of Halifax and the other larger centres. Population was further augmented after 1764, when the Acadians returned to the Chaleur Bay region and as New England settlement continued to move into the region.

Nova Scotia emerged from these political and military realignments with two distinct economies. The garrison town of Halifax looked to the British fleet and to the mercantile and outfitting duties that connection promised. Its view was across the Atlantic and to the

West Indies. It was imperial in perspective, and the powerful merchant fleets of Massachusetts were its main rivals. The outports and farms, however, were largely isolated from imperial economic development. Massachusetts was not so much their rival as it was their metropolis, a primary source of supplies and the home of their families. This position of simultaneously competing with and relying on the more advanced economies to the south remains an important theme of Maritime economic history today.

29

Conclusion

Newfoundland's early economic development is clearly and unambiguously tied up with its staple export. As the late Keith Matthews wrote,

> The fishery first drew men to Newfoundland; the fishery shaped the policies of the nations concerned in it; the fishery both created and limited the way of life of the colonists; and the fishery, through its fluctuating prosperity, its assumed value to Europe and the conflicts it caused, determined when, where, in what numbers, and under what conditions the colonists should settle.[9]

The situation in the Maritimes was quite different. There, war accomplished in a few short years what two centuries of fishing activity had not; it created the basis for permanent European settlement of what are now Canada's Maritime provinces. The contrast with Newfoundland in this respect is striking and provides an early warning of the limits of the more naïve version of the staples theory. Neither the largely subsistent economy of the Acadians nor the garrison economy of Halifax fits neatly into that framework. Political factors, first those stranding the Acadians and then those establishing Nova Scotia as an outpost of the British empire, figure at least as prominently in the early economic history of the region as do the characteristics of the cod fisheries.

NOTES

1. D.B. Quinn, "The Argument for the English Discovery of America Between 1480 and 1494," *Geographical Journal* 112 (1961): 277–85.
2. The best description of financing is found in Gillian T. Cell, *English Enterprise in Newfoundland, 1577–1660* (Toronto: University of Toronto Press, 1969), 6–18. Harold A. Innis, *The Cod Fisheries: The History of an International Economy*, rev. ed. (Toronto: University of Toronto Press, 1954), 18–23, also has useful information on the organization of the French trade. The following paragraphs are taken primarily from these two sources.
3. W. Gordon Handcock, *Soe longe as there comes noe women: Origins of English Settlement in Newfoundland* (St. John's: Breakwater Books, 1989), table 3.1, 56–57.
4. C. Grant Head, *Eighteenth Century Newfoundland: A Geographer's Perspective* (Toronto: McClelland & Stewart, 1976), 82.
5. Handcock, *Soe longe as there comes noe women*, 92.
6. Keith Matthews, *Lectures on the History of Newfoundland, 1500–1830* (St. John's: Breakwater Books, 1988), 96.

7. This section draws on Head, *Eighteenth Century Newfoundland.*
8. The resident population is usually defined to be the total winter population, made up of masters, men-servants, wives of masters, women-servants, and children. Handcock further distinguishes between temporary and permanent population. Using a quote by a naval captain in 1664 to the effect that "soe longe as there comes noe women they are not fixed," he calculates the permanent population as equal to two times the number of females plus the number of children. The temporary population is then the difference between the total winter population and the estimated permanent population. He estimates that the permanent population was about 30 percent of the total winter population in 1713, rising to about 45 percent by 1765. See Handcock, *So long as there comes noe women,* figure 5.1, 97, and accompanying text.
9. Matthews, *Lectures on the History of Newfoundland, 1500–1830,* 10.

FURTHER READING

Buckner, Phillip A., and David Frank, eds. *Atlantic Canada Before Confederation.* The Acadiensis Reader, vol. 1. Fredericton: Acadiensis Press, 1985.

Buckner, Phillip A., and John G. Reid, eds. *The Atlantic Region to Confederation: A History.* Toronto: University of Toronto Press, 1994.

Cell, Gillian T. *English Enterprise in Newfoundland, 1577–1660.* Toronto: University of Toronto Press, 1969.

Handcock, W. Gordon. *So longe as there comes noe women: Origins of English Settlement in Newfoundland.* St. John's: Breakwater Books, 1989.

Head, C. Grant. *Eighteenth Century Newfoundland: A Geographer's Perspective.* Toronto: McClelland & Stewart, 1976.

Innis, Harold A. *The Cod Fisheries: The History of an International Economy.* Rev. ed. Toronto: University of Toronto Press, 1954.

Matthews, Keith. *Lectures on the History of Newfoundland, 1500–1830.* St. John's: Breakwater Books, 1988.

Rowe, Frederick W. *A History of Newfoundland and Labrador.* Toronto: McGraw-Hill Ryerson, 1980.

Chapter Three

New France

NEWFOUNDLAND'S TRANSIENT settlers notwithstanding, Samuel de Champlain's arrival at Quebec in 1608 marked the beginning of permanent and officially recognized European settlement in what would become Canada. It also marked the beginning of the transition of the continent's economy from one based on the Native population's tradition of communal landholding and egalitarian tribal government to one based on private property and the concept of the state. By the time New France fell to the British a century and a half later, the eastern half of the continent would be dominated by Europeans and European economic practices.

Like that of Atlantic Canada, New France's economic development in this period was a product of the interaction between external forces and North American endowments. In this case, the external forces were French colonial policies. That may seem an unremarkable statement, but, as J.F. Bosher noted, there is a tendency among historians to look to New France as "an early chapter in the history of Canada."[1] Taken too far, this tendency leads to an underrating of the interrelationships of the colony with the mother country. New France was a small centre of settlement throughout its existence and, for the first 50 years, was little more than a trading post — a tiny extension of the Old World's commercial and religious interests to the New World. Over time, it evolved a more complex society and economy, but even at the time of the conquest by the British in 1759 the European population was just over 70 000. Specie was scarce, capital accumulation was limited, and the range of production, though much expanded in recent years, still fell far short of that of the English colonies to the south.

Instead, New France was a colony that, throughout its existence, was dependent on the staples trade. This dependence is the second crucial characteristic of the economy. The fur trade, especially the beaver trade, dominated commercial transactions from the colony's beginning to its end. Initially, furs were its only export product. Later, efforts were made to diversify exports and a rising population did allow some economic diversification, with limited exports in foodstuffs and with a growing range of locally produced goods to meet domestic demand. However, furs provided the initial reason for the colony's establishment and dominated its trade.

The Early Fur Trade and New France to 1649

In the long interlude between Jacques Cartier's voyages in the 1530s and Champlain's settlement in 1608, Europeans maintained sporadic contact with the St. Lawrence region.

Fishermen visited the gulf and the mouth of the St. Lawrence regularly. A sporadic trade with coastal Native peoples sprang up, and various European goods worked their way inland in exchange for furs heading eastward. Instability in Europe due to the wars of the Reformation and the absence of sufficient economic incentive in the St. Lawrence region, however, meant that the continued contact did not lead to any efforts at settlement in the area.

The situation was different by the early seventeenth century. The French crown was consolidating its power and, more importantly, transatlantic trade of some significance involving furs now looked possible, a result of changes on both the demand side and the supply side. The economic situation now made settlement seem attractive to influential forces within French government and business circles.

Key to this development was what was happening to the European fur trade. The fur trade was dependent on European fashion. Exotic furs had been used for luxury items of clothing or trim for centuries. The pelt most crucial to the evolution of the North American trade, however, was the beaver. By the sixteenth century, the beaver's inner coat was used in the making of the increasingly popular felt hat. By 1600, not only was the felt hat popular, but changing fashion led to widened brims and thus an increase in the amount of beaver fur required per item produced. Up to this time, the demand for beaver pelts had been met from European, primarily Russian, sources. By the time Champlain set sail, however, those supplies were dwindling due to overtrapping. European fur prices rose in response, inducing merchants to look to alternative sources of supply.

North America was well situated to meet this new demand. The vast lakes and rivers of the continent from the forested eastern woodlands to the far western Pacific slope created an ideal habitat for the beaver and other fur-bearing animals. The next two and one-half centuries of European exploration and expansion in what is now Canada was, to a large extent, dictated by the pursuit of furs. To the merchants of France's western ports the extent of the resource was not known, but the trade prior to 1600 led them to expect that there was much to be gained in converting this casual trade into an ongoing business.

If the trade were to succeed, however, the French needed access to the Native hunters and trappers who could provide the furs. The French had neither the labour nor the skill to bring in the furs themselves. As it turned out, they were fortunate in their timing. Until recently, the St. Lawrence had been occupied by the powerful Iroquois. As Cartier's experiences attest, the presence of such a significant group would have put early French colonization in a precarious position. By 1600, however, the Iroquois tribes of the region had been pushed south of the Great Lakes. The St. Lawrence valley below Montreal was thus largely an empty land. At no time in the history of New France did French settlement seriously encroach upon occupied tribal lands.

In effect, the French inserted their settlement among three main tribal groups. To the north were the Montagnais and Algonquin peoples. They were nomadic and depended on the hunt. They were also excellent trappers and would be important to the French fur trade. To the west were the Huron. When Champlain arrived they were the most powerful group in the region, with a population of nearly 30 000. Champlain's early alliance with the Huron put them in the enviable position of being intermediaries in the fur trade. They were the people who had direct access to French technology, and they had the power to prevent Native peoples farther west from acquiring equivalent access. The Huron passed along French goods (with suitable profit) to interior tribes, while returning furs from those tribes (with suitable profit) to the French.

The power and location of the Huron also had one other very important result. Champlain considered the Huron as the key to a successful trade and, in order to cement the Huron alliance, he, as early as 1609, had taken part in a raid on an Iroquois village. Thus, from the beginning, New France not only depended upon the Huron but became the enemy of the Iroquois. Moreover, the long-standing intertribal warfare increased in intensity with the arrival of European settlement. The Iroquois had good reason to wish to deny their Huron enemies access to the French. These reasons were reinforced when, in 1613, the Dutch established a colony at the mouth of the Hudson River (present-day New York) and, soon after, a trading post upriver, at Albany. The Iroquois assumed the same role for the Dutch fur trade as that of the Huron in trade with the French. Both groups wished to displace their rivals and to gain a monopoly of access to European goods. For the next 30 years, the Huron and Iroquois battled for supremacy in the region.

With these developments, a staples (or commodities) trade was born, one that would be of considerable importance throughout the history of New France and beyond. Indeed, the staple (fur) was such a powerful force that its characteristics, together with French colonial policy, did much to shape colonial development in early Canada.

The first characteristic of the industry was that both demand and supply were unpredictable and highly volatile. The amount supplied in any period depended on the needs and fortunes of many individual traders and tribes, on access through middlemen, on the weather, and on many other variables. Demand was equally difficult to predict, depending as it did on the vagaries of fashion. Tastes changed, brims widened and narrowed. Good times in Europe increased the demand for hats, while bad times decreased it. In the short run, at least, both demand and supply were relatively unresponsive to changes in price. Thus, unless regulated in some manner, these shifts in demand and supply meant wild swings in fur prices.

For these reasons, there was an understandable tendency on the part of European merchants, in New France as later in the Canadian West, to try to gain some control over the fur trade. One technique was to try to gain the exclusive right to trade with the Native peoples. Such a position would allow merchants to control the number of North American furs reaching European markets each year, and, at the same time, to prevent the Native hunters and trappers from using competition among traders to drive up the price of furs relative to that of trade goods. But the fur trade was not an easy industry to control in this manner. Anyone with a knowledge of the country and the ability to handle a canoe could attempt trapping or trading furs. Thus, other means of control had to be found.

Control over transportation of the furs to Europe was one technique. So too were control over the supplies coming in as trade goods from Europe and understandings with the tribes that supplied the furs. Whatever the technique, merchants in this mercantilist age could look to governments for assistance. Thus, from the beginning of settlement, officials in both France and New France either sanctioned private attempts to control the fur trade or, when these failed, used the powers of the state directly. Meanwhile, there were subjects of New France and other countries who had reasons to subvert monopoly control.

The second characteristic of the fur trade was its tendency to expand over a large geographical area. Local supplies of furs were quickly exhausted, and new areas had to be found. The trade moved inland rapidly. Because furs can be characterized as "high value, low bulk"; that is, a relatively small quantity of furs is worth a great deal, transport costs were a relatively low factor in the overall cost of doing business. Even the interminable travel time over vast distances involved in regular seventeenth-century crossings between Quebec and France were considered worthwhile. Within North America, this meant that such practical local forms of transportation as the birchbark canoe, used by and adopted from the Native peoples, were efficient means of carrying on the trade.

34

Of course, the farther afield one went, the greater the costs, through the participation of ever more middlemen and increased transport costs. In principle, then, there was at any time an identifiable feasible area of exploitation whose extent depended on the costs of transporting the product from the interior to Europe and on the price of furs relative to that of trade goods. In reality, of course, the situation was not that simple. Neither European nor Native traders operated as if they were conscious of where the feasible margin lay. Still, the pursuit of profit meant a historical tendency toward continual expansion seeking new areas of supply. Thus the fur trade was instrumental in encouraging the European exploration of large parts of North America.

This characteristic helps explain the evolution of the territory of New France. W.J. Eccles has accurately noted that New France possessed a frontier configuration that was unique and differed radically from the one in British settlement colonies to the south.[2] For the British, the line of agricultural settlement and the colony's boundaries were more or less the same; however, such was not the case for New France. Instead, New France evolved as what has been termed a "river empire," with long tentacles of economic, political, and military influence stretching thousands of miles beyond the area of settlement. As Map 3.1 indicates, even by 1750 the settled portion of New France was confined to a stretch of land running from just below Quebec City to Montreal. The population was a mere 50 000. Yet, this same colony's influence extended through the Great Lakes to the Prairie west, southward into the Mississippi and Ohio river basins, and all the way to the Gulf of Mexico.

This unusual expansion was made possible by the river systems. Champlain had established his settlement on the waterway that provided the best access into the interior of the continent. The St. Lawrence–Great Lakes system provided a natural transportation route, extending thousands of miles west, northwest, and, with relatively short portages, south as well. In contrast, access was much more restricted for the English colonies to the south. Only New York's Hudson–Mohawk system provided anything like the easy transportation the French enjoyed. It was indicative of the future of New France that, within a few years of their arrival, the French routinely travelled more than 500 km inland from Quebec, visiting their allies, the powerful Huron, located between Georgian Bay and Lake Simcoe.

The importance of the Native peoples to the economic structure of New France cannot be overemphasized. In the first half-century after the Europeans landed, the French colony was, in many ways, an insignificant thing. Fifteen years after Champlain established his settlement, there were still fewer than 70 settlers in New France. There was no agriculture other than a few plots to feed the garrison, and there were practically no families. It was, in the words of W.J. Eccles, not really a settlement at all, but a mere "commercial outpost" to facilitate the gathering of furs. The fur trade was, in effect, an international trade. The French empire extended as far as Quebec, where it dealt with the independent Native groups. Only because the Native hunters and trappers supplied the skill and labour to exploit the beaver trade was there any trade at all.

State policy also helps explain the slow growth of New France in the early years. The king of France may have wanted a flourishing settlement in North America, but, as was the case with other governments, he was loath to commit his nation to large expenditures for risky overseas ventures. As a substitute, therefore, the state turned over the responsibility for settlement to private companies. The idea was that the state could limit the drain on its revenues if it gave special trading privileges in the New World to some company. In return, the company would underwrite and manage the costs of exploration and subsequent settlement. This was the technique under which Champlain had settled Quebec and, indeed, though the companies would change, it was the technique used to underwrite the

Map 3.1 New France as a "River Empire," c. 1750

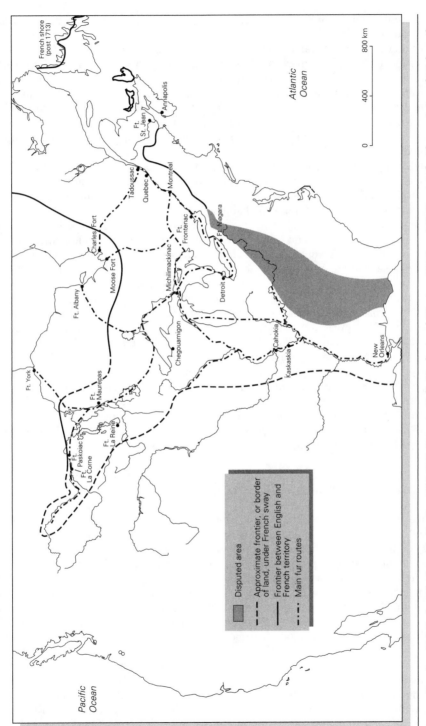

Source: Based on W.J. Eccles, *The Canadian Frontier, 1534–1760* (Toronto: Holt, Rinehart and Winston, 1969), p. 169. Reprinted with permission of Wadsworth, an imprint of the Wadsworth Group, a division of Thomson Learning. Fax 800-730-2215

Quebec venture until 1663. New France was, then, legally as well as figuratively, a commercial outpost.

This status created several problems. The monopoly companies that were formed on the basis of royal charters, as one recent business history has noted,[3] were far from perfect structures for the task at hand. Old systems of court favouritism, invited participation, and short-term loyalties proved inadequate to the task at hand. The establishment of the colony was a very expensive form of business endeavour, after all, and the right to the fur trade carried with it the obligation of settlement and missionary work. Not surprisingly, the history of early New France includes repeated corporate collapse and inability to support the needs of colonization.

The second and related problem was that company and crown interests did not always coincide. Critics argued that the companies allowed settlement to languish while they pursued profits. Defenders of the companies pointed to arbitrary court interventions, uncertain jurisdictional lines, and frequent changes of government policy. The fact was that the sustenance and growth of an agricultural colony in a relatively harsh climatic environment such as that of the St. Lawrence required significant, continuous subsidies. Such subsidies were more than most companies could afford. Company monopoly was certainly not the optimum means to promote settlement, but its use was a symptom rather than a cause of the lack of growth.

The real problem was that there was no economic reason for the colony to grow beyond a rather minimal size in the absence of massive subsidization. The fur trade did not require a large French population. The small population, together with the arduous task of clearing the lands, the repeated clashes with the Iroquois, and the unlikelihood that any crop grown in New France could find an export market, prohibited much agricultural development. As late as 1660, the European population of all of New France was only about 3000 people. The three communities of Quebec City, Trois-Rivieres, and Montreal were little more than villages. Most of the land along the St. Lawrence remained wilderness, and only around Quebec was there sufficient cultivation for it to be called an agricultural community. As Marcel Trudel has so aptly put it, "There was the constant feeling that at any moment everyone might pack up and go back to France."[4]

A Period of Transition, 1649–1670

Quebec was, however, on the eve of momentous change. Two major developments brought about these changes and would finally allow the colony to be established on a firm footing. The economy would, in the process, become more complex. Furs would remain important, but a growing population would create meaningful agricultural settlement and even more ambitious schemes for growth.

One major change came from a shift in the balance of power among the Native groups, causing the French to take an increasingly active role in the fur trade. For some decades, individuals (known as *coureurs de bois*) had ventured out into the wilderness to explore, to establish contacts with more distant tribes, and, as entrepreneurs, to undertake a little trade and transport of furs themselves. The governments of the day had often condemned these independents. Still, the practice continued and even flourished, as the same river networks that had made the colony dominant in the fur trade allowed people easy access to the interior, though the bulk of furs continued to be supplied by the Native peoples.

In 1649, the Iroquois launched a successful assault on the Huron nation, dispersing its people and thereby ending the Huron dominance of the fur trade. They then turned on the French and the Ottawa, who threatened to replace the Huron. Although the Iroquois ultimately failed to gain a dominant position themselves, they did cause chaos in the transportation system over the next 15 years. In the process, the middleman role of the Native peoples was considerably weakened. The Ottawa, Algonquin, and Montagnais tribes would all have liked to assume the role taken by the Huron — as, for that matter, would the Iroquois — but none was able to. Instead, the French took over the role. Over the next 30 years, there was a tremendous expansion of French presence and influence.

The second major change occurred in 1663, when the French government finally abandoned the concept of the company monopoly and made New France a royal colony. The government of the colony became, in theory at least, like that of any other French province, responsible, in this case, to the Ministry of Marine. Decision making was increasingly centralized (though distance always imposed limits), and the French government took a much more serious interest in the colony. The immediate result was an infusion of military support (the Carignan–Salières Regiment) to suppress the Iroquois threat, increased financial aid, and energetic though relatively short-term support for immigration. Members of the Carignan–Salières Regiment were encouraged to settle, and some 400 did. Immigrants were subsidized to come across, and groups of artisans and women (known as *filles du roi*) were given additional incentives. Within a decade, the population increased from 2600 to 7000. For the first time, the population was large enough that the colony was stable, and activities other than the fur trade began to take on importance.

The newly established royal colony of New France was put under the energetic direction of Jean Colbert. For Colbert, and for the king he served, two key principles guided the formation of policy. The first was theological: for reasons that had much to do with recent French history, Louis XIV wanted to ensure that the powerful and influential religious presence in New France was kept under control. Second, and most relevant to New France's economy, Colbert and the king wanted to integrate New France more closely into the overall economy of the French empire. This integration was to proceed along the lines of the favoured French economic policy of mercantilism.

The challenge for Colbert was to use mercantile policy to develop New France (and the lucrative West Indies) by encouraging more fruitful trade within the empire. The New World should be more of a buttress to the Old World and, along the way, the New World's economy would become more developed. The fur trade would continue, of course, but it should be joined and strengthened by other activities. It was with these principles in mind that Colbert created a new official for New France, the intendant. The intendant was Colbert's personal representative in the colony and the individual in charge of economic development.

What Colbert and his initial appointee to this new post, Jean Talon, wanted to do was reasonably straightforward. First, they wanted to diversify the economy. Far too many basic supplies had to be brought over from France. The colony could not even feed itself, much less provide surpluses that might help meet imperial needs elsewhere. All too often, ships returning from New France did so in ballast because there were no cargoes for export. All too often, as well, those same ships had been in New France, supplying grains or artisanal products that, seemingly, the colony itself should have been able to produce.

The model to emulate existed to the south. Rapidly growing English colonies such as Massachusetts (under the Massachusetts Bay Company, founded in 1629) had established a successful series of trade connections both with the home country and with the British West Indies. The British system seemed to Colbert an ideal to which the French colonial system could aspire. New France, while exporting furs to France, might send wheat, fish, or timber to the West Indies. Sugar from the West Indies could go either to France or to New France. Of course, France would continue to export manufactured and luxury goods

A shipyard in New France. The first appointee to the post of intendant of New France, Jean Talon (shown on the left in this romanticized picture), embarked on a number of ventures intended to diversify the economy of the colony. One was the foundation of the first Canadian shipyard.

Confederation Life Gallery of Canadian History.

to the colonies, but colonial prosperity and a larger colonial population would considerably increase the French market there. All of this trade would also, in good mercantilist fashion, be restricted to French shipping and thereby encourage the growth of the French merchant marine.

In an effort to achieve the development of these potential export industries, the French crown, through Colbert and Talon, put considerable effort and funds into various schemes.[5] It has been estimated that, in its first years, the considerable annual sum of 200 000 livres was invested in the colony.[6] None of the ventures was very successful. Although agriculture did develop to a degree, an export market for foodstuffs was not achieved until much later. The fisheries remained marginal and could never really compete in outside markets with the French fleets in the Atlantic fishery. Colonial shipbuilding and ancillary activities such as rope and sail production were never able to compete with production in France itself.

By the early 1670s, the enthusiasm of the French crown for its North American colony had waned. The problems had proved more intractable than expected, and the costs higher. Yet, there is a danger of dwelling too much on the failure of shipbuilding or other industries. Most important to the colony of New France was the influx of military support, capital, and civilian population that occurred in these years. Though the real impetus lasted only a decade, it allowed the colony to become something more than a fur-trade outpost, though it was always in the shadow of that export-oriented trade. The fur trade itself was on the verge of tremendous expansion and, with it, the frontiers of New France. Neither of these developments would have been possible without the strengthened economic and population base.

Agricultural Expansion, 1663–1713

What distinguished the post-1663 colony was the emergence of landholding and farming as increasingly important activities. More and more people moved out onto the land, especially after the Iroquois threat was lessened. Thus, the system of landholding and its implications, largely irrelevant up to that point, began to take on added significance.

As was the case in most colonies, the system of land title was derived from the home country. For New France, this meant that the seigneurial system, based upon the Custom of Paris, was the standard from the time that agricultural land-granting began.[7] It was a feudally based system in which the crown granted land to certain nobles or seigneurs who, in return, swore allegiance to the crown. The seigneurs then allotted portions of their land to those who farmed it, known as censitaires or, as became common in New France, habitants. In contrast to practice under the British freehold system, the censitaire did not own the land outright but had it as part of a feudal relationship in which he owed allegiance and certain duties to the seigneur, just as the seigneur owed certain responsibilities to the censitaires.

In New France, the landholding system of the seigneury also took on special characteristics. The first of these was the result of geography. The St. Lawrence River was the natural (and, for decades, the only) highway in the colony. Access to the river was thus crucial, and the design of landholdings reflected that. In order to maximize the number of individuals with this important access to the river, the allocations to censitaires tended to be narrow but deep (see Figure 3.1). Eventually, as the population grew and the seigneury filled up, a second row would be settled. In the early years of the royal colony, however, this scheme was largely hypothetical, as most seigneuries had yet to open even a significant portion of their prime waterfront lands. Many had no cleared land at all.

The river gave the landholding patterns of New France yet another characteristic. As the population settled along the riverbank, there developed a long, thin ribbon of population that stretched intermittently along the St. Lawrence. There were no villages in any traditional sense, in that there were no real dividing points that distinguished the "centre" of a community from its periphery or from the countryside. Only the forest at the back of a settlement gave it definition. Thus, the importation of a European system of landholding led, under different geographical circumstances, to a radically modified dispersion of population and activities.

The slow growth in population meant that the seigneurial system only gradually overlay the forested lands. The number of seigneuries granted by 1663 was relatively small, and large gaps existed between them. Even these gaps, however, seriously understate the amount of wilderness that still existed in the St. Lawrence valley. As late as 1700, after considerable additional population growth, one estimate concludes that perhaps only 5 percent of seigneurial land was actually cleared. Only well into the eighteenth century is it possible, therefore, to talk of the St. Lawrence valley as a settled agricultural community.

A more realistic idea of the progress of agricultural development is given by Map 3.2, which shows the distribution of people along the St. Lawrence valley some 30 years after the establishment of the royal colony. Even then, as can be seen, wilderness dominated much of the St. Lawrence valley. The only really extensive continuous settlements occurred near Quebec City (downriver for approximately 30 km, and on the Île d'Orléans) and near Montreal (primarily on the south shore). Huge stretches, especially on the south shore, remained unsettled.

This slow growth, even after the establishment of a royal colony, says much about the difficulties that faced would-be seigneurs and censitaires. The St. Lawrence valley was

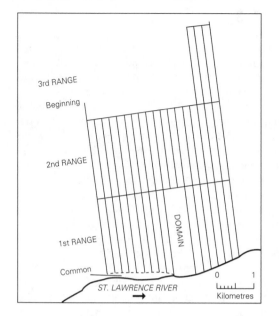

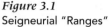

Figure 3.1
Seigneurial "Ranges"

Source: Adapted from R. Cole Harris, *The Seigneurial System in Early Canada: A Geographical Study*, 2nd ed. (Montreal and Kingston: McGill–Queen's University Press, 1984), p. 175.

heavily treed and, in this preindustrial age, the process of clearing the land was extremely time-consuming and expensive. The costs and the time involved depended, of course, on the availability of labour and on the nature of the forest the settler faced. One estimate, however, concludes that, on average, a farmer could clear only about two arpents (two-thirds of a hectare) a year! It was, thus, several years before a farmer could clear sufficient land to feed a family, much less provide any sort of potential cash surplus.

Also, given the agricultural techniques and crops of the era, the St. Lawrence valley was a far from ideal agricultural region. Its growing season was shorter than France's, the soil was relatively sandy, and the lowland character of much of the region made drainage a problem. Along much of the north shore, the rocky surface of the Laurentian Shield reached almost to the river. "All in all," as Cole Harris concluded, "the soil sources of early Canada were scanty."[8]

One of the questions that has been discussed by historians is whether the seigneurial system itself retarded settlement. The system was encumbered by certain economic obligations for both parties. The seigneur was expected to provide a grist mill and a modicum of protection, in addition to other administrative responsibilities. The censitaire, or habitant, had to pay rent to the seigneur (*cens et rentes*), undertake labour for a fixed number of days on the roads or bridges in the seigneury (the *corvée*), grind his grain at the seigneur's mill (the *banalités*), and pay a fee to the seigneur upon the sale of his property (*lods et ventes*).[9]

The impact of these encumbrances should not be overstated. Estimates of the burden to the farmer indicate that the seigneurial system "never represented an overwhelming proportion of the economic surplus produced by the average farm family."[10] There were good reasons for this situation, for though New France was a hierarchical society, it was much less so than France itself. The availability of cheap land and the seigneur's desperate need to attract people to that land contrasted sharply with the situation in the home

Map 3.2 Canadian Settlement, 1692 and at the End of the French Regime

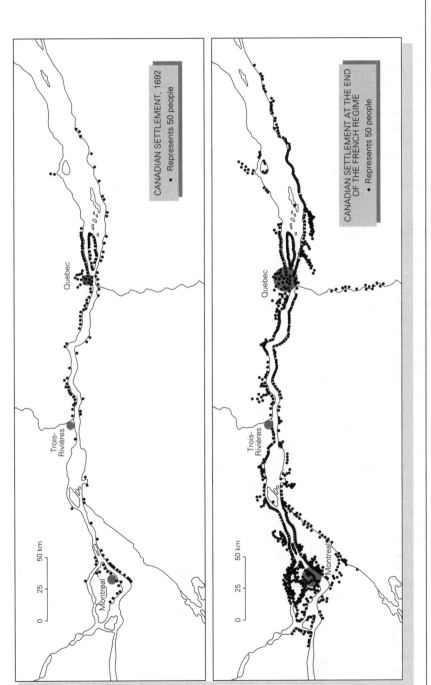
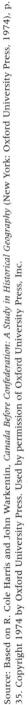

Source: Based on R. Cole Harris and John Warkentin, *Canada Before Confederation: A Study in Historical Geography* (New York: Oxford University Press, 1974), p. 35. Copyright 1974 by Oxford University Press. Used by permission of Oxford University Press, Inc.

country. The net effect was a levelling of incomes and social status relative to those in France. As visitors to New France repeatedly noted, seigneurs were poorer and had less power than did their counterparts in France, while the habitants had more relative wealth and a greater ability to influence events. New France in the seventeenth century provides a classic example of what can happen to social and economic structures when the relative values of various commodities — in this case, land and labour — change.

Overall, the years after the establishment of royal government did bring serious agricultural settlement to New France. It is useful to remember that for most subjects farming, not furs, provided the basic means of earning a livelihood. The influx of population and capital also allowed a degree of diversification and urban development. Neither Montreal nor Quebec City was exactly a rival to Paris. As late as 1744, Quebec City's population was only 4600, and that of Montreal (founded in 1642) only about 3500. Trois-Rivières, the other "urban" community, had reached only 400. Still, the colony of New France was now firmly established as more than a commercial outpost. The Native population would no longer be able to challenge the French for control of the St. Lawrence valley.

The Expansion of the Fur Trade, 1663–1713

In spite of this agricultural expansion and the other developments, the fur trade remained, throughout these years, the central economic activity of the colony, so far as the international trading system was concerned. Animal pelts in one form or another accounted for more than 90 percent of the exports of New France well into the eighteenth century.[11] For all the plans of Talon and Colbert, furs remained the one really valuable resource in which New France (and the Native lands around it) had a distinct economic advantage. Thus, the establishment of a royal colony, though it brought diversification, also saw a tremendous expansion of the fur trade.

The 1670s and 1680s saw the most dramatic territorial expansion of the fur trade that was to take place in the history of New France. In 1673, Frontenac established Fort Frontenac on the site of present-day Kingston, while René-Robert Cavelier de La Salle explored southward, reaching the mouth of the Mississippi within a few years. Exploration was followed or accompanied by new alliances, the opening of new fur regions, and a tremendous inflow of furs to the warehouses in New France, greatly increasing the personal gain of La Salle and Frontenac. There was also expansion to the northwest, albeit on a less dramatic scale, as coureurs de bois made new contacts and broadened their trade areas to the west of Lake Superior. By the 1680s, the French "river empire" had expanded over thousands of square kilometres and extended over much of the eastern half of the continent.

This expansion had several effects. First, it altered the nature of the fur trade. Initially, the role of trader and transporter had belonged either to the Native peoples or to the highly independent coureurs de bois. As the trade expanded westward, however, the journeys grew longer and the time between the purchase of trade goods and the ultimate return on that investment increased. In this way, credit became increasingly important. Those larger-scale merchants with access to both began to dominate the trade. There was still a place for the habitant who wished to make a living in the trade, but it was more often as a hired paddler and agent, a voyageur, than as an independent small businessman.

The second effect of expansion was oversupply. W.J. Eccles estimated that, between 1675 and 1685, given the prices that existed, "twice as much beaver was shipped to France as the French market could absorb."[12] In those years, exports of furs doubled. By the late

1690s, they had doubled again. Inevitably, the price declined. Instead of fewer furs coming in in response, however, there were more. This result could be explained in part by the effort of traders to maintain income by increasing quantity and in part by government decisions to maintain a relatively high price for furs. It also reflects, however, a particular response of some Native groups. Many of them were nomadic, and the accumulation of goods presented real difficulties. Extra pots or pans could be burdensome during the journeys from place to place. There was, in other words, a fixed number of goods desired by many Native traders. The higher the price for their furs relative to that for trade goods, the fewer furs would be necessary to supply their wants. In times of lower prices for furs, however, more would be needed and more would be supplied.[13]

For whatever reasons, the decline in prices was accompanied by an increase in the number of furs. From an average annual output, between 1675 and 1685, of some 40 000 kg, production rose to an amazing peak of 135 000 kg by the end of the century. The glut continued to grow so that, by the late 1690s, there was some ten years' worth of beaver pelts stocked in warehouses. The situation was so desperate that the French government ordered the West closed to the fur trade and the majority of posts abandoned. The trade would, henceforth, occur only when Native traders brought pelts to the French along the St. Lawrence or at Fort Frontenac. Even that did not resolve the problem, however; over the next few years, there were several reorganizations of the fur-trading monopoly, new restrictions on the trade, several bankruptcies, and considerable overall economic hardship for the colony. By 1705, one report indicated that every pelt brought to France was being sold at a loss.[14] Not until 1714 did the restrictions finally have the desired effect of eradicating the surplus inventory of pelts.

The third consequence of the expansion of the trade was to intensify old rivalries. Neither the English nor the Iroquois were willing to stand by and watch the French expansion. The Iroquois faced the danger of being outflanked by the French in the fur trade and thus having their source of supplies for trade to the English cut off. By 1680, the Iroquois launched attacks on the Illinois tribes to the west. Over the next several years, they expanded their attacks on the Native allies of the French. By 1689, the French themselves were coming under attack. In August of that year, the Iroquois virtually destroyed the village of Lachine, burning it to the ground and taking numerous prisoners. Not until 1700 was any sort of longer-term peace achieved between the Iroquois, on the one hand, and the French and their Native allies, on the other.

For the English colonies, the French presence in the interior meant two things. First, like the Iroquois, English fur-trade merchants were concerned about future sources of supply. If ever-more tribes were connected to the French alliance system, it became doubtful whether the English would be able to maintain adequate supplies for themselves. Such concerns, however, affected only a small number of English colonists, largely in New York.

Second, and more important was what French expansion seemed to imply in terms of geographical control. The dominance of the French in the interior seemed to threaten the future expansion of British colonies. As of the late seventeenth century, the need to settle the trans-Appalachian west was not a pressing matter, but the giant crescent of French influence that now surrounded the English colonies seemed a very real threat. Map 3.1, though depicting a somewhat later state, indicates the pattern that was developing.

The French also had cause to fear the English. The primary reason was the establishment, in 1670, of the Company of Adventurers Trading into Hudson's Bay (the Hudson's Bay Company). The French began to fear a pincer movement by the English. This English presence was especially important for the fur trade, as posts on the bay could draw Native traders northward and thus divert furs from the French system. The New York traders were already enough of a threat in this regard, and it was with some concern, therefore, that the French watched this English attempt to gain access to the Native groups that, so far, had been mostly removed from English competition. Over the next 40 years, French and English would try combinations of competition, diplomacy, and armed assault to gain control of the bay.

Ultimately, the French lost. In 1713, the Treaty of Utrecht recognized English claims over Hudson Bay. This was a case of military victory following economic victory. The English were successful in developing an integrated system between the bay posts and the British metropolitan fur market. The French, however, seemed to view their activities around the bay merely as counters to the English and as a buffer for more important trade activities occurring elsewhere. Their system in the bay area was never fully integrated and never very efficient.

The conflict over the bay was only part of the growing clash in North America between the two great imperial powers. By 1690, the French were convinced that the English were actively supporting the Iroquois in their ways. In response, New France raided a series of smaller English settlements in the northern English colonies. The English colonists, predictably, retaliated. This marked the beginning of an on-again, off-again war for dominance in North America. In fact, the next 80 years would see almost as many years of war (1690–97, 1701–13, 1744–48, 1755–63) as years of peace. Before this period was over, the conflicts between the colonies began to take on a life of their own, overshadowing and eventually precipitating conflict between the parent countries.

The details of the conflicts are beyond the scope of this study. As a general proposition, however, it is worth noting that the continual wars had a significant effect on the economy of New France. Indeed, many historians have argued that the warfare was as important as the fur trade in shaping both the society and the economy of the colony. The payroll for troops (regular or militia), the policies of the French government, the alliances with the Native tribes, and a host of other factors that emerged from war affected the economy.

Overall, the effect of war on the economy of New France was negative, despite the addition of the military payroll. To the extext that it was oriented toward war, the French government did not put its resources into peaceful economic development. The war also exacerbated the colony's fiscal and monetary problems. Each year, governments were spending far more than their income, and each year, as well, the insufficiency of the bullion supply became more and more apparent. The result was a series of expedients. The most famous of these was "card money," so called because it involved the issue of playing cards, stamped and signed by government officials as paper money. First used in the late seventeenth century, this method became an increasingly common way of dealing with lack of specie through the simple expedient of creating an alternative medium of exchange. Throughout the rest of the war, New France thus limped along with a barely solvent government, depressed trade, and a monetary system that was flimsy at best.

Yet, the colony was important to France and becoming ever more so. It was increasingly being seen as an integral part of imperial strategy. France's overall desire for hegemony in Europe was to have effects on its small colony across the Atlantic. In particular, the French government had abandoned Colbert's idea of consolidation of the colony and had more or less accepted the more grandiose visions of officials in New France. In a dispatch of 1701, Louis XIV favoured using the extension and consolidation of the French river empire as a means of hemming in the growing British colonies to the south. This vision gave the colony a purpose beyond the fur trade and gave the French government reason to put increased effort (when it could afford to) into the strengthening of New France. It also reversed priorities along the frontier. As W.J. Eccles noted, a colony that previously had rested on the economic cornerstone of the fur trade now found the fur trade often used as an instrument of imperial strategy.[15] The logic was simple. Alliances with western tribes became valuable as part of the consolidation of the frontier against English expansion. Good prices for furs would help cement those alliances.

The logic was simple, but several things made success difficult. Foremost was the fact that the British traders out of New York were able to provide a more attractive range of goods and to do so more cheaply. Only the barrier of the Iroquois had prevented the western tribes from turning to the English with increasing frequency. This points to the second problem: by 1700, the Iroquois were considerably weakened. The long war with the French and their allies had taken its toll. They were unlikely to act as a barrier much longer and, indeed, they made various moves in the first years of the eighteenth century indicating that they might be willing to facilitate rather than hamper the trade between the English and other Native groups. This the French could not allow, for reasons of state. In response, therefore, the government began to offer increasingly valuable gifts and to subsidize the price of furs with key allied tribes. The vast frontier to the west, opened for the sake of the trade, had now become an end in itself, and the fur trade, though still very much profit-oriented in general, was now a subject of state policy.

Growth, Diversification, and Conflict, 1713–1750

In 1713, the War of the Spanish Succession came to an end. France lost Acadia and its claim on the Hudson Bay regions. The future of the French empire in North America had suffered a severe blow. Yet, New France itself was, after a long period of stagnation, about to enter an era of unprecedented growth and prosperity. The best estimates indicate that the gross domestic product of New France more than doubled in the two decades after the Treaty of Utrecht.[16]

There are several reasons for the growth. The first was the extended period of peace, lasting some 30 years. With peace, shipping increased, financial circumstances stabilized (though not immediately), and attention could be turned from war to development. Second, rising demand for beaver in European markets coincided with the end of the war. The revival of the fur trade, as might be expected, created a new optimism among both the average citizens and the merchants who hired them. Increases in the value of the fur exports improved trade balances and brought more consumption goods into the colony.

Some of the forces encouraging prosperity had little to do with New France. Most importantly, Europe was emerging from a long period of economic stagnation. In what Miquelon called the "metamorphosis of the seventeenth century into the eighteenth,"[17] inflows of gold and silver, in the generation after 1680, eased the monetary shortage and trade revived. For its part, France, after running large deficits in the war and after a postwar financial and speculative scandal, put its own financial house in order. Together, these changes yielded impressive results. From the depressed years immediately after the Treaty of Utrecht through to the early 1740s, French trade with its colonies increased sevenfold.

The bulk of that increase was not with New France but with the West Indies. Nevertheless, there were events in the North Atlantic that benefited New France. Foremost of these was that, in response to the loss of Acadia, the French government constructed the fortress town of Louisbourg on what is now Cape Breton Island. The town reached a population of more than 2000 by the 1730s. This might not seem to be a significant addition to the economy of the region until one remembers that at this time Quebec City had a population of only about 5000 — after one and a third centuries of settlement. Louisbourg provided a significant new market for the agricultural and forest products of New France. In addition, the growing market in the West Indies meant that shipments of grains, fish, timber, and other products did begin to go, though less regularly, from New France to the West Indies. New France finally achieved a diversified, if still limited, export market (see Table 3.1).

Table 3.1 Exports from Quebec, 1736

	France	Île Royale	West Indies
Total value (livres)	954 000	123 900	97 400
Percentage of total trade	81%	11%	8%
Fish and other	6%	—	19%
Victuals	—	99%	71%
Furs	32%	—	—
Beaver	43%	—	—
Hides	19%	—	—
Timber	—	—	10%

Source: Derived from R. Cole Harris, ed., *Historical Atlas of Canada*, vol. 1 (Toronto: University of Toronto Press, 1987), plate 48.

This export trade was reflected in the domestic growth of the colony's economy. The fur trade was and would remain the primary activity of the colony, but the revival of trade and the demand for local products encouraged new land settlement, new immigration, and new ventures. In part, this diversification was brought about by local population growth. By the 1740s, a high birth rate and increased immigration had pushed the population to 50 000 and, by the 1750s, to something over 60 000, a tremendous rate of growth compared with that of earlier decades.[18] Moreover, as the colony developed, work became more specialized. There was now a meaningful urban population. By 1740, Quebec City had a population of 5000 and Montreal 3500; by 1760, population in these settlements had reached 8000 and 5000, respectively. Many of the residents were engaged in commerce, finance, and education and did not grow their own food. They therefore provided a market for agricultural surpluses.

The growing population encouraged more than merely agriculture. In 1734, a small forge at St. Maurice began production of stoves and iron. It was natural to look at producing such goods locally, given their weight and the consequent costs of transportation from France. However, the plant required to undertake such production involved an expensive outlay. Thus, in perhaps the first of several instances in Canadian history, capital costs seemed to prevent the development of an enterprise deemed essential to the community. That, at least, was how energetic promoters presented their case for government support. They succeeded and were able to obtain ever-larger loans and grants from the government of New France. In the end, the forges produced almost half a million kilo-grams of iron, and then, in 1741, promptly went bankrupt.[19]

The St. Maurice ironworks is an index of both the growth of the economy by the later stages of the regime and the limitations to that growth. These major areas of diversification were matched in dozens of smaller ventures — new grist mills on the seigneuries, new artisan shops in the towns, greater activity by merchants, sealing along the north shore. There were even revivals of plans for shipbuilding and other grandiose attempts to create major new economic activities.

New France on the Eve of Conquest

These developments raise two basic questions about the economy of New France in the years between the Treaty of Utrecht and the fall of the colony. The first concerns the agricultural sector. Were the patterns of mature settlement different from those of the seventeenth century, and did these differences affect the relationship between seigneur and habitant?

Certainly, by the mid-eighteenth century, the agricultural landscape of the St. Lawrence valley had changed. By now, there were some 250 seigneuries, ranging from the well-established to the largely uncleared ones on the edge of agricultural settlement. Also, in distinct contrast to the earlier period, the St. Lawrence valley had been more or less continuously settled by Europeans from below Quebec City to above Montreal. Along the south shore, that settlement stretched considerably east of Quebec. It was also beginning to spread southward along the Richelieu River system. The shape of settlement had not changed, however. The combination of a narrow band of fertile soil with the continued desirability of access to the St. Lawrence had created an agricultural New France that was a long narrow strip of settlement, straggling along the banks of the rivers. As one eighteenth-century observer commented, "It could really be called a village, beginning at Montreal and ending at Quebec, which is a distance of more than one hundred and eighty miles."[20]

The question, however, is whether economic and social relationships had changed, even though the shape of settlement had remained the same. Some have argued that class distinctions were widening and that, if there ever had been a frontier egalitarianism, it was now passing.[21] Others have emphasized the permanency of the earlier situation. What had been done could not be undone, according to this argument. The eighteenth-century habitant was wealthier and more independent than was his peasant counterpart in France. The seigneur was not the equivalent of an old-country aristocrat.

These viewpoints are not mutually exclusive. Land was still less valuable than that in France, but it was more valuable than it had been a half-century before. Especially in wealthier and more productive seigneuries, there was an increased surplus to be taken off the land and, therefore, an increased advantage to the seigneur. For some seigneurs, the income derived from the various dues would have been meaningful by this time. One estimate is that one-half to two-thirds of the seigneurs were wealthy enough that much of the manual work on their farms would have been done by employees.[22] On other seigneuries, subsistence farming or pioneer conditions left little for the seigneur to extract.

It is also important to take time into account. Both yield and prices varied considerably from year to year, and crop failures were far from unknown. Alternative sources of income as well as personal capital could, thus, be of great importance to the seigneur. Large institutions, such as the church, or wealthy individuals were better able to weather the downturns and to maintain themselves as their aristocratic status demanded than were those who depended on the yearly income of the seigneury.

The other, and even more contentious, question surrounding the economy of New France in the eighteenth century concerns commerce. There has been considerable debate as to the extent and nature of the bourgeois class in New France. The debate has been particularly contentious because it has strong political overtones. Traditional anglophone interpretations have argued that New France, however heroic and interesting, was a backward colony of a backward system. Only after the British conquest, this argument continues, was there significant growth of a commercial class, and this class was British. Recent years have brought variations on this argument from both francophone and anglophone historians, but the argument remains essentially the same. New France was never sufficiently developed to have a meaningful merchant class, nor was the outlook of this preindustrial colony designed to encourage one.

In contrast, the Quebec nationalist school of historians began, in the 1940s, to argue that the extent of the bourgeoisie in New France had been underestimated. The colony was moving toward a more complex and more complete economy when the conquest by the British in 1760 stunted the development. In an argument known as the decapitation theory, this school concluded that the conquest caused the wealthiest and most educated in the colony to return to France, thus "decapitating" the social structure of the colony by removing its most powerful and innovative members. A vacuum was created, into which English and Scottish merchants moved. It is a politically evocative image of a "proto-nation" whose destiny was forever and tragically altered by military conquest.

The political controversy surrounding these two schools has ensured that, over the last generation, a great deal of attention has been paid to the question of the bourgeoisie and of business in New France, especially in its later days. It is thus possible to come up with a more detailed reconstruction of commerce under the old regime than otherwise would have been the case.

The trade with New France was shaped by certain characteristics that were the result of the age and the distances involved.[23] First, trade was dependent on credit, and the duration of that credit could be quite long. In the autumn, a fur trader in New France might purchase a cargo of trade goods on credit. The next spring, those goods would be parcelled out and sent inland in the care of the various groups of voyageurs and traders. After a summer of trading, they would return in the fall to sell their furs and repay their debt. A year would have passed, and frequent problems in timing meant that a two-year delay was not uncommon. Second, the transatlantic trade was a risky one. Voyages could take from fewer than 30 to more than 120 days, and ships were regularly lost at sea. The frequent wars of the age added to the risks — though, of course, they also tended to add to the profits of those ships that survived the hazards.

Considerable resources were needed to engage in the transatlantic trade with any success, and, for that reason, among others, the control of the transatlantic trade remained in France. The colonial merchants simply did not have the financial strength or the connections to take it over themselves. In particular, as Figure 3.2 shows, the trade was dominated by merchants in one or two ports. Most important was La Rochelle, which had the longest and steadiest connections to New France. Bordeaux provided competition, and other ports, such as Rouen and Nantes, entered the picture on occasion. Overall, however, it was a concentrated trade, with one or two ports receiving the furs and providing the merchandise to the colony. Indeed, through much of the period, trade was more concentrated than that, as in many decades two or three families controlled the great bulk of the transatlantic trade with New France. Two other features of the shipping patterns should be noted. First, there is the tremendous increase in shipping from 1720 to the conquest. Second, though La Rochelle may have dominated the trade through much of the colony's history, that was not the case by the final years. Bordeaux and others had now become important in the transatlantic trade.

The merchants from La Rochelle and elsewhere carried out their trade in various ways. In many instances, they had an agent or factor living in Quebec. This person would take orders from smaller retailers, fur traders, and others, and then dispense the goods that arrived on the ships from France. Sometimes these orders were handled strictly on a commission basis. The merchant obtained and shipped the good for a fee. At other times, the merchant sent the good over and his agent in Quebec sold it on his behalf. There was also a third variant, used by less-established companies, in which no permanent agent existed; instead, a cargo would arrive and be sold on the spot by itinerant merchants, often the captain of the ship that transported the goods in the first place.

There was some local wealth: some had accumulated considerable fortunes in trade; others had had success in the local carrying trade with Louisbourg, or in seal fisheries and other enterprises. Most important, however, was the fur trade. By the mid-eighteenth century, some twenty outfitters, almost all Canadian-born, dominated the trade.[24] Even for these, however, the transport of furs to France, and their sale once there, depended on those same La Rochelle and Bordeaux merchants. The size of their fortunes, moreover,

Figure 3.2 Origins of Shipping to New France, 1680s–1744

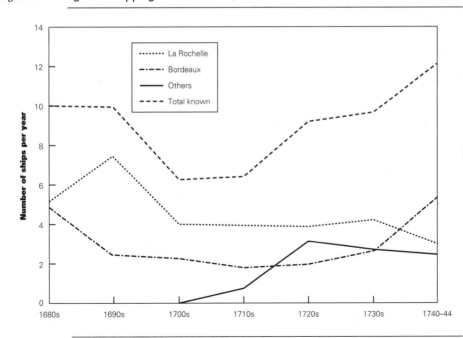

Source: Derived from J.S. Pritchard, "Ships, Men and Commerce: A Study of Maritime Activity in New France," Ph.D. thesis, University of Toronto, 1971, cited in Dale Miquelon, *New France, 1701–1744* (Toronto: McClelland & Stewart, 1987), p. 128.

while important in a small colony, was usually quite meagre compared with those of the French merchants with whom they dealt.

Overall, this situation can be characterized as a classic metropolitan–colonial relationship. The bourgeoisie was divided between France and New France, both by wealth and by function. The powerful and wealthy export–import business remained in metropolitan hands, as did credit facilities and capital. The lesser commercial enterprises, those of storekeeper and merchant, were in local control. However, the business in the interior belonged to the citizens of New France. Metropolitan control could not penetrate that far inland, and considerable business activity thus concentrated in the rising city of Montreal, foreshadowing its eventual dominance over Quebec City.

This picture has implications for the way in which the conquest is depicted. When the British captured Quebec City in 1759 and gained the whole of New France by treaty in 1763, they did disrupt the normal business, but the way in which they did so was affected by the dualism in the nature of the bourgeoisie. The Canadian-born fur traders and local intermediaries were not likely to head to France. Montreal, after all, was their home. Likewise, the average storekeeper or trader had neither the means nor the will to leave. In other words, to the extent that there was a local bourgeoisie, it remained more or less intact. If there was a decapitation, it was a transatlantic one. It was the merchant class of La Rochelle and elsewhere, along with their agents, who found the trade of New France cut off. Before long, local merchants found alternative suppliers in merchants from New England or Scotland, and thus the internal (as opposed to external) business structure of the colony was not severely disrupted.

Conclusion

The exact size or nature of the bourgeois class did not determine the fate of New France, however, population did. New France's orientation toward the fur trade as well as the limits imposed on agriculture by soil and climate had kept the population small, however vast the territory. In contrast, to the south, the English colonies had grown steadily, both in number and in population. By 1756, when the Seven Years' War broke out, the English population was more than 2 million, compared with New France's 60 000. With each passing year, the disparity of populations had grown, and by the mid-eighteenth century, the British colonies had reached a size that threatened to overwhelm that of any combination of the French and the Native peoples. Ultimately, the French could not be defeated in the wilderness, and their alliances with the Native tribes remained intact to the end. It didn't matter, however. The one settled portion of New France fell to the British, and in 1763 the whole territory was ceded to the English. A new era in the society and economy of North America was about to begin. The French river empire, with its fur-trade staple, was now joined with the British settlement empire and its agricultural staples.

NOTES

1. J.F. Bosher, *The Canada Merchants, 1713–1763* (Oxford: Oxford University Press, 1987), 3.
2. W.J. Eccles, *The Canadian Frontier, 1534–1760* (New York: Holt, Rinehart and Winston, 1969).
3. Graham Taylor and Peter Baskerville, *A Concise History of Business in Canada* (Don Mills, ON: Oxford University Press, 1994), 23.
4. Marcel Trudel, *The Beginnings of New France, 1524–1663* (Toronto: McClelland & Stewart, 1973), 270.

5. On these various schemes see W.J. Eccles, *Canada Under Louis XIV, 1663–1701* (Toronto: McClelland & Stewart, 1964), 46–58.
6. Eccles, *Canada Under Louis XIV*, 52.
7. The standard work on the seigneurial system remains R. Cole Harris, *The Seigneurial System in Early Canada: A Geographical Study*, 2nd ed. (Montreal and Kingston: McGill–Queen's University Press, 1984).
8. Harris, *The Seigneurial System in Early Canada*, 17.
9. The *banalités* could include other seigneurial revenues, but the grist mill was the only one to achieve widespread effect in New France.
10. Morris Altman, "Note on the Economic Burden of the Seigniorial System in New France 1688–1739" Historical Reflections 14(1) (1987): 135. Louise Dechêne, "L'évolution du régime seigneurial au Canada: le cas de Montréal aux XVIIe et XVIIIe Siècles," *Recherches Sociographiques* 12 (Mai–Aôut 1971): 37–48, sees the overall burden as more significant.
11. R. Cole Harris, ed., *Historical Atlas of Canada*, vol. 1 (Toronto: University of Toronto Press, 1987), plate 48.
12. Eccles, *Canada Under Louis XIV*, 110–11.
13. This traditional view of Native behaviour in the fur trade has been questioned by Ann Carlos and Frank Lewis. Their argument rests on evidence of depletion of beaver supplies. Competition between English and French traders resulted in higher prices for furs, which led to increased harvests by the Native peoples, which led to depletion. In areas where the Hudson's Bay Company had a monopoly, prices were lower and the beaver population was maintained at levels consistent with maximum sustainable yield. See "Indians, the Beaver and the Bay: The Economics of Depletion in the Lands of the Hudson's Bay Company, 1700–1763," *Journal of Economic History* 53 (1993): 465–94.
14. Dale Miquelon, *New France, 1701–1744* (Toronto: McClelland & Stewart, 1987), 16–17, 58, 67.
15. Eccles, *The Canadian Frontier*, 131–33.
16. Morris Altman, "Economic Growth in Canada, 1695–1739: Estimates and Analysis," *William and Mary Quarterly* 45 (October 1988): 702.
17. Miquelon, *New France*, 83.
18. The best work in English on family formation and population growth in this period is H. Charbonneau et al., *The First French Canadians: Pioneers in the St. Lawrence Valley* (Newark, NJ: Delaware University Press, 1993). For a more purely statistical treatment see Jacques Henripin, *La population canadienne au début du XVIIIe siècle* (Montreal: 1975).
19. Michael Bliss, *Northern Enterprise: Five Centuries of Canadian Business* (Toronto: McClelland & Stewart, 1987), 65–66.
20. The traveller was Peter Kalm, a Swedish botanist; this quote is from Miquelon, *New France*, 190.
21. Allan Greer, *Peasant, Lord and Merchant: Rural Society in Three Quebec Parishes 1740–1840* (Toronto: University of Toronto Press, 1985).
22. Miquelon, *New France*, 196–97.
23. The following paragraphs are drawn from Bosher, *The Canada Merchants*; Dale Miquelon, *Dugard of Rouen: French Trade in Canada and the West Indies* (Montreal and Kingston: McGill–Queen's University Press, 1978); and Miquelon, *New France*.
24. Miquelon, *New France*, 157.

FURTHER READING

Altman, Morris. "Economic Growth in Canada, 1695–1793: Estimates and Analysis." *William and Mary Quarterly* 45 (October 1988): 684–711.

Armstrong, Robert, *Structure and Change: An Economic History of Quebec*. Toronto: Gage, 1984.

Crean, J.F. "Hats and the Fur Trade." *Canadian Journal of Economics and Political Science* 28 (1962): 373–86.

Dechêne, Louise. *Habitants and Merchants in Seventeenth Century Montreal*. Kingston and Montreal: McGill–Queen's University Press, 1992.

Eccles, W.J. *The Canadian Frontier, 1534–1760*. New York: Holt, Rinehart and Winston, 1969.

Harris, R. Cole. *The Seigneurial System in Early Canada: A Geographical Study*. Montreal and Kingston: McGill–Queen's University Press, 1984.

Innis, Harold A. *The Fur Trade in Canada*. New Haven: Yale University Press, 1962.

Miquelon, Dale. *New France, 1701–1744*. Toronto: McClelland & Stewart, 1987.

Part Two

The British Mercantile Era, 1763–1846

Beginning of Long Reach, a painting by George Neilson Smith.

This New Brunswick landscape, with Saint John River in the fore-

ground, was painted in 1839. New Brunswick Museum, Saint John,

N.B., Canada/John Clarance Webster Canadiana Collection/W412.

54

IN 1763, when France ceded its North American possessions to England, there was great rejoicing, both in England itself and in the American colonies. The great struggle for a continent had ended, and a threat to existence had been removed from north of the American colonies. The British now controlled all of North America except for two tiny islands off the coast of Newfoundland. For the next 90 years, until the granting of responsible government, the political fortunes of the British North American colonies were directed from London. Equally important, for the next 90 years the economic fortunes of these areas would be bound up with the tenets of British mercantilism. In short, the age of imperial rivalry gave way to the British mercantile era.

The economic future of these new possessions was not a matter of high priority for the British government in the early years. Although fishing was an important business, Quebec added very little to the established fishing resources of the Atlantic colonies. As for the interior, Quebec was noted for its presence in the fur trade and little else.

Politics, not economics, dominated British considerations in the new colony. Specifically, the British government faced two challenges. First, it had to placate the French population. After years of war and a period marked by corruption among French officials, there was an opportunity to win the loyalty of a population that had traditionally been an enemy of the British empire. Second, and equally important, the British had to convince the many Native peoples allied with the French that there was no reason to resist the British presence. This task would be especially difficult, since the French policy in past years had been to subsidize the fur trade for the sake of Native support. If the British cut back on such subsidies and on outright grants too quickly, the restiveness would only be made worse. This possibility was demonstrated clearly in 1763, when Chief Pontiac and a coalition of tribes led a widespread revolt against new British rule. It would take two years before peace was restored along the frontier.

On the economic front, the British had to try to incorporate their new possessions into their already diverse American empire. Some economic means had to be found to give form and purpose to an economy that ranged from the sugar plantations of the West Indies to the far-flung fur trade of the French, from the frontier settlements of the western Carolinas and of the trans-Appalachian regions to the highly complex and wealthy New England area and the fishing outports of Newfoundland and the Maritimes.

The British had earned a measure of success on the political front by the time of the American Revolution (1775–83). The Quebec Act of 1774 meant that British rule was at least tolerated. By restoring much of its traditional hinterland and by establishing a structure of government and religion supported by Quebec elites, the act did much to give the colony a sense of security within the empire. Certainly there was no particular reason for the French to look to the rebellious American colonists. In the West, the Native peoples not only had accepted the British presence but fought as their allies against the American colonists.

The British had little or no success integrating and developing the North American colonial economies, however. The home government and the American colonies could not agree on the principles of economic policy, much less on its details. As for what was to become British North America, little or nothing had been done in terms of policy except to reunite the old fur-trade hinterland under the Quebec Act. There had been considerable movement of opportunistic Scottish and American colonial merchants into the niches and vacancies of Quebec commercial society. They had begun to be a presence in the fur trade and had always been involved in the provisioning of local garrisons. In general terms, however, the structure of Quebec society — as for those of Newfoundland and the Maritimes — was much the same in 1775 as it had been at the time of the conquest. Before any significant changes could take place in Britain's northernmost colonies, full-scale rebellion was to dismember Britain's American possessions.

The uprising in the American colonies that began in 1775 would take eight years to resolve. The conflict was, in many ways, a civil war, as Americans fought to decide whether their future lay in independence or in the British empire. In some colonies, such as Massachusetts and Virginia, the leadership and populace were overwhelmingly rebels, while in others, such as New York, up to half the people actively supported the British. It was a fierce struggle, with families divided and with the basic principles of nationhood and human rights at stake. In the end, of course, the Americans won their independence. The British could not sustain a war at such distance, especially as the English people were themselves increasingly war-weary. Thus, in 1783, thirteen of Britain's colonies became independent.

From the beginning, there were close cross-border contacts in trade and immigration between the United States and the British North American colonies. Over the decades, such contacts would grow until they became a central fact in the Canadian economy. But rivalry was important too. British North America and the United States were heirs to the long-standing contests between New France and the American colonies for dominance of a continent, a situation unaffected by the changes in political allegiance or in the products being developed. Continental contact and continental rivalry, set against a background of political animosity and distrust, were yet another general theme running through the evolution of British North America. Indeed, the political instability that marked North America between 1763 and 1815 indicates that, in many ways, the struggle for mastery of a continent that had dominated during the previous period continued. Only after the end of the War of 1812 did that unresolved struggle settle into anything resembling stability.

With the end of the American Revolution, Britain was left with a remnant of its once massive North American empire. Composed of a naval garrison at Halifax, numerous fishing villages scattered along the Atlantic shoreline of Nova Scotia, the small settlements of Newfoundland, the French Roman Catholic regions of the St. Lawrence valley, and the thinly populated wilderness beyond, it was a diverse and largely empty region that had been of little consequence to overall British economic planning before 1776. An earlier board of trade report had neatly summarized the importance of British North America by noting that "the Newfoundland fishery as a means of wealth and power" was worth more than Quebec.[1] So, too, were the important sugar islands of the West Indies. The remaining colonies in British North America were thought to be largely irrelevant to Britain's own economic prosperity, though both Quebec City and Halifax had a certain military significance in the minds of British strategists.

However marginal these colonies might be to the British in 1783, the economic development of Quebec (after 1791, Upper and Lower Canada), the Maritimes, and Newfoundland over the next 60 years would nevertheless be shaped, to an important degree, by British economic thinking. This outlook continued firmly in the mercantilist framework, which, as we have seen, influenced policy during early British experiences in North America and French ones in New France. The British still believed in state aggrandizement, while recognizing the importance of commerce as its key.

As befitted the general principles of this creed, Great Britain's mercantilist policy emphasized two related themes. The first was a continuation of the Navigation Acts, which put a series of prohibitions and restrictions on any foreign ship carrying merchandise into

England. The details were complex, but the net effect was to reserve to British ships the entrepot trade into the wealthy and increasingly large English market while restricting those who could carry goods within the colonial network. One of the complaints of New England seamen had been that the acts operated against colonial interests. One of the great hopes of Nova Scotians at the end of the American Revolution was that those same acts would now allow Halifax to supplant Boston in the West Indies trade.

The second general strategy of mercantilism rested on the long-standing belief in self-sufficiency and encouraged the empire to draw its raw materials from its own territories. That general principle was no more absolute after 1763 than it had been previously, however, and there were continuing shifts in the details of the policy. In some instances, it would work on a truly imperial basis, and in British North America's favour. Thus, Britain set out in the early nineteenth century to encourage a timber industry in Canada, even though it was possible to buy from Baltic sources more cheaply. On other occasions, there were contradictions. Not all members of the empire were created equal, as the Americans had long complained, and the developing British North American colonies would have to compete with favoured home interests that often sought protection and regulation at the expense of fellow British subjects in the colonies.

The British Navigation Acts and the general policy of self-sufficiency had been in action before. Both would continue to be important, especially to the Maritime colonies. Newly important to British North America in the nineteenth century, however, was a series of tariffs, trade barriers, and outright prohibitions known as the Corn Laws ("corn" is the British term for wheat). These laws varied tremendously over the period of their existence (1660–1846, repealed in 1849), but their principles remained sufficiently constant that it is possible to generalize.

Mercantilism continued to provide the policy framework for these years, but it is only part of the story. It is all too easy to discuss both the policies of the colonial power and the economic development of the colonies as if the home country was nothing more than the issuer of regulations. It was much more than that, of course; it was the major market for colonial goods, the supplier of most manufactured products, and the main source of savings, labour, and entrepreneurship.

Given this fact, it is significant that this period of colonial development paralleled one of the greatest events in economic history — the British industrial revolution. Britain was undergoing one of the most tumultuous periods of change and growth in its history. Both its population and its wealth were increasing rapidly. In the decade after the American Revolution, Britain's population increased by 10 percent, and much greater increases occurred in the following decades. The colonies were, thus, tied to a nation that had an abundance of sophisticated goods to export, savings to invest, and a rapidly growing population that could serve both as a market for colonial produce and as a source for colonial immigration. Obviously, then, the generally rapid development of British North America in these decades was affected by the industrialization taking place in Britain.

There is another important factor to take into account in looking at mercantilism, one that distinguishes this period from the previous one. Mercantilism was a policy and a philosophy increasingly under challenge. New theories of trade, of the economy, and of the role of the state were already present. Adam Smith's anti-mercantilist *Wealth of Nations* had been published in 1776. Though Smith's economic thinking was not adopted immediately, his impact on the shape of the future empire was almost as great as that of the American Declaration of Independence, which was signed the same year. Smith, and those who followed in his footsteps, mounted a widespread assault on the principles of state involvement and protectionism so prevalent in mercantilist thought.

Nearly three-quarters of a century passed before the principles inherent in Smith's 1776 work were fully developed in British policy. When that time came, in the 1840s, it would be one of the events that closed this second era of British North American development. Long before the final collapse of mercantilism, however, the effect of free-trade thinking began to show up in policy. To understand British North American development in this period, therefore, it is important to remember that the development was a product not just of British mercantilism but of the erosion over time of that mercantilist policy.

The final great influence on British North America was the United States. Established through revolution, the young American nation began as a straggling set of thirteen states loosely bound together under a constitution known as the Articles of Confederation. Very quickly, however, the Americans developed a powerful economic presence on the basis of strong colonial economies. In 1789, a new and more meaningful constitution was established. Thereafter, the Americans continued to jockey with Britain for supremacy on the continent. The Americans were British North America's greatest trading partner, most significant economic rival, and potential (occasionally all too real) military foe throughout this period. Yet ultimately the two economies were inextricably linked— bound by geography, similar cultures, and a common North American experience.

To summarize, three threads external to British North America affected its economy in the period between 1736 and the 1840s. The first of these was mercantilism and its gradual erosion. The second was the ongoing industrial revolution in Great Britain — a revolution that would make Britain, by the end of this period, the world's most powerful industrial, financial, and commercial nation. Finally, there was the often annoying and often indispensable presence of the rising former American colonies. In this period, they were small in wealth and power, compared with the mother country. However, they grew rapidly in population and wealth and became an increasingly important market for Canadian products. All of these threads must be understood in relation to the particular circumstances of time and place that shaped each region. This part discusses the development of the various colonies.

NOTE

1. Cited in Gerald Graham, *British Policy and Canada, 1774–1791* (London: Longmans, Green, 1930), 9.

Chapter Four

The Atlantic Colonies

THE PERIOD from 1763 to 1850 is arguably the most dramatic in Atlantic Canada's economic history. At the period's outset, Newfoundland and the Maritimes barely qualified as permanent settlements. Newfoundland was still an important base for migratory fishermen from Britain, although the permanent population had been growing slowly since the early part of the century. There were perhaps 7300 individuals residing over the winter in Newfoundland in the 1750s, and about the same number of summer visitors. The settlements clung precariously to existence, without formal British sanction and with only the most rudimentary of governmental systems.

The position of the Maritimes was not much stronger at the time. There were only a few thousand residents — fishermen, subsistence farmers, soldiers, and a few traders and merchants.

The position of the Atlantic colonies was much different 90 years later. Newfoundland then had a permanent population of 120 000. Fishing still dominated the economy, but now it was almost exclusively a residentiary activity. There was some diversification into the spring seal fishery and into shipbuilding, shipping, and trading. Politically, the island had been granted colonial status in 1824 and representative government eight years later.

The change in status was even more pronounced in the Maritimes. Now there were three colonies, with a combined population of nearly 534 000 — 277 000 in Nova Scotia, 194 000 in New Brunswick, and 63 000 in Prince Edward Island. Fishing was still a key sector, but the economies had diversified considerably. Shipbuilding and shipping and trading were important activities in each colony. As well, Prince Edward Island produced a net agricultural surplus, New Brunswick was an important timber exporter, and Nova Scotia boasted some mineral production. Small-scale manufacturing activities had grown up in the larger centres. The economic development was matched by political evolution; all three colonies had attained responsible government by the 1850s.

These developments are readily explained as the products of the forces identified in the introduction to Part Two: the application of British mercantile policy to the colonies, the rising American presence, and the changes wrought by the industrial revolution. A new factor is the role played by residents, especially the merchants and other business lenders.

Newfoundland

The return of peace in 1763 brought predictable consequences for the Newfoundland economy. The migratory fishing trade regained some of its earlier importance (see Figure 2.1) as markets in Europe opened up again and as the transatlantic voyage became safer.

The permanent population of the island fell slightly from its wartime levels at first, but rose again in the ensuing decades (see Figure 4.1). The introduction of the potato at this time provided a local substitute for imported flour and bread, easing one of the perennial difficulties of the residentiary fishery.

The American Revolution and the subsequent exclusion of the thirteen colonies from the British mercantile system had significant implications for Newfoundland's economic development. The effects were mixed, since New England was, at the same time, a competitor with Newfoundland and one of its most important suppliers. As a competitor, the island stood to gain from any British measure to exclude New England fishing ships from Newfoundland waters and New England fish from European markets. There was also some hope that St. John's might pick up some of the fish, molasses, and rum trade with the West Indies from New England. But the island relied on imports of foodstuffs and other supplies from New England, and any attempt to curtail this trade would raise the cost of supplies and thus affect the population adversely.

The immediate consequence of the revolution was prosperity, as New England boats were excluded from the fisheries by the powerful Royal Navy. Total production rose, and, in keeping with historical patterns, the migratory trade rebounded (Figure 2.1). Eventually, though, the adverse consequences of the American Revolution outweighed the positive ones for the island. The Navigation Acts forbade the importation of food and other supplies from New England. Substitutes from British colonies were inadequate and

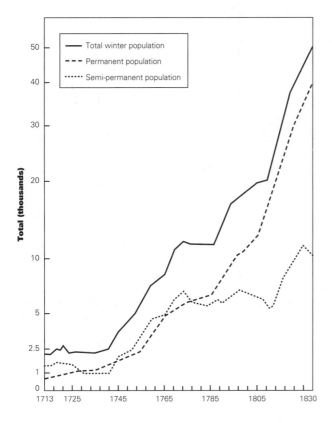

Figure 4.1
Newfoundland Population
Changes, 1713–1830

Source: W. Gordon Handcock, *Soe longe as there comes noe women: Origins of English Settlement in Newfoundland* (St. John's: Breakwater Books, 1989), p. 97.

more expensive, putting a squeeze on the residentiary fishery. This pressure on settlement was compounded by renewed attempts by British officials to discourage the residentiary fishery, apparently as a means of interfering with the commercial activities of the newly independent Americas. Population, which had risen to nearly 20 000 in the late 1780s, fell to fewer than 12 000 by 1797. Total catch in the same year was only 375 000 quintals (1 quintal equals 112 pounds), or 40 percent of the 1788 level.[1]

War broke out again in Europe in 1793 and ran, with some interruption, to 1815. These hostilities imposed great hardship on the Newfoundland fishery. The important Spanish market was closed from 1797 until 1809. This loss left Gibraltar and Portugal as the main European markets, and in these countries Newfoundland faced stiff competition from Norway and the United States. Prices for fish fell and remained low. In some years, the poor quality of the catch added to the woe; 1797 was judged by contemporaries as the worst year since the American Revolution. Fears of starvation led in 1803 to permission to import food from New England. Beginning in 1804, however, conditions turned around, and, by 1815, catches of more than 800 000 quintals were being recorded (see Figure 2.1).

These disruptions were hard on the industry as a whole, but especially so on the migratory fishery. In the late 1780s and early 1790s, residents accounted for about one-half of the total codfish catch; by 1815, virtually the entire catch was local (Figure 2.1). This shift to a residentiary fishery was the final step in a process that had been occurring since the first fishermen wintered over centuries earlier and that had been well underway since 1730. It had been stopped only temporarily by the prohibition on the importation of New England food and other supplies. These regulations were suspended in stages as the other British colonies proved unable to meet the needs of the island, and with the relaxation the residentiary fishery regained its competitive edge.

This period has been described as a "watershed" in Newfoundland history. As historian Shannon Ryan put it, "Newfoundland, which had always been a fishery based around an island, would finally become a colony based on a fishery."[2] Another Newfoundland scholar, economic historian David Alexander, adds to the point by noting that, while it is customary to claim a history for Newfoundland of several hundred years, it is more appropriate to view it as one of the countries of nineteenth-century European settlement.[3] Even the British government finally yielded, as noted earlier, granting the island colonial status in 1824. No act can better symbolize Newfoundland's unique economic history: after more than 325 years of continuous economic activity, to be formally recognized as a colony!

The economic fortunes of the new colony depended crucially on the level of activity in the two branches of the fishery: the bank fishery and the inshore fishery. Chapter 2 noted that the British had been active on the banks since the early part of the eighteenth century. They held a near monopoly on this trade in many of the Napoleonic War years. With the end of the war, however, the Newfoundland–British presence on the banks began to diminish, and by the 1840s it had largely disappeared. One report in 1848 noted 360 French vessels on the banks, with up to 17 000 men. The American fleet was at least as large; Newfoundland was not represented in this count.[4]

It is commonplace to attribute the demise of the British–Newfoundland presence in the bank fishery in this period to competition from French and American vessels. French fishermen returned to the North Atlantic fishery after 1815, encouraged by a system of bounties introduced by their government. They made the island of St. Pierre the centre of this resurgence, and its population, together with that of neighbouring Miquelon, rose tenfold between 1820 and 1870, from only 500 to more than 5000. Like the French, the Americans benefited from generous government subsidies and from protected domestic markets.[5]

The inshore fishery underwent some adjustments of its own. The technology remained much as it had for centuries. Fishermen went out in small boats each day during the summer months, bringing back the catch for light salting and drying on shore. The main changes were the opening of new fishing areas and the development of a new product. East Coast fishermen, particularly those from Conception Bay, had moved into the north shore areas during the Napoleonic Wars, practising their own brand of migratory fishing. When the French returned in 1815, the Newfoundland fishermen moved farther north to exploit the Labrador fishery. This process was like the early history of Newfoundland in miniature, in effect. Some fishermen, called stationers, established themselves on shore, catching and curing the fish in one place. Others — floaters — operated from on board their ships and moved from one fishing area to another.

The Labrador fishery was not feasible by itself, given the great distances involved. It was profitable, however, when combined with a new staple activity, the spring seal fishery. Ships first sailed from Newfoundland after 1793 in search of seal herds. Exports of seal oil jumped during the Napoleonic War years and remained high to midcentury. In 1827, there were 290 ships and 5418 men involved in the industry; by 1857, these figures peaked at 370 ships and 13 600 men.[6]

The inshore fishery underwent a change in the pattern of ownership in this period. Up to the 1820s, the activity was largely carried out by individuals, known as planters, who owned buildings, boats, and equipment and who fished by using hired crews. By the 1840s, however, this class of operators had largely disappeared and had been replaced by independent fishermen. Now the same individual who owned the boat and equipment also supplied the labour, usually assisted by family members.

Until the beginning of the nineteenth century, British firms dominated commercial life on the island. The roots of this control lay in the migratory fishery. British shipowners and captains from the West Country ports left caretakers on the island to look after their interests over the winter months. As the migratory fishery declined, these caretakers evolved into agents and clerks of the British firms, still located in the outports. They provided local fishermen with the necessary supplies in the spring, typically on credit. They received dried fish and cod oil in exchange, which the firms then marketed in Europe. Out of the proceeds, the merchants paid wages and other costs and advanced a winter supply to the planter.

During the Napoleonic Wars, firms from St. John's became involved in supplying fishermen and marketing the product in Europe. Their mode of operation was different from that of the British firms, however. Rather than deal with the fishermen directly, they supplied local traders, who would in turn supply the outport fishermen. This practice put them into direct competition with the British outport firms. Over time, aided by the fact that the principals were resident on the island year-round, the St. John's firms prevailed and the British companies gradually withdrew. The process had proceeded so far by the mid-nineteenth century that a contemporary observer identified St. John's as the "emporium of the Island."

The Newfoundland fishery entered a long period of relative stagnation after 1815. The trend is shown in Table 4.1. Salt cod exports, which had averaged more than 1 million quintals between 1815 and 1819, declined to fewer than 800 000 in the 1830s, before recovering again to around 950 000 quintals in the 1840s. Prices declined as well; they averaged $3.90 per quintal in 1815–19 but did not rise above $3 again until 1865–69. Gross export value fell from about $3 million in 1815–19 to $2.5 million in 1845–49. Recognizing that population more than doubled over the same period, it is clear that per capita output, in both physical and value terms, fell significantly.

The international trade in dried cod was growing. The problem was that Newfoundland did not maintain its share. Exports from the island to Portugal and Italy remained roughly constant in absolute terms, with competitor nations picking up most of the new demand in these countries. Exports from Newfoundland to Spain actually fell substantially, mainly to the benefit of Norway, which had emerged as a major competitor after the Napoleonic Wars. There was little change in the absolute volumes sent to the West Indies. The only new market developed was Brazil, which had opened up after 1808 and by 1848 was taking over 100 000 quintals.

In part, Newfoundland's relative decline was unavoidable. Competitors such as Norway were certain to emerge in the nineteenth century as technology advanced and shipping costs fell. In part, though, the problems seem to have been self-imposed.[7] There is substantial evidence that Newfoundland fishermen paid less attention to the curing of the fish in this period, giving rise to problems of quality control and a reputation for inferior products that exacerbated the competition problem. Just why they would allow this to occur is unclear, although some writers have linked it to the shift from planters to independent fishermen, with the attendant loss of skilled and specialized labour in the curing process.

There were spinoff activities from fishing and sealing beyond the commercial developments. The Newfoundland economy relied heavily on shipping services — to harvest the cod and seal, to carry these products to market, and to distribute supplies to the outports. At first, the ships and the shipping services were obtained from Europe, primarily Britain. Gradually, however, Newfoundland began to produce and operate some of its own vessels, giving the island an important backward linkage from its main staple exports. This development was possible as the scope of the trade grew and as local merchants developed the expertise and capital to invest in these activities. They concentrated on the fishing and coastal trades, building schooners and other smaller craft. Newfoundlanders owned and operated larger ships as well, but these were typically purchased offshore, in part from other British North American colonies.

These other activities notwithstanding, Newfoundland by mid-century was still a highly specialized economy. A census taken in 1858 showed that 89 percent of the labour force was employed in fishing, 4 percent in agriculture, and 1 percent in lumbering (the cutting and preparing of forest timber, used for carpentry, shipbuilding, etc.), with the remaining 6 percent designated as mechanics or professionals and merchants. In another census in 1869, fishing still occupied 84 percent of the labour force, agriculture 4 percent, and lumbering and mining 1 percent each. Secondary workers now made up 9 percent of the total, and service-sector workers the remainder.[8]

In sum, Newfoundland had come a long way since 1763. It was firmly established as a colony by 1850, something it had not been even 50 years earlier. Though it had developed considerably, there was a consistency dating back to the first West Country fishermen. Its economy remained highly specialized, dominated by one export industry to an extent unrivalled in any other North American possession. It continued to be a classic example of an economy based largely on staple production. Virtually the entire life of the community revolved around the fortunes of the export trade — from the fishermen to the boatbuilders scattered across the island, to the traders in the outports, to the merchants in St. John's.

The Maritimes

The Maritimes developed very little economically between the end of the Seven Years' War and the American Revolution. The population of Halifax, for example, fell to about 1500 in 1755, from 5000 five years earlier, as military fears waned and as fishing bounties were

Table 4.1 Quinquennial Averages of Salt Cod Exports for Newfoundland: Volumes, Prices, and Gross Export Values, 1815–1819 to 1930–1934

Period	Volume (000 quintals)	Price ($ per quintal)	Gross Export Value ($ thousands)
1815–19	1 018	3.90	2 968
1820–24	883	2.46	2 175
1825–29	923	2.08	1 942
1830–34	763	2.42	1 840
1835–39	788	2.78	2 193
1840–44	944	2.79	2 637
1845–49	963	2.66	2 547
1850–54	955	2.61	2 454
1855–59	1 205	3.33	4 008
1860–64	1 172	2.65	4 218
1865–69	969	3.86	3 731
1870–74	1 273	3.93	5 026
1875–79	1 134	3.88	4 354
1880–84	1 460	3.82	5 582
1885–89	1 192	3.66	4 316
1890–94	1 101	3.60	3 957
1895–99	1 224	2.89	3 549
1900–04	1 302	4.19	5 562
1905–09	1 574	n/a	n/a
1910–14	1 346	5.66	7 583
1915–19	1 517	9.35	15 650
1920–24	1 499	8.67	13 265
1925–29	1 398	8.37	11 587
1930–34	1 179	5.90	7 010

Source: David Alexander, "Newfoundland's Traditional Economy and Development to 1934," in James Hiller and Peter Neary, eds., *Newfoundland in the Nineteenth and Twentieth Centuries* (Toronto: University of Toronto Press, 1980), p. 20.

reduced. Several hundred Ulster Irish arrived in the colony, some redirected from New England, and an advance guard of what was ultimately to be a large migration of Scots came in 1773. The newly acquired regions of Cape Breton and St. John's Island (renamed Prince Edward Island in 1798) fared no better. There were only 271 inhabitants in the latter in 1768, rising to about 1000 by 1773, with just a few soldiers and fishermen in Cape Breton. With the defence motive gone, the colony possessed no real attraction beyond access to the fisheries and the availability of land for largely subsistence agriculture.

The region's economic problems at this time lay partly with the inappropriate policies of the imperial government. Restrictions were placed on the export of coal from Cape Breton, and forests were reserved for the Royal Navy. Land policies were more controversial yet. Cape Breton and Prince Edward Island were divided into 20 000 acre lots in 1763. Four years later, the entire area of the latter colony was disposed of by lottery to British nobility in the form of 64 land grants. The object was to make the colony self-financing by having the landlords sponsor settlement and pay rents to cover administrative expenses. They met neither of these responsibilities with any regularity, and the resulting conflict between the resident elites and the absentee landowners, known as the "land question," dominated economic and political life in Prince Edward Island for the next century. Similar types of land grants were issued in Nova Scotia proper to a much lesser extent, but with the same lack of success.

The main problem, though, was that Nova Scotia's economic endowments put it in direct competition with New England for a place in the British mercantile system, and Nova Scotia simply could not compete with its more established neighbour. Nova Scotia did not have the requisite timber and agricultural surpluses to send to the West Indies and lacked the expertise in shipping and shipbuilding to compete even in the carrying trade. New England was able to produce cheaper and better-quality supplies of timber (used for carpentry, shipbuilding, etc.) and agricultural supplies. Only the fisheries were naturally competitive, as the long presence of New Englanders along the Nova Scotia coasts attested. As long as the colonies to the south were part of the British empire, it seemed, the Maritimes were destined to be tributary to them.

When the American Revolution broke out, there was some scattered sympathy with the revolutionaries but never any serious threat that the "neutral Yankees of Nova Scotia" would secede. The British naval presence is only part of the explanation. More fundamentally, unlike the thirteen colonies, Nova Scotia could look to the mercantile system as a source of support rather than constraint. With the American colonies on the other side of the Navigation Acts, Nova Scotia might be able to take up the role that natural competitive disadvantage had until then denied it.

Three developments of particular importance stemmed from the American Revolution. Most immediately, the British navy turned to the pine forests of Nova Scotia for the masts that it had been securing from New England. This was not a large-volume trade but it was a high-value one, and it did set the stage for the developments in the timber industry that were to follow.

More important, at least potentially, was the decision by the British in 1783 to end what had been an effective exemption of New England from the terms of the Navigation Acts. With this step — one not taken lightly, given the importance of New England to the British mercantile system — the West Indies trade was reserved for the British North American colonies. The potential this development opened up was enormous. Fish from the region were already going to the sugar plantations; with New England excluded from this trade, the British North American colonies could expect their share of this market to grow. Agriculture could be developed to supply the foodstuffs previously coming from New England farms, and timber would be available for construction and barrels. Further, as these materials had to be shipped to the islands and the sugar and molasses taken to Britain, a stimulus would be provided to the shipping interests in the port communities and to the shipbuilders who would supply them with vessels.

The revolution also did what economic considerations alone could not: they provided an important influx of population into the region. Several thousand Loyalists came to the region during the war, although many of them subsequently left. The wave that came in 1783 consisted mainly of farmers. They took up land in the river valleys on the western side of the Bay of Fundy. This influx and the resulting rivalries between newcomers and the Halifax elite led to the creation of New Brunswick as the "Loyalist" colony in 1784. Others settled in Nova Scotia proper, others in Cape Breton (another new colony), and a few in Prince Edward Island. Another wave came in 1784, when it became clear that the Navigation Acts were to be applied to New England. These were mainly merchants and traders, settling in Halifax, Saint John, and other coastal towns. In all, the population of the Maritimes approximately doubled in a short time with these arrivals.

Because the western side of the Bay of Fundy was very lightly populated territory, the refugees had a significant impact. This newly bustling region around Saint John created a second centre of settlement in Nova Scotia, a rival to Halifax. Geographic distinctiveness as well as political differences led, in 1784, to the creation of New Brunswick, which became for many years thereafter a colony dominated by a Loyalist elite.

Like migrant groups throughout history, the Loyalists had a dual effect on the local economy. In the short term, they provided new markets for the produce of the population that was already there. Recent research has traced the development and subsequent specialization of agriculture on the Bay of Fundy— the old Acadian lands — to the arrival of the Loyalists and the markets they provided.[9] In the longer term, they added to the labour force, increasing the potential output of the economy. The farmers, fishermen, loggers, shippers, and sailors contributed to the Maritimes' new economic status in the British mercantile system.

If the hopes for the region in these years were high, the reality was something less. Simply put, the Maritime colonies were unable to fill the role handed to them. Fishing progressed satisfactorily enough, and there was some development of shipbuilding and of the carrying trade. The main obstacles to supplanting New England in the mercantile system continued to be the lack of a surplus of timber and of cheap agricultural supplies. Sawmills were established near harbours soon after the revolution, and timber was produced for export. As the most accessible stands of timber were cut, however, costs rose dramatically. Nor did agriculture develop as planned. The Halifax area produced only a small surplus of beef and flour. Settlers continued to come to Prince Edward Island — the population had grown to about 4400 by 1798 — but whatever surplus they provided was taken by the other colonies. New Brunswick and Cape Breton provided virtually no sustainable surpluses.

The consequences of these failures were predictable. Plantation interests in the West Indies began to lobby for the re-entry of New England suppliers, just as the fisheries of Newfoundland had. Partly in response to these pressures and partly out of a desire to create good will with the United States in its war with France, the imperial government began to grant re-entry. American breadstuffs were made legal traffic in 1786. Jay's Treaty of 1794 effectively re-established New England as the main supplier of produce and shipping services to the British plantations. The British North American colonies were still involved in the trade, but now only as an offshoot of New England activity. All direct trade between Nova Scotia and the West Indies had virtually ceased by 1804. The lack of success in taking over New England's role, combined with an unfortunate decision in 1790 not to make further land grants (which was expected to be temporary but, in fact, lasted for seventeen years), led to substantial outmigration from the colonies.

The outbreak of war in 1793 brought a second chance to the region, and this time the inducements were enough to bring about a notable response. The threat to British shipping posed by Napoleon's blockade caused a tighter enforcement of the Navigation Acts, leading, in 1803, to a partial withdrawal of New England's West Indies privileges. This advantage was accentuated in 1807, when the United States passed the Embargo Act, prohibiting all commerce with Europe out of American ports. This measure was replaced in 1809 by the Non-intercourse Act, which freed Americans to trade with other countries, but imposed even tougher regulations on trade with Britain and France.

Colonial merchants jumped at the opportunities this embargo provided. Trade with the West Indies grew dramatically after 1807. Nova Scotia doubled its trade in the period between 1808 and 1811, compared with that of the previous four years; New Brunswick doubled its trade in one year, 1811, alone. Whatever local produce was available was sent directly to the islands. The remainder of the demand was met by picking up supplies from New England, obtained by smuggling or by open defiance of U.S. law. Cargoes from

Europe were imported into Nova Scotia, for re-export to the Caribbean. Nova Scotia merchants seemed finally to have delivered on their earlier claim that, with the proper inducements, they could replace New England in the British mercantile system. The real test would come, however, when more normal times returned.

By stimulating the carrying trade in this manner, the American Revolution and the Napoleonic Wars also contributed to the development of an activity that would define the Maritimes' economy for the next century and beyond. Until the 1780s, shipbuilding was largely a small-scale, local activity geared to the fishery. As in Newfoundland, fishermen mainly built and operated their own vessels. The influx of Loyalists into the colony created a demand for the services of small coastal vessels, which also tended to be built locally. At this time, however, these two activities were relatively small-scale, more in the vein of a "preindustrial craft".[10]

The impetus to shipbuilding as an industrial activity came from the West Indies carrying trade. The growth of bilateral trade between the Maritimes and the plantation economies created a demand for the services of sailing vessels that could make this journey. Britain could not meet this demand, and the Americans were excluded from doing so by the British Navigation Acts and by their own government's legislation. Thus the merchants turned to local suppliers. Already by the late 1780s, Maritime shipyards were turning out several dozen vessels each year, and this total grew significantly in the following decades. Nova Scotia led the way in this endeavour, but the other colonies contributed as well. Generally, the ships were owned by the merchants, meaning that shippers were also shipowners.

The economic repercussions of the Napoleonic Wars on the Maritimes extended well beyond the West Indies trade. The blockade of the Baltic ports interrupted the supply of timber to Britain. With its economic and military power thereby threatened, Britain turned to the colonies. Exports of squared timber (logs squared roughly with a broadaxe in the forest after felling) from British North America jumped tenfold between 1805 and 1809. This opening was only temporary, however, unless some form of preferential access to the British market could be negotiated. The low-value, high-bulk nature of squared timber meant that transport costs made it impossible for North American supplies to compete on equal terms with the more accessible Baltic supplies.

The British government agreed to requests for protection. A differential duty between foreign and colonial timber was already in effect, but it was less than the extra transportation charges from North America. Duties were raised as a wartime measure in 1809. One year later, all temporary and permanent tariffs were doubled, and they were raised another 25 percent in 1813. Since duties on foreign wood were much higher to begin with, these proportionate increases widened the advantage given to colonial products significantly. Already, by 1811, the tariff preference clearly exceeded the transport-cost differential, and the 1813 increase just added to the advantage. Capital and labour were drawn to the industry, and British North America had another staple export.

Timber operations followed waterways closely, since water transport was the only economical means to get this high-bulk, low-value product to market. Nova Scotia lacked good river access to the interior, so, once the most accessible coastal stands were cut, the potential for further expansion was limited. What production there was from the Atlantic coast area went mainly to Britain, while that from the Bay of Fundy region went to the West Indies. Newfoundland and Prince Edward Island figured even less in the timber trade than did Nova Scotia, and the industry was even less important to the local economies. In all three colonies, once the most accessible stands were taken, wood was cut mainly as an input into shipbuilding.

New Brunswick's geography was ideally suited to the trade, however, and timber quickly came to dominate the economy. Vast reserves of pine and spruce were accessible via the several rivers that led into the interior. As the preferential duties were imposed, New Brunswick was transformed into a giant lumber camp. Figure 4.2 shows timber and lumber exports from New Brunswick from 1800 to 1850. Exports of squared timber rose twentyfold between 1805 and 1812, to reach nearly 100 000 tons. They fell off slightly for a year but, by 1815, had surpassed their 1812 level. As the Napoleonic Wars ended, the trade was firmly established in the colony.

The organization of the squared-timber trade took shape quickly. Work gangs of four to six men — usually local farmers and often from the same family — ventured into the woods in the fall. They selected and cut trees, squared them with a broadaxe, and dragged them to the river. There the timbers were made into rafts and floated to the port cities, where they were bought by one of the British timber firms that had set up subsidiary operations there, and sent to England. In England, the timber was cut into planks for naval use or, after 1815, for general construction.

The development of a timber trade with Britain created a demand for the services of ships that could carry this cargo across the ocean. There was considerable incentive, for natural competitive reasons as well as the specific tenets of British mercantilism, to produce some of this capacity in British North America, particularly in New Brunswick. The Navigation Acts excluded foreign shipping from most colonial routes. Further, ships built in the colonies faced no duties on entering Britain. These two features favoured shipbuilders in British North America over their foreign competitors.

Figure 4.2 New Brunswick Timber and Lumber Exports, 1800–1850

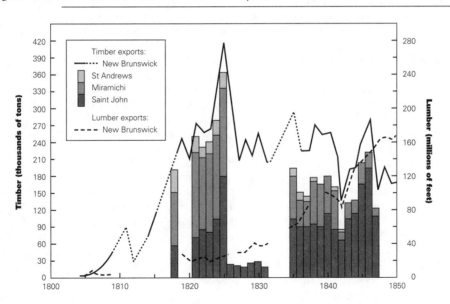

NOTE: THE DATA ON WHICH THIS FIGURE IS BASED ARE DERIVED FROM A WIDE RANGE OF SOURCES. IN SEVERAL YEARS, THE FIGURES USED ARE BEST ESTIMATES DERIVED FROM CONFLICTING REPORTS.

Source: Graeme Wynn, *Timber Colony* (Toronto: University of Toronto Press, 1981), p. 34.

There was a further factor yet. A ship built in the colonies could be loaded with timber, and both cargo and ship could be sold in Britain. Since transport costs were a significant portion of the total cost of colonial timber landed in Britain, piggybacking on the timber trade in this manner gave colonial producers a competitive advantage over their competitors in Britain. In this way, timber preferences gave an indirect stimulus to the shipbuilding industry in British North America. Since New Brunswick was the leading timber producer, it was natural that it would also become the leading colonial exporter of ships to Britain. This activity was still quite limited as the Napoleonic Wars ended, but it would grow very quickly thereafter.

The effect of these developments on New Brunswick's economy was immediate. The harvesting of timber was a labour-intensive process, creating employment and thereby attracting immigrants. The colony's population nearly tripled, from 25 000 in 1805 to 74 000 in 1824, at the time of the first official census. The timber trade also had linkages to other sectors of the economy. New businesses sprang up to service the timber industry and the attendant growing population. Shipping increased dramatically out of Saint John, and that city, in particular, saw considerable growth in businesses oriented both to exports and to local consumption.

The combination of revolution, war, American retaliation, and mercantile policy with respect to the Navigation Acts and timber preferences gave the Maritimes a start in its economic life. Historically, the period from 1815 to the 1840s is one of attempts to parlay this hothouse beginning into a permanent economic base. Success or failure depended on several things. Would the fisheries be reserved for local fishermen, or would the Americans obtain renewed access to them? Would the Navigation Acts be applied consistently, or would New Englanders work their way back into the trade? Would timber preferences be maintained after the war? Would the kick start to shipbuilding translate into a natural competitive advantage, or would it remain dependent on mercantile policy? In all cases, to what extent would these beginnings, however artificial their origins, lead to self-sustaining economic growth?

The first challenge came, as expected, in the fisheries. Britain responded to pressure from Nova Scotia and sent naval ships to keep the Americans outside the three-mile limit and away from ports and landing sites. Negotiations led eventually to the Convention of 1818, under the terms of which American fishermen renounced all rights to fish within three miles of any "coasts, bays, creeks, or harbours" of the colonies. They could, however, land for shelter or repairs, as long as existing property rights were respected. In exchange, they gained fishing rights on the south and west shores of Newfoundland and off Labrador. The provisions were sufficiently vague, however, that disputes were more or less continuous until a temporary resolution was reached with the Reciprocity Treaty of 1854.

The West Indies carrying trade was also at stake after 1815. The Maritimes had prospered greatly by the wars and the American Embargo Act of 1807, which essentially forbade trade out of American ports, but the area had not yet evolved to the point where it could be an effective replacement for New England. The problem continued to be the lack of a surplus of cheap agricultural and timber products. Predictably, New England sought access to this trade after 1815, plantation interests on the islands supported this relaxation of the Navigation Acts, and merchants in Nova Scotia and elsewhere had to lobby for their continuation.

The Navigation Acts were intended to reserve the trade for British North America. The United States responded to them by passing its own Navigation Act in 1818, closing American ports to British vessels coming from or going to the West Indies. The British retaliation was the Free Port Act of the same year, wherein a wide range of American products could be imported into the British North American colonies in either American or British ships, something not previously possible under the Navigation Acts. The intent was to reroute this produce to the West Indies, using the ships and trading facilities of the now free ports of Halifax, Saint John, and St. Andrews. This provision had its intended effect, causing the Americans to react with even stricter legislation, which, in turn, invited British retaliation, and so on; finally, a compromise "reciprocity agreement" was reached in 1830 wherein New England was given parity in regard to British vessels with the West Indies carrying trade. The Maritimes' position was protected, in part, by the imposition of a duty on products being brought into the islands from New England, which was waived for products from the colonies. Thus, while the merchants of the area were unable to retain the privileged position they had had during the Napoleonic Wars, they did manage to secure enough of it to keep themselves in relative prosperity.

Predictably, timber duties came under attack after the war. Pressure to remove them by consumers in Britain encountered the opposition of shipowners and colonists, who defended them, often using traditional mercantilist arguments to bolster their case. The latter groups won out, and the duties were made permanent in 1816, although the levy on colonial timber was increased slightly in 1821 and that on foreign timber lowered. Opposition to the duties never let up, and there was a nearly continuous succession of hearings and investigations that merged with the growing chorus of general anti-mercantilist sentiment. Not until the 1840s, however, did the first reduction come.

Timber dominated the New Brunswick economy after 1815, surpassing fishing and agriculture in importance. As British population increased, so, too, did the demand for construction materials. Exports of squared timber from New Brunswick alone rose from 100 000 tons in 1812 to 240 000 in 1819, and to their all-time peak of 417 000 tons in 1825 (see Figure 4.2). They fell thereafter, and averaged around 200 000 tons until the early 1840s. The industry was very volatile. Aside from that of 1812, there were recessions in 1821, 1826–27, and much of the 1830s. Part of the instability stemmed from the supply side, as the amount and quality of timber that ended up in the ports varied from season to season. More important, though, was the fact that lumber, being tied to the cyclically prone construction industry, was one of the first activities to suffer in a general recession.

As the industry became established, the production of deals (sawn planks) became increasingly important. In staples-theory (principal commodity or article of trade) terms, a forward linkage developed out of the timber trade. Logs were floated to sawmill sites, where they were cut into planks. Deals made better use of the logs than did squared timber, and they provided more value added to the resource before export. Most sawmills were located at waterpower sites, although a steam operation was in place in Saint John in 1821. Some of the output was used locally, and more went to Britain, where it overtook Baltic imports by 1835. American capital began to penetrate New Brunswick timber lands in the 1830s in search of supplies, but, in the main, that market would not be significant for another decade.

The shipbuilding industry boomed after 1815 (see Figure 4.3). Between 1815 and 1860, more than 2.2 million tons of shipping was built in the three Maritime colonies. This figure compares to 5.2 million tons built in the United Kingdom, the world's premier maritime power, in this period.[11] Sager and Panting justly conclude that "British North America had become one of the world's major shipbuilding centres."[12] About half of the tonnage built in these years was exported to Britain, much of it in conjunction with timber exports as noted above. Not surprisingly, New Brunswick dominated this activity. The remainder was a variety of types of vessels for a variety of uses: fishing, the coastal trade, and the West Indies trade, and in these activities the other colonies were more prominent.

70

Table 4.2 shows the number and tonnage of ships on registry at Atlantic Canadian ports in 1830, 1840, and 1849. Newfoundland accounts for between 20 and 22 percent of the ships registered, but for less than 20 percent of the tonnage, reflecting the preponderance of small coastal vessels. Around 55 percent of the vessels were registered in Nova Scotia, as were between 38 and 51 percent of the tonnage, showing again the importance of the coastal trade. Prince Edward Island accounts for 6 to 8 percent of both. The pattern in New Brunswick is opposite that of Nova Scotia and Newfoundland; its share of the tonnage exceeds that for the number of ships. The concentration on the transfer trade, with its linkages into timber, is evident.

Agriculture remained the relatively underdeveloped sector of the Maritime economies after 1815. Immigrants developed the rich soils of Prince Edward Island, the absentee-landlord situation notwithstanding, but its area was too small to support much export trade. About 85 percent of what was sent went in small ships to neighbouring colonies. Oats was the principal earner of credit, supplemented by shipments of potatoes, grains, and livestock. Many Prince Edward Island farmers added to their income by spending the winter cutting timber in New Brunswick and Maine.

It has been standard to describe the agricultural sector in Nova Scotia at mid-century as small-scale, largely subsistence-oriented, and a minor contributor to the colony's total output. More recent research shows that this characterization is too simplistic.[13] The

Table 4.2 Number and Tonnage of Vessels on Atlantic Canadian Registry, Various Years

Region	1830		1840		1849	
	Number	*% of Total**	*Number*	*% of Total**	*Number*	*% of Total**
Newfoundland						
Vessels	465	20	702	22	970	22
Tons	28 846	18	43 949	16	59 501	17
Nova Scotia						
Vessels	1 299	56	1 727	53	2 467	55
Tons	83 981	51	103 871	38	153 051	43
Prince Edward Island						
Vessels	135	6	195	6	301	7
Tons	7 661	5	15 696	5	28 587	8
New Brunswick						
Vessels	434	19	608	19	775	17
Tons	43 532	27	109 003	40	117 475	33
Total						
Vessels	2 333		3 232		4 513	
Tons	164 020		272 519		358 614	

*MAY NOT ADD UP TO 100.0 DUE TO ROUNDING.

Source: Derived from Keith Matthews, "The Shipping Industry of Atlantic Canada: Themes and Problems," in Keith Matthews and Gerald Panting, eds., *Ships and Shipbuilding in the North Atlantic Region* (St. John's: Memorial University Press, 1978), appendix I, p. 9.

Figure 4.3 British–American Shipbuilding, by Province, 1785–1905

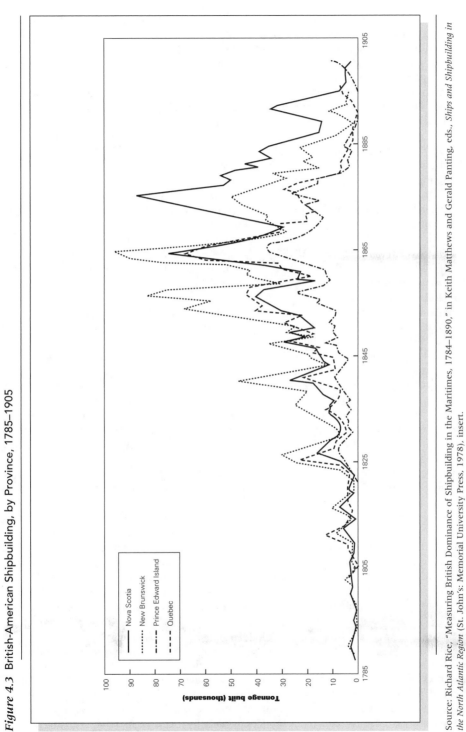

Source: Richard Rice, "Measuring British Dominance of Shipbuilding in the Maritimes, 1784–1890," in Keith Matthews and Gerald Panting, eds., *Ships and Shipbuilding in the North Atlantic Region* (St. John's: Memorial University Press, 1978), insert.

authors identify three distinct zones of economic activity: a farming zone in the northern regions, with branches extending into the Bay of Fundy area and into Cape Breton, occupied mainly by farmers producing surpluses for local markets, for Halifax and other larger centres, and occasionally even for export to other colonies or Boston; a fishing zone along the coastline, where farms were small and definitely second to the fishery; and a lumbering zone covering most of the colony, where farming was carried out alongside lumbering. Farm size, productivity, product mix, and degree of market orientation varied significantly among these three zones, and even within the farming zone.

The traditional picture of New Brunswick agriculture in the colonial period is equally critical. The apparent failure to develop an agricultural surplus is commonly attributed to the drawing power of the other staples, particularly timber. In an early version of a phenomenon that, in the 1970s, came to be labelled "the Dutch disease," New Brunswick's very success in one natural-resource product is said to have worked against the growth of a more diversified economy. Lumber drew capital and labour out of the more sedentary agriculture and into the more speculative but potentially more profitable trades. The parallel with the fur trade and agricultural development in New France is obvious.

This explanation is not entirely satisfactory, however. In principle, agriculture and timber were complementary activities. Indeed, they are usually portrayed as such in the Ottawa valley timber trade. Farmers could attend to their land in the spring and summer and go into the woods in the fall and winter to cut timber to supplement their income. In New Brunswick's case, however, it is alleged that the activities overlapped. There were often problems in getting the timber to market in the spring in time to return to the land; when schedules did permit, the prices were often so low that the farmer found himself in debt. Inevitably, agriculture lost out. Just why this should have been so in New Brunswick but not in Upper and Lower Canada was never explained.

Fortunately, this picture of New Brunswick agriculture has been clarified.[14] Much the same picture emerges as that for Nova Scotia sketched above. Where soil and climate conditions permitted and where local markets existed, New Brunswickers rationally concentrated on agricultural pursuits and produced surpluses for sale. Where conditions were less propitious, they concentrated their energies elsewhere. The timber trade and its ancillary activities, rather than suppressing agriculture as traditionally supposed, appear to have stimulated it by providing the major markets for agricultural surpluses. Like Nova Scotia, there was wide variation across the colony in average farm size, productivity, crop mix, and orientation to market.

Nova Scotia developed a small mining industry in this period. The Duke of York's mineral rights for Cape Breton coal were taken over in 1826 by the General Mining Association of London, which began to develop the property as a source for exports to the other colonies and the United States, and as a coaling station for North Atlantic steamships. Access to the United States was restricted by high duties, though, and in the other British North American colonies Cape Breton supplies had to compete with British coal that came in as ballast on timber ships. Thus, the activity remained small in scale.

Two types of manufacturing developed in the region. Sawmills, shipyards, and flour mills were direct spinoffs of the staples trades, either as backward linkages providing inputs to the export sectors or as forward linkages further processing the output. As well, such relatively small enterprises as tanneries, iron foundries, furniture shops, carriage works, and breweries served the local market and were protected by transport costs from imports from Britain and the United States. Halifax and Saint John, the largest centres in the region, were the most important manufacturing locations. These cities also saw developments in financial and commercial services, usually by the same merchants engaged in the main staples trades. Like manufacturing, some business was directly involved with the staples trades and some existed to provide services to the resident population.

Tables 4.3 and 4.4 provide an overview of the Maritime economy at midcentury. The data in Table 4.3 can be summarized in various ways but perhaps are most revealing when organized by province. Nova Scotia had the most geographically diversified trading pattern of the group. The bulk of its exports — nearly two-thirds — went to other North American colonies or the West Indies. The United States took another 21 percent, other foreign nations 11 percent, and the United Kingdom less than 5 percent. The United Kingdom was the dominant supplier, however, followed by the United States, other North American colonies, and other foreign nations.

Britain took more than three-quarters of New Brunswick's exports, in contrast to Nova Scotia's very limited shipments, reflecting the importance of the shipbuilding and timber sectors. The United States and other North American colonies were second, and about equally important, at around 11 percent; other sales were negligible. New Brunswick was the most dependent of the three Atlantic colonies on British suppliers, at nearly 50 percent, with the United States providing another 34 percent of its imports.

Prince Edward Island was the most linked by trade to the other North American colonies. Fully 50 percent of its total exports and the same percentage of imports were accounted for by intercolonial sales. The island relied most, in proportional terms, as well, on other foreign markets for sales (31 percent), although, in absolute terms, the volumes were not very large. The United Kingdom purchased less than 20 percent of the island's exports, and other markets were negligible. Prince Edward Island depended to about the same extent as did Nova Scotia on Britain for imports, but apparently purchased little from the United States.

The composition of trade by region is given in Table 4.4. In 1853, Nova Scotia's largest export was fishery products, at 36 percent, followed by agricultural products, at 22 percent; forest products, at 16 percent; manufactures, at 11 percent; and mineral products, at 9 percent. Manufactures were the largest component of imports, at 45 percent; followed by agriculture products, at 36 percent. More than 82 percent of New Brunswick's exports

Table 4.3 Trade of the Maritime Colonies by Origin and Destination, 1851

Trading Partner	Nova Scotia		New Brunswick		Prince Edward Island	
	Imports	*Exports*	*Imports*	*Exports*	*Imports*	*Exports*
	(% of total)		*(% of total)*		*(% of total)*	
United Kingdom	38.9	4.3	46.8	75.4	38.0	18.7
British Possessions	19.2	63.8	16.7	11.5	49.1	50.8
North America	18.5	38.1	16.4	9.4	49.1	50.3
West Indies	0.7	25.7	0.1	1.6	—	0.5
Other	—	—	0.2	0.5	—	—
Foreign	41.9	31.9	36.5	13.1	12.9	30.5
United States	25.2	20.8	33.7	10.8	—	—
Other	16.7	11.1	2.8	2.3	12.9	30.5

Source: S.A. Saunders, *The Economic History of the Maritime Provinces* (Fredericton: Acadiensis Press, 1984), appendix: table I, p. 99.

Table 4.4 Trade of the Maritime Colonies by Product, 1853

Product	Nova Scotia Imports (% of total)	Nova Scotia Exports (% of total)	New Brunswick Imports (% of total)	New Brunswick Exports (% of total)	Prince Edward Island Imports (% of total)	Prince Edward Island Exports (% of total)	Province of Canada Imports (% of total)	Province of Canada Exports (% of total)
Agricultural	35.9	21.9	34.2	2.9	17.8	65.0	13.9	48.1
Fishery	8.0	35.9	2.3	5.3	3.0	10.1	1.2	1.8
Forest	0.7	16.2	2.8	82.1	0.2	18.1	0.3	48.2
Manufactures and miscellaneous	44.5	10.9	53.6	6.7	70.9	6.8	80.2	1.2
Mineral	1.7	9.4	2.6	2.0	1.2	—	1.9	0.6
Wines and liquors	9.2	5.7	4.5	1.0	6.9	—	2.5	0.1

Source: S.A. Saunders, *The Economic History of the Maritime Provinces* (Fredericton: Acadiensis Press, 1984), p. 103.

were classed as forest products, with no other sector accounting for more than 7 percent. Manufactures made up 54 percent of imports; agricultural products, another 34 percent. Of Prince Edward Island's foreign sales, 65 percent were of agricultural products, 18 percent forest products, and 10 percent fishery products. Manufactures accounted for 71 percent of imports; agricultural products, 18 percent.

The ambiguity associated with applying staples theory to Maritime economic development in this period remains. In many ways, growth was predicated on the appearance of new staples, and the form it took followed from the nature of the export. New Brunswick, with its timber economy, is perhaps the clearest example. Yet, much is left unexplained by the approach, as the reference to the connection between timber and agricultural development in New Brunswick suggests. Other examples could be cited, but the point remains that, in contrast to the case of Newfoundland, reference to staples activities is a necessary but far from sufficient condition for understanding the economic histories of the three Maritime provinces.

One further point bears stressing here. As we have seen, the Maritime economies began life as a response to revolution, war, and British mercantile policy. After 1815, they were forced to deal with continuous pressure to remove whatever advantages they had secured, whether in the fisheries or with respect to the Navigation Acts and timber preferences. They also experienced some diversification of activity beyond these staple trades, most notably into shipping and shipbuilding. The question facing the region in the 1840s, then, as the mercantile provisions were ending and as industrialization was spreading to North America, was whether the economy had matured enough to survive and prosper from these changes.

Conclusion

In summary, by midcentury, the Maritimes looked vastly different from the way it had in 1760. From a few thousand fishermen, soldiers, suppliers, and subsistence farmers at the earlier date, population had grown to more than 533 000, or 22 percent of the total of all British North American colonies at the time (excluding Newfoundland). The economies were dominated by the production of a few products for sale abroad. Fishing was a key sector, especially in Nova Scotia. The main market was still the West Indies, followed by the United States, the Spanish West Indies, the Mediterranean countries, and South America. Timber was prominent in New Brunswick. Britain took the bulk of the exports in the form of square timber, with ancillary sales of sawn timber to the West Indies and the United States.

Prince Edward Island was the only region to have developed a small agricultural surplus for export. In the other economies, agriculture was ancillary to lumbering, fishing, and other activities, and food imports were common. There was some mineral production, mainly in Nova Scotia. Shipbuilding was the main processing activity, with output going to the local coastal trade, to offshore markets, and, increasingly, to local merchants and traders. The other processing activities produced for the local market, behind the natural protection of distance. Shipping and trade were the main service activities. The next decades would prove the strength of this economic base.

NOTES

1. Shannon Ryan, "Fishery to Colony: A Newfoundland Watershed, 1793–1815," in Phillip A. Buckner and David Frank, eds., *Atlantic Canada Before Confederation*, The Acadiensis Reader, vol. 1 (Fredericton: Acadiensis Press, 1985), table II, p. 141.
2. Ryan, "Fishery to Colony," 148.
3. David Alexander, "Newfoundland's Traditional Economy and Development to 1934," in James Hiller and Peter Neary, eds., *Newfoundland in the Nineteenth and Twentieth Centuries: Essays in Interpretation* (Toronto: University of Toronto Press, 1980), 19.
4. Cited in Shannon Ryan, *Fish Out of Water: The Newfoundland Saltfish Trade, 1814–1914* (St. John's: Breakwater Books, 1986), 56.
5. Presumably, although this point is never spelled out, the argument is that the new supplies from the subsidized fleets drove prices in Europe below average costs for the non-subsidized British–Newfoundland bank fleet.
6. Shannon Ryan, "The Newfoundland Salt Cod Trade in the Nineteenth Century," in Hiller and Neary, eds., *Newfoundland in the Nineteenth and Twentieth Centuries*, 45.
7. See the discussion in Ryan, *Fish Out of Water*, chapter 2.
8. David Alexander, "Newfoundland's Traditional Economy and Development to 1934," in Hiller and Neary, eds., *Newfoundland in the Nineteenth and Twentieth Centuries*, table 4, 28.
9. Graeme Wynn, "Late Eighteenth Century Agriculture in the Bay of Fundy Marshlands," in Buckner and Frank, *Atlantic Canada Before Confederation*, 44–53.
10. Eric W. Sager with Gerald E. Panting, *Maritime Capital: The Shipping Industry in Atlantic Canada 1820–1914* (Montreal and Kingston: McGill–Queen's University Press, 1990), 23.
11. Sager and Panting, *Maritime Capital*, 29.
12. Sager and Panting, *Maritime Capital*, 29.
13. Robert MacKinnon and Graeme Wynn, "Nova Scotia Agriculture in the 'Golden Age': A New Look," in Douglas Day, ed., *Geographical Perspectives on the Maritime Provinces* (Halifax: Saint Mary's University, 1988), 47–59.
14. See T.W. Acheson, "New Brunswick Agriculture at the End of the Colonial Era: A Reassessment," and Beatrice Craig, "Agriculture in a Pioneer Region: The Upper St. John River Valley in the First Half of the 19th Century," both in Kris Inwood, ed., *Farm, Factory, and Fortune: New Studies in the Economic History of the Maritime Provinces* (Fredericton: Acadiensis Press, 1993).

FURTHER READING

Acheson, T.W. *St. John: The Making of a Colonial Urban Community.* Toronto: University of Toronto Press, 1985.

Buckner, Phillip A., and David Frank, eds. *Atlantic Canada Before Confederation.* The Acadiensis Reader, vol. 1. Fredericton: Acadiensis Press, 1985.

Buckner, Phillip A., and John G. Reid, eds. *The Atlantic Region to Confederation: A History*. Toronto: University of Toronto Press, 1994.

Hiller, James, and Peter Neary, eds. *Newfoundland in the Nineteenth and Twentieth Centuries: Essays in Interpretation*. Toronto: University of Toronto Press, 1980.

Inwood, Kris, ed. *Farm, Factory, and Fortune: New Studies in the Economic History of the Maritime Provinces*. Fredericton: Acadiensis Press, 1993.

MacNutt, W.S. *The Atlantic Provinces: The Emergence of Colonial Society, 1712–1857*. Toronto: McClelland & Stewart, 1965.

Matthews, Keith. *Lectures on the History of Newfoundland, 1500–1830*. St. John's: Breakwater Books, 1988.

Matthews, Keith, and Gerald Panting, eds. *Ships and Shipbuilding in the North Atlantic Region*. St. John's: Memorial University Press, 1978.

Ryan, Shannon. *Fish Out of Water: The Newfoundland Saltfish Trade, 1814–1914*. St. John's: Breakwater Books, 1986.

Sager, Eric W., with Gerald E. Panting. *Maritime Capital: The Shipping Industry in Atlantic Canada, 1820–1914*. Montreal and Kingston: McGill–Queen's University Press, 1990.

Saunders, S.A. *The Economic History of the Maritime Provinces*. Edited and with an introduction by T.W. Acheson. Fredericton: Acadiensis Press, 1984.

Wynn, Graeme. *Timber Colony*. Toronto: University of Toronto Press, 1981.

76

Chapter Five

Quebec and Lower Canada

IN 1759, Quebec City fell to the British. Four years later, the end of the Seven Years' War confirmed by treaty what had occurred in conflict: New France was ceded to Great Britain. The people of the region were faced with new challenges and an uncertain future. Not the least of these challenges was the political and economic place of the newest colony within the British empire.

The British got at least three things when they gained possession of Quebec. First, and foremost, they removed a threat on their colonies' northern frontier. Second, they gained a monopoly on the North American fur trade. Finally, they acquired a colony that was predominantly rural, with a population primarily dependent on subsistence agriculture. This population was also French and Roman Catholic, with its own history, culture, laws, and institutions. The removal of the threat and control of the fur trade were important gains; however, the presence of a large population of French Roman Catholics was problematic.

The combination of political demands (to avoid French resistance to British rule), economic policy (British mercantilism and imperial interests), and the internal forces developing in Quebec shaped the evolution of the colony's economy for the first 80 years of British rule. These factors pertain to the entire history of Lower Canada. Still, sufficiently important changes occured that it is possible to characterize the economic development of Quebec (and, after 1791, Lower Canada) as having three distinct phases.

The first phase, from the conquest to the early nineteenth century, was marked by considerable growth and opportunity. The traditional staple, furs, continued to be central to the economy, while a market for wheat seemed to be opening up in Britain. Living standards rose as the rapidly increasing population was matched by an economy that grew even more rapidly. Economic performance in the second era, beginning in the early nineteenth century and continuing through to the early 1830s, was more mixed. The importance and viability of staples shifted dramatically. New ones, such as timber, became important as old ones collapsed or experienced tremendous fluctuations from year to year. There was, thus, both growth and considerable dislocation. Finally, in the 1830s, dislocation and growth were replaced with stagnation and decline. No new area of growth had yet appeared, while existing staples were either effectively finished (furs), in a state of crisis (agriculture), or no longer experiencing growth (timber).

This depiction of events has, itself, created some controversy. The question has been raised as to whether emphasizing a few resource staples is a sufficient basis for understanding the nature of the economic circumstances in Lower Canada. Does over-reliance on one theme lead to the exclusion or subordination of others? This warning must be kept in mind. Still, the dominant importance of staples cannot be set aside, even though alternative sources of growth must also be explored.

Adjustment to the New Regime, 1760–1802

The British were well aware that they faced a major challenge if they were to successfully integrate the new colony into the existing empire. This task was especially difficult because the fabric of the whole North American empire seemed about to tear apart. The English colonies to the south had become increasingly restive under British rule, and the removal of the threat of New France made them feel they had no further need for British protection. Disputes over tax laws led to civil disobedience, violence, and, in 1775, the outbreak of the American Revolution. Before long, armies would once again be invading Quebec; this time the invaders would be American.

Because Britain's attempt to deal with its recent conquest took place in an era of upheaval and war, the political approach to the Quebec problem was dictated by the need to maintain some internal stability. The French Roman Catholics had to be won over to the British crown, or, at the very least, brought to the point where they were unlikely to join their troublesome neighbours to the south. The result was a series of experimental and oft-changing laws and systems. English and French law competed for pride and place, as did the English and French religious establishments.

Most fundamentally, the basic institutions of government were in flux. Initially, the British ran the colony by means of a military government. This temporary measure, expedient in the midst of war, was abolished when the colony was formally ceded to England and the British issued the Proclamation of 1763. Faced with contradictory pressures from the residents of Quebec, from the Native peoples to the west, and from the American colonies to the south, the British reduced the boundaries of Quebec to little more than the St. Lawrence valley. The vast river empire that had been so much a part of the French experience and economy in North America was excised. Then, only eleven years later, the British reversed themselves. In the Quebec Act of 1774, Quebec's boundaries were extended to include much of the old hinterland of New France. The unity of the fur trade was thus reasserted.

Finally, after the American rebellion, and with the southern part of the old territory lost to the newly formed United States of America, the British implemented the Constitutional Act of 1791. The St. Lawrence valley–Great Lakes region was split in two. The western portion became Upper Canada; the eastern portion— the settled portion of what had been New France — became Lower Canada. Also, for the first time, Lower Canada and the French Roman Catholics who represented the vast majority of its population were granted a legislative assembly. However, that concession did not end the political turbulence. Divisions of class and language combined with tensions in the constitutional system of Lower Canada to exacerbate relations between French and English. By 1837, the colony was in a state of rebellion, and before long the constitution would be suspended and authoritarian rule once again in place, albeit temporarily.

These political approaches were paralleled by British attempts to integrate Quebec into the British imperial economy. The first era opened with economic upheaval that flowed from the constitutional disruption brought by the conquest. Metropolitan–hinterland relationships and practices built up over the past century were suddenly torn apart. The Rouen and Bordeaux merchants were gone. Local French businessmen and agents were cut off from their backers and suppliers. Many inhabitants found themselves holding worthless card money or IOUs from the former regime. Louisbourg, the one steady export market for agricultural products in previous years, was now destroyed. There was no certainty as to how the trade structure of the St. Lawrence valley, and of the fur trade beyond it, would fit into the imperial system of the new government of the region, that of the British empire.

It was not long before British merchants, financiers, and investors moved in to fill the vacuum. Merchants from the American colonies had accompanied the army into Quebec in 1759, and many remained once the war was over, hoping to supply the garrisons and to sell to the population of Quebec. As was true during the French regime, however, it was not local merchants, French or English, who dominated trade. Rather, large London-based partnerships, such as those headed by Brook Watson and Gregory Rashleigh, emerged with the capital and connections necessary to assume control of this new market. Like their French predecessors, they used local agents to promote their interests and handle affairs on site.

Powerful individuals did emerge in Quebec itself. For example, George Allsop acted as an agent for such people as Brook Watson but was also active in his own right in both the merchandise and the fur trades. Other, less wealthy, merchants brought goods in by the shipload or worked with ship captains to carve out a niche for themselves. Still, until well after the end of the American Revolution, the bulk of the import–export trade and of the provisioning of army garrisons was controlled by those large-scale operators centred in London or, to a lesser degree, Boston or New York. As one historian has said of the transition from the old to the new regime, "The names changed but the structure remained intact."[1]

Local capital did develop, and, not surprisingly, one of the first places it did so was in the traditional staple area of the fur trade. After the conquest, the fur trade went through considerable adjustment. First, there was the disruption of financial and supply arrangements resulting from the conquest. Then, a two-year Native resistance known as Pontiac's Rebellion swept much of the western frontier. Third, the American Revolution again disrupted trade to the southwest. By the 1780s, however, the trade out of Montreal had been renewed, as new groups of fur traders emerged. The fur trade entered a new era of geographical expansion as access to cheaper trade goods from Britain extended the feasible margin of exploitation. It remained an important economic activity, still accounting for more than three-quarters of the exports of Quebec in the late 1760s, and between two-thirds and three-quarters of those exports in most of the years before 1790.[2]

During these transitional years, French Canadians continued to control much of the trade. They were, after all, the experts, and through the 1760s, they owned 80 percent of the canoes heading west. Finances matter, however, and there was not the savings in the colony to handle the large investments and the long-term gap between outlay and return. Thus, British capital became increasingly influential. By the 1780s, more and more of the furs from the West came through the businesses of Scottish merchants such as the McGills and the Frobishers. When the smaller partnerships began, in the 1780s, to come together under the large North West Company syndicate, control rested firmly in the hands of the interconnected Scottish clans. The work force continued, as before, to be drawn from the French-Canadian Roman Catholic habitant class, but now the line between management and worker was increasingly an ethnic and linguistic one as well.

The tremendous impact of the English and Scottish merchants on Quebec in these years implies that the historical emphasis should be on discontinuity brought about by an ascendant British presence in the region. Yet, in many areas, there were strong elements of continuity in spite of the changes. For one thing, the British consciously sought to prop up many of the institutional and social characteristics of the *ancien régime*. The seigneurial system remained intact until 1854, and, until 1791, the British routinely granted new lands in the colony on a seigneurial basis. Further, the non-representative institutions that existed before 1791 enabled the British to look to the seigneurial class as the natural representatives of the French-Canadian population, while tending to ignore the bumptious merchants. Thus, the French-Canadian Roman Catholic elite was propped up by continued access to government power and patronage. Nor should the fact that Quebec was under an authoritarian form of government be overlooked. The failure of the British to give Quebec the representative government typical in other parts of the continent was anomalous, but it also meant that there was a degree of continuity between old and new regimes.

Economic and social continuity as well existed for most of the residents. Merchants and government officials might have found their careers and lives in flux, but more than 80 percent of the population of Quebec lived in rural areas, and for these small storekeepers and parish priests — and, especially, for the habitants — life did not change dramatically. New monetary stability was felt almost immediately, but the daily rhythms of life went on as before. Patterns that appeared in the final decades of New France continued without interruption in the postconquest years.

The most dramatic of these patterns was demographic. After a long period of slow population growth, New France had, in the final decades of its existence, begun to experience rapid population growth. This change was largely attributable to natural increase. Birth rates went up, and death rates, which had always been relatively low, declined. This pattern continued without interruption after the conquest and, indeed, accelerated. Very rarely in the late eighteenth and early nineteenth centuries did the birth rate fall below 50 per 1000. (In comparison, during the famous baby boom of the 1950s, Canadian birth rates were in the order of 24 to 28 per 1000.) Aided by rising English immigration, population rose phenomenally[3] — from a little more than 60 000 people in the 1750s to approximately 165 000 by 1790, to more than 300 000 by 1815. In two generations, the population increased fivefold! By 1840, it would double again, to 600 000.

Intermittent bursts of significant immigration abetted this process and, more importantly, altered the linguistic and religious balances of the colony. During and after the American Revolution, thousands of Loyalist refugees headed northward toward British North America. Most of them settled in Nova Scotia or Upper Canada, but some settled in what became Lower Canada. The area known as the Eastern Townships was largely opened and settled by Loyalists and later British immigrants. In the cities, there was also a steady influx of anglophones, so that, by the early nineteenth century, 40 percent of the population of Quebec City and 33 percent of that of Montreal was anglophone.[4] Still, the cities were small, and by 1815 these inflows, rural and urban, had brought the anglophone population of Lower Canada to only about 15 percent.

This population growth transformed the countryside. The small, straggling population of New France hugging the St. Lawrence was replaced by a population expanding quickly into new agricultural areas. Existing seigneuries were pushed back from the St. Lawrence, while new seigneuries were opened at a regular rate; after 1791, freehold tenure was established for new lands. The edge of settlement receded toward the Laurentian mountains to the north and up the Ottawa valley at the western edge of the colony. Though the rivers would long be at the centre of the colonial transportation system, their impact was lessened by the development of more extensive road systems.

The rapid rise in population also brought to an end the "one continuous village" that had characterized eighteenth-century New France. The number of villages and towns began to increase. Centred on the parish church, local stores, and artisans' shops, these villages were largely service centres for the surrounding agricultural community. Most had a population of fewer than 1000, however, and did little to change the overwhelming dominance of agriculture outside of Quebec City and Montreal. In fact, estimates of population indicate that Quebec was more rural in 1810 than it had been in 1760. From being more than one-quarter of the population in 1787, the urban population of Lower Canada fell to less than one-sixth of the total by the end of the War of 1812 and to perhaps one-tenth before the trend began to reverse itself.

A demographic shift of this magnitude raises an obvious question. Was this population growth independent of economic opportunity, in which case one would expect, a la Malthus, to see living standards in New France falling? Or, conversely, was the population growth a response to a rise in economic opportunity? The best evidence available indicates that, at least in the years before 1800, the standard of living in Quebec was not only maintained but improved and that, therefore, economic growth must have been faster than population growth. The question thus arises: what caused this economic growth?

Though there are numerous explanations, two or three major changes in the Lower Canadian economy seem central. First, there were direct expenditures by the British government. The army brought with it considerable amounts of specie. Behind the specie lay new possibilities for work with the British garrisons. Though the largest suppliers of the garrisons were merchants from outside the colony, there were still numerous opportunities for local profits on a smaller scale. Troops were billeted in homes, for example, and although this imposition was not always welcome, it did provide cash to the homeowner. Likewise, contracts to supply local garrisons with firewood, fresh produce, and other such materials added to the opportunities for profit.

There were dramatic changes in farm production as well. Agricultural output grew sufficiently to feed all those new mouths and, in fact, generated surpluses. After experiencing some lean years in the 1760s, the agricultural sector produced increasing quantities of wheat, potatoes, peas, flax, and some animals.[5] Much of this production, of course, went to feed the expanding population, for the subsistence economy still largely shaped the average habitant farm. Still, such was less the case in 1800 than it had been in 1750, as habitants in many parts of the province devoted an increased percentage of their efforts to commercial production and exports of wheat.

These wheat exports reflected the growth of Britain and the British West Indies as export markets. Initially, this trade was sporadic and reasonably small-scale, although the amount could occasionally be significant. Thus, in 1774, nearly half a million bushels of wheat were exported. By the 1780s, exports had become established, and farmers geared production to the possibilities overseas. By the early 1790s, exports were between 400 000 and 600 000 bushels a year (see Table 5.1). In the better years, agricultural exports rivalled those of the fur trade in importance. Certainly, given the high percentage of the Lower Canadian population that depended on agriculture, this growth in exports was, as Fernand Ouellet has noted, the central overall pattern of economic development in Lower Canada in these years.[6]

Though the precise figures are debatable, the trends indicated in Table 5.1 are clear enough. From at least the early 1790s to the end of the first decade of the nineteenth century, wheat exports were a consistent part of the economy of Lower Canada. Further, studies of habitant life have concluded that this same period saw a more consistent appearance of cash in the countryside.

The growing population and the increased amount of cash in rural areas provided opportunities for ancillary activities. It was now possible for artisans and small merchants

Table 5.1 Wheat Exports from Lower Canada, 1793–1810

Year	Amount (000 minots)*	Year	Amount (000 minots)*
1793	542	1802	1151
1794	483	1803	438
1795	449	1804	273
1796	25	1805	115
1797	101	1806	152
1798	139	1807	334
1799	201	1808	399
1800	318	1809	—
1801	663	1810	—

*1 MINOT = 1.07 BUSHELS.

Source: Figures from T.J. Le Goff, "The Agricultural Crisis in Lower Canada," *Canadian Historical Review* 55(1) (March 1974): 22.

to expand their operations. Villages that developed with the rising population were logical locations for these merchants and artisans, who, in turn, were supplied by larger wholesalers and merchants (some English and some French) operating out of Montreal and Quebec. All in all, this meant several things. First, the domestic market for products was gaining in importance. Second, the links were thus drawn somewhat more closely between town and country than had been the case in the *ancien régime*. Finally, subsistence farming declined as farmers took advantage of the new export market.

It is important to realize, however, that participation in the emerging wheat economy was not uniform across the colony, for two main reasons. First, some lands were more suited for wheat than others, just as the size of some landholdings were better suited for efficient production. Second, there existed strong traditions of mixed farming in Lower Canada. Oats, potatoes, corn, and peas were standard crops, though none was as important as wheat, which, in 1815, accounted for roughly 75 percent of all field crops.[7] In addition, there was an increasing number of livestock in the colony by the end of the eighteenth century. Most farms had at least a few cattle, some sheep and poultry, and some hogs. Dairying was a growing industry.[8] Lower Canada never became a monoculture in which farmers specialized in wheat at the expense of all else — not even in the best wheat years.

Mixed farming was traditional in subsistence agriculture. The tendency of peasant families to provide much (never all) of the goods to feed and clothe their families required an eclectic mixture of crops, livestock, and dairy animals. The type of farming that appeared in the late eighteenth and early nineteenth centuries, however, was not representative of a system in which wheat was uniformly supplanting an older tradition of peasant agriculture. Mixed farming was also becoming more market-oriented and, thus, represented a parallel or alternative strategy to a concentration in wheat. Local village and urban markets now existed for the products of mixed farming. There was a degree of specialization among farmers; one concentrating in, say, dairy products might supply another concentrating in something else. Here, as elsewhere, the cash economy was gradually eroding the isolation of the countryside.

Agricultural Adjustment and New Staples, 1815–1840

In the early nineteenth century, the forces that had been building up in the economy led to some dislocations and dramatic changes. Older key sectors, such as furs and agriculture, ceased to be areas of growth, while new sources of economic activity, from timber to financial institutions, became important parts of the colony's economic activity.

AGRICULTURE

In the late eighteenth century, Quebec seemed to be emerging as a significant exporter of grain. Table 5.1 illustrates that these exports continued for nearly a decade into the nineteenth century. Thereafter, however, Quebec ceased to be a wheat exporter, and, indeed, by the 1830s, if not earlier, it was clear that it had become a significant importer of wheat.

Though wheat remained an important crop through to the 1830s, it did not increase as quickly as did total cultivated land population. Rather, mixed farming increased, and beef and dairy cattle, in particular, became more and more numerous, as did sheep. The number of cattle, for example, increased ninefold between 1784 and 1831, and sheep 6.5 times. In contrast, the number of horses increased more slowly, at a rate roughly comparable to the population increase. In other words, more and more farmers were moving into new areas of specialization, while wheat declined in relative importance. Overall, it has been estimated that between 1800 and 1831 wheat fell from 60 percent to 21 percent of all agricultural produce.[9]

The problem for economists and historians, then, has been to discover what happened between the time of those rising exports at the turn of the century and the situation in the 1830s. Why did Quebec switch from being a net exporter to being a net importer of wheat? The various attempts to answer this question have generated some of the most heated debate in Canadian economic history.[10] Since the debate itself is interesting, and since its resolution has important economic and political implications for Quebec's history, it is worth reviewing in some detail.

There are three basic explanations of Quebec's shift from net wheat exporter to net wheat importer. One view can be summarized as follows: there was a market in Britain for North American wheat throughout the first half of the nineteenth century; this market represented the best allocation of resources for Quebec farmers; but, for a variety of reasons, they were unable to take advantage of it. The most controversial version of this position is that the Lower Canadian habitant was simply a bad farmer. Initially, the new soils of frontier lands made up for the backward and inefficient farming techniques. As the farms matured, however, the weaknesses in farming practices became critical. Ouellet estimates, for example, that wheat production per family declined from between 100 and 200 minots in the 1760–1802 period to fewer than 50 minots by 1831.[11]

Others see the failure in the quantity and quality of the land. They point to the rapid growth of Quebec's population at this time. The filling up of good areas, the division of farms through inheritance until they were too small to be efficient, and the simple necessity of feeding their families drove farmers back toward subsistence agriculture with some side trade in the local communities. As one historian put it, "It was not so much that wheat production had declined after the record highs of 1801–2, it was simply that it stagnated after this date near its earlier levels while population continued to rise, steadily and inexorably."[12] Reinforcing this viewpoint is the argument that wheat was always a marginal crop for the St. Lawrence valley and that conditions (for example, farm size and soil) had to be optimal for it to be competitive.

In one way or another, these viewpoints (and variants on them) see an economy in crisis. After a century or more of basic subsistence farming, the habitants and seigneurs of the St. Lawrence valley began to develop an export market — first, in Louisbourg, under the old regime, and then, under the British, in the West Indies and Britain itself. The exports could not be sustained, however, and Lower Canada entered a period of economic uncertainty and even crisis that would continue to the 1840s.

The second explanation is that there was a market in Britain for North American wheat throughout the first half of the nineteenth century, but this market did not represent the best allocation of resources for Quebec farmers, and they therefore, quite rationally, allocated their resources elsewhere. The key fact in this argument is the uncertainty of the Atlantic trading system and of the British market for wheat in particular. Demand was erratic and undependable. There were some good years, but after a time farmers found it not worth their while to continue growing for the British market. Instead, in a conservative but rational process, they returned their production to a more mixed type of agriculture to meet the needs of the local population. In this view, there was no agricultural crisis, and the standard of living in the agricultural sector may actually have improved in the first part of the nineteenth century.[13]

Marvin McInnis has provided a variation on this interpretation.[14] He first discounts the various versions of the supply failure thesis. He argues instead that there was no reliable market in Britain for wheat from Quebec or anywhere else in North America until the 1840s. High transport costs and Corn Law ("corn" is the British term for wheat) duties precluded such exports in all but the poorest of harvest years in Britain. The price that Quebec farmers could obtain for their grain in Britain in most years was below their supply price, which was set by the interaction of demand and supply for wheat in Quebec. Thus Quebec exported wheat in periods when the British wheat price less transport costs and import duties was still higher than the price of wheat in Quebec. Otherwise they profited from disposing of their supplies internally, as was generally the case after the first decade of the nineteenth century.

McInnis adds a third explanation. As the more suitable wheat lands of Upper Canada opened up, farmers there were able to produce wheat more cheaply than were their Lower Canadian counterparts, and these supplies (and any American supplies that found their way down the St. Lawrence) began to flow into Quebec, forcing an adjustment on farmers there. This competition, along with the clear problems with pests and diseases in the 1830s, transformed Quebec into a net wheat importer. The market for agricultural products other than wheat did not grow rapidly until after mid-century, so this argument is consistent with the position that Quebec farmers faced some hardship in the 1830s and 1840s.

The debate over the agricultural state of Lower Canada goes far beyond the state of habitant prosperity. John McCallum argued that the failure of Quebec commercial agriculture, and of wheat in particular, set back the entire economic development of the region relative to Upper Canada.[15] Local wealth accumulated more slowly, and thus the movement into secondary production was more difficult, at least east of Montreal. Economic power thus gravitated westward as, eventually, did population.

The economics of agriculture have also been linked directly to the turbulent politics of the period, specifically to the rebellions of 1837. The most important statement of this link came from Fernand Ouellet in 1966. Ouellet argued three basic points. First, there was an agricultural crisis in the early part of the nineteenth century. Second, a self-serving group of professionals (mainly doctors and lawyers) sought to take advantage of French-Canadian nationalism to gain support for their bid for political power by using the new British institution of the elected assembly. Third, the two events merged because the combination of declining economic circumstances and a patriotic appeal proved irresistible. The Patriote party of Louis-Joseph Papineau drew support from devastated farmers and, instead of responding constructively to circumstances, headed down the road that led to rebellion.[16]

In response to Ouellet, several alternative viewpoints and modifications have emerged. One of the best-known of these proceeds from the belief that there was no particular crisis in agriculture in the early nineteenth century, though it may not have been the rapid-growth sector it had been in previous years. Further, according to this position, agriculture should not be isolated from the broader economy. An absence of agricultural growth does not mean an absence of growth overall. New sectors of the economy opened, and the French-Canadian bourgeoisie as well as the average person adapted quite well to these altered circumstances. By the time the transition was complete, a new and modern market economy had emerged from the structures of the *ancien régime*. This interpretation, as its best-known supporters recently said, "suggests rather a dynamic and entrepreneurial view of Lower Canada at the turn of the nineteenth century."[17]

The failure of wheat as a staple meant that, whether there was an agricultural crisis or successful adaptation by farmers, wheat exports were not a primary force in driving the economy. The economic growth necessary to sustain an increasing population would have to come from another quarter.

THE FUR TRADE

Lower Canada's economic growth would no longer be supplied by the traditional staple of the region, the fur trade. For Montreal, the heyday of that trade was over. The merger in 1804 of the North West Company and the XY Company, both based in Montreal, marked the realization that supply lines were becoming longer and that profits were more difficult to achieve in the face of fierce competition from the Hudson's Bay Company. It was still an important trade for those engaged in it, but it was a much smaller part of Lower Canada's economy than it had been a half-century before, if for no other reason than that the population was so much bigger. Even before the War of 1812, fur exports had shrunk to less than 10 percent of the Lower Canadian total.[18] By 1821, the trade would disappear from the St. Lawrence valley altogether. A tradition lasting two centuries was coming to an end.

TIMBER

A new staple developed in these years, however — timber cut from the vast forests of Upper and Lower Canada and exported to Great Britain for the building and carpentry trades. Within a few short years, the timber trade changed from being a minor and specialized activity to become Lower Canada's most important export. It would remain vital to the economy through much of the century. It is also perhaps the best example of the way in which an imperial policy had a direct and immediate effect on the British North American economy.

Local businessmen and colonial governments had, for years, tried to turn the vast resources of the North American forest into an exportable good. As far back as the 1660s, Colbert and Talon had included lumbering in their ambitious program for New France. That plan failed, but on various occasions thereafter the idea was revived. There were even some occasional exports, but generally it was difficult for local entrepreneurs to compete with European sources. Baltic suppliers were much closer to both France and Britain. Still, a minor trade had slowly developed. In the years after the conquest it accounted for between 5 and 20 percent of Quebec exports. Overall, however, British North American timber exports served only a small fraction of the vast British market, where Baltic sources still dominated.[19]

The early nineteenth century saw the high politics of war and trade affect imperial timber policy. During the Napoleonic Wars, the British moved to find new and more secure sources of supply. Thus, in 1805, they raised the tariff on foreign timber to 25 shillings a load, and in 1809, to more than 39 shillings. In Canada, as in New Brunswick, the timber trade exploded. By the end of the decade, Lower Canada alone accounted for more imports into Britain than did all the Baltic sources. As early as 1810, timber was a more important export for Lower Canada than were fur and wheat combined. By the 1820s, more than 100 000 tons of squared pine, 20 000 tons of squared oak, and millions of individual "deals" (softwood planks) and staves (curved pieces of wood) were exported annually from the St. Lawrence valley. This new trade was reflected in seaport traffic, as a

Timber raft on the St. Lawrence, c. 1838. Unlike other staples, timber provided its own transportation. Squared-off timber, lashed together to form a makeshift raft and with a cabin or tent for the crew, was floated downstream to the St. Lawrence and, ultimately, to Quebec City.

National Archives of Canada/C-40326.

tremendous increase in shipping into the St. Lawrence took place. From an average volume of less than 15 000 tons in the late eighteenth century, shipping rose to 137 000 tons by 1810.[20] As Figure 5.1 indicates for the Port of Quebec, there was a direct correlation between the dramatic rises in shipping and in the timber trade. Lower Canada had found its new staple.

The timber trade was quite different in its characteristics and requirements from both farming and the fur trade. Farming was carried on within the frontiers of settlement, and the fur trade well beyond it. The timber trade, however, was carried out on its edges. Because it was a high-bulk, low-value product, transport costs were an important determinant of the feasible margin of exploitation. Water was a cheap way to transport timber, and thus the trade thrived along the numerous rivers feeding into the St. Lawrence from the Canadian Shield — most importantly, along the Saguenay and up the Ottawa valley, where huge stands of prime timber were available for the axe and where rivers acted as highways to carry the product to the ships that would transport it to Europe.

The rhythm of the trade was, as with so much else in preindustrial society, seasonal. In the winter, crews based on tumbledown shanty camps worked long, arduous days, cutting the timber and hauling it to the nearest body of water suitable for use as a means of transportation. Then, when spring breakup came, the interior camps became quiet as the crews either disbanded or moved downstream with the wood.

In the first years of the trade, the bulk of timber exports were in the form of squared timber (pine or oak). This primitive form of processing fitted the frontier conditions and also allowed the trade to develop one of its most characteristic features, the timber raft. Once on larger rivers, such as the Ottawa or Saguenay, the timbers could be lashed

Figure 5.1 Timber Exports and Total Shipping, Port of Quebec, 1808–1812 to 1838–1842

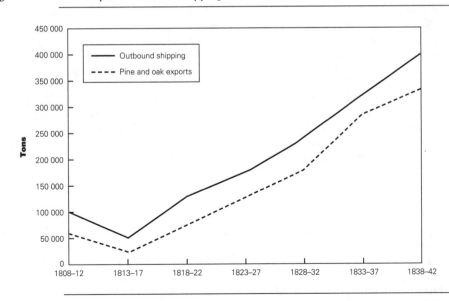

Source: Derived from Fernand Ouellet, *Lower Canada, 1791–1840: Social Change and Modernism* (Toronto: McClelland & Stewart, 1980), p. 352. Used by pemission of the Canadian Publishers, McClelland & Stewart.

together to form a makeshift raft. The raft was then floated downstream to the St. Lawrence and, ultimately, to Quebec City. Tents or makeshift cabins erected on the rafts provided shelter for the crew that tended them.

As the trade developed, the export of deals increased and, thus, the number of sawmills connected to the timber trade. In staples-theory terms, this further processing of the staple product was a forward linkage. Cheap power — water power, in this instance— was an important element of this new activity. Deals were a higher-value product relative to weight than was squared timber, so transport costs were less of a factor and the feasible market area was expanded. This further processing of timber, using a cheap natural-power source, elementary as it was, was a forerunner of the great wood-products industries of today.

The hard life of winter in the camps and spring and summer on the move created an especially volatile lumbering society. As one historian noted, the "lumber trade was not one designed to produce the clean-cut, all-round, all-Canadian personality."[21] For one thing, the trade operated in a strictly hierarchical and authoritarian society. Lumber communities were divided, especially in their earlier years, between the lumber "barons" who dominated the region and the men who worked at a hard job for poor wages. The barons of the Ottawa region, for example, initially consisted of such Americans as Philemon Wright, Braddish Billings, and Ira Honeywell. Later, Scottish and English merchants joined them in the race to exploit the riches of the region.

In many cases, these men ruled over quite large concerns, involving hundreds, even thousands, of men. Through much of the period, the workers comprised a mixture of recent Irish immigrants and French Canadians. Cut off from the wider community during much of the year, they returned to settled areas often for a spree of heavy drinking and lavish spending. The ethnic mix of French and Irish was often a volatile one — a drink too much, a hostile word, anything might set off dangerous and occasionally fatal clashes between the two groups. Canada's frontier society was not always, as myth would have it, all that peaceable.

It would be a mistake, however, to portray lumbering as the exclusive preserve of large groups of rough transients. Indeed, the seasonal nature of cutting and hauling meant that lumbering, especially hauling, was often a part-time activity for farmers in the vicinity of the trade. Like the fur trade before it, the timber trade provided them with an opportunity to obtain cash. This incentive was especially significant because the trade was carried out on the fringes of settlement, where farms were often not yet fully established; the winter activities of the timber trade carried families over the early years while their farms were being developed. Moreover, for some, the trade was more than a transitory activity. Much of the farmland of the Saguenay and of the Ottawa valley was less than ideal for farming. Thus, there developed a kind of symbiosis between the marginal farms of the region and the trade. The marginal farms provided labour to assist in the trade; the trade allowed the marginal farmer to survive on his land.

In communities such as Hull and Bytown, along certain parts of the Saguenay, and in other spots on the Shield, the timber trade was the lifeblood of the community. More difficult to evaluate, however, is the impact of the trade on the larger society of Lower Canada. How important was it? To what degree could a resource trade along the edges of civilization act as an alternative for continued agricultural growth or for the nascent industrial developments of the region?

First, the trade did generate a significant demand for labour. As we have indicated, lumbering required thousands of men at certain times of the year and thus provided work for new immigrants such as the Irish or for those French Canadians who could not make a living on the farm. It was not only the habitant who benefited. Many seigneurs suddenly found that all that unwanted forest was a more valuable asset than agricultural land. Later, as the trade moved from squared timber to deals, seigneurs or other entrepreneurs found that additional money could be made in the development and operation of sawmills.

Second, the trade also had an important impact on urban centres in Lower Canada, particularly Quebec City. Quebec was the financial and shipping and shipbuilding centre of the entire Canadian trade. In that sense, the colony of Upper Canada was tributary to its Lower Canadian counterpart. As Figure 5.1 indicates, the trade enlivened the port activities of Quebec to an unparalleled degree. Numerous "coves" sprang up, as local timber merchants and forwarders built wharves, employed clerks and labourers, and arranged for the buying, selling, and oceanic transportation of the timber.[22] Also a part of this metropolitan side of the trade were the fortunes made in it. Wealth accumulated not only to the barons on the Ottawa but also to the merchant traders of Quebec. Other business activities and a degree of economic diversification thus resulted, as it was supposed to, from the pursuit of this staple resource.[23]

Marvin McInnis posited an interesting new angle on Lower Canada's timber industry.[24] He believes that Lower Canada was dependent on wheat exports from Upper Canada quite early in the nineteenth century, and goes on to ask how Lower Canadians paid for these shipments. His answer: from timber receipts. The timber industry thus permitted a degree of efficient interregional specialization that would not have been possible otherwise. David Ricardo could not have found a better example of comparative advantage: by specializing in timber production and engaging in international trade, Lower Canada was able to consume more wheat per capita than it would have been able to if it had attempted to meet its needs internally.

Overall, then, between the early 1800s and approximately 1830, elements of the Lower Canadian economy underwent significant transition. Not only, as many historians have argued, was the market economy more fully developed than previously, but the staples trade changed. The fur trade, which had been central to the economy of New France, became peripheral to Lower Canada's. In the meantime, the agricultural sector, though perhaps not in crisis, did not assume the fur trade's old mantle as a staple economy. This would have been a serious problem for the overall trade balance of the colony as well as for any prospects of diversification had it not been for the fortuitous decision of the British to develop a colonial timber trade. While the trade did not always promote the most desirable social structures and its effects were unevenly distributed across the regions of Lower Canada, it did provide the colony with a major export and the people in the colony with new jobs.

It is short-sighted to look at Lower Canada in these years only in terms of commercial activities. Considerable change had undoubtedly taken place as the old fur staple collapsed, as the new staple of wheat was tried and abandoned, and as the population grew dramatically. Yet the vast population of the colony were farmers, and for them daily life had hardly changed at all. Even the timber trade, important though it was, affected the work patterns of only certain parts of the colony— mainly the Ottawa valley. Those settled in that area were probably more tied to the market economy than their grandparents had been and their standard of living may have been a little higher or a little lower. But overall, the patterns of daily work and the human relationship to the land and the seasons had altered little.

Agricultural Crisis and Metropolitan Commerce, 1830–1846

Between the grandfather who had farmed immediately after the conquest and the grandson who took up farming around 1830, one important thing had changed. For the former, expectations had been high. British currency and a rising demand for wheat seemed to indicate prosperity for the future. This was not the case by 1830. A series of blights hit the Lower Canadian wheat crop. Wheat midge, in particular, devastated crops in several years. From at least 1833 onward, there was a recurring agricultural crisis in the colony. Several regions reported widespread hunger, even starvation, and the agricultural population experienced a serious decline in its standard of living. The colony that had, in the late eighteenth century, hoped to become a major wheat exporter was, by the 1830s, dependent on imported crops to feed itself. The 1830s brought home the fact that agricultural production directly affected the majority of the population. Only so many people could be absorbed into forest work or into the shipyards of Quebec. The vastness of the rural agricultural population overwhelmed any employment possibilities in the timber trade.

The immediate crisis in Lower Canada's agricultural sector would pass, but the transformation was permanent. By the 1840s, two things were clear. First, there was no immediate likelihood of any significant expansion of agricultural opportunity. Second, farmers had abandoned wheat as a major crop in favour of the mixed agricultural style that had begun to emerge in the first decades of the century. In some instances, this new style of farming led to the development of an urban-oriented and successful agricultural strategy. In many other instances, however, the cash sales were small supplements to what was essentially subsistence farming. Moreover, with the good farm lands settled, new arrivals would have to be accommodated elsewhere.

What choices did the offspring of the Lower Canadian farmer have? As was the case where other types of land were scarce, they had to decide whether to remain within the limited economic horizons offered by their own community or to move. Family and friendships vied with economic opportunity. For Lower Canadians, the choice was especially difficult because to leave the colony implied being absorbed in the sea of English Protestantism that surrounded them. Even the cities of Lower Canada seemed a threat, with their large English-speaking populations and their foreign world of commerce. Over the next decades, clergy and government would urge farmers to locate on the marginal lands of the Shield rather than see them lost to the traditions of their forefathers.

Ultimately, however, exodus was the choice of thousands. Interestingly, that exodus was not mainly to new agricultural frontiers, though some did head off to the frontier regions in the United States. Instead, the attraction was to the cities and towns. In particular, a long-term trend emerged that saw the population go southward, across the border to the United States. Beginning in the 1820s, French Canadians had moved off to New England and elsewhere to take advantage of the embryonic industrial economy developing to the south. As the agricultural crisis worsened and as the pace of New England's industrial development quickened, the rate of emigration from Lower Canada increased. By the 1840s, New England was probably the primary frontier (albeit an industrial one) for the agricultural population of the St. Lawrence valley. It would remain so through much of the century.

This exodus raises the question of the urban alternatives in Lower Canada, for there is a danger that, in the emphasis on staples, the significance of the urban centres and their contribution to overall economic development will be overlooked. By midcentury,

Montreal was clearly the dominant city in British North America and would be the centre of industry and commerce well into the twentieth century. Quebec City was the centre of the timber trade, and a local and very wealthy elite had sprung up in the region. What, then, was happening in these two urban centres in the first four decades of the nineteenth century, and to what extent must they be taken into account in understanding the economic evolution of the colony?

Certainly their place in the overall economy was much less significant than it would become by the latter part of the century. Lower Canada actually became more rural in the late eighteenth and early nineteenth centuries. Only toward the end of this period, at the height of the agricultural crisis, did this tendency reverse itself. Montreal, with a population of up to 20 000 in 1820, had just overtaken Quebec City and would, over the next decades, assume a dominant position. In these years, however, both cities still exhibited the standard characteristics of rather small pre-industrial centres of population. Neighbourhoods were largely undifferentiated ethnically, and types of residence hardly at all. It is not possible to talk of residential, commercial, and institutional quarters of the city; they were intermixed.[25]

Of the two cities, Quebec had the less complex economy. Both its social and its economic structure remained reasonably constant between the War of 1812 and the 1850s. In particular, the economy centred on two forces. The first was the timber trade, with its linkages to shipping and shipbuilding. The second was the significant institutional presence of a large military garrison, several church institutions, and, until the union of the Canadas in 1841, the seat of government for Lower Canada. In addition, it acted as a supply and service centre to the well-settled agricultural hinterland around it.

Montreal's economy was more dynamic and went through several complex changes in the period from 1800 to the beginnings of industrialization in the 1850s. In the late 1700s, the city's economy was dependent, as it had been for the previous century, on the fur trade. The richest merchants were those who dominated that trade. For these merchants, the dominance of half a continent seemed the natural destiny of their city. They, like the French government before them, looked to the St. Lawrence system as a giant highway from which might be drawn the wealth of North America. Their ideal was, as Donald Creighton termed it, that of an empire of the St. Lawrence.[26]

With the new century came an important transition, and it was Montreal's success in making this transition that would eventually propel it to dominance. Specifically, Montreal was successful in becoming the metropolitan centre for the growing settlements of the Great Lakes region. Its geographical location on the natural transportation system and as the closest city to the new frontier meant that, as the region developed as a settlement frontier, Montreal was the natural metropolitan centre in which to locate government and business activities. Only gradually would new Upper Canadian metropolitan centres, particularly Toronto, assert their own influence. As one historian has noted, until about 1820, Upper Canada was in many ways a colony of Lower Canada.[27]

The role played by Montreal in Upper Canadian activities flowed naturally from the fur trade. The big fur traders had, after all, long supplied European manufactured goods to the interior in return for staples. As the Native population of the interior was supplemented by a growing European and agricultural population, many of the fur-trade firms simply found themselves expanding their business. And along with supplies to the Native peoples would go those destined for new settlements at Niagara or Kingston. Along with furs from the interior would come supplies of potash, wheat, and other commodities. As the new staples grew in importance and as the fur trade declined, the emphasis could be shifted accordingly.

Of course, such a brief description underestimates the difficulties involved in such a transition. These shifts involved dislocations of accustomed business practices and demanded a readiness to adapt to new circumstances. Networks of merchant storekeepers had to be established across Upper Canada (and in Lower Canada as well) to act as the distributors to the new population, while transportation facilities had to be improved to handle the much bulkier staples of the agricultural frontier. Along the way, a good many Montreal wholesalers and shippers failed. For the group as a whole, however, the advantage of having a growing frontier next door facilitated a transition away from the fur trade.

The movement into the commodity trade points out something else about the evolution of Montreal commerce— its diversification. The fur trade brought considerable wealth into the hands of a Montreal elite, which was successful in taking that wealth and moving into new ventures. The Upper Canada trade was a prime example of this type of activity, but there were others. Thus, for example, John Molson founded his fortune on the inevitable demands for beer. By the early nineteenth century, however, he was moving into shipping and was, in fact, the owner of the first steamship to be built in the Canadas, the *Accommodation*. Steamship construction soon developed, as the demand for the new technology increased. In a slightly later instance of the same investment of capital, the Redpath fortune, earned in construction, was turned to sugar-refining and other activities.[28]

The presence of a large and wealthy community of businessmen also meant that Montreal led the way in developing the financial infrastructure necessary for modern business. In 1817, the Bank of Montreal, which still exists, was founded, and over the next twenty years the now-defunct Bank of Canada, City Bank, and Banque du Peuple followed. Other examples could be given, but the point is that the fur trade had, early on, made Montreal the centre of finance and wealth in British North America. The movement of that capital into new areas of endeavour — from wholesaling through shipping, and, eventually, manufacturing — reinforced Montreal's position in the economy, accumulated more capital for it, and allowed the city to emerge as the predominant business centre with a hinterland that would eventually be transcontinental.

The expansion of that hinterland is especially connected to the improvement of transportation. The demands of the new staples trade led businessmen to form the first major canal company in the Canadas. In 1819, the Lachine Canal Company was created to overcome the rapids that had halted Cartier's trip inland back in 1534 and that now added greatly to the costs of shipments in and out of Upper Canada. Eventually, as in so many

Canada's first bank. The oldest bank in the country, the Bank of Montreal opened in 1817. In 1819, it moved into its first permanent home, on St. James Street, Montreal, site of the bank's present-day headquarters.

Bank of Montreal Archives.

other instances of Canadian development, the company was taken over by the government. Still, a canal was finished in 1824.[29]

This first Lachine canal was rudimentary and, for what it accomplished, expensive. Over the next two decades it and other canals between Montreal and Lake Ontario would become a source of contention between political factions, would drain the colony's tax dollars, and would remain unsatisfactory for the needs of the merchants. It would be the late 1840s before a complete and relatively efficient system of locks allowed shipment from the Great Lakes to the Atlantic. Nevertheless, the very fact that investors and the colony were willing to begin such a daunting prospect is important. Each improvement expanded Montreal's hinterland and furthered the city's growing desire to assert both a transcontinental and transoceanic presence. In a way, the Lachine canal was the beginning of a series of infrastructure improvements that culminated in the Canadian Pacific Railway and a truly transcontinental transportation system.

One other point needs to be made about both cities. As the stereotype would have it, the English were, indeed, concentrated in the cities. One estimate concludes that, in 1825, about 33 percent of all the English in Lower Canada lived in the three main centres of population, compared with about 5 percent of the French.[30] Likewise, what had drawn the English there, to a large extent, was the commerce. Still, it would be dangerous and simplistic to conclude from this that business was a purely English activity. The continuity of French bourgeois activities was strongest in the area of merchandising. The disadvantages of capital were outweighed here, in many instances, by a common language and by a network of ties through the smaller rural villages. The penetration of consumer goods into the countryside provided a new outlet for the wholesaler and retailer in the years after the American Revolution. Thus, in many instances, especially at the retail level, the chief businessmen were French Roman Catholics.

This urban concentration had two implications. First, as recent studies have shown, wealth generated from business activities in the cities would increasingly be invested in diverse pursuits as the city's economic base broadened. French Canadians were active by the 1840s in such areas as banks, property, and insurance. Second, however, the orientation of French-Canadian Roman Catholic businessmen toward the local retail trade meant that, as Montreal's influence expanded to become continental, they were less involved than were their English counterparts. The national business image of Montreal, well established by the later nineteenth century, was English-speaking in spite of a continuing francophone business community.

Conclusion

By the time of the union with Upper Canada in 1841, Lower Canada was on the eve of a new era. The preindustrial society, with its rural predisposition and traditional values, was about to be overtaken by industrialization. The dynamic sectors of the province would shift to the cities, especially Montreal, and there the roots developed in the early part of the century would soon explode in a series of new business ventures and industrial activity. None of this was apparent in the late 1830s, however. Open rebellion had torn the community apart, while the repeated recent failures of the wheat crop had lowered the standard of living for the agricultural community and, indeed, for much of the colony. The political unrest had frightened the English business community and discouraged immigration and new investment. The growth and economic optimism of the late eighteenth century seemed a long way off.

93

NOTES

1. Linda Kerr, "Merchant Activity in Quebec: The Decade After the Conquest," unpublished paper presented at the North American Conference on British History, Coeur d'Alene, Idaho, October 1988, 3. For a good summary of merchant activity see Jose Iguarta, "A Change in Climate: The Conquest and the Marchands of Montreal," *Canadian Historical Association Papers* (1974): 115–34.
2. Fernand Ouellet, *Economic and Social History of Quebec, 1760–1850* (Toronto: McClelland & Stewart, 1980), 83.
3. These figures on French-Canadian Roman Catholic population are from T.J.A. Le Goff, "The Agricultural Crisis in Lower Canada, 1802–1812: A Review of the Controversy," *Canadian Historical Review* 55(1) (March 1974): 1–31.
4. Gilles Paquet and Jean-Pierre Wallot, *Lower Canada at the Turn of the Nineteenth Century: Restructuring and Modernization*, CHA Historical Booklet No. 45 (Ottawa: Canadian Historical Association, 1988), 5.
5. Ouellet, *Economic and Social History*, 84–89.
6. Ouellet, *Economic and Social History*, 8.
7. Serge Courville and Normand Sequin, *Rural Life in Nineteenth Century Quebec*, CHA Historical Booklet No. 47 (Ottawa: Canadian Historical Association, 1989), 10.
8. Fernand Ouellet, *Lower Canada, 1791–1840: Social Change and Nationalism* (Toronto: McClelland & Stewart, 1980), 4.
9. Ouellet, *Lower Canada*, 120.
10. For a flavour of the controversy see Le Goff, "The Agricultural Crisis"; Gilles Paquet and Jean-Pierre Wallot, "The Agricultural Crisis in Lower Canada: Mise au point — A Response to T.J.A. Le Goff," and T.J.A. Le Goff, "A Reply," both in *Canadian Historical Review* 56(2) (June 1975); and R.M. McInnis, "A Reconsideration of the State of Agriculture in Lower Canada in the First Half of the Nineteenth Century," in Donald Akenson, ed., *Canadian Papers in Rural History*, vol. 3 (Gananoque, ON: Langdale, 1983).
11. Ouellet, *Lower Canada*, 120.
12. Le Goff, "The Agricultural Crisis," 22.
13. Gilles Paquet and Jean-Pierre Wallot, "Crise agricole et rensions socio-ethniques dans le Bas Canada 1802–1812: éléments pour une réinterprétation," *Revue d'histoire de l'Amerique française* 26 (September 1972): 185–207.
14. McInnis, "A Reconsideration."
15. John McCallum, *Unequal Beginnings: Agriculture and Economic Development in Quebec and Ontario until 1870* (Toronto: University of Toronto Press, 1980).
16. Ouellet, *Economic and Social History of Quebec*.
17. Paquet and Wallot, *Lower Canada*, 3.
18. Paquet and Wallot, "Crise agricole," 54.
19. The figures of 5 percent and 20 percent are from R. Cole Harris and John Warkentin, *Canada Before Confederation: A Study in Historical Geography* (New York: Oxford University Press, 1974), 86.
20. The standard work on the British timber trade is A.R.M. Lower, *Great Britain's Woodyard: British America and the Timber Trade, 1763–1867* (Montreal and Kingston: McGill–Queen's University Press, 1973).
21. Ouellet, *Economic and Social History*, 38. For export figures see Ouellet, *Lower Canada*, 352.
22. Michael Cross, "The Lumbering Community of Upper Canada, 1815–1867," in J.M. Bumsted, ed., *Canadian History Before Confederation: Essays and Interpretations*, 2nd ed. (Toronto: Irwin–Dorsey, 1979). The general description of social life in the trade is drawn largely from this article.
23. Lower, *Great Britain's Woodyard*, chapter 17.
24. See R.M. McInnis, "The Early Ontario Wheat Staple Reconsidered," *Canadian Papers in Rural History VIII* (Gananoque, ON: Langdale Press, 1992), 17–48.
25. For a good representation of this at a slightly earlier date, see R. Cole Harris, ed., *Historical Atlas of Canada*, vol. 1 (Toronto: University of Toronto Press, 1987).

94

26. Donald Creighton, *Empire of the St. Lawrence* (Toronto: Macmillan, 1956).
27. Ouellet, *Economic and Social History*, 157.
28. The best discussion of the Montreal business community at the end of the Lower Canadian era is in Gerald Tulchinksy, *The River Barons: Montreal Businessmen and the Growth of Industry and Transportation, 1837–1853* (Toronto: University of Toronto Press, 1977).
29. On the canal and the controversy surrounding it see Creighton, *Empire of the St. Lawrence*, 197–211; see also Ouellet, *Lower Canada*, 133–35, on the Lachine and other early canals.
30. Harris and Warkentin, *Canada Before Confederation*, 97.

FURTHER READING

Armstrong, Robert. *Structure and Change: An Economic History of Quebec.* Toronto: Gage, 1984.
Greer, Allen. Peasant, Lord and Merchant: *Rural Society in Three Quebec Parishes, 1740–1840.* Toronto: University of Toronto Press, 1985.
Lewis, Frank, and Marvin McInnis. "The Efficiency of the French-Canadian Farmer in the Nineteenth Century." *Journal of Economic History* 40(3) (September 1980): 497–514.
Lower, A.R.M. *Great Britain's Woodyard: British America and the Timber Trade, 1763–1867.* Montreal and Kingston: McGill–Queen's University Press, 1973.
McCallum, John. *Unequal Beginnings: Agriculture and Economic Development in Quebec and Ontario until 1870.* Toronto: University of Toronto Press, 1980.
McInnis, R.M. "A Reconsideration of the State of Agriculture in Lower Canada in the First Half of the Nineteenth Century." In Donald Akenson, ed., *Canadian Papers in Rural History*, vol. 3. Gananoque, ON: Langdale Press, 1983.
Ouellet, Fernand. *Lower Canada, 1791–1840: Social Change and Nationalism.* Toronto: McClelland & Stewart, 1980.
Paquet, Gilles, and Jean-Pierre Wallot. "The Agricultural Crisis in Lower Canada: Mise au point — A Response to T.J.A. Le Goff." *Canadian Historical Review* 56 (June 1975): 133–55.

Chapter Six

Upper Canada

UPPER CANADA, as the area would become in 1791, was initially very much on the periphery of the empire. It was the hinterland of a hinterland, and even in the remnant of North America left to the British after the American Revolution it initially played a marginal part. Newfoundland, with its valuable fish trade; Nova Scotia, with its strategic value; and the St. Lawrence valley, with its relatively large population, ranked ahead of this wilderness in importance to the British. Yet within 50 years it was to become the most important of all Britain's North American possessions. Strong economic development was crucial to the growing importance.

The economic development of Upper Canada/Canada West from the American Revolution to the abolition of the Corn Laws in 1846 can be divided into three phases. The first phase, from 1783 to about 1815, involved the development of a generally simple pioneer economy, tributary to both Great Britain and Montreal. The second stage, from 1815 to the late 1830s, saw growth of output and population as well as considerable cyclical volatility. It also saw the increasingly active intervention of the government and of investors to facilitate commerce, in general, and staple exports to Great Britain, in particular. Considerable progress was made, but fiscal strain and the inadequacy of local savings and governmental institutions soon became apparent. The third stage, from the late 1830s to the abolition of the Corn Laws in 1846, brought better economic times and a more secure fiscal base. Continuing immigration permitted the rapid development of a mature agricultural-commercial colony. This final phase also prepared the way for the beginnings of industrialization.

Throughout these three phases, though, the patterns that shaped the growth of Upper Canada remained fairly consistent. This was a colony, and its early development was intertwined with British mercantile policies. Changes of direction in Britain could, as we will see, create dramatic rhetoric in Upper Canada. They also required the economy to adjust to new circumstances shaped by the metropolis across the Atlantic. To a lesser extent, other economic centres, from New York to Montreal, also had their impact, bringing possible opportunities or disasters for those involved in this emerging economy. Overall, however, the adaptations were successful. A strong and varied resource base, an increasingly diversified and experienced colonial elite, and a growing population all propelled Upper Canada past the frontier stage of economic development in a relatively short period of time.

The Pioneer Economy, 1783–1815

The dominant feature of Upper Canada at the beginning of the American Revolution was its wilderness state. The French had established some fur-trading posts and defensive forts during their regime, however, as with so much of the frontier of New France, these were but a series of way stations in the wilderness. They were designed to encourage the trade and support of the real rulers of the territory, the Native peoples. Even the small settlement that sprang up near the present-day city of Windsor did not change the fact that the economy of this region was much as it had been 50 years before. Simply put, the area was beyond the feasible margin for all economic activities except the fur trade.

The American Revolution brought the first change to the region. Military factors did what economic ones could not: draw population to this wilderness area. Loyalists, threatened at home, sought a refuge during the conflict. Throughout the revolution, groups from the frontier of New York state fled north to find a secure base for families and non-combatants, while military groups, such as Butler's Rangers, moved back and forth across the frontier as circumstances demanded. These concentrations of people thus had characteristics reminiscent of refugee camps, military encampments, and communities in their first years. During the war, few were certain they would not be returning south. Crops and farming remained secondary to military activities, and these communities could not have survived without the assistance of the British military, which supplied both the weapons of war and the necessary food.

As the revolution neared its end, Loyalist units and communities realized that what had been a military base was now likely to become a permanent home. Two military groups, one under the leadership of Colonel William Butler at Niagara and the other under the Johnsons at the eastern end of Lake Ontario, established communities based on what had previously been military groupings. There was a great deal of movement in and out during the first months and years. Loyalists drifted westward from the area around the Richelieu, while others, unsuited for the wilderness life, returned to the United States or left for England. There were no customs houses to contact or complicated forms to be filled out, and thus many came in unannounced and unnoticed by the officials. Generally, however, the best estimate is that the Loyalist population of what were still the western reaches of Quebec was somewhere around 6000 by the end of the American Revolution. A region that was still beyond the frontier of settlement and had come into existence for military reasons now had to develop some permanent existence and some means of livelihood for its newly arrived people. For most Loyalists, there was no returning home. They had no choice but to try to create a livelihood on the frontiers of settlement of North America.

Certain disadvantages were faced by those who hoped to see their new homeland prosper and grow. Most obviously, the colony was across the border from a new nation that regarded the British presence in North America as an unmistakable threat. Further, it was initially a part of an even more distinctive British colony, French-speaking Roman Catholic Quebec. This status had an obvious effect on the region. In its founding years, government, financial influence, and goods emanated from Quebec, and especially from Montreal. Even after the region became a colony in 1791, Upper Canada remained tied for a long time to the merchants, forwarders, and bankers of Montreal. London was thus twice removed. Montreal provided the route of transportation, the source of credit, and the access to goods and power needed by the infant colony. Subservience to and, later, rivalry with that metropolitan centre and that French-speaking Roman Catholic population would do much over the years to shape both the economics and politics of the lower Great Lakes communities.

The main difficulty, however, was the feature noted above: in these years, the region was beyond the feasible margin for all economic activities except the fur trade. The timber trade was not yet a viable economic activity even in the more favourably situated and endowed Maritimes and Lower Canada. Agriculture was a more obvious option, but here

98

Pioneer life in Upper Canada: one of the earliest Loyalist settlements. Loyalist refugees from the American Revolution found a wilderness that was practically unsettled by Europeans. Yet, in 50 years, Upper Canada was to become the most important of all Britain's North American possessions.

National Archives of Canada/C-23633.

too basic economics worked against the region. At this time, Upper Canada was beyond the feasible margin of commercial agriculture. To see this point, and to understand why the disadvantage was ultimately overcome, it is useful to consider the simple economics of homesteading.

Individuals will leave their homelands to take up agricultural land elsewhere for one basic reason: to improve their lot and that of their families. If the motive for leaving is a quest for political or religious freedom, as it often is, they will go to where these attributes seem greatest as long as there is land available and it can provide for their basic needs. If the motive is more purely economic, they will go to the destination that promises the greatest expected economic gain over their lifetime. This very simple point suggests three factors to look at in explaining the timing of agricultural migration to a particular area such as Upper Canada: the expected gains from establishing a farm, the expected costs of doing so, and how the net returns from this location compare with those available in the next most likely destination.

One obvious determinant of expected returns in agriculture is secure access to suitable land, which focuses attention on such issues as climate, fertility, and land disposition and tenure systems. Is the soil fertile and the climate forgiving? Is the land available for settlement? Can property rights to the land be established, and are they thereafter secure? The other factor is the price the migrant expects to receive for each unit of output produced. The relevant price here is the farm-gate price, defined as the price the product sells for in its final destination minus any tariffs or other such charges and minus all transport costs.

The main costs of bringing a farm into production are the price of the land and the cost of tools, equipment, and hired labour (if relevant) needed to prepare and then work it. The net return each year is equal to total revenue minus total costs (where lump-sum expenditures such as those for land or machinery are amortized over a number of years). The calculation over a lifetime (or longer, if the farm is to be bequeathed to children) is important because losses in early years will not deter migration if the expectation is that they will be offset by future returns.

It is worth stressing two important points here. First, expected lifetime net returns need not just be positive. They must be larger than those available from the next best option for the migrant, which means comparing them with those available in the country of origin and in all other feasible destinations. For Upper Canada at this time, the main competition was with U.S. land. Second, the focus is on expected returns, which is simply a recognition of the fact that economic decisions are generally made on the basis of incomplete and imperfect information, especially in historical settings.

Seen in these terms, Upper Canada was not an attractive destination for agricultural migrants in the late eighteenth century. Certainly, suitable potential agricultural land was available. Estimates vary, but it is unlikely that the European population of Upper Canada was more than 14 000 when it became a colony in 1791 (see Table 6.1). The sparse settlements begun by the ex-Loyalist units had expanded somewhat with sporadic immigration. Occasionally there were relatively large groups, such as the 520 Scots Roman Catholics who settled in Glengarry in 1786.[1] More often, smaller numbers of people drifted in from Quebec, Nova Scotia, Scotland, and even the United States. Yet, much of the lakeshore remained empty and the back concessions were still untapped.

Suitable land may have been there, but it was not always available, or at least available on secure terms. From the beginning, there were contradictions in the approaches to land and settlement in what would become Upper Canada. In particular, two things would plague its government and people over the next few years. The first was a question of the nature of land ownership. As part of the province of Quebec, land in this new frontier was presumably to be held on a seigneurial system, something confirmed in instructions to Governor Frederick Haldimand in 1783.[2] Yet, for the Loyalists who flooded north during and after the American Revolution, the seigneurial system was foreign, mystifying, and unacceptable. To them, land ownership meant land ownership and nothing else. Moreover, many colonial officials agreed, sensing that the land system would have to be

Table 6.1 Population of Upper Canada, 1785–1848

Year	Population	Year	Population
1785	6 000	1824	118 000
1790	12 000	1826	166 000
1791	14 000	1831	237 000
1794	25 000	1836	374 000
1805	46 000	1842	487 000
1811	60 000	1848	726 000
1817	83 000		

Source: Douglas McCalla, *Planting the Province: The Economic History of Upper Canada, 1784–1870* (Toronto: University of Toronto Press, 1993), p. 249. © Queen's Printer for Ontario, 1993. Reproduced with permission.

altered if immigrants were to be attracted. Thus, over the next several years the settlers acted, to all intents and purposes, as if they were operating under a freehold system. Land was exchanged, sold, and purchased as if it were freehold, even though, in fact, it was held under seigneurial tenure.

In 1791, the problems of uniting a new English-speaking Protestant population and an existing French-speaking Roman Catholic system led to the division of Quebec into Upper Canada and Lower Canada. This division also meant that the seigneurial system was abolished in Upper Canada. Even then, however, problems continued. In fact, not until 1796 was the Upper Canadian government sufficiently organized to implement a straightforward system through which a would-be settler could progress, in a more or less orderly manner, from arrival to clear title. As one historian has noted, "The most telling evidence against the land-granting system in Upper Canada before 1796 is that in 1796 only a very small proportion of settlers of the province had patents or any other legally valid title to lands which had been granted to them in the past thirty-five years."[3]

The land system, as it had evolved to 1795, was really two systems, both based on freehold tenure. The first involved what were termed "official" settlers: those granted lands, without condition, on account of service or position. The great majority of such settlers were Loyalists and military officials who had served in the American Revolution. The precise size and distribution of grants varied over time, but generally they ranged from 5000 acres (2000 ha) for field officers to 200 acres (80 ha) for privates and for civilian Loyalist males. These land grants were intended for settlement purposes but did not have to be occupied to be retained. In many cases, they became assets, held not for development but for speculation against the future worth of land in the colony.

The other class of settlers was the immigrants whose right to land came not from service to the crown but from their potential role in developing the colony. They also had the opportunity to acquire 200 acres (80 ha) of land, but only under certain conditions. Initially, they were given a location ticket to the land. In order to convert that location ticket into clear title, they had to fulfil certain requirements — to live on the land, clear the roadway allowance, build a home, and fence and clear a certain portion of the land. Once that was done (and it often took much longer than the optimistic twelve months that the government set down as the standard), a patent could be issued.

The existence of the two groups of settlers, "official" and "immigrant," created the second and much more persistent problem for the development of Upper Canada. The aims and interests of the two classes of settlers were often at odds. Many official grantees settled on the land and improved it in the same way that settlers fulfilling requirements would. Others, however, saw land as a speculative asset to be held, but not occupied, until increasing population pushed the value up. The existence of speculative landholding contradicted the general government policy, set out by Governor John Graves Simcoe and his successors, of encouraging agricultural development and population growth. Empty lands in prime locations sat vacant, while bona fide immigrants were forced to more remote locations. To compound this problem, the government did not open all lands for settlement. In each township, one-seventh of the land was set aside as a clergy reserve to support the Church of England, and another one-seventh as a crown reserve. Not only was the immigrant likely to find vacant speculative lands nearby, but vacant church and government lands as well. In a colony with a small, scattered population, this meant less likelihood of adequate schools within reasonable range and adequate roads anywhere but on the main routes set out by Simcoe.

The main obstacle to settlement in Upper Canada at this time, however, was the high cost of transporting products to market and bringing in equipment and supplies. Adding to the barrier of high ocean freight rates was the fact that a farmer contemplating locating in Upper Canada had first to get his product to an ocean port. This involved an arduous journey by land to a lake port. To carve roads through the wilderness would be a particular concern of Simcoe, the first governor of the colony, but it would be more than 60 years before there was more than the most rudimentary and limited access to the interior. Then the product had to journey along a Great Lakes–St. Lawrence waterway replete with rapids and other obstacles. To illustrate the problem, in this early period, the cost of shipment of British goods from Montreal to Prescott, the head of navigation on Lake Ontario, was greater than the cost of shipment from Liverpool to Montreal.[4]

There was no real push to improve transport facilities at this time because there were still adequate supplies of better-situated land elsewhere. New York's expanding frontier of settlement had not yet reached Canada (see Map 6.1). The Eastern Townships of Quebec, not Upper Canada, attracted the majority of the few American immigrants. Nevertheless, by the time the government regularized the procedures for land titles the population had reached almost 25 000 individuals, and it was possible to talk of something approaching settled communities in the Niagara district, in the eastern counties of the colony, and around York, the new capital.

Map 6.1 Upper Canada and New York Frontier of Settlement, 1790

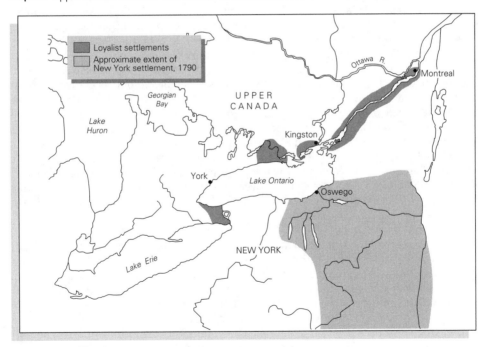

Source: Based on Sam B. Hillard, "A Robust New Nation, 1783–1820," in Robert D. Mitchell and Paul A. Groves, eds., *North America: The Historical Geography of a Changing Continent* (Totowa, NJ: Rowman and Littlefield, 1987). p. 168. Copyright 1990 by Rowman & Littlefield Publishers. Used with permission of the publishers.

In the late 1790s, the American movement into Upper Canada began in earnest. Niagara, which until that time had been a rather isolated community, separated from the natural frontier pushing westward from Quebec, now found itself at the edge of the aggressive, expanding American frontier. The result was dramatic, particularly in the large unsettled areas that stretched inland from Niagara. Township after township opened up to meet the demand of American settlers. Upper Canada's population expanded accordingly, reaching approximately 50 000 by 1806 and 80 000 by 1814.

The tradition in Canadian economic history is to link this surge of migration to two factors: the filling up of competing land in the United States and an increase in the expected returns to agriculture, stemming from the appearance of a market in Britain for North American grains, particularly wheat. The first factor is undeniably relevant. New York state still had, at the end of the American Revolution, many areas of undeveloped land along its northwestern frontier. The state's population grew rapidly, however, from 340 000 in 1790 to 959 000 by 1810. Such growth pushed the western frontier to the borders of British North America. The border proved a small deterrence and, given Native restiveness along the American frontier, a positive incentive for many.

The link of migration to wheat exports is much less certain, however, for two reasons. First, recent literature has recognized that commercial farming, while ultimately the basis of colonial development, was, before the War of 1812, peripheral to most individuals and to the colony. Establishing a farm took time. This was a heavily treed region, and clearing the land, first of trees and then of stumps, was not only backbreaking labour but a slow task. Estimates are that a farmer could clear about 1 ha a year. Thus, it would take a lifetime to establish a moderate-size farm unless the settler had sufficient capital to hire clearing crews. Most did not; thus surplus could come only over time. About 1 ha (or one year of labour) was needed just to feed the average-size family.[5]

Even if sufficient land were cleared to produce a surplus, other obstacles to commercial agriculture existed, especially in the first years of settlement. No outlets existed in transport grain to distant markets, nor were there local mills to produce flour. Until the late 1780s, there were only two flour mills in the entire colony: one on the Bay of Quinte and the other near Niagara. Most immigrants did their milling by hand, and an evening's labour might produce only enough for the next day's needs. There was, in other words, a considerable lag between the time a family occupied a piece of wilderness land and the time that sufficient crops could be grown for any significant or regular sales to take place. Likewise, there was a considerable lag between the time of initial settlement and the time that Upper Canada was able to produce a staple for export. It was 1794 before the first wheat from Upper Canada came through Montreal, and 1800 before those shipments became even sporadically significant.

The second reason to question the traditional link between settlement and wheat exports comes from the demonstration by Marvin McInnis[6] that the market in Britain for North American wheat, from Upper Canada or elsewhere, was highly erratic at this time. The combination of high transport costs and Corn Law duties (as mentioned earlier, "corn" is the British term for wheat) meant that in all but the poorest of harvest years in Britain it simply did not pay to ship wheat across the Atlantic. The farm-gate price, as defined above, was below the farmer's cost of production. Transport costs from farm to ocean port were lower in Lower Canada than they were in Upper Canada at this time, so it is not surprising that when British wheat prices were high, as they were in the first decade of the nineteenth century, it was the former province that sent the grain.

Potash was produced more quickly because it was acquired as a by-product of the clearing process. There are two perspectives on the potash trade, however, and opinions on the significance of the trade will vary depending on the perspective taken. From a macro-economic perspective, it is unlikely that potash was ever very important to the foundation of the colony's economy. The trade was a transitory one for settlers and, as wheat cultivation replaced land-clearing, it invariably fell off. In any given year, therefore, only a certain percentage of settlers were involved in the trade, and the overall export figures were only rarely significant to the colony. From the perspective of the individual settler, however, potash was very important, providing a cash return in the early years of settlement.

If wheat exports to Britain did not support settlement in these early years, what did? Since settlers were not entirely self-sufficient, how did they pay for imports of equipment and supplies? Transfers from external sources is one answer. Foreign exchange came into the colony in three ways: via the British government, from money brought by immigrants, and through trade. These inflows allowed a pioneer society without any significant export and without, as yet, the means of livelihood for people who were still attempting to become farmers to purchase the necessary goods to sustain itself.

Particularly important was the role of the British government. The Upper Canadian economy received considerable support from the mother country. The British contribution to the region came in two main forms. First, the government of London recognized the claim of the Loyalists on it. They had fought for the empire in a bloody civil war, and many had lost homes, businesses, and income in the effort. Aside from the land grants already mentioned, the Loyalists got assistance in a number of other ways, depending on time and locality. Food, clothing, implements, building materials, and seed were typical items of distribution. From 1783 to 1788, Loyalist families thus depended on direct handouts from the British government. The importance of these grants is revealed by the fact that, when the subsidies ended in 1788–89, the year became known locally as "the hungry year" as unprepared families found it difficult to get by without British assistance.

In addition to these supports, there were the "Loyalist claims." Those Loyalists who had suffered losses of income or property as a result of their loyalty to the crown were able to submit a claim to the British government and to ask for compensation. At the very least, these claims were driven to their maximum figure by a sense of grievance for wrongs suffered. Most likely, they were rife with deliberate exaggeration. In either case, however, British payments of Loyalist claims average £178 per claim, an amount sufficient to live on for a year, and acted as a further transfer of British resources to the wilderness of Upper Canada.

In the short run, these direct payments and indirect subsidies were extremely important. In effect, the British government subsidized the initial stages of settlement in Upper Canada. It also meant that there was profit to be made by merchants who could supply these immigrants. The initial fortunes, whether large or small, of a new commercial class rested on the most readily available source of income — British reparations for a lost war.

The Loyalist grants were important, but they were temporary. The other major contribution of British government funds to the new colony was to last somewhat longer and was probably even more important than the subsidies. The end of the American Revolution in 1783 did not end the struggle between the United States and its old parent for supremacy in North America. In many ways, in fact, little beyond the independence of the actual thirteen colonies was resolved. In the West, the British remained in control of thousands of square kilometres of the old French hinterland, even though the land was now recognized by both as U.S. territory. In British North America, there was optimistic (and vain) talk of using this control as a means to gain additional territory. Along both borders, there was a fear of what might come, and, as a result, there was a need to reinforce the boundaries on the map with military force.

104

British garrisons, in the West and in the emergent Upper Canada, were important not only for whatever sense of security they gave but, even more so, for the income they created in a local economy. In the case of the Niagara region, for instance, or that of Kingston, the impact was considerable. Whether providing the British with materials from the local market or acting as the agent to import them from Montreal or England, local entrepreneurs, such as Niagara's Robert Hamilton, found British military contracts to be a key to success on the frontier. For the more modest citizen, the garrison provided an important market to which one could sell (through such people as Hamilton). Pork was the garrison's major purchase from the local community, but farmers also looked to the garrisons for cash for the first crops of wheat, vegetables, or even occasional fruit. The presence of the forts also provided work, such as baking, brewing, hauling, carpentry, and other tasks that could not be handled internally.[7]

Unfortunately, it is impossible to be precise about the amount spent by garrisons in Upper Canada. Military accounts on the cost of the garrison, inexact in themselves, do not distinguish between money spent locally and that sent out for imported supplies. One estimate concludes that between £54 000 and £77 000 was spent annually in Upper Canada in each of the years 1795–1805.[8] Especially in the early years, when the population was small and before wheat exports became significant, the impact of the garrisons on the colony would have been crucial. In 1795, for example, such estimates indicate that the British spent £2 for every resident of Upper Canada. Even as late as 1805, the annual expenditure might very well have amounted to £1 per capita. These estimates are very rough, but for many settlers still struggling to move beyond subsistence, the expenditures by the British military in Canada were probably one of the few means of acquiring currency.

The colony had two other apparent sources of revenue at this time. Wheat was shipped down the St. Lawrence as early as 1794. Some of this produce may have gone on to Britain, but most of it probably remained in Lower Canada. Initally, these shipments were both small-scale and sporadic. Douglas McCalla estimated that in 1803 the average returns to farmers from such sales were between £5 and £6. Although such sales "do not seem to represent a large income for a farm family,"[9] they are worth noting for two reasons. First, even small sums of cash were important to largely self-sufficient farmers. Second, such shipments were harbingers of things to come. In the decades to come, downriver shipments of wheat would play an increasingly important part in Upper Canada's economy.

Compared with the garrisons and Loyalist claims and wheat sales to Lower Canada, the old activity of the fur trade, still so important to Montreal in the late eighteenth century, was not very significant to Upper Canada. When Governor Simcoe proclaimed in 1792, "I consider the fur trade on its present foundation to be of no use whatever to Upper Canada," he was simply reflecting the reality about the marginal importance of that trade to Upper Canada.[10] True, considerable portaging took place to the southwest in the 1780s and early 1790s. For such people as Hamilton, the supply of the fur trade was yet another lucrative possibility for business on the frontier. Yet, two things stand out about this trade. First, it is unlikely that it had much impact beyond the immediate localities of the portages. Second, whatever impact it did have was lessening by the mid-1790s. The British had in 1794 agreed to hand over their western posts to the United States, and the southwest fur trade was unlikely to remain dominated by British capitalists for much longer. The northwest trade was still expanding, but many of the supplies for that went up the Ottawa River and not through the settled portion of Upper Canada at all. The fur trade was an activity in which Montreal was dominant, and Upper Canada was largely irrelevant, even in its early days.

If the fur trade was marginal to the economic well-being of the average settler, the settlers themselves were central to the economic well-being of the colony. The settlers that came to Upper Canada between 1791 and 1812 were relatively common folk, but most, nevertheless, had some means. This was not the famine migration of later years. "Immigration," grumbled one Scot who was left behind, "is a glorious thing for them that have the money."[11] The average per capita wealth of those coming from the United States was likely even greater than that of the Scots. Many of these, by the later 1790s, were established farmers who had sold previous holdings to move on.

Most settlers, therefore, had funds, and all had to spend a considerable amount for tools, provisions, clothing, and other items in order to establish a farm. Financing purchases on the instalment plan was common, and long-term credit was crucial. As that farm was being developed, there were also linkages to other sectors of the economy. Sawmills sprang into being to house the population and, given the similar technologies, often provided the basis for grist mills. Initially, the sawmill would help house the developing population. As settlement and construction moved beyond the region, flour milling would assume greater importance. Flour milling, further, was naturally linked to distilleries, given the latter's need for grain. There was also a growing market in key goods provided by an expanding population. For example, two men who founded a sawmill near York early in the nineteenth century soon found themselves milling flour and distilling grain into whisky. Messrs. Gooderham and Worts thereby established a long-lasting business that rested directly on the demands of a growing population.

For the shopkeepers and forwarders, external spending gave them their livelihood at a time when the earnings of the local farmers were still relatively small. Expenditures by the garrisons, by Loyalists, and by incoming immigrants went through their hands and, to a degree, back out of the colony, to suppliers in Montreal and beyond. British exports to the Canadas between 1800 and 1812 averaged £376 671 annually between 1800 and 1812; so, at least a portion of the funds that came over from the home country went back to its growing industrial sector. Available figures indicate a large net flow of funds (primarily cash) from Britain to Canada through the entire period from the American Revolution to 1812.

All of this means that, at least in its earliest phase, Upper Canada did not have a staple-based (or commodity-based) economy. The assistance to Loyalists, the economic importance of the British garrisons, and the amount of income flowing into the colony by means of immigration provide a better understanding of the nature of economic growth in its earliest period than does any attempt to link this activity to wheat exports.

The end of this initial stage, sometime soon after the end of the War of 1812, left the colony with three economic characteristics. First, and most important, was the straightforward fact that the land, empty in 1783, was now much more populated. The 1811 population of 83 000 was hardly a large one compared to Lower Canada's 300 000, but now there were sufficient people to allow a continuous line of settlement along the north shore of Lake Ontario, from Prescott to Niagara. Settlement was also pushing westward from the Niagara region, and Lake Erie was the destination of small but growing numbers of pioneers. To the north, in the Ottawa valley, lumbering had penetrated the region, but settlement in areas distant from the major water arteries was still largely in the future and access to the "back country" still difficult. The Niagara region, the Bay of Quinte, and the territory immediately around the capital of York were the only places where population was at all large.

The second characteristic of the economy at this time was the establishment of sectors that were eventually to emerge as important export industries. Timber had been important from 1806, though less to Upper than to Lower Canada, and its impact affected only eastern Upper Canada. Agriculture was also on the verge of becoming an important export sector. By 1817, 326 000 acres (130 000 ha) of land were under cultivation and wheat exports to Lower Canada neared 200 000 bushels.[12] Upper Canada began to be seen as a region with great potential in wheat. The dependence on primary resources was reflected in the third characteristic of the economy. Even more so than Lower Canada, Upper Canada was overwhelmingly rural. Urban centres were insignificant. The Town of York, the capital of the colony, had fewer than 1700 people as late as 1824; Kingston, the largest town in the colony, had a population of 2300 in 1820. The population was over 95 percent rural.[13] This pattern would continue well into the next stage of colonial development. Only in the 1840s would any sort of rapid urban growth develop in this small agrarian colony.

Immigration and Settlement, 1815–1841

The period after the War of 1812 ushers in the second phase in Upper Canadian development. Areas around Kingston, Niagara, and York had now been settled for nearly two generations. Farms and villages there had moved beyond the first phase of clearing and rough subsistence farming to a more established and commercially oriented type of farming. Merchants had established the necessary links to permit a steady flow of the growing exports of the colony downriver to Montreal. By now, it was no longer a matter of opening up a wilderness along the lower Great Lakes; that had already been accomplished. Now the structure was different (see Map 6.2). Established farms and villages along the lake were backed by an inland hinterland just entering the pioneer stage of development. Over the next generation the gaps along the lakefront filled in, the good regions inland went through the pioneer stage, and commercial elites sought to establish the legal and financial infrastructure to facilitate their business. Along the way, friction developed within the constitutional system, between farmers and merchants, and between inland and waterfront regions. A rebellion in 1837 and the restructuring of government in 1840 would be a part of the structural change that was taking place.

Other changes distinguish the pre- and postwar patterns. One of these was immigration. Before the War of 1812, the U.S. frontier of settlement accounted for most Upper Canadian immigrants. There had been immigration from the British Isles, but that had been secondary. After 1815, the proportions reversed. American immigration slowed, for two reasons. First, the frontier of open land in the United States had moved westward. Native resistance having been eliminated in the previous decades, the rapid expansion of American agriculture moved beyond the shores of Lake Erie and Lake Ontario to new lands in the Ohio region and beyond. Indiana became a state in 1816; Illinois, in 1818. Upper Canada was no longer in the direct path of those heading to the frontier of settlement.

There were also institutional impediments that were the result of the postwar suspicions, including various measures on the part of the Upper Canadian and British governments to make land ownership more difficult for American citizens. In 1815, for example, the colonial secretary issued instructions to refuse grants of lands to any American immigrant.[14] This regulation would later be modified, but other provisions and uncertainties, including uncertainties as to the rights of "aliens" to obtain lands, meant that, for the next several years, immigration from the United States was severely restricted.

Map 6.2 Distribution of Population, Upper Canada, 1794, 1824, and 1840

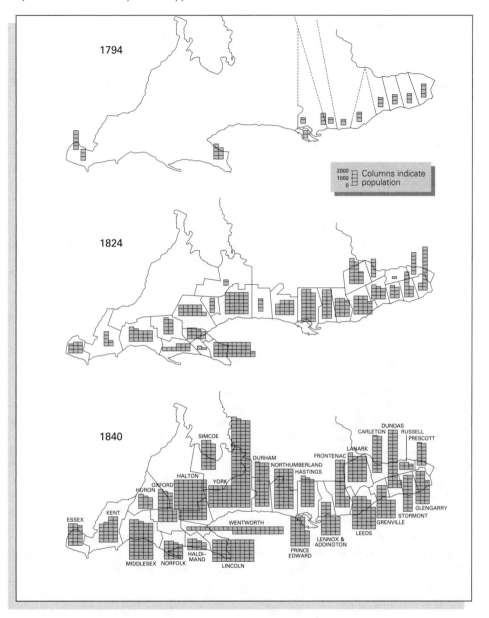

Source: Based on J. David Wood, "The Population of Ontario," in Roger Hall, William Westfall, and Laurel Sefton MacDowell, eds., *Patterns of the Past* (Toronto: Dundurn Press, 1988), p. 57. © Ontario Historical Society, 1988. Used with permission of the publisher.

108

Forces across the Atlantic meant that an ample supply of immigrants could offset the decline of American settlement. Most importantly, the population of Great Britain was growing at a tremendous rate. In 1700, England's population had been just over 5 million, representing a growth of approximately a million people in the previous century. By the time of the conquest in 1759, that population had grown another million; by the end of the American Revolution, by another million; and by the turn of the century, by another million and a half. By 1821 it would be nearly 3 million larger than it had been in 1801.[15] This accelerating growth was the result, to a large degree, of a decline in mortality rates, dating from the middle of the eighteenth century.

In response to concerns over rapidly rising population, increasing unemployment, and the subsequent cost of relief given to the poor, the British government initiated measures to assist would-be emigrants to settle in British North America. The measures varied considerably, depending on the time and place, but from 1815 to 1825 a series of schemes sought both to relieve the economic situation at home and to develop the colonies by means of state-assisted emigration. Typical was the 1815 scheme that provided some 700 emigrants with 100 acres (40 ha) of land, rations for eight months, and implements.

Over the next several years, other groups followed and, with government assistance, began to open up new districts of Upper Canada. Historians who have assessed these schemes have tended to see them as disappointing, if not outright failures. From the British government's point of view, the expense was greater than had been anticipated. Certainly, assisted emigration was no solution to overpopulation at home. From the point of view of overall level of emigration, moreover, assisted emigration was relatively unimportant. Even at the height of British support for migrants, unassisted emigration remained much more important. It was for these reasons and others that the British government abandoned the idea of assisted emigration in 1825.

Yet, assisted emigration did have positive aspects. First, there seems to have been a relatively high success rate among assisted emigrants. A good number did stay, at least long enough to clear their land and obtain the patent. Second, the fact that the immigrants were under an arrangement with the government meant that they could, to a degree, be directed to the lands that the government wanted to see opened. Many such groups were thus instrumental in opening up new townships away from Lake Ontario. For example, British military settlement schemes opened the Perth region to settlement between 1817 and 1822. By the latter date, some 4000 people had taken up land in this area, which otherwise would have remained empty. Also, all too typical was the fact that when immigrants arrived in Upper Canada, they were directed, as was the 1815 group, to some remote district to which, as one Canadian historian noted, "they had to cut their way through twenty miles of unbroken bush."[16]

When the assisted-emigration scheme was abandoned in 1825, it was replaced by a plan based on private enterprise. John Galt had been one of a number of officials appointed by the British government to investigate civilian losses during the War of 1812. Along the way, he came up with a scheme to create a privately owned land company to assist in immigration and settlement. The proposal was timed perfectly, for the British were tired of their direct involvement in assisting emigration. This seemed like a suitable alternative, and in 1826 the Canada Company, as it was known, began operations.

The basis of the company's plans was a 1 million acre (400 000 ha) tract of land stretching west from the present-day city of Guelph to Goderich. Known as the Huron Tract, this wedge-shaped parcel had been bought from the crown and was to be developed by the company as a means of attracting immigrants. Over the next years, development did take place and immigrants were brought in. The land was, however, west of the current frontier of settlement, and the London-based directors found, as had the British government before them, that immigration was an expensive business.[17]

British assistance helped increase the flow of immigration. So, too, did the Canada Company. Far more important than either, however, were the economic factors that drew thousands of individuals to seek to improve their economic well-being by migrating to Upper Canada. Although completely accurate figures do not exist as to the rate of immigration, Figure 6.1 gives a reasonable estimate of emigration to British North America. It shows how British immigration increased from practically nothing to some 23 000 by 1819, and to an average of more than 12 000 annually through the 1820s. There is little doubt about the trend of settlement: Upper Canada was an increasingly popular destination after 1815, with an average annual population growth of 9 percent a year between 1817 and 1826. Economic cycles, political circumstances, and other factors might affect the actual immigration in any given year, but the trend was upward.[18] The population of Upper Canada reflected this immigration, growing from 83 000 in 1817 to 237 000 by the beginning of the 1830s, and 487 000 by 1842. In a generation, it had more than quintupled (see Table 6.1).

Many of these immigrants were undoubtedly motivated by much the same considerations as their predecessors: expecting to be able to provide a better life for their families by meeting most of their own needs on the farm, supplemented occasionally by cash sales. For these new arrivals, life often differed little from that of their predecessors. Even government assistance and the Canada Company made little difference to the harsh routine of settlement. It was still a matter of saving sufficient funds to take care of transportation, fees for land claims, and rations until crops could be grown. Credit was still essential for

Figure 6.1 British Emigration to British North America, 1815–1840

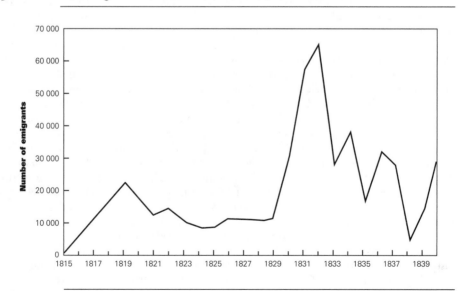

Source: Derived from Helen Cowan, *British Emigration to British North America* (Toronto: University of Toronto Press, 1961), appendix.

survival. The pioneer experience was not all that different from that of the earlier generation who had come out when Upper Canada was but an adjunct of Quebec.

There was a real opportunity to improve their social and material standing over time. The standard of living of an Upper Canadian farmer owning a piece of cleared, fertile land was considerably higher than most could have realized in anything like an analogous social position in England, Scotland, or Ireland. The degree to which that improvement could be realized depended, as always, on a combination of skill, luck, and hard work. It also depended on the savings that immigrants could invest in their new piece of land. The well-off, for example, might avoid the wilderness site in the woods and buy an accessible piece of land from one of the numerous speculators. Others would be able to move to a productive position even more quickly by purchasing an improved farm from some pioneer who wished to sell out and move on.

Yet, for all the similarities in the experience of the pre- and post-1812 pioneer, commercial possibilities in the agricultural sector were considerably brighter after the war. Increasingly, a rudimentary pioneer economy, based on land appreciation and the inflow of immigrants, ran parallel to an increasingly productive agricultural sector. Agricultural produce, and not just the potential of the future, was becoming important to the shape of the Upper Canadian economy after 1820.

The growth of agriculture after the War of 1812 was not without difficulties. The war had kept prices high for farmers who were fortunate enough not to have their farms in the line of marching armies or foraging raiders. After the war, prices remained high for a while, in part as a result of continued purchases by enlarged British garrisons and a high demand for wheat in Great Britain. It was not long before army garrisons and, therefore, army purchases, began to shrink. Within a few years, the boom times (and inflation) of war had come to an end.[19]

Over time, however, the demand for Upper Canada's wheat surplus came from two other sources. Lower Canada was now producing less wheat than it had in the past. By the 1830s, wheat coming from the west to Montreal accounted for nearly three-quarters of net exports from the Canadas.[20] By the period 1824–31, the quantities of wheat coming into Montreal from the west were greater, on average, than the total exports from the St. Lawrence system. In other words, western wheat not only dominated the export trade but increasingly fed Lower Canada.

The British market for wheat and flour was a great lure to Upper Canadians as well, but here they faced two obstacles: import duties and transport costs. The import duties were set out in the Corn Laws, which, as we saw earlier, were designed to provide agricultural interests in the United Kingdom with protection from offshore competition. Inroads were being made on protectionist thought in Britain, however, and the exclusion of colonial wheat only increased the force of the challenge. Over the next few years, British Corn Law regulations underwent a series of modifications that had the net effect, by 1827, of turning a strong protectionist and exclusionist system into a moderate tariff preference for British farmers (see Figure 6.2). Any reduction in the British duty on wheat would be mainly reflected in a higher farm-gate price in Upper Canada, so these changes to the Corn Laws certainly favoured the expansion of agriculture in the colony.

Whatever the import duties, however, an export trade in wheat from Upper Canada could only develop if transport costs were lowered. The first stage in this process was the distance between farm and lake port. To move away from the waterfront was to encounter the vast forest, an obstacle to both farming and movement. There were, it was true, a few roads: Yonge Street, running north from York, and Dundas Street, which went west from the head of the lake, were opened by Governor Simcoe before 1800 for the dual purposes

Figure 6.2 Corn Law Tariff Structure, 1822–1825 and 1827–1842

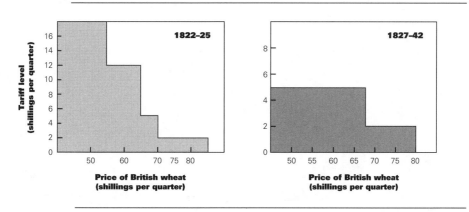

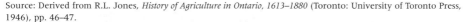

Source: Derived from R.L. Jones, *History of Agriculture in Ontario, 1613–1880* (Toronto: University of Toronto Press, 1946), pp. 46–47.

of defence and colonization. Both were mere strips through the wilderness, however. Trees were cleared to the point where an axle could pass over the remaining stumps. These conditions would remain unchanged for many years to come, except for the ruts that passing traffic wore along the forest track. Gradually the regions were settled, and as farmers took up land other local roads appeared, usually of the same primitive variety.

These realities imposed certain limitations and rhythms on the movements of the farmer in this period (see Figure 6.3). A great deal of travel took place immediately after harvest in the fall. Grain was moved to the mill, supplies bought for the winter, and a break taken to mark the completion of another growing season. This was the time to visit the town and to look to whatever purchases of clothing, materials, or other "luxuries" might be affordable. An even better time for movement was in the dead of winter. Travel by sleighs running over snow was invariably superior to that over the best roads that Upper Canada had to offer. When the snow melted in some untimely winter thaw or with the coming of spring, the muddy tracks became impassable for a wagon, and the movement of heavy goods ceased. By midsummer, roads had dried out enough that another round of purchases, movement of supplies, and visits could take place before the busy harvest season began.[21]

The primitive road system and its inherent problems meant that water continued to be the key method of transportation for bulk goods over long distances until the coming of the railway at midcentury. This fact was both the great advantage of Upper Canada and, paradoxically, one of its great burdens. The advantage came from the fact that the St. Lawrence–lower Great Lakes system had provided this inland colony with access to the sea. People and goods were able to move back and forth with an ease that would have been impossible had there been no direct water route. The burden was that the natural state of the St. Lawrence–Great Lakes system was far from ideal. It was one thing for fur traders to portage their goods at several points. Furs were high value-to-bulk goods that could be shipped profitably in spite of transport costs. Wheat was a bulk good, however, and the costs of transshipment were a significant burden.

Figure 6.3 Cycle of Wheat Delivery to Yonge Mills, 1834

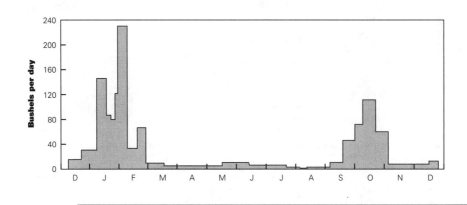

Source: Thomas McIlwraith, "The Adequacy of Rural Roads in the Era Before Railways: An Illustration from Upper Canada," *Canadian Geographer* 14(4) (Winter 1970): 357.

If wheat was to be exported along the Great Lakes–St. Lawrence system, therefore, improvements had to be made, which at this time meant canal construction. Lower transport costs would increase the farm-gate price of wheat, which in turn would mean both higher returns to existing farmers and an expanded feasible area for commercial agricultural production. In the absence of better transportation alternatives for their grain, farmers in Upper Canada would tend to support canal projects.

The geography of the region was such that the new feasible agricultural area created by an improved Great Lakes–St. Lawrence waterway would lie partly in Canada and partly in the United States. Thus, while farmers were only concerned that their grain travelled to tidewater as cheaply as possible, the merchants and forwarders wanted it to do so along this particular waterway. They were not interested just in Upper Canadian wheat but in the dominance of a vast hinterland stretching through Upper New York state, the Ohio country, and the new territories to the west.[22] Just as Robert Hamilton and his compatriots had done much of the supplying of fur traders in this region in the late eighteenth century, so those who succeeded Hamilton wanted to ensure that it was they who shipped American wheat to England and supplied the growing back-country population of both British North America and the United States with the latest luxuries and manufactures from the United Kingdom.

The problem for the Canadian merchants was that there were also U.S. merchants, shippers, forwarders, and financiers with their eyes on the growing produce of this transborder frontier region. The need for improved transportation facilities to supply the west led New York to counter the natural advantages of the St. Lawrence waterway. In 1825, the Erie Canal was opened, connecting Lake Erie to the Hudson–Mohawk river system and thence to New York. Three years later, the Oswego feeder connected the Erie system to

Lake Ontario. These improvements captured not only the American agricultural frontier, but also much of the Canadian one. These farmers now had their improved waterway to tidewater. They were therefore less likely to support the merchants in their attempts to construct a parallel one north of the border.

Improvements in the Canadas began nonetheless. In 1819, St. Catharines businessman William Merritt began work on the Welland Canal between Lakes Erie and Ontario. Developed in part because of Merritt's need for more abundant supplies of water for his milling operations, the Welland was an ambitious project that, once completed, would overcome one of the longer portages in the Great Lakes system. At the other end of the system, a group of Montreal businessmen had begun work on the Lachine Canal near Montreal.

At this point, differences between the state of development in New York and that in the Canadas became apparent. New York was a heavily populated region with an increasingly diverse economy. It had a population of well over a million people and considerable wealth. Therefore, it had little trouble financing the Erie system. The Canadian economy was still in an early stage of development and did not possess any significant amount of savings. It is, therefore, not really surprising that both the Welland and the Lachine canals soon ran into financial trouble.

In Upper Canada, the importance of the grain trade and of the aspirations to commercial hegemony over the American West soon became apparent. Merritt went, cap in hand, to government, and, in 1826, the government purchased some £25 000 in stock. Once in, it could not easily get out, and other stock purchases and grants soon followed the first one. As H.G. Aitken noted in his study of the canal, by 1827 the "Welland Canal Company was already degenerating into a privately controlled institution for the disbursement of public funds." By 1834 the government recognized its irrevocable stake in the canal when, as part of another grant, it insisted on the right to appoint three of the seven directors of the canal company. By 1839, it was moving to take over the canal completely.[23]

In Lower Canada, the fate of the Lachine was much the same. The original investors could not make a go of it, and the legislative assembly of Lower Canada had to take over. There were two differences in the pattern, however. First, the collapse of the original company meant that, unlike Welland, the Lachine became a government operation by 1821. Second, political divisions between the predominantly English-Canadian merchant class and French-Canadian professional and farm interests meant that the legislative assembly became hostile to further canal development. It was to be many years later, under different political circumstances, that canals were built to circumvent the other rapids on the upper St. Lawrence.

There was a third canal project. In 1826, the imperial government funded the construction of the Rideau Canal system to assure military supply movements in the event of another war with the United States. When completed in 1832, it ran from Kingston through the Rideau waterway to the Ottawa River at Bytown (now Ottawa) and provided a minimum depth of 4.5 feet (1.4 m) for boats running from Montreal to Lake Ontario. Together with the Welland, this canal provided direct access from Montreal to the interior and marked a significant improvement upon the natural transportation system of the Great Lakes. It is thus fair to see the transportation infrastructure improving parallel and in response to the rise of a significant wheat-export sector.

Yet, the improvements were of limited use. The Rideau Canal was a circuitous way to get from Kingston to Montreal. The very thing that made it attractive to the military — its distance from the vulnerable upper St. Lawrence — hampered its effectiveness as a commercial supply system. Further, the depths in the system varied from the 4.5 feet (1.4 m) of the Rideau to the 8 feet (2.4 m) of the Welland. Ships plying the Great Lakes were unlikely to be able to proceed through the Rideau. Boats or barges with a shallow enough draft to ply the Rideau were unlikely to venture out on the stormy Great Lakes. Transshipment was still necessary. Over the next twenty years, the development of the St. Lawrence canal system and its ongoing rivalry with American transportation routes was a central theme in the welfare of farmers, merchants, and government. It would also be a severe financial strain. As early as 1829, three-quarters of the government's debt to the Bank of Upper Canada was related to expenditures on Welland Canal.[24]

Several years ago, Aitken coined the phrase "defensive expansionism" to sum up the policy of development represented by the Welland and other canals. In brief, he argued that the development of the canal system was necessary because of the American moves to capture the grain trade. Yet, as Merritt quickly discovered, Upper Canada did not possess the savings to undertake such a project, and investors elsewhere were not likely to be enthusiastic about such a dubious scheme. In other words, the project was crucial to the aspirations of the colony but was not a viable private market venture. The only alternative was government involvement as an agent of development. It is a pattern that has been a constant characteristic of Canadian economic development.

There was one additional complication. Under the Navigation Acts, American wheat coming through Canada or ground into flour in Canada counted as Canadian supplies. While the merchants favoured this provision since it increased the likelihood that American farmers would ship their wheat to Britain via the Canadian system, Canadian farmers resented it since the influx of American grain tended to depress domestic prices. Until 1831, this effect was moderated by a Canadian tariff on American wheat. In that year, however, the British government abolished all duties on American agricultural products entering Canada. This move was a great benefit to Canadian merchants and forwarders because they got to carry all of that American wheat as well as Canadian. Indeed, the shifts in attitudes toward imports of American flour and wheat reveal the rise of a merchant class whose views did not always coincide with those of farmers.

The combination of a more accessible British market, lower transport costs, and the growing market for wheat in Lower Canada allowed a recovery from the agricultural recession of the early 1820s. In 1826, some 599 000 acres (240 000 ha) of land were "under culture." By 1829, that figure had grown to more than 717 000 acres (287 000 ha), and, by 1832, to 916 000 acres (366 000 ha). Parts of the province, such as Niagara and the areas immediately adjacent to Kingston and to York, were, by the latter date, well-established agricultural communities with farms far removed from the pioneer stage.

The impact of this developing agricultural sector is shown as well by the export figures for wheat. As was mentioned above, wheat from the western United States and from Upper Canada flowed through Montreal in ever-larger amounts during the 1820s. As the records do not separate American from Upper Canadian produce, it is not possible to make any exact statement on the growth of wheat exports. Overall, however, the movement of western wheat through Montreal increased from an 1817–22 mean of 281 000 bushels to an 1824–31 mean of 534 000 bushels. In 1831, more than 1 million bushels of wheat from the west moved down the St. Lawrence (see Table 6.2). Given the opening of alternative outlets for western wheat in the Erie Canal (see page 120) and given the tariff that was imposed on American wheat and flour coming into Canada in the 1820s, there is nothing to indicate that this growth was disproportionately the result of American shipment through Canada.

Table 6.2 Shipments of Wheat from West to Quebec and Overseas, 1817–1847

Year	Amount (000 bushels)	Year	Amount (000 bushels)
1817	219	1833	1177
1818	229	1834	400
1819	78	1835	109
1820	416	1836	(unknown)
1821	421	1837	(unknown)
1822	326	1838	644
1823	(unknown)	1839	1045
1824	240	1840	2943
1825	186	1841	3438
1826	371	1842	(unknown)
1827	627	1843	(unknown)
1828	517	1844	3271
1829	337	1845	3791
1830	931	1846	4593
1831	1069	1847	5757
1832	(unknown)		

Source: John McCallum, *Unequal Beginnings: Agriculture and Economic Development in Quebec and Ontario until 1870* (Toronto: University of Toronto Press, 1980), table S.1, p. 124.

Wheat was Upper Canada's most important agricultural product, but it was not the only one. The Upper Canadian frontier was still, in many respects, a pioneer economy where farmers provided themselves and their families with a range of foods, even as they concentrated the majority of their land on one or two key crops. Likewise, livestock of various sorts, from hogs through chickens and cattle, were used as food for the family and for cash sales to local towns or to British garrisons.

There was also an element of gender specialization that showed up in these different farming activities. Many, though not all, of these non-wheat activities were the responsibility of women. The fact that some of these activities do not find their way into the marketplace has often caused historians to underestimate their importance, and thereby, to undervalue the importance of women's contributions. Yet, these activities were vital to the well-being of the farm operation. For one thing, a good part of the family's food and clothing on even the relatively commercialized nineteenth-century wheat farm was home-grown or home-made. The kitchen garden was not a hobby but a vital source of food, as was the milk obtained from farm cows. Common, as well, was the mixing of these operations as a part-cash, part-self-provisioning activity. Thus, in many cases, milk or eggs would provide a small cash sale to the local village or town. As these operations could be started relatively rapidly, income from them often predated significant sales of wheat and, thus, like potash or work for the local garrisons, provided crucial funds during the first years. Even after the farm was established, these ancillary activities were vital to the farming operation.[25]

116

Particular parts of the province also concentrated on particular crops. After 1820, as wheat prices slumped, a number of farmers in Essex and Kent counties began to grow tobacco. It was a labour-intensive crop that was also lucrative and, by the time wheat prices recovered, many farmers in the region had become sufficiently specialized that they did not return to wheat.[26]

Nevertheless, in only a few regions were specialized crops such as tobacco important. Wheat created capital, brought in people, and allowed the development of commerce and manufacturing. Wheat was undoubtedly the dominant crop in Upper Canada. The growth of the wheat economy in the period from the early 1820s through the later 1830s has led some economists and historians to argue strongly that wheat provided the central impetus to growth in the sense that this was implied by traditional staples theory.[27] As one author put it, "A more classic case of staple production would be difficult to imagine."[28]

Others, while admitting the obvious importance of wheat, note that it is very difficult to relate wheat exports to overall economic prosperity and growth in the colony. High wheat exports are not easily matched with the attraction of immigrants or, at least in the short term, to commercial prosperity.[29] There is general consensus, however, both that wheat was the key to the agricultural sector in Canada and that agricultural production was central to the continued prosperity of the economy through the later 1820s and early 1830s.

Economic Diversification, 1815–1840

What linkages, if any, did the export grain economy have with other facets of Upper Canadian economic development? Did agricultural requirements lead to other developments within the economy? In other words, did the export grain economy have linkages that helped diversify and develop the Upper Canadian economy, as classical theories about a successful staple would have it? This is a difficult question to answer, at least for the period before 1840. There were some linkages, of course. The small metropolitan centres existed mainly to serve the attendant farm communities. The merchant community stocked its wares and planned its budget according to the rhythms of farm life. Equally, it has been argued that the presence of a viable farm hinterland was central in the 1830s to the assertion of pre-eminence by the city of Toronto by mid-century. The existence of Yonge Street, stretching north to Holland Landing, and the presence of a fertile and accessible hinterland gave Toronto an opportunity for growth.[30] Between 1826 and 1841, the population of the city grew from 1719 to more than 14 000. It was not exactly a major urban centre yet, but it was, by 1841, significantly larger than any of its Upper Canadian rivals.

It is also possible to argue that the period before 1840 saw the beginnings of a distinct merchant-capitalist class and that such a class was directly or indirectly dependent on agricultural exports. There is disagreement on this point, however, and more work needs to be done before any final conclusions can be drawn. Still, various pieces of evidence point to the period between 1820 and 1840 as being crucial in this regard. First, it was in this period that the financial infrastructure necessary for regular merchant and financial activities came into being. In 1821, the first bank in the colony, the Bank of Upper Canada, was chartered by the legislature. Strongly interlinked with the government clique known as the Family Compact, the bank was able to secure favour over rival interests in Kingston and to force a withdrawal of the Bank of Montreal from many parts of the province.

A comparison of the state of the bank at the time of its formation with its state at the time of the 1841 union of Upper and Lower Canada reveals much about the development of capital in Upper Canada. Initially the bank was required by the legislature to have £20 000 in deposits before it could begin business. Even with the backing of the Family Compact, and even though it was the only bank in the colony, it could not raise the money. The requirement was lowered to £10 000. That was still too much. One estimate is that it had only £8000 on opening day. Only an illegal advance from the army chest allowed it to meet minimum requirements. To the degree that this reflects the resources in the provincial capital, it indicates the absence of any significant capitalist class.

The subsequent years stand in sharp contrast. As population poured into the province and as the grain trade developed, so, too, did savings. The bank paid regular dividends through the 1820s and soon had branches in Niagara, Cobourg, Kingston, and Brockville. By 1840, in spite of the financial crisis that hit the colony in 1837–38, the bank remained a prosperous and viable institution — a fact reflected in the £38 000 in dividends that it had paid out over the years.[31]

Thus, there was, by the 1830s, an emerging class of entrepreneurs who, though tied to the political elite of the colony, were distinct forces in their own right. Such people as William Allen, the first president of the Bank of Upper Canada, were involved in a range of business activities ranging from life insurance to the Welland Canal. Along the way, Allen and others, such as grain forwarder Isaac Buchanan and merchant James Newbigging, amassed considerable financial resources and developed intercolonial and even transatlantic connections. These resources would prove important when the colony moved to the expensive venture of railway development a few years later.[32]

The rise of a business class distinct from that of Montreal also had implications within the colony. More and more it was the grain distributors, the merchants, and the bankers in Toronto and Hamilton that stepped into the place of Montrealers. As they gained wealth and strength, they also gained autonomy from Montreal, often dealing directly with New York or London. At the same time, they asserted their dominance over the surrounding region. Small communities were increasingly oriented toward Toronto or Hamilton. The process was not complete by 1840, but, however much other lakefront communities might spin dreams of their own glorious prospects, the "golden horseshoe" was beginning to take shape.

The rise of Toronto and Hamilton is clearly reflected in the patterns of settlement after 1820. The established districts around Kingston remained static or declined in terms of share of the provincial population. So, too, did the fertile Niagara region. This fact has been attributed to poor soil in the hinterland, in the case of Kingston, and to an absence of free land, in the case of Niagara. That may be the case, but it is revealing that the frontier London and western regions saw little or no relative population growth in the later 1820s. In the 1830s this situation changed somewhat, but even by 1840 this whole frontier of open and available land had increased its portion of the provincial population by only a little more than 3 percent.

What grew, in relative terms, was the area immediately adjacent to the communities of Toronto and Hamilton. The Town of York, as Toronto was called before 1834, may have been small, but the population dependent on it was increasing rapidly. The Home District increased its population from 18 400 in 1826 to 78 900 by 1841. The District of Gore increased from 13 000 to 56 400 in the same period. Together, their share of the provincial population increased by more than 10 percent in this fifteen-year period. By 1814, one

The town of York in the early 1830s, looking east along King Street East. Although the town was small, the population dependent on it increased rapidly. By the time of the union of Upper and Lower Canada, one in five Upper Canadians lived within 75 miles of the city of Toronto, foreshadowing that city's importance in the colony.

Toronto Reference Library (T.P.L.)/J. Ross Robertson Collection: T10248.

in five Upper Canadians lived within 75 miles (120 km) of Toronto. This was a shift of some importance and, when combined with the rising Toronto merchant class, clearly foreshadowed that city's pre-eminence within the colony. By the time the provincial government left the city in 1841, it was no longer crucial to Toronto's survival. It had been transformed from an administrative centre to a commercial city. It was not yet able to challenge Montreal's farflung resources or to dream, as Montrealers had long done, of commercial supremacy over wide swaths of the continent. Such challenges and dreams were only a few years away, however.

The urban centres, whether Toronto, Kingston, Hamilton, or small farming towns, also had an increasingly diverse economic profile. Tanners, blacksmiths, carpenters, brick makers, and so on all had come into being to serve the growing population and an economy increasingly based on cash transactions. Newspapers sprang up like weeds in this very political age. Every place that had pretensions to being a town soon carried a paper of some political stripe and varying quality. By 1841, Toronto alone had twelve papers and Kingston five.[33] There were even some 1300 places listed as factories by this time, though the great majority in this pre-industrial age were small operations — potash works, tanneries, furniture makers —aimed at serving the local market and protected from outside competition by the very high costs of transportation. Still, the variety of enterprise indicates the way in which the agricultural prosperity of the province had permitted the development of a considerable range of activities. Before long, these small industries would begin to challenge agriculture and commerce for an important place in the overall economy.

The Beginnings of a New Economic Order, 1840–1846

119

For all the progress and growth that had occurred, Upper Canada was in trouble by the mid-1830s. Wheat prices in Britain had collapsed, and many farmers found themselves facing an increasingly uncertain future. Immigration fell off by the middle of the decade, as the British ceased to leave their homeland in such great numbers. Certainly the absence of a significant demand for wheat made pioneer life in the colonies a less attractive proposition.

Things were equally difficult for the government. Revenues for a colonial government in this period were always precarious. Some British grants could be counted on, as could some excise taxes. The largest single item of government revenue, however, was customs duties — tariffs on goods entering the country. The great majority of goods entering Upper Canada, however, cleared customs and paid the attendant duties not in the province but at Montreal. Throughout the years, this fact had been a source of controversy between Upper and Lower Canada and, though both the British and the Lower Canadian governments accepted in principle the right of Upper Canada to have a share of these revenues, the difficulties remained.

One part of the problem with Lower Canada was political. The control of funds was a major focal point of the battle between reformers and conservatives in that province. There was also a natural desire to hold on to as much as possible. Upper Canada complained loudly and often that it never got its fair share. The other part of the problem was the simple fact that Upper Canada contained the primary settlement frontier for British North America. It was this province, therefore, that had the most rapidly growing population. In 1814, Upper Canada's population was only 28 percent of that of Lower Canada. By 1831, it was 43 percent, and, by the union of 1841, was probably approaching 70 percent, in spite of Lower Canada's high birth rate. Such rapid change meant that, by the time an agreement was made with Lower Canada on the basis of population, it was outdated.

The frontier position of Upper Canada also created difficulties on the expenditure side. The Family Compact and the rising merchant class of the colony were firm believers in the necessity of extensive growth. People had to be attracted, exports had to increase, and investments had to be made. To do this, financing was necessary, and, as the Welland Canal experience illustrates, Upper Canada soon found itself directly involved in the heavy costs of development. Even if revenues had been more equitably distributed and external depressions and financial crises had not intruded, it is likely the government would have found itself overextended by the late 1830s. As it was, it nearly went bankrupt. The crisis resulting from political division, government overexpenditure, and farm discontent led to a tripling of government debt between 1834 and 1838. By the troubled year of 1837, depression had settled over the province, and government and financial circles began to fear for the soundness of Upper Canada's young banking system. In the spring of that year, a series of economic and political events in the United States caused the New York banks to suspend specie payments. The suspension soon spread to other American banks, and the panic reached across the border. In Lower Canada, the Bank of Montreal suspended specie payments in the spring, and by June the legislature allowed the banks in Upper Canada to follow suit.[34]

All of this was serious enough, but the rebellions in both Lower and Upper Canada at the end of the year created an image of political instability that threatened to prevent recovery. The government remained in a precarious financial state. Indeed, by 1839, Sir George Arthur, the lieutenant-governor of Upper Canada, noted with chagrin that "the public debt of this province ... involves an expenditure in interest nearly equal to the whole revenues of the colony." Immigrants were naturally hesitant to come to a land plagued by depression, rebellion, and recurring postrebellion border incidents. Whereas some 12 000 immigrants landed at Quebec in 1836, only 990 did so in 1838, and 1586 in 1839. External intervention would be necessary if the economic and fiscal soundness of the colony were to be restored within a reasonable time.

That external assistance came in two forms. First, the British government moved to unite Upper and Lower Canada. One motive was political. It was hoped that a growing English population would eventually dominate and assimilate the existing French-Canadian Roman Catholic population. There was also an economic motive. The creation of the single Province of Canada was very much an attempt to create a rational economic unit with a strong fiscal base for future development.

The economic motivation of the British government was clearly reflected in the special report by Lord Durham, who had been sent in the wake of the rebellions to advise upon remedies for the future. For Durham, the key to happiness and loyalty, at least among the English colonials, was prosperity. Those measures that developed the economy were henceforth to be seen as a part of the great imperial effort to bring contentment to this part of the empire. Charles Poulett Thompson (soon to be Lord Sydenham), the first governor-general of the united Province of Canada, symbolized the new attitude of Britain. Unlike past governors, who had had professional military and diplomatic backgrounds, Thomson, a former president of the British Board of Trade and former member of Parliament from the industrial city of Manchester, was focused on economic growth. Outside assistance was also provided to promote development and to gain support for the efforts of Sydenham. The British government guaranteed a £1.5 million loan to the new province. Provincial loans raised under this guarantee would have all the prestige and financial security of the British government. Canada would be able to raise money in Britain once again to undertake rapid development.

The British efforts as well as the return of political stability in Canada had the desired effect. Immigration picked up, population increased, and wheat exports rose to record levels. There was also a considerable infusion of spending directly from the government, as it used the British guarantee to develop a canal system with a depth of 9 feet (2.75 m), from Lake Erie to the Atlantic. With a reorganized Board of Works spending the £1.5 million and more, and with up to 6000 labourers employed on canal works, the colonial government became, for the first time, a significant enough spender to have a direct effect on the economy.

The commercial possibilities of the new Province of Canada depended, as always, on the health of the primary-resource sector, in general, and on the export markets for timber and wheat, in particular. The state of the latter staple was potentially a problem. From the early 1830s, farmers had been unhappy with British policies, which seemed to favour commercial interests. Since the mid-1830s, farmers had faced uncertain wheat prices in Britain and had been frustrated by the protective remnants of the Corn Laws. To some degree, the rebellions of 1837 reflected the agrarian discontent with the trends of recent years.

The continuing erosion of mercantilism helped Canadian farmers in this instance. In the Canada Corn Act of 1843, the British government agreed to accept Canadian wheat in

Britain, regardless of local prices, for the nominal duty of 1 shilling per quarter (1 quarter = 8 bushels). Canada, for its part, had responded to British and agricultural concerns the year before by levying a duty of 3 shillings per quarter on all American agricultural produce coming into Canada. It was a situation with something to please everyone. The duty was not high enough to prevent Americans from taking advantage of the Corn Act by shipping along the St. Lawrence, and the merchants could thus look forward to expanded business. At the same time, Canadian farmers finally had a concrete price advantage over their American competitors in dealing with wholesalers.

None of these policy decisions would have had any dramatic effect had there not been demand for Canadian products. Fortunately for Canada, there was. In timber and wheat, there was a generally strong demand in Britain and a still small but growing market in the United States. Wheat exports from Canada were, by 1840, higher than they had ever been before. By 1846 and 1847, even that record amount had almost tripled. In the latter two years, the total exports were greater than those of the entire period from 1817 to 1839. Over the next decade, such orders of magnitude were not at all uncommon. Prosperity was reflected in population growth and in urban development. The actual rates were remarkable, surpassing by far those of the home country at the peak of its demographic explosion. Canada West increased from a total population of 300 000 in 1840 to 721 000 by 1851. Toronto grew from a mere 14 000 people at the time of the union to 23 500 by 1848, and to nearly 31 000 by 1851. It was, by then, a city with a significant hinterland. Wholesalers now had the connections, the money, and the volume to import directly from New York or London. They, in turn, were the distributors for many smaller urban centres in Ontario.[35]

In Canada East, the population growth was encouraged not only by a healthy inflow of immigrants but also by a continuation of the high birth rate and low mortality rate. A population of around 600 000 at the time of the union grew to 890 000 by 1851. Montreal, which despite Toronto's growth was still the commercial and financial centre of the province, experienced the benefits of the commercial prosperity of the first half of the decade. Its population grew from approximately 40 000 at the time of the union to more than 57 000 by 1851. In spite of such a healthy growth rate, however, Canada East did not grow as quickly as did Canada West. There was simply not as much cheap fertile land as there was in Canada West, and the agricultural output was mixed at best. By 1851, Canada West had surpassed Canada East in population, an event that was to create considerable political unrest over the next years.

Conclusion

The changes of the 1840s also brought Canada to the threshold of a new era. Rapid immigration had allowed the settlement of large tracts of land, so that, by midcentury, settlement was pretty much complete in large parts of southern Canada West. A population of a few thousand in 1783 had grown to almost a million in fewer than 70 years. Only on the northern fringes of settlement, where fertile land met the Canadian Shield, and in the area west of London was there still any significant amount of homestead land. Before long, these too would be gone. The agricultural frontier was about to move beyond the Province of Canada.

The new era was also coming because of revolutions in the imperial system. The Canada Corn Act, which had been so praised, was but another manifestation of the British movement away from mercantilism. In 1846, as a result of famine in Ireland, the Corn

Laws were suspended and then abolished. Henceforth, an economic system that had grown up under assumptions predicated on mercantilism would have to adjust to the new world of open trade. For many Canadians, especially millers and forwarders, it was not a comforting thought.

122

Finally, a new economic era was about to begin because of changing technology, especially in the era of transportation. Steam power had come to the Great Lakes earlier in the century. Now, by the later 1840s, steam power was about to lessen the importance of the lakes as a transportation route. Canada was on the verge of the railway era, and this would have massive implications not only for transportation but for the nature of finance, the distribution of wealth, the degree of capital accumulation, and the overall structure and diversity of the economy.

Transportation, the legislative framework within which the economy operated, and the impending passing of the agricultural frontier thus marked the end of one stage of Canadian development. The next stage would see Canada move to a much larger political base, partly to facilitate further economic development. It would also see increasing diversity in the economy and the movement, at least in the central regions, away from a simple staple economy. Confederation and the beginnings of industrialization were keys to the economic developments of the years after 1846.

NOTES

1. J.M. Bumsted, *The People's Clearance, 1770–1815* (Edinburgh: University of Edinburgh Press, 1982), 73.
2. T. Regehr, "Land Ownership in Upper Canada, 1783–1796," *Ontario History* 55 (1963): 37.
3. Regehr, "Land Ownership," 46.
4. T.W. Acheson, "The Nature and Structure of York Commerce in the 1820's," *Canadian Historical Review* 50(4) (1969): 406–28.
5. Peter Russell, "Upper Canada: A Poor Man's Country? Some Statistical Evidence," *Canadian Papers in Rural History*, vol. 3 (Gananoque, ON: Langdale Press, 1978), 136–37.
6. R.M. McInnis, "The Early Ontario Wheat Staple Reconsidered," *Canadian Papers in Rural History VIII* (Gananoque, ON: Langdale Press, 1992), 17–48.
7. See John Philip, "The Economic and Social Effects of the British Garrisons on the Development of Western Upper Canada," *Ontario History* 41 (1949): 37–48; Bruce Wilson, *The Enterprises of Robert Hamilton* (Toronto: University of Toronto Press, 1983).
8. Douglas McCalla, "The 'Loyalist' Economy of Upper Canada," *Social History* 16(32) (November 1983): 291.
9. Douglas McCalla, *Planting the Province: The Economic History of Upper Canada, 1784–1870* (Toronto: University of Toronto Press, 1993), 24.
10. Simcoe to Henry Dundas, April 28, 1792; cited in E.A. Cruikshank, ed., *The Correspondence of Lt. Governor John Graves Simcoe*, vol. 1 (Toronto: Ontario Historical Society, 1931), 141.
11. Cited in Helen Cowan, *British Emigration to British North America* (Toronto: University of Toronto Press, 1961), 25. See also, on the question of capital, Bumsted, *The People's Clearance*.
12. McCalla, *Planting the Province*, appendix B, tables 3.2, 3.4.
13. McCalla, "The 'Loyalist' Economy."
14. M.L. Hansen and J.B. Brebner, *The Mingling of the Canadian and American Peoples* (New Haven: Yale University Press, 1940), 95.
15. From E.A. Wrigley and R.S. Schofield, *The Population History of England* (London: Edward Arnold, 1981), table 7.8. Figures are less certain for Scotland and Ireland, but indicate that Scotland's growth rate was approximately that of England. Ireland's may have been even higher.
16. Cowan, *British Emigration*, 43.

17. On the Canada Company see Clarence Karr, *The Canada Land Company: The Early Years* (Toronto: Ontario Historical Society, 1974).
18. Cited in Cowan, *British Emigration*, appendix B.
19. McCalla, *Planting the Province*, 34.
20. Some of that wheat was American. Since the figures are not consistent, it is impossible to separate wheat of U.S. origin from that of Upper Canadian origin. The irregular figures indicate, however, that Upper Canada was the supplier of most of this wheat. See John McCallum, *Unequal Beginnings: Agriculture and Economic Development in Quebec and Ontario until 1870* (Toronto: University of Toronto Press, 1980), appendix S1.
21. See Thomas McIlwraith, "The Adequacy of Rural Roads in the Era Before Railways: An Illustration from Upper Canada," *Canadian Geographer* 14(4) (Winter 1970): 344–60; and T.W. Acheson, "The Nature and Structure of York Commerce in the 1820's," in J.K. Johnson, ed., *Historical Essays on Upper Canada* (Toronto: McClelland & Stewart, 1975).
22. The classic statement of this merchant outlook is Donald Creighton, *Empire of the St. Lawrence* (Toronto: Macmillan, 1956).
23. H.G. Aitken, *The Welland Canal Company: A Study in Canadian Enterprise* (Cambridge, MA: Harvard University Press, 1954), 41–42.
24. Acheson, "The Nature and Structure of York Commerce," 189.
25. On the earliest stages of farming in Upper Canada see Janice Potter, "Patriarchy and Paternalism: The Case of Eastern Ontario Loyalist Women," unpublished paper presented at the Canadian Historical Association annual meeting, June 1988. See also Alison Prentice et al., *Canadian Women: A History*, 2nd ed. (Toronto: Harcourt Brace, 1996), 69–70.
26. The most straightforward case for the application of the staples theory to Upper Canadian wheat is seen in McCallum, *Unequal Beginnings*.
27. McCallum, *Unequal Beginnings*, 4.
28. Douglas McCalla, "The Wheat Staple," *Canadian Historical Association Historical Papers* (1978): 34–46.
29. Acheson, "The Nature and Structure of York Commerce."
30. Carol Vaughan, "The Bank of Upper Canada in Politics, 1817–1840," *Ontario History* 60 (December 1968): 185–204; and Peter Baskerville, ed., *The Bank of Upper Canada* (Ottawa: Carleton University Press, 1987).
31. See Peter Baskerville, "Entrepreneurship and the Family Compact, 1822–1855," *Urban History Review* 3 (February 1981): 15–34. For a good example of the rise of an Upper Canadian business in the 1830s and after see Douglas McCalla, *The Upper Canada Trade, 1834–1872: A Study of the Buchanans' Business* (Toronto: University of Toronto Press, 1979).
32. McCalla, *Planting the Province*, appendix B, table 6.11.
33. Angela Redish, "The Economic Crisis of 1837–1839 in Upper Canada: Case Study of a Temporary Suspension of Specie Payments," *Explorations in Economic History* 20 (1983): 402–17.
34. Cited in Cowan, *British Emigration*, appendix B.
35. D.C. Masters, *The Rise of Toronto* (Toronto: University of Toronto Press, 1987).

FURTHER READING

Craig, Gerald. *Upper Canada: The Formative Years, 1784-1841*. Toronto: McClelland & Stewart, 1963.

Johnson, J.K., ed. *Historical Essays on Upper Canada*. Toronto: McClelland & Stewart, 1975.

McCalla, Douglas. "The 'Loyalist' Economy of Upper Canada." *Social History* 16(32) (November 1983): 279–304.

McCalla, Douglas. *Planting the Province: The Economic History of Upper Canada, 1784–1870*. Toronto: University of Toronto Press, 1993.

McCallum, John. *Unequal Beginnings: Agriculture and Economic Development in Quebec and Ontario until 1870*. Toronto: University of Toronto Press, 1980.

Wilson, Bruce. *The Enterprises of Robert Hamilton*. Toronto: University of Toronto Press, 1983.

Chapter Seven

The Western Economy, 1713–1870

THE ECONOMIC HISTORY of western British North America before the transfer of the region to Canada has two important characteristics. First, like that of so many other parts of Canada before Confederation, the commercial economy rested on the exchange of European manufactured trade goods for the primary resources of the region; in this case, the trade was such items as tools, clothing, blankets, weapons, and cooking utensils for various types of furs. These furs were used for two purposes in Europe: a luxury trade in fur coats and other apparel; and the primary felt trade, which had been the same since the time of Champlain, and for which the fur of the beaver was the essential ingredient.[1]

The second characteristic distinguished the western region from other parts of North America. In those regions, this exchange was carried on primarily between an ocean-based or an agriculturally based community of European origin and the Europeans themselves. The settlement and development of the region accompanied the economic process. In the West, however, the years before 1870 saw the dominant exchange take place between indigenous non-European peoples and Europeans —who, throughout most of the period and most of the region, never controlled or even attempted to control the overall social and political or even economic structures of the region. Settlement and development came, but slowly, for it was not a necessary part of the economic activity of western North America to either party involved.

Other subordinate themes must be traced in tandem with dominant ones. The first is that the tendency toward concentration in the fur trade, evident already in the early years of New France, was more important than ever in this period. Small firms quickly got absorbed into larger ones, and competition, when it existed, took the form of strategic interaction among a few rivals. The reasons for the tendency to concentration were the same: the inherent riskiness of the industry, the need for financing due to the delay between expenditures and receipts, and the benefits of being able to control the supply of furs going to Europe and the supply of trade goods going inland to the Native trappers.

There is also a point of some importance concerning the dual role of the Native peoples in the fur-trade process. Until recently, the Native population had tended to be seen as a passive part of the whole trade, perhaps exploited or perhaps treated fairly, but little able to control their own destiny. More recently, however, excellent works by historians, economists, and geographers have demonstrated that this was far from the case. The Native participants had a very active role in the trade and were, especially in the years before 1850, often able to control the directions of the trade better than were their European suppliers. It was their own land and their own society; they knew how to exploit it better than did the interloper.

Finally, however, the system broke down. The resource was seriously depleted in large parts of the West. European interlopers were increasingly able to penetrate the region and to dictate the terms of trade. Further, by the final decades of the Hudson's Bay Company charter, the social and economic structure of the region was changing. Agriculture was appearing on the eastern periphery, and from the southern United States settlement hemmed in the tribes. The economy was in transition and, as is often the case in such instances, the economic power in the region shifted accordingly.

The Era of the Middleman, 1713–1770s

The pattern of trade that existed through much of the eighteenth century rested on three elements. The first was the Hudson's Bay Company. Forts Albany, Churchill, and York on Hudson Bay provided depots for European goods and collection points for the furs brought from the interior. Those bringing the furs, the Cree and Assiniboine, provided the second central element in the trade. Finally, there were the French traders. These interlopers, as they were known, competed with the Hudson's Bay Company in the Port Albany catchment area throughout the eighteenth century and in the York Factory area beginning in the late 1730s. The Churchill fort enjoyed a virtual monopoly throughout the period, however, due to its great distance from the St. Lawrence. Guns, hatchets, blankets, knives, chisels, tobacco, and liquor formed the staples of the trade. Determining the precise value of the trade at any given time is difficult. It was a valuable one, however, and large enough to attract the massive capital and effort required to broach the interior of North America far ahead of the settlement frontier.

Yet, there is one important qualification to be made. For the European, the health of the western economy in the eighteenth century would be assessed in terms of the fur trade. A high demand for furs and a ready supply would mean economic prosperity. Still, it would be false to impose the fur-trade companies' concept of the trade cycle on the western interior. For the Native peoples, economic prosperity throughout this period depended less on the fur trade than on the state and movements of wild game. This was still a nonmonetary economy, dependent for its well-being on the hunt. European technology and European trade had an impact but did not alter this fact in any fundamental way until much later.

Early in the eighteenth century, French military incursions against Hudson's Bay Company posts had been resolved by the 1713 Treaty of Utrecht. Under this treaty, the French relinquished all claim to Hudson Bay. Therefore, until the fall of New France, the fur trade was divided between the great North American powers on the basis of geography — the French operating out of Montreal, and the English from the bay.

The most important characteristic of the fur trade, the one that defines this era in the history of the western economy, was the effective control of the trade by key middlemen tribes. By the mid-eighteenth century, the Cree and Assiniboine were able, as were the Ottawa and Algonquin earlier, to dominate the exchange of goods between the Europeans and the Native peoples of the interior. This control put them in a very powerful position, both economically and politically, because they could decide to what degree European technology would filter inland, and at what price. They could also determine what furs, and in what quantities, went to each of the European companies. It was a good position to be in, and the territories they controlled expanded accordingly.

Central to their power were the costs and difficulties of transportation to both Europeans and the Native peoples. The northwest was a vast territory with a small population.

126

Transportation was difficult and, if the timing relative to seasons was wrong, highly dangerous. It was extremely unattractive for Native traders in the distant interior to travel thousands of kilometres to one of the bay forts — especially given the limited needs of a nomadic people. This was an area where the Cree and Assiniboine could perform a useful service.

These two groups were located in a strategic position geographically. Scattering along forest and parkland to the south and west of the bay, they were the first Native peoples who had regular contact with the Hudson's Bay Company traders. They were also in a good position to take advantage as the French traders began to push west, past the Ottawa tribe, who had for so long in the past acted as middlemen. Located between the forest and what is now mid-Saskatchewan, these people could make the trip to the bay in relative ease, if one can describe a 300 to 1200 km trip by canoe in those terms. They could also save more distant Native traders the difficulties of transport by buying their furs and, in return, selling them Hudson's Bay Company or French goods.

None of this is to imply a selfless service on the part of the middleman. The markup for such a service could be considerable. For example, a gun purchased at York by a Cree trading group would sell to the Blackfoot, a Cree enemy, for three and a half times the purchase price. Knives could jump ninefold in price.[2] Nor were these goods new. The traditional practice was for the middlemen to use the implement or weapon for a while and then to pass it off at high prices to tribes in the interior. Further, where the distances involved did not dissuade interior tribes from heading toward the bay, a show of force might. The access to guns by the middleman made this show of force somewhat more persuasive.

By the early eighteenth century, the fur-trade system was in place. The Cree and Assiniboine had established themselves between the fur resources and the European traders, and, much like the merchants of Montreal, profited by facilitating the exchange of these resources. This system lasted a long time; not until late in the century did anything disturb it. The French, it was true, did penetrate beyond the Great Lakes to the Prairies by the 1730s. All that did, however, was bring them into the lands of the Cree and Assiniboine and, thus, make it easier for the middlemen. These two groups had what has been described as a "virtual monopoly" over the supply of furs to the Europeans. Counts done at York Factory in the late 1750s indicate that practically "all the Indians coming to the post were either Cree or Assiniboine."[3]

There are two other striking things about the eighteenth-century fur trade. First, as the presence of the middlemen indicates, this trade was more controlled and dominated by the Native peoples than by the Europeans. The Hudson's Bay Company sat, for the most part, on the coast of Hudson Bay, and, from their trade centres at such places at Fort Albany, Fort Churchill, and, most importantly, Fort York, acted as collectors of furs brought from the interior by Native bands. The Europeans' knowledge of the inland territories and their control of economic events therein were scant. Even when the French began to push on to the Prairies in the 1730s, they affected only the edge of the fur trade. The collection depots moved a little closer to the trading bands, but the fundamental principles remained the same.

It was the Europeans who had to adapt to a large degree if they wished to succeed in the region. Trade practices had to alter to conform to the patterns of Native life. For example, currency had little meaning or purpose for the interior tribes, and the Hudson's Bay Company and French traders could not rely on their pricing system accordingly. Instead, a barter accounting system on the basis of MB (made beaver), which denoted the rate of exchange based on a prime beaver pelt, became the standard usage of the company. The failure of a European currency system to penetrate the country indicates the degree to which the indigenous population retained economic dominance in the region.

Map 7.1 Tribal Distribution in the Canadian West, c. 1750

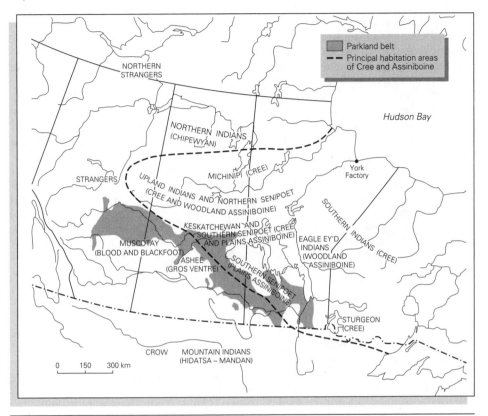

Source: Based on A.J. Ray, *Indians in the Fur Trade: Their Role as Hunters, Trappers, and Middlemen in the Lands Southwest of Hudson Bay, 1660–1870* (Toronto: University of Toronto Press, 1974), p. 20. Reprinted with permission.

Most peculiar to the fur trade, however, was the attitude of the Native peoples toward trade goods. The Europeans found in the West, as they had earlier found in much of the East, that Native traders wanted only so much in terms of kettles, axes, guns, and the like. Once they had these goods, better prices or more attractive durable goods would not produce a change in supplies. Indeed, at times when the demand for beaver was especially high, the European traders were often dismayed to find that the Native traders would bring fewer rather than more furs to trade. The reason was simple: they could obtain their required trade goods (once estimated at about 70 MB a year). Only when Native traders were enticed with ephemeral goods, such as liquor, or easily transportable ones, such as beads, could the pattern be broken.[4]

There was another Native economic practice to which Europeans had to adjust. Native traders routinely made ritual exchanges of goods between themselves. Band meeting band would give presents as a token of friendship and good will. When the Europeans arrived, they found it expedient to adopt this practice. When a group of traders arrived at a Hudson's Bay Company fort, a ceremony occurred in which the leading officials at the fort would welcome the leading Native representatives and gifts would be exchanged. Only after a due amount of ceremony could trading begin, usually the next day.

This institutionalized gift-giving has led to the argument that the Native economy should not be seen in market terms at all. In preindustrial societies, the argument goes, security of person and of group became paramount. Exchanges of goods were, therefore, based not on expectations of profit or loss but on intergroup exchanges for reasons of alliance, or at least of non-interference. "The coming of the market system," according to this view, "had still to await the development of peaceful conditions, adequate and reliable policing, and a common legal framework."[5]

There is an element of truth in this assertion. There is no doubt that the ritual gift-giving was derived from such a diplomatic practice. It is one thing, however, to say that the Native economy was different from that of the European in its precise behaviour. The loosely based system of kinship and alliances as well as the nomadic lifestyle ensured that would be the case. It is quite another to say that it was not a market economy. The Native population was interested in using goods to secure friendship and security, of course. These were independent peoples, and there was no arbiter to turn to should peaceful understanding break down. Nothing in the practice contradicts the existence of a market economy, however, any more than the modern ledger entry under "good will" should imply a lack of interest in profit. Gift-giving was a natural outgrowth of the state of the country. For the Hudson's Bay Company and the Native traders alike, it was just one more cost of doing business.

The Era of Renewed Competition

Beginning in the mid-eighteenth century, the dynamics of the economy of the interior underwent a series of changes. First, in the late 1750s, the French traders disappeared. New France was about to fall to the English, and their sources of supply, and soon of capital, were collapsing. For a few years, the Hudson's Bay Company once again had a monopoly in the region. The use of liquor was cut back, and the price given for furs was lowered, at least to a degree.

Then, within a decade, new traders began to spread westward from the Great Lakes. These were the so-called pedlars operating once again out of Montreal. In many cases, the canoemen and traders were men familiar with the business from before the fall of New France. This time, however, they were backed by English and Scottish capital, and the expeditions were headed by the representatives of the new British merchant class moving into Montreal. As the Hudson's Bay Company would quickly discover, the change of rulers at Quebec did not alter the fundamental rivalry between the two major routes to the West, the St. Lawrence River and Hudson Bay. Indeed, the two systems were about to enter into a period of especially fierce competition that would end with one of them being absorbed by the other.

Initially, the pedlars out of Montreal were small outfitters, but the nature of the fur trade encouraged combination. The formation, re-formation, and merging of outfits in the period from the 1760s through the 1790s is bewildering, given the sheer number of events, but only two events demand attention here. The first is that there did emerge, by the 1780s, a dominant syndicate out of Montreal, known as the North West Company.[6] Headed by the Scottish merchants of the McTavish and Frobisher clans and held together by a series of partnership arrangements, the North West Company had the resources and desire to challenge the Hudson's Bay Company head-on.

The second point to note is that, while the advantages of combination might be very clear, there was no easy way to ensure that some new interloper did not appear on the scene. Through this entire period, both the Hudson's Bay Company (which considered the North West Company an interloper) and the North West Company were harassed by the appearance of new fur-trade partnerships out of Montreal. If these new companies could be driven out of business, then all was well. If not, the best practice, at least as far as the North West Company was concerned, was to absorb them.

This characteristic of the trade was shown most clearly in the greatest challenge to the North West Company. In 1794, the British signed Jay's Treaty with the United States, handing over thousands of square kilometres of British-occupied territory south and west of the Great Lakes. The southwest fur trade was thereby reserved for American citizens. Various merchants and traders turned their eyes north and west of the Great Lakes. In 1798, two new Montreal firms emerged to challenge the supremacy of the North West Company. This challenge grew more serious when the Sir Alexander Mackenzie Company, or the XY Company as it was popularly known, had both the resources and the determination to challenge the supremacy of the North West Company.

The rivalries that sprang up in the northwest after 1770 had a marked effect on the nature of the fur trade. The Montreal companies quickly expanded their operations to territories never visited by the French before the conquest. By 1778, Peter Pond of the North West Company had a post on Lake Athabasca, and, by 1793, Alexander Mackenzie, then still of the North West Company, had journeyed overland to the Pacific. By the early 1800s, as the three-cornered rivalry between the North West, XY, and Hudson's Bay companies reached new heights, scores of posts sprang up along the rivers of the parkland and forest belt.

This rapid penetration inland brought major changes in the economic activity of the interior. The first change was on the part of the Hudson's Bay Company. For more than a century, the company had maintained a strategic position on the bay. The Native middlemen had made the trek to it. As the Montreal traders penetrated the Saskatchewan River system and then the Athabasca River, however, the Native traders found it less and less necessary to make the arduous trip to the shores of Hudson Bay. The traders would come to them.

The result was that the company began to lose its share of the trade. York Factory, for example, saw a rapid decline as the central entrepot of the fur trade. Whereas some 25 000 to 40 000 MB per annum went through the post in the first half of the eighteenth century, the number was down to 18 000 by 1768 and to a mere 8000 by 1773. Overall, one estimate is that, by the 1780s, the Hudson's Bay Company was doing only about £30 000 worth of trade, while, in contrast, the Montreal traders garnered somewhere between £165 000 and £245 000. The company that, only a few years before, had enjoyed a monopoly in the interior was, in other words, doing only about 15 percent of the fur-trade business.[7]

The company had to respond or face bankruptcy. When it became obvious that Native traders were no longer making the trek to the bay, the company decided to move inland. In 1774, it established Fort Cumberland on the Saskatchewan River, about 400 km southwest of York Factory. From there, it spread westward along the Saskatchewan system and its tributaries, until, in 1795, it established Fort Edmonton. In the early nineteenth century, the system would continue to expand, westward to the Rockies and northward into the Athabasca system.

To supply this growing network of posts, the company instituted another innovation. Increasingly, in the early nineteenth century, it hauled its goods not by the traditional *canot du nord* but by York boat. This 12 m boat required the same number of crew as a *canot du nord* (six to eight), but carried twice the cargo. The efficiency of such loads more than made up for the difficulties in portaging and in loading and unloading. The use of the York boat, in combination with the efficiency of transporting goods to the interior via Hudson Bay, was the greatest strength of the Hudson's Bay Company. With every kilometre inland that the Montreal merchants extended their network, the transportation advantages of the bay become more obvious. The York boat only accentuated those advantages.

In contrast, one of the great disadvantages faced by the Hudson's Bay Company was of its own making. The North West Company rested on a series of partnerships and incentives that tied the success of the company to the income of senior personnel. Most important in this regard was that a good portion of the company was owned by the wintering partners (so called because they wintered over in the territories). The experts in the actual day-to-day operations of the trade in the field thus had both incentive and involvement in policy. Their ideas made the North West Company innovative and tremendously expansionary. This setup also meant that knowledge of the interior was regularly conveyed to those back in Montreal, and new schemes resting on first-hand experience could be developed. Conversely, the Hudson's Bay Company was rigidly centralized. Wages were determined in London, and there was little flexibility for those acting in the territories. This policy of centralized authority and rigid personnel practices reflected the same caution that had led the company to sit on the bay for more than a century. Only when pushed by its competition did it begin to change policy.[8]

In 1770, a system of bonuses was developed for Hudson's Bay Company employees. Over the years, these would be extended to the point where they could become a significant part of an individual's annual salary.[9] Salary was only a part of the problem, however, and the lack of consultation, centralized decision making, and rigid practices continued to plague the company well into the nineteenth century.

In spite of the move inland by the Hudson's Bay Company and in spite of that company's growing transportation advantages, the Montreal merchants remained dominant in the fur trade into the nineteenth century. The Montreal merchants, undaunted by the countermoves of their rivals, simply pushed their network farther afield, competing with one another as well as with the Hudson's Bay Company. Between 1789 and 1805, some 325 new posts were built in the thinly populated interior.[10] When, in 1804, the North West Company merged with the XY Company, that dominance seemed all the greater. So weak was the Hudson's Bay Company position that, in 1808, with problems accentuated by European wars, it suspended dividends. It seemed only a matter of time until the English-based company succumbed before the onslaught from Montreal.

The most dramatic aspect of this expansion was the movement of the North West Company into the transmountain west and what is now British Columbia. Alexander Mackenzie's trip to the Pacific had been a daring example of exploration, but competition within the fur trade led, over the first decade or so of the nineteenth century, to the addition of thousands of square kilometres of rugged mountainous areas, valleys, and Pacific coastline to the already huge areas covered by the trade. The expansion also created problems and pointed to the limits faced by the North West Company in its drive for supremacy.

Initially, the trade developed slowly. The traders found that both the geography and the Native population of British Columbia posed problems. The geographical difficulties are fairly obvious. In what was later termed "the sea of mountains," it was extremely difficult to find an easily travelled river route that would permit the ready transport of furs, trade goods, and supplies. Not until about 1811 was the Columbia River route sufficiently well known that it provided that link — a link that was, of course, but a thin ribbon travelling through a vast and segmented geography. Even so, by the War of 1812, the expansionary mood of the age had led to a series of posts throughout the interior. In 1813, the North West Company used the War of 1812 and a nearby British warship to coerce the American Fur Company into "selling" Fort Astoria on the Columbia River, and the network was complete.

A modification of Native trade practices was also required. The North West Company was never able to develop a series of stable trade relationships with the tribes of the far west. The reasons may have been related to numbers, for this region was much more heavily populated than the Prairies, or to the different types of band and tribal relationships that had grown out of the geography and culture of the region. Various approaches were taken, including the use of members of eastern bands as trappers, but the solutions were never really satisfactory.[11] Even in the first stages of European contact, the economy of British Columbia proved to have a unique character that required considerable changes in technique.

The vast expansion of the Montreal trade network created problems not only for the Europeans, whether of the Hudson's Bay or the North West Company, but also for the Native population. The extension of the European trading networks rapidly destroyed the privileged position of the Cree and Assiniboine. Interior bands could now trade directly with any of two or three companies without making the arduous journey to the bay and without paying the high markup demanded by the Native middlemen. "Henceforth, the trading post moved with the Indian trappers; access to it could no longer be controlled by native trades."[12] The European presence now extended over much of the western half of British North America.

The inland expansion of the fur companies also brought new opportunities for the Native peoples. The ever-growing numbers of Europeans inland required food supplies for their extended network of forts. Thus, the exchange of European technology for local animal pelts became a more complex economic operation, involving support services rendered by the local community. From the various regions of the interior, but especially from the buffalo regions of parkland and prairie, a series of new trade patterns developed. Cree and Blackfoot groups sent provisions northward to fur-trade posts along the well-travelled Saskatchewan River and Lake Winnipeg routes.

These supply movements were far from peripheral to the economy of the West. The requirements of each post were sizable. Arthur Ray has estimated that, at one medium-sized post on the Pembina River, nearly 150 buffalo were killed, more than 1000 fish caught, and 325 bushels of potatoes required to provide basic food supplies for one year. In 1813, the North West Company contracted for 644 bags of pemmican meat, each bag weighing 40 kg. This amount filled more than 200 canoes.[13] Before long, some of the largest posts in the interior, such as Fort Edmonton, would exist as bases for the exchange of food supplies rather than as fur-trade centres.

The Cree in the parkland/prairie region of the west and the Assiniboine found a new role for themselves. As their middleman role disappeared, they moved quickly into the role of suppliers to the various fur-trade companies. As early as 1790, Alexander Mackenzie could comment of the Assiniboine that "they are not beaver hunters. ... They confine themselves to hunting buffalo and trapping wolves, which cover the country."[14] This transition had been aided by the adoption of the horse by the plains tribes over the past century, which made the buffalo hunt much more efficient and the transport of meat both easier and faster. The Cree, the Assiniboine, and, less regularly, the Blackfoot thus became the major suppliers of the new network of posts springing up in the interior. The same event that took one livelihood away quite fortuitously provided another.

131

There were also significant economic changes taking place among the Europeans in the West. The ailing Hudson's Bay Company had been vulnerable to a takeover for some time, and the Earl of Selkirk was able to take control of the company. Then, in 1811, he persuaded the company to grant him a large tract of land south of Lake Winnipeg, where he founded the Red River settlement. Selkirk's primary purpose was to assist the dispossessed Scottish Highlanders. Yet, his timing and his choice of site were bound to be viewed as less than philanthropic by the North West Company. The settlement, established at the confluence of the Red and Assiniboine rivers, lay along one of the primary supply routes to the northern posts. It also lay near the main transportation route from eastern Canada. To the North West Company, the Red River settlement was but another move in the escalating competition between the bay and the river.

Over the next few years, the Red River colony inflamed the already intense competition between the two companies. The government of Red River interrupted pemmican shipments to the interior, thus threatening starvation to a good many North West Company employees in the interior. The Nor'Westers tried to entice the settlers away and, when that effort failed, turned to the emergent *bois-brûlé* or Métis people, who saw their interests as allied with those of the North West Company. The climax came in 1816, when confrontation between settlers and Métis at Seven Oaks left 22 dead. Competition had turned to harassment, and harassment to something approaching open warfare.

The violence at Red River brought the chaos in the interior of North America to the attention of officials in London. Pressure was put on the two organizations to find a means of resolving their dispute. An incentive was also given: if a resolution could be achieved, the British government was prepared to guarantee the resulting organization an exclusive licence to trade in the region. In other words, if this battle could be resolved, the British government would pledge itself to see that no new competition arose.

The companies were surprisingly compliant. For all the enmity that had built up over the years, there was a recognition that competition had been ruinous to all involved. Overbuilding of posts and overstaffing in the interior had led both to a glut of furs and to dangerous depletion of the resource in some areas. Increasing use of liquor had damaged the morale of the Native trappers and, from the companies' point of view, had led to an unstable relationship with the Native population.

Yet this raises an interesting question, one that cannot be fully answered. Only a decade or so earlier, the North West Company had been confident of its hold on the trade and equally confident of its ability to take over or destroy the Hudson's Bay Company within a few years. Yet, as the merger took shape, it was the Hudson's Bay Company that survived, albeit in somewhat altered form. What had happened to the dominance of the Montreal traders?

By 1821, the large and impressive North West Company was much weaker than it appeared. The reason most commonly offered for this depletion of strength is the vast cost of running a transcontinental transportation system from Montreal. Within a few decades, the company had added thousands of square kilometres of new territory to its operations, had expanded over the mountains into British Columbia, and had undertaken its vast building program to undercut the Hudson's Bay Company. The distance from tidewater to the trapper in the field simply became too enormous. Indeed, by the end of the period, the coastal regions of British Columbia were being supplied by ship rather than overland. Even so, the interior of the region and the vast prairie and subarctic areas were still supplied by ship and canoe all the way from Montreal — a trip, in some instances, of almost 5000 km.[15] There were other problems as well, including administrative ones in the accounting and capitalization system of the company. Specifically, no provision was made for capital renewal, and all profits were distributed to the partners. Reserves, therefore, did not exist, and costs had to be met out of operating revenues. Undercapitalization and tremendous costs thus came together to create what, in modern parlance, would be termed a liquidity crisis just as the competition reached its peak.

In these speculations as to the collapse of the North West Company, it is also worth considering the effects of sheer fatigue and profit taking on the part of the Montreal proprietors. The North West Company had always seen a degree of tension between its Montreal partners and those wintering in the interior. It is possible that, in later years, some of the aging senior partners were willing to take a cash settlement to leave the troublesome winterers behind and turn to other pursuits. McTavish and Company, representing the Montreal partners, got a generous settlement, worth some 30 percent of the new company.[16] As we have seen, by the 1820s, the St. Lawrence and lower Great Lakes offered many opportunities for the diversification of business. The new staples trade and export–import businesses to supply the growing population of the Canadas would attract many ex-fur traders over the next years. Few of the great proprietors of the old North West Company would succeed, however, and many disposed of their stock to pay off debts or to make investments in other ventures. By the mid-1820s, the partnership of 1821 had effectively been dissolved. The winterers had been absorbed into the Hudson's Bay Company and the Montreal proprietors forced out.[17]

The new company created by the 1821 merger reflected the strengths of both of the former institutions. On the one hand, the bay, not the river, would be the future supply line to the northwest. Henceforth, the economy of the fur trade and the economy of the rest of British North America were to operate largely independently of each other. On the other hand, the new Hudson's Bay Company had to find some way of absorbing the wintering partners of the North West Company. The merger reflected the strength of a system that had integrated those with experience and skill in the interior into the management of the company. Thus, in 1821, the company adopted what was known as the deed poll. Some 85 shares (about 40 percent of the company's stock) were distributed among the wintering partners. Chief factors, the senior officials at major posts, each received two of these shares, and each chief trader (the level below factor) received one share. In good times, these shares could be worth a great deal. For example, in 1855, as the fur trade prospered, a chief factor's share of the profits amounted to well over £800, an amount comparable to that earned by the top rank of civil servants in the Province of Canada at the time.[18]

All in all, it was a restructuring that gave the new company the best of both worlds. It had the transportation advantages of the Hudson's Bay Company, some of the entrepreneurial drive of the North West Company, and a legal monopoly from Great Britain. The trick now was to take advantage of these operations in the field. Order had to be restored, redundant posts abandoned, excess personnel retired — all would take time and skill.

The Company Monopoly

The merger of 1821 and subsequent events altered the economic structure of the west as profoundly as had the earlier penetration of the North West Company. The fur companies of the eighteenth and early nineteenth centuries have been described accurately as "premodern" or, alternatively, as an "anachronism" in their structure and approach to the trade.[19] The North West Company was a loose syndicate of partnerships, unwieldy in size and bizarre in its accounting procedures. The Hudson's Bay Company rested, of course, on the concept of the chartered monopoly, a creature of the seventeenth century existing into the nineteenth.

The way in which the fur-trade companies waged competition in the interior also reflected an approach to commerce different from that of the modern era. As had been the case under Elizabeth I, when part-pirate, part-merchant, part-naval officers sailed the oceans for the empire, the fur-trade companies freely mixed commerce with aspects of sovereign authority and with sheer theft. Thus, for example, both companies used an old law that gave Canadian justices of the peace jurisdiction in the northwest as a means of harassing and arresting opponents. Violence and semimilitary activities were adopted, as had been used in Seven Oaks and in Selkirk's subsequent employment of Swiss mercenaries to seize North West Company supplies and furs at Fort William.

These premodern approaches also extended into other areas. Inventory management was non-existent, while family relationships and personal status often took precedence over the profitability of the firm. The makeup of new outfits rested more on tradition than on demand, as identical supplies were ordered year after year, even if certain items had been shown not to be in demand. Likewise, staffing policy rested on a combination of paternalism, tradition, and nepotism, once again indicating that profitability and efficiency took second place in the planning of the two organizations.

All this was in the process of change with the merger of 1821. Indeed, many of the changes had begun in the Hudson's Bay Company in the years immediately before the merger. Faced with the struggle for survival against the North West Company, the new Hudson's Bay Company owners, under the leadership of Selkirk, had introduced personnel reductions, stricter financial accountability, and other cost-reduction measures. Within two years, they turned the company's annual operations from a loss to a profit.

It was with the merger that the real changes came, however. These were facilitated by two facts. The first was that the merger had left redundant posts, over-staffing, and redundant inventory. As one historian has commented,

> The sudden end of rivalry made nonsense of the trading structures which the two companies had built. There were surplus posts and personnel, and over-lavish trading practices. Prices paid to the Indians had risen during the years of competition, and alcohol traded with irresponsible abandon. Trapping had been carried out at all seasons, of young as well as of adult animals, and many areas were now denuded of furs.[20]

Even under the most traditional management, change would have been necessary.

Traditional management was not what they got. George Simpson, the man appointed by London to oversee the reorganization of the company, was an individual who put the corporation ahead of kinship, and modern efficiency ahead of tradition. The "Little Emperor," as Simpson was known, moved, over the next few years, to reduce costs and personnel as quickly as possible. Within five years, staff was cut by almost two-thirds, the number of posts was reduced to 45 (about 325 had been built between 1789 and 1805), and the use of liquor was reduced tremendously. The power of the wintering partners declined while Simpson's increased. The faraway London board increasingly trusted his judgement and left the day-to-day operations in the field to their man on the spot. Within a very few years, the ungainly operation left by the merger of two companies had been reshaped into a well-organized unit.[21]

The merger also brought changes to the economy of the region as a whole. Most immediately, Red River became both a residence for redundant employees and a centre for those who would attempt economic diversification in the region. Attempts included the Buffalo

Wool Company, the Tallow Company, and experiments with flax and hemp. All were failures. With no local market and with the colony isolated from metropolitan centres, these results were not surprising.[22]

What Red River did become was a focal point for the surrounding territory. Fur traders and their families increasingly joined the original Scottish settlers — as, ironically, did the Métis, who had initially seen the colony as a threat. Moreover, the settlement did have a distinct economic purpose: supplying provisions to the fur-trade posts throughout the interior. It was located on a major supply route and thus became a natural site for the collection and transshipment of such supplies as pemmican and buffalo meat. Further, as agriculture in the region developed, the surpluses could be used to vary the provisions sent out to the posts.

Finally, the developing Métis community used Red River as a base from which to set out on the semiannual buffalo hunts that supplied both their own food and goods for the provisioning trade. Strange though it might seem to consider a colony of 6000 people as a metropolitan centre, that is exactly what Red River became. It was the centre, moreover, for a vast area running from the Shield on the east to the Rockies on the west, and well into the parkland regions to the north. Of course, its influence was weaker than that of similar urban–rural relationships in more settled areas, but there was certainly no other metropolitan centre to challenge it.

The role of Red River has been much discussed in the histories of the region. There was a feeling, dating back to the Nor'Westers, that such an agricultural settlement in the midst of a fur-trading region was threatening. Agriculture and settlement, the argument went, were hostile to the fur trade. This argument was, in turn, picked up and expanded upon by later economic historians who, looking back at the rise of free trade in the 1840s and the development of the West as an extension of the Canadian agricultural frontier, saw the colony as "a vulnerable point in the defences of the company."[23]

To a degree, this argument depends on the benefit of hindsight. As will be argued, the rise of free trade and the eventual agricultural settlement of the West had much more to do with forces external to the region than with the presence of Red River. Indeed, Red River was a natural, even essential, development. Once the Europeans began to assert a permanent presence inland, there was a need for a centre of settlement that reflected European social and economic practices, even if modified to meet the demands of the country. Red River provided such a place.

One of the most dramatic examples of the relationship between the settlement and the country came in the coalescence of the Métis community in the years after the founding of the colony. The Métis, or mixed bloods, were descendants of unions between French fur traders and Native women. What gave them a distinct identity, however, and what brought them together as a community, was their sense of being indigenous to the country but distinct from the Native communities of their mothers. Indeed, many of mixed parentage were never Métis in any meaningful sense, in that they adopted the economic and social practices of their Native mothers.

The Métis' sense of distinctiveness was shaped by cultural factors (such as the use of the French language), by religion (Roman Catholicism), and by a distinct economic role in the northwest. In one sense, they were in an awkward position. Class and social barriers meant that it was extremely difficult for them to rise very far in the ranks of the fur trade. Most Métis men remained canoemen or casual labourers. Further, they were not routinely the actual trappers of furs, as were the Native peoples. The Métis were far less nomadic than the Native peoples and thus had both a greater interest in and a greater need for European goods on a larger scale. Somehow, they had to find a niche in the economy of the northwest.

They found that niche in the nineteenth century by playing an important role in the provisioning trade. Even more than the Cree, the Métis depended for their well-being on the demands of the fur trade for buffalo meat. Every summer there were large and well-organized commercial hunts, followed by the preparation of pemmican and its transport to the outlying posts. The buffalo hunt, as a commercial operation, both gave them their primary distinctiveness as a community and provided them with their main source of cash in the first half of the nineteenth century.

Yet, this depiction of the Métis as buffalo hunters must be qualified. The Métis were not a purely nomadic people, following the buffalo. Rather, at Red River and in other isolated sites around the region, they developed a mixed economy of small-scale farming, seasonal employment with the Hudson's Bay Company, and the provisioning of the trade. They were, thus, neither a purely peasant society rooted to a single spot nor a nomadic people dependent on the cycle of game; rather, they stood somewhere between the two. Later English observers would be critical of them for failing to follow agriculture more aggressively. In these years, however, the Métis' activities made sense both traditionally, in terms of their own culture, and economically. The combination of activities was their best means of taking advantage of the opportunities created by the Europeans' continued penetration of the interior.

A new period of stability thus developed in the West between 1821 and the 1840s, brought on initially by the absence of competition among European fur traders. Without competition, the Hudson's Bay Company could regularize its practices without sacrificing profitability. By the mid-1820s, dividends had reached 10 percent; they stayed at that level or higher for the next several years. A trader with one share in the deed poll would, it has been estimated, receive an average of £400 per annum in profits through the 1820s.[24]

The stability after 1821 also reflected the fact that other groups in the region had made the necessary economic transition to a world where the European fur traders were present throughout the interior. The Cree and Assiniboine found, as did the Métis, at least a partial substitute for their middleman role in the provisioning trade — as, to a lesser degree, did the Blackfoot confederacy. The Cree supplemented their provisioning with trapping and, of course, with a continued reliance on the hunt and fishing. The Métis supplemented their provisioning with hunting for personal consumption, small-scale agricultural production, and labour for the company. Red River, after a period of turbulence during its founding years, became a centre for both Europeans and Métis. The end of expansion and the development of monopoly seemed to have returned stability to the western economy.

The Hudson's Bay Company was very much aware of the advantages of monopoly and followed a policy of actively preserving it through a practice known as a "frontier policy." In this procedure, certain areas of the company's trading regions were designated both vulnerable and expendable. When outside competition appeared in these areas, the company was willing to pursue ruthless competitive means to ensure that this competition did not expand into the heartland of company operations. For example, the company waged a price war with American fur traders in the territory west of Lake Superior for several years in the 1820s and 1830s. The company traded at a loss in a deliberate attempt to drive the intruding companies into bankruptcy. In another case, also in the late 1820s, Peter Skene Ogden of the company headed south to the Snake River country. American trappers and traders had been pushing westward and appeared to endanger the fertile Oregon region. Ogden therefore "trapped out" the region, deliberately wiping out the fur-bearing animals. A trappers' desert was thus interposed between expanding American businessmen and the operations the company considered important.[25]

The Intrusion of New Forces

The stability was temporary. The absence of expansion on the part of the company did not alter longer-range trends brought on by the European presence in the region. In various ways, forces were gathering that would upset the balance in the region. The economy of exchange in the region rested largely on two natural resources, furs and buffalo. The balance in the region rested on the ability of both the Métis and the Native population to enter into profitable trade with the Hudson's Bay Company without falling into too vulnerable a position. Both the resource base and the balance between groups were being undermined, even during the relatively calm period of the monopoly years. Within twenty years of the merger, new and fundamental shifts occurred in the economy and society of the region. As Gerald Friesen noted, "The 1840s can stand as a dividing line between one era and another."[26]

During the period of three-cornered competition, the endangered resource in the region had appeared to be the beaver. Indeed, Simpson and other officials made balanced trapping a priority after 1821. As it turned out, however, it was not the beaver but the buffalo that proved the more serious problem as time went on. In the early years of the Red River settlement, it was possible in some years to see buffalo from the Red River colony. By the 1840s, it was necessary to travel hundreds of kilometres westward to find the herds. Throughout the region, reports indicated that the great buffalo herds were in decline.

The exact reasons for the decline are still a matter of discussion among historians. Various forces seem to have played a part. First, and perhaps most important, was the long-term impact of the horse. By the end of the eighteenth century, buffalo hunting on foot had been replaced by the horseback raid that was so common in later European imagery of the West. What the horse did, however, was to make the Native or Métis hunter more efficient. The chance of a kill was greater and, most significantly, the hunter had the speed and mobility to bypass the undesirable bull to kill the cow.

This increased efficiency in the hunt had a greater effect on the herds because of ancillary factors. First, though the statistics are necessarily absent, indications are that the Native and Métis population of the West was increasing throughout the late eighteenth century and into the nineteenth. There were more mouths to feed, so more buffalo had to be hunted. Also, aside from the demands of band and family, there was the opportunity to supply the fur-trade companies with buffalo meat. Finally, it may also be that disease, possibly transmitted by European animals introduced into the region, affected the herds by the 1840s. The herds thus had an increasingly difficult time replenishing themselves.

The diminished herds may also have been brought about, in part, by an apparent increase in the demand for European goods on the part of the Native peoples of the Prairies. Previously the great bulk of Native purchases had been of metal-based implements, from pots and pans to weapons. By the 1840s, however, new goods were in great demand: cloth, flour, molasses. Basic food and clothing were now sought not from the land but from trade with Europeans. The independence that had previously characterized Native relations with the European fur traders was being replaced by a new vulnerability. The rhythm of hunting and fishing, which had been the real determinant of the western economy in the eighteenth century, was gradually being replaced by an economy dependent on the exchange of goods between the Europeans and the Native population of the region. In 1840, the process was sufficiently under way that it hinted of the transformation to a modern agricultural economy over the next generation.

138

Until this time, the Hudson's Bay Company had always relied on economic means to retain its monopoly. Distance, effective transportation systems, economies of scale, and the willingness to take a loss in one region to protect another had allowed the company to preserve control of the region. There had long been a group of freelance trappers and traders among the Métis and others in the West. However, they, like the Native traders, had usually found it advantageous to trade at company stores. In effect, their activities differed little from the traditional business of the company. The American frontier of settlement was drawing ever closer, however, and with it came an advance guard of fur traders determined to siphon off some of the business of the Hudson's Bay Company. The first challenge appeared at Pembina, just south of the border. Norman Kittson, an American fur trader, established a post there and had sufficient capital backing to challenge the Hudson's Bay Company. Before long "free traders" from the Red River area were making the trek south to Kittson's post. The isolation of the region was coming to an end.

In response, the company abandoned its strongest weapon — the economic position it held — and resorted to its weakest — its legal position under the charter and the exclusive licence to trade. Various measures were attempted but, except for a brief period in 1846–48, when British troops were stationed in Red River, all failed. Although the company tried to assume many quasi-governmental functions in the territories, it was, ultimately, a commercial concern; it had no military power to back up its edicts, and its powers to imprison or fine people who considered themselves eligible for the full privileges accorded a British subject were of dubious legitimacy. Every action taken led to screams of tyranny, and when, at the famous Sayer trial in 1849, the Métis community at Red River made it apparent that they would no longer tolerate pretences to monopoly, the whole legal strategy of the company collapsed. The period of monopoly was now over. Those who came into possession of furs, whether by trapping or trading, could now look to whomever they wished.

Overall, then, the 1840s brought the West into a state of transition once again. The collapse of the company's monopoly, the changing trade practices of the Native and Métis communities, the receding buffalo herds, and the approach of the American frontier of settlement created new forces that signalled the erosion of a regional economy based on an important but small number of activities: the fur and provisioning trade, hunting, and trapping. Continental and international events were impinging on the region now and would do so with ever-greater effect in the next generation. The West was about to be overtaken by the greatest force in colonial North American economic development, the agricultural frontier. The questions now were, who would develop that frontier and what would happen to those whose economic livelihood rested on the old order?

Expansionism

Borders provide an interesting complication in the study of economic development. Economists and historians like to emphasize the transcendent reality of economic forces, whatever borders or artificial government creations may exist. Thus, for example, the charter of the Hudson's Bay Company could not prevent the leakage of furs south of the border once the American presence at Pembina took hold. Equally, the early settlement of Upper Canada was to a large degree the result of its being in the path of the natural frontier of settlement westward from New York. The border had little effect on this movement, in spite of the enmity between Britain and the United States at the time.

Yet, borders can have an important effect. Tariff policies, import quotas, government projects, and other measures are obvious examples of this. In the case of the northwest, between 1850 and 1870, the presence of a border, even one represented on the northerly side only by a commercial concern, did make a difference. Red River was, by the 1850s, in the path of an expanding American frontier of settlement. The Minnesota territory, established in 1849, was becoming an influential presence in Red River and beyond. By 1860, it would have a population of 172 000, more than that of the entire Hudson's Bay territories. In 1859, the first steamboat on the Red River, the *Anson Northrup*, tied the major settlement of the region directly into the American commercial system. In a move that symbolized the changing commercial poles of the area, the Hudson's Bay Company decided to supply Red River from the United States rather than the bay. Politically, a group of enthusiasts in Minnesota looked with covetous eyes on the region as a natural place for future commercial and political development.[27]

For all this, the territory was not swallowed up, as was Oregon, in 1846, by American settlers. The ability of the border to withstand the pulls from the United States was increased first by the U.S. Civil War (1861–65), which slowed settlement, and second by a Sioux uprising in northern Minnesota in 1862, which drove back outlying settlers and further slowed settlement in that particular direction. In the meantime, the Province of Canada, its own agricultural expansion halted by the marginal lands of the Canadian Shield, could use the common British flag to its advantage. Enthusiastic expansionists pressed for the transfer of the region as a means of providing a new hinterland for development. When Confederation came in 1867, the political structure finally existed that could allow transcontinental development. In 1870, the northwest was transferred to Canada and, though the fur trade continued to exist, especially in more northerly regions, agriculture was to be the new staple resource of the region.

The transfer to Canada and the replacement of the fur trade with agriculture had profound effects on the economic relationships in the region. It is possible, indeed, to see the economic development of the region until the late nineteenth century in terms of the relationships between the major population groups. Successive stages were marked by a growing presence of the European population, until, in the years after 1870, that group became the only significant economic power in the region. The Native and Métis populations would be forced into a position of economic and social marginality that contrasted sharply with their dominant position through the first century of the fur trade and even with the combination of growing material dependence and cultural distinctiveness that marked the period after 1840.

The hegemony of the European economy would have come regardless of the response of the indigenous peoples. Once the wave of population of the agricultural frontier reached the West, it was inevitable that the small and scattered population of the region would either assimilate into the new system or be displaced economically. Ironically, however, the hegemony of the new economic order may have come more rapidly and with more devastating effect because of the particular economic response of the Native and Métis peoples during the 1860s and 1870s.

For years, a trade in buffalo robes had been carried on by the Hudson's Bay Company. Almost all the robes were sold in North America, and the great majority of these were used as sleigh blankets. Through the 1840s and 1860s, the robe trade had provided Métis and Native provisioners with a useful sideline. It was generally a minor activity, however. The demand for robes was more or less constant, and the robe was "worth only about as much as a common fox skin."[28] The trade may thus have contributed in a small way to the depletion of the herds through the 1840s and 1850s, but it was not likely a crucial factor.

Then, beginning in the later 1860s, there was a sudden and sharp shift in the demand for furs. The average Hudson's Bay Company price for a robe rose from $4.82 in 1866 to

$8.82 in 1870 and would remain near that level for several years thereafter.[29] The expansion of the American rail and steamboat network also meant that the costs of transporting the bulk robes declined. The robe trade was suddenly a very attractive proposition.

It was also a trade that, given the circumstances, invited destruction of the resource on which it was based. For one thing, the buffalo herds were already under severe pressure. For another, the Hudson's Bay Company was no longer, if it ever had been, in a position to control the harvesting of the resource. Indeed, the company's role in the trade had always been secondary to that of American frontiersmen operating out of such places as Fort Benton in Montana. Also, these American traders operated, to a degree, on a speculative basis. The prices offered and the supplies they acquired made economic sense only if the boom in robes continued for years to come. Perhaps they even sensed how their own economic activity was creating an ever-scarcer resource, and they were stockpiling against the future. That is conjecture, but, whatever the reason, there is no doubt of the tremendous inventories acquired in a short period of time.

This trade had numerous effects. First, the use of whisky by some of the traders and some notorious incidents in the early 1870s caused the Canadian government to assert its control more quickly over the Prairies. This move would facilitate the development of new economic activity. Second, the Métis and Native peoples, such as the Cree and Blackfoot, responded to the opportunity by shifting much of their energy to the buffalo-robe trade. Finally, however, all of this meant that the basic staple of the plains tribes was being hunted in greater numbers than ever before. The herds had had trouble replenishing themselves since the 1840s. In the 1870s, increased hunting north and south of the border turned an ecological imbalance into a slaughter.

This destruction was the final step in a series of steps that marked the end of the old economic order in the West, one that had rested on the game resources of the region. Game had been both the basis of independence from the Europeans and the basis of trade with them. Independence was tied to the ability of a Native band to live off the land by hunting or fishing. European technology was a source of convenience and comfort long before it was a necessity to the tribes of the Northwest. It was the basis of trade, of course, in that both the fur and the provisioning trades rested on the continued demand for the furs of the region. Long before 1870, however, the balance was beginning to shift. The commercial ties to the Europeans were becoming closer, and the dependence on trade goods greater. The Europeans and the Métis, for their part, were increasingly present in the interior. Both the Métis buffalo hunt and the crops grown at Red River diminished the importance of the Native provisioning trade. In the meantime, the buffalo on which provisioning rested were becoming scarcer.

Then, in the 1870s, two things happened that destroyed the economic basis of the old order. First, the isolation of the region came to an end as first the American and then the Canadian frontier reached the area. Second, the already tenuous balance of economic power among the various groups in the region (Native, Métis, European) was shattered. The European population of the region grew more in the five years after the transfer than it had in the previous 200! Much of this population still resided in the eastern part of the region, but the direction was clear: henceforth, Canadian and western European economic structures and practices would shape the region.

The third, and final, event was the destruction of the buffalo. Eventually, the Native population and the Métis would have been forced to abandon the hunt anyway. The concept of the communal territory over which hunters might roam conflicted too sharply with the demands of agriculture for protection of crops and with the European concept of private property. The destruction of the herds, south as well as north of the border, however, left the Native population with no economic basis with which to resist European hegemony. By the late 1870s, the buffalo was nearly extinct and tribes of the region had no choice but to accept the treaties offered by the Canadian government and to move onto reservations.

The great commonality of land and the dual use of game resources for trade and subsistence, which had been the basis of western economy before the arrival of the Hudson's Bay Company, were forever gone, to be replaced by the more complex structures of an agricultural/industrial society. Both the people and the activities of the old order became marginal to the existence of the new.

141

Conclusion

In the two centuries from the arrival of the Hudson's Bay Company in 1670 until the transfer in 1870, the West had undergone slow but significant economic change. The penetration of European technology and trade goods led to significant changes in the role of tribes. The rise of the Métis people created a new social and economic dynamic in the region as did the founding of the Red River colony. By the time of the transfer, European goods and a complex European–Native interaction had taken hold throughout the region. Yet much remained of the former way of life. Barter predominated over the use of currency. The majority of the population were still nomadic. The population of the region was still much more dependent upon hunting and trapping than upon agriculture. Private property was a notion confined to only a minuscule percentage of the total land available. Within the next twenty years all of this was to be swept away. For the West was about to experience more change in a generation than it had in two centuries.

NOTES

1. Gerald Friesen, *The Canadian Prairies: A History* (Toronto: University of Toronto Press, 1985), 46.
2. Arthur J. Ray, *Indians in the Fur Trade: Their Role as Hunters, Trappers, and Middlemen in the Lands Southwest of Hudson Bay* (Toronto: University of Toronto Press, 1974), 69.
3. Ray, *Indians in the Fur Trade*, 61.
4. See note 13 in Chapter Three, however, which cites some literature that questions this interpretation of Native behaviour in the period 1700–63.
5. Abraham Rotstein, "Trade and Politics: An Institutional Approach," *Western Canadian Journal of Anthropology* 3(1) (1972): 1.
6. The North West Company emerged from a series of temporary partnerships between outfitters. Initially, these partnerships were short-lived. Thus historians might choose different dates for the formation of the company. The first partnership was in 1776; a second, in 1779. In 1780, the first multiyear arrangement was made.
7. Friesen, *The Canadian Prairies*, 62.
8. Ann Carlos and Stephen Nicholas argue that the company maintained fixed-price standards, in spite of the inflexibility they introduced, partly because these standards reduced the possibility of their agents cheating on the company. In this way (along with other techniques), they overcame the classic problem of any overseas firm: how to ensure that agents abroad work for the benefit of the company and not in their own self-interest. See "Agency Problems in Early Chartered Companies: The Case of the Hudson's Bay Company," *Journal of Economic History* 50(4) (December 1990): 853–76.
9. Harold Innis, *The Fur Trade in Canada* (Toronto: University of Toronto Press, 1970), 157.

10. Graeme Wynn, "On the Margins of Empire," in Craig Brown, ed., *The Illustrated History of Canada* (Toronto: Lester and Orpen Dennys, 1987), 235.
11. R. Cole Harris and John Warkentin, *Canada Before Confederation* (New York: Oxford University Press, 1974), 290–91.
12. Friesen, *The Canadian Prairies*, 39.
13. Ray, *Indians in the Fur Trade*, 130–32.
14. Cited in Ray, *Indians in the Fur Trade*, 133.
15. Innis, *The Fur Trade in Canada*, chapter 9; W.T. Easterbrook and H.G.J. Aitken, *Canadian Economic History* (Toronto: Macmillan, 1956), 173.
16. Innis, *The Fur Trade in Canada*, 280.
17. Gerald Tulchinsky, *The River Barons: Montreal Businessmen and the Growth of Industry and Transportation, 1837–1853* (Toronto: University of Toronto Press, 1977), 4, 108–10, refers to some of these new investments. See also "Edward Ellice," *Dictionary of Canadian Biography*, vol. 9 (Toronto: University of Toronto Press, 1976), 233–39.
18. Innis, *The Fur Trade in Canada*, 284–85.
19. Michael Bliss, *Northern Enterprise: Four Centuries of Canadian Business* (Toronto: McClelland & Stewart, 1987), 105; J. Foster and D. Richeson, *The Fur Trade in Canada Since 1867* (Ottawa: Museum of Man, 1986), 6.
20. Glyndwr Williams, "The Hudson's Bay Company and the Fur Trade: 1670–1870," *The Beaver: Magazine of the North*, Outfit 314(2) (Autumn 1983): 51.
21. J.S. Galbraith, *The Little Emperor: Governor Simpson of the Hudson's Bay Company* (Toronto: Macmillan, 1976).
22. On the various experiments see E.E. Rich, *The Fur Trade and the Northwest to 1857* (Toronto: McClelland & Stewart, 1967), 250–52.
23. Innis, *The Fur Trade in Canada*, 330.
24. Innis, *The Fur Trade in Canada*, 337.
25. On the general policy of the company see J.S. Galbraith, *The Hudson's Bay Company as an Imperial Factor, 1821–1869* (Berkeley: University of California Press, 1957), 88–96.
26. Friesen, *The Canadian Prairies*, 91.
27. Alvin Gluek, *Minnesota and the Manifest Destiny of the Canadian North-West* (Toronto: University of Toronto Press, 1965).
28. On the buffalo robe trade see Bob Beal, "The Buffalo Robe Trade," in John Foster, ed., *The Métis Hivernant Settlement at Buffalo Lake, 1872–1877: An Historical Report Prepared for the Department of Culture* (Edmonton: Government of Alberta, 1987).
29. Beal, "The Buffalo Robe Trade," 88.

FURTHER READING

Carlos, Ann. "The Causes and Origins of the North American Fur Trade Rivalry, 1804–1810." *Journal of Economic History* 41(4) (December 1981): 777–94.

Carlos, Ann. "The Birth and Death of Predatory Competition in the North American Fur Trade, 1810–1821." *Explorations in Economic History* 19 (1982): 156–83.

Carlos, Ann, and Stephen Nicholas. "Agency Problems in Early Chartered Companies: The Case of the Hudson's Bay Company." *Journal of Economic History* 50(4) (December 1990): 853–76.

Galbraith, John S. *The Little Emperor: Governor Simpson of the Hudson's Bay Company*. Toronto: Macmillan, 1976.

Innis, Harold. *The Fur Trade in Canada*. Toronto: University of Toronto Press, 1970.

Ray, Arthur J. *Indians in the Fur Trade: Their Role as Hunters, Trappers and Middlemen in the Lands Southwest of Hudson Bay, 1660–1870*. Toronto: University of Toronto Press, 1974.

Part Three

The Economic Background to Confederation, 1846–1867

The wood-burning Lady Elgin, Engine No. 1, of the Ontario,

Simcoe and Huron Railroad, on an early track in the Toronto area.

Rail transportation and travel had a profound impact on the

Canadian economy in the nineteenth century. National Archives of

Canada/PA-13682.

144

THE BRITISH NORTH AMERICA ACT received royal assent on March 29, 1867. The preamble to the legislation described it as "An Act for the Union of Canada, Nova Scotia, and New Brunswick, and the Government thereof; and for Purposes connected therewith," and went on to declare:

> Whereas the Provinces of Canada, Nova Scotia and New Brunswick have expressed their Desire to be federally united into One Dominion. ... And whereas such a Union would conduce to the Welfare of the Provinces and promote the Interests of the British Empire. ... And whereas it is expedient that Provision be made for the eventual Admission into the Union of other Parts of British North America. ...

Section 3 of the act stated that "the Provinces of Canada, Nova Scotia, and New Brunswick shall form and be One Dominion under the Name of Canada." Three months later, on July 1, 1867, the Dominion of Canada joined the world of nations.

Many accounts look at Confederation almost as an accident of history. Political deadlocks in the Province of Canada, unusual political combinations in the Maritimes, and the crisis of the American Civil War, it is alleged, drove separate colonies into a union that was, in one famous phrase, "a carpentering rather than a smelting" of the parts.[1]

Without denying the importance of the short-term crises, the fact is that Confederation was a predictable political response to a set of economic forces that had been building for many decades. The roots of the change went back a century, to the beginning of the industrial revolution. The literature on this complex phenomenon is vast, but it generally agrees on a number of points. First, the industrial revolution began in Britain around the middle of the eighteenth century and had spread to the continent and to North America by the middle of the nineteenth century. Second, it is most aptly described as a period of "accelerating and unprecedented technological change."[2] Third, this technological change was primarily in four main areas: power technology (the steam engine), metallurgy (iron), textiles, and a miscellaneous category that includes machine tools, ceramics, glass, papermaking, and rudimentary chemicals. Fourth, the industrial revolution is associated with the rise of factory production, even if the nature of the link is subject to debate.

The effects of the industrial revolution on economic life were profound, and these economic changes forced adjustments in government. The rise of industrialism accelerated the transfer of effective political power from the land-owning classes to those involved in the production, transport, and sale of the products of the industrial age. As such groups gained power and influence, they naturally sought governments that could provide reasonably efficient fiscal and legal structures for the new emerging economies. Remnants of the feudal era became increasingly incapable of meeting the new demands, and the nation state, already well developed in some areas, came to dominate even further.

In Europe, Italy was welded into a single state in 1849, more than 1200 years after the Roman empire had disintegrated. In 1870, an even more powerful nation came into being when Prussia ushered a collection of states and principalities into the new nation of Germany. It was no coincidence that this new nation was already well on the road to industrialization.

In the United States, industrialism also led to nation building, though in a slightly different way. In the years after the War of 1812, the Americans had begun a slow and steady march toward industrialization. Industrial output increased twelvefold in real terms between 1815 and 1860.[3] Manufacturing made up less than 5 percent of GNP in 1810, but more than 15 percent in 1860. Cotton textiles, concentrated in the New England states, were the leading sector. Factory production replaced handicraft methods, slowly at first, and then rapidly after about 1815. New England cotton-industry output stood at 2.4 million yards in 1815 and at 857.2 million yards in 1860 — an annual growth rate of nearly 15 percent — making it the largest manufacturing industry in the nation in 1860. Production of wool, silk, linen, and other textiles complemented this development. Iron production was another important sector, especially as it came to be linked with the great expansion in railway mileage.

By 1860, therefore, every sign was that the United States was on the verge of becoming a significant industrial power that, like Germany, would soon challenge Britain's pre-eminent position. First though, America had to assert the power of the nation over regional interests. The American Civil War of 1861–65 did just that. By 1865, the industrializing north had ensured that the nation would survive intact as one of the largest and wealthiest domestic markets for the growing economy.

The situation in British North America was different, but not as much as one might think. It was different, of course, in that Canada was not yet an industrial power. Nevertheless, industrialization affected Canada both directly and indirectly. Directly, Canada experienced the first taste of industrialism when it embarked on an ambitious spate of railway building in the 1850s. The cost requirements of such vast projects soon demonstrated the inadequacy of existing institutions and structures of government. The indirect effects were equally profound. Britain abandoned the mercantilist notions that had shaped Canadian economic life for nearly two centuries, while the rapid economic expansion underway south of the border offered both unparalleled opportunities and some degree of threat of annexation by the United States. Changes would have to be made.

From an economic perspective then, Confederation must be seen as part of a quarter-century adjustment that paralleled events elsewhere in the Atlantic world. The adjustment began in the mid-1840s, as the British mercantile system began to unravel; it took its political shape in 1867, with Confederation and the British North America Act; and it culminated with the subsequent expansion into the West and John A. Macdonald's "National Policy" of 1879. Together, these changes were Canada's response to an industrializing world, and preparation for its own incipient industrialization process.

We explore these links in this part. Chapter Eight examines the development of those sectors of the economy (forestry, agriculture, and shipping and shipbuilding) most directly affected by the end of the British mercantile system. Chapter Nine looks at railways and early industrialization in British North America. Chapter Ten reviews the events leading up to Confederation in 1867, examines briefly the main economic provisions of the British North America Act, and concludes by discussing the rounding out of Confederation.

NOTES

1. Frank Underhill, *The Image of Confederation*, The Massey Lectures, 1963 (Toronto: Canadian Broadcasting Corporation, 1964).
2. Joel Mokyr, *The Lever of Riches: Technological Creativity and Economic Progress* (New York and Oxford: Oxford University Press, 1990), 82.
3. Gerald Gunderson, *A New Economic History of America* (New York: McGraw–Hill, 1976), 156.

Chapter Eight

Adjustment to the End of Mercantilism

THE BRITISH MERCANTILE system unravelled quickly once the process began. Timber duties were the first to be affected, with the initial cuts coming in 1842 and the last of the differential duties gone by 1860. The Navigation Acts were repealed in two steps, in 1849 and 1854. Thereafter, British ports were open on equal terms to vessels of all nations. Agricultural duties ended as well. The Irish famine of 1845–46 forced the British government to admit offshore wheat freely. Notice was given the following year that, effective as of 1849, grain could be imported into the United Kingdom upon payment of a nominal duty, and even this small levy was removed in 1869.

Trade liberalization proceeded beyond agriculture. An estimated 1150 items carried duties in 1840, but fewer than 50 did by 1860. Britain was a free-trade nation in practice as well as in doctrine.

If the dismantlement of the British mercantile system created some unease in the British North American colonies, the reaction is understandable. In the minds of many contemporaries, the colonial economies owed their very beginnings to the Navigation Acts, the timber preferences, and the Corn Laws. Now, all were going, raising doubts about future economic prospects. Would squared timber still find a market in the United Kingdom if forced to compete on equal terms with supplies from the Baltic? Could Canadian grains still find a market in Britain? Even if they could, would these supplies, and those from adjacent U.S. lands, continue to travel there via the Great Lakes–St. Lawrence forwarding system? To what extent did Atlantic Canada's carrying trade and shipbuilding activity still depend on the Navigation Acts and timber preferences?

This belief that the end of the British mercantile system spelled economic disaster for the North American colonies rested on two assumptions: the aggregate prosperity of the colonial economies depended directly on the success of a few export industries; and the success of these industries depended directly on preferential access to the United Kingdom. By extension, the fears would be unwarranted if either assumption proved false. Even if the export industries required the mercantile system to become established, they may have moved beyond this infant industry status to become internationally competitive. Alternatively, even if the aggregate economic performances of the colonial economies did depend on a few export activities in the beginning, they may have become sufficiently diversified that this direct dependence no longer held.

Timber

Initially the concerns of North American politicians seemed justified. In 1843, exports of squared timber fell by more than 25 percent, and unemployment spread through the timber camps and ports associated with the trade. Yet by the 1850s wood products were a growing export, more than doubling between 1850 and 1854. They fluctuated around this 1854 figure until 1862, when they increased to a new level that was maintained to 1867. At the time of Confederation, wood exports in value terms were two and one-half times greater than they were in 1850. Clearly, timber exports did not disappear from the Canadian economy following the removal of the British timber preferences.

To understand the developments in the wood industry in this period, it is important to distinguish among three types of wood exports: squared timber; deals, which were thick planks (3 inches [7.5 cm] or more) of fairly high quality in terms of both material and manufacture; and planks and boards. It is also important to distinguish the two export markets for Canadian products in this period: Britain and the United States.

The majority of the exports of the early timber trade were in squared timber. British North America had exported some deals to Britain as far back as the 1790s, although the trade was miniscule until about 1820. It rose steadily thereafter, surpassing supplies from the Baltic in the early 1830s and remaining ahead of them until about 1860.[1]

An export trade in deals required two prior developments: sawmills capable of meeting the relatively strict quality requirements; and a means to transport the product to tidewater, for, unlike squared timber, deals could not simply be floated downriver. The colonies were blessed with abundant fast-flowing rivers, so a power source was no problem. Small mills catering to local demand had been a feature of the timber industry from the beginning, and they served as a source of skilled labour. By 1842 there were 982 sawmills in Canada West alone, and by 1851 there were more than 1500.[2] With the advent of canals, the transportation problem was alleviated. The Ottawa River became the centre of the deals industry, with additional capacity in New Brunswick and along the St. Lawrence to Lake Ontario. The first steam-powered mill appeared in Saint John in 1821, but it was after mid-century before this technology became dominant. Steam power, together with the railway, freed the industry from its locational dependence on river sites.

If preferences were essential for the industry's survival, then timber and other wood product exports should have declined more or less continuously in the 1850s, and end in 1860 when the last duties were removed. In fact, as Marvin McInnis shows, exports grew in value terms, and in 1867 were 27 percent higher than they were in 1850. Thus, while we cannot know how squared-timber exports might have fared if British preferences had been maintained, the removal of these duties clearly did not spell the death knell for the activity.

Several factors are clearly important for the activity's survival after the tariff cuts in 1842, however.[3] First, as already noted, differential duties were reduced in 1842 but not completely removed until 1860. Thus, North American timber enjoyed preferential treatment in Britain for nearly two decades after the initial cuts, albeit at a decreasing rate. Second, ocean freight rates on British North American timber were falling in this period,[4] a development of particular importance to this relatively high-bulk, low-value product. Third, British timber demand was generally high in the 1850s and 1860s as a result of booms in building and shipbuilding. Marvin McInnis argues that the British market was able to absorb increasing timber supplies from the Baltic without displacing those from British North America.

Another reason for the survival and growth of Canada's forest industry after the loss of preferential treatment in the British market was the American demand for forest products. From 1850 to 1890, New Brunswick exported most of its forest products to Britain with exports of sawn lumber replacing the shipment of squared timber. Ontario and Quebec also exported forest products to Britain, but after mid-century the major source of growth in exports was planks and boards to the United States. Given the much larger size of the forest sector in Ontario and Quebec than in New Brunswick and Nova Scotia after 1850, the emergence of the United States as an alternative market was clearly an important reason for the survival and growth of the Canadian forest industry. Marvin McInnis estimates that, in 1850, wood exports to the United States accounted for only 20 percent of total wood exports. By 1870, the value of forest products exports to the United States was 80 percent of the value of forest products exported to Britain. While the value of forest products exports from Ontario and Quebec to Great Britain was roughly equal to the value of forest products exports to the United States, the degree of processing of the timber differed between the destinations. Over 75 percent of the value of exports to United States was from planks and boards produced in Ontario and Quebec, whereas over 70 percent of the value of Canadian exports to Britain was accounted for by deals and pine timber.[5]

The lumber trade with the United States developed in this period for a number of reasons. The U.S. economy was growing rapidly, as was the urban population, so the demand for lumber was expanding. Reciprocity, the Civil War, and the fact that the forests of the eastern United States were largely depleted by this time deflected this demand toward Canada. On the supply side, Canadians had the timber resources, water-power sites, and labour skills necessary to allow them to begin to respond to this demand. As saw-milling technology improved, they were able to bring their production costs down. The development of canals, and then railways, meant that transport costs, always an obstacle in this industry, came down significantly. As with deals, steam-powered mills and railways freed the industry from its locational dependence on river systems.

Wheat

We have already questioned the notion that the agricultural sector in British North America was driven by wheat exports and that success in exporting wheat to Britain depended in the main on preferential access under the Corn Laws. Atlantic Canada never depended on wheat exports, and Quebec did only for about two decades after 1790. Ontario is the exception, although shipments to Britain only became important in the 1840s, long after agriculture was well established in the province. Still, it is revealing to ask what happened to this activity after 1846, when the British market was thrown open on an equal basis to all nations.

In fact, exports of wheat from Ontario continued to grow after 1846, due to a generally buoyant international economy. Estimates vary, but the trend is clear. After a slight downward slump in 1846–47, wheat exports recovered. It was in the 1850s, though, that the most dramatic growth occurred. At the beginning of the decade, Canada West exported approximately 4.3 million bushels of wheat. A decade later, the figure had increased to 11.1 million bushels, or 61 bushels for every man, woman, and child in the province.[6]

Not only did wheat exports from Ontario continue to grow after 1846, but so too did the share of wheat in total agricultural output. The gross value of agricultural production in the province increased from $36 million in 1851 to $89.2 million in 1860, and to $93.9 million in 1870. Wheat accounted for 30 percent of this total in 1851 and 36 percent in 1860, before falling to 15 percent in 1870.[7]

The actual process of harvesting grain had changed little in the past century. It was slow, labour-intensive, and severely limiting to the size of farming operations. By the 1850s, however, mechanical reapers were beginning to appear in the province. These implements reduced the time and labour necessary to cut the crop. With the development of the self-rake reaper by the 1860s, another tedious step in the harvesting process was made more efficient. Good grain prices in these years encouraged farmers to move to the reaper more quickly than otherwise might have been the case, and the adoption of the reaper made farmers able to respond to the opportunities for increased grain production. By 1871, nearly 37 000 mowers and reapers operated in Ontario alone.[8]

Clearly, the removal of the Corn Laws had little effect on Canada's ability to compete in British markets, and, apparently, on the return to Ontario farmers from wheat relative to other products. The mid-1850s were the peak years of this staple trade, and exports were still substantial as late as 1866. Only in 1869 did Canada as a whole become a net importer of wheat and flour.[9] As Ontario's dependence on wheat exports lessened, it did so partly as a result of supply problems and partly because farmers were drawn to more profitable uses for their resources. The domestic demand for fruit and vegetables, dairy products, and meat increased as population and income grew. Demand for these products was growing in the United States as well, and here reciprocity and the U.S. Civil War deflected some of this demand north of the border. The advent of railways brought transport costs on these products down, and hence farm gate prices up, increasing the attraction of this market.

The St. Lawrence–Great Lakes Carrying Trade

Wheat farmers may have had a relatively smooth transition after the abolition of the Corn Laws, but the same was not true for some of the activities linked to wheat exports. When Britain moved to abolish its Corn Laws in 1846, it ended the longstanding aspirations of the merchants of the Province of Canada to be the forwarders of a large hinterland draining into the Great Lakes. Huge investments had gone into canal building as a means of competing with the United States, as entrepreneurs responded to the opportunities provided by the Canada Corn Act and other legislation.

The most obvious examples of business responding to imperial legislation were the investments in flour mills along the St. Lawrence in the 1840s. American wheat could come into Canada without significant duty, but American flour could not. Yet, all flour shipped out of the Canadas could benefit from the imperial system. It thus benefited Americans to ship their wheat to Canada and have it ground into flour. With the opening of the British wheat market to all nations on an equal basis, Canada found itself with far too much flour-milling capacity. From the resulting bankruptcies, a ripple effect occurred, as workers were let go, banks declared loans to be in default, and carters and haulers found their business with the mills down drastically.

Another group affected were the shippers and forwarders who depended on the carrying trade from the United States. Aside from contending with the abolition of the Corn Laws, they had to adjust to the passage of the Drawback Acts by the United States in 1845 and 1846. These acts permitted goods in transit through the United States to be carried in bond. Henceforth, Canadian wholesalers purchasing from Britain, and Canadian farmers exporting their product, could look to either the St. Lawrence or the American system for the best rates.

In such an open competition, the Americans had an advantage. Canadian shipping rates through the Great Lakes were lower than those along the American Erie Canal system. One optimistic report estimated that advantage to be as much as $4 per ton from Detroit. The problem was that the inland Canadian route led to Montreal, and the American one to New York. The former was a seasonal port far up a river noted for stretches of tricky navigation. The other was an ice-free port with ready access to the open ocean. Lower rates from New York to Liverpool more than compensated for higher American rates inland. Canadian shippers could still compete, but it would henceforth be much more difficult to do so. Many feared the worst, and clamoured loudly that the home country had betrayed imperial necessity and, not incidentally, Canadian pocketbooks.

Depression in trade along the St. Lawrence followed. Exports via the St. Lawrence fell from a figure of £2.7 million in 1845 to a low of £1.7 million in 1848. Government revenue from the expensive canal system also tumbled, the Welland's tolls falling some 60 percent between 1846 and 1848.[10] With its finances already overextended by the construction of the canal system, the government soon found itself facing yet another fiscal crisis. Fears of bankruptcy and difficulties on the British credit market added to the sense of panic and instability that existed.

Finally, adding to the woes was the vast immigration of 1846–48. The same famine that had acted as a catalyst for the suspension of the Corn Laws drove more than a million Irish out of their homeland between 1846 and 1851.[11] British North America received almost a quarter of a million of these refugees at the very time that the economy was adjusting to the dismantlement of the British mercantile system.[12] Where previous waves of immigration had been in response to opportunities (pull factors) arising from the economic growth in the British North America colonies, the arrival of this wave of Irish immigrants was in response to the desperate conditions (push factors) in Ireland. The economy of the colonies was ill-prepared to absorb the immigrants into their labour force. As Canadians reacted to the arrival of a flood of poor and often diseased refugees, the traditional view of immigrants as the lifeblood of the colonies changed, at least temporarily. The Irish, the prejudices of the time would have it, were a benighted people who would never be anything but a drain on the land. The problems of Europe, it was feared, were being sent to North America.

Famine migration, financial ruin, imperial desertion, and government impecuniousness thus mark the traditional view of the period from 1846 to 1850. Yet, it is difficult to posit too gloomy a scenario. The panic of these years was, to a large degree, a reflection of human psychology rather than economic collapse. That psychology emanated from a sincere belief by a circle of businessmen and politicians (often the same individuals) who had consistently overestimated the importance of, and therefore the effect of the absence of, the imperial system to Canadian development. Their mood was made worse by the assertion of power by the Reform Party and by the controversial 1849 Rebellion Losses Bill, which compensated certain rebels from 1837. It was climaxed by a short-lived but emotional campaign for annexation to the United States.

In fact, the years from 1846 to 1850 were ones of commercial adjustment rather than of any fundamental depression in the Canadian economy. In 1847, a record amount of wheat went downriver from Canada West, and most of it went overseas. Thus, the actual effects of the commercial upset were specific, in terms of both occupation and region. Farmers were not as hard hit as were merchants. The merchants of Canada West were seemingly not as hard hit as those Montrealers whose livelihood rested on the St. Lawrence trade. Canada West as a whole does not seem to have experienced the same sense of panic as the business community of Canada East.

Even among the commercial class of Montreal, the serious problems resulting from 1846 were short-lived. By 1850–51, there was a strong recovery under way, fuelled by international prosperity, and the Province of Canada entered a period of rapid economic growth that belied the pessimism both business and government had shown only a couple of years earlier. Such rapid growth underlines the fact that the basic strengths of the economy were not seriously undermined by the British movement away from a mercantile structure.

Shipping and Shipbuilding

Since shipping and shipbuilding were closely tied to British mercantile policy, there was understandable concern about how they would fare in the absence of timber duties and the Navigation Acts. As it turned out, the industry continued to expand until Confederation. In 1843, one year after the first reduction in the British timber preference, 262 vessels were built in the Maritime provinces, totalling slightly more than 26 000 tons (23 600 t). These figures then increased, with some annual fluctuation, to 1856, when 388 vessels totalling nearly 151 000 tons (137 300 t) were built. Construction then dropped to 295 vessels and 59 200 tons (53 800 t) in 1858 before climbing to its historic peak in 1864, when 586 vessels were built, totalling more than 210 000 tons (191 000 t).[13] The numbers of ships constructed more than doubled, and the tonnage they represented increased more than eightfold in two decades after 1842. Clearly, any initial advantage that had been derived from participation in the British mercantile system had long since been transformed into a natural competitive advantage, resting on the skills and resource endowments of the region.

The trend in shipping more or less paralleled that for shipbuilding. Tonnage on registry in Atlantic ports fell off slightly in the mid-1840s, but then climbed more or less continuously and peaked in the early 1880s. This period, beginning around 1850 and lasting for about five decades, was the "golden age of sail" for the Maritime provinces.[14] The main business was carrying American staple products — grain, cotton, and tobacco — to British and European markets. In 1863–64, this trade made up over 70 percent of the voyages of vessels on registry in four of the ports. The West Indies contributed another 10 percent, with the remaining trade distributed around the world.[15] As in the case of shipbuilding, whatever initial advantage the region had derived from the British mercantile system had been parlayed into a natural competitiveness.

The Reciprocity Treaty

The end of the British mercantile system may not have been the economic catastrophe for the resource sectors that some had predicted in 1846. Nevertheless, a vision that had propelled ambitious merchants and shaped government policy had collapsed. Canadians thus looked for alternative places to send their products and, after 1846, politicians and businessmen increasingly focused their enthusiasms south of the border. If Canada could not capture the American carrying trade, perhaps it could sell some of its produce to the Americans.

The attraction of the United States as a market was possible because of the tremendous changes that had taken place over the past couple of decades. When Upper Canada was created in 1791, the United States had a population of 4 million. By 1850, that population had increased to 23.4 million, much of it in states along, or close to, the British North American border. Moreover, recent years had seen the beginning of meaningful industrialization in New England and other areas. The demand for raw materials to build the factories and the houses of the growing cities, to feed the machines and the increasingly urban population, grew rapidly through the 1840s. By 1850, nearly $5 million worth of such goods as timber, sawn planks, fish, and other primary and semiprocessed resources were going south annually. American consumption of British North American products was still much smaller than was British consumption, but it was growing. Given such figures, it was natural that the United States emerged as an alternative export market.

Once Canada became interested in the American market, the idea of free trade followed naturally. A special arrangement with the United States might help restore some of the certainty about access to markets for resource products lost with the end of the British mercantile system. The reverse side of the coin was the fact that the United States had heretofore used tariff barriers to discourage key British North American products. For example, Canada's biggest export, timber, was taxed at an ad valorem rate of 20 percent. Other key products faced similar barriers. British North American exporters were thus at a disadvantage in trying to compete with American producers. Lowering American barriers might permit them to develop this new market.

A reciprocity agreement with the United States also offered British North Americans more than a new market. With preferential access to the British market under mercantilism, the British North American colonies developed under free trade conditions. The B.N.A. colonies could not protect the home markets against British manufactures, though the British protected the B.N.A. colonies against American manufactures. Under these arrangements, the colonies earned income on exports but they remained highly specialized in the production of only a few staples. Reciprocity with the United States offered a new opportunity as the British North American colonists had some power to negotiate the terms of the Agreement. In particular, unlike free trade with England, reciprocity with the United States primarily included natural products on the free list. The B.N.A. colonies were able to use tariffs to protect manufacturers. As such, reciprocity promised not only income from exports, but also the potential to industrialize and diversify the colonies of British North America.

As each B.N.A. colony could set its own tariffs, and to the extent that the economies and economic conditions in each of the colonies differed, the move towards reciprocity with the United States began with each colony taking its own initiative. The reciprocity movement had its origins in Canada West. For many years, the American market had been looked upon covetously by businessmen such as William Hamilton Merritt of Welland Canal fame. Then, when the abolition of mercantilism led to the short-lived annexation movement in Montreal, Canadian businessmen and politicians began to consider some sort of trade arrangement with the United States as an alternative. Such an arrangement would provide the benefits of commercial access to the neighbour to the south while avoiding the extreme action advocated on behalf of the Canadian government. Reciprocity was an alternative to annexation; it was also, from the more material point of view, seen as good business. Thus, from the late 1840s onward, talk of reciprocity began to be heard more and more frequently in Canada.

The first formal move in the Atlantic region came in 1849, when New Brunswick organized a conference on the reciprocity question. Prince Edward Island was the first colony to move explicitly, passing a bill in 1849 providing for free trade for a specified list of commodities if the United States reciprocated. Similar measures were enacted by Nova Scotia and New Brunswick in 1850. Only in Newfoundland was there little interest in the proposal. Opinions in the Atlantic region shifted, beginning in 1852. By then, it had become apparent that the Americans would demand access to the offshore fisheries of the Maritime colonies as part of any package. Such competition would seem to cut into the profitability of the Maritime fishery. Nova Scotia became the most outspoken critic of the idea of concessions, and found support in New Brunswick and Prince Edward Island. Interestingly, Newfoundland, which had been indifferent until this point, remained out of step with the other provinces by suddenly pressing for an agreement.

The result of this interest in North American trade liberalization was the Reciprocity Treaty of 1854. The negotiations for the treaty provided an almost casebook lesson concerning two North American realities. First, it was the smaller party —Canada — that was most interested in the treaty. American interest was confined to certain specialized sectors and was countered by suspicion or apathy on the part of most politicians and businessmen. Thus, it was up to Canada to find a means of gaining acceptance in the United States. (More than 130 years later, a similar pattern developed during the Canadian–American free-trade negotiations of the 1980s.)

Second, the treaty illustrated both the regional differences that are so much a part of Canadian history and the realities of power when such regional differences clash. Strict British enforcement of boundary regulations concerning fishing in Maritime waters led to a series of confrontations between American fishermen and British naval patrols. Diplomacy was now becoming enmeshed in trade policy. The Americans were apathetic about trade with the Province of Canada, but the dual desire to avoid diplomatic confrontation with Great Britain and to gain access to the Maritime fisheries began to alter their view.

There was one complication. Several of the Atlantic colonies, with Nova Scotia at the forefront, were nervous about opening their waters to the American fishermen, even in return for access to American waters. It mattered little, however. By this time both Canada and Great Britain were interested in pursuing the treaty for diplomatic and economic reasons. Nova Scotia was pressured into accepting the 1854 Reciprocity Treaty. The tactic was simple: Britain threatened to withdraw its patrol boats, thus making American encroachment likely, with or without a treaty. The Province of Canada was not to be denied in 1854; neither would it be denied in 1867, under a much more important economic and political arrangement.

The Reciprocity Treaty, signed in June 1854, reflected the orientations of the British North American economies toward primary resources. Articles I and II of the treaty provided for reciprocal access, with some exceptions, to the coastal fisheries. Article III provided for free importation into each country of a range of products, from grains and breadstuffs through animals and animal products to fish, timber, and minerals. Altogether, the items covered accounted for approximately 90 percent of the existing trade across the British North American–U.S. border. The treaty was to last for ten years and, thereafter, for twelve months following an announcement by the Americans, in 1865, of their intention to terminate it; the treaty came to an end on March 17, 1866.

The traditional view of the Reciprocity Treaty stresses its contribution to the economic growth of the colonies in the 1850s and 1860s. Certainly, casual examination of the data suggests such a correlation. Trade between British North America and the United States increased in the period covered by the treaty, and the United States gained in relative importance as an export market. Total Canadian exports to the United States rose fourfold, from $8.6 million in 1854 to $34.8 million in 1866, or from 40.7 percent of total exports at the beginning of the treaty to 69.2 percent at the end. The change in imports was less marked, rising from $15.5 million to $20.4 million over the same period, with the share remaining constant at 38 percent.

The problem, of course, is that there were many other important developments in this period in Canada, the United States, and abroad that might have affected trade between the two nations at least as much as did the treaty. To determine the effect the treaty actually had, two questions need to be posed and answered. First, what was the impact of the

154

Reciprocity Treaty on the volume of trade between Canada and the United States? Second, whatever impact there was on volume, how did these changes in trade flows contribute to real economic gains?

The first question can be addressed with the aid of some data assembled by Officer and Smith for their influential study of the Reciprocity Treaty, presented in Table 8.1. The obvious place to start is with changes in trade patterns in the initial year of the treaty and in the year after its termination, since these can be more confidently ascribed to the treaty than can figures stretching over a decade and a half. Looking at exports first, Officer and Smith's data show that shipments of items covered by the treaty increased by more than $8 million in 1855 from what they were in 1854, or by 96 percent. They rose again in 1856, fell off to about 50 percent above their pretreaty level for three years, and then jumped again during the Civil War.

This result certainly suggests that the treaty was effective. To be certain, however, other possible explanations need to be ruled out. One possibility is that the measured increase in trade reflected that more trades were reported once tariffs were eliminated. For example, where smuggling was practiced, the existence of tariffs would reduce the reporting of trade, not necessarily the amount of trade. Another possibility is that Canadian reciprocity items were more attractive (i.e., cheaper) for reasons that had nothing to do with reciprocity — abundant harvests or transportation improvements coming on stream, for example. If so, however, exports of the same items to the rest of the world should have increased as well. In fact, they fell in value terms from 1854 to 1855 by $3.9 million, or 37 percent. The apparent conclusion is that the treaty did divert some primary products from offshore to American markets. Whatever effect there was, however, was temporary. By 1856, exports of reciprocity items to the rest of the world were back to their 1854 levels.

Another possible explanation for the 96 percent increase in the export of reciprocity items to the United States in 1855 is that American demand for Canadian products increased for reasons that had nothing to do with reciprocity — a relative inflation or a general disruption in production, such as that experienced later during the Civil War, for example. If so, however, all Canadian exports to the United States should have increased, not just reciprocity items. In fact, shipments of non-reciprocity items declined slightly, by $8000, or 3.4 percent, again suggesting that the treaty must have had some initial effect. However, since this decline in exports of non-reciprocity items to the United States is less than the $556 000 (26.6 percent) registered in the same category for the rest of the world, some change in the U.S. economy unrelated to reciprocity was possibly under way as well.

The situation with respect to imports is similar. Imports of reciprocity items from the United States increased nearly fourfold in 1855 over 1854 figures, or by $5.8 million. Sales from the rest of the world fell slightly at the same time, as did imports of nonreciprocity items from both the United States and abroad, so the explanation cannot be a general deterioration of Canadian competitiveness. Imports remained at the 1855 level until 1862, when they jumped significantly for two years before dropping back to 1855 values.

The figures for the termination of the treaty are less conclusive. There was a large drop in exports of reciprocity items from Canada in 1867, although this drop is largely explained by the fact that the 1866 figure was abnormally high. There was a glut of shipments going ahead of the announced reimposition of tariffs. Imports of reciprocity items from the United States fell by 43 percent, while imports of non-reciprocity items rose by 21 percent, which is consistent with what abrogation of the treaty would imply. But imports of reciprocity goods from the rest of the world fell by 13 percent and those of non-reciprocity items rose by 18 percent as well; clearly, other factors were at work.

Officer and Smith go on to examine the impacts of the treaty on particular sectors.[16] They find little effect on the trade in timber, animals, wool, and barley, and some possible

Table 8.1 Canadian Trade Statistics, 1850–1868

| | Imports into Canada of | | | |
| | Reciprocity Articles from | | Non-reciprocity Articles from | |
Year	U.S. *($ thousands)*	Rest of World *($ thousands)*	U.S. *($ thousands)*	Rest of World *($ thousands)*
1850	1 238	187	5 358	10 197
1851	1 039	355	7 325	12 713
1852	940	453	7 536	11 355
1853	1 281	657	10 499	19 543
1854	1 976	855	13 556	24 141
1855	7 726	649	13 102	14 608
1856	8 083	1 083	14 621	19 797
1857	8 642	1 025	11 582	18 183
1858	5 565	1 036	10 070	12 407
1859	7 106	1 424	10 487	14 538
1860	7 069	1 407	10 204	15 766
1861	9 981	1 316	11 088	20 670
1862	14 431	1 700	10 742	21 727
1863	12 339	1 667	10 770	21 188
1864*	4 876	657	5 551	12 799
1865	9 132	1 851	10 457	23 180
1866	8 752	2 213	11 672	31 165
1867	6 114	1 925	14 159	36 852
1868	5 461	1 451	16 993	33 343
1850	4 756	5 684	196	1 324
1851	3 860	7 188	212	1 704
1852	6 048	6 672	236	1 100
1853	8 696	10 524	340	2 452
1854	8 412	10 508	236	2 092
1855	16 508	6 652	228	1 536
1856	17 776	10 400	204	1 428
1857	12 912	10 640	296	1 600
1858	11 656	9 190	274	909
1859	13 625	8 455	297	725
1860	18 096	12 787	332	1 146
1861	13 972	18 646	414	1 685
1862	14 566	15 289	498	1 326
1863	17 573	16 608	2 477	2 689
1864*	6 769	4 118	953	1 067
1865	20 567	13 994	2 372	2 675
1866	31 337	13 245	3 433	2 242
1867	22 051	16 108	3 533	3 278
1868	19 376	15 516	4 974	4 672

*DATA AVAILABLE FOR JANUARY 1 TO JUNE 30 ONLY; 1850–63 DATA FOR YEAR ENDING DECEMBER 31; 1865–68 DATA FOR YEAR ENDING JUNE 30.

Source: Lawrence Officer and Lawrence Smith, "The Canadian–American Reciprocity Treaty of 1855 to 1868," *Journal of Economic History* 28 (December 1968): 600. Reprinted with the permission of Cambridge University Press.

adverse consequences for the Canadian cheese industry. Wheat, oats, and flour probably benefited. Overall, however, the impact of the treaty on trade flows pales in comparison with those of the U.S. Civil War, railway construction, and general income and population growth in the two countries.

The final issue is what impact even these small trade-flow effects had on economic welfare. Officer and Smith conclude that the trade that was affected— that in grains — was largely convenience trade, meaning that the way grain supplies were shipped to markets in the two countries was altered to save on transport costs. Since relative price differences were, therefore, likely small prior to the trade, the welfare effects would be minimal. Reciprocity added little to real income growth in Canada in this period.

While Officer and Smith conclude that the overall gains from reciprocity for the British North America colonies were modest at best, Marilyn Gerriets and Julian Gwyn[17] argue that the agreement had a significant impact on the Nova Scotia economy. First, the agreement complemented the earlier movement towards freer trade that the colony had shown. They show that Nova Scotia's economy responded to the increase in exports to the United States by shifting resources into production activities where the province had a comparative advantage; away from wheat and pork and towards products like potatoes, coal, and dairy products. Further, while the overall gains from reciprocity were not dramatic, the removal of tariffs gave the coal mines and mackerel fishery a substantial stimulus.

Conclusion

Generally, the resource sectors and the shipping and shipbuilding industries of the British North American colonies adjusted fairly well to the rather abrupt end of a system that had, for so long, shaped their economic and political development. Existing activities survived and even prospered for a time, and new products were developed and new markets found. The relative ease of the transition would have surprised those generations of colonial politicians and businessmen who had lobbied so hard and so long in London for the retention and extension of imperial privileges.

NOTES

1. A.R.M. Lower, *Great Britain's Woodyard: British America and the Timber Trade, 1763–1867* (Montreal and Kingston: McGill–Queen's University Press, 1973), 260.
2. Douglas McCalla, *Planting the Province: The Economic History of Upper Canada, 1784–1870* (Toronto: University of Toronto Press, 1993), appendix B, table 6.1.
3. R.M. McInnis, "Canada in the World Market for Forest Products, 1850–1895," unpublished manuscript, Queen's University, 1988.
4. C. Knick Harley, "Ocean Freight Rates and Productivity, 1740–1913: The Primacy of Mechanical Invention Reaffirmed," *Journal of Economic History* 48(4) (December 1988): 851–76.
5. Plate 38: The Forest Industry, 1850–1890, in R. Louis Gentilcore, ed., *Historical Atlas of Canada Vol. II, The Land Transformed* (Toronto: University of Toronto Press, 1993).
6. McCalla, *Planting the Province*, appendix B, table 5.2. For an estimate that gives somewhat higher export figures see Donald Akenson, *The Irish in Ontario: A Study in Rural History* (Montreal and Kingston: McGill–Queen's University Press, 1984), 29.
7. John McCallum, *Unequal Beginnings: Agriculture and Economic Development in Quebec and Ontario until 1870* (Toronto: University of Toronto Press, 1980), table S.4, 127.

8. Richard Pomfret, "The Mechanization of Reaping in Nineteenth Century Ontario," in Douglas McCalla, ed., *Perspectives on Canadian Economic History* (Toronto: Copp Clark Pitman, 1987), 81–95.

9. Marvin McInnis, "The Changing Structure of Canadian Agriculture, 1867–1897," *Journal of Economic History* 42(1) (March 1982): 194.

10. Province of Canada, Department of Public Works, *Annual Reports*, 1846–50 (Ottawa: Department of Public Works).

11. D.H. Akenson, *The Irish in Ontario: A Study in Rural History* (Montreal and Kingston: McGill–Queen's University Press, 1984), 29.

12. Akenson, *The Irish in Ontario*, 32.

13. Richard Rice, "Measuring British Dominance of Shipbuilding in the 'Maritimes,' 1787–1890," in Keith Matthews and Gerald Panting, eds., *Ships and Shipbuilding in the North Atlantic Region* (St. John's: Memorial University, 1978), 109–55, appendix 1.

14. Eric W. Sager and Gerald E. Panting, *Maritime Capital: The Shipping Industry in Atlantic Canada, 1820–1914* (Montreal and Kingston, McGill–Queen's University Press, 1990), 88.

15. Eric W. Sager and Lewis R. Fischer, "Atlantic Canada and the Age of Sail Revisited," *Canadian Historical Review* 63(2) (1982): 125–50 (figure 1).

16. Lawrence Officer and Lawrence Smith, "The Canadian American Reciprocity Treaty of 1855 to 1866," *Journal of Economic History* 28 (December 1968): 598–623.

17. Gerriets, Marilyn and Julian Gwyn. "Tariffs, Trade and Reciprocity: Nova Scotia, 1830–1866." *Acadiensis* XXV (2) (Spring 1996): 62–82.

FURTHER READING

Ankli, R.E. "The Reciprocity Treaty of 1854." *Canadian Journal of Economics* 4 (February 1971): 1–20.

Head, C. Grant. "Plate 38: The Forest Industry, 1850–1890." In R. Louis Gentilcore, ed., *Historical Atlas of Canada, Vol. II: The Land Transformed, 1800–1891*. Toronto: University of Toronto Press, 1993.

Masters, D.C. *The Reciprocity Treaty of 1854*. Carleton Library No. 9. Toronto: McClelland & Stewart, 1963.

McCalla, Douglas. *Planting the Province: The Economic History of Upper Canada, 1784–1870*. Toronto: University of Toronto Press, 1993.

McCallum, John. *Unequal Beginnings: Agriculture and Economic Development in Quebec and Ontario until 1870*. Toronto: University of Toronto Press, 1980.

Officer, Lawrence, and Lawrence Smith. "The Canadian American Reciprocity Treaty of 1855 to 1866." *Journal of Economic History* 28 (December 1968): 598–623.

Pomfret, Richard. "The Mechanization of Reaping in Nineteenth Century Ontario." In Douglas McCalla, ed., *Perspectives on Canadian Economic History*. Toronto: Copp Clark Pitman, 1987.

Sager, Eric W., and Lewis R. Fischer. "Atlantic Canada and the Age of Sail Revisited." *Canadian Historical Review* 63(2) (1982): 125–50.

Sager, Eric W., and Gerald E. Panting. *Maritime Capital: The Shipping Industry in Atlantic Canada, 1820–1914*. Montreal and Kingston: McGill–Queen's University Press, 1990.

Tucker, G. *The Canadian Commercial Revolution, 1845–1851*. Carleton Library No. 19. Toronto: McClelland & Stewart, 1970.

Chapter Nine

Railways and Early Industrialization

THE TRADITIONAL SECTORS of the British North American colonies underwent profound change in the years from the union in 1841 to Confederation in 1867. The pioneer economy of Canada, with its heavy dependence on human and capital inflows, was replaced by a more mature agricultural and commercial system. Atlantic shipping and shipbuilding moved from being a small offshoot of the fishing industry and of the Navigation Acts to become a significant presence in their own right. Equally important to this era, though, and very much a portent of the future, was the development of more complex production techniques locally, including the beginnings of industrialization. As British North America grew in population, wealth, and skills, its economy was able to employ more advanced technologies derived from advanced industrial nations.

Railways

The impact of technology on the economy was demonstrated most clearly in the area of transportation. Railways, operational as practical vehicles of transportation in Europe since the 1830s, transformed the nature of business in the colonies, the structure of cities and villages, and the life of the average citizen. To enthusiasts, they were almost supernatural in their potential:

> Poverty, indifference, the bigotry or jealousy of religious denominations, local dissensions or political demagogueism may stifle or neutralize the influence of the best intended efforts of an educational system but that invisible power [steam] ... will assuredly overcome the prejudices of mental weakness or the design of mental tyrants.[1]

Railways were essential to the development of British North America because of the great distances involved in moving people and goods. As was true in the United States, transportation costs assumed enormous proportions as the frontier of settlement moved farther and farther inland. The expensive canals developed during the 1840s had been intended to meet this problem, but canals had their limitations. First, they could improve the movement of goods only along natural waterways; they could do nothing to assist inland settlements. Further (and this provided the second great attraction of railways), canals were subject to the tyranny of the Canadian winter. From late fall through spring each year, the transport of goods ground to a near halt as the waterways froze over. Railways, in contrast, were relatively immune to the effects of winter and could reach beyond the waterways to wherever potential traffic justified their presence. Finally, they were faster than water transportation and, in comparison with any other type of land transport, much less likely to damage the goods in transit. For the settler who wished to break out of social and economic isolation, for the merchant who hoped to deliver goods more efficiently, for the promoter who wished to sell off lands, and for the nationalists and enthusiasts, the technology of the steam railway seemed the answer.

Yet, the vast distances and scattered population that made the railway so important to British North America also created problems. Railways were tremendously expensive, much more so than canals and than any other project undertaken in British North America until this time. There was not sufficient speculative capital in the colonies to undertake such risky ventures. Thus, with the exception of a successful but short railway line along the Richelieu River, built in 1836, British North Americans continued to plan, dream, and promote, but not to build, railways through the 1830s and 1840s. Government-supported canals remained the focus of transportation planning through the 1840s, even as the United States expanded its railway network from about 160 km in 1830 to 14 000 km by 1850 and approximately 50 000 km by 1860.

By 1850, however, circumstances were becoming more favourable for would-be railway-builders. First, Great Britain's stock of private investment funds was growing rapidly. The success of the industrial revolution had generated tremendous amounts of income, and ever-greater percentages of it were available for investment. In the 1830s and 1840s, the great enthusiasm of British investors had been for domestic railways, but, by 1850, the initial boom of British railway construction was slowing and opportunities for domestic investment declined. To the evolving financier class in Great Britain, overseas investments were more attractive than they had been a decade or so earlier.

Even so, the small colonies of British North America were not all that attractive as a destination for British capital; speculative railway ventures by unknown Canadian promoters were even less so. Something would have to be done to encourage private investment, and the only body powerful enough to have any meaningful influence was the government itself. If railways were to be built in British North America, governments would have to get involved, as they had earlier with canals. From the outset of the railway era and up to the present, Canadian railway projects and government would have close relationships. This feature of Canadian economic development contrasts with that of the American experience where governments distanced themselves from infrastructure investments.[2] This time, however, the government authorities were determined to avoid direct public ownership and sought, instead, to make private-investment schemes more attractive.

The Province of Canada proceeded by throwing its credit behind railway ventures. In 1849, it passed the Railway Loan Guarantee Act, which stipulated that, if railways met certain conditions, they could have the interest on their bond issues guaranteed by the Government of Canada. The Municipal Loan Act of 1852 provided an alternative channel to the same end. Provincial credit was made available to those municipalities that wished to get involved in the game of railway subsidization. Many did, and towns and villages soon joined the rush to spread the magic of the steel rail into their community. To a society both enthusiastic about and often directly involved in railway ventures, it made eminent sense. To the Canadian politician whose personal investment in railways often meshed conveniently with his enthusiasm for such legislation, a chance for personal profit was enhanced. Most important to the British investor, it reduced the risks sufficiently to make British North American railways a worthwhile venture.

As it turned out, the Canadian government was nearly driven to bankruptcy. Municipalities foundered on the rocks of ill-conceived investments, and British investors found their loans disappearing into the pockets of Canadian contractors and promoters. Nevertheless, it was fortunate for Canada's transportation system that such events were not foreseen. The commitments were made, the investment came in, and the railways were built.

From 1850 through 1857, the Province of Canada underwent a boom in railway construction. Financing came not only from British capitalists but from private Canadian sources, from the United States, and from municipalities. Major completions included the St. Lawrence and Atlantic Railway, operating between Montreal and Portland, Maine, by 1853; the Great Western Railway, from Niagara through Hamilton and London to Detroit, by 1855; and, in the same year, the Ontario, Simcoe and Lake Huron Railway (later the Northern Railway), from Toronto to Collingwood (see Map 9.1).

All of these were feeder lines, designed to tie the farming hinterlands of Canada to urban centres along the Great Lakes and St. Lawrence. More ambitious was the Grand Trunk Railway, which used British engineering skills and British capital to run from Quebec City in the east to Sarnia in the west by 1859. It tied together the major cities of the province and cost more than $67 million to complete.[3] When it was completed, the

Map 9.1 Rail Lines in the Province of Canada, 1860

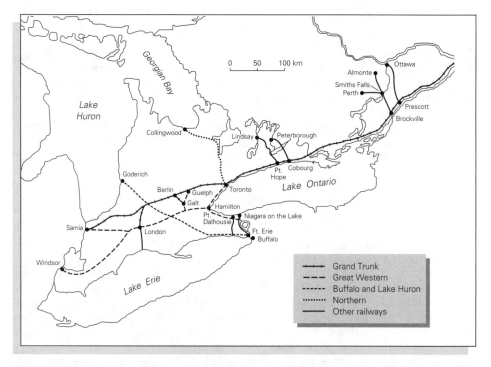

Source: Based on R. Cole Harris and John Warkentin, *Canada Before Confederation: A Study in Historical Geography* (New York: Oxford University Press, 1974), p. 155. Copyright © 1974 by Oxford University Press, Inc. Used by permission of Oxford University Press, Inc.

Grand Trunk Railway was not only the largest railway in Canada; it contained the longest railway line in the world. Something of the enormous expense of railways can be comprehended when it is realized that this sum alone was greater than all the money spent on public works — canals, bridges, roads, buildings — by the Province of Canada between the Act of Union in 1841 and Confederation.

By 1857, the boom was over. The province had gone from 100 km of railway in 1849 to 2900 km by the time the Grand Trunk reached Sarnia. The traffic generated often could not bear the costs of operating the railway, much less its capital investment. Time after time, the government had to step in to rescue collapsing railways, to pay interest on bond defaults, and to explain why politicians with large investments in railways always seemed to be willing to pour good government money after bad.[4] How the railway builders financed investment also created problems for the viability of the railways. Carlos and Lewis show that, in the late 1850s, the Grand Trunk Railway had a large, increasing debt load. Where a debt-to-equity ratio of 1 is considered appropriate for financing a project like the Grand Trunk mainline construction, the Grand Trunk Railway had a ratio of 3 in the late 1850s and as high as 25 by 1872. This reliance on debt finance, over equity finance, was likely encouraged by the expectations of British investors that the Canadian government would bailout the railway company, if necessary. Henceforth, at least until the annexation of the West provided new temptations, railway construction proceeded much more cautiously.

The economic impact of the railways was enormous in several ways. First, the railway construction boom of the 1850s accounts for much of the prosperity of those years (see Table 9.1). Millions of dollars of foreign investment flowed into Canada, largely from Britain, generating employment for the huge work forces necessary for railway survey and construction.

Table 9.1 New Railway Miles in Operation and Net Capital Formation Resulting from Railway Transport and Telegraph, Province of Canada, 1850–1862

Year	Railway Miles Opened	Net Capital Formation *($ millions)*
1850	12	1.3
1851	63	2.5
1852	118	6.2
1853	444	13.7
1854	332	13.3
1855	335	16.7
1856	441	9.2
1857	103	7.3
1858	150	10.3
1859	520	4.5
1860	44	5.2
1861	9	1.8
1862	0	1.5

Source: Lawrence Officer and Lawrence Smith, "The Canadian–American Reciprocity Treaty of 1855 to 1868," *Journal of Economic History* 28 (December 1968): 603, 609. Reprinted with the permission of Cambridge University Press.

The coming of the railways also had a major impact on the metropolis–hinterland relationship in the colony. Urban centres that were at the terminus of key railways could expand their own hinterlands and increasingly tighten their economic control of the regions around them. Village artisans, small industries, and local wholesalers, previously protected by the costs of transport, now found themselves vulnerable to more cheaply made goods sent by train from the larger urban centres. Local newspapers began their long slide into obscurity as the larger, flashier, and more powerful newspapers of the cities penetrated the countryside by means of railway. The Toronto *Globe*, for example, was able to extend its range of influence over much of Canada West. Its political views, centred in Toronto, now helped shape the thinking of a large portion of the district.

The railway thus allowed Montreal, Toronto, Hamilton, and a few other centres increasingly to dominate smaller communities. The Great Western, which extended its line to Toronto in the later 1850s; the Grand Trunk; and the Ontario, Simcoe and Huron (later the Northern) meant that Toronto businesses now had easy access for their goods to all of what is now southern Ontario. Likewise, the St. Lawrence and Atlantic and the Grand Trunk gave Montreal increased dominance over the other towns and villages of Canada East. The process would take a generation, but the configuration of railways meant that, by 1860, the trends were set.

There was a certain relentless logic to it all. It was because a few centres were larger than others that the railways gravitated toward them. That gravitation, in turn, confirmed the dominance of those centres and allowed them to increase the range and variety of their influence. Population movements then responded to new opportunities in these larger cities. Montreal grew from 40 000 inhabitants at the time of the union to 115 000 by 1871; Toronto, from a mere 14 000 to 59 000. The former would almost double, and the latter almost triple, its 1871 population in another twenty years. Railways also affected the nature of manufacturing and the structure and location of industries, and were instrumental in creating new industries.

There was one thing railways did not do, however: they did not supplant canals or natural waterways as the primary transportation system for bulk goods. Water transport remained cheaper than rail, and the canal system of the Canadas continued to carry most of Canada's export goods for many years to come. One contemporary set of figures estimated that only 6.6 percent of grain reaching Montreal in 1862 came by rail and that only 5.3 percent going seaward from Montreal did so.[5] Railways supplemented the canal system, acted as feeders to it, and operated more quickly and without regard to season. For the farmer and merchant, what the railways did was extend the reach of, and make more flexible, the existing transportation system of the Canadas. They did not replace it.

In the Maritimes, railway fever caught hold as it had in the Province of Canada, but, as it turned out, the construction of such expensive projects was even more difficult for these smaller colonies. Those strongly in favour of railway construction in the Maritimes had two objectives in mind. The first was to consolidate the hold of the main urban centres — Saint John and Halifax, essentially — over their own hinterlands. The second was to establish the region as the entrepôt (central warehouse) of trade between the continent and Europe, which meant constructing a trunk line to Quebec, or to Maine, or, in the most ambitious scheme, to both.

Plans to tap the trade of the continent, and the difficulties in doing so, are best illustrated by the main proposals vying for financing in the 1840s. The Halifax and Quebec line was to run from Halifax through eastern New Brunswick to Quebec. The European and North American project (one of the more grandiose titles ever bestowed upon a railway project) was intended to proceed from Halifax, through southern New Brunswick, to

Grand Trunk Railway locomotive no. 21303, c. 1860. The Grand Trunk Railway, which tied together the major cities of the province, cost more than $67 million to build. The line from Toronto to Montreal opened in 1856; by 1859, it ran from Quebec City in the east to Sarnia in the west. The Grand Trunk Railway was later taken over by the government and was eventually absorbed into the Canadian National Railways system.

Grand Trunk Railway Locomotive No. 21303, Mimsy No. 23. National Gallery of Canada, Ottawa.

Portland, Maine, linking to Canada from there via the St. Lawrence and Atlantic Railway. The British government was unwilling to finance a line through U.S. territory, however, while the governments of Nova Scotia and New Brunswick fought over routing within the region. No resolution was found.

In the meantime, construction of lines within the region proceeded, albeit slowly. The government of Nova Scotia built a line from Halifax to Truro, with a branch to Windsor, in the 1850s. In 1867, the line was extended to Pictou, giving Nova Scotia a total of 230 km of railway by 1867. In New Brunswick, the old St. Andrews and Quebec project, dating back to the 1820s, was resurrected in 1847 as the New Brunswick and Canada, and, from that date in 1867, 200 km of track were laid between Saint John and Woodstock. Another line of 170 km was completed between Saint John and Shediac.

By Confederation, the Maritimes had only about 600 km of track in operation, and no trunk lines to either Canada or the United States. They had managed to link Halifax to both the Bay of Fundy and the gulf region, and Saint John to the gulf. They had also, in the process, amassed a considerable debt that was weighing on the slim resources of the colonial governments. Both this debt and the desire to secure links to the interior were instrumental in pushing the colonies toward Confederation.

Early Industrialization

The linkages to heavy industry promoted by railways point to an important but as yet open question in Canadian economic development. Was British North America moving toward industrialization in the 1850s? To pose this question is not to imply that it became a full-fledged industrial power before Confederation; primary resources clearly remained the source of livelihood for the great majority of Canadians. Rather, it is a question of whether the population growth, prosperity, and linkages resulting from railway construction in the 1850s prompted the Canadian economy to diversify into a range of manufacturing goods previously imported from outside the colony and changed the nature of production, moving from smaller "cottage" operations to larger factory systems.

Before that issue can be addressed, two preliminary points have to be made. The first is that there was always a range of cottage industries and small ventures catering to the local market, finding niches in the trade network from the metropolitan centres. There were no significant economies of scale in the artisan stage of production, and local firms were protected from distant competitiors by high transport costs. Both conditions would change during the nineteenth century, however.

The development of such activities in Halifax and St. John's was noted earlier. New France had its share of ventures, and, by the 1780s, in Quebec, a considerable range of activity — commercial, financial and industrial — was being carried on. As the frontier expanded into what became Upper Canada, a range of activities soon followed. Sawmills and grist mills were there from the beginning, and they would remain the largest employers in the manufacturing sector until midcentury. Distilleries and breweries were not far behind. Tanneries, saltworks, and even ironworks had come into being before the War of 1812. As well, local service industries —such as the baker, blacksmith, and harness maker — could often grow from a one-person operation to a small industry as local population developed. From the 1820s to the 1840s, operations grew more complex: papermaking appeared by 1830, shipbuilding grew with the increasing trade along the Great Lakes, and, by the 1851 census, a marine railway and shipyard in Toronto employed some 50 workers.[6] Agricultural-implement companies evolved to meet the needs of the still-dominant farming population and would, within another generation, develop into one of Canada's leading manufacturing exports.

None of these industries was very large. Even by midcentury, only a few employed more than a score of workers. Further, their presence does not change the fact that all of the British North American colonies depended on the sale of raw and semiprocessed primary resources. Nor were the basic trade patterns of a colonial society altered. The flow of goods from Britain was dominated by manufactured goods and by luxury items; that from Canada, by primary resources or semiprocessed goods. Such small industries, however, were a necessary prerequisite to more significant industrialization, for, in the successful merchandising, forwarding, tanning, distilling, and myriad other operations, an entrepreneurial instinct was being developed, as were a skilled work force, the technology, and the pools of savings that could respond should the opportunity arise.

The second point is that, quite aside from these small industries, the colonies were capitalist and commercial long before they were industrial. From the shippers and traders in the Atlantic region through the Hamiltons, McTavishes, and Molsons in Canada, there was a strong orientation toward business from the beginning. By the time of Confederation, Halifax, Saint John, Toronto, and Montreal were, above all, cities of "merchants, tradesmen and artisans."[7]

In the years between the conquest and the beginning of the nineteenth century, Canadian merchants were faced by a military–government elite that held the business of trade and profit making in disdain. The confrontation was shortlived, however, for there was not and could not be a strong enough landed gentry to counter the power of the businessmen. Indeed, the largest landowners were often active businessmen. By 1800, if not before, the values of commerce and growth had triumphed in Upper Canada.

In Lower Canada, the complex relationships among language, religion, and occupation made the issue more difficult to resolve. As the early governors found, however, the business class of Montreal, French or English, did not accept a limited role in society. Certainly by 1840, if not before, the old aristocratic and anti-commercial social attitudes of Lower Canada were an anachronism. Profit, loss, extensive growth, efficiency, and a myth of individualism pervaded the Canadian economy and the Canadian political scene by the early nineteenth century. Values and political institutions were geared to the move to industrialism. When the opportunity came, there would be no great difficulties posed by either the social climate or the political structures. Indeed, when the British appointed a former president of the Board of Trade as governor general in 1841, they were, in a symbolic way, recognizing the hegemony of the capitalist system in the new Province of Canada.

The profits earned by the commercial class also prepared the way for industrialization. Success in commerce led to pools of savings that became available for entrepreneurial applications of technology to production. It was John Molson, using new wealth acquired from the thirst of Canadians, who, in 1809, built the first steamboat in the Canadas. It was John Frothingham of Montreal who first gained wealth as a hardware merchant and then used his income to begin his own industrial productions.[8] Peter McGill of Montreal began in the fur trade before the War of 1812 and moved from there into timber, shipping, sawmills, and the Marmora ironworks.[9] There was, thus, by the time of the union, a considerable business class with the outlook and the income to be ready when circumstances dictated changes in the Canadian economy. In this, as in so many other ways, the Canada of the union was quite different from what it had been even a generation before. Diversification was a natural process, as successful merchants and manufacturers ventured into new areas.

Appropriate governmental policies, social institutions, entrepreneurial values, and available capital prepared the way for industrialization. Also necessary was a labour force. One of the most striking features of the New World had been the relative abundance of resources and scarcity of people. Labour-intensive activity could, therefore, be hampered by high wage rates and an absence of suitable skills. Certainly travellers from Europe, throughout the nineteenth century, were struck by the affluence of Canadian workers and by the high wages they commanded.

Any discussion of labour history is fraught with debate. The role of class, the relationship between classes, and the degree of exploitation or benefit derived from class relationships are always contested issues, in the history of Canada no less so than elsewhere. There does seem to be agreement, however, that between 1840 and 1860 there developed in Canada a significant non-landowning working class. The presence of such a class both differentiated the Canada of Confederation from that of a half-century before and was central to the development of manufacturing.

Changing opportunities and options for immigrants were crucial to the evolution of the working class. On the one hand, it became increasingly expensive for new arrivals to homestead. Some have argued that there was a deliberate government policy designed to create a labour force. Others see the outcome as incidental to the increase in population and the receding of the frontier of settlement. Population increased dramatically with the high immigration of the 1840s. Moreover, the absence of savings on the part of many of the Irish famine immigrants meant that there was less opportunity to take up settlement opportunities.[10] Certainly, by Confederation, there existed a significant "class" of individuals who owned no agricultural land, and often no real property of any sort, but who followed opportunities to earn wages where they could.

Yet, it is simplistic to see the creation of a landless work force as something arising from the misery and desperation of famine immigration. Recent works have shown that a high percentage of the Irish did have some means and did settle on the land. Also important, therefore, were those forces attracting individuals away from the settlement process.

In this instance, both the 1840s and the 1850s were important. The drive that began after the union to complete the canals required large numbers of labourers. Little industrial technology was applied to the construction of canals, and it was not uncommon in the 1840s to have more than 6000 people employed during peak seasons. As the canal boom ended in the late 1840s, the railway boom came along. Much work has yet to be done on whether the same workers moved from site to site and from canals, to, say, logging, to railway construction, or whether successions of workers moved through the labour camps to eventually settle on the land. Whichever case proves most correct, however, the fact is that, at least from the 1840s, a permanent work force existed. Government began to concern itself with such issues as unemployment and with civil disturbance from groups of workers on canal and railway sites, and other such matters. That is not to say that there was, as yet, a large number of factory wage-earners, in the modern sense. Such a development would not come until later. The development of a landless class, however, provided the possibilities for the evolution of a wage-earning factory class to come into being once it was required.

The presence of the necessary prerequisites to industry meant that, as opportunities developed, it was possible to take advantage of them. Initially, as might be expected, economic diversification in the Canadas was not designed to compete in the international marketplace with British, European, or American firms. Rather, as with the earlier grist mills, the industries of the 1840s and 1850s arose as adjuncts to other sectors of the economy. Once developed, however, the technology and expertise were in place. As firms developed, it was increasingly possible to supplant foreign suppliers.

Typical in its origins, though not in its tremendous success, was the Massey Company. Hart Massey had typified the Upper Canadian settler of the first phase of development. He made money as much, or more, by clearing land and reselling it as by any of the crops he grew. Then, on a trip to the United States, he saw one of the earliest mechanical threshers and began to assemble them for the Canadian market. Expertise and profits followed, and by the later 1840s, he moved into the manufacture of the implement. An American import was replaced by the Canadian-made machine, both serving the dominant agricultural sector. As well, a firm began that was soon to be one of the world leaders in agricultural-implement production.[11]

Similar stories of assembly, repair, and then manufacturing could be recounted for steam engines, to meet the growing demand for steamers along the Great Lakes; for tanning, to meet local demands; or for the progress from sewing imported materials into clothes to the rise of a textile industry. Most dramatic of all, however, was the impact of the railway on Canadian industry. For, if companies were to operate the ultimate technology of the industrial revolution, they needed to import all those aspects of industrialism that supported such technology. A railway could not run without freight cars, locomotives, and the hundreds of parts and materials that were required to keep such complex machinery in operation.

Initially, these materials were imported, but repair facilities were necessary on site, and these facilities soon developed production capabilities. The result was that the larger railways, such as the Grand Trunk and the Great Western, soon developed their own industrial plants. These plants quickly became among the largest in British North America. By 1871, for example, the Grand Trunk operations at Pointe St-Charles, Quebec, employed 790 employees, and those of the Great Western, at Hamilton, nearly 1000 (see Table 9.2). Rolling mills, steel foundries, and related activities were either established directly by the companies or came into existence because of the opportunities to supply the railways.[12] Several other plants were owned separately from the railways but existed to supply

Table 9.2 Major Railway Equipment Manufacturers in Canada, 1871

Firm	No. of Employees	Annual Wages ($)
Great Western: Hamilton	984	500 000
Grand Trunk: Pointe St-Charles shops	790	250 000
Northern: Toronto	561	215 808
Grand Trunk: Brantford car and locomotive shops	315	182 000
W.P. Bartley Engine Works and Foundry: Montreal	222	49 200
St. Lawrence Foundry Machine and Car Shop: Toronto	200	100 000

Source: Excerpted from Paul Craven and Tom Traves, "Canadian Railways as Manufacturers, 1850–1880," in D. McCalla, ed., *Perspectives on Canadian Economic History* (Toronto: Copp Clark Pitman, 1987), pp. 127–28.

railway needs. So impressive is the impact of the railways on manufacturing that it is tempting to argue that railways brought heavy industry to Canada.

Railways also brought the techniques that would permit other industrialization to proceed more smoothly. Such large enterprises as the Grand Trunk or Great Western demanded sophisticated (and politically connected) financial stuctures, a hierarchical and often far-flung management system, and other appurtenances of the industrial age. They also required international financing and, most importantly, access to the wealthy British financial markets. Government guarantees helped overcome some of the nervousness of British investors, make up for the absence of local financial expertise, and give those involved experience. Of course, the bad experience of many Grand Trunk bondholders also gave people an experience of Canadian industrialism in a different and negative sort of way.

The government could help in other ways as well. With industry came cries for protection and support of that industry. This was a natural attitude for businessmen to take as they sought to maximize profits and reduce competition. The myth of free and open competition seems never to have blunted the drive for advantage. It was also natural that the cries would get a positive reception in Canada. It was a small colony, dependent on primary resources, and economic diversification had a great appeal. As early as 1847, Conservative politician Robert Baldwin Sullivan complained, "I do not like to see hatters importing hats, shoemakers selling foreign shoes; and tanners offering foreign leather as superior articles."[13] As manufacturing became a greater force, so, too, did the cries that foreign competition must be discouraged.

This changing attitude first showed up as policy in the Galt-Cayley tariff changes of 1858–59. The average duty on 353 tariff items rose from 8.54 percent to 12.11 percent.[14] This protection applied not only to foreign nations, such as the United States, but to the British as well. The home country was not pleased but had to accept the fact that, having gone its own way over colonial protests in 1846, it could hardly turn around and insist that the colonies now act for the greater empire. Canadian officials, sensitive to free traders in England and at home, emphasized the need to raise revenue to cover the disastrous outlays to railways and argued that any protection to manufactures was incidental. There is little doubt, however, that protection and not just revenue was crucial in the minds of the policy makers.[15]

There is also a convincing case to be made that the imposition of duties in 1858–59 resulted in an expansion of manufacturing output. One cannot reach this conclusion simply by comparing imports of manufactured goods before and after the tariff changes, since other factors were not constant. One solution, adopted by D.F. Barnett,[16] is to compare imports of inputs with those of finished products before and after the changes. The Galt–Cayley schedule lowered duties on primary products, raised them only slightly on intermediate items, and raised them substantially on tertiary products. Thus if the tariff changes were effective in protecting an industry, one would expect to see a rise in its input–output import ratio. Barnett finds this pattern to be true for 1860–62 compared with 1856–58, providing convincing evidence that the Galt–Cayley tariff changes affected Canadian manufacturing activity.

Industrial production also grew in importance in the Maritimes before Confederation. Wood-processing and shipbuilding industries dominated, understandably. Beyond these activities, there was the usual range of small concerns producing mainly for the domestic market behind the natural protection provided by transport costs. Saint John, for example, was described as an "important manufacturing centre" in 1850.[17] In addition to shipbuilding and sawmilling, the city hosted tanneries, flour mills, iron and brass foundries, furniture shops, carriage-makers, and breweries. These activities grew over the next two decades until, in 1871, manufacturing output in New Brunswick rivalled that of Ontario and Quebec in per capita terms. The decline of the region occurred later.

Grand Trunk Railway erecting shops, Pointe St-Charles, 1860. Larger railways required repair facilities on site, and these soon developed production capabilities. Grand Trunk developed its own industrial plant, which quickly became among the largest in British North America. By 1871, the Grand Trunk operations at Pointe St-Charles employed nearly 800 people.

National Archives of Canada/PA-138678.

One contrast with the Province of Canada in this early period of industrialization is worth noting. While merchants in Canada moved into industrial pursuits as opportunities opened up, it has been argued that in the Maritimes the two pursuits were competitive rather than complementary.[18] In Saint John, for example, the merchants played essentially no part in industrial developments before 1840. They remained free traders as the British mercantile system collapsed, stoutly opposing any attempts by local farmers and industrialists to secure a degree of protection from American and British imports. Industrialization did proceed after 1850, T.W. Acheson concedes, but the actions of the merchants delayed this development by two crucial decades.

Conclusion

The arrival of railways, the development of some industry, the rise of key urban centres, and protectionist policies such as those of Galt and Cayley raise the question of whether British North America in general, and the Province of Canada in particular, underwent a profound and crucial shift between 1850 and 1867. Many historians and some economists have argued that the series of events mentioned above sowed the seeds for a fundamental reorientation both in Canadian economic thinking and in the direction of Canadian development.

According to this argument, three things came together. First, the railways created a need for a broader financial base for the government, as canals had a generation earlier. They also provided the transportation systems that allowed urban centres such as Montreal and Toronto to seek wider hinterlands. Second, the extensive growth of the prosperous and crucial agricultural frontier was threatened, even as wheat farming reached new levels of value. Simply put, the agricultural frontier that had fuelled development in Upper Canada/Canada West from the beginning was coming to an end. In Canada East, the opportunities for new settlement had been limited since the 1830s. Overall, by the late 1850s, with Canada West filling up, there was little good crown land available for settlement left south of the Canadian Shield. Farming was also changing, and, by Confederation, wheat was no longer a dominant staple.

Third, and finally, the Province of Canada saw great possibilities for commercial, financial, and, most ambitious of all, industrial development. All of these things were considered dependent on continued growth in the traditional sources of economic strength — the exploitation of primary resources and the immigration of people and capital. New minerals, new timber stands, and, most of all, a new agricultural frontier would be necessary if the growth of past decades was to continue.

As a result of these concerns, the politician-businessmen, the nationalists, and the enthusiasts of the Province of Canada began to seek ways to break out of the confines of the St. Lawrence valley and to continue the extensive growth that had been so central to Canadian economic development. To the east lay the Maritime colonies, well settled and prosperous. To the west lay the vast untapped resources of the Hudson Bay territories. Only some new political arrangement, however, could allow the province to realize its economic ambitions. In this light, it is significant that one of the first to propose the idea of expansion to the west and of a federal system for all British North America was Alexander Galt, author of Canada's first protectionist tariff. The policies, purposes, and effects of Confederation on all of British North America thus cannot be divorced from the economic development that had taken place by 1867.

NOTES

1. Thomas Keefer, *The Philosophy of Railroads* (Toronto: University of Toronto Press, 1972 [1849]), 11.

2. Ann Carlos and Frank Lewis, "The Creative Financing of an Unprofitable Enterprise: The Grand Trunk Railway of Canada, 1853–1881," *Explorations in Economics History* 32(3) (1995): 273–301.

3. Michael Bliss, *Northern Enterprise: Five Centuries of Canadian Business* (Toronto: McClelland & Stewart, 1987), 184.

4. See Ann M. Carlos and Frank Lewis, "The Profitability of Early Canadian Railroads: Evidence from the Grand Trunk and Great Western Railway Companies," in Claudia Goldin and Hugh Rockoff, eds., *Strategic Factors in Nineteenth Century American Economic History* (Chicago and London: University of Chicago Press, 1992), 401–26, for estimates of the private and social returns to early Canadian railroads.

5. H.Y. Hind, T.C. Keefer, J.G. Hodgson, Charles Robb, M.H. Perley, and Rev. William Murray, *Eighty Years' Progress of British North America* (Toronto: L. Nichols, 1864), 207.

6. J. Spelt, *Urban Development in South-Central Ontario* (Toronto: McClelland & Stewart, 1972), 72.

7. Peter Goheen, *Victorian Toronto 1850 to 1900* (Chicago: University of Chicago Press, 1970), 50. Goheen's quote refers to Toronto, but the statement is equally correct for the other cities.

8. Bliss, *Northern Enterprise*, 161; Gerald Tulchinsky, *The River Barons: Montreal Businessmen and the Growth of Industry and Transportation, 1837–1853* (Toronto: University of Toronto Press, 1977), 12–13.

9. Tulchinsky, *The River Barons*, 21.

10. On the former view see Leo Johnson, "Land Policy, Population Growth and Social Structure in the Home District, 1793–1851," in J.K. Johnson, ed., *Historical Essays on Upper Canada* (Toronto: McClelland & Stewart, 1975), 32–57; and Gary Teeple, "Land, Labour and Capital in Pre-Confederation Canada," in Gary Teeple, ed., *Capitalism and the National Question in Canada* (Toronto: University of Toronto Press, 1972), 43–46.

11. Details from Claude Bissell, *The Young Vincent Massey* (Toronto: University of Toronto Press, 1981), 8–9.

12. Paul Craven and Tom Traves, "Canadian Railways as Manufactures, 1850–1880," in D. McCalla, ed., *Perspectives on Canadian Economic History* (Toronto: Copp Clark Pitman, 1987), have done some excellent work in establishing the importance of such railway-related operations.

13. Cited in A. Den Otter, "Alexander Galt, the 1859 Tariff and Canadian Economic Nationalism," *Canadian Historical Review* 63(2) (June 1982): 158.

14. D.F. Barnett, "The Galt Tariff: Incidentals or Effective Protection?" *Canadian Journal of Economics* 9(3) (August 1976): 389–407, table 1.

15. The protective effect was achieved partly by raising average duties overall and partly by increasing the effective rate of protection, to use the term that it is known by today. Average duties were lowered on primary products, raised only slightly on intermediate items, and raised substantially on tertiary items. This cascading tariff structure increases the spread between the price of final products and the cost of purchased inputs. Thus, the more processed the product, the greater is the degree of protection. See Barnett, "The Galt Tariff," for details and calculations.

16. Barnett, "The Galt Tariff."

17. T.W. Acheson, "The Great Merchant and Economic Development in Saint John, 1820–1850," in Phillip A. Buckner and David Frank, eds., *Atlantic Canada Before Confederation*, The Acadiensis Reader, vol. 1 (Fredericton: Acadiensis Press, 1985), 177.

18. Acheson, "The Great Merchant and Economic Development," 177.

FURTHER READING

Barnett, D.F. "The Galt Tariff: Incidental or Effective Protection?" *Canadian Journal of Economics* 9(3) (August 1976): 389–407.

Craven, Paul, and Tom Traves. "Canadian Railways as Manufactures, 1850–1880." In D. McCalla, ed., *Perspectives on Canadian Economic History.* Toronto: Copp Clark Pitman, 1987.

McCalla, Douglas. "An Introduction to the Nineteenth-Century Business World." In T. Traves, ed., *Essays in Canadian Business History.* Toronto: McClelland & Stewart, 1984.

Chapter Ten

Confederation and the British North America Act

FOR DECADES, British North Americans had discussed the desirability of greater autonomy within the British empire and had, on occasion, even flirted with the idea of leaving the empire altogether. For a time the British had resisted this tendency, but the changing philosophies toward colonial possessions that accompanied the demise of mercantilism, as well as the growing stridence of colonial demands, led to a reversal of policy. In 1848, the British had granted the colonies responsible government, which effectively gave British North Americans control over their domestic affairs. Confederation was the next logical step in the process of devolving control over the colonies. It was also a response to particular concerns of the 1860s, including political stalemate in the Province of Canada and fear of the forces emanating from the Civil War in the United States.

Without denying the importance of these political motives, it is possible to argue that Confederation was equally, perhaps even primarily, the product of two sets of economic forces. First, Confederation was an institutional arrangement designed to bring about a more complete integration of the existing colonial economies. The integration was sought because the British mercantile system was now history, and the main alternative, the Reciprocity Treaty with the United States, would soon end. Confederation gave the colonies a political structure with which to remove all tariffs and other restrictions on trade among themselves, erect a common tariff on trade with other countries, and plan for joint transportation facilities.

Second, Confederation was an institutional arrangement designed to make transcontinental economic expansion possible. The perception was that commercial prosperity and industrial success were linked to an expanding resource frontier. By the mid-1860s, that resource hinterland had been extended to include the fertile plains of the Canadian west. Reaching that frontier, however, involved a commitment well beyond the means of the colonies in their present state. In this sense, then, as Vernon Fowke has written, "the national policy predated the creation of a national government in Canada and envisaged the establishment of such a government as one of its indispensable instruments."[1]

Economic Integration Before 1867

Ironically, the first explicit attention to the question of economic integration in British North America arose as a result of a political separation. The Constitutional Act of 1791 divided Quebec into two colonies: Upper and Lower Canada. In so doing, however, it linked them into an arrangement that today would be referred to as a customs union. All trade between the colonies was to be free of duties and other restrictions, and there was to be a common set of tariffs on trade with other nations. These latter tariffs might well distinguish among imports from Britain, other British colonies, the United States, and the rest of the world, but the schedule was to be the same for the two colonies.

This arrangement led to considerable subsequent dispute between the two colonies. The first problem concerned the division of tariff and excise revenue. All imports from overseas landed first in Lower Canada, where they were taxed. If the products were intended for consumption in Lower Canada, there was no problem. If they were to be forwarded to consumers in Upper Canada, however, the tariff revenue properly belonged to that legislature. Officials thus had to determine what proportion of total imports went to each colony and to allocate revenue accordingly. To make matters even more difficult, Upper Canada was growing more rapidly than Lower Canada, so the formula had to be revised continuously. This issue only disappeared with the union of the Canadas in 1841.

The other challenge to the customs union arrangement came from the fact that tariffs and excise duties were the main revenue source for the colonial governments. If revenue needs differed, tariff rates that were appropriate for one colony might be inappropriate for the other. Officials in one colony, seeking additional revenue, would press for higher tariff and excise taxes, only to be opposed by officials of the other, content with their revenue and worried about a possible political backlash. Because of its more ambitious economic development plans, Upper Canada typically was in the former position.

As long as most imports came up the St. Lawrence and no duties on intercolonial shipments were possible, there was little Upper Canada could do about this situation. As overland trade with the United States began to develop, however, the situation changed; Upper Canada began to levy these duties directly. At first, efforts were made to keep the rates identical to those in Lower Canada, but eventually this objective was lost. Free trade between the colonies remained, but the common external tariff structure disappeared. Once again, this situation was only reversed in 1841.

In the 1840s, with the end of the British mercantile system in sight, pressure renewed for the increased economic integration of the North American colonies. The Colonial Office pushed for a customs union along the lines of the German *Zollverein*. In 1847 Nova Scotia offered to admit the products of other colonies free of duty, provided that they did the same, and in 1848 New Brunswick offered free trade in all products but spirits. Canada offered a more limited list of items for reciprocal free trade, mainly excluding manufactured products, so this initial venture languished. In 1850, however, the colonies did offer each other free trade from a list of foodstuffs and raw materials.

Opposition by Canada and Prince Edward Island to free trade in manufactured products stalled further progress, and the colonies turned their attention to reciprocity with the United States. Alexander Galt put forth a plan for complete reciprocity on behalf of Canada in 1859, only to have the idea rejected by the British Board of Trade as being discriminatory. By 1861, the British attitude had softened, and the following year a conference was held to explore the possibility. Officials were unable to settle on a common external tariff structure (the Maritimes balked at adopting Canada's higher tariff rates), however, and the idea languished until 1864, when it became subsumed in the larger Confederation negotiations.

The push for greater economic integration involved more than just tariffs, however. Nova Scotia and New Brunswick were active early on in planning railway projects that would link the two colonies to each other and to Canada. The first proposal for a rail line running from Saint John to Quebec appeared in 1827, and a preliminary reconnaissance of the route was completed in 1835. Joseph Howe appeared to have an agreement for a line linking Halifax to Quebec in 1851, but it eventually failed. The three colonies continued to negotiate among themselves and with the British government. Sandford Fleming was appointed in 1864 to undertake a survey of the route for what was to be the Intercolonial Railway, and he submitted his report the following year. Further action, however, had to await Confederation.

The Colonial Economies at Confederation

Some important differences existed among the colonial economies at Confederation, but there were also many similarities. For example, the colonies seemed to have experienced roughly similar aggregate growth rates in the 1850s and 1860s. Table 10.1 shows population totals for Canada and the provinces for the census years 1851–71. In the absence of data on GDP, population can serve as a measure of extensive economic growth. Ontario's population grew most quickly in the 1850s, increasing by 47 percent in the decade, compared with 25 percent for both Quebec and the Maritime provinces as a group. In the 1860s, Ontario's population growth actually lagged slightly behind that of Nova Scotia and Prince Edward Island. Overall, the distribution of population changed very little between 1851 and 1871. The shares fell very slightly for each of the Maritime provinces, declined somewhat more for Quebec, and rose for Ontario.

Canada's population was about 80 percent rural in 1867. Montreal was, by far, the largest city, with 100 000 inhabitants. Quebec City followed with a population of 60 000, and then Toronto, with about 50 000. Halifax had slightly fewer than 30 000 residents in 1867, and Saint John about 700 fewer than Halifax. The remainder of the 3.5 million Canadians lived in small villages and towns, in lumber camps, and on farms.

The basic economic structures of the colonial economies were quite similar. Nearly one-third of Canada's GDP in 1870 came from services, such as construction, transportation, government services, and wholesale and retail trade.[2] Given the local nature of most service-sector activity, it is unlikely that these activities varied much among regions. The remaining two-thirds came from commodity production, including agriculture, forestry, hunting, trapping, fishing, mining, and manufacturing. These outputs differed among regions, but less than one might think, given the tendency in Canadian economic history to focus on staple exports to the neglect of other sectors.

Table 10.2 shows the sectoral distribution of income from commodity production in 1870 for Canada as a whole and for Nova Scotia, New Brunswick, Quebec, and Ontario. Agriculture was by far the largest sector, accounting for 54 percent of commodity income for Canada as a whole. Ontario was most dependent on farm production, relying on it for nearly 60 percent of total commodity income. This feature is not unexpected, given the success that Ontario farmers had early on in producing wheat for export and then switching to a more diversified set of products as new markets developed. More surprising, perhaps, is the importance of agriculture in the other three provincial economies. This sector accounted for 49 percent of Quebec's commodity income, 47 percent of New Brunswick's, and 46 percent of Nova Scotia's.

These figures capture a feature of the Canadian economy at this time that is often masked by the attention given to staple exports: most mid-nineteenth-century Canadians, regardless of where they lived, spent most of their time engaged in agricultural pursuits. When physical and economic conditions were right, as in parts of Ontario, there were surpluses for sale in distant markets. Most agriculture was not this commercially oriented, however. More typically, farmers produced cereals and animal products for themselves

Table 10.1 Population of Canada and the Provinces to 1871: Growth from Previous Decade and Percentage of Total, 1851–1871

Region	1851			1861			1871		
	Population (000)	Growth (%)	% of Total	Population (000)	Growth (%)	% of Total	Population (000)	Growth (%)	% of Total
Nova Scotia	276.9	36.7	11.4	330.9	19.5	10.2	387.8	17.2	10.5
New Brunswick	193.8	24.1	8.0	252.0	30.4	7.8	285.6	13.0	7.7
Prince Edward Island	62.7	33.2	2.6	80.9	29.0	2.5	94.0	16.3	2.5
Maritimes	533.3	31.4	22.0	664.4	24.6	20.6	767.4	15.5	20.8
Upper Canada/Ontario	952.0	95.5	39.1	1396.1	46.6	43.2	1620.9	16.1	43.9
Lower Canada/Quebec	890.3	31.9	36.5	1111.6	24.9	34.4	1191.5	7.2	32.3
British Columbia	55.0	*	2.3	51.5	*	1.6	36.2	*	1.0
North-West Territories	5.7	*	—	6.7	*	0.2	48.0	*	1.3
Manitoba	—	*	—	—	*	—	25.2	*	0.7
Total	2436.3		100.0	3229.6		100.0	3689.3		100.0

*NOT APPLICABLE— BOUNDARIES CHANGED.

Source: M.C. Urquhart and K.A.H. Buckley, eds., *Historical Statistics of Canada* (Toronto: Macmillan, 1965), series A2–14; and S.A. Saunders, *The Economic History of the Maritime Provinces* (Fredericton: Acadiensis Press, 1984), p. 105.

Table 10.2 Sectoral Distribution of Income, Canada, 1870

Region	Farm	Factory	Forestry	Mines	Fish
Canada	54%	33%	10%	2%	1%
Nova Scotia	46	27	7	12	7
New Brunswick	47	39	11	1	3
Quebec	49	37	12	1	1
Ontario	59	32	9	1	0

Source: Derived from Kris Inwood and James R. Irwin, "Canadian Regional Commodity Income Differences at Confederation," in Kris Inwood, ed., *Farm, Factory and Fortune: New Studies in the Economic History of the Maritime Provinces* (Fredericton: Acadiensis Press, 1993), table 2, p. 102.

and their families, selling small surpluses locally where markets existed. In some cases, farmers also fished or cut timber.

Prosperous and complex agricultural sectors existed in all four provinces, not just in Ontario. T.W. Acheson has recently challenged the stereotype of New Brunswick agriculture as largely subsistence-oriented, existing as a sideline to lumbering.[3] He argues that there was no single provincial agriculture. Rather, New Brunswick's agriculture at mid-century featured a wide range of producing farms, a significant degree of specialization, a growing market for agricultural produce in the province, and farms that were at least as efficient as those in other jurisdictions with similar geographic conditions. Nova Scotia's agricultural performance in the decades before Confederation has also come under considerable scrutiny recently, with the conclusions apparently emerging that agricultural income in the province grew throughout the period and that farmers continued to experience at least "modest prosperity."[4]

Manufacturing was the second-largest commodity-producing sector in Canada as a whole, as well as in each of the provincial economies. It was most important in New Brunswick, at 39 percent of total output, a figure that mainly reflects the relative importance of wood and shipbuilding industries in the economy. Quebec was next at 37 percent, followed by Ontario at 32 percent, and Nova Scotia at 27 percent.

There was more variation among provinces in their resource industries. Not surprisingly, Quebec and New Brunswick were the most dependent on forestry, at 12 percent and 11 percent of total commodity income, respectively. The figure for Ontario was 9 percent, and for Nova Scotia 7 percent. Nova Scotia, with its coal-mining sector in Cape Breton, was the only economy to report any significant mining activity. Fishing was relatively most important in Nova Scotia and contributed as much to commodity output for that province as forestry. New Brunswick reported some fishing activity as well, 3 percent of total output.

The trading profiles of the provinces differ, as might be expected (see Table 10.3). Nearly 40 percent of Nova Scotia's exports in 1865 were fishery products, followed by agricultural products at 18 percent and minerals at 16 percent. Manufactures made up only 12 percent of exports, but 58 percent of imports. Two-thirds of New Brunswick's export trade was in forest products, followed by 13 percent in manufactures. Manufactured goods were the largest import (47 percent) for that colony in 1865, followed by agricultural products at 40 percent. Three-quarters of Prince Edward Island's exports were classed as agricultural, with another 18 percent coming from the fisheries. Manufactures made up more than 50 percent of the island's imports; agricultural products, another 24 percent. Agricultural

Table 10.3 Composition of Trade, Maritimes and Canada, 1865

Product	N.S. Imports (% of total)	N.S. Exports (% of total)	N.B. Imports (% of total)	N.B. Exports (% of total)	P.E.I. Imports (% of total)	P.E.I. Exports (% of total)	Prov. of Can. Imports (% of total)	Prov. of Can. Exports (% of total)
Agricultural	29.6	18.4	39.5	6.8	24.2	73.0	31.2	51.9
Fishery	2.7	39.3	1.5	7.5	4.6	17.6	1.2	2.1
Forest	1.8	8.8	1.0	66.3	6.8	8.4	1.3	40.3
Manuf. and misc.	57.8	11.7	47.4	13.3	55.3	0.5	57.9	3.9
Mineral	1.7	15.5	3.6	5.1	3.5	0.3	5.3	1.6
Wines and liquors	6.4	6.3	7.0	1.0	5.6	0.2	3.1	0.2

Source: S.A. Saunders, *The Economic History of the Maritime Provinces* (Fredericton: Acadiensis Press, 1984), p. 103.

products were the leading export of the Province of Canada (52 percent), followed by forest products (40 percent). Manufactures (58 percent) and agricultural goods (31 percent) were the dominant imports.

Table 10.4 illustrates that regional economic disparities were already a feature of the Canadian economy at Confederation. Ontario was the richest economy, with per capita commodity income 20 percent above the national average. Quebec was next at 86 percent of the national average, followed by New Brunswick at 83 percent and Nova Scotia at 75 percent. The differences are largely explained by the relative performances of the agricultural sectors, as might be expected, given the importance of this activity in each economy. Income per farm in Ontario was 30 percent above the national average, and more than twice that in Nova Scotia. As Inwood notes in summarizing the data, "Eastern and northern Canada was poor because fishing, mining and forestry were unable to compensate for the relatively low levels of agricultural income".[5]

Table 10.4 Income per Capita, Agricultural Income per Improved Acre and per Farm, and Share of Improved Acreage Devoted to Pasture and Hay, Canada, 1870

Region	Income per Capita	Income per Farm	Imp. Acres per Farm	Income per Imp. Acre	Imp. Acres in Pasture and Hay
Canada	100%	100%	100%	100%	51%
Nova Scotia	75	58	78	74	76
New Brunswick	83	70	78	91	61
Quebec	86	81	100	81	55
Ontario	120	130	110	119	43

Source: Derived from Kris Inwood and James R. Irwin, "Canadian Regional Commodity Income Differences at Confederation," in Kris Inwood, ed., *Farm, Factory and Fortune: New Studies in the Economic History of the Maritime Provinces* (Fredericton: Acadiensis Press, 1993), tables 2, p. 102, and 3, p. 105.

Confederation

The idea of a political union of the British North American colonies emerged in an unusual manner. In the Maritimes, there had been long-standing discussions of Maritime union. In 1864, New Brunswick, Nova Scotia, and Prince Edward Island agreed to hold a conference at Charlottetown to discuss the idea. In the meantime, internal politics in the Province of Canada had led to the creation of a coalition government pledged to try to end a political deadlock that had created unstable ministries and fruitless elections. One way out of the deadlock was to abolish the legislative union of Canada East and Canada West in favour of some sort of federal system, perhaps including the other British North American colonies. Thus, when the Canadians heard about the Charlottetown conference, they asked for the right to present their own thoughts on the future of the British North American colonies. In the face of their enthusiasm, the original idea of Maritime union, which had never really generated much excitement, was swept aside, and the idea of Confederation came to the fore.

The Charlottetown conference had dealt only in principles. In September 1864, a follow-up conference at Quebec City hammered out the basic terms of what would become, with some modifications, the British North America Act. Now the various colonies could see more precisely what this grandiose idea implied. As it turned out, some were not as enthusiastic as others.

Newfoundland showed little interest, early on, in the idea of Confederation, or even of Maritime union. The colony was represented at the Quebec conference in 1864, and the delegates returned with some enthusiasm for the idea. Two major groups on the island opposed any such moves, however. Roman Catholics did so because they were predominantly Irish, and Confederation smacked of British conquest. Merchants opposed it because they saw it (correctly, it might be added) as leading to higher tariffs on supplies to the fisheries and a financial commitment to a government primarily obsessed with furthering the defence and economic-development interests of the central provinces. Opposition waned in the mid-1860s in the midst of recession, but economic conditions had improved somewhat in 1869, when an election on the issue was held. The anti-confederates won, and Confederation for Newfoundland had to await another 80 years and another set of circumstances.

Prince Edward Island shared many of these fears and was, as well, mired in local political rivalries that involved personality, old wounds left by absentee landlords, and, most genuinely, a realization of just what a small power this province would be in a Canadian federation. A sense of local pride, concern for the loss of identity, and internal politics caused Islanders to turn their backs on the initial proposal.

Positions were not so clear-cut in the Maritimes. Proponents of Confederation in Nova Scotia and New Brunswick saw two main advantages to union. Ports such as Halifax and Saint John could serve as year-round, ice-free outlets for Canadian —and perhaps even American— products on their way to Europe. The large and growing central Canadian market beckoned as well, for everything from coal to manufactured goods. Both objectives required rail connection to Montreal and Toronto, an expanded branch-line network within the region, and free movement of goods among the colonies. All requirements were more easily met through coordinated action.

Opponents of Confederation in Nova Scotia and New Brunswick varied, depending on time and place. It was possible to trot out well-remembered tales of Upper Canadian betrayal, especially on earlier plans to build an intercolonial railway, and to point to the violence-prone nature of Canadian politics dating back to 1837. Most common, however, was the fear that Canada would threaten the Maritime economy with a high tariff structure and with a high debt charge from profligate canal and railway construction.

The main enthusiasm for political union lay in central Canada. Here, though, hope rested less on what integration promised from expanding economic contacts among existing economies than on what it seemed to make possible in the way of establishing new ones. Central Canadian business interests were as confident of capturing Maritime markets for primary and manufactured products as were their counterparts of the reverse, to be sure. The real prize, though, lay in establishing a transcontinental economy along the lines of the obviously successful one to the south. Development of the resource potential of the West, broadly defined, would provide the country with a new staple for export and a new frontier of investment. As W.L. Morton put it, central Canada wanted to "break out" of the confines of the St. Lawrence.[6] Canadians, as the Toronto *Globe* stated as early as December 10, 1856, were "looking for new worlds to conquer."

Transcontinental expansion was difficult, however. Most obviously, the plains area had to be made part of Canada. Then, a rail line had to be built in time to preempt American expansion into the area. That task required financing beyond the resources of the colonies. Political union would create a larger fiscal base with which to attract British investors. Confederation would also give the new Dominion greater control over tariff and immigration policies, the former to help finance rail expansion onto the plains and the latter to guide settlers to them. As Vernon Fowke argues, settlement was the goal; railways, tariffs, and land and immigration policies were the means; and Confederation was the major constitutional instrument.[7]

The British North America Act

Canada was constituted as a federation by the British North America (BNA) Act in 1867. Two orders of government were created: federal and provincial, each with a designated set of powers and each deemed sovereign in its spheres of jurisdiction. The choice of a federal arrangement is revealing, given that otherwise the constitution was to be "similar in Principle to that of the United Kingdom": Parliament was given clear responsibility for defence, the workings of the economic union, and national economic development. The legislatures were to look after more purely provincial and local matters.

The preamble to section 91 empowers Ottawa to make laws for the "Peace, Order and good Government of Canada," in all matters not specifically assigned to the provinces. A list of specific responsibilities is then included, "for greater Certainty." Of particular interest for economic development are the regulation of trade and commerce, the raising of money by any mode or system of taxation, the postal service, the census and statistics, defence, navigation and shipping, seacoast and inland fisheries, currency and coinage, banking, weights and measures, bankruptcy and insolvency, patents, copyrights, and the criminal code.

Section 92 contains no general preamble such as that for section 91, but rather proceeds directly to delineating the exclusive powers of the provinces. They were to be responsible, in the words of section 92.16, for "Generally all Matters of a merely local or private Nature." Jurisdiction over property and civil rights is set out explicitly, a move that subsequent analysts have seen as an attempt to give control of "culture" to the provinces. Provincial responsibilities of most interest for subsequent economic development are those over direct taxation within the provinces for revenue purposes, the management and sale of public land, hospitals, municipalities, local works and undertakings, and property and civil rights.

The act contains some other provisions that were important economically at the time, or have become so since. Section 93 assigns responsibility for education to the provinces. Section 95 provides for concurrent powers over agriculture and immigration. Section 109 states that all lands, mines, minerals, and royalties belonging to the several provinces in 1867 shall continue to belong to them. Section 121 states that all articles of the "Growth, Produce, or Manufacture of any one of the Provinces shall ... be admitted free into each of the other Provinces." Section 125 states that no lands or properties belonging to one level of government shall be liable to taxation by another. Parliament is given authority over treaties with foreign powers in section 132. Section 145 (repealed in 1893) compelled Parliament "to provide for the Commencement, within Six Months after the Union, of a Railway connecting the River St. Lawrence with the City of Halifax in Nova Scotia." Finally, section 146 provides for the admission into the union of Newfoundland, Prince Edward Island, British Columbia, and Rupert's Land.

Rounding Out Confederation

The formal declaration of a new Dominion on July 1, 1867, even with all the details of the BNA Act, still left several administrative problems unresolved. The establishment of a new government where none existed before and the transfer of powers from one level of government to another required a series of regulatory and practical steps. In the case of Canada, the major transfer of powers did not flow from Britain to the Dominion. That would occur gradually, through precedent. Instead, the immediate problem was to transfer powers that had previously existed within the colonies to the new federal government. In effect, this meant that the provinces (as they now were) lost powers and the Dominion government acquired them.

The nature of the restructuring is relevant to the Canadian economy. Government establishes the rules under which an economy functions. Even in the relatively simple governmental world of the nineteenth century, everything from currency to property rights to trade systems were determined by government laws and regulations. This was an important, if less well known, part of the Confederation process. As we have seen, much of the motivation behind Confederation was economic development. It was thus imperative that the rules of the new economy be established quickly and in such a way as to facilitate trade.

THE INFRASTRUCTURE OF GOVERNMENT

The development of a Dominion civil service proved relatively straightforward. The new capital of Canada was to be Ottawa, the capital of the old Province of Canada. This was symbolic, for it is only a slight simplification to say that the Province of Canada continued and flourished in the new Dominion government. Most of the civil service and the parliamentary staff, not to mention the prime ministership, were transferred to the new Dominion. Intrusions by Nova Scotians and New Brunswickers began immediately, of course, but it took time and considerable patronage before the Maritimes developed a significant presence in the civil service. The situation for the provinces varied. Ontario and Quebec were faced with creating many government structures from the ground up. Some civil service staffs, such as those dealing with crown lands and education, derived from the

Province of Canada. Others had to be developed as needed. In Nova Scotia and New Brunswick, of course, the process was simpler. The core of the old government remained in place.

Two major forces shaped Confederation-era economic regulations. First, of course, British precedent and practice carried considerable influence. The BNA Act notwithstanding, Canada was subject to British jurisprudence in general and to centuries of particular British precedents. The highest court of appeal was not in Canada but overseas in the Judicial Committee of the Privy Council. Canada was not merely going to replicate Britain, however. It had its own precedents and practices. It was one thing, for example, for an advanced industrial nation like Britain to adopt free trade. Canada was more likely to continue to seek special reciprocal arrangements, or, as would eventually happen, to retreat behind the walls of high tariffs. The second great influence came from the Province of Canada. In several areas, early Dominion policy was borrowed directly from the Province of Canada.

The most important and most controversial of these borrowings involved the tariff. As noted earlier in the chapter, the main obstacle to further economic integration of the colonies before 1867 was their inability to agree on a common external tariff. The Maritimes were reluctant to adopt the higher Canadian tariffs on trade with other countries. Canada adopted a new tariff structure in 1866, in anticipation of Confederation. Duties on manufactured goods were reduced to bring them closer to those of the Maritimes. The act also restored duties on the items that had been admitted free under reciprocity. The Dominion's initial tariffs were more or less taken directly from its provincial predecessor.[8]

Less contentious, but perhaps even more important, was the development of Dominion banking legislation. For the first two years after Confederation, the Canadian government had problems framing banking legislation. Then it turned to Francis Hincks, a former premier of the Province of Canada and a man considered to have one of the best financial minds in the country. By 1871, Hincks had established both the banking and the currency systems of the new Dominion, with one eye to precedent set by the Province of Canada and the other to the need of the new Dominion government to assert a stable financial regime. The precedent came in the currency. Canada retained the decimal currency system based on the dollar that Hincks himself had introduced in 1854. The adaptation to new circumstances came in the compromise reached between the banks and the Dominion on note issue. Banks would have the right to issue notes $4 and above, and the Dominion the monopoly over small denominations. Something of a mix between old and new came in the Bank Act of 1871. Many of its provisions were based on earlier legislation from the Province of Canada. There were also changes, however, designed to recognize the nature of transcontinental banking. Most importantly, Hincks encouraged national branch banking, something that distinguished Canadian practice from American and has remained central to the Canadian banking structure ever since.[9]

Banking was among the more complex pieces of a legislative and regulatory puzzle that fell into place between 1867 and the early 1870s. Patent law, weights and measures, and hosts of other mundane but necessary rules and regulations were quickly borrowed from British precedent, taken directly from the Province of Canada, or adapted to the new national expanse.

The fiscal arrangements set out in the act deserve mention, given their importance throughout Canadian history. Giving Ottawa unlimited powers to tax, while restricting the provinces to direct levies, meant that the federal government took over customs and excise duties, which contributed 85 percent of total government revenue at that time. Provinces were left with spending responsibilities that exceeded their capacity to tax. This fiscal gap was covered by Ottawa's agreeing to make annual per capita grants to the provinces, to provide a cash subsidy in support of government and legislatures, and to assume all provincial debts. New Brunswick received a special ten-year grant in recognition of its special financial needs, and the same provision was extended retroactively to Nova Scotia in 1869.

Three features of these fiscal arrangements should be noted, less for their immediate relevance than for their role in political and constitutional debates many decades later. First, the clear intent was to make an economic union out of the British North American colonies. The prohibition on indirect taxation by provinces complemented section 121 of the act in preventing the erection of tariff-like barriers to interprovincial trade. Second, there was a clear commitment to offset fiscal gaps so that each level of government could carry out its constitutionally assigned functions effectively. Statutory payments were set to balance taxation powers and expenditure responsibilities. Finally, there was a commitment to rough fiscal equity across provinces and a recognition that responsibility for achieving it rested with the federal government. Equal per capita grants were implicitly equalizing, while special payments to the two poorer provinces were explicitly so.

GEOGRAPHY

Geographically, the new Dominion of Canada was only a partial success in 1867. Both British and Canadian enthusiasts had hoped to incorporate all of British North America into the new Dominion, yet Newfoundland and Prince Edward Island remained aloof. The Hudson's Bay Company territories were not yet incorporated and, without them, British Columbia could not even be approached.

Crucial to the economic development of the Dominion was the way in which most of these geographical limitations of 1867 were overcome. The first territorial expansion was also the greatest. Now that Confederation was in place, the new governmental and fiscal base allowed the long-sought expansion to the West. By the time of Confederation the British, the eager Canadians, and the Hudson's Bay Company officials recognized that the days of the old order were finished. The fur-trade frontier was about to yield to the agricultural frontier, and a form of government appropriate for this new stage of economic development was imperative. In 1869 an agreement reached between Britain, Canada, and the Hudson's Bay Company provided for compensation to the fur-trade corporation in exchange for the transfer of their territory.

Unfortunately for all involved, nobody had thought to consult the residents of Red River. In response, Louis Riel led what became known as the Red River resistance. Not until the summer of 1870 was the resistance broken and Canadian authority established in the region. The incident serves as a sharp political reminder of the economic implications of the transfer. The Métis in the West had developed a distinct economic role for themselves by hunting buffalo and, in more recent years, by acting as carters and traders within the Hudson's Bay Company economic system. Their resourcefulness in overcoming the earlier crisis, however, did not ease their concerns about the transfer. They knew that the new firms crowding into Red River, with their Ontario ties and English language, were likely better poised to gain the business of the growing Canadian community in the West. Nor did it take much to foresee that the buffalo hunt, long an integral part of the Métis economy and culture, would suffer as thousands of farmers poured into the country.

Economic as well as cultural threat thus triggered the Red River resistance. In the end, the Métis forced the Dominion to create a new province, Manitoba, and obtained guarantees for their language and religion. The guarantees, however, could not stop the transformation of the West into an English-speaking Protestant region. They did not even begin to address the economic shifts that would transform the Prairies and the people who lived there over the next generation.

Important though these changes were for the Métis, the real economic significance of the transfer was that it shaped Canadian economic policy for nearly 50 years. In 1871, agriculture was the most important economic sector in the nation. Not surprisingly, therefore, the acquisition of a vast new area of arable land was seen as the key to the growth of the new Dominion.[10] Not only the farmers would prosper under this vision. The growing western hinterland provided a ready market for the emergent manufacturing sector of eastern Canada. Montreal and Toronto manufacturers, wholesalers, and transportation companies could all gain by acting as primary suppliers to this vast new frontier. Such an expanding internal market also made it easier for the government to move toward tariff protection. Canada would export primary materials to the world; it would try to preserve its own frontier for itself.

Such an economic policy also had tremendous regional implications. The notion of a protected central Canadian industry supplying a western agricultural hinterland set off a train of policies, from high tariffs to subsidized rail rates on the haulage of wheat (the Crow rates). These policies and the whole notion of regional specialization led to long-running and often acrimonious debates about regional equity, federal–provincial rights, and intersectoral struggles for influence.

The transfer of the prairie West to Canada opened up the possibility of an even more distant acquisition, British Columbia. Previous European involvement in British Columbia had, for the most part, been tied to the transcontinental fur trade. The structure of the economy had been changing, however. In 1857, gold was discovered in the interior near Fort Hope. That year alone some 30 000 people, mainly from the United States, flooded into the colony in search of instant riches. Given that the main Hudson's Bay Company settlement, Fort Victoria, had a population of only about 300 at the time, the numbers take on a greater meaning.[11]

This gold rush, as with others before and after it, did not last. By 1863 the rush was "played out," as the phrase went, and many of the adventurers departed. Nonetheless, the gold rush had transformed British Columbia in several ways. First, the influx of population had forced the British government to act, since administration by a fur-trade company was insufficient. In 1859, the British created the new colony of British Columbia, consisting of the modern-day mainland. Vancouver Island would remain a separate colony until 1866. Second, the influx of miners tipped the population balance. Although the Native population was still large, the European economy and social system were now dominant on southern Vancouver Island, on the lower mainland, and in parts of the interior.

Finally, the gold rush began the restructuring of the economy. British Columbia was no longer merely a fur-trading outpost, so far as the Europeans were concerned. For one thing, the gold rush had required access to the interior, and initial primitive trails were developed into wagon roads with the help of the Royal Engineers. Even before Confederation, roads ran from the coast inward to the Fort Hope–Yale region and along the southern Okanagan. These roads facilitated settlement and trade in the years that followed the gold rush. The growth in European settlement also encouraged diversification. By the 1860s, ventures were being developed that, although small in scale, gave an indication of the future of the region; timber, sawmilling, and fishing. Victoria had evolved from trading post to genuine settlement.

Initially, these events had little to do with the new Dominion of Canada. The decline of the fur trade, in fact, severed the east–west economic connections that had previously

184

existed. British Columbia's future seemed to rest across the Pacific or, even more likely, down the coast in the growing markets of Oregon and California. The latter potential, though, gave politicians in Victoria, Ottawa, and London concern. The British had already lost the Oregon Territory in 1846 and feared that British Columbia would be tempted into the expansionist arms of the Americans. Connection to Canada, therefore, was a natural alternative. The colony should be tied into a transcontinental economy based on an east–west axis. In 1871, the deal was completed and Canada acquired its Pacific province. In return, Canada undertook to make the east–west connection meaningful. It would provide a railway to British Columbia within a decade.

The Canadian Pacific Railway (CPR) was actually completed in 1885. In the interval, British Columbians would complain loudly about central Canada's failure to do them justice. Central Canadians, for their part, would occasionally rue their promise of a railway. The endless squabbles, however, are less informative than the principle behind the decision to build the railway. Once again politics dictated economic policy. In the sense that the CPR was designed to entice British Columbia, it is another example of "defensive expansionism." Public investment was committed because a project was deemed essential, but private funds were not forthcoming.

The final nineteenth-century acquisition came in 1873, when Prince Edward Island was enticed into Confederation. In this instance the issue was also a railway, but here the marketplace was correct and the government overenthusiastic. Prince Edward Island had developed railway fever in the 1860s and set out to build a railway across the island. It is doubtful the market ever existed to support such an undertaking, but the government underwrote the enterprise anyway. To make matters worse, the route became increasingly circuitous as various politicians and local organizations ensured that the railway ran through their own areas. Construction standards were poor, some of the contractors negligent, and cost overruns became endemic. By 1873, to make a complex story straightforward, the island faced a simple choice. It could go bankrupt trying to support its poorly built railway, or it could accept Confederation and have the railway taken over by the federal government. This is what it did. Canada was more than willing to absorb such a small railway — it had already agreed to the Intercolonial and the Canadian Pacific, after all — in return for a new province.

Conclusion

Confederation was dictated by many things, including politics, fear of the United States, and French–English relations. Economic development, however, had to be among the most important factors. The reordered North American structure provided, as Fowke has said, the wherewithal in constitutional and financial terms for British North America to continue to develop. It allowed central Canada to reach toward a transcontinental hinterland. It provided a crucial new frontier of settlement and thereby continued to attract population. It also implied many things that would shape economic development in the next decades: an east–west trade system, a federal system that would occasionally hamper the trade and development it was designed to encourage, and a nation in which one region would dominate politically and economically for the foreseeable future. All of these issues would, in turn, do much to determine Canadian politics in the decades to come. Indeed, many of the issues of Confederation remain an essential part of the Canadian political and economic landscape well over a century later.

Confederation also demands a different perspective on the evolution of economic history for the post-1867 period. No longer is it possible to cast the story in terms of several distinct and isolated colonies tied, however loosely, to British mercantile policy and to the fortunes of their main staple products. Now, there is a national economy to deal with and a national focus to bring to bear on economic and political issues. Regional differences did not disappear by an act of the British Parliament, however, so the national perspective must always be complemented by the regional ones. Nor is reference to staples activities sufficient to explain economic development, if indeed it ever was. The industrial revolution is an important new theme. As with the political change, though, it adds to an existing one rather than supplanting it.

NOTES

1. Vernon C. Fowke, "The National Policy — Old and New," in W.T. Easterbrook and H.G.J. Aiken, eds., *Approaches in Economic History* (Toronto: McClelland & Stewart, 1967), 239.
2. M.C. Urquhart, "New Estimates of Gross National Product, Canada, 1870–1926: Some Implications for Canadian Development," in Stanley L. Engerman and Robert E. Gallman, eds., *Long-Term Factors in American Economic Growth*, National Bureau of Economic Research, Studies in Income and Wealth, vol. 51 (Chicago and London: University of Chicago Press, 1986), table 2.13, 42.
3. T.W. Acheson, "New Brunswick Agriculture at the End of the Colonial Era: A Reassessment," in Kris Inwood, ed., *Farm, Factory and Fortune: New Studies in the Economic History of the Maritime Provinces* (Fredericton: Acadiensis Press, 1993), 37–60.
4. Kris Inwood and Phyllis Wagg, "Wealth and Prosperity in Nova Scotia Agriculture, 1851–1871," *Canadian Historical Review* 75(2) (June 1994): 242.
5. Kris Inwood and James R. Irwin, "Canadian Regional Commodity Income Differences at Confederation," in Inwood, ed., *Farm, Factory and Fortune*, 103.
6. W.L. Morton, *Canada 1857–1873: The Critical Years* (Toronto: McClelland & Stewart, 1964), 21.
7. Fowke, "The National Policy."
8. Graham D. Taylor and Peter Baskerville, *A Concise History of Canadian Business* (Toronto: Oxford University Press, 1994), 242.
9. "The Banking System of Canada," in Adam Shortt and Arthur Doughty, eds., *Canada and Its Provinces*, vol. 10, *Industrial Expansion II* (Toronto: Glasgow Brook, 1914), 627–35.
10. Doug Owram, *Promise of Eden: The Canadian Expansionist Movement and the Idea of the North West, 1856–1900*, 2nd ed. (Toronto: University of Toronto Press, 1992), 115–24.
11. Jean Barman, *The West Beyond the West: A History of British Columbia* (Toronto: University of Toronto Press, 1991), 61–62.

FURTHER READING

Buckner, Phillip A. "The Maritimes and Confederation." *Canadian Historical Review* 71 (1990): 1–45.
Creighton, D.G. "Economic Nationalism and Confederation." In D.G. Creighton, ed., *Towards the Discovery of Canada*. Toronto: Macmillan, 1972.
Fowke, Vernon C. "The National Policy — Old and New." *Canadian Journal of Economics and Political Science* 18(3) (August 1952): 271–86.
Martin, Ged, ed. *The Causes of Canadian Confederation*. Fredericton: Acadiensis Press, 1990.
Morton, W.L. *Canada, 1857–1873: The Critical Years*. Toronto: McClelland & Stewart, 1964.
Simeon, Richard, and Ian Robinson. *State, Society, and the Development of Canadian Federalism*. Toronto: University of Toronto Press, 1990. Parts I and II.

Part Four

A National Economy
Established, 1867–1913

Mrs. Sophie Hrynchuk, a Ukrainian settler, in Redwater, Alberta, in
1912. In the late nineteenth and early twentieth centuries, population on the Prairies increased rapidly. Glenbow Archives/NA-2497-18.

CANADA'S ECONOMIC PERFORMANCE from Confederation to World War I is marked by two prominent features. First, the period divides naturally into two distinct periods. For three decades after 1867, the BNA Act's promise that "Union would conduce to the Welfare of the Provinces" seemed a hollow one. The western frontier proved incapable of attracting much settlement, and the central and eastern provinces were pale shadows of the robust industrial economy south of the border. Immigrants came to Canada, but in many cases only to continue on to the United States, joining the thousands of native-born who were making the same move.

This situation changed, beginning in 1896 and continuing to the outbreak of war in 1914. Suddenly, prairie land agents could not keep up with the influx of homesteaders seeking to file claims. Workers were drawn to remote mines, forests, and hydro-electric sites. Manufacturing and service industries boomed, and firms grew in size and sophistication. Cities grew even faster than the rural areas. Foreign capital poured into the country. Most visibly perhaps, Canada became the first choice for thousands of international migrants, including, in an interesting reversal of the experience of the previous three decades, many Americans.

The contrast in performance between the two periods is clear from Figure P4.1, which plots annual values of real GNP from 1870, the earliest year for which reliable GNP data are available,[1] to 1913. Casual inspection of the figure suggests that economic growth was more rapid after 1896 than it was in the preceding quarter century. Real GNP grew at a compound annual rate of 2.38 percent between 1870 and 1896, and at a rate of 6.48 percent between 1896 and 1913. On balance, statistical analysis of the GNP series that accounts for cyclical influences on the GNP series shown in Figure P4.1 provides support for Malcolm Urquhart's observation that "the Canadian economy developed in fundamentally different ways after 1900 than it had before," largely due to much higher rates of capital formation.[2]

Population is another common measure of aggregate economic growth. It is an especially useful indicator for an economy such as Canada's, in which international migration is important. Net inmigration generally signals that real income in Canada is growing relative to those both in sending countries and in other potential destinations. Conversely, net outmigration signals relatively slow economic growth in Canada.

Table P4.1 shows population change by decade for Canada for the census years 1871–1911. Total population increased by 17.2 percent in the 1870s, by 11.7 percent in the 1880s, by 11.1 percent in the 1890s, and by a staggering 34.2 percent in the first decade of the twentieth century. The differences among the decades are almost entirely accounted for by net international migration rather than natural increase. Net migration was equal to 21.5 percent of 1871 population in the 1870s (i.e., net outmigration). This figure rose to 23.4 percent of the population in the 1880s, fell back slightly to 22.7 percent in the 1890s, and then switched to net inmigration equal to 15.1 percent of the population in the period 1901–11.[3]

Real GNP and population are measures of extensive economic growth. They indicate how the economy is performing in aggregate terms, but not how real incomes are changing. The latter requires a measure of intensive economic growth, real GNP per capita. Figure P4.2 plots the values of this variable for the period 1870–1913. Interestingly, it

Figure P4.1 Real GNP, Canada, 1870–1913

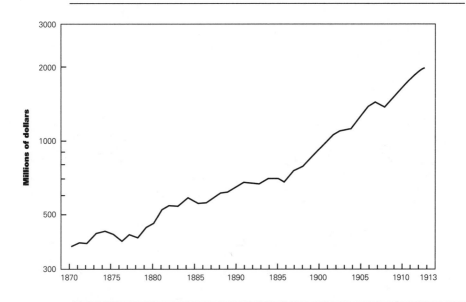

Source: Adapted from M.C. Urquhart, "New Estimates of Gross National Product, Canada, 1870–1926: Some Implications for Canadian Development," in Stanley L. Engerman and Robert E. Gallman, eds., *Long-Term Factors in American Economic Growth*, National Bureau of Economic Research, Studies in Income and Wealth, vol. 51 (Chicago: University of Chicago Press, 1986), table 2.9, pp. 30–31.

Table P4.1 Population and Growth Rates, Canada, 1871–1911*

Decade	Pop. at Beginning of Decade (000s)	Rate of Pop. Increase by Decade (%)	Rate of Natural Increase (%)	Rate of Net International Migration (%)
1871–1881	3689	17.2	18.7	–1.5
1881–1891	4325	11.7	15.1	–3.4
1891–1901	4833	11.1	13.8	–2.7
1901–1911	5371	34.2	19.1	15.1
1911	7207			

*ALL RATES ARE A PERCENTAGE OF POPULATION AT BEGINNING OF DECADE.

Source: M.C. Urquhart, "Canadian Economic Growth, 1870–1980," Department of Economics, Queen's University, discussion paper no. 734, 1988, table 1, p. 6.

exhibits much the same pattern as real GNP. Real GNP per capita rose over the entire period, but with a discernible break in 1896. It grew at a compound annual rate of 1.06 percent between 1870 and 1896, and at a rate of 3.95 percent between 1896 and 1913.

Figure P4.2 Real GNP, per Capita, Canada, 1870–1913

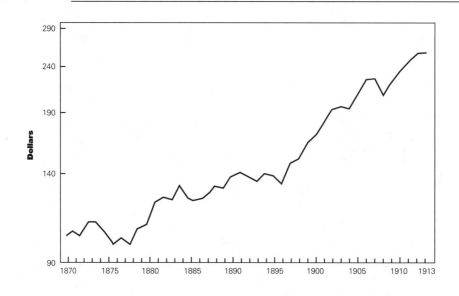

Source: Adapted from M.C. Urquhart, "New Estimates of Gross National Product, Canada, 1870–1926: Some Implications for Canadian Development," in Stanley L. Engerman and Robert E. Gallman, eds., *Long-Term Factors in American Economic Growth*, National Bureau of Economic Research, Studies in Income and Wealth, vol. 51 (Chicago: University of Chicago Press, 1986), table 2.9, pp. 30–31.

The acceleration of aggregate economic growth in Canada after 1896 was matched by an increase in average living standards.

Another way to gain some perspective on an economic growth record is to compare it with that of other economies. For Canada, the obvious first comparison is with the United States. Table P4.2 shows rates of growth of population, real GNP, and real GNP per capita for the two countries for the four decades between 1871 and 1910. The American population increased significantly faster than Canada's in the 1870s, and nearly twice as fast in the 1880s and 1890s. The pattern reversed after 1900, however, when the Canadian population increase was well above that to the south.

The pattern for real GNP growth was slightly different from that for population. Real output in the United States grew substantially faster than did Canada's in the 1870s, but only slightly faster in the following two decades. After 1900, the Canadian growth rate was nearly double the American one. The figures for real per capita GNP suggest that the American standard of living rose more than three times faster than Canada's in the 1870s, but that the opposite situation held for the next three decades, with the greatest difference in Canada's favour coming between 1900 and 1910.

In comparison with other "new" countries of settlement, Australia and Argentina, Canada's strong economic performance from 1900 to 1913 becomes clear. Whereas Canada's economy had slow growth from 1870 to 1895, Australia's economy grew somewhat faster over the 1870s, but at the same rate of Canada's over the 1880s. In 1870, Australia had the world's highest per capita income economy with an income 1.5 times that of the United States. By 1890, Australia and the United States had the same per capita

Table P4.2 Comparative Growth Rates of Canada and the United States, 1871–1910*

Years	Population		Total Real GNP		Real GNP per Capita	
	Canada	U.S.	Canada	U.S.	Canada	U.S.
1871–80	1.6	2.3	2.6	5.7	1.0	3.3
1880–90	1.2	2.3	3.2	3.5	2.0	1.2
1890–1900	1.0	1.9	3.5	3.6	2.4	1.7
1900–1910	2.8	2.0	6.0	3.8	3.2	1.8

*ALL GROWTH RATES ARE COMPOUND RATES GIVEN AS A PERCENTAGE PER ANNUM.

Source: M.C. Urquhart, "New Estimates of Gross National Product, Canada, 1870–1926: Some Implications for Canadian Development," in Stanley L. Engerman and Robert E. Gallman, eds., *Long-Term Factors in American Economic Growth*, National Bureau of Economic Research, Studies in Income and Wealth, vol. 51 (Chicago: University of Chicago Press, 1986), table 2.10, p. 32.

income. In contrast, from 1870 to 1895, Canada's per capita GDP was 60 percent of the United States' GDP. By 1913, Canada's income had risen to 80 percent of the United States' per capita GDP.[4] Thus, the economic performances of Canada and Australia diverge substantially after 1895. Alan Taylor shows that, from 1900 to 1913, Canada's GDP per capita grew by 3.3 percent per year whereas Australia's per capita GDP grew by 1.14 percent per year. Taylor also shows that another wheat exporting nation, Argentina, had growth in per capita GDP of 2.47 percent per year from 1900 to 1913.[5] Both Canada and Argentina benefited from investment booms over that period whereas capital formation in Australia was more modest. After World War I, when Argentina's economy went into a long-run decline, Canada's continued to close the gap on U.S. per capita incomes.

Canada was a net loser of population in the three decades before 1900 — the only new country to be so — but was a significant receiving country in the following decade. The inflow after 1900 was, however, still small in relative terms; Canada received fewer than 10 percent of the total international migrants in this decade, about one-seventh of what the United States did. Canada was not even the second most popular destination after 1900: Argentina was, with about 50 percent more migrants; it was followed by Canada and then closely by Brazil. Still, the pattern in comparison with that of other new countries of settlement is consistent with the conclusion reached above: that Canada's relative economic position changed favourably at the turn of the century.

The second general feature of the Canadian economy in this period is its notable structural change. Figure P4.3 shows the distribution of GDP by broad sector for the years 1870–1910. The immediate impression from the graph is the large and consistent fall in the relative importance of agriculture in the economy, and the equally large and consistent rise in the importance of the service sector. Agriculture was the largest activity in the economy in 1870, accounting for 37.1 percent of total value added. Yet, by 1910, this share had fallen to 21.6 percent. Services (including construction and utilities) were second to agriculture in 1870, at 36 percent of GDP. This share had risen to 50 percent by 1910. There were some fluctuations in the shares of other primary products and of manufacturing, but virtually no changes in relative importance over the four decades.

As usual, we must look for the roots of Canada's experience in the international economy. The period was marked by two major developments. First, it witnessed the shift

Figure P4.3 Percentage Distribution of GDP, Canada, 1870–1910

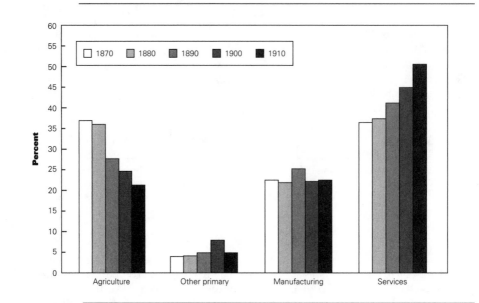

Source: Adapted from M.C. Urquhart, "New Estimates of Gross National Product, Canada, 1870–1926: Some Implications for Canadian Development," in Stanley L. Engerman and Robert E. Gallman, eds., *Long-Term Factors in American Economic Growth*, National Bureau of Economic Research, Studies in Income and Wealth, vol. 51 (Chicago: University of Chicago Press, 1986), table 2.9, pp. 30–31.

of industrial supremacy from the early leader, Britain, to the later-industrializing nations of Germany, France, and the United States. The period 1873–96 used to be known as the Great Depression in Britain, with that term understood to imply an actual contraction of real output or, at least, a dramatic reduction in the rate of increase relative to that of preceding decades. However, it now seems clear that the period was less a depression than a deflation. Wholesale prices fell every year but one between 1873 and 1896, after remaining roughly constant or even rising slightly from 1850 to 1873.[6] Still, Britain's relatively slow growth to the mid-1890s signals, as David Landes notes, "the evening of the industrial revolution" in that country.[7]

The disruption and dislocation brought about by this shift of industrial leadership led, predictably, to a return to protectionism, reversing the progress toward freer trade that had been under way since the 1850s. An alliance between "rye and iron" in Germany led to the imposition of duties on industrial and agricultural products in 1879, with the rates raised considerably in the 1880s. The French raised agricultural tariffs in 1885 and 1887, and moved to a comprehensive system of duties in 1892. Similar strategies were adopted in most other European nations. Britain resisted these pressures, even though, in relative terms, at least, it was losing the most ground.

The victory of the North in the U.S. Civil War also encouraged a trend toward protectionism in that country. The defeat of the South had weakened agrarian interests and allowed an emerging northern industrial economy to have unprecedented influence in Congress. This was symbolized by the 1866 cancellation of the North American Reciprocity

Treaty. Over the next decades, the United States experienced considerable industrialization, behind high tariff walls. On the eve of the Civil War, half of American commodity output originated in agriculture and only one-third in manufacturing; by 1900, the positions were exactly reversed.[8] By the beginning of World War I, the United States' economy was the world's leader.

Britain's Depression (or deflation) of 1873–96 provides some explanation for the slow growth in per capita incomes in Australia and Canada, as both countries' economies were closely tied to the British economy. Also, as a substantial portion of the external investments in Canada, Australia, and Argentina were from British sources, the availability of capital depended on financial conditions in England. Thus, as industrial leadership passed from England to the United States, the economic fortunes of Canada shifted from those of Australia and Argentina to Canada's proximity to and strengthening of ties with the United States.

The second major development in this period was the emergence of what has since become known as the second industrial revolution, a series of technological developments — or improvements, since the steps that actually led to commercial application were merely the final ones in a process of invention and innovation that had begun much earlier. Like the first industrial revolution, it is impossible to date this one precisely. Most accounts, however, place the beginnings in the 1880s and early 1890s, with development in full force by the turn of the century.

Perhaps the most visible symbols of the second industrial revolution were the advances in the production and use of steel. The Bessemer process and the Siemens–Martin furnace increased the quality and uniformity of steel and reduced fuel requirements. Further developments increased the scale of furnaces and mechanized the loading and handling processes. The real cost of steel fell as a result, and it began to be substituted for other materials in everything from construction (the completion of the Eiffel Tower in 1889 being the most dramatic demonstration of this potential) to bridges and shipbuilding.

Parallel advances in the measurement and working of steel had even more dramatic impact. The initial developments were in response to a growing demand for high-velocity firearms, sewing machines, cash registers, typewriters, complex farm machinery, bicycles, motors, and other such goods. As the procedures developed, the technological basis was laid for the internal-combustion engine, the automobile, and the airplane. There were French, German, and British automobiles on the road by the turn of the new century, but these developments paled when compared with what was about to happen to the auto industry in the United States. Airplanes, by contrast, developed rather more quickly in Europe than in North America up to the start of World War I. The economic impacts of both inventions were just beginning to be felt at the turn of the century. Their effects would be enormous and, indeed, are still being felt.

Developments in the chemical industry were of great importance as well. A shift to a new production process for soda brought down the costs of dyes and other products, benefiting the textile industry in particular. The range of medicines available to doctors increased. The rise in automobile use prompted advances in petroleum refining and distillation. Plastics was an established branch of the chemical industry by 1900, and the use of cellulose nitrate in photographic film in the 1890s laid the basis for the motion-picture industry. Other cellulose products were the main constituents in synthetic fibres.

Developments in electricity were at least as spectacular and far-reaching in their ultimate economic and social impacts. The properties of electricity were understood early on, but not until nearly the end of the nineteenth century had that knowledge advanced to the point where electricity could be produced, transmitted, and utilized cheaply and effectively.

194

With the capacity to supply electricity improved, the only remaining requirement was to develop ways of using it efficiently. Developments were under way that would make electricity competitive with gas in the lucrative commercial and domestic lighting markets. The perfection of alternating current and the development of an alternating-current motor by the early 1890s opened the way for the use of electricity in providing motive power to industry and the home. Finally, developments in metallurgy at this time spawned the close association between refining and cheap electricity.

Technological advances made the new products and techniques possible. That these advances were taken up when they were, on the scale they were, is explained by changes on the demand side. Prices turned up in the mid-1890s, after nearly two decades of more or less continuous decline. Gold supplies were augmented by discoveries in South Africa, Australia, and the Klondike, and this increase in the world's money supply led to general inflation. Agricultural prices increased relative to manufactured ones as the booming U.S. economy absorbed more and more of its own grain production. Real interest rates were at historic low levels in the 1890s as well, adding to the incentive to invest in new capital equipment.

This part looks at how these international developments interacted with such domestic influences as resource endowments and government policies to determine the course of Canadian economic development between 1867 and 1913. The discussion centres on three questions. First, why was economic growth in the period between 1896 and 1913 so robust, and in particular why was it so much more robust than that experienced in the preceding three decades? Unlike other turning points in Canadian economic history (the end of British mercantilism, or, still to come, a worldwide depression and two world wars), there are no obvious international events to explain this sudden transformation. Second, what accounts for the economic growth that did occur before 1896, particularly for the notable rise in living standards? Finally, why did Canada's economic structure alter as it did?

NOTES

1. These historical GNP estimates were prepared by Professor M.C. Urquhart and colleagues at Queen's University over a period of many years. They begin with the first census after Confederation and end in 1926, when the official Statistics Canada series begin. See M.C. Urquhart, *Gross National Product, Canada 1870–1926: The Derivation of the Estimates* (Kingston & Montreal: McGill-Queen's University Press, 1993).
2. M.C. Urquhart, "New Estimates of Gross National Product, Canada, 1870–1926. Some Implications for Canadian Development," in Stanley L. Engerman and Robert E. Gallman, eds., *Long-Term Factors in American Economic Growth*, National Bureau of Economic Research, Studies in Income and Wealth, vol. 51 (Chicago and London: University of Chicago Press, 1986), 35–36. Kris Inwood and Thanasis Stengos, "Discontinuities in Canadian Economic Growth, 1870–1985," *Explorations in Economic History* 28 (1991): 274–86. Lewis T. Evans and Neil C. Quigley, "What Can Univariate Models Tell Us about Canadian Economic Growth 1870–1985?" *Explorations in Economic History* 32 (1995), 236–252. Evans and Quigley challenge whether the statistical model used by Inwood and Stengos can definitively identify the wheat boom as a "structural break" in Canadian economic development. Evans and Quigley show that other plausible statistical models reveal other events like the Great Depression of the 1930s and oil price shocks as important events, but not the wheat boom. Alan G. Green and Gordon R. Sparks, "Population Growth and the Dynamics of Canadian Development: A Multivariate Time Series Approach," *Explorations in Economic History* 36 (1999): 56–71.

3. Marvin McInnis argues that these conventional figures seriously misrepresent both immigration and emigration in the period 1871–1901. He estimates that actual immigration was about 35 percent of that reported for the 1870s, 27 percent of that for the 1880s, and 58 percent for the 1890s. His estimates of emigration are correspondingly lower as well, especially for the 1880s. See Marvin McInnis, "Immigration and Emigration: Canada in the Late Nineteenth Century," in T. Hatton and J.G. Williamson, eds., *Migration and the International Labour Market, 1850–1913* (London: Routledge, 1994).

4. David Greasley and Les Oxley, "A Tale of Two Dominions: Comparing the Macroeconomic Records of Australia and Canada since 1870," *Economic History Review*, LI, 2 (1998): 294–318.

5. Alan M. Taylor, "External Dependence, Demographic Burdens, and Argentine Economic Decline after the Belle Epoque," *Journal of Economic History* 52(4) (December 1992): 907–936.

6. S.B. Saul, *The Myth of the Great Depression, 1873–1896,* 2nd ed. (London: Macmillan, 1985), 12.

7. David S. Landes, *The Unbound Prometheus: Technological Change and Industrial Development in Western Europe from 1750 to the Present* (Cambridge: Cambridge University Press, 1969), 235.

8. Gerald Gunderson, *A New Economic History of America* (New York: McGraw–Hill, 1967), 305.

Chapter Eleven

Agriculture

THE LOGICAL PLACE to begin a discussion of Canada's economic performance in the period 1867–1913 is with the agricultural sector. Developments in this sector provide at least partial answers to two of the questions posed in the introduction. First, the marked acceleration in aggregate economic growth after 1896 coincides almost exactly with the boom phase of prairie settlement. Second, economic growth before 1896 was still respectable, partly because agriculture elsewhere in the economy managed to adjust and adapt quite successfully to the changing economic times.

The Prairie Wheat Economy

Of all the economic developments in Canada's first half-century, the prairie wheat boom is perhaps the most dramatic. Certainly it is the most studied. There are at least three reasons for its central role. First, as seen in the part introduction, plans to develop the plains for agricultural settlement were a large part of the motive behind Confederation itself and were basically the entire focus of the national policy. Thus, prairie settlement became the most viable barometer of the success of the new federation — the basis for the doubt and pessimism to 1896 and the exuberance and confidence thereafter.

Second, when settlement did come, it did so with dramatic effect. There were fewer than 75 000 people living in Manitoba and the Northwest Territories in 1871. By 1891, this figure had risen to around 250 000, two-thirds of whom were in Manitoba. By 1911, the three Prairie provinces had a combined population of 1.3 million, and Saskatchewan was the largest. Railways criss-crossed the Prairies, with two more transcontinental lines in the process of completion. Most of the arable land was at least thinly settled as settlers queued up to purchase land that could not be given away fifteen years earlier. From being a minor factor in world markets, Canada had grown to be a major presence; in 1909, Winnipeg handled more wheat than any other centre in the world.[1]

Third, the settlement of the Prairies affected more than just that region, as indeed was the hope of Canadian politicians and business leaders from the outset. Wheat transformed more than just the Prairies and more than just the economy. Canadians far removed from the region earned their livelihood by preparing the region for settlement, supplying the equipment needed to produce the grain, transporting the grain to its markets, and providing for the needs of the farm families. Wheat also created two new provinces and a regional identity and political perspective that has continued to the present.

PLANNING FOR PRAIRIE SETTLEMENT

With the land transfer of 1870, the Hudson's Bay Company gave up its claim to the region, contained in the 1670 charter, in exchange for a lump-sum payment of £300 000 (worth about $34 million in 2001), land in the vicinity of its trading posts not to exceed a total of 2000 ha, and one-twentieth of the fertile belt. The term "fertile belt" was understood to be that area bounded "on the south side by the United States boundary, on the west side by the Rocky Mountains; on the north by the northern branch of the Saskatchewan River; on the east by Lake Winnipeg, Lake of the Woods, and the waters connecting them."[2] The Red River resistance led to a further 560 000 ha being set aside for "half-breed residents." The remainder of the land was retained by the government of Canada (meaning that the newly created province of Manitoba would not have the same constitutional status as the four original provinces), to be administered "for the purposes of the Dominion."

There were considerable variations within that fertile belt. Aside from local differences in quality of soil and availability of water and wood, major geographical features distinguished the region. The northern portion was "parkland," a treed and relatively well-watered region with mixtures of flat and rolling terrain. To the south were the true prairie grasslands, flat and open, although often traversed by sharp coulees and similar features. These features affected contemporary views, and there was a belief in the 1870s that not all of the fertile belt was really suitable for settlement. Specifically, the most likely pattern of settlement was thought to extend from Red River in a northwesterly direction, through the Touchwood Hills to the area of what is now Saskatoon and Battleford. From there, it extended westward, to Fort Edmonton, and southward along the east side of the Rockies. In contrast, the southern region, known as Palliser's Triangle, would be settled only marginally. Before long, promoters would drop such qualifications, but events would prove the initial analysis a reasonably accurate one.

What really mattered was that Canada now had a continuous agricultural frontier to replace the one that had been filled in Ontario. Settlement could spread westward from the small core in the Red River–Winnipeg region to the vast prairie beyond (see Map 11.1). Moreover, the open landscape and the relative absence of trees assisted in opening the region. The slow process of clearing that affected pioneer operations in the Canadas was a minimal problem throughout much of the Prairies.

LAND POLICY

One prerequisite to settlement was the surveying of the land, and, in this process, the open terrain also assisted rapid progress. A system was formally approved in 1869, based on townships divided into 36 sections (see Figure 11.1), with each section containing 640 acres (256 ha), like those in the United States and unlike the 800 acre (320 ha) sections in central Canada. Two sections of each township were designated as school lands, to be sold by auction by the Department of the Interior, with the proceeds going to the province or territory for education spending. Other portions went to the Hudson's Bay Company as part of the purchase arrangement, were left for free homesteads of 160 acres (64 ha) each, or were set aside as railway land grants. Halfbreed claims, as they were called at the time, were handled through a special system of grants and script. There were also provisions for road allowances, correction lines, and areas set aside for colonization companies.

There were, as a consequence of this system, a variety of ways prospective immigrants could obtain land in the Canadian Prairies. The most important type of land acquisition

Map 11.1 The New West, Canada, 1891–1931

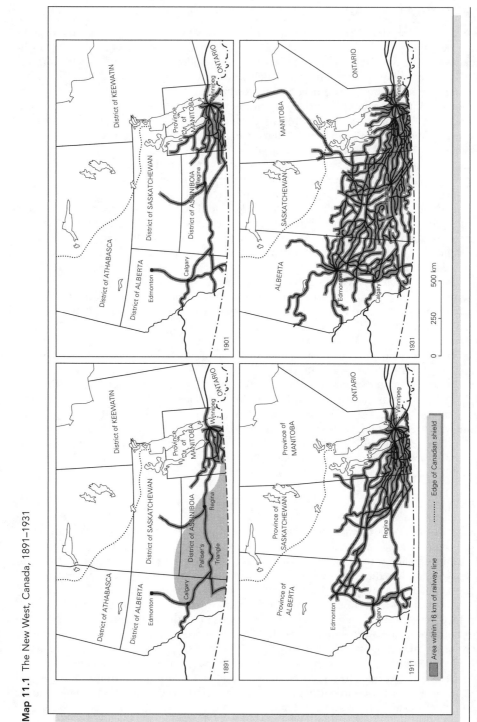

Source: Based on *John Warkentin, Canada: A Geographical Interpretation* (Toronto: Methuen, 1968), p. 412.

was that of free homesteads. The first Dominion Lands Act, in 1872, provided for home-steads of one-quarter section for a fee of $10 ($215 in 2001) and a minimum of three years' residence, but only outside a belt of 20 miles (32 km) on either side of a proposed transcontinental rail line. Government land within the block was to sell for $2.50 per acre (0.4 ha). Since no farmer could haul grain 20 miles by wagon, this measure put all free land at an uneconomic distance from any transport facility, but since, at the time, there were no rail lines in any case, the effects of such distances were negligible.

Free-homestead policy changed as the prospect of a transcontinental rail line came nearer. An order-in-council in 1879 narrowed the restricted belt to 10 miles (16 km) (but raised the price of government lands therein to $6 per acre (0.4 ha)). Even-numbered sections outside this belt were available for free homestead, and a price structure was devised for odd-numbered sections. The most important change came in 1882, when all even-numbered sections were thrown open for free homestead, even those within the CPR belt. Thereafter, the main changes related to the possibility of taking out a second homestead (allowed in 1883 and abandoned three years later) and to tightening the definitions of the residence requirement and improvements necessary for patenting.

Next to free homesteads, the railway land grant was the pillar of Dominion land policy. The idea, borrowed from the United States, was simple. As part of its subsidy, a company was given title to blocks of land in the areas through which its line would pass. Railways were, thus, in the land as well as the freight business. The hope was that, with land to sell, the companies would set freight rates to encourage settlement; or, conversely, with freight to haul, they would price the land and promote it for quick settlement. In short, the railway land grant was seen as an incentive system that made the railways' interests identical with those of the government.

The railway land grant idea was part of Canadian land policy from the beginning. Every proposal for a Pacific railway included grants of land as part of the subsidy; only the amounts varied. The grant actually made to the CPR amounted to 25 million acres (10 million ha). Dozens of rival projects — colonization railways —then sprang up, most of which received land as part of their charter as well. Closely related were the colonization companies proper, who received land in exchange not for building rail lines but for promising to bring settlers to the Prairies.

For the remainder of the land, essentially the odd-numbered sections the railways passed over, the government experimented with a variety of sales techniques. Provision was made in the 1872 Dominion Lands Act for homesteaders to purchase up to 640 additional acres (256 ha), but it was withdrawn in 1881. Beginning in 1874, a homesteader could "pre-empt" an unclaimed adjoining quarter-section at the government price, once

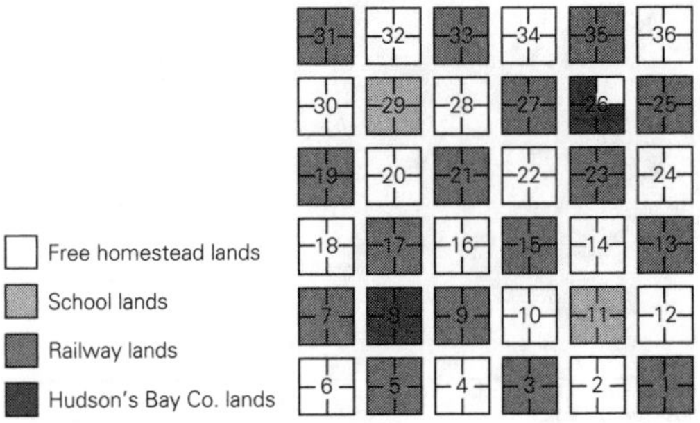

Free homestead lands

School lands

Railway lands

Hudson's Bay Co. lands

Figure 11.1
A Survey of a Standard
Prairie Township

Source: D.G. Kerr, ed., *Historical Atlas of Canada* (Don Mills, Nelson, 1981), p. 62.

patent to the homestead was issued. There was much concern, however, that pre-emption led to speculation, and it was withdrawn in 1890.

Pre-emptions and purchased homesteads were reintroduced in 1908, partly out of concern that 160-acre (64-ha) farms were too small, but mainly because the government wanted the revenue to finance railway grants. Homesteaders located next to odd-numbered sections not taken by railways could purchase a quarter-section from the government for $3 per acre (0.4 ha). Those having no contiguous quarter-section available could purchase one elsewhere, again for $3 per acre. Both provisions were in effect until 1918, when they were withdrawn to make land available to returning veterans of World War I. Overall, nearly 118 million acres (47 million ha) of prairie land were granted under Dominion administration, in the proportions shown in Figure 11.2.

Land policy came under considerable scrutiny at the time of settlements, and has attracted the attention of researchers more recently. The administration of school lands is almost universally praised. Martin speaks of it as "Dominion policy at its best."[3] The Hudson's Bay Company is almost as universally condemned for doing much the same thing as did the Department of the Interior — speculating on timing and using a reservation price in an attempt to maximize sales revenue. The beneficiaries of the revenue were different, but the effects on the rate of settlement must have been quite similar. Who benefited is thus one criterion that has been used to judge the worth of the system.

Railway land grants have been both criticized and praised. Homesteaders did not like them, seeing them as part of what they termed "land-lock." More generally, however, they have been heralded as a wise and essential part of settlement policy, although a distinction is sometimes drawn between the CPR and the other companies. Tying the railways' interest to those of the government — ensuring that both would be interested in rapid and

Figure 11.2 The Disposal of Prairie Lands, Canada 1870–1930

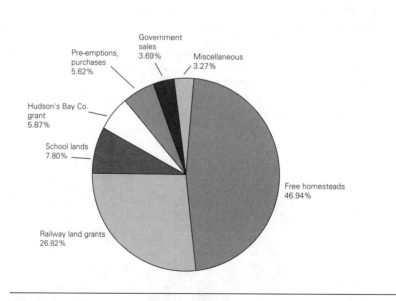

Source: Calculated from Chester Marin, *Dominion Lands Policy* (Toronto: McClelland & Stewart, 1973), pp. 228–29. Used by permission of the Canadian Publishers, McClelland & Stewart.

extensive settlement of the Prairies — made the companies important agents of the national policy. They assisted in advertising the region, subsidizing immigrants, and disseminating agricultural techniques. Having railway sections next to free-homestead ones meant that farmers generally had an empty contiguous quarter-section they could purchase when they wished to expand their operation to 360 acres (144 ha). Even the selection process is sometimes seen as a virtue. Freezing land until railway sections were completed allowed settlement of the poorer and drier areas to be at least postponed.

The traditional view of free homesteads is that although some undeniable waste and inequities were associated with them, by promoting rapid and extensive settlement they served the purposes of the Dominion well. More recent research has tended to argue that it was not necessary to give away land to attract settlers and that the waste and inefficiency involved in doing so were probably much greater than is realized. Free land did not attract many settlers before 1900; after that date, sales were consistently as robust as free-homestead entries. The waste referred to came from premature settlement.[4] Since homesteads were allocated on a first-come, first-served basis, settlers were forced to claim them before they were economically viable. They had to work them to retain the claim, so capital and labour were committed prematurely.

The concept of premature settlement has some appeal, but evidence in support of it is mixed at best. For example, Frank Lewis finds no support for the view that farm settlement on the Canadian Prairies was premature. Lewis finds that rising wheat yields and railway branch line construction that provided lower transportation costs resulted in an increase in profitable farmland.[5] This insight helps to explain why land sales were as robust as free-homestead entries when settlement did occur. Tony Ward concurs that rapid settlement of the Canadian Prairies after 1896 reflected the fact that the profitability of wheat farming on the Canadian Prairies improved by the 1890s due to changes in wheat farming technology and weather. In particular, Ward argues that short-term climatic variation in the 1870s and 1880s reduced temperatures, rainfall, and the length of the growing season to the point that wheat farming outside of the long-settled Red River Valley was not profitable. Thus, while the national policy was appropriate to induce settlement, but not so sufficient to induce growth, Ward concludes that much of the settlement that did occur before 1900 was premature.[6]

A TRANSCONTINENTAL RAILWAY

Some sort of rail connection was obviously necessary if the Prairies were to be developed. The distances were vast, and there was no artery transportation equivalent to the one that the St. Lawrence–Great Lakes system had provided for eastern settlement. Construction of the Northern Pacific Railway in the United States in the late 1860s meant that Canada had to start soon if the entire area was not to become part of the American frontier. The promise to British Columbia created a final impetus to construction.

Besides the enormity of a Canadian transcontinental railway, political and nation building considerations increased the project's risk and diminished its profitability. To head off American expansion north of the 49th parallel, the Canadian railway would have to be built all at once and ahead of demand. The Canadian government also required that the railway have an all-Canadian route, passing north of the Great Lakes through the Canadian Shield, a region of low population and high construction costs. The Canadian government recognized that without an all-Canadian route, the likely beneficiaries of the Canadian wheat trade would be the American railways and manufacturers. For this reason, the Canadian government required that the owners of the transcontinental railway be Canadian, i.e., not American.

These considerations meant that the Canadian government would have to provide a considerable subsidy to encourage the construction of the project. The Grand Trunk was the obvious candidate to build the line, but even with a considerable government subsidy, the company refused to build a transcontinental railway under the Canadian government's terms. The Grand Trunk counter offered to build rail lines on the Canadian Prairies but insisted on linking the western Canadian rail lines with U.S. lines rather than constructing an all-Canadian route. The Grand Trunk also had no intention of building the line all at once and ahead of demand — the construction of western Canadian rail lines would be done incrementally as those areas were settled. Despite approaching the Grand Trunk on more than one occasion, the Canadian government ruled out granting the transcontinental charter to the company because of its refusal to accept the government's terms of construction.[7]

The account of the Canadian Pacific Railway has become one of the better-known stories of Canadian history. Well-known engineer Sandford Fleming was commissioned to survey the route in 1871, a task he completed over the next several years. A charter was drawn up in 1873 authorizing the Canadian Pacific Railway Company — an amalgam of two earlier contenders — to construct a line from Lake Nipissing to some point on the Pacific Ocean. In return, the company was to receive a grant of $30 million and 50 million acres (20 million ha) of land, with additional land for branch lines. That plan broke down with the resignation of the Macdonald government in 1873 over a scandal involving political contributions from the railway's silent American backers.

The Liberal government of Alexander Mackenzie (1873–78) was unable to interest another company in the project, and ended up constructing pieces between waterways and American lines. By 1880, more than 1100 km (683 miles) of lines were either completed or under contract.

Macdonald resumed the search for a company to build the line, and in 1880 an agreement was reached with the Canadian Pacific Railway Company, controlled by George Stephen, James Hill, and Donald Smith. In exchange for constructing a line of Union Pacific quality from Montreal to the Pacific Ocean via the Yellowhead Pass, the CPR received numerous incentives from the government. The most important were $25 million and 25 million acres (10 million ha) of land. The land was to be in alternate sections of 640 acres (256 ha) each (the odd-numbered ones) in a belt 24 miles (38 km) deep, on either side of the railway between Winnipeg and Jasper. The land had to be "fairly fit for settlement," meaning that acreage in the railway belt deemed unfit could be exchanged for better land elsewhere. In addition, there were less-valuable concessions, including exemption from taxation for the railway and its grounds and buildings, and similar exemption for the land grants for twenty years. No company could build a line south of the main line for twenty years, existing government lines in the West were handed over to the company, and lines currently under construction were to be completed by the government and then handed over.

Construction of the line began almost immediately and was completed in 1885, with the last spike being driven in by the Honourable Donald Smith at Craigellachie, B.C., on the morning of November 7. The main line did not follow that laid out by Sandford Fleming, but rather took a more southerly route through Winnipeg, Regina, Moose Jaw, Calgary, and Kicking Horse and Rogers passes, en route to Vancouver. Branch lines were built quickly, though not quickly enough to satisfy the settlers who depended on them. Before the century was out, track ran south from Winnipeg to the American border; north from the main line to Saskatoon, Prince Albert, and Edmonton; and south from Calgary to Fort Macleod. In the east, the CPR, through purchase and construction, extended the line to Toronto and Montreal and established connections through American railways to Portland, Maine. Shortly thereafter, a "short line" was built through Maine to Saint John, giving the company access to Atlantic Canada.

The CPR was a tremendously successful company, and its founders were lionized in the business journals of the day as the epitome of business acumen. There is a certain irony in this, for two reasons. First, these businessmen were successful in part because of the vast government subsidies that underwrote the railway. Second, at the time of construction, and for a while after, few thought much of the railway's prospects. As the well-known British magazine *The Economist* said on February 9, 1881, the CPR could expect "a long and dreary season of unprofitableness."

The contrast between the low expectations and the rapid success of the company has led to considerable discussion about the large subsidy that it was given at the time. Was it necessary to subsidize the company at all, or would a railway have been built anyway as the prospects for settlement improved? If a subsidy *was* necessary— to pre-empt American expansion northward and meet the deadline imposed by British Columbia's terms of union — was the amount excessive, reflecting the close links between the government and the railway promoters rather than economic necessity? Research suggests that some subsidy was indeed necessary if a railway were to be built much before the turn of the century, since the actual rate of return earned by the CPR between 1886 and 1895 was below that available on other investments. But the same calculation suggests that the subsidy was substantially in excess of what was needed to make up the difference, at least if the riskiness of the venture is ignored.[8]

To infer that the Canadian government gave too large a subsidy to the CPR syndicate is too strong a conclusion. Because the railway had to be built all at once, the project was an "indivisible" investment. As much of the investment would be in building roads, bridges, and tunnels, much of it was irreversible. Under these conditions, the holder of the transcontinental railway project had an incentive to delay the investment when the project's future profits were uncertain. The option to delay construction had value for the company. Thus, to encourage earlier construction of the railway, the Canadian government had to include some subsidy to compensate the CPR syndicate for the early exercise of the project's option value. The size of the necessary subsidy for this option value reflected the perceived risk of the project. Calculations that account for the option value of the railway project show that even at low levels of project risk (as measured by the expected variance of railway profits) it is unlikely that the subsidy paid to the CPR was excessive.[9]

Free land and a transcontinental railway notwithstanding, there was no wheat boom before 1896. Free homestead entries rose briefly in the early 1880s, with the construction of the CPR, but fell off for the next decade. In some of these years, cancellations exceeded entries, and the stock of homesteads actually declined. The lands of southern Manitoba were gradually settled and the population of that province reached 150 000 by 1891. West of this, however, settlement was thinly scattered, with vast areas still untouched by the plough one generation after the transfer.

THE WHEAT BOOM

Suddenly, in the mid-1890s, the situation changed. Figure 11.3 illustrates just how dramatic the turnabout was. Of the total stock of homesteads taken out to 1930, only 8.8 percent were recorded by 1885, and only 20 percent by 1900. Yet, this proportion had reached over 50 percent just six years later, and nearly 90 percent by the outbreak of World War I.

Figure 11.3 Net Accumulated Homesteads in Each Year, Canada, 1875–1930

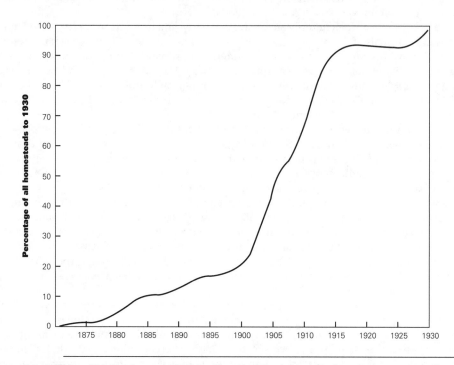

Source: Calculated from M.C. Urquhart and K.A.H. Buckley, eds., *Historical Statistics of Canada* (Toronto: Macmillan, 1965), series K34–41.

This rapid geographical spread of settlement is reflected in other statistics. In 1901, there were 55 000 farms on the Prairies, occupying 15.4 million acres (6.2 million ha). About one-third of this acreage (5.6 million acres [2.2 million ha]) was improved and 3.6 million acres (1.4 million ha) of it were under field crops. By 1911, the number of farms and the area occupied had increased more than 3.5 times, to 200 000 farms and 58 million acres (9 million ha). Improved acreage was four times greater, at 23 million acres, and the area under field crops nearly five times as great, at 17.7 million acres (7 million ha).[10]

What changed in the mid-1890s? Why had nearly three decades of efforts to populate the Canadian West achieved so little when, suddenly, they seemed so spectacularly successful? The general answer is that Canada was able to capture an increasing share of a secularly rising world wheat trade. Why the international trade in grain increased steadily after the mid-nineteenth century is well understood. Why Canada suddenly entered it so effectively after 1896 when it could not before is still a source of some disagreement.

The main markets for export grains in the nineteenth century were in Europe, particularly Britain. From a position of virtual self-sufficiency in the 1840s, imports grew by the outbreak of World War I to account for nearly 30 percent of total supplies for Europe as a whole and for nearly 75 percent of consumption in the United Kingdom. Demand grew in these countries, but the main factor behind the shift to international specialization was a dramatic decline in the costs of getting grain from the farm gate to Liverpool. Ocean rates fell as steel replaced iron and wood in ships, as the vessels became larger, as marine engines improved in efficiency, and as associated port costs fell. Inland rates declined as steel rails were introduced and as engines and rolling stock were improved. With the gap between export and import prices reduced in this manner, Liverpool prices could fall in nominal terms from the 1850s to the 1890s. This fact, together with rising incomes and populations, accounts for the rise in British demand, while prices at the export points could rise more or less continuously, which accounts for the increase in supply from frontier regions.

Canada was a relative latecomer to this growing international wheat trade. The Black Sea area and the United States together effectively accounted for the entire export trade in wheat in 1865–69 and for more than 80 percent as late as 1895–99. Canada supplied only 4 percent of the trade at the turn of the century, about the same as India and about one-half of what Australia did. Yet, this share had quadrupled to 16 percent just fifteen years later, ranking Canada with the United States and Argentina and well ahead of India and Australia.[11]

Canada's lag in entering this trade is puzzling. The Rowell–Sirois Commission wrote of a favourable conjuncture of circumstances after 1896 that suddenly made wheat production in Canada profitable, and this interpretation quickly became the standard account. Prairie agricultural land was now attractive because transport costs had declined, cereal prices had risen, the costs of inputs to agriculture had fallen relatively, interest rates were at their lowest level in recorded history, international capital and labour flows were increasing, the technology to farm the Prairies and to store and transport the product to market was now available, and last, but for the commission certainly not least, Dominion land, transportation, and immigration policies were supportive.

The problem for the commission's explanation is that, while these factors certainly explain why there was settlement on the Canadian Prairies at all, they cannot explain why the bulk of it took place in the fifteen years after 1897. Transport costs and prices of farm inputs had been falling for some time, wheat prices were higher in the late 1870s and early 1880s than they were after 1897, and the technology needed on the Canadian plains was basically the same as that associated with the Dakota boom of the 1870s and 1880s. Capital and labour were invested around the world prior to 1900; they just were not attracted to Canada. Finally, the provisions of the national policy were the same in 1896 as they had been a decade or more earlier.

Much has been made of the impact of railway freight rates, the Crow rates in particular, on the development of the prairie grain economy. In 1897, Ottawa agreed to provide a subsidy of $11 000 per mile ($6875 per kilometre), up to a maximum of $3.6 million, to allow the CPR to build a line from Lethbridge through the Crow's Nest Pass to Nelson, B.C., to tap the rich mineral resources of that area. The company, in turn, agreed to reduce "in perpetuity" its rates on grain destined for export and on incoming settlers' effects, such as agricultural implements and construction materials. Known as the Crow's Nest Pass rates, the cuts were made in stages, coming into effect fully in 1899. The rates were suspended during World War I and then reimposed by statute in 1925 at the level agreed to in 1897, where they stayed until the 1980s.

There is a general belief that, by lowering the cost of getting prairie wheat to port, this agreement speeded up the rate of settlement and extended it into areas it would not otherwise have reached. This probably overstates the case, however. Freight rates were falling anyway, and, in fact, an agreement between the Manitoba government and the Canadian Northern Railway led the CPR to reduce its rates below the Crow's Nest levels in 1902, and they remained below this ceiling until well into World War I, when the agreement was temporarily suspended. Others have argued that the level of rates was less important than the promise contained in the "in perpetuity" clause. The binding of the rate-setting behaviour of the CPR in this manner, it is hypothesized, assured would-be settlers that the railway would not resume monopoly behaviour once they were established on the land.

Immigration policy is sometimes credited with a key role. The Dominion had assumed control of its own immigration policy in 1867, and the first Immigration Act was passed two years later. Generally, the policy throughout the remainder of the nineteenth century was one of laissez faire.[12] The overriding objective was to attract population, especially to the farmlands of the West. Only paupers and indigents were unwelcome, as regulations of 1879–80 and 1891 made clear, although colour loomed large unofficially. Otherwise, the government joined with the CPR and other companies in mounting promotional campaigns in Europe and the United States. There were some successes, such as the arrival of Icelandic settlers in Manitoba in 1873. In general, however, results were disappointing. More people left Canada (mainly to go to the United States) than arrived in the latter half of the nineteenth century.

Settlement policy was clearly administered more energetically after 1896, with Clifford Sifton in charge of the Department of the Interior. Expenditures on advertising and promotion rose significantly, and particular efforts were made to attract American farmers. Sifton also removed several of the obstacles to settlement. Administration of the Homestead Act was improved, and railways were pressured to patent land owed to them in order to free up the remainder for homesteading. Efforts were also made to develop the irrigation potential of the drier areas and to promote ranching and forestry operations. It is difficult to judge how much impact these efforts had in promoting settlement, relative to all the other changes under way at the time. But like the Crow rates, Clifford Sifton is firmly associated with the wheat boom, whatever the evidence.

The explanation for the timing of prairie settlement rests rather on some combination of new cultivation techniques, technical change, and perhaps changes in climate that contributed to increased wheat yields.[13] Except for the small region in southern Manitoba that was already settled by the mid-1880s, either the land was too dry or the growing season too short to support grain farming before 1896. The solution to the moisture problem came in the late 1880s with the development of cultivation techniques suitable for semi-arid land. Developments in farming techniques and equipment allowed farmers to cultivate a larger area in the short growing season available, thereby increasing returns to farming. The development of Marquis wheat, in widespread use in the region by 1909, expanded the feasible area of cultivation further. Tony Ward shows that climate change is also an important piece of the puzzle. Just as the Prairies were opened up by the construction of the CPR, there was a substantial adverse fluctuation in climate. While temperatures, rainfall, and the length of growing season increased slowly through the 1880s, it was not until after the turn of the century that they returned to typical levels.[14] With these advances, together with lower railway costs, induced railway branch-line construction, and higher wheat prices after 1896, the Canadian Prairies were brought within the feasible region of cultivation, and large-scale settlement began.

WHEAT AND PRAIRIE DEVELOPMENT

Settlement before World War I was marked by distinct stages. In the early couple of decades, settlement reflected the assumptions of early scientific analysis, which argued that the best land ran in a crescent shape, northwestward from Winnipeg to Edmonton and then southward along the foothills of the Rocky Mountains. Early settlements thus began in the relatively accessible region around Winnipeg, spreading in sporadic fashion northwestward to towns like Prince Albert and Edmonton. Then, after 1885, the newly completed CPR drew settlement southward. Cities like Calgary and Regina began to emerge. After 1896, the crescent-shaped wedge thickened, as homesteaders took up land in the colder northern fringes and in the drier Palliser's Triangle region of southwestern Saskatchewan and southeastern Alberta. By 1913, less than two decades after migration began in earnest, the entire prairie region was at least thinly settled.

The surge in settlement spurred new railway development. William Mackenzie and Donald Mann had been involved in railway construction since 1886. By the 1890s, they had begun to buy up railway charters, often with land grants attached to them. In 1896, they purchased the charter for the Lake Manitoba Railway and Canal Company and built a link to the CPR main line. By 1900, they had extended the track into Saskatchewan. Other charters from the federal, Manitoba, and Ontario governments allowed them to begin to build from Winnipeg to Port Arthur, on Lake Superior. Over the next few years, encouraged by the economic boom on the Prairies, the company began in earnest to complete a transcontinental line through construction and purchase. By 1905, the only gaps remaining were Ottawa to Port Arthur, in eastern Canada, and Edmonton to the Pacific. Both sections were completed by 1915, with the western section following Sandford Fleming's route from Edmonton through the Yellowhead Pass to Vancouver.

The expectations of the time also attracted a railway that, 30 years earlier, had refused to participate in the transcontinental scheme under the government's terms at the time. In 1902, amidst the prairie settlement boom, the Grand Trunk Railway put forward a proposal to build west to the Pacific. The attraction of merging the Canadian Northern with the Grand Trunk was not lost on the government. Negotiations failed, however, and construction proceeded on both. The government agreed to build a line from Winnipeg through the northern clay belts of Ontario to the Maritimes. This it did, completing the project in late 1913. Named the National Transcontinental, the line was to be leased to the Grand Trunk rent-free for three years and then at 3 percent of the cost of construction for the next 47 years. The Grand Trunk Pacific, a subsidiary company created expressly for the purpose, built a line from Winnipeg through Edmonton and the Yellowhead to Prince Rupert on the Pacific, opening in September 1914. The Grand Trunk refused to lease the National Transcontinental upon its completion, so Canada's third line operated as a hybrid private–public venture.

Each company built branch lines in addition to their trunk lines. The total length of track on the Prairies doubled, from around 3000 km in the mid-1880s to 6000 km in 1899. Construction continued until, by 1913, there were about 18 000 km of track in the three provinces. Most homesteaders could thus be assured that their farm either was already served by a railway spur or soon would be.

Wheat was the dominant field crop from the beginning. It accounted for more than 70 percent of the farmland in 1901, with oats making up most of the remainder. Wheat's share fell slightly, to 63 percent, in 1960, and to 59 percent by 1911, although its total area increased, from 2.5 million acres (1 million ha) in 1901 to 10 million acres (4 million ha) in 1911. Total production in 1911 was 208 million bushels, which represented 91 percent of total Canadian output for that year.[15] Oats took up 28 percent of the area in 1911 and flaxseed, at 7 percent, had overtaken barley. Manitoba and Saskatchewan were the most specialized in wheat; Alberta the least.

Not all who came west came to farm, however. Of the prairie population, 18 percent were classed as urban in 1891, with the term "urban" defined to include incorporated villages and towns as well as cities. This figure rose to 25 percent by 1901 and to 35 percent by 1911. Put differently, the rural population rose by 2.7 times between 1901 and 1911, from 316 000 to 859 000, which is the popular image of the Prairies at this time, but the urban one rose by 4.6 times, from 103 000 to nearly 500 000.[16]

The pattern of urban development was a classic hierarchical one, based on the needs of the wheat economy. The main determinant of location on an otherwise essentially flat, featureless plain was the railway. Farmers located as close to it as possible to minimize transportation costs, drawing, in turn, the entire range of distribution and service activities. First in line were the villages and small towns that sprouted at regular intervals along the line to gather the grain and to meet the most immediate needs of the settlers. More than 600 centres with population greater than 100 sprang up after 1900, with hundreds of smaller centres scattered in between.

These smaller centres, in turn, were serviced by larger rural centres such as Brandon, North Battleford, and Red Deer. They were distinguished by their larger populations and greater range of service industries. Above them came the five big prairie cities of Winnipeg, Regina, Saskatoon, Calgary, and Edmonton, spread roughly equidistantly across the Prairies. They were service centres to the service centres, so to speak. In addition, they featured some small-scale manufacturing, and were the sites of provincial capitals and universities. Rivalry among them was intense, as each used whatever means available to promote population growth and economic development.

Winnipeg was the undisputed apex of the prairie urban hierarchy in the years before 1914.[17] Its 1891 population of just over 27 000 had grown to nearly 45 000 by 1901, and to nearly 150 000 by 1911, making it, at that time, Canada's third-largest city. Geography dictated that all east–west lines be funnelled through one point in southern Manitoba, while local politics determined that this point would be Winnipeg rather than Selkirk or some other centre. It was also the first centre established, which gave it a head start on the other four big cities. In addition to its status as Manitoba's urban centre, Winnipeg was the location of much of the manufacturing and service activity attracted to the Prairies. A grain and produce exchange was established in 1887, and a wheat-futures market ten years later. Banks, brokerage houses, shippers, insurance agents, consultants, and wholesalers located in the city to serve the regional and occasionally the national markets. Manufacturing output increased fivefold between 1881 and 1901, and nearly quadrupled in the next decade. Grain-processing, meat-packing, and the production of construction materials dominated.

While Winnipeg experienced some economic diversification, there was little in the region as a whole. Agriculture dominated, although the mix varied somewhat across the Prairies. Saskatchewan quickly became the quintessential wheat producer. Other grains, animals, and animal products were relatively more important in Manitoba and Alberta. Manufacturing development was small-scale and specialized —some milling, some packing, some production of farm tools and equipment, some production of building supplies. The limited manufacturing development meant that, in a relative sense at least, services— banking, insurance, wholesale and retail trade, personal services, education, and government — were important employers outside of agriculture.

THE WHEAT BOOM AND THE NATIONAL ECONOMY

The wheat boom affected more than just the prairie economy, as the framers of the national policy had hoped and planned for decades earlier. British Columbia lumber came across the mountains for use in building the homes, businesses, and grain elevators of the Prairies. Ontario and Quebec manufacturers were able to use the protection provided by the national-policy tariffs and the facilities of the transcontinental railways to ship their manufactured products to the region. Backward linkages from the wheat economy included production of steel rails, railway rolling stock, and agricultural implements and supplies. A flour-milling industry developed at transshipment points such as Port Arthur and Montreal to process that grain not directly exported. Producers in all sectors profited from being able to supply the many consumer demands of the new population, from household items and clothing to financial and insurance needs.

While the wheat boom clearly played a significant role in Canadian economic development after 1896, the exact contribution it made is the subject of considerable uncertainty. One common view is that wheat was a perfect staple, in both an economic and a political sense. The dramatic rise in wheat exports pulled Canada out of a recession, if not a depression, and it vindicated the dreams and plans of the framers of Confederation after three decades of frustration.

The most vivid version of this account is, again, that of the Rowell–Sirois Commission. To them, settlement of the West in such short order after 1896 brought "prosperity and rapid economic expansion to the rest of Canada," and, in this atmosphere, "Canadians began to believe themselves to be a great people. Their work in creating the West gave them that sense of common achievement which marks a nation."[18] Easterbrook and Aitken echo this theme when they write that "Canada's whole economic development hinged on this wave of prairie settlement" and that "the east–west economic and political alignment of the country, the linking together of its various regions, was greatly strengthened by the growth of industry in the central provinces."[19]

The logic of this received view is pure staples theory, tempered by a healthy respect for the role of the national policy. Farmers needed machinery and equipment and other inputs to grow the grain, elevators and other terminal facilities to grade and store it, rail lines and lake freighters to transport it, mills to process some of it, and ports to ship it to markets abroad. They required food, clothing, furniture, utensils, and other consumer goods for their own consumption. They needed the services of lawyers, bankers, realtors, teachers, and clergy.

Some of these ancillary industries located near the farms, spurring the growth of the prairie villages, towns, and cities noted above. But the prairie market by itself was too small, and its resource endowments too limited, to support the larger-scale, more sophisticated operations. These items had to be imported, which is where the national policy comes in. Federal railway policy ensured that grain would move east, through Canadian handling and distribution facilities, and on Canadian rail lines, rather than south, to join American supplies. Tariffs ensured that Canadian manufactured goods could compete with imported ones, providing not just revenue to central Canadian businesses but also return traffic for the railways. In the words of Rowell–Sirois, "The resolute application of these policies directed the growing demands for capital equipment, for manufactured goods, for distributive and commercial services into Canadian channels, thus bringing expansion in other parts of the Dominion."[20]

As seen above, aggregate or extensive economic growth, as measured by population and GNP, was definitely greater after 1896 than in the preceding three decades, and it is the close association of this growth with the opening of the Prairies that suggests the Rowell–Sirois view. Correlation does not imply causality, however, so it is still legitimate to ask what role the wheat boom played in this acceleration. Two points, in particular, suggest that some modification of the more simplistic staples interpretation is needed. The first is the simple observation that there were several other developments of importance under way in other resource industries and in manufacturing and services, and they certainly had some role in the overall record.

The second qualification comes from the observation that the economic boom was well under way before wheat exports became significant. Net exports of wheat and flour were 10 million bushels in 1896. They rose to 39 million bushels in 1903 before falling back to 24 million bushels in 1904 and just 20 million bushels in 1905. Exports recovered to 47 million bushels in 1906, and rose thereafter to equal 62 million bushels in 1911 and 135 million bushels in 1914.[21]

Figure 11.4 makes it clear that investment spending, and not exports, led economic growth after 1896. Gross fixed capital formation accounted for 11.5 percent of GNP in 1896. This figure then rose more or less continuously, reaching a peak of 34.1 percent of GNP in 1912 before falling off very slightly in 1913. Total exports, on the other hand, declined from just over 19 percent of GNP in 1896 to 13 percent in 1911, and were still less than 16 percent in 1913. Much of the new capital formation undoubtedly anticipated the eventual appearance of wheat exports. With this modification, the association of Canadian prosperity after 1896 with the wheat boom remains credible. As Urquhart concludes, "The evidence of our data supports most strongly the presumption that the growth and many of the changes in the Canadian economy were a consequence of the settlement of the Prairies."[22]

Canadians clearly could not have supported investment of this magnitude out of their own savings. Foreign capital inflows equalled 2.1 percent of GNP in 1897. They rose

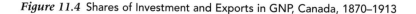

Figure 11.4 Shares of Investment and Exports in GNP, Canada, 1870–1913

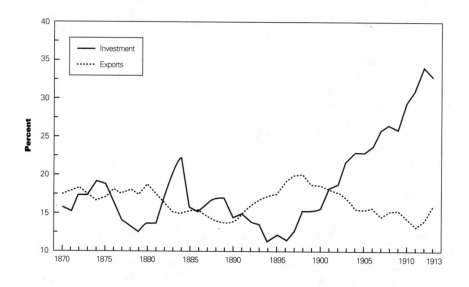

Source: Adapted from M.C. Urquhart, "New Estimates of Gross National Product, Canada, 1870–1926: Some Implications for Canadian Development," in Stanley L. Engerman and Robert E. Gallman, eds., *Long-Term Factors in American Economic Growth*, National Bureau of Economic Research, Studies in Income and Wealth, vol. 51 (Chicago: University of Chicago Press, 1986), table 2.11, pp. 33–34.

steadily thereafter, to reach a high of 17.7 percent in 1912, before falling off slightly the following year. This net financial inflow (equal to the deficit on current account) allowed Canadians to utilize more final goods and services each year than their economy was producing. The connection between financial flows and current account balances in this period was the subject of a famous study by the Canadian economist Jacob Viner many years ago, and it continues to interest theorists and historians today.[23]

The boom after 1896 was not restricted to population and GNP, it will be remembered; per capita output increased at a faster rate as well. If the wheat boom is associated with the extensive growth, it is natural to ask what its connection was to this apparent increase in average living standards. Specifically, how much better off was the average Canadian on the eve of World War I as a consequence of the wheat boom?

Chambers and Gordon took up the issue in 1966 in an article that is justly regarded as heralding the introduction of "new" economic-history techniques in Canada.[24] Their method was appropriately counterfactual. The wheat boom's contribution to living standards, by definition, is equal to real per capita income in Canada as it actually was in 1911, minus what it would have been in that same year if the development had never taken place. Knowing what actual income was in 1911 poses no conceptual problems, although the task of getting satisfactory estimates is subject to all the uncertainties of working with historical data. Obtaining estimates of its hypothetical value — that is, what real per capita income would have been in some state of the world that never actually existed— is more problematic. This is precisely the type of challenge that illustrates both the power and the limitations of the new economic history.

Chambers and Gordon use a very simple general equilibrium model to estimate what real per capita income would have been in 1911, in the absence of prairie settlement. They conclude that the wheat boom added 1.94 percentage points of the observed 23.6 percent growth in real per capita incomes between 1901 and 1911. At most, then, by their model, the wheat boom accounted for just under one-twelfth, or 8.4 percent, of the observed rise in the standard of living. More than 90 percent came from increases in the value of manufactured goods, technological changes in manufacturing, and from other exogenous factors.

These conclusions, running counter, as they did, to the popular perception of the wheat boom as the engine of Canadian economic growth in this period, not unexpectedly attracted considerable attention. An early exchange highlighted the tendency of staples theorists to think in extensive- rather than intensive-growth terms, but added little else beyond pointing out that Chambers and Gordon failed to include some tariff revenue in their estimate. Another contribution disputed their estimate of one of the important pieces of data, arguing that, even by their own model, the wheat boom contributed more to growth. Other authors questioned the very structure of the model, and provided revisions that doubled the contribution, moving it from the status of minor to major contributor to real income growth in this period.[25]

A consensus on the wheat boom and Canadian economic growth would run as follows. It definitely contributed to the extensive growth of the economy between 1896 and 1913, although probably less so than some of the more enthusiastic accounts suggest. As will be shown in the following two chapters, there was considerable strength elsewhere in the economy in this period, providing an impetus that is often overlooked by focusing on the more dramatic settlement of the Prairies. Its contribution to living standards likely lies somewhere between the estimates of Chambers and Gordon and those of their more enthusiastic revisionists.

Agriculture in Other Regions

Because of the great drama surrounding the prairie wheat boom, agricultural develop-ments elsewhere in the country in this period tend to be neglected. To do so, however, means missing an important part of the story of Canada's economic performance. As Table 11.1 indicates, wheat contributed just 14 percent of final agricultural output at the turn of the century, about the same share as each of the preceding three decades. The prairie set-tlement boom only becomes evident in the data a decade later, when wheat's share rises to 24 percent.

The shift from wheat to mixed farming after the mid-1850s is evident from Table 11.1. By 1870–71, animal products accounted for over 60 percent of final agricultural output in Canada, while wheat contributed just under 16 percent. This transformation was reversed temporarily in the middle to late 1870s, as Ontario underwent what McInnis has termed a "mini" wheat boom.[26] Low-cost cattle from the American South and Southwest began appearing after 1870, driving down prices in eastern U.S. markets and, as a result, returns to Canadian farmers. Some turned to the British market, although this trade was not very substantial until the next decade. Others apparently shifted back into wheat production; between 1875 and 1882, the value of wheat output nearly doubled and its share of final agricultural product rose to nearly 20 percent. Supply outstripped local demand, and Canada was again a net wheat exporter by 1879.

The long-term trend was re-established in the 1880s. Wheat prices fell as low-cost sup-plies from the American Midwest appeared on the world market. Wheat acreage and pro-duction fell back to pre-1871 levels, and animals and products rose in relative importance. While wheat contributed just 14 percent of total final agricultural output at the turn of the century, animal products made up 65 percent. The motives behind the shift back to mixed farming in Ontario have been the subject of some inquiry. The question is whether the reallocation was a predictable response to changing relative product prices, or whether farmers came to view wheat production as equally profitable but inherently more risky and withdrew from it in favour of more secure products. The consensus of those who have studied the issue appears to favour the former explanation.[27]

Farmers found markets for their animal products at home and abroad. Beef exports to the United Kingdom climbed in the 1880s, with eastern supplies augmented by shipments from western ranches. Butter and cheese, in particular, grew in importance. Cheese was the fastest-growing agricultural output after 1880, with the British the primary market. Two-thirds of the cheese produced in 1881 was exported, and by the mid-1890s this figure had risen to 80 percent. Some writers have referred to cheese as a new staple, although its absolute output was never really large enough to warrant such a leading role. Butter output was consistently much larger in volume terms, for example, but was produced mainly for the domestic market.

The other development of note after 1890 in central Canadian agriculture was the growth of hog production. Canada lacked a cheap food source for pigs before 1890, and production was mainly for on-farm and local use. The situation changed after 1890 as a U.S. tariff on barley drove feed-grain prices down, and as whey, a by-product of cheese production, became available as feed. Canadians also adapted their product to the leaner breed of animal preferred in the British market. Bacon transported relatively well, and Ontario produce began to appear on breakfast tables in Europe.

The agricultural changes taking place in central Canada had important social implica-tions, especially when viewed in conjunction with the simultaneous rise of factories. One of the most important of these concerned the role of women in agriculture. For as long as

Table 11.1 Final Agricultural Product and Its Composition, Canada, 1870–1871 to 1912–1913

Years	Total Product	Dairy Products	Other Animal Products	Wheat	Other Field Crops	Other Outputs
			Millions of Current Dollars			
1870–71*	139	24	60	22	17	16
1878–79 to 1882–83	172	35	57	33	26	21
1888–89 to 1892–93	186	49	65	27	23	22
1898–99 to 1902–03	235	66	88	33	22	26
1908–09 to 1912–13	444	95	154	106	51	37
			Percentage of Total			
1870–71	100.3	17.3	43.2	15.8	12.2	11.5
1878–79 to 1882–83	100.0	20.3	33.1	19.2	15.1	12.2
1888–89 to 1892–93	100.0	26.3	34.9	14.5	12.4	11.8
1898–99 to 1902–03	100.0	28.1	37.4	14.0	9.4	11.1
1908–09 to 1912–13	100.0	21.4	34.7	23.9	11.5	8.3

*CENSUS YEARS ONLY.

Source: R.M. McInnis, "Output and Productivity in Canadian Agriculture, 1870–71 to 1926–27," in Stanley L. Engerman and Robert E. Gallman, eds., *Long-Term Factors in American Economic Growth*, National Bureau of Economic Research, Studies in Income and Wealth, vol. 51 (Chicago: University of Chicago Press, 1986), table 14.2, p. 749.

farming had taken place, women had an active role in supporting the farm business. Sometimes, as in the pioneer economies, this had meant working alongside their husbands daily. In other situations, as in large-scale wheat farming, women had left the major commercial crop to the men and had concentrated, instead, on vegetable gardens, animal care, and other operations designed to increase farm income and provide food directly for the farm table.

As Quebec and Ontario farmers moved to a concentration on commercially oriented mixed farming, the place of women in the operation was inevitably altered. In a dramatic example, women were displaced from their traditional roles as milkers and producers of cheese and butter. In other areas of production, the trends were not always so dramatic but, as Marjorie Cohen has shown, the ability of women to earn direct income and to participate equally in the farm business probably declined after Confederation.[28]

This changing role of women on the farm reflected a more general trend. A high percentage of farm operations in central Canada were now efficient operations with specialized functions, albeit in a mixed-farming economy and with considerable mechanization. This tendency would continue over the next two generations, and each improvement in crop technique, each additional piece of machinery, meant that more food could be produced with less labour. This changing technology reduced the need for farm labour, whether male or female. Both the sons and daughters of farmers or farm labourers moved on, seeking opportunity on the frontier or in the rising factory and service sectors of the cities. Between 1891 and 1901, the number of males involved in agriculture declined in both Ontario and Quebec. The data on women are less readily available, but every indication is that their numbers in this sector declined as well. The drop continued at an accelerated rate in the first decade of the twentieth century, giving rise to a great deal of concern about the undermining of a way of life. From an economic point of view, however, what took place was a natural response to an increasingly efficient industry.

Clearly, part of the reason why Canada before 1896 fared better economically than was believed is that the established agricultural sector was innovative and flexible. Farmers adopted new technologies as they became available, and they adjusted their mix of outputs in response to changing market opportunities. Traditional accounts, in their insistence on linking economic growth to staple production, overlooked this facet of our economic history.

Conclusion

These developments in agriculture are an important part of the story of Canada's economic development in the years from Confederation to the outbreak of World War I. The timing of the prairie wheat boom coincides almost exactly with the pattern of aggregate economic development more generally. The success that farmers in other regions had in adjusting to new products and new technologies is surely part of the explanation for Canada's respectable economic performance before the boom that occurred after 1896.

Yet focusing on agriculture is not enough. As noted in the introduction, this sector's share of GNP declined every decade after 1870. Clearly, something else was happening in the economy at the same time. The following chapter discusses these events.

NOTES

1. Paul Voisey, "The Urbanization of the Canadian Prairies, 1871–1916," *Histoire Social/Social History* 8 (May 1975): 77–101.
2. Chester Martin, *Dominion Lands Policy*, edited and with an introduction by Lewis H. Thomas, Carleton Library No. 69 (Toronto: McClelland & Stewart, 1973), 24.
3. Martin, *Dominion Lands Policy*, 100.
4. See C. Southey, "The Staples Thesis, Common Property, and Homesteading," *Canadian Journal of Economics* 11(3) (August 1978): 547–59.
5. Frank D. Lewis, "Farm Settlement on the Canadian Prairies, 1898 to 1911," *Journal of Economic History,* Vol. 41, No. 3 (September 1981): 517–535.
6. Tony Ward, "Climate Change and the National Policy," *Canadian Journal of Economics* XXIX (Special Issue) (April 1996): S344–S348.
7. G.P. de T. Glazebrook, *A History of Transportation in Canada* (New York: Greenwook Press, 1969).
8. See P.J. George, "Rates of Return in Railway Investment and Implications for Government Subsidization of the CPR: Some Preliminary Results," *Canadian Journal of Economics* 1(4) (November 1968): 740–62.
9. J.C. Herbert Emery and Kenneth J. McKenzie (1996), "Damned If You Do, Damned If You Don't: An Option Value Approach to Evaluating the Subsidy of the CPR Mainline," *Canadian Journal of Economics* XXIX, 255–270.
10. V.C. Fowke, *The National Policy and the Wheat Economy* (Toronto: University of Toronto Press, 1957), 73.
11. See C. Knick Harley, "Transportation, the World Wheat Trade, and the Kuznets Cycle, 1850–1913," *Explorations in Economic History* 17(3) (July 1980): 218–50.
12. Alan G. Green, *Immigration and the Canadian Economy* (Toronto: Macmillan, 1976), 14.
13. Kenneth Norrie, "The National Policy and the Rate of Prairie Settlement: A Review," *Journal of Canadian Studies* 14(3) (Fall 1979): 63–76. For a more recent review see Tony Ward, "The Origins of the Canadian Wheat Boom, 1880–1910," *Canadian Journal of Economics* 27(4) (November 1994): 865–83.

14. Tony Ward, "Climate Change and the National Policy," *Canadian Journal of Economics* XXIX (Special Issue) (April 1996): S344–S348.
15. Fowke, *The National Policy*, 75.
16. Paul Voisey, "The Urbanization of the Canadian Prairies, 1871–1916," *Histoire Sociale/Social History* 8 (May 1975): 77–101.
17. Alan F. Artibise, "An Urban Economy: Patterns of Economic Change in Winnipeg, 1879–1971," *Prairie Forum* 1(2) (November 1976): 163–88.
18. Royal Commission on Dominion–Provincial Relations, *Report*, Book 1: *Canada, 1867–1939* (Ottawa: King's Printer, 1940), 68, 79.
19. W.T. Easterbrook and H.G.J. Aitken, *Canadian Economic History* (Toronto: Macmillan, 1965), 484, 485.
20. Royal Commission on Dominion–Provincial Relations, *Report*, 68.
21. Calculated from M.C. Urquhart and K.A.H. Buckley, eds., *Historical Statistics of Canada* (Toronto: Macmillan, 1965), 363–64.
22. M.C. Urquhart, "New Estimates of Gross National Product, Canada, 1870–1926: Some Implications for Canadian Development," in Stanley L. Engerman and Robert E. Gallman, eds., *Long-Term Factors in American Economic Growth*, Vol. 51 (Chicago and London: University of Chicago Press, 1986), 64.
23. See Trevor J.O. Dick and John E. Floyd, *Canada and the Gold Standard: Balance of Payments Adjustment, 1870–1913* (Cambridge: Cambridge University Press, 1992); and Georg Rich, *The Cross of Gold: Money and the Canadian Business Cycle, 1867–1913* (Ottawa: Carleton University Press, 1988).
24. E.J. Chambers and Donald F. Gordon, "Primary Products and Economic Growth: An Empirical Measurement," *Journal of Political Economy* 74 (August 1966): 315–22.
25. Richard Pomfret provides an intelligible review of this literature in *The Economic Development of Canada* (Toronto: Methuen, 1981), "Appendix: The Wheat Boom's Contribution to Economic Growth," 157–64.
26. Marvin McInnis, "The Changing Structure of Canadian Agriculture, 1867–1897," *Journal of Economic History* 42(1) (March 1982): 195. Much of the discussion here is based on McInnis's research.
27. See William L. Marr, "The Wheat Economy in Reverse: Ontario's Wheat Production 1887–1917," *Canadian Journal of Economics* 14(1) (February 1981): 133–45; and Robert E. Ankli and Wendy Millar, "Ontario Agriculture in Transition: The Shift from Wheat to Cheese," *Journal of Economic History* 42(1) (March 1982): 207–15.
28. Marjorie G. Cohen, *Women's Work, Markets, and Economic Development in Nineteenth-Century Ontario* (Toronto: University of Toronto Press, 1988).

FURTHER READING

Bertram, G.W. "The Relevance of the Wheat Boom in Canadian Economic Growth. "*Canadian Journal of Economics* (November 1973): 546–66.
Chambers, E.J., and Donald F. Gordon. "Primary Products and Economic Growth: An Empirical Measurement." *Journal of Political Economy* 74 (August 1966): 315–22.
Cohen, Marjorie G. *Women's Work, Markets, and Economic Development in Nineteenth-Century Ontario.* Toronto: University of Toronto Press, 1988.
Drummond, Ian M. *Progress Without Planning: The Economic History of Ontario.* Toronto: University of Toronto Press, 1987. Chapter 3, "Agriculture, 1867–1941," 29–51.
McInnis, Marvin. "The Changing Structure of Canadian Agriculture, 1867–1897." *Journal of Economic History* 42(1) (March 1982): 191–98.
Norrie, Kenneth. "The National Policy and the Rate of Prairie Settlement: A Review. "*Journal of Canadian Studies* 14(3) (Fall 1979): 63–76.
Ward, Tony. "Origins of the Canadian Wheat Boom, 1880–1910." *Canadian Journal of Economics* 27(4) (November 1994): 865–83.

Chapter Twelve

Resources and Manufacturing

FOR ALL ITS DRAMA, the prairie wheat boom was essentially a product of the technology of the first industrial revolution: railways, steamships, steel ploughs, and the like. Concurrent with the wheat boom, however, was another set of influences that was very much part of a new wave of technological advances. The second industrial revolution, described in the introduction to this part, had a profound effect on Canada. It meant the end of some traditional activities, forced others to adjust and adapt in order to survive, and brought entirely new industries into being. These economic changes, in turn, brought about major adjustments in Canadian social and political life.

General Determinants of Manufacturing Growth

When considering the determinants of manufacturing growth, it is useful to distinguish between two broad types of activities. The first involves the further processing of agricultural and natural-resource products. Sawmilling and planing, pulp and paper production, flour milling, cheese production, and smelting and refining are examples of this type of activity. These are often referred to as primary manufacturing activities,[1] since the dividing line between growth or extraction and further processing is often unclear. Sometimes, as in cheese and butter production or sawmilling, both activities are carried out by the same individual or firm.

Most of these activities have little in common beyond a tie to a natural-resource base. On the demand side, some turn out final products (cheese), while some produce intermediate goods for further processing (pulpwood, metal refining). Some produce mainly for the local market, although most export a substantial portion of their output. On the supply side, some (cheese making) employ very simple technology, while others (pulp and paper production, smelting and refining) are capital intensive and relatively complex. In general, Canada's success in primary-manufacturing activities is easily explained by its rich natural-resource endowment, sometimes coupled with access to cheap power.

The other broad type of manufacturing activity features the production of more finished goods, such as iron and steel, leather, transportation equipment, clothing, textiles, printing and publishing, chemicals, tobacco, miscellaneous industries, rubber, chemicals, and electrical products. It is sometimes referred to as secondary manufacturing. Some food and beverage production, such as breweries and distilleries, are included in secondary manufacturing as well. Some of these industries turn out products intended for household consumption, in which case demand depends on population, income, and the prices of domestic goods relative to those of imports. In other cases, output is intended for use by other firms in the economy, so demand generally depends on the rate of business investment and expansion. Occasionally, output is exported, in which case demand depends on Canada's international competitiveness.

The determinants of the domestic supply of secondary manufacturing products are less obvious. In earlier decades, as we have seen, local firms enjoyed the benefits of natural protection due to high transport costs. This advantage was rapidly disappearing by Confederation, however. Success thereafter depended on how successful Canadian-based firms were at competing with manufactured imports from the United Kingdom and the United States, in particular. In general, the ability of domestic firms to compete depended on the terms of access to intermediate inputs, the supply of capital, the skills and prices of labour services, the presence of entrepreneurial talents, the transport costs incurred in assembling inputs and distributing outputs, the size of the domestic market relative to that required for minimum economies of scale, and foreign and domestic policy initiatives.

One such policy instrument in this period, in Canada as elsewhere, was tariffs and excise duties. Canada did not begin life as a highly protectionist nation; the new Dominion adopted the 1866 tariff schedule of the Province of Canada. These rates were raised, for revenue purposes, in 1870, but the hike was rescinded the next year. The basic duty was raised by 2.5 percentage points in 1874, bringing the average tariff to about 20 percent. Rates then remained virtually unaltered for the next four years.

Canada retained this relatively liberal policy for the first years of Confederation for a number of reasons. The Maritime provinces opposed tariffs, and duties were kept low and even lowered in some cases to placate them. There was also considerable philosophical support for freer trade in Canada. Also, the Dominion was doing quite well on the trade front, given reconstruction and post-Civil War inflation in the United States, so pressure for protection was not strong. Finally, often forgotten is the fact that Canadians never really gave up on the idea of securing a new reciprocity arrangement with the United States and hoped to signal this interest by keeping existing rates down.

Sentiment toward tariffs changed over the 1870s, however. In part, Canada followed the rising tide of protectionism worldwide, and in part the motivation was more local. Demand for manufactured goods grew more slowly in the 1870s than it had in the first few post-Confederation years, and certainly more slowly than had been anticipated. Local firms faced increasing competition as technological change and declining transport costs made imports cheaper. Manufacturing interests began to organize to lobby for increased protection, and found politicians open to their demands. Established interests in the Maritimes and the West opposed tariffs, but the political influence of the former was waning and that of the latter was, so far, negligible. The opposition Conservatives recognized a winning electoral strategy and based their successful 1878 campaign on a promise to introduce a national policy of wide-ranging protectionism.

The tariff increases put in place by the Macdonald government in 1879 were avowedly protectionist. The general rate was raised from 17.5 percent to 20 percent. Duties were restored on a range of agricultural products, such as oats, wheat, and barley, presumably to give farmers the impression that protection was intended for them as well. Coal and coke, iron and steel, machinery, hardware, and textiles were given special protection, either through higher rates or the imposition of specific duties (a flat rate per unit of the product imported) as opposed to ad valorem duties (a percentage of the landed price of the import). The apogee of protectionism came later, in 1887, after duties were raised even further, especially on iron and steel, farm machinery, and textiles.

218

Even in the midst of imposing these new and higher duties, the government did not give up hopes of securing some type of reciprocal free-trade arrangement with the United States. The 1879 schedule, for example, listed certain articles that would be admitted duty-free from the United States, should they reciprocate. Efforts to negotiate an arrangement continued throughout the 1880s and into the 1890s, but the two countries were never able to draw up a mutually agreeable list of commodities to be covered. Also, in a flash-back to the 1840s and 1850s, American access to the Atlantic fisheries became part of the package, adding yet another complication.

The election of a Liberal government headed by Wilfrid Laurier in 1896 did not spell the end of industrial protectionism, whatever campaign rhetoric might have led voters to believe. Some changes were made on individual items in 1897, but the overall level of protection was altered very little. O.J. McDiarmid noted in his classic study of Canadian commercial policy[2] that the average duty was 23 percent in 1879; 32 percent in 1891; 30 percent in 1896 on the eve of the Liberals' election; and still 27 percent in 1903, after seven years of their administration. In 1879, 70 percent of items were free of duty, whereas only 61 percent were in 1896, and 60 percent in 1903. The Liberals extended the use of bounties and of drawbacks on duty paid on imported components and, in 1904, introduced what has been called the first anti-dumping clause in tariff history.[3]

One of the more notable moves of the Laurier government was the reestablishment of a broad British preferential system in 1897, after nearly a half-century absence. Effective in 1898, products from Britain and British colonies faced duties 25 percent lower than those on imports from all other nations. In 1900, the preference was raised to one-third. No reciprocal advantage was secured, however, much to the chagrin of some Canadian exporters. A third "column" was added to the tariff structure in 1907 as a basis for negotiating special arrangements with other countries, but it remained effectively dormant until 1935.

The final stage in the development of Canadian commercial policy prior to World War I began in 1910, when the idea of a reciprocal trading arrangement with the United States was broached yet again. This time, however, negotiators were able to draw up a list of items and duties satisfactory to both countries. Most natural products were to trade freely between the two countries. Duties on processed agricultural products and farm machinery were lowered, and there were special provisions to cover a range of other products. The agreement passed both the House and the Senate in the United States after short but lively debate. Opposition to it was much greater in Canada, however. In the September 1911 election, the Liberals were defeated soundly by the Conservatives, who appealed to protectionist interests and imperial sentiment under the slogan "No truck nor trade with the Yankees."

Wilfrid Laurier's defeat in 1911 has been interpreted as Canada's rejection of reciprocity in favour of a commitment to protectionism and an assertion of Canadian nationalism and loyalty to her British connections. With the rejection of reciprocity a Canada–U.S. preferential trade agreement left the agenda for over twenty years. In one of those ironies that make history so interesting, 78 years after campaigning against reciprocity, a Progressive Conservative government introduced a comprehensive free-trade agreement with the United States over the strenuous objections of a Liberal Opposition.

Did Canada reject reciprocity in 1911? Eugene Beaulieu and Herb Emery find that other than pork packers, Canadians were supportive or indifferent to reciprocity in 1911 which suggests that Laurier's defeat in 1911 was not based on a rejection of open trade relations with the United States.[4] This result supports Judith MacDonald, Anthony O'Brien, and Colleen Callahan's contention that Canada was not headed in a protectionist direction prior to America's imposition of the Smoot-Hawley Tariff in 1930.[5]

Overview of Manufacturing Development

As noted earlier (refer to Figure P4.3), the manufacturing sector's share of gross national product remained nearly constant in the period under review. Manufacturing accounted for 22.5 percent of GDP in 1870, virtually identical to its share 40 years later. These aggregate numbers obscure some important shifts within the sector, however. The period 1867–1913 witnessed the decline of some long-standing manufacturing activities, change and adaptation in several others, and the emergence of a number of new industries.

Figure 12.1 shows the relative shares of the main manufacturing activities in 1870. A clear hierarchy of activities is apparent. Wood products (mainly planks and boards) are at the top, accounting for over one-fifth of total manufacturing value added. Next in the hierarchy is a group of three activities — iron and steel products (agricultural implements, foundry and machine-shop products, boilers and engines, cutting and edging tools, pumps and windmills, sewing machines, wire); leather products (footwear and harness); and foods and beverages (flour and grist mills; butter, cheese, and meat products; breweries and distilleries) — each contributing around 15 percent of value added.

Transportation equipment (ships, carriages, railroad equipment) and clothing make up a third tier, with their shares of 7 percent being one-half the level of those activities in the second tier and one-third that of wood products. A fourth tier comprises textiles (mainly cotton and woollen goods), non-metallic minerals (clay and stone products), and printing and publishing, with about 3 percent each. The remaining activities, grouped at the bottom, account for 2 percent or less.

This mix of manufacturing activity changed notably over the next four decades. Figure 12.2 shows the share of total value added in manufacturing in 1900 relative to that in 1870 for each manufacturing category, with the sectors presented in descending order of their

Figure 12.1 Percentage Distribution of GDP, Manufacturing, Canada, 1870

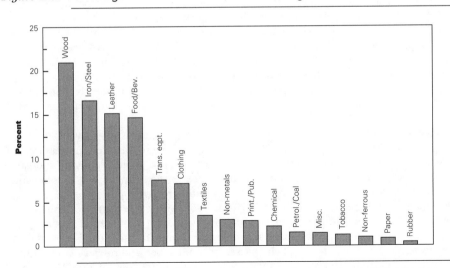

Source: Adapted from M.C. Urquhart, "New Estimates of Gross National Product, Canada, 1870–1926: Some Implications for Canadian Development," in Stanley L. Engerman and Robert E. Gallman, eds., *Long-Term Factors in American Economic Growth*, National Bureau of Economic Research, Studies in Income and Wealth, vol. 51 (Chicago: University of Chicago Press, 1986), table 2.18, p. 60.

Figure 12.2 Share of GDP, Manufacturing, Canada, 1900 Relative to 1870

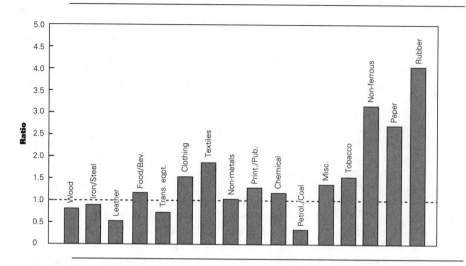

Source: Calculated from M.C. Urquhart, "New Estimates of Gross National Product, Canada, 1870–1926: Some Implications for Canadian Development," in Stanley L. Engerman and Robert E. Gallman, eds., *Long-Term Factors in American Economic Growth*, National Bureau of Economic Research, Studies in Income and Wealth, vol. 51 (Chicago: University of Chicago Press, 1986), table 2.18, p. 60.

share of manufacturing GDP in 1870. A number above 1.0 in this graph means that final product in that sector grew at a faster rate than manufacturing output as a whole over the decade, while a number below 1.0 shows the opposite situation. Figure 12.3 shows the same information for 1910 compared with 1900. By separating the information in this manner we can see whether manufacturing developed differently in the boom years compared with the period of relatively slow growth to 1896.

Figure 12.2 shows that eleven manufacturing industries grew at a rate above that for the sector as a whole in this period, while five grew more slowly. What is particularly striking is the relatively slow growth rates of the largest industries. The dominant manufacturing activity in 1870, wood products, grew at just 80 percent of the sectoral average. Two of the three second-tier activities identified in Figure 12.1 (iron and steel and leather products), and one of the two third-tier activities (transportation equipment) grew more slowly.

With the exception of food and beverages and clothing, the fastest-growing manufacturing activities in the period 1870–1900 were ones that were relatively unimportant in 1870. Yet, aside from being relatively small in 1870, these rapidly growing industries cannot be classified in any easy manner. Some belong to the resource sector, some could benefit from tariff protection, and others could not. Tariff protection prompted the growth of several manufacturing activities between 1870 and 1900. Meatpackers and clothing and textile manufacturers were amongst the pro-tariff constituencies at the time the national policy tariffs were introduced. In other cases, technological change in production processes and materials resulted in rapid growth of chemicals, pulp and paper, and rubber manufacturing.

Figure 12.3 illustrates the nature of industrial growth in the boom period. Nine manufacturing industries grew faster than the manufacturing sector as a whole, seven grew less rapidly, and one (petroleum and coal products) just held its share. The industries that were

Figure 12.3 Share of GDP, Manufacturing, Canada, 1910 Relative to 1900

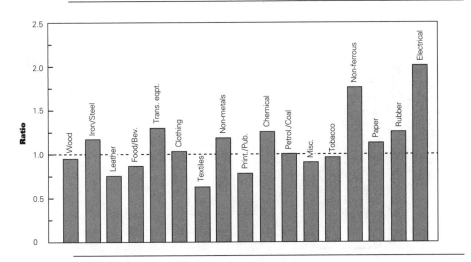

Source: Calculated from M.C. Urquhart, "New Estimates of Gross National Product, Canada, 1870–1926: Some Implications for Canadian Development," in Stanley L. Engerman and Robert E. Gallman, eds., *Long-Term Factors in American Economic Growth*, National Bureau of Economic Research, Studies in Income and Wealth, vol. 51 (Chicago: University of Chicago Press, 1986), table 2.18, p. 60.

largest in 1870 continued to lose ground relatively. Wood products grew at just 94 percent of the sectoral average, food and beverages at 86 percent, and leather products at just 75 percent. The exceptions to this pattern were iron and steel products from the second tier, and both third-tier activities, clothing and transportation equipment.

By 1910, as a consequence of these changes, the hierarchy of manufacturing activity had flattened out considerably from what it had been in 1870 (see Figure 12.1). As Figure 12.4 illustrates, a group of four industries shared top spot in terms of share of manufacturing GDP in 1910: iron and steel products, wood products, food and beverages, and clothing. The drop in percentage points of share to the next-most-important category (transportation equipment) is quite marked, but thereafter the rankings fall off more or less continuously.

Case Studies

At this point, it is most useful to look at a number of case studies of Canadian manufacturing development in this period. We begin with a long-standing activity that did not make the transition to the new economic environment, then look at some examples of ones that did manage to adapt, and conclude with some examples of entirely new industries.

SHIPBUILDING

Canada's wooden shipbuilding industry goes back to at least the eighteenth century, although the golden age began only after the Napoleonic Wars. The historic peak of the Maritime shipbuilding industry was reached in 1864, when 586 vessels, totalling nearly

222

Figure 12.4 Percentage Distribution of GDP, Manufacturing, Canada 1910

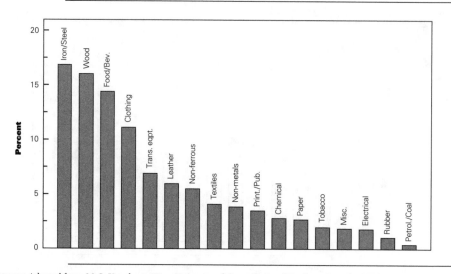

Source: Adapted from M.C. Urquhart, "New Estimates of Gross National Product, Canada, 1870–1926: Some Implications for Canadian Development," in Stanley L. Engerman and Robert E. Gallman, eds., *Long-Term Factors in American Economic Growth*, National Bureau of Economic Research, Studies in Income and Wealth, vol. 51 (Chicago: University of Chicago Press, 1986), table 2.18, p. 60.

211 tons (192 t), were built. The number of ships constructed fluctuated between 282 and 393 between 1870 and 1878, but fell to 203 in 1880. By 1890 this figure had declined to 169, and by 1896 only 96 ships, totalling 6 tons (5.5 t) were built.[6] The golden age of Maritime wooden shipbuilding was over, a casualty of the shift to steam and iron ships elsewhere in the world that had been underway for decades.

This fall in shipbuilding was accompanied in the 1860s and 1870s by a surge in shipowning. Early accounts of this latter trend pictured it as something forced on the region's shipbuilders by the decline in demand in Britain for wooden ships. Left with the vessels, shipbuilders were forced to operate them to cut losses. This adherence to a technology and an industry that was so obviously in decline was often cited as evidence of the economic difficulties of the region.

A more recent account, however, argues that the surge in registrations was a continuation of a trend that had begun much earlier and that parallels a similar trend in the United Kingdom. Investment in shipping was not an unpropitious gamble but rather a "finely judged attempt to seize expanding opportunities, and then to maintain rates of return as demand for sailing ship services fell."[7] It was a rational act, since rates of return to shipping at that time were likely at least equal to those available in other sectors. Owners went to great lengths to improve the productivity and performance of their vessels to maintain profits. Thus, it was a noble and enterprising group that faced the end when it came, and not the myopic builders-cum-inadvertent-owners of "floating coffins" that is sometimes supposed.

The mystery of the failure of Maritime shipbuilding to adjust to new technologies is not solved, but one prime candidate is apparently banished. If shipbuilders and shipowners were as calculating and entrepreneurial as this research indicates, the fault cannot have been with lack of local expertise in the industry. Individuals and firms capable of maintaining a profitable living out of a declining wooden-ship industry certainly must have been capable of operating in the new environment, given a fair chance.

FORESTRY PRODUCTS

223

The wood products industry was in a state of flux at Confederation. Exports of squared timber were still growing absolutely but were falling in relative importance to those of more processed products — primarily deals, planks, and boards — which represented 70 percent of exports in 1867. Markets were changing as well, largely but not entirely reflecting the shift in the composition of output. Exports to Great Britain were substantially higher in absolute terms in 1867 than they had been in 1850; yet in the latter year they represented about 50 percent of total exports, while in the former they had been more than 80 percent.

These trends continued in the immediate post-Confederation period.[8] Exports of forest products were exceptionally strong in the first half-dozen years after. Total shipments in 1873 were up nearly 80 percent over what they had been six years earlier, with the U.S. market being particularly strong. Then came the international slowdown in 1873. Wood exports were especially hard hit by the downturn, most notably those going to the United States. The British market remained reasonably firm, falling only in the late 1870s, and then only for a brief time. The U.S. market collapsed, however. Exports fell from $12.5 million in 1873 to $4.3 million in 1879, when recovery began. For four years, 1875–79, Britain took between 65 and 73 percent of total exports, compared with the 47 percent it had taken in 1873. By 1881, Canadian wood exports had regained their very high levels

West Head Mills, Saint John, N.B. Although New Brunswick's early timber trade was predominantly in squared timber, eventually lumber, the product of sawmills, increased in importance. It included deals, planks, and boards, and was mainly pine and spruce.

New Brunswick Museum, Saint John, N.B., Canada.

of the early 1870s, as recovery proceeded in both major markets. Thereafter, though, the trend was flat until 1897.

The gradual loss of the British market is easiest to explain. There was a general decline of demand for wood products in Britain as construction slowed and as shipbuilding in wood wound down. What demand remained shifted increasingly to Baltic suppliers. The sluggishness of the U.S. market is more problematic. McInnis found no obvious explanation in his reconstruction of the data for the period. Dwindling supplies do not appear to have been the problem that some earlier accounts have suggested, and McInnis posited that growing domestic demand may have been an important factor.[9] Urbanization and industrial growth in Canada took an increasing share of the output.

The trend toward processing timber in Canada before export began to be reversed in the 1890s. The explanation for the reversal was partly geographical and partly political. The gradual shift of the trade to the upper Great Lakes region made it cheap to cut logs in Canada and float them across the lakes to sawmills in the United States. Exports of logs, which had averaged around $250 000 in the early 1880s, jumped tenfold by 1895. The political component came in the form of a graduated U.S. tariff. Logs entered freely, while processed lumber products faced duties. The federal government had attempted, in the 1880s, to encourage processing in Canada by imposing export duties on unprocessed logs, but these had been removed in 1890 in exchange for a lowering of the U.S. tariff on sawn lumber. American policy became more protectionist in 1897, when the Dingley Tariff imposed a duty on sawn lumber but left the import on unprocessed logs free. The duty was constructed in such a way as to rise automatically if Canada reinstituted the export tax on logs.

With the export tax rendered useless as a countermeasure, Canadian lumber companies turned their attention to the provincial governments. There was a precedent: British Columbia had instituted an embargo on the export of unprocessed logs from crown lands in 1891. Ontario now adopted a similar measure. Effective April 30, 1898, all pine timber from crown land had to be made into sawn lumber in Ontario. The restriction to timber from crown lands skirted the constitutional issue nicely, since the policy came under the power of the province to manage its natural resources.

On the surface, at least, the export embargo appeared to be effective. The export of logs fell off, and that of lumber continued to grow — $33 million in lumber exports were recorded in 1913, compared with $25 million in 1897.[10] It is not clear, however, how much of the success was attributable to the policy per se and how much was simply the result of the natural advantage Canada had in sawmilling. Plentiful stands of cheap timber, together with inexpensive hydro-electric power, gave the industry a base in Canada that could not be matched in the United States. It has often been remarked that provincial governments found the political will to implement these measures and to make them stick in the face of lobbying efforts only because economics was on their side.

The contribution to economic growth of Canada's vast forest reserves was renewed in the new century with the development of a new set of uses for wood. Until well into the nineteenth century, paper production, in Canada as elsewhere, was based on inputs of rags, grasses, and straw. Operations were small and oriented to the local market, and the product was relatively expensive. Technology was to change all that. The important breakthrough was the isolation of the cellulose component of wood and its substitution for rags and grasses. There were two main stages to this operation. Wood was first either ground or treated with chemicals to produce wood pulp. The pulp was then further processed into paper of various kinds. Ground pulpwood, being relatively coarse, was ideal for further working into newsprint, while chemical pulps were required for the production of the finer grades of paper.

Canada possessed vast tracts of spruce that were ideal for processing into wood pulp. This endowment was reinforced by the fact that pulp production, mechanical or chemical, along with some of the further processing, required vast amounts of power. The simultaneous development of the hydro-electric capacity of central Canada provided this very advantage. North American demand was growing rapidly as well, for newsprint in particular. U.S. newspaper circulation rose by more than 80 percent between 1870 and 1909, as a result of growing populations and relatively falling prices.

Firms responded to the possibilities early on.[11] Canada's first groundwood pulp mill opened in Valleyfield, Quebec, in 1866. The first mill to use hydro-electric power appeared in Georgetown, Ontario, in 1888, beginning the close association of those industries that continues today. The Canadian market was too small to absorb much output, so producers naturally turned to the much larger American one. At first, American producers had adequate supplies of pulpwood close to the major consuming centres and imports were minuscule. As supplies were used up, wood prices rose, and Canadian resources became competitive. As producers turned to this market, they found a familiar obstacle — a cascading system of duties that allowed pulpwood to enter free but put increasing levies on wood pulp, newsprint, and processed paper. As it had with the timber provisions, the American tariff increased in the presence of a Canadian export tax on pulpwood.

Canada's cost advantage in wood-pulp production was apparent, given cheap hydro power and vast spruce forests, so lobbying efforts to overturn the American barriers were successful. The main actors, again, were the provincial governments. Ontario passed an order-in-council in 1900, this time without even much fanfare, extending the "manufacturing condition" to pulpwood. Henceforth, all spruce cordwood taken from crown lands had to be manufactured into mechanical or chemical pulp in Canada. The measure was not immediately effective, because U.S. companies could still draw on their own resources and because Quebec refused to follow suit. Eventually, however, Quebec followed Ontario's lead (in 1909), and the two provinces' superior resource endowments prevailed.

As Burley noted,[12] data for the early years of the pulp industry are scattered and unreliable. There were 2.1 million cords of pulpwood cut in Canada in 1913, half of which was exported. This figure declines constantly thereafter, as none of the product is processed domestically before export. Wood-pulp output, the next stage of the process, stood at 363 000 tons (330 000 t) in 1908, the earliest year for which data are available, and had grown to 855 000 tons (777 000 t) in 1913. One-half to two-thirds of production was exported in these years.

With wood pulp attended to, Canadian attention turned to shifting the newsprint industry north of the border as well. Here, the support of an important ally was key. Newsprint costs in the United States were rising steadily, making access to cheaper Canadian supplies ever more attractive to large U.S. newspapers. Their lobbying efforts were successful, representing one of the few instances in which an interest group was able to have tariffs removed. President William Howard Taft lowered the rates on newsprint in 1911, and, in the Underwood schedule of 1913, those on mechanical pulp and newsprint were removed entirely. The stage was set for the development of a major Canadian industry, one that remains important today.

IRON AND STEEL

The manufacturing category labelled iron and steel products encompasses a wide variety of activities. Output in 1870 was mainly of secondary products, using scrap or imported iron as inputs. Much of the product was intended as inputs into other sectors (agricultural implements, machinery, structural steel, hardware and tools, wire), so demand would be correlated with investment activity. Not surprisingly, this sector grew most rapidly in the 1880s and in the decade 1900–10, when investment spending was rising as a share of GNP, and declined relatively in the other two decades.

There was some primary iron production in Canada in this period as well. Charcoal iron production predated Confederation.[13] The activity persisted in the face of competition from coke iron because of the abundance of cheap wood and the fact that its properties were such that producers of railway vehicles and agricultural implements, both of particular importance in Canada, were willing to pay a premium price for it. Charcoal iron output declined more or less continuously through the 1870s and 1880s, with the exception of a couple of output spikes in 1882 and 1886. Inwood attributes this trend to the fact that production costs in charcoal iron did not fall fast enough to allow the product to compete with coke iron and steel, both of which were improving in quality and falling in price.

Surprisingly, charcoal iron production rebounded, beginning in the early 1890s. Output more than trebled in the two years after 1891 and doubled again by 1899. The peak production year was 1913. Inwood explained this development as a combination of two factors. New techniques in smelting and in the preparation of charcoal meant lower production costs. These techniques were available in the United States earlier, but were only adopted in Canada after 1890, when the domestic market was large enough to accommodate production of the requisite scale.

The more significant developments in iron and steel production, however, came with the new technologies. Nova Scotia had ample deposits of coal and reasonably accessible supplies of iron ore, so it was in that province, not unexpectedly, that this branch of the primary iron-and-steel industry was first established. Beginning in the 1870s as an operation to manufacture iron products from scrap material, Nova Scotia Steel cast Canada's first steel ingots at Trenton in 1883. Shortages of scrap iron and the encouragement given by the "iron tariff" of 1887 led to the establishment of blast furnaces at Ferrona and Londonderry. The capital for these early ventures came from local merchant families, although control of the Londonderry ironworks soon passed to Montreal. Expansion continued, as Nova Scotia Steel acquired ore deposits on Bell Island, Newfoundland, and collieries on Cape Breton and erected a new steel plant in Sydney Mines. It was, by then, a fully integrated operation, owning blast and open-hearth furnaces, rolling mills, forges, foundries, and machine shops.

A second venture in Nova Scotia was larger yet. Boston and Montreal investors formed the Dominion Coal Company in 1893 to refinance several Cape Breton collieries. In 1899, the Dominion Iron and Steel Company erected a steel works at Sydney, and soon the company was the largest in Canada. Its most important product, by far, was steel rails, and its own rail plant took most of the output.

Iron and steel production in central Canada followed shortly, helped by the fact that technological changes had gradually reduced the amount of raw-material inputs needed per unit of output, freeing the sector from the need to remain at resource sites and allowing it to draw closer to markets. Quebec had numerous secondary operations but no significant primary production. A group of Hamilton capitalists founded the Hamilton Blast Furnace Company in 1895, the first modern iron-making plant in Ontario. Ore was shipped in from Minnesota and coal from Pennsylvania via Lake Erie and the Welland Canal. In 1899, the company merged with Ontario Rolling Mills to form the Hamilton

Steel and Iron Company. The first steel output was in 1900. Another blast furnace was added in 1907. In 1910, the Steel Company of Canada, eventually the nation's premier steel-maker, was formed when the primary iron-and-steel plant at Hamilton was merged with most of the rolling and finishing companies in Ontario and Quebec.

The final operation came in 1901, at Sault Ste Marie, under the initiative of the American promoter Francis Hector Clergue. Algoma Steel was formed at the turn of the century as one of a number of ambitious projects by Clergue in the Sault Ste Marie region. The location was chosen because it was near the Helen Mines ore deposits of Northern Ontario and advantageously situated to supply western Canada's demand for steel rails. The project was encouraged by a contract from the Laurier government for steel rails, the first given to a Canadian firm. Production began in 1902, and the first rails were rolled, but work on the iron furnaces lagged behind. The company collapsed in 1903, mainly because of mismanagement, but was resuscitated that same year as the Lake Superior Corporation. Coal was imported from West Virginia and, for a time, ore from Minnesota. Problems were gradually overcome, and the company prospered, as the demand for steel rails in the West grew.

Thus by early in the twentieth century, after considerable consolidation, the Canadian steel industry was marked by three features. First, it was now dominated by four firms (Algoma, Stelco, Scotia Steel, and Dosco). Second, it was concentrated in Ontario and Nova Scotia. Third, it was highly unstable. Financial pressures would lead, by 1920, to the merger of the two Nova Scotia firms into Besco and threaten one or other of the companies with bankruptcy at various points in their history.[14]

AGRICULTURAL IMPLEMENTS

The agricultural-implement industry is another interesting case study of Canadian industrialization.[15] Prior to Confederation, and for a considerable time thereafter, the sector was characterized by numerous small-scale operations, producing a wide variety of tools and implements for local farmers. The more enterprising members of the group, notably the Massey Company and the Harris Company, made regular trips to the United States, often returning with the rights to manufacture the new machines in Canada.

The industry began to change in the 1880s. The tariff on agricultural implements was raised from 17 to 25 percent in 1879, and to 35 percent in 1883, in an apparent attempt to promote a Canadian industry. Output did increase significantly in the ensuing decades, and production became more concentrated. There were 221 firms in 1891, producing $7.5 million. In 1901, 114 firms produced $9.6 million, and 88 firms produced $20.7 million in 1910. Employment nearly doubled over the period, and the value of capital increased more than fivefold. The main concentration took place in Ontario. That province hosted only 55 of the total of 88 Canadian plants in 1906, but together they produced 92 percent of the value of output.

The domestic market soon became constraining. Both Massey and Harris began to sell farm equipment overseas in the late 1880s, giving Canada one of its few secondary-manufactured-goods exports of the time. The two first merged in 1891 to form the Massey-Harris Company and, in the same year, absorbed the newly merged Patterson-Wisner complex. In 1910, Massey-Harris opened a plant in the United States, giving Canada one of its early multinational companies. The American giant International Harvester established a subsidiary in Canada in 1902. International Harvester, together with Massey-Harris and the smaller Canadian company Cockshutt, dominated the Canadian scene for decades.

228

Wire mill of the Dominion Iron and Steel Company, Sydney, N.S. The steel works at Sydney were built by the Dominion Iron and Steel Company in 1899; soon, the company was the largest in Canada. Its most important product, by far, was steel rails, with its own rail plant taking the bulk of the output.

National Archives of Canada/PA-17696.

MINERALS AND REFINING

Interest in Canada's mineral wealth dates back to 1604, when an engineer accompanying Champlain reported the presence of iron, silver, and copper at St. Mary's Bay in Nova Scotia.[16] For nearly three centuries thereafter, though, the only deposits to attract much attention were those containing gold and silver, coal seams, iron ore, fuel peat, and construction materials such as gypsum and cement. Gold and silver were valuable as precious metals and could be uncovered and extracted with relatively simple techniques. Coal was used as a fuel for heating purposes, and as an input, along with iron ore, in the production of iron and products. Structural materials were relatively ubiquitous, and again could be extracted and processed simply. Other materials were known to exist, but either there was no significant demand for them or they could not be extracted with the techniques of the time.

This situation changed after the mid-1880s. Figure 12.5 shows the annual value of total mineral output from 1886, when consistent statistics become available, to the eve of World War I. Figure 12.6 shows the relative importance of the broad categories of minerals in the same period. Total output doubled between 1886 and 1895, from $10 million to $20 million, trebled again in the next five years, and then doubled again by 1913. During the boom years after 1897 it was minerals, especially in British Columbia, and not agriculture

Figure 12.5 Value of Total Mineral Output, Canada, 1886–1913

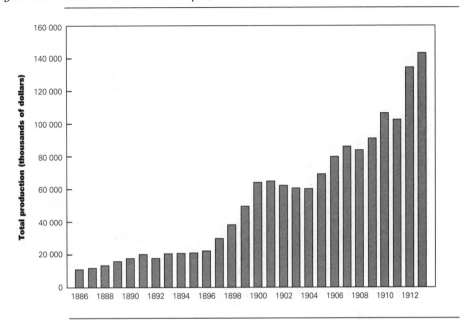

Source: Canada, Dominion Bureau of Statistics, *Canadian Mineral Statistics, 1886–1956*, cat. no. 26-501 (Ottawa: Dominion Bureau of Statistics, 1957), p. 48. Reproduced by authority of the Minister of Industry, 1995.

or manufacturing, that attracted the bulk of British investment in Canada. Structural materials consistently accounted for about one-fifth of the total value of output throughout these years. This category includes such items as clay products, cement, sand and gravel, and sandstone. The economics of these cases is relatively uncomplicated. Deposits are located relatively ubiquitously across the country, and are exploited for the local market in step with construction activity. Thus, while structural materials were obviously important as a source of local income and employment, there is little national drama to be found in the figures.

Non-metallic minerals were the least-important category in 1886, at 12.3 percent of the total output, and declined to about 5 percent of the total by the outbreak of World War I. Absolute value of output rose, nevertheless, from $1.3 million to $7.4 million. With the exception of asbestos, these are the least well-known of the minerals. Phosphate was the leading material in this category in 1886, at about 25 percent of the total, with salt, sulphur, asbestos, and gypsum being other important commodities. There was little change in these patterns over the period.

Fuels are a more important and more familiar category. Total output was $4.4 million in 1886 and, by 1913, had risen to more than $41 million. They accounted for more than 40 percent of total mining activity until the turn of the century, when their share slipped below 30 percent, where it remained until 1913. Coal was the dominant commodity throughout in this category, ranging from 82 percent of fuel output in 1895 to nearly 95 percent in 1913. Nova Scotia was the dominant producer. Production and exports from that province grew until the 1920s. A new export activity opened up in the 1880s, and

Figure 12.6 Share of Mineral Output by Main Category, Canada, 1886–1913

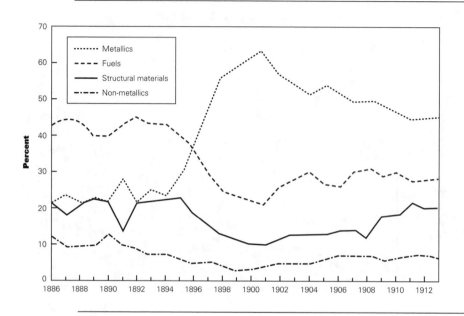

Source: Canada, Dominion Bureau of Statistics, *Canadian Mineral Statistics, 1886–1956*, cat. no. 26-501 (Ottawa: Dominion Bureau of Statistics, 1957), p. 48. Reproduced by authority of the Minister of Industry, 1995.

especially after 1900, as coal from Vancouver Island began to go to the San Francisco and district market. Petroleum from Ontario captured 12 percent of the fuels market in 1886, but fell to near oblivion in the twentieth century as the oilfields ran dry. Natural gas grew in importance, by contrast, as the plentiful reserves of Alberta began to develop.

Metallic minerals are the main story of this period, in terms of economic importance as well as of political excitement. Gold is far and away the most spectacular of the lot. This precious metal comes in three forms, and each was important in what was a succession of gold booms. Alluvial gold, that found by panning rivers and lakes, is the most familiar. Canada's first gold rush began in 1858, when deposits were discovered in the Fraser River in British Columbia. Hordes of prospectors arrived immediately, many from the overcrowded California fields. They followed the rivers into the interior, eventually entering the Cariboo District and bringing to this vast wilderness a short-lived but frantic boom.

The next phase of the gold industry was more spectacular yet. News that gold of immense value had been found on the Klondike River brought miners from around the world to this isolated and inhospitable area. Success was immediate, for some at least, and gold production soared. Dawson City grew from a small outpost to a city of over 30 000 in just a few years. The boom could not last, and it did not. By 1910, Yukon gold production virtually ceased, and Dawson City reverted to an outpost.

Gold is also found in ore bodies, either as the principal component or secondary to other minerals. The economics, in either case, is very different from that for alluvial gold. The ore must be mined, and the gold extracted through smelting and refining. Thus, large companies with access to capital and metallurgical expertise replaced solitary prospectors with mules and gold pans. In this respect, at least, gold was a mineral very much like the other metals. Deposits became viable only as chemical methods were developed to separate the ores into their constituent parts and as cheap power sources became available.

Gold production of this third type began in the Rossland area of British Columbia in the 1890s, with the ore initially being shipped to the United States for smelting. More important developments took place in Ontario, as the vast deposits of the Porcupine and Kirkland Lake areas were opened up. Production from these areas in one year, 1913, exceeded that for all previous years together, and output doubled, then doubled again, after that.

Silver was the metal most sought after, next to gold. Some relatively small production had occurred in the Lake Superior region around the time of Confederation, but the major phase began twenty years later, when important silver deposits were discovered in British Columbia. The ore was so rich that it paid to pack it out by horse and ship it by water or rail to the United States for reduction. Activity spread and grew more diversified as metallurgical advances opened up more deposits, and the development of cheap power drew smelting activities north of the border. British Columbia dominated the sector for twenty years, until the silver deposits near Cobalt were opened up and Ontario became an important producer as well.

Unlike precious metals, there was little use for base metals before the late nineteenth century. Only as industrialization in Europe and the United States proceeded did such metals as copper, zinc, and lead take on any real value. The discovery that steel could be made much stronger by adding nickel alloy was a key development. Reinforced steel was in great demand by the building trades and armament manufacturers. With the prospects of a market established, Canada's vast resources of zinc, copper, nickel, cobalt, and other base metals were of considerable value. Early metallurgical techniques were imported, but Canadian-based companies such as Cominco were quick to extend them to overcome their own problems and to expand the range of feasible deposits.

The early progress of Canada's base-metals industry was impressive. Copper production increased slowly but steadily from the mid-1880s. Output in value terms was 8 times its 1886 level in 1900, and 30 times that amount in 1913. Lead production rose from a value of a few thousand dollars in the late 1880s to $2.8 million by the turn of the century. Production fell off slightly for a couple of years, and then remained roughly constant until a new flotation process developed by Cominco during World War I laid the basis for a strong postwar expansion. The first reported zinc production was 788 000 pounds (358 000 kg) in 1898, for a value of $36 000, and even this had virtually disappeared until World War I demands led to a spectacular recovery.

Nickel is perhaps the most interesting case study of mineral development in this period. Early on, production from a small mine in the Eastern Townships of Quebec was used locally for costume jewellery and tableware. The rich deposits of the Sudbury area were discovered in the course of constructing the CPR, but at first the nickel was considered an impurity to be removed to get at the more valuable copper and other metals. As demand for nickel grew, a consequence of its use in hardening steel, companies began to experiment with techniques for recovering the metal. The Orford Copper Company obtained a U.S. naval contract to work with the Sudbury ores, and production began. A smelting operation was constructed in Copper Cliff to produce nickel matte. The matte was then sent to a refinery in New Jersey for upgrading into nickel, whence it went to U.S. steel companies. Its main competitor, the Canadian Copper Company, sold its ore to Orford for smelting. In 1902, the two companies joined to form the International Nickel Company of Canada (Inco Ltd.). Production of nickel rose from practically nothing in 1886 to 7 million pounds

(3.2 million kg) by 1900 and to 37 million pounds (16.8 million kg) by 1910. By the eve of World War I, production had reached nearly 50 million pounds (22.7 million kg).

Issues in Canada's Industrialization, 1870–1913

The way in which manufacturing developed after 1870 had many implications for future generations of Canadians and for future political debates. Three issues, in particular, stand out. The first concerns the efficiency of at least some of the manufacturing ventures that emerged in this period. Tariffs, it is often alleged, created not just a secondary manufacturing sector in Canada but a high-cost, inefficient one. The broad protection offered by the tariffs meant that industry in Canada developed as a "miniature replica" of that in the United States. There were too many firms, producing too many product lines, in too small a market. All could operate only because of protection, which guaranteed that tariffs would be a long-time feature of the Canadian industrial scene. Canadians would pay the price for this inefficiency in the form of real incomes that were lower than they otherwise could be, and by being saddled with a manufacturing sector that remained sluggish and conservative compared with those in other western industrial nations.

Foreign ownership is the second issue. It is often alleged that tariffs are responsible for the very high levels of foreign control of Canadian industry, in that they created trade barriers sufficiently high that foreign firms, primarily American ones, were induced to establish branch plants in lieu of exporting. As Michael Bliss noted, however, to the extent the claim is true, it ranks as one of the bitter ironies of the national policy. Businessmen and politicians of the day anticipated this development; indeed, they sought it. American branch plants, located behind the tariff to provide for the Canadian market, would provide industry and employment in a nation hungry for industrial development.[17]

Ownership of the plants was not the issue. However, where the work was being done was very much a matter of policy. Both the Dominion and the provincial governments actively pursued policies that encouraged the development and processing of Canadian materials in Canada. Ontario was especially active in this regard and pursued various royalty and other arrangements that were, in effect, attempts to raise the cost of exporting raw materials and, thereby, encourage manufacturing of those materials within the province. As one businessman put it, "We should decide to sell them our paper, but not one stick of spruce".[18]

The final issue concerns the location of manufacturing activity in Canada. In 1870, Ontario hosted 52 percent of manufacturing activity, measured by value of output; Quebec hosted another 35 percent; and the remainder was in the Maritimes. By 1900, when the western provinces appear in the data, Ontario's share was still above 50 percent, while Quebec's had fallen to 32 percent and the Maritimes' to 10 percent. Ontario's relative position held firm through the boom after 1900, while those for Quebec and the Maritimes slipped further. The West's share went from essentially nothing in 1870 to about 13 percent in 1910.[19]

The trends are more revealing when primary and secondary activities are distinguished. Ontario's constant overall share was the result of a significant decline in its relative position as a primary producer, offset by a notable increase in its share of secondary activities. Quebec lost, in a relative sense, on both counts, and about evenly so. The Maritimes slipped in both categories as well, although, in their case, the decline was proportionately greater in secondary products. The relative decline in primary products in all three established regions reflects the fact that most manufacturing activity in the western provinces centred on processing resources.

These aggregate data illustrate the development over this period of an industrial heartland in Canada, centred in Ontario and, to a lesser extent, in Quebec. It was not that manufacturing output in total grew more rapidly in central Canada than elsewhere. Indeed, over the period 1870–1910, Ontario actually lost a little of its lead as the western economies developed, and Quebec lost a lot. It was, instead, the specialization that arose across regions in the type of manufacturing that gave rise to an industrial heartland. The outlying regions of the country concentrated on primary manufacturing, usually the simple processing of resources. These activities were oriented to resource sites because there was significant weight loss in the initial stages of production or because electricity was a key input. One exception was clothing, a labour-intensive industry that was drawn to the Maritimes by the relatively low wages there. Atlantic Canada, the Prairies, and British Columbia hosted, as well, small-scale secondary activities, serving the local market and protected naturally by distance.

Ontario and Quebec, by contrast, attracted a disproportionate share of secondary activities — in some cases (such as machinery and autos), representing virtually the entire national production. In essence, the central provinces were the natural location in Canada to host these industries. Their population was larger and more geographically concentrated, and incomes were generally higher. The region was just across the Great Lakes from one of the most advanced and rapidly industrializing regions of the world. As well, in these matters, growth begets growth. The more industrial activity there is in an area, at least up to a point well beyond Ontario and Quebec in these years, the more likely other sectors are to locate there to take advantage of interindustry linkages, pools of skilled labour, and specialized business services.

The concentration of protected industry in southern Ontario and Quebec is sometimes ascribed to tariffs, but this claim is incorrect. Tariffs may have induced industry to locate in Canada rather than export over the tariff, but, once this decision was taken, the choice of where to situate in Canada was strictly a business one. The heartland, with its relative natural advantages, inevitably won out.

Eric Jones argues that industrialization is symptomatic of an economy's wealth rather than the cause of that wealth.[20] In the case of Ontario, John McCallum links the wealth that Ontario accumulated from the wheat boom through the mid-nineteenth century as an important source of capital for the development of industrial firms and the infrastructure, such as railways, that would foster industrialization. In contrast, Quebec lacked as robust an agricultural sector as Ontario and failed to develop the wealth and local capital necessary to encourage the capital intensive, high value added industry of Ontario.

More legitimately, the tariff was seen by many as a means of redistributing income from the periphery to the centre. The farmers of the Prairies, the loggers of British Columbia, and the fishers of the Maritimes received little or no protection. Indeed, they needed none, as their industries were internationally competitive. Yet, they paid tariff-inflated prices for the tools and implements of their trades and for the clothing, furniture, and comforts they provided for their families. The benefits went to central Canadians, in the form of jobs and higher profits in the protected industries. However correct these claims are, and analysis of them is very complex, they remain a prominent feature of political debate today.

One obvious, but often overlooked, point should be made here: it is misleading to refer to Ontario and Quebec as the emerging industrial heartland. In fact, most of the two provinces was, and indeed remains, more like the periphery of the country in terms of economic structure, depending on lumber, pulp mills, mines, and hydro-electric projects for its livelihood. The real heartland was a group of industrial cities stretching from Windsor, through Southern Ontario and along the Great Lakes, to Montreal. There were even important differences between the industrial areas of Ontario and Quebec. The former province specialized much more obviously in producer goods, while Quebec drew more consumer goods such as clothing and textiles.

234

Conclusion

Though the rapid growth of prairie settlement captured the lion's share of attention at the time, the so-called "wheat boom" era was also marked by considerable activity in the manufacturing sector, both primary and secondary. Canadian cities like Toronto and Montreal became centres of a growing urban work force, and the Canadian economy made ready use of emerging technologies to promote development. Yet, even in this era of rapid growth, there was considerable dislocation as old industries stagnated and as newer industries, such as steel, seemed to exist in an almost permanent state of flux. Overall, however, as the flattening of the industrial hierarchy indicates, by 1913 the Canadian economy was considerably more diversified than it had been at the turn of the century. Much of the growth of these years would, in turn, be instrumental in the role Canada played in World War I.

NOTES

1. See Gordon Bertram, "Historical Statistics on Growth and Structure of Manufacturing in Canada, 1870–1957," in J. Henripin and A. Asimakopulos, eds., *Conference on Statistics, 1962 and 1963* (Toronto: University of Toronto Press, 1964), 93–146, for further discussion of this distinction.
2. O.J. McDiarmid, *Commercial Policy in the Canadian Economy* (Cambridge, MA: Harvard University Press, 1946), 205.
3. McDiarmid, *Commercial Policy*, 217.
4. Eugene Beaulieu and J.C. Herbert Emery, "Pork Packers, Reciprocity and Laurier's Defeat in the 1911 Canadian General Election," *Journal of Economic History.*
5. Judith A. McDonald, Anthony Patrick O'Brien, and Colleen M. Callahan, "Trade Wars: Canada's Reaction to the Smoot-Hawley Tariff," *Journal of Economic History* 57, No. 4 (1983): 802–826.
6. Richard Rice, "Measuring British Dominance of Shipbuilding in the 'Maritimes,' 1787–1890," in Keith Matthews and Gerald Panting, eds., *Ships and Shipbuilding in the North Atlantic Region* (St. John's: Memorial University, 1978), appendix 1, 148–51.
7. Eric W. Sager and Lewis R. Fischer, "Atlantic Canada and the Age of Sail Revisited," *Canadian Historical Review* 63(2) (1982): 125–50.
8. The following material is derived from R.M. McInnis, "From Hewn Timber to Sawn Lumber: The Canadian Forest Industry in the Latter Half of the Nineteenth Century," unpublished paper, Queen's University, 1988.
9. R.M. McInnis, "Canada in the World Market for Forest Products," unpublished paper, Queen's University, 1988.
10. M.C. Urquhart and K.A.H. Buckley, eds., *Historical Statistics of Canada* (Toronto: Macmillan, 1965), series K176-183, 337.
11. See Trevor J.O. Dick, "Canadian Newsprint, 1913–1930: National Policies and the North American Economy," *Journal of Economic History* 42(3) (September 1982): 659–87; and Kevin Burley, "Introduction," in Kevin Burley, ed., *The Development of Canada's Staples 1867–1939*, Carleton Library no. 56 (Toronto: McClelland & Stewart, 1987), part four, 332–40.
12. Burley, "Introduction," 333.
13. See Kris Inwood, *The Canadian Charcoal Iron Industry, 1870–1914* (New York and London: Garland, 1986).

14. Craig Heron, *Working in Steel: The Early Years in Canada, 1883–1935* (Toronto: McClelland & Stewart, 1988), 16–29.

15. See W.G. Phillips, *The Agricultural Implement Industry in Canada* (Toronto: University of Toronto Press, 1956); and Michael Bliss, *Northern Enterprise: Five Centuries of Canadian Business* (Toronto: McClelland & Stewart, 1987).

16. See Canada, Dominion Bureau of Statistics, *Canadian Mineral Statistics, 1886–1956* (Ottawa: Queen's Printer, 1957); and Burley, *The Development of Canada's Staples.*

17. Bliss, *Northern Enterprise.*

18. H.V. Nelles, "The Problem of Resource Development," in Donald Swainson, ed., *Oliver Mowatt's Ontario* (Toronto: Macmillan, 1972), 201.

19. Bertram, "Historical Statistics."

20. E.L. Jones, *Growth Recurring: Economic Change in World History* (New York: Oxford University Press, 1993).

FURTHER READING

Altman, M. "A Revision of Canadian Economic Growth 1870–1910 (A Challenge to the Gradualist Interpretation)." *Canadian Journal of Economics* 20 (February 1987): 86–107.

Armstrong, Christopher, and H.V. Nelles. *Monopoly's Moment: The Organization and Regulation of Canadian Utilities 1830–1930.* Philadelphia: Temple University Press, 1986.

Bertram, Gordon. "Economic Growth in Canadian Industry, 1870–1914: The Staple Model and the Take-off Hypothesis." *Canadian Journal of Economics and Political Science* 29(2) (May 1963): 159–84.

Bliss, Michael. *Northern Enterprise: Five Centuries of Canadian Business.* Toronto: McClelland & Stewart, 1987.

Brown, R.C., and G.R. Cook. *Canada, 1896–1921: A Nation Transformed.* Toronto: McClelland & Stewart, 1974.

Caves, R.E. "Economic Models of Political Choice: Canada's Tariff Structure." *Canadian Journal of Economics* 9 (May 1976): 278–300.

Dick, Trevor J.O. "Canadian Newsprint, 1913–1930: National Policies and the North American Economy." *Journal of Economic History* 42(3) (September 1982): 659–87.

Easton, S.T., W.A. Gibson, and C.G. Reed. "Tariffs and Growth: The Dales Hypothesis." *Explorations in Economic History* 25 (April 1988): 147–63.

Emery, George. *Noxons of Ingersoll, 1856–1918: The Family and the Firm in Canada's Agricultural Implements Industry.* Ingersoll: Ingersoll Historical Society, 2001.

Inwood, Kris. "Maritime Industrialization from 1870 to 1910: A Review of the Evidence and Its Interpretation." In Kris Inwood, ed., *Farm, Factory and Fortune: New Studies in the Economic History of the Maritime Provinces.* Fredericton: Acadiensis Press, 1993, 149–70.

Nelles, H.V. *The Politics of Development: Forest, Mines and Hydroelectric Power in Ontario, 1849–1941.* Toronto: Macmillan, 1974.

Sager, Eric W., with Gerald E. Panting. *Maritime Capital: The Shipping Industry in Atlantic Canada, 1820–1914.* Montreal and Kingston: McGill–Queen's University Press, 1990.

Chapter Thirteen

Utilities, Services, and Government

THE FOURTH BROAD economic sector of the Canadian economy, services, was second in size only to agriculture in 1870, and grew in relative importance every decade thereafter. By 1910, services accounted for over 50 percent of gross domestic product.

In spite of their obvious importance, relatively little is known about this set of economic activities. In part, this situation reflects the relative lack of understanding of service activities in any economy, for any period.[1] In part, however, it is an unfortunate legacy of the traditional focus in Canadian economic history on the staples-theory concept. In this approach, service activities tend to be cast as derivative to the resource and resource-processing sectors. They exist to collect the staples and transport them to market, to distribute manufactured products to consumers, and to provide non-tradeable products in local markets.

This characterization may be accurate for some service industries, but it is definitely not so for others. As this chapter illustrates, the service sector covers a wide range of economic activities, each of which made a unique contribution to Canada's economic development in this period. We begin with a brief overview of this sector, followed by a closer look at some of the individual activities.

Overview

Figure 13.1 shows the shares of gross domestic product accounted for by each of the activities in this sector for the census year 1870, ranked in order of importance. The largest sector, with 7.4 percent of total value added, was community, business, and personal services. This broad category includes such diverse activities as all manner of recreation services, professional services to businesses, professional services to households, laundries, and accommodation and food services. Four other activities ranked next in importance, each with 5–6 percent of GDP: wholesale and retail trade, residential rents, construction, and transportation and communication. The public sector, including education and public-sector resource royalties, was next with 4 percent, followed by banking and finance at 2.1 percent.

Clearly, this category includes a wide variety of economic activities. In considering them, it is useful to make at least three distinctions. The first concerns the ultimate disposition of the products. In some cases, the output is intended mainly for use by households. Residential rents is the most obvious example, as it represents the value of housing services consumed by households. Urban transportation, passenger rail transportation, household utilities, personal banking and financial services, retail trade, and a wide range of personal services such as haircuts and entertainment are other examples.

Figure 13.1 Service Sectors as Percentage of GDP, Canada, 1870

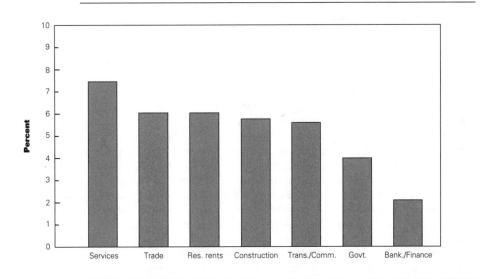

Source: Calculated from M.C. Urquhart, "New Estimates of Gross National Product, Canada, 1870–1926: Some Implications for Canadian Development," in Stanley L. Engerman and Robert E. Gallman, eds., *Long-Term Factors in American Economic Growth*, National Bureau of Economic Research, Studies in Income and Wealth, vol. 51 (Chicago: University of Chicago Press, 1986), table 2.13, p. 42.

In these cases, demand for the service in any period depends on population, personal income, and relative prices. As the economy grows, both in extensive and intensive terms, demand for services will generally grow as well. Since demand for these products is generally assumed to be income elastic (that is, a 1 percent increase in income, all else being equal, will give rise to a greater than 1 percent increase in demand), consumption will tend to increase relatively faster than income.

In other service industries, output is an intermediate good, destined for use as an input into further production elsewhere in the economy. Non-residential construction, freight transportation, industrial use of light and power, business banking and finance, wholesale trade, and legal and accounting services to businesses are obvious examples.

These services are more complex to analyze, since they are both a consequence and a determinant of economic growth. They are a consequence to the extent that demand for them rises as the business sector expands. Thus demand for banking and financial services or legal and accounting services will rise as commodity production expands, and fall as it contracts. But as a cost of business, sometimes an important one, they are also a determinant of economic growth. For example, as noted in the previous chapter, access to cheap electricity was an important factor in the success of the pulp-and-paper and metal-refining industries after 1895. Banking and finance are other examples.

The second important distinction is on the supply side. Many of the activities included in this category are produced privately, in response to the normal profit considerations. Wholesale and retail trade, business and personal services, and construction are obvious examples. In some instances, domestic firms will have to compete with foreign suppliers, in which case success depends on Canadian competitiveness, much as in commodity production.

Some of the services are produced privately, but with substantial government involvement and regulation. Banking and finance, transportation, and electrical utilities are obvious examples. Analysis of supply-side responses is more complex in these instances, since one needs to take explicit account of government involvement. When do governments choose to operate the activity itself, and when are they content merely to regulate private-sector companies? Electric utilities and railways are obvious examples. How are regulations set and enforced, and to what economic effect?

Still other outputs in this sector are produced directly by governments. Classic public goods such as defence, public safety, and justice are the most obvious examples. The post office, some types of utilities, and some transportation facilities are also examples of government activities. Analysis of supply-side responses is different again in these cases. Why did governments carry out the functions they did in any given period? How were these responsibilities divided among federal, provincial, and municipal governments? How were they financed? What effects did these choices have on economic growth and development?

A third distinction is between tradeable and non-tradeable outputs. Some services are inherently non-tradeable, or at least they were in the nineteenth and early twentieth centuries. Haircuts and personal banking services come to mind. In these cases, output prices will reflect local demand and supply conditions. Other services are tradeable, at least potentially. Financial and other professional services to businesses are obvious examples. In these cases, prices depend on Canadian competitiveness and on the degree of government protection afforded the industry through entry regulations and other barriers.

Figure 13.2 shows the share of each service sector in GDP in 1900 relative to that in 1870, while Figure 13.3 does the same for 1910 relative to 1900. A number above 1.0 in these graphs indicates that the activity grew relatively faster than the economy as a whole

Figure 13.2 Shares of Service Sectors in GDP, Canada, 1900 Relative to 1870

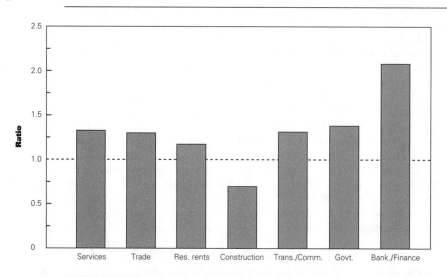

Source: Calculated from M.C. Urquhart, "New Estimates of Gross National Product, Canada, 1870–1926: Some Implications for Canadian Development," in Stanley L. Engerman and Robert E. Gallman, eds., *Long-Term Factors in American Economic Growth*, National Bureau of Economic Research, Studies in Income and Wealth, vol. 51 (Chicago: University of Chicago Press, 1986), table 2.13, p. 42.

over the period in question, while a number below 1.0 indicates that it grew more slowly. The reason for distinguishing the two periods is to see if there is any difference in service-sector growth before and after 1896. Figure 13.4 shows the shares of the service sectors in 1910, ranked in order of their relative importance in 1870.

Figure 13.2 reveals that all sectors but construction increased their share of GDP between 1870 and 1900. Banking and finance increased the most rapidly, more than doubling their share in this 30-year period. The other activities expanded at a fairly even pace. Construction is a highly cyclical industry, so its decline almost certainly reflects the relatively slow growth in the economy at the end of the nineteenth century.

Figure 13.3 reveals a somewhat different pattern for the boom decade. Electric light and power trebled its share of GDP over this decade, in part because it began from a very low base. The construction industry increased twice as fast as GDP as a whole, reflecting its cyclical sensitivity and the fact, noted earlier, that the economic boom of 1896 was largely investment driven. The next most robust expansion was wholesale and retail trade, reflecting the settlement of the Prairies and urbanization elsewhere. Transportation and communication grew relatively rapidly as well, again likely an effect of the prairie wheat boom. With the exception of business and personal services, the other sectors grew at the same rate as the economy as a whole.

Like the manufacturing sector discussed in Chapter Twelve, the most useful way to proceed at this point is to look at some specific examples of service-sector growth and development in this period. Drawing on the supply-side distinction made above, we look first at a purely private activity (wholesale and retail trade), then at three activities that were mixed public and regulated private (banking, finance, and hydro-electricity), and finally at purely public-sector activities.

Figure 13.3 Share of Service Sectors in GDP, Canada, 1910 Relative to 1900

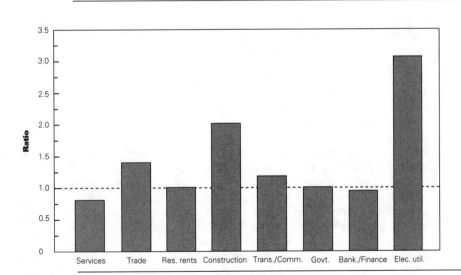

Source: Calculated from M.C. Urquhart, "New Estimates of Gross National Product, Canada, 1870–1926: Some Implications for Canadian Development," in Stanley L. Engerman and Robert E. Gallman, eds., *Long-Term Factors in American Economic Growth*, National Bureau of Economic Research, Studies in Income and Wealth, vol. 51 (Chicago: University of Chicago Press, 1986), table 2.13, p. 42.

Figure 13.4 Share of Service Sectors in GDP, Canada, 1910

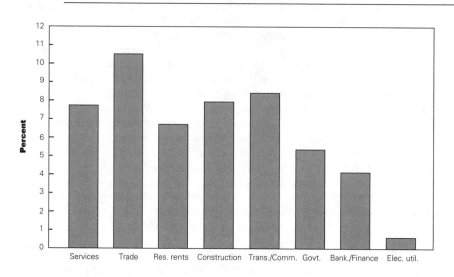

Source: Calculated from M.C. Urquhart, "New Estimates of Gross National Product, Canada, 1870–1926: Some Implications for Canadian Development," in Stanley L. Engerman and Robert E. Gallman, eds., *Long-Term Factors in American Economic Growth*, National Bureau of Economic Research, Studies in Income and Wealth, vol. 51 (Chicago: University of Chicago Press, 1986), table 2.13, p. 42.

Wholesale and Retail Trade

A rising standard of living through much of the nineteenth century meant that whole sections of society could now become consumers on a routine rather than an essential basis. On the other side, manufacturers catering to this growing market developed mass-produced goods more cheaply than could have been done under earlier craft traditions. They also produced a wider range of goods. In effect, this involved both a displacement of earlier economic activity and the creation of a new market. The displacement came as goods previously made locally, or at home, were increasingly the products of centralized factories. The new market came because the rising standard of living allowed people who, in earlier generations, had been able to own, say, one good outfit to buy several over the course of a lifetime. In addition, they now owned things that, before industrialism, would have been reserved for a higher income class. It was "the democratization of luxury."[2]

The changes in consumption led to a dynamic and widespread revolution in retailing during the nineteenth and early twentieth centuries.[3] Small general stores could no longer carry the range of goods necessary to meet the public demand, especially in larger centres. Thus two tendencies occurred: the first was specialization, as general stores gave way to shops concentrating on dry goods, groceries, hardware, and so forth; the second, and most dramatic, was the rise of the large department store in the nineteenth and twentieth centuries. Here the answer to consumer demand was not specialization but economies of scale. The department store specialized within itself and, because of its size, could often deal with manufacturers directly, thus saving the mark-up that would otherwise have been paid to wholesalers. It could also offer customers a range of choice not available in smaller stores. The next step for many of these stores was to expand beyond a single site, creating stores wherever a sufficiently large urban population existed. Finally, there was the possibility of selling where there was not even a store. Mail-order catalogues would prove one of the most revolutionary and important means of bringing department-store quality to a thinly spread rural population.

Once we recognize the impact of mail-order catalogues, the rise of e-commerce through on-line Internet shopping at companies like Amazon.com does not seem so revolutionary. As Robert Gordon points out, e-commerce has not been an introduction of new services; it is an alternative to the mail-order catalogue shopping introduced in the 1870s. Even when they offer on-line shopping, many retailers continue to issue their paper catalogues to prospective customers.[4]

The first department stores appeared in the United States in the 1840s, and soon after Confederation, Morgan's in Montreal employed 150 clerks and had several specialized departments. In Toronto, Timothy Eaton opened a store in 1869 and within a decade had expanded to ten "departments." By the 1880s, he would move to new premises of some 2300 m^2 and be equipped with the latest product of science, electricity. He also began a catalogue business that would, by the beginning of the twentieth century, make Eaton's a national name.

The prosperity of the period after 1897 completed the shift in retailing. There were tremendous profits to be made, and stores like Simpson's, Morgan's, and, most of all, Eaton's, moved to take advantage of the times. As well, the Hudson's Bay Company responded to the growing western population by expanding across the Prairies from its small stores in Winnipeg and Vancouver. A fur trade company was, in the process, transformed into a retail chain.[5] Stores like Eaton's, in the meantime, had moved backward in the chain of production, doing their own wholesaling, shipping, and, in some instances, manufacturing.

Statistics concerning the retail trade for this period are difficult to come by. Indeed, as late as 1930 the Dominion Bureau of Statistics complained of "this gap in the national statistics."[6] Nonetheless, the impression remains of a dynamic sector of the economy, adapting to new possibilities and growing in response to a rising standard of living. Between 1897 and 1909, for example, Eaton's employees increased from 1600 to 8775. By 1914, the company's sales were more than $50 million annually.[7]

Banking and Finance

The financial sector has two main functions in any economy.[8] The first function is that of financial intermediation, or transferring funds from those with savings to those wishing to borrow these savings. Savers can be households, businesses, even governments upon occasion, and they can be domestic and foreign. Borrowers, likewise, can be households, businesses, or governments, and they too can be domestic and foreign. Intermediation can mean simply bringing the saver and borrower together, as solicitors frequently did in historical times. Most often, however, the financial intermediary itself collects the savings (by accepting deposits, for example), and then makes them available to borrowers (by issuing loans, for example).

While financial intermediation channels savings into investments, the importance of financial intermediation and economic growth for a small open economy like Canada remains unresolved. In a small open economy, the availability of foreign sources of capital means that there is no necessary link between domestic savings and aggregate capital formation. If the supply of domestic savings rises, then the effect may be to "crowd out" capital from external sources from the domestic economy. Thus, even if financial institutions in Canada were responsible for mobilizing savings in Canada and channeling the savings into capital investments, the financial sector may have no influence whatsoever on economic growth. This is not to say that financial institutions have no impact on the standard of living. To the extent that income accruing to domestically-financed capital remained in Canada, a larger share of income remains in Canada. Further, if the nature of the investments (such as in the transportation infrastructure) differs between capital financed from domestic versus foreign sources, then domestic savings mobilized by financial institutions may be important for the developing infrastructure to capture linkages from staples exploitation. Finally, governments interested in borrowing to finance public spending may benefit from having access to a pool of domestic savings rather than relying on foreign lenders if the domestic lenders can provide more favourable terms.

Researchers have established that financial sector development and economic growth are positively correlated, but the causal relationship between the financial sector development and economic growth has not been identified. Thus, it is possible that an emerging financial sector in nineteenth-century Canada was symptomatic of rising incomes and savings rather than the reason for growth. Would capital formation in Canada have been less than it was in the absence of sufficient banking and financial institutions?[9] Canada's proximity and access to British and U.S. financial markets makes this question difficult to answer. Argentina may provide the best counter-factual for Canada. Like Canada, from 1890 to 1913, Argentina's rapid economic growth was fuelled by British capital. In both countries the financial sectors showed strong development during this period of high growth. After 1913, British capital retreated from both economies as Britain's position as banker to the world was weakened by the costs of World War I. After 1914, Canada's economy and financial sector remained strong whereas Argentina's economy entered a period of long-term stagnation. Where Canada accessed U.S. sources of capital, Argentina found no substitute for the retreat of British capital after 1913. As Alan Taylor argues, "The retreat of foreign capital in the interwar period emphasized the need for local finance, but the response was disappointing: domestic financial development from 1914 to 1939 was only weak, fragile and tentative."[10] If Argentina's experience is counter-factual for Canada, then it would follow that the development of a domestic financial sector is reflective of growth, rather than a cause, or at least, that a domestic financial sector is a poor substitute for foreign capital in fuelling economic growth.

There are two broad types of financial intermediaries: banks and non-banks. Banks are distinguished by the fact that their liabilities serve as a medium of exchange, or money. Historically, this meant notes as well as deposits, but now it only includes the latter. A wide variety of institutions qualify as non-banks: savings banks, life insurance companies, fire and casualty insurance companies, building societies, trust companies, consumer finance companies, mutual funds, credit unions and caisses populaires, and pension funds.

In pioneer times, the process of financial intermediation was as simple as the act of a merchant extending credit to a farmer until the harvest was complete. As the economy grew in size and sophistication, so too did the need for new institutions. Thus, banks emerged in the early nineteenth century to accept deposits, issue notes, discount bills, and trade in foreign exchange. The Bank of Montreal commenced operations in 1817, and by the time of Confederation Canada had 35 chartered banks. Private non-bank institutions developed at different times. The first fire and casualty company appeared in 1809, the first savings bank in 1819, the first life insurance company (the Canada Life Assurance company) in 1847, the first trustee pension plan (a contributory pension plan for clerical and indoor staff of the Grand Trunk Railway) in 1874, the first trust company in 1882, and the first credit union in 1900.[11]

The other function of the financial sector is that of financial brokerage, or facilitating the transfer of financial claims among units in an economy. Stock markets and stock brokers are the most obvious examples of this type of institution, but the definition also covers underwriters, jobbers, and foreign-exchange dealers.

FINANCIAL INTERMEDIATION

The Canadian financial system developed dramatically between Confederation and World War I. Total assets of financial intermediaries in current-dollar terms rose from $142 million in 1870 to $290 million in 1880, to $499 million in 1890, to $832 million in 1900, and to $2.3 billion in 1913. The average annual growth rate between 1870 and 1910, in current-dollar terms, was 6.5 percent, and in constant-dollar terms 6.1 percent. Since these rates are substantially higher than those for goods and services in total, the ratio of financial assets to GNP rose significantly, reflecting the growing sophistication of the Canadian economy in this period.

Table 13.1 shows the relative sizes of the various types of financial intermediaries in this period. Chartered banks dominated the sector in 1870, with 73 percent of total assets. Private non-banks, together, held another 19 percent, with building societies and mortgage-loan companies being the most prominent of these. The remainder of the assets were public, consisting mainly of Dominion notes.

The situation changed markedly between 1870 and 1896. Chartered banks grew more slowly than the sector as a whole, and by 1896 they controlled less than half of the total

Table 13.1 Share of Total Financial Assets by Sector, Canada, 1870–1913

Sector	1870	1880	1890	1900	1913
	(% of total)				
Chartered banks	72.6	55.4	49.5	52.6	57.4
Private non-banks	18.9	34.2	39.5	37.3	34.2
Quebec savings banks	3.7	3.1	2.6	2.5	1.9
Life insurance companies	2.4	3.4	8.6	13.1	14.1
Fraternal benefit societies	—	—	0.3	1.0	1.9
Fire and casualty insurance companies	3.2	3.1	3.5	3.3	3.1
Building societies and mortgage-loan companies	9.6	24.6	24.5	16.2	10.6
Trust companies	—	—	—	1.2	2.6
Public	8.4	10.3	11.0	10.1	8.3
Dominion notes	5.2	4.9	3.1	3.4	5.7
Post office and government savings	3.2	5.4	7.9	6.7	2.4
Federal annuity, insurance, and pension account	—	—	—	—	0.2

Source: Calculated from E.P. Neufeld, *The Financial System of Canada : Its Growth and Development* (Toronto: Macmillan, 1972), appendix table B, pp. 612–32.

assets. Private non-banks more than doubled their share over the same period, to 41 percent of the total. The major growth came from life insurance companies, accounting for 13 percent of the assets in 1896, and building societies and mortgage loan companies, accounting for nearly 22 percent. Public-sector assets rose slightly as well, with a large rise in post office and government savings offsetting a fall in the share of Dominion notes.

244

This situation reversed somewhat in the boom years from 1896 to 1913. The share of chartered banks in total assets rose, to reach over 57 percent in 1913. Private non-banks fell in relative importance, with the bulk of this decline coming from building societies and mortgage-loan companies. Life insurance companies continued to grow in relative importance, albeit more slowly than in the previous period. The share of public-sector assets declined as well, even though the share of Dominion notes grew.

Chartered Banks

Under the BNA Act of 1867, the Dominion government assumed responsibility for currency and coinage and for banking. There was some pressure to structure the financial system along the free-bank lines of the United States and of the Province of Canada's Free Banking Act of 1850, but the proposal was opposed by the banks (other than the Bank of Montreal) and the idea died. The gold standard was retained. The British one-pound coin (sovereign) and the U.S. ten-dollar coin (eagle) were declared to be legal tender, and the Canadian dollar was fixed in terms of gold at the rate of one American dollar equals one Canadian dollar, and one British pound equals $4.867 Canadian dollars.

The Dominion Notes Act of 1870 restricted the chartered banks to issuing notes of a minimum denomination of $4, giving the government monopoly control over $1 and $2 bills. Dominion notes were legal tender and were redeemable in specie upon demand. The government was required to hold a minimum reserve against outstanding Dominion notes. Although bank notes were not legal tender, they were popular with the public; they were redeemable on demand in specie or Dominion notes. There was no legal minimum reserve requirement against the notes and deposits of the chartered banks beyond a tie to the value of paid-up capital, although for prudent business reasons they maintained sufficient reserves of gold, Dominion notes, and deposits and call loans in New York and London.

The first formal legislation governing banking was the Bank Act of 1871, which largely restated existing provisions with respect to the chartering of banks, the minimum subscribed capital, the conditions for note issue, and other regulations.

Canada's banking system took shape in the years after Confederation. This period saw the emergence of a large branch-banking system, dominated not by small regional private banks but by national corporations. The 35 active banks in 1867 increased to a peak of 51 in 1874, and then fell more or less continuously thereafter. There were 37 active banks in 1896 and 24 in 1913. The number of branches grew significantly over the same period. For example, there were fewer banking corporations in 1911 than there had been in 1900, yet there were 1846 more branches.[12] The Bank of Montreal was far and away the largest chartered bank in 1870, with 28.3 percent of total bank assets. By 1910, its share had dropped to 18 percent, and the Canadian Bank of Commerce now had 12.4 percent of the assets and the Royal Bank 7.5 percent.

These statistics were also reflected in the fortunes of individual firms. Once again, the pattern was consolidation, both structurally and geographically. The Bank of Nova Scotia was chartered in Halifax in 1832, moved to Toronto in 1900, and absorbed the Bank of New Brunswick in 1910. The Bank of Commerce began operations in Toronto in 1867, and in 1900 it took over the Bank of British Columbia, which had operated in that province since 1862. The Merchants' Bank of Halifax was founded in 1869, becoming the Royal Bank of Canada in 1901 and moving to Montreal five years later. The Bank of Toronto opened in 1853; the Dominion Bank, in the late 1860s.

The implications of this structure for Canada's economic development in this period is unclear. On the plus side, the concentration meant that the banking system was remarkably stable. Bank failures do not figure prominently in Canada's economic history. Others, however, have argued that the relative lack of competition meant a cautious and conservative lending policy, a feature that has been to the detriment of the economy more generally.

On one critique at least, the evidence does seem quite clear. It has long been alleged that the banks' lending policies discriminated against manufacturing firms, and against borrowers in the Maritimes and the West. The bias against manufacturing is allegedly responsible for the high degree of foreign ownership in this sector, while the bias against the outlying regions supposedly reinforced their hinterland economic status. However, a detailed look at the lending practices of the Bank of Nova Scotia between 1900 and 1937 finds no evidence to support either of these hypotheses.[13]

Private Non-Banks

The real story of this period was the growth of the private non-bank activities. Together, they doubled their share of financial assets between 1870 and 1913. Nearly all the growth came from building societies and mortgage loan companies and from life insurance companies. Banks were restricted in the real estate they could take as collateral for loans, which left a niche in the market for firms willing to take on these longer-term commitments. Life insurance companies grew dramatically, as sales representatives from Canadian companies spread across the country and eventually around the world. New companies sprang up, many to become household names — Ontario Mutual (1871), Sun Life (1871), London Life (1874), and Manufacturers Life (1887), among others. Canadian companies wrote 50 percent of the business in 1870, and 65 percent in 1900. Some, like the Canada Life Assurance Company, were in the very top rank of Canada's financial institutions.[14]

FINANCIAL BROKERS

Financial brokers began to appear, as the supply of government debt, chartered-bank stock, railway bonds, and stocks and other financial instruments grew. A board of brokers was formed in Montreal in 1863. In 1872, it began calling itself the Montreal Stock Exchange; in 1874, it received a charter under Quebec law. The Toronto Stock Exchange went through a number of guises before becoming officially incorporated in 1878. This activity was not limited to central Canada, though. The Winnipeg Stock Exchange was established in 1903, the Vancouver Stock Exchange in 1907, and the Calgary Stock Exchange in 1914. As Taylor and Baskerville remind us, however, these markets remained fairly local and small until at least the 1920s. Large-scale underwriting requirements still looked to the London markets or, increasingly, to New York.

Hydro-Electricity

Hydro-electricity affected Canadian economic and political life most profoundly. Economically, "hydro" has come to symbolize the transition from the "old" industrialism of the nineteenth century, wherein Canada was at a distinct disadvantage internationally, to the "new" industrialism of the twentieth, with its great promise for this nation. Politically, the campaign for public power and the intention to use it to promote economic diversification at the provincial level set a pattern that has continued to today.

246

By 1880, after a series of prototypes, generator technology was sufficiently advanced that electricity could be produced cheaply and in great quantities. The next major step was the development by Thomas Edison of the central electric system. With this innovation, electricity could be produced at one central site, for use by different consumers at different places, and for different purposes. Transmission was the next hurdle. Electricity could be transmitted long distances only at high voltages, yet safe domestic use required low voltages, such as the 110 volts Edison eventually settled on. The solution came with the development of the transformer. With it, electricity could be stepped up to high voltage for transmission and reduced again for distribution.

These developments meant that electricity generation could take place in a few large plants, far removed from consumption sites. Specifically, distant rivers could now be used to turn turbines, with the output transmitted to urban and industrial areas. Large-scale production from cheap hydro sources meant taking advantage of economies of scale, which, in turn, meant that electricity prices fell significantly. Canada was well endowed with water power, so the stage was set for a major new industry producing cheap power for a range of new products.

The initial developments in hydro-electricity generation were not made in Canada, however, but rather in Niagara Falls, New York. A plant was opened there in the summer of 1895, supplying power first to Buffalo and then to a host of electrochemical industries that were quickly drawn to the power site. This demonstration of the potential of hydro-electricity to promote industrial development, together with the obvious potential for such production in Canada, led to pressure to begin development of the resources north of the border.

Quebec, Ontario, Manitoba, and British Columbia led the way in hydroelectricity development.[15] Five major producers came to dominate the Quebec scene, although only two

London Life headquarters, 1905. Life-insurance companies and other private non-bank activities grew dramatically between 1870 and 1913, doubling their share of financial assets. Canadian life-insurance companies wrote 50 percent of the business in 1879, and 65 percent in 1900.

London Life Archives.

were in operation as World War I began. Shawinigan Water and Power was the first off the mark. The entrepreneurial initiative for the venture came from a group of Boston financiers, with some Canadian representation added as the company got started. Construction began at Shawinigan Falls, on the St. Maurice River, in 1899, and the first power was delivered in 1903. Financing was an early problem, but, with the initial delivery contracts honoured, the company found it much easier to peddle its bonds in American and British markets.

The progress of the Shawinigan company is especially interesting in that it is instructive of the type of economic activity that came to surround hydro-electricity. Its first contract for hydraulic power was in 1899, with the Northern Aluminum Company, which proposed to locate in the area to use electricity for bauxite reduction and aluminum fabrication. By 1906, this operation was one of the largest aluminum producers in the world. A second contract for hydraulic power, this time with Belgian capitalists looking for a location for a pulp mill, followed one year later. A newsprint mill was added in 1904, and capacity was expanded in 1906. The first big contract for electricity came in 1902, in an arrangement with the Montreal Light, Heat and Power Company. The Shawinigan Carbide Company began production in 1904, becoming the second major consumer of electricity. By 1908, this enterprise was controlled by the Shawinigan company, and, by 1909, was a wholly owned subsidiary of it. Further Montreal sales of electricity were negotiated in 1907 with Montreal Street Railway and with Vulcan Portland Cement, indicating the range of linkages to hydro.

Demand for electricity was growing so rapidly by this time that, after 1908, the Shawinigan company declined to make further contracts for hydraulic power, and earlier contracts were bought back. A second powerhouse was completed in 1911, and a second transmission line to Montreal was put into service. The Wabasso Cotton Company of Trois-Rivières located a thread mill in Shawinigan in 1909, shipping the output to the parent company for weaving into cloth. Two transmission lines to Trois-Rivières served firms producing iron, bags for cement, and pulp and paper, along with other smaller concerns. Power was also sent via submarine cable to the asbestos and manufacturing industries south of the St. Lawrence. The company also looked to the retail market and, by 1907, was distributing power to 40 communities.

The other significant electricity operation in prewar Quebec was the Montreal Light, Heat and Power Company. Formed out of a series of mergers of small gas and electric companies, Montreal Light, Heat and Power was in complete control of the Montreal market by 1903. Steam provided a significant portion of the generating capacity early on, but hydro gradually replaced it, especially after 1909, when a new plant at the Soulanges rapids was opened, by which time the company was operating three stations. Its output was sold entirely in the city, for residential, urban transportation, and general manufacturing purposes.

The pattern of development in Ontario took quite a different turn from that in Quebec. There was some early interest in the Welland River, but the real prize was Niagara Falls. In 1892, the Canadian Niagara Power Company, a wholly owned subsidiary of the parent across the river, obtained an exclusive lease to produce power on the Canadian side of the falls. The failure of the company to meet the terms of the lease, and the mounting public concern this neglect was causing, led the Ontario government to renegotiate in 1899, removing the monopoly provision. A second lease was granted to a group of Buffalo industrialists, organized as the Ontario Power Company, in 1900. A third concession — the first to Canadians —was granted in 1903 to the Electric Development Company. The first two firms began construction in 1902; the third, in 1904.

By the turn of the century, though, public ownership was emerging. In 1902, the smaller towns and cities of the southern part of the province began to talk about banding together to secure for themselves cheap and reliable supplies of hydroelectric power to enhance their manufacturing bases. The idea quickly took root among the business interests of the region. Some proponents of public power urged the provincial government to get involved, while others pushed for permission for a consortium of municipalities to construct and operate their own system. Although Premier George William Ross resisted provincial involvement, he did establish the Ontario Power Commission in 1903 and had it undertake to study the feasibility of a municipal consortium taking charge. The refusal of the existing companies to guarantee a supply of electricity quickly turned the movement into one for public power.

Political pressure led the government to establish the Hydro Electric Commission of Enquiry in 1905, with Adam Beck as its chairman. Its 1906 report recommended the establishment of a publicly owned distribution network. The government responded by creating a permanent hydro-electric power commission, charged with regulating the private utilities and determining the means for distributing electricity to the municipalities.

Opposition to the plan for a provincial role, and to the alternative one for a joint municipal venture (proposed by the Snider Commission at the same time), came, predictably, from private companies and other business interests. A furious political battle was waged, with public-power proponents emerging victorious in the municipal elections of 1907, when ratepayers authorized their administration to enter into contracts with the Hydro-Electric Power Commission to deliver electricity to the towns at specified prices. Hydro then moved to sign a contract with the Ontario Power Company for delivery of power at Niagara, and the municipalities, in turn, signed their final contracts with the commission. In 1908, a contract was let by the commission to construct a transmission line connecting Niagara Falls with these municipalities. Ontario Hydro, as the commission became known, was finally in business; its first "switching on" occurred in October 1910.

Hydro-electric power station, Niagara Falls, Ontario, 1907. Niagara Falls was the first source in North America to generate hydro-electric power on a large scale. This new source of light and power had an impact on the economy and politics of Ontario comparable to that of the coming of the railway 50 years earlier.

Hydro One Networks Inc., Archives/HP1243.

Developments in the western provinces were smaller-scale, understandably, given their smaller populations and economies. By 1900, the Winnipeg Electric Street Railway Company, headed by William Mackenzie of railway fame, had an effective monopoly on gas, electric, and public-transit facilities in Winnipeg. In 1902, the company entered into an arrangement with the Ogilvie Milling Company (a large user of power) to develop a hydro-electric site on the Winnipeg River. As that project neared completion, in 1906, Winnipeg ratepayers approved the construction of a $3.25 million plant, also on the Winnipeg River. Construction began in 1909, and Winnipeg Hydro, as the second company was known, began delivering electricity in competition with the Winnipeg Electric Street Railway Company in 1911.

Developments in British Columbia began much the same way. The British-owned British Columbia Electric Railway (BCER) dominated utilities in the major centres. Vancouver Power, organized in 1898 to develop a waterpower site, soon came under the control of the BCER. The potential of the province was quickly acknowledged, and the first delivery of hydro-electricity was made in 1903. Unlike what had occurred in Ontario and Manitoba, interest in a municipal venture went nowhere, and BCER retained its monopoly position until some time after World War I.

Hydro capacity in Canada grew quickly, once development began. Unfortunately, it is difficult to be very precise about the early progress of the industry because comprehensive statistics are available only from 1917 on. Figure 13.5 shows the record for hydraulic-turbine installation in Canada from 1890 to 1914. Because hydraulic power used directly in the pulp-and-paper and other industries is included in the data, hydro-electricity generation is overstated somewhat in this figure. Nevertheless, the growth is impressive. From 72 000 horsepower of hydraulic-turbine installation in 1890, capacity increased 25 times by 1900; it increased by that amount again by 1905; doubled once more, to 977 000 horsepower, by 1910; and stood at nearly 2 million horsepower in 1914. Ontario and Quebec accounted for the bulk of this capacity — 80 percent in 1900, and about that figure in 1914.[16] In 1914, Ontario had 44 percent of Canada's installed-turbine capacity and Quebec

Figure 13.5 Hydraulic-Turbine Installations, Canada, 1890–1914

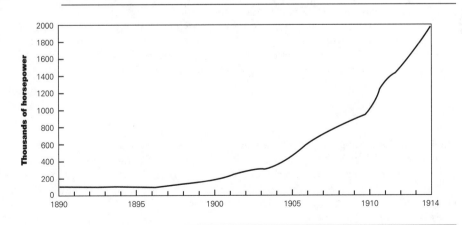

Source: M.C. Urquhart and K.A.H. Buckley, eds., *Historical Statistics of Canada* (Toronto: Macmillan, 1965), series P75, p. 454.

had 34 percent. British Columbia was a distant third, at around 10 percent; Manitoba next, at less than 5 percent; and the others' proportion was inconsequential.

It is difficult to know even approximately the impact of the development of "white coal" on Canada's economic fortunes. Hydro developments were important economic events, in and of themselves. Building the dams, installing the turbines, and constructing the transmission lines absorbed a significant amount of the young nation's capital resources and provided employment to many workers. Cheap electricity also attracted a host of power-intensive industries to these regions and gave Canada a comparative advantage in a range of industries it has retained to the present day. Some activities used the power directly in the production process, while others used it to drive machinery. (Examples of links to aluminum, carbide, and pulp and paper were discussed above, and more will be outlined below.)

A further effect, more difficult to quantify but potentially among the most important of all, is the impact of the availability of a cheap and reliable power source on secondary industry more generally. Canada was disadvantaged in terms of a nineteenth-century industrialism based on coal. The only deposits of this fuel were in Nova Scotia and the Prairies, far removed from the country's natural centres of manufacturing. Hydro could not compete with coal in terms of supplying heat, but it could in terms of motive power. As the potential of Niagara Falls and the St. Lawrence River and its tributaries was developed after 1900, Canadian industry could locate near both cheap power and its main markets. The old disadvantage had disappeared. As an early and influential study of the industry concluded, "Hydroelectricity has been a prerequisite to Central Canada's industrial growth."[17]

Cheap electricity also transformed the lives of ordinary Canadians in untold ways, many of which had economic impacts. Electric tramways were among the first users of the new resource. With commuting costs reduced, people could live farther away from their jobs, meaning that the shapes of cities began to change. Electrical gadgets reduced the drudgery of everyday chores in the home. Stoves, refrigerators, vacuum cleaners, and, most of all, reliable methods of lighting began to penetrate at least the middle-class environment by World War I.

Finally, politicians and business leaders were quick to note the connection between cheap power and industrial development. Control of the resources thus came to be seen as an essential part of what Nelles termed "the manufacturing condition,"[18] and what in another current terminology would be called "province-building." Thus, throughout its history, hydro has always been more than just another sector. The nearly mythical role sometimes ascribed today to Ontario Hydro and, especially, Hydro-Quebec in the economic development of their respective provincial economies in fact goes far back in time.

Government Services

The British North America Act was designed to give the federal government responsibility for defence and development, while leaving all matters of a more local concern to the provincial governments. On the revenue side, the federal government could raise revenue by any form of taxation, while provincial governments were restricted to direct taxes. Ottawa paid annual statutory subsidies to the provinces to balance revenues and expenditures among orders of government.

Total federal government spending rose from less than 5 percent in 1870 to reach 9 percent in 1885, before falling back to the 5–7 percent range until World War I.[19] These figures mask a certain tension in Canadian society at the time as to how large government spending should be. The nineteenth-century notion of the appropriate role for government was much different from that which would develop through the course of the twentieth century.

Clearly there were some functions that the government should be responsible for, such as roads, justice, and defence. It also recognized that certain areas occupied the border between private and public good. Thus, for example, the Canadian state assumed responsibility for "common carriers" by setting rules and regulations for railways.

Further, as we have seen, the Dominion was an active participant in shaping the Canadian economy. Government policies shaped western land ownership, immigration, and tariffs, all of which affected Canadian economic development. Irwin Gillespie characterizes the federal government's main objectives to attract people and build the union. There was also more direct subsidization of economic growth than is often realized. Railways were the favourite recipients of government grants. Together the Canadian Pacific, the Intercolonial, and Prince Edward Island systems absorbed large percentages of government expenditure through the latter decades of the century. Canals remained expensive, though less burdensome than they had been in colonial days. Drydocks, fishery wharves, and a host of other economic services completed the picture. As Figure 13.6 indicates, by far the largest expenditure was tied to Canada's geography and past politics, including railway subsidies, canal upkeep, and similar costs.

Figure 13.6 Distribution of Government Expenditures, Canada 1900–1910

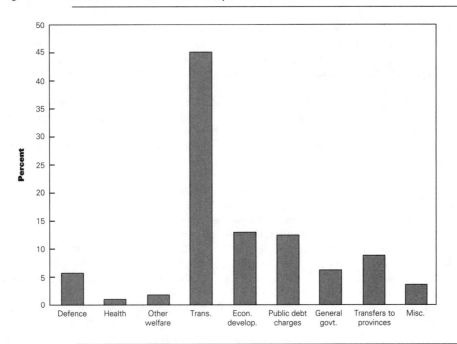

Source: Derived from Statistics Canada, *Historical Statistics of Canada*, 2nd, ed., cat. no. 11-516E (Ottawa: Supply and Services Canada, 1983), tables H19–34. Reproduced by authority of the Minister of Industry, 1995.

What was missing in federal government spending relative to recent decades was the Dominion's role as a social assistance agency. Welfare was a provincial responsibility, and this assignment was taken literally in the years before World War I. Ottawa spent nothing at all in that area.

252

Prior to 1930, and certainly before 1914, the only role any level of government in Canada provided for social assistance or welfare was a residual one.[20] Municipal governments were responsible for providing relief, or assistance, during times of economic hardship. Social assistance was only available for those families or individuals who had no savings or family to help them through hard financial times. James Struthers describes how public relief was thought of as a last resource for aiding the poor and the unemployed. Public assistance was kept discretional, minimal, and degrading so as to discourage dependency and encourage individual self-reliance. Canadians in need were not expected to starve, but they were expected to learn to save, to economize (particularly on luxury items, such as liquor), and to plan for the future.[21]

Cultural attitudes also governed the definition of who was considered deserving, or in need, of government assistance. Hardship due to unemployment was viewed as a moral failing of the individual rather than as a legitimate condition. Before 1914, even though year-round employment was not the norm for most sectors of the Canadian economy and every winter most workers were out of work, the workers were expected to save some of their income from the summer months to see them through the winter. Further, as Struthers argues, unemployed workers were thought to be able to find employment at any time so long as they would accept a lower wage. Thus, there was no legitimate reason for any able-bodied worker to experience prolonged involuntary unemployment. Anyone who remained unemployed and who would need public assistance was not only improvident, but also lazy.[22]

Before 1914, providing public assistance to the poor and unemployed was also at odds with the federal government's nation-building agenda that centred on western settlement. As Canada sought to attract immigrants to settle the vacant land on the Canadian Prairies, there seemed to be no reason why a Canadian should be unable to find work. Struthers points out that "abnormal" unemployment was viewed as the result of too many Canadians being lured away from their true vocation on the land for the bright lights of the city and its prospects for "easy" work. By not providing public assistance, governments were encouraging workers "back to the land" where they belonged.[23]

The absence of government spending on social security should not be interpreted as an absence of protective arrangements against economic hardship for Canadian households. A wide range of institutions and strategies were available to households that in contrast to today's centralized administration of government programs with compulsory participation, typically had de-centralized administration with voluntary participation. For example, in the pre-1914 period, the major cost of illness and accidents for a worker was lost wages rather than the costs of hospitalization and medical care. The most important providers of sickness insurance were "friendly" societies, like the Independent Order of Odd Fellows and the Knights of Pythias. Members of these organizations typically received cash benefits if they were sick and unable to work and, in some cases, they also received treatment from a lodge doctor. Households also used savings, accumulated wealth, and labour earnings from children to manage the costs of the household breadwinner's illness or accident.[24]

In the absence of government pensions, or financial support, for workers too old to work (or unwilling to continue working), aged Canadians relied on family and accumulated wealth and assets to support them in their old age. Brian Gratton argues that in the

United States, family economic strategies, in particular intrafamilial exchanges, promised the elderly considerable security.[25] Catharine Wilson describes how in nineteenth-century Ontario, many tenancy contracts resulted in a rental contract between father and son. The contract provided the older generation of the family with security and gave the younger generation access to the land. Rather than just transfer ownership of land to the son, the retention of ownership and control of the property by the elderly, with the promise of inheritance, was used as a leverage to induce children to support their elderly parents.[26]

The Dominion government financed its expenditures with a mixture of taxation and debt. Ottawa's tax sources were relatively limited. Customs and excise duties accounted for over 85 percent of total federal government revenue in 1868. By 1900, these two sources still contributed nearly 79 percent of total revenues, a figure that did not change much until World War I. There were no federal sales taxes or personal or corporate income taxes in these years. Irwin Gillespie argues that this was due, in part, to fears that higher taxes than in the U.S. would discourage labour and capital from locating in Canada.

Overall though, federal government philosophy during these years favoured debt.[27] Ottawa ran a deficit every year from 1868 to 1902, and showed only six surpluses before 1914.[28] A small nation with a vast frontier could reasonably expect that economic subsidies were investments in future growth. It only made sense, therefore, that this hypothetical larger, more prosperous nation of the future would be easily able to repay the earlier debts. Total Dominion debt rose from less than 1 percent of GNP in 1870 to nearly 18 percent by 1890.[29] By then, the persistent failure of the West to live up to expectations became a lively political issue. Through the early 1890s, civil servants were laid off, projects delayed, and operations trimmed. Capital expenditures were especially hard hit, falling by some 50 percent between 1890 and 1893. Debt as a percentage of GNP rose to 22.1 percent in 1896, before falling back to 7.6 percent in 1913.[30]

The concern about debt through the 1890s meant two things. First, government behaviour in the recession was cyclical, thus exacerbating the situation rather than countering it. This would not be the last time that government responded to economic recession and debt concerns by cutting back, though the overall role of government in the 1890s was sufficiently small that any effects were local rather than national. Second, the mood of the 1890s diminished the already small government relative to the economy. When the economy turned around in 1897, total federal government spending was only 5.6 percent of GNP.

The federal government, with its high-profile economic development efforts, was the most visible government entity in the decades after Confederation. Yet this situation was beginning to change as the new century opened. The rapid growth of the Laurier years created new demands on government, most of which fell on the provincial and municipal levels. Industrialization made unemployment more cyclical and more obvious than had been the case in an agricultural economy. Urbanization created a demand for a broader set of public goods. Publicly owned street railways, slum clearance, new sewers, health and sanitation, crime control, and, by implication, social reform, all became issues. As the cliché of the time went, disease did not respect class or neighbourhood.

One important example of the shift in the role of provincial governments is social policy. The provinces had been left with responsibility for welfare and education under the British North America Act because of the desire to preserve local identities, especially in francophone Quebec. Certainly at the time it did not seem an onerous proposition, fiscally. Public welfare consumed only a small portion of provincial costs, and even education was a relatively small burden in an age when most children left school before grade 8. Yet by the twentieth century both areas were becoming more important. As society urbanized

253

and industrialized, the demand for improved education continued to increase. By 1913, education was the largest single area of provincial expenditure and, by itself, absorbed more than the entire provincial revenue just fifteen years before. Every indication was that costs were just beginning to escalate.

The provincial role extended beyond these areas, however. In spite of their small fiscal bases, provinces could play an important role in economic development. Several provinces caught railway fever and nearly bankrupted themselves in the process. In other cases, especially in Ontario and Quebec, governments used a combination of regulation and enticement to try to draw industry into their jurisdictions.[31] Aided by a friendly Dominion tariff, they were often successful, especially in attracting American branch plants and resource industries.

The changes in provincial requirements forced changes in taxation. If the revenues of the Dominion government were small by current standards, those of the provinces were infinitesimal initially. In the early years after Confederation the provinces had extremely limited revenue sources. Even rich and powerful jurisdictions like Ontario derived almost half their revenue from Dominion subsidies. New Brunswick received more than 90 percent of its income from that source.[32] Licence fees, land sales (denied to the Prairies), and a mixed bag of small revenue sources made up the local taxation base.

Not surprisingly, the first response to the growing provincial responsibilities after 1900 was to look to increased federal subsidies. In this way, the political unpopularity of taxation could be carried by another jurisdiction and, for the poorer provinces, federal subsidy was in effect a transfer of revenue from the wealthier parts of the country. The boom made it relatively easy for the Dominion to respond, and in 1906 Dominion subsidies increased by approximately one-third. Even so, the share of federal transfers in total provincial revenues continued to decline, going from 54 percent in 1868 to 39 percent in 1890, and to 26 percent in 1910.[33]

Provincial and municipal governments resorted to a wide range of taxes to fund their growing expenditures. All provinces had succession duties and corporation taxes in place before World War I. British Columbia introduced a personal income tax in 1876, and Prince Edward Island followed suit in 1894. Prince Edward Island introduced the first corporation income tax in 1894, with British Columbia this time following in 1901. In both these cases, the other provinces were much later in tapping these sources. Municipalities in all provinces relied on real property taxes. Interestingly from a present-day perspective, many municipal governments also levied personal income taxes and poll taxes.[34]

Competition Policy and Labour Unions

Structural economic change requires institutional adaptation. Sometimes, as in the case of the fiscal demands on the provinces, these adaptations are obvious; in other cases, they are more subtle but nonetheless vital. If they are not made, the social disruption of economic change is magnified, often to the broad detriment of society as a whole.

One of the features of industrial development in the years after 1900 was concentration of industry into ever-larger establishments. In addition, company-owned and -operated establishments were increasingly displaced by joint-stock companies. Both of these tendencies, as well as industrialization, led to increased unionization. Although the union movement in Canada can be traced back to some small pre-Confederation craft unions, unionization and large-scale industry more or less grew together in the late nineteenth and early twentieth centuries.

The rise of unionism was not smooth, and its course provides a clear demonstration of the need for government to adjust to new economic structures. The initial reaction of employers was that unions violated individual liberty— theirs, and that of the worker who did not wish to join. The fact that they were forming "trade associations" and fixing prices at the same time was not seen as a contradiction. Employer resistance and union militancy led to some bitter strikes. Railways, as the largest employer of the nineteenth century, were the scene of some of the most bitter confrontations, such as the Grand Trunk strike of 1876. Ten years later a royal commission on labour received embittered testimony about the state of employer–employee relations in the nation, and the pattern continued. As the century drew to a close, there were plenty of examples of confrontation in mines, railways, and factories.

Early examples of union activity can be traced to the first decades of the nineteenth century. These were isolated and usually transient examples, however, and significant unionization was, to a large degree, a product of industrialism. Specifically, the period from 1850 through the 1870s saw the rise of many individual unions and a series of "associations," in which various unions in a city or region developed an umbrella organization to co-ordinate affairs and provide mutual support, among other activities. The Toronto Trades Assembly, which was established in 1871, included some fourteen area unions and typified the efforts to link union activities. In 1873, a national organization, the Canadian Labour Union, was formed. Though national in design, it cannot be said to have represented anything like all of the unions that existed at that time.

In these early years there was no fixed pattern of union organization. Some unions, such as the British Amalgamated Society of Carpenters and Joiners, were affiliated with British unions. Others, such as the Railway Conductors, were associated with American unions. Still others, such as the Nova Scotia coal miners' Provincial Workmen's Association, were purely local responses to the needs of workers and had no international affiliations. Most, but not all, were craft unions (tied to a particular skill, such as carpentry). The one thing they did have in common was the difficult task of asserting the power of workers in an era that glorified the myth of individualism and looked with suspicion on associations of workers as antithetical to the spirit of individual initiative.

Perhaps the most interesting, and certainly the most powerful, example of union organization in the years before 1900 is the Knights of Labor. This American-based union (formed 1869) spread to Canada in the mid-1870s and was, by the late 1880s, the most powerful union organization in Canada.

The Knights were an unusual organization, combining trade-union activity with much of the ritual and social life of fraternal lodges, such as the Masons. It was also a completely open union, interested in representing all workers, regardless of skill or gender. Its open policy on membership and its tremendous success also meant that it was little loved by traditional craft-union organizations. These craft unions, increasingly dominated by American internationals, grew relatively stronger by the end of the century, partly because of the strong support they received from their American headquarters and from the American Federation of Labor.

By the early twentieth century, the international unions were sufficiently strong to assert their control over the Canadian national association, the Trades and Labor Congress (TLC). In Berlin (now Kitchener), Ontario, in 1902, the internationals supported a series of resolutions at the annual TLC convention that banned dual unionism and gave AFL-affiliated unions primacy in any dual-union controversy. The net effect was to destroy the already declining Knights of Labor and to make many Canadian unions into miniature replicas of their American counterparts. The continental integration that was taking place in business was thus paralleled, even exceeded, by that emerging in unionism.

256

The rise of unions caused much controversy. Blood was shed in bitter strikes, panicky politicians vied to condemn this threat to the established order, and union leaders reciprocated with militant rhetoric drawn from the more radical politics of European socialism that often belied their own weakness and moderate goals. Businessmen, the most vociferous of all, condemned the restraint of trade that unionism represented, while conveniently forgetting their own associations and price-fixing arrangements. In fact, however, the rhetoric did not reflect reality. The union movement in the early twentieth century was hardly a threat to the social order, nor does it appear to have altered in any significant way the economic structure of Canadian industry. Indeed, unionism in the decade and a half before the war was declining in numbers and power, and whatever assistance it may have been able to give individual workers, it cannot be said, in these years, to have altered the course of Canadian economic development, however much Canadian businessmen might have lamented.

Part of the strife in these years was the result of the fact that the state was initially ill-equipped to deal with the new phenomenon of massed labour against the powerful employer. State regulations and attitudes had to catch up to economic developments. This would take decades to complete, but the years of the Laurier boom saw the groundwork laid. William Lyon Mackenzie King, the future prime minister, served as the first deputy minister of labour in the Laurier government and subsequently as minister of labour. He had observed the growth of bitter strikes in Britain and the United States, and moved to create a groundwork of state-supervised rules for conciliation, arbitration, and collective bargaining.[35] They were rudimentary and, as the Winnipeg General Strike of 1919 would demonstrate, labour strife could still threaten the nation's stability. Nevertheless, they were one more case of institutional adaptation to the emerging industrial society.

COMPETITION POLICY

The trend to business concentration in both manufacturing and services not unnaturally attracted the attention of some in the economy, particularly small businesses, farmers, and consumer groups. There were allegations of price-fixing, predatory pricing, price discrimination, and misleading advertising. A spate of publicity in the 1880s led to the establishment of a select House of Commons committee on combines, and Canada's first Anti-combines Act was passed in 1889. There was little support for interference into what were generally seen as necessary and justifiable actions by businesses to ensure a fair return. Michael Bliss concluded that "the 1889 law was pious anti-monopoly posturing that had no effect on anything."[36]

Conclusion

These service-sector developments point to three general conclusions. First, the Canadian economy clearly grew in complexity and sophistication, as well as in size, in the four decades following Confederation. Second, staple products are a necessary but far from sufficient part of the story. Some service-sector growth derived from resource activities, and thus fits the traditional interpretation of the period. The wholesale and retail networks that sprang up to support the prairie wheat economy are the most obvious examples. But other developments had more independent origins, and acted to reinforce and promote aggregate economic growth. Third, virtually all the activity originated in the private sector, the considerable attention typically given to government policies in this period notwithstanding. Government as we know it today was one depression and two world wars away.

NOTES

1. One obvious problem is the difficulty of measuring output for many service activities. For example, what is the output of the legal profession or the education sector? For an overview of some recent work on the service sector in Canada see Herbert G. Grubel and Michael A. Walker, eds., *Service Industry Growth: Causes and Effects* (Vancouver: Fraser Institute, 1989).

2. Joy I. Satink, *Timothy Eaton and the Rise of His Department Store* (Toronto: University of Toronto Press, 1990), 43.

3. Satink, *Timothy Eaton*, 39.

4. Robert J. Gordon, "Does the 'New Economy' Measure up to the Great Inventions of the Past," *Journal of Economic Perspectives* 14(4), 2000, 49–74.

5. David Monod, "Bay Days: The Managerial Revolution and the Hudson's Bay Department Stores, 1912–1929," *Canadian Historical Association Historical Papers* (1986): 176.

6. *Canada Year Book* (Ottawa: King's Printer, 1931), 613.

7. Satink, *Timothy Eaton*, appendix.

8. See E.P Neufeld, *The Financial System of Canada: Its Growth and Development* (Toronto: Macmillan, 1972).

9. D. Mole, "Financial Development and Capital Formation," in M.H. Watkins and H.M Grant, *Canadian Economic History: Classic and Contemporary Approaches* (Ottawa: Carleton University Press, 1993).

10. Alan M. Taylor, "Argentina and the World Capital Markets: Saving, Investment, and International Capital Mobility in the 20th Century," *Journal of Development Economics* 57 (1998): 147–184.

11. Neufeld, *Financial System of Canada*, table 2:1, p. 35.

12. Michael Bliss, *Northern Enterprise: Five Centuries of Canadian Business* (Toronto: McClelland & Stewart, 1987), 268.

13. L.T. Evans and N.C. Quigley, "Discrimination in Bank Lending Policies: A Test Using Data From the Bank of Nova Scotia, 1900–1937," *Canadian Journal of Economics* 23(1) (February 1990): 210–25. See also Neil C. Quigley, Ian M. Drummond, and Lewis T. Evans, "Regional Transfers of Funds Through the Canadian Banking System and Maritime Economic Development, 1895–1935," in Kris Inwood, ed., *Farm, Factory and Fortune: New Studies in the Economic History of the Maritime Provinces* (Fredericton: Acadiensis Press, 1993), 219–50.

14. Peter Baskerville and Graham Taylor, *A Concise History of Canadian Business* (Toronto: Oxford University Press, 1994), 253.

15. The following material is drawn from J.H. Dales, *Hydroelectricity and Industrial Development in Quebec, 1898–1940* (Cambridge, MA: Harvard University Press, 1957); H.V. Nelles, *The Politics of Development: Forests, Mines and Hydroelectric Power in Ontario, 1849–1941* (Toronto: Macmillan, 1974); and Christopher Armstrong and H.V. Nelles, *Monopoly's Moment: The Organization and Regulation of Canadian Utilities 1830–1930* (Philadelphia: Temple University Press, 1986).

16. Dales, *Hydroelectricity*, 35.

17. Dales, *Hydroelectricity*, 180.

18. Nelles, *Politics of Development*, chapter 2.

19. W. Irwin Gillespie, *Tax, Borrow and Spend: Financing Federal Spending in Canada, 1867–1990* (Ottawa: Carleton University Press, 1991), table C-3, 287.

20. D. Guest, *The Emergence of Social Security in Canada* (Vancouver: University of British Columbia Press, 1980).

21. James Stretchers, *No Fault of Their Own: Unemployment and the Canadian Welfare State 1914–1941* (Toronto: University of Toronto Press, 1990).

22. James Struthers, *No Fault of Their Own*. For a discussion of programs other than unemployment relief, see James Struthers, *The Limits of Affluence: Welfare in Ontario, 1920–1970* (Toronto: University of Toronto Press, 1994).

23. James Struthers, *The Limits of Affluence*, 8.

24. George Emery and J.C. Herbert Emery, *A Young Man's Benefit: The Independent Order of Odd Fellows and Sickness Insurance in the United States and Canada, 1860–1929* (Kingston and Montreal: McGill-Queen's University Press, 1999).

258

25. Brian Gratton, "The Poverty of Impoverishment Theory: The Economic Well-Being of the Elderly, 1890–1950," *Journal of Economic History* 56(1), March 1996: 39–61.
26. Catharine Anne Wilson, "Tenancy as a family strategy in mid-nineteenth century Ontario," *Journal of Social History* 31(4), 1998: 875–896.
27. See Stanley L. Winer and Walter Hettich, "Debt and Tariffs: An Empirical Investigation of the Evolution of Revenue Systems," *Journal of Public Economics* 45 (1991): 215–42.
28. Gillespie, *Tax, Borrow and Spend*, table C-2, 284–86.
29. Gillespie, *Tax, Borrow and Spend*, table C-3, 287–89.
30. Gillespie, *Tax, Borrow and Spend*, table C-3, 287–89.
31. Nelles, *Politics of Development*.
32. Donald Creighton, *British North America at Confederation* (Ottawa: King's Printer, 1940), 94.
33. A. Milton Moore, J. Harvey Perry, and Donald I. Beach, *The Financing of Canadian Federation: The First Hundred Years* (Toronto: Canadian Tax Foundation, 1966), table 29, 119.
34. Gillespie, *Tax, Borrow and Spend*, table A-2, 260.
35. Paul Craven, *Impartial Umpire: Industrial Relations & the Canadian State, 1900–1911* (Toronto: University of Toronto Press, 1980).
36. Bliss, *Northern Enterprise*, 362.

FURTHER READINGS

Armstrong, Christopher. "Making a Market: Selling Securities in Atlantic Canada before World War I." *Canadian Journal of Economics* (August 1980): 438–54.

Armstrong, Christopher, and H.V Nelles. *Monopoly's Moment: The Organization and Regulation of Canadian Utilities 1830–1930*. Philadelphia: Temple University Press, 1986.

Bliss, Michael. *Northern Enterprise: Five Centuries of Canadian Business*. Toronto: McClelland & Stewart, 1987.

Evans, L.T., and N.C. Quigley. "Discrimination in Bank Lending Practice: A Test Using Data From the Bank of Nova Scotia, 1900–1937." *Canadian Journal of Economics* (February 1990): 210–25.

Gillespie, W. Irwin. *Tax, Borrow and Spend: Financing Federal Spending in Canada, 1867–1990*. Ottawa: Carleton University Press, 1991.

Lindert, Peter. "The Rise of Social Spending, 1880–1930." *Explorations in Economic History* 31(1) 1994, 1–37.

Neufeld, E.P. *The Financial System of Canada: Its Growth and Development*. Toronto: Macmillan, 1972.

Rich, G. *The Cross of Gold: Money and the Canadian Business Cycle, 1867–1913*. Ottawa: Carleton University Press, 1988.

Part Five

The Turbulent Years, 1914–1945

Women working in a railway yard during World War II. As a result of the labour shortage during this era, women were encouraged to work outside the home. National Film Board of Canada/National Archives of Canada/C-79525.

260 **THE DOMINANT FEATURE** of the Canadian economy in the period 1914–45 is one of continuous adjustment to a series of major and prolonged shocks. First came a world war in 1914, then demobilization, then the fragile North Atlantic economy of the 1920s, then the massive international depression of the 1930s, and finally another world war in 1939. Each of these events posed major challenges both to individual Canadians and to their governments. In dealing with the challenges, institutions were transformed, economic structures changed, and human psychology altered. Contemporary Canada is, in no small measure, the direct product of this era of challenge and response.

Figure P5.1 illustrates the great economic volatility that characterized this period. The value of real output fell slightly in 1914 as the Laurier boom slowed. This trend was reversed the following year as wartime production began. Real GNP peaked in 1917, after which the economy sank into a postwar depression that lasted until 1921. Real output at the trough of this depression was below its level of ten years earlier. The economy then expanded continuously throughout the 1920s, peaking in 1929 with real GNP equal to 1.7 times its value in 1921.

The greatest volatility was yet to come, as Canada entered its worst depression ever. From 1929 to 1933, the value of real output fell by 30 percent. The economy began to recover in 1933, with a pause in 1937–38, but real output did not reach its 1929 value

Figure P5.1 Real GNP, Canada, 1913–1945

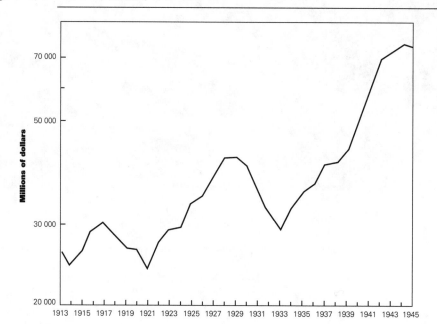

Source: M.C. Urquhart, "Canadian Economic Growth, 1870–1980," Department of Economics, Queen's University, discussion paper no. 734, 1988, table 2.

again until 1939. The effects of World War II are evident in Figure P5.1. Real GNP rose every year to 1944 and then declined slightly in 1945. At its peak in 1944, real GNP was 1.7 times its value in 1939.[1]

Figure P5.2 demonstrates that the volatility in intensive economic growth was more severe yet. Real GNP per capita fell in 1914, and then rose each year until 1917. The decline to 1921 was very pronounced, with real output per capita falling to a level last seen in 1905. At the peak in 1928, one year earlier than for GNP, real per capita GNP was 1.5 times its 1921 value. The collapse to 1933 is very evident in the graph, with real per capita output in that year only 65 percent of its 1928 value, and, indeed, only marginally above what it was in 1921. It was 1940 before this series regained its 1928 value, but by 1944 real per capita output was 1.6 times its value in 1939.

Canada's economic record between 1913 and 1945 reflects more graphically than ever this nation's dependence on international events. Victory in the Great War, 1914–18, rested as much on the efficient application of technology and on mass production as on military strategy. Thus governments on both sides of the conflict faced an economic challenge as much as a military one. Aggregate output had to be expanded, even as workers were being drafted into military service and as international capital flows were drying up. The mix of output had to be shifted as well. Government demands on the economy had to take precedence over private demands, particularly those of individual consumers. All sectors, from farming to banking, had to learn to meet the military needs for food, clothing, transportation, and, most of all, instruments of destruction.

Figure P5.2 Real GNP per Capita, Canada, 1913–1945

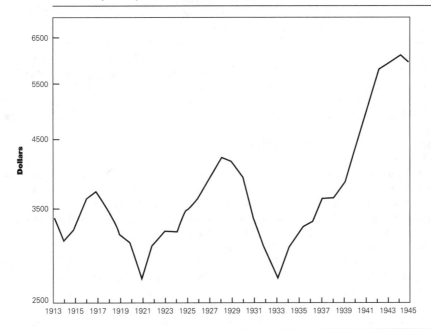

Source: M.C. Urquhart, "Canadian Economic Growth, 1870–1980," Department of Economics, Queen's University, discussion paper no. 734, 1988, table 2.

262

As the war ended, the reconstruction task began. The war-torn nations of the continent faced the greatest challenge, given the great loss of life and the damage to land, buildings, and machinery and equipment. Nations that were spared this destruction still had to reverse the restructuring processes they had gone through as hostilities began. Labour markets had to absorb great numbers of new entrants in the form of returning veterans, and the structure of production had to be shifted back to meet peacetime demands.

The immediate postwar period brought an economic boom to the Atlantic economy. Aggregate demand in most nations was strong as firms sought to replenish inventories, consumers drew down some of the savings they had accumulated during the war, and expenditures by governments came down only slowly. This brief boom turned to depression in 1920–21 as government spending declined and as authorities reacted to the burgeoning inflation by implementing restrictive monetary policies. The U.S. economy began to recover in the second half of 1921 and expanded steadily thereafter until mid-1929. The British economy grew throughout this period as well, albeit more slowly.

Conditions were more chaotic on the continent. The defeat of the German empire interrupted its economic growth and left that former industrial power under massive obligations of foreign debt and war reparations. Eastern Europe faced great economic and political dislocation. Imperial Russia had never been a major industrial nation, but its size, natural resources, and large population had made it important economically before the war. The war, however, brought massive losses to Russia and, in 1917, culminated in the Russian revolution. For years thereafter, the nation was torn apart by civil strife and its economy was a shambles.

Political decisions stemming from the war made matters more rather than less difficult. An example is the question of reparations. Reparations were a plan to make Germany pay for at least a portion of Allied war costs. They followed from the Allied position that Germany was morally responsible for the war. The plan was based on appealing but ultimately simplistic logic. The guilty should be punished, and the punishment could assist war-shattered economies, while enabling Allied governments to avoid implementing excessively high taxes. Moreover, and especially important to war-ravaged France, the continual drain on Germany's financial strength would hinder any attempts by the country to regain great-power status. In pursuit of these aims, the Allies had demanded and received a £1 billion interim payment during the initial peace negotiations. Then, in 1921, the Allies presented a bill to Germany for £6.5 billion worth of goods and services, to be paid in regular instalments over the next decades.

The reparations issue was mixed in with that of Allied war debts. Britain and France had borrowed massively in order to finance their own war effort. The U.S. treasury alone had lent the two countries some $7.7 billion. Now, as the United States recoiled from its involvement in European affairs, it was politically popular in that country to take a hard line and demand repayment. The Allies protested that such repayments should be forgiven as another American contribution to the war effort, since the United States had joined so late, and pointed out, further, that such a drain on western Europe would only hinder the restoration of economic stability. The Americans were not impressed.

The American insistence on Allied repayment made German reparation payments crucial to the Allies. In effect, Allied debtors hoped to avoid undue strain on their own economies by using a portion of German reparation payments to mollify the Americans. German payments would flow to France and Britain, and then to the United States. Americans would then, presumably, invest overseas to strengthen the international community.

There were several flaws in this scheme. For one thing, the German economy and economic will were not up to bearing the burden of reparations in the immediate postwar period. The entire German monetary system collapsed soon after reparations were begun. Hyperinflation in 1921–22 made the Deutschmark worthless and forced the Allies, led by the Americans, to slow down reparations payments to something approaching a bearable rate. Second, American investment did not flow abroad, in either the direction or the amount that would have allowed it to assume the role taken by British capital before the war. Thus, throughout the first part of the decade, the international financial community remained in considerable turmoil.

By the mid-1920s, there was some stabilization. The American expansion has already been noted. The Dawes plan, which combined rescheduled reparation payments with American loans to Germany, helped recovery in Europe. The German economy prospered after mid-1926, largely financed by foreign borrowing. The French economy boomed beginning in 1927, helped by a return to the gold standard that featured an 80 percent devaluation. Britain returned to the gold standard in 1925. The decision to retain the prewar rate meant that its currency was overvalued, which was responsible at least in part for that nation's relatively slow economic growth for the remainder of the decade.

This short period of prosperity ended in 1928–29, as the industrial world began its slide into what would turn out to be the greatest economic collapse of modern times. The downturn began in the late 1920s, when, as Peter Temin noted, "the Atlantic economy ... was in the grip of deflationary policies."[2] This situation was a result of deliberate policy action in the United States, transmitted to other countries by the operation of the recently re-established international gold standard. American monetary policy turned increasingly contractionary in 1928 and 1929 in an attempt to curb speculation on the New York Stock Exchange. The resulting high interest rates drew capital from Europe, forcing monetary authorities there to deflate in order to protect their currencies. The British were having to deflate anyway, to defend the overvalued pound. The undervalued French franc was drawing gold and foreign-exchange reserves to that country, creating further deflationary pressures in other economies.

There are a number of reasons why this deflation in the late 1920s turned into the Great Depression. The primary impetus seems to have come from the fact that monetary and fiscal policies in the United States and Germany remained tight in 1930 and 1931, in the face of pressures on their currencies. The U.S. Federal Reserve raised the discount rate in September 1931, in response to the currency crises in Europe and Britain's abandonment of the gold standard. The German central bank maintained interest rates in that country well above those in New York and London, in an attempt to stem the outflow of gold. Thus adherence to the rules of the gold standard dictated a tightening of monetary conditions in 1930 and 1931, when precisely the opposite policy was called for.

Monetary shocks alone do not explain the severity and duration of the Depression in the United States, however. Other contributing factors include the simultaneous downturn in other countries in the late 1920s, which reduced the market for American exports; the stock-market crash of October 1929, which lowered private wealth by about 10 percent and added to consumer-spending uncertainty, particularly with respect to the purchase of consumer durables; the downward rigidity of nominal wages, which resulted in the cost of labour rising as deflation proceeded, causing unemployment to rise; deflationary expectations, which meant that real interest rates were above nominal rates, further depressing business investment; bank failures; and crop failures.[3]

As the Depression continued, nations sought to cushion themselves against its worst effects. In their efforts to do so, they often made things worse. In particular, there was a

263

general move to high levels of protectionism. The theory was that at least the domestic market could be preserved for local producers. Instead, the rise of tariff walls around the world only hastened the shrinkage of international trade and put barriers in the way of any easy recovery. By the beginning of 1931, the value of international trade had declined to less than two-thirds of what it had been at the beginning of 1929.[4]

Once the Depression hit, it fed upon itself. Collapsing expectations, financial crises, shrinking international trade, and increasingly restrictive trade barriers sent the international economy into the most drastic collapse of the industrial era. By 1933, the bottom of the Depression, international trade had declined to one-third of what it had been at the beginning of 1929. Unemployment skyrocketed, nations were destabilized, and an industrial world used to economic progress settled into an era of stagnation.

The Great Depression reached its nadir in the United States in 1933. The recovery that began in that year, Temin argued, was a rapid response to the new policy regime introduced by the new president, Franklin D. Roosevelt, who took the necessary steps to devalue the American dollar.[5] New Deal spending added a further expansionary impetus to policy. Finally, the Federal Reserve loosened monetary policy. These measures triggered an immediate increase in stock-market prices, and soon thereafter increases in business investment and consumer spending. It would be several years yet, and one temporary setback in 1937, before the level of economic activity returned to pre-Depression levels, but at least the downward spiral had been reversed.

In an ironic and tragic way, however, the Nazis were responsible for ending the Depression not just in Germany but internationally. Their aggressive foreign policy eventually forced a response from other European nations, and led, of course, to World War II. With the coming of war, the final great shift of these years took place. As had been the case in 1914–18, modern industrial war demanded that the full productive capacity of the engaged nations be utilized. The Depression ended, and western economies underwent tremendous growth. Equally important, World War II also brought an end to the tremendous volatility ushered in by World War I. For out of this war came a new concern with the stability of international trade. Better currency and trade systems were established, while the United States adopted a series of policies calculated to encourage stability in international trade. The short, sharp fluctuations of the past quarter-century would be replaced by longer-term cycles of prosperity and growth.

NOTES

1. GNP is an imperfect measure of economic welfare at any time, but it is especially problematic in a wartime economy. Much of this output increase was material destined to end lives in Europe.
2. Peter Temin, *Lessons from the Great Depression* (Cambridge, MA: MIT Press, 1989), 25.
3. See Barry Eichengreen, "The Origins and Nature of the Great Slump Revisited," *Economic History Review* 65(2) (May 1992): 213–39.
4. William Ashworth, *A Short History of the International Economy, 1850–1950* (London: Longmans, Green, 1952), 203; C.P. Kindleberger, *The World in Depression: 1929–1939*, 2nd ed. (Berkeley, CA: University of California Press, 1986), 172.
5. Temin, *Lessons from the Great Depression*, 100.

Chapter Fourteen

World War I, 1914–1918

IN AUGUST 1914, after years of rising tension, the nations of Europe went to war. For the next four years, the British empire, allied with the French and the Russians, was to be pitted in conflict with the German and Austro–Hungarian empires. This massive conflict, known to contemporaries simply as the Great War, profoundly affected the Canadian economy. In the short term, the war exacerbated an economic slowdown already underway. In the medium term, it brought renewed prosperity and economic restructuring as Canada drew on its new economic strengths to become a major supplier of food and material to the Anglo–French war effort. Canadian wheat and Canadian bacon fed the soldiers at the front, while Canadian-made uniforms clothed them. Canadian ammunition would, after a while, be used to kill the enemy. In the longer term, no part of the Canadian economy, private or public, was left unmarked by the war experience.

The causes of World War I were rooted in the same forces that encouraged European expansion around the globe centuries earlier. Economic and political rivalries between European monarchies and nation states contributed to unstable political and economic conditions. Leonard Dudley argues that, as early as the 1870s, Europe was in a state of political disequilibrium. With industrialization, England, France, Germany, and other major European states had surplus resources to allocate for military purposes and expansive foreign policy. Where France and Great Britain had world-wide empires to absorb their military expenditures, Germany did not and the amount of resources it could mobilize for military purposes greatly exceeded what it needed to defend its own territory. Further, the introduction of railway and telegraph technologies enhanced Germany's capacity to deploy its military resources. In this sense, it was inevitable that Germany would plan a European expansion and that "Europe would not find stability until these resources (economic surplus for the military) were either fully committed to territorial control or destroyed."[1]

John Keegan[2] argues that in a continent in which a handful of powers exercised control over a number of subordinate peoples who made demands for wider democracy, and from which England and France ruled much of the rest of the world, fear of war in the abstract was ever present, but no one knew when war might break out or what form it might take. Efforts had been made to encourage peaceful coexistence between the various political entities of Europe through credit arrangements between countries, inter-marriage between royal families of different countries, and negotiations for co-operation in limiting military expenditures. Thus despite attempts by leaders such as Russia's Tsar Nicholas II to encourage the nations of Europe to search for means to avert conflict, the age old quest for security in military superiority guided European policy on this question at the start of the twentieth century.

Keegan views the Germans, who resented their lack of colonies, as provoking the worst of the European rivalries through Germany's decision in 1900 to build up its naval fleet to be capable of engaging England's Royal Navy in battle. England responded and by 1906, the race to outbuild Germany in modern battleships held a dominant place in British public policy. France, with a population of 40 million, decided to match the number of German soldiers even though Germany's population numbered 60 million. Thus, well before 1914, an arms race was underway. Finally, as Keegan points out, armies plan. In Germany, the Kaiser and the army informed the Prime Minister in 1912 of the central war plan that they had been preparing since 1905. In June 1914, the unstable and volatile conditions in Europe escalated with the assassination of Archduke Franz Ferdinand, heir to the throne of the Austria-Hungary throne, by a group of five Serbs and a Bosnian Muslim in Sarajevo.

By 1918, Germany had two million war dead, representing 13 percent of Germans born between 1870 and 1899. France, with a smaller population, also suffered two million war dead. Britain had 744,000 war dead and its empire contributed another 225,000 to that total. Canada's war dead numbered at 60,000. The number of wounded, mutilated, and disabled soldiers increased the casualty total further, for example, 170,000 members of the Canadian Expeditionary Force (CEF) were wounded. Added to the human costs of World War I were the enormous military costs even for the victorious Great Britain. From 1915 to 1918, British military expenditures absorbed 25 to 30 percent of the British GNP. In addition to the direct costs of World War I, we must also add that the costs of World War II, 1939 to 1945, were attributable to the economic conditions of the peace settlement of 1919 and the Treaty of Versailles, designed to prevent Germany from re-arming, but left Europe no closer to political-territorial equilibrium than it had been in 1871.

The Economic Impact of the War

The initial effect of the war was to make the slowdown that had occurred in 1913 worse. Capital imports, such an important part of the economy before the war, all but collapsed by 1915. The already shaky industries that depended so much on investment were hit immediately. Construction continued its collapse from the previous year, hitting bottom in 1915. Railways, already overextended and in trouble, were forced to cut back operations. Workers were let go in large numbers. By 1915, there were 50 000 fewer employees in railway and related activities than there had been only two years earlier.

As the war continued, the excess capacity disappeared, and access to enough goods and services became the problem instead. Most immediately, the war meant that Canadians could no longer borrow abroad on a net basis to supplement domestic output. Net capital imports, which had been as high as 17.7 percent of GNP as recently as 1912, fell to 2.5 percent of GNP in 1915 and to less than 1 percent in 1916. In 1917 and 1918, Canada actually became a net capital exporter. In a dramatic reversal of the wheat boom pattern, Canadians were producing more goods and services in total than they themselves were using, and the surplus output was transferred abroad in support of the Allied war effort.

Supply constraints were also felt in the labour market. War-fuelled production increased the demand for labour, while on the supply side the army took tens of thousands of individuals out of the labour force. Also, the long-standing inflow of immigration into Canada slowed to a trickle as the war disrupted the normal patterns of resettlement. The number of immigrants to Canada declined from a high of more than 402 000 in 1913 to fewer than 145 000 by 1915 and only a little more than 48 000 in 1916. Unemployment effectively ended by 1915; in much of the country, there was a serious shortage of workers by midwar.

Figure 14.1 illustrates just how much the structure of production was altered as a result of the war. Exports expanded dramatically, rising from 18.5 percent of GNP in 1913 to a peak of 41 percent of GNP in 1917. In absolute terms, this amounted to a tripling of merchandise exports, from $421 million in 1913 to $1.34 billion by 1918. Imports, which stood at $633 million in 1913, fell to $522 million in 1914 and to $516 million in 1915, before rising again to reach $953 million in the final year of the war.[3]

Government spending on goods and services rose from 10 percent of GNP in 1913 to 14.5 percent in 1914 and remained in this range until 1920. While these numbers are smaller than the export shares, this change still represents nearly a 50 percent increase in the size of government in the economy. Investment spending declined in relative terms, returning to a share of GNP more like the share it had at the turn of the century as the wheat boom was getting underway. Foreign capital inflows were negligible in 1916 and became negative (i.e., net capital outflows) in 1917 and 1918.

Figure 14.2 shows these structural changes in a slightly different manner. Agriculture maintained its relative share of GDP in this decade, for the first time since the 1870s. Other primary industries grew at the same pace as the economy as a whole as well, maintaining their share of 5 percent of total production. Manufacturing activities grew slightly faster

267

Figure 14.1 Shares of Investment, Exports, and Government in GNP, Canada, 1913–1945

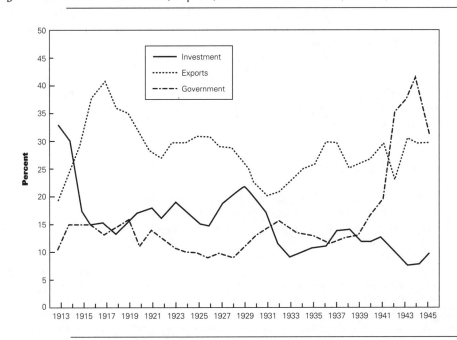

Source: M.C. Urquhart, "Canadian Economic Growth, 1870–1980," Department of Economics, Queen's University, discussion paper no. 734, 1988, table 4.

268

Figure 14.2 Distribution of GDP by Main Sector, Canada, 1910–1950

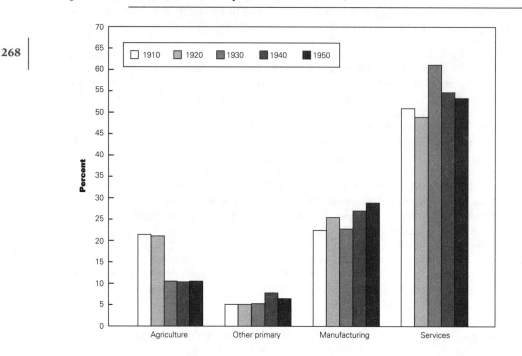

Source: M.C. Urquhart, "Canadian Economic Growth, 1870–1980," Department of Economics, Queen's University, discussion paper no. 734, 1988, table 10.

than GDP, rising to contribute over one-quarter of final output in 1920. Service industry output rose relatively slowly, on the other hand, with the result that its share of GDP declined for the first time.

The Role of Government

The government faced two separate, but related, challenges in converting the economy from a peacetime to a wartime basis. First, it had somehow to lay claim to the goods and services it needed to conduct its war effort. With aggregate capacity at its limit, the only recourse was to increase its share of domestic output at the expense of private demands, particularly private consumption spending.

At the outset, the Canadian government assumed that the war would be a short one, and it began its war effort with a modest $50 million appropriation. The war was not short, however, and the $50 million did not fuel government defence expenditures even to the end of 1914. Soon, the government found itself spending on a completely unprecedented scale. Even in 1914, expenditures rose to $246 million. By 1917, they would be $574 million and, by their peak in 1919, $740 million. In just five years, the expenditures of the Dominion had tripled!

During much of the war, the government's position was that this additional expenditure should be financed largely through debt. This view was partly pragmatic, given the limited experiences with different types of taxation and the fear that the recession-mired economy of 1914–15 could not handle additional taxation. It was also partly philosophical. Finance minister Thomas White had this to say about it in 1916: "We are justified in placing upon posterity the greater portion of the financial burden of this war, waged as it is in the interests of human freedom, and in their benefit in equal if not in greater degree than our own."[4]

Traditionally, Canadians had looked abroad to wealthier and more developed pools of capital to handle their debt requirements. The railways and many of the other great projects of the Dominion had drawn their funds from the seemingly limitless British investment markets. Thus, in 1914, the Canadian government turned there once more, raising some $60 million soon after the war began. Inevitably, however, the British market was a limited source of war funding. It was not long before the British war effort absorbed all domestic capital. The Canadian government then looked to the second great capital market of the world — New York. A war loan for $45 million was first floated there in August 1915, and further loans would be floated throughout the duration of the war.

With access to foreign borrowing (and thus to foreign-produced goods and services) limited, the federal government had no choice but to appropriate a larger share of domestic output. There were three ways that it could do this: domestic borrowing, increased taxation, and printing money. Each option involved a significant new exercise of power.

In the prewar era, the budgets of the Dominion government had certain striking characteristics. First, by any modern standard, they were minuscule. In 1913, the Dominion spent approximately $185 million, up from the $136 million spent in 1911. Second, in spite of occasional grumbles from British investors, overall Canadian debt was small. From 1900 on, the Dominion government regularly ran surpluses on operating accounts and, in spite of the heavy commitments to railways in recent years, the per capita debt in Canada was lower in 1913 than it had been in the 1880s.[5]

Nor was taxation onerous. The Dominion, in 1913, did not have, nor had it ever had, any corporate or personal income tax. Instead, revenue came from indirect taxation — customs duties, excise taxes, and non-tax receipts, such as those of the post office. Of these, by far the most important were customs duties, which, as Figure 14.3 indicates, accounted for just a little less than two-thirds of all revenue. The heated debates that raged over tariff policy in the earlier years of the nation's history are more understandable, given this figure. Tariffs were the tax that most directly affected average Canadians in the years before World War I.

No one had suspected that the savings of Canadians could finance government borrowing needs on any great scale. After all, Canadian governments and Canadian entrepreneurs had looked abroad for funds ever since William Merritt had found that there were insufficient savings in Upper Canada to finance the Welland Canal. This idea had never really been challenged over the years. Indeed, Canadian governments had never tried to raise significant funds domestically. No bond issue in the history of the Dominion had been for more than $5 million.[6]

When war came, therefore, domestic loans were not seen as a meaningful source of funds. "The gross amount would be quite small," concluded White, in 1915, of any possible bond issue in Canada.[7] He was wrong. When the government did turn to the domestic bond market in 1915, White called for $50 million from the Canadian public — and subscribed $100 million! This set the pattern for the rest of the war, as issue after issue

270

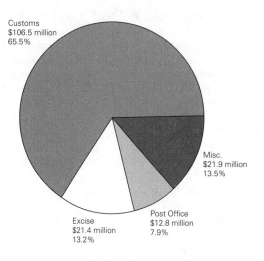

Customs
$106.5 million
65.5%

Misc.
$21.9 million
13.5%

Excise
$21.4 million
13.2%

Post Office
$12.8 million
7.9%

Figure 14.3
Sources of Dominion Government
Revenue, Canada, 1913

Source: W. Irwin Gillespie, *Tax Borrow and Spend:
Financing Federal Spending in Canada, 1867–1990*
(Ottawa: Carleton University Press, 1991, table
C-2.

was floated and the Canadian public responded. By the time the war was over, Canadians had funded the vast war effort out of their own savings to the amount of $2 billion, ten times what had been secured abroad.

Though the majority of war costs were handled through borrowing, the government found itself under increased pressure, as time went on, to implement new taxes. In part, this was the result of the feeling that at least a portion of the costs should be borne out of current revenue. More important, however, were the building political forces. Many corporations and individuals had made considerable profits during the war. As the sacrifices of the general public mounted, there was a growing cry to ensure that the burden of the war was distributed among all classes in society. New taxes aimed at the well-off could ensure at least a symbolic redistribution.

In response to growing fiscal and political demands, the government moved into direct taxation. In 1916, a business profits tax was introduced, with revisions the next year. Most important to the future fiscal management of the government and to future Canadian citizens was the imposition in 1917 of the Dominion Income War Tax. To say that it was an important wartime measure makes sense only with the advantage of hindsight. At the time, it was seen neither as an important revenue-gatherer nor as a very onerous tax. Even by 1919, after the rates had been twice revised upward, a married man making $2500 (a quite comfortable salary at the time) paid only $20 in income tax. The vast bulk of the population paid no tax at all (see Table 14.1). Finally, the government promised that the income tax had been introduced only because of the dire necessities of war. Once the war was over, the tax would be repealed.

Perhaps not surprisingly, the income tax was never repealed. The responsibilities and costs of the government could not be returned to the levels of prewar days. First of all, since the war had been financed largely through the use of debt, the government had to increase its revenue, at least to the point where it could handle the service charges on that new debt. By 1920, those debt charges had risen to $164 million. Second, there were other long-term costs associated with the war. The most important of these was the commitment to veterans in disability allowances, pensions, and other payments. Before the war, such

Table 14.1 Dominion Income War Tax Payable, Canada, 1917 and 1919

Income ($)	1917		1919	
	Single ($)	*Married ($)*	*Single ($)*	*Married ($)*
1 500	—	—	20	—
2 000	20	—	40	—
2 500	40	—	60	20
3 000	60	—	80	40
5 000	140	80	160	120
10 000	420	360	662	620
20 000	1320	1260	2132	2090

Source: Robert Craig Brown and G. Ramsay Cook, *Canada, 1896–1921: A Nation Transformed* (Toronto: McClelland & Stewart, 1974), p. 232. Used by permission of the Canadian Publishers, McClelland & Stewart.

payments had not even existed. By 1920, they had reached $76 million. Thus, debt service and pensions alone were greater than all government expenditures in 1913. The clock would never be turned back, though to do so remained a heartfelt yearning among certain politicians and civil servants of the 1920s and later.

Finally, the federal government financed a portion of its wartime expenditures through the simple expedient of printing money. The Finance Act, 1914, contained four important provisions with respect to war finance. First, the federal government suspended the redemption of Dominion notes in gold, thereby taking Canada off the international gold standard. Second, the chartered banks were allowed to meet their liabilities to the public with their own note issue instead of gold or Dominion notes. Third, the chartered banks could use the excess circulation privilege year round instead of just during the harvest season. Fourth, the government could advance Dominion notes to chartered banks upon the pledge of satisfactory securities.

With these provisions in place, the Dominion government was able to increase its issue of Dominion notes. It advanced $16 million of new Dominion notes to the Canadian Northern and Grand Trunk Pacific railway companies against the deposit of securities. A further $30 million in Dominion notes were issued to cover government outlays, to bring the total new note issue to $46 million. Finally, in 1917, Ottawa advanced a loan of $50 million in new Dominion notes to London.[8] With this expanded note issue, the government was able to finance part of its wartime expenditures in the form of a free loan from the Canadian public. The expansion of the money supply occasioned by this note issue, coupled with the increase in bank loans that the Finance Act made possible, was partly responsible for the wartime inflation.

Meeting Wartime Needs

The government was concerned with more than just its share of total domestic production, however. It also needed to alter the composition of output to meet wartime needs. Market incentives, in the form of higher prices and greater profit opportunities, brought about some reallocation naturally. But some hands-on attention was needed as well, particularly in the case of manufacturing.

MANUFACTURING

Until 1914, Canadian manufacturing had been the protected "infant" of the Canadian economy. While wheat, timber, and other resources were traded internationally, most Canadian manufacturing business was done within the highly protected domestic economy. As late as 1913, only about 7 percent of Canadian secondary manufactured goods were sold overseas.[9] Moreover, manufacturing, as was the case in other areas of the economy, was in a slump at the beginning of the war. The question for contemporaries, then, was whether Canadian manufacturers could improve their performance sufficiently to meet the wartime demands.

Manufacturing faced serious problems early in the war. While Canadian workers remained unemployed and Canadian factories operated at low capacity, the British sent war orders to the neutral United States. Canadian businesses complained that they were not getting their fair share of war orders. The British were not just being perverse, however. The simple fact was that Canadian industry in 1914–15 was often incapable of meeting the high technical standards required by military purchasers, especially in munitions. Rumours of corrupt dealings on the part of those politically connected to the minister of militia, Sam Hughes, only added to the tainted image. All in all, it was a shabby beginning for Canadian wartime manufacturing. By May 1915, some $170 million in orders had been received for various Canadian munitions, but only $5.5 million had been delivered.[10]

By late 1915, things began to change. Canadian companies were learning the necessary skills and adopting the techniques required by meticulous military purchasers. The British, their own capacity now stretched to the limit, were willing to look to the capable Canadian firms.

The most significant single British decision affecting Canadian manufacturing came in November 1915. The British government asked Canadian packing-house magnate Joseph Flavelle to head a purchasing agency known as the Imperial Munitions Board (IMB). Responsible to the British government, this board was headed by a Canadian, and most of its staff were located in Canada. Within weeks, hundreds of new contracts were pouring into Canadian companies to supply the shells, casings, fuses, and other instruments needed to continue the war of attrition in France.

The activities of the IMB were massive. As early as February 1916, the IMB was spending $5 million a week. The British orders for the first half of 1917 alone were $250 million, and the IMB was the nation's largest employer. New companies had to be created by Flavelle when existing ones either could not meet specialized requirements or could not keep up with demand. By 1917, the board was so successful that "something between one-quarter and one-third of all the ammunition used by the British artillery in France, [and] more than one-half the shrapnel" came from Canada.

Although the IMB's activities were dramatic, similar trends, if not of the same scale, occurred in all manufacturing sectors affected by the war. Estimates of Ontario production in 1915 indicate that war production accounted for at least a quarter of all trade in activities as diverse as tent- and sail-making, the manufacture of boilers and engines, and the production of automobiles, explosives, steel and iron, plumbing equipment, and woollen goods and yarns.[11] Perhaps two figures most clearly sum it up: first, total wages and salaries in manufacturing increased by more than $300 million between 1915 and 1918; second, while 7 percent of Canadian manufactured goods were sold overseas in 1913, the figure rose to 40 percent by 1918.[12]

AGRICULTURE

The other key sector of the economy during the war was agriculture. Central to agricultural exports in recent years, of course, had been the West. At the beginning of the war, however, the West was in desperate economic shape. Construction had collapsed, building companies folded across the region, and investment in urban centres was withdrawn by overextended eastern and British investors. Unemployment rose dramatically, with the building trades leading the way. In Winnipeg, unemployment among some building trades has been estimated to have been as high as 90 percent by the winter of 1914–15.[13]

Farmers were only marginally better off. For various reasons, they, too, were extremely vulnerable to any economic downturn. From about 1910 on, there had been a movement, urged on by the Dominion government, into the marginal wheat lands of the Palliser Triangle. Thousands of new farms had been established in areas of southeastern Alberta and southwestern Saskatchewan on lands that, only a few years earlier, had been dismissed as unsuited for settlement. As was true of the marginal Laurentian lands in Quebec and the Canadian Shield in Ontario, such regions were capable of supporting a farm family only in the best of times. It was not one of those times in 1914. Further, the rapid growth of the West and the buoyant optimism of the era had encouraged farmers to take on more

Women munitions workers at Vancouver Engineering Works Ltd., 1917. Within weeks of the appointment of Canadian packing-house magnate Joseph Flavelle to head the Imperial Munitions Board, hundreds of new contracts were pouring into Canadian companies to supply ammunition used by the British artillery in France. By 1917, between a quarter and a third of all ammunition, and half of the shrapnel, came from Canada.

Vancouver Public Library Special Collections/VPL 910.

and more debt to establish themselves quickly. They were, thus, not in a position to survive any extended weakness in agricultural markets. Finally, farmers found that they had to face a mediocre harvest as well. The 1914 crop year was one of the poorest in recent history. Average wheat yields plunged to fewer than 16 bushels an acre after having been at 20 per acre in 1913. Nor did price compensate, as there were only two slight upward movements.

The recovery of agriculture during World War I showed parallels to that of manufacturing. The turnaround came in late 1915. Good weather created a record crop — a phenomenal 360 million bushels of wheat — that year. Moreover, there was a demand for it. The war was disrupting shipment of supplies from Russia and other parts of Europe, and the large armies in France had to be fed. Thus, prices held in spite of the large crop, and the agricultural sector produced a greater value of products than ever before.[14] Farmers found themselves on the road to recovery.

For the duration of the war, wheat reigned supreme. Any doubts about marginal farm lands or overextended credit disappeared as wheat prices continued to rise. In 1917, when the British said they would take all the wheat Canada could deliver, the price of wheat rose to $2.21 a bushel. Acreage sown to wheat increased by 50 percent from 1914 to 1917, while new farmsteads were created and existing holdings expanded in spite of the choking off of immigration. It was a joke among agricultural students at the University of Saskatchewan that their classes were full of former real-estate agents, caught in the crash of 1913, who now sought to make their fortunes in the new area of fast money — wheat.[15]

The extraordinary circumstances of war had two results. First, farmers who had been in such dire straits in 1913–14 were, by 1917, riding the crest of a wheat bonanza. The good price they were getting for their wheat not only brought in immediate income but led to rapid increases in the value of their property. Prices for prime wheat land rose as high as $90 an acre by the end of the war. For those unfortunate enough to buy at the height of the land boom, it would be the end of another world war before values returned to their 1918–19 levels.[16] Many took advantage of the increased value of their land and sold out to others who wished to operate on a larger scale. Thus, farm size increased steadily throughout the latter part of the war.

Among those who resisted the temptation to sell, the tendency was to put the profits of these years not into debt retirement or savings but into capital equipment. Tractors were not yet common, but trucks and automobiles made their appearance in ever-larger numbers throughout the war and immediate postwar years. Standing gasoline engines, a variety of mechanized aids to production, and, of course, improvements to houses and barns were common in these prosperous years. In hindsight, many would rue the failure of the farmer to hunker down, eliminate debt, and prepare for the storm that was to come. Given the record of prairie prosperity, 1913–14 notwithstanding, prairie farmers were reacting in a rational manner, seeking to maximize both capital assets and operating profits. Nothing in the past generation of prairie development suggested they should do anything else.

The abnormal conditions of war changed the role of the government in the marketing of grain. Since 1899 and the Manitoba Grain Act, government had been involved in questions of grading, transportation, and storage of grain. Until the war, however, the involvement had been at arm's length, with the Dominion trying to ensure that the various parties involved — elevator companies, grain exchanges, farmers, and overseas customers— operated according to understood rules of behaviour. The grain business was still essentially a free-market operation in 1914, albeit one hedged in by rules.

During the war, the free market no longer operated in agriculture. As early as 1915, the Canadian government commandeered 13 million bushels of wheat for war purposes. As time went on, the demands of war increasingly meant that Canadian farmers were selling their wheat not to British wholesalers but to the British government. By 1917, as mentioned above, the British government asked for every surplus bushel that Canada could produce. In response, the Canadian government stepped in to ensure that the marketing of grain was orderly. In June of that year, the government established the Board of Grain Supervisors, giving it the right to fix prices and to handle all bulk overseas sales. In 1919, the Canadian Wheat Board took over responsibility for the marketing of grain. Though the government saw this as a temporary wartime measure and abandoned the experiment in 1920, farmers saw it as the long-sought response to their demands for direct government involvement in the grain business. The political and economic pressure to resume that involvement would ultimately prove irresistible.

Agriculture was not just a western activity. Ontario produced a greater value of agricultural produce than any other province, and agriculture was Ontario's most important industry.[17] Quebec, it might be added, was also a major producer, ranking just behind Ontario and Saskatchewan in field-crop production in 1914. In the central and Maritime provinces, as in the West, people responded to the opportunities of the war.

For Ontario, Quebec, and the Maritimes, things were quite different from what they were in the West, however. The West was oriented toward the production of export staples, especially wheat. In the eastern provinces, the agricultural activities were more mixed, and the picture during World War I was more complex. This is especially true of central Canada, where farming had for a long time been largely directed at domestic markets. Garden produce, cattle, dairy products, hogs, and sheep were all important in the region. Central Canada had ceased to be an important supplier of wheat in the previous century, though there was a temporary revival of wheat production in Quebec as farmers sought to cash in on wartime demand. In general, however, local markets remained an important destination for eastern agricultural produce throughout the war. Overseas demand thus affected eastern farmers less dramatically than it did those in the West.

This emphasis on domestic markets does not mean that the export market was irrelevant. Butter, beef, and, most of all, hog production responded to wartime demands. Bacon was easily preserved and was, therefore, an important part of every soldier's rations throughout the war. The average hog price rose from $6.62 in 1911 to nearly $20 by 1919. Canadian exports multiplied ninefold between 1913 and 1919. Those Canadian farmers lucky enough to have large herds at the outbreak of the war stood to make windfall profits. Over the next four years, herds increased, especially in Quebec and Alberta, as farmers sought to profit from wartime demand.

The wartime prosperity and the longer-range trends inherent in modern agriculture were bringing about changes on central Canadian farms, as they were on western ones. Though eastern farms were small by western standards, they, too, were getting larger, on average. The smallest farmers, those with fewer than 10 acres (4 ha), were disappearing. There was no real place for the subsistence farmer in a business that was increasingly efficient in operation. This efficiency was aided by the introduction of machinery. As in the West, tractors were still scarce. Even in prosperous Ontario, only 1 farm in 30 possessed a tractor by 1921. In Quebec and the Maritimes, they were even more scarce. Automobiles and trucks were becoming common, however. More than eight times as many farmers in Ontario had trucks as had tractors by 1921.[18] As trucks became more numerous, the number of horses began to decline. The Ontario horse population reached its peak in 1916

The Garneau Bros. threshing outfit, Edmonton. Because such machines as this steam-driven thresher were so expensive, threshing crews of fifteen to twenty men moved with the machinery from farm to farm at harvest time, several farms thus sharing the expense.

Provincial Archives of Alberta/B270.

and then began a permanent decline. In the East, as in the West, land values appreciated, though more so in Ontario than in the Maritimes or Quebec.

There is still much detailed research to be done on eastern agriculture in the war years. The information that does exist, however, leads to the tentative conclusion that the war was less important to the shape of agriculture in Ontario than to that in any agricultural province and that, overall, the East (and British Columbia's small agricultural sector) was less affected by the war than were the Prairies. Longer-term trends dominated the changes taking place, while, in spite of the buoyant overseas market, local markets remained central to farm prosperity. Regional and interprovincial disparities did not seem to have been significantly altered, though the abandonment of marginal farms may have been delayed by wartime demand.

The Long-Run Economic and Social Consequences of the War

For Canada, the Great War is often held up as a defining event equal to, if not more powerful than, Confederation as a nation-building force. Given the challenges of wartime, Canadians had proven to the world, and more importantly, to themselves, to be capable soldiers and industrial producers. Socially, the War was an assimilating force that allowed ethnic minorities to surrender their own identities for membership in a Canadian community that was homogeneous in belief and outlook.[19] Further, mythology surrounding who fought in the war stereotyped Canadian soldiers as either rugged frontiersmen or tortured aesthetes.[20]

Johnathan Vance argues that this view of the war as a nation-building force is overly optimistic because the mythical society it described was too often contradicted by the realities of peacetime. Exclusionary and racist rhetoric remained the order of the day as new Canadians, not of British stock, even ex-soldiers, were not considered equal to Canadians of British stock. Immigrant workers were fired in the post-War rush to hire ex-soldiers and the Naturalization Act was amended in 1919 such that it was virtually impossible for aliens to become naturalized. British stock Canadians who could not forget Quebec's opposition to conscription created and perpetuated the characterization of French Canadians "as the only white race of quitters" despite statistical evidence to the contrary. Vance points out that French Canada's human contribution to the War reflected more on the demographic characteristics of French-Canadian society and inept recruiting methods than on disloyalty or lack of attachment to Canada.

Desmond Morton takes on the stereotype of Canadian soldiers as robust, free spirited pioneers who had worked on farms or on the edge of the wilderness. By the end of the War, farmers, hunters, fishermen, and lumberjacks were only 22.4 percent of the Canadian Expeditionary Force (CEF). White-collar workers were more numerous in the CEF than farmers and 36.4 percent listed their occupations as industrial. Further difficulties with the "frontiersmen" stereotype of the Canadian soldier emerge when one recognizes that most of the CEF were not Canadian born. Morton highlights that the Canadian Expeditionary Force, as one of Canada's first great national institutions, was dominated by the foreign born. Far from a melting pot, most of the CEF was British born and British bred. Almost 80 percent of the CEF soldiers were single and the average age at enlistment was 26.3 years.

Michael Edelstein notes that the high rates of voluntary enlistment in the Dominions like Canada surprised the British government and people. Morton's description of the CEF suggests that the high rates are not so surprising once one recognizes that in large part, it was British emigrants who were enlisting. As Morton argues, as "an immigrant people, Canadians wisely put more stock in commitment than in birthplace." The fact that the Canadian born were only a majority of the CEF by 1918 suggests that Canadian interests in the War were similar to those of Americans who did not enter the conflict until 1917.

The view of World War I as a nation-building event can also be seen as an interpretation of the economic effects of wartime. Three long-run effects of all this wartime activity are worth noting. The first is the importance of the war to Canada's industrial development. The second is the alleged regional inequities of this industrialization, particularly in western Canada. The third is the alleged destructive tendencies of the war on western agriculture.

On the first point — the significance of manufacturing during the war — the traditional view has been optimistic. "By the end of the war Canada was launched as a significant industrial nation," concluded historian Donald Creighton in the 1960s.[21] Others have echoed similar sentiments. Canada, the argument went, surprised itself with its ability to produce highly sophisticated manufactured materials in the pursuit of the war effort. Employees responded to the demand for war products and moved to the new industries. Plants opened and exports increased. Although the recession at the end of war was an inevitable consequence of the end of war production, the war was nevertheless important to the development of a modern industrial economy.

In general terms, this argument holds, though some important qualifiers must be added. There is little doubt that the war spurred manufacturing. What is more important, however, is the long-term effects of the changes of these years. If the period from 1910 to the mid-1920s is looked at, rather than the 1914–18 period, it is possible to distinguish in at least a general way between the short-term demands of the wartime economy and the longer-term effects of the war experience on the Canadian economy.

In the manufacturing sector, the use of a longer time frame does have an effect. As Figure 14.4 indicates, the constant-dollar value of manufacturing did increase significantly, whether shorter- or longer-term figures are used. The relative position of manufacturing, however, increased considerably during the war years, only to recede after the war. The recession of 1921 did much to wipe out the recent gains, revealing the temporary nature of many wartime effects. Similarly, the relative place of manufacturing increased during the war, from 22.5 percent of GDP in 1910 to 25.1 percent in 1920. By 1926, however, it had dropped to 21.1 percent.

278

The impact of the war and subsequent recession was particularly dramatic in the area of employment. Employment in manufacturing in 1921 was nearly 70 000 fewer than in 1910. The two recessions (1913 and 1921), in other words, had a more powerful effect than the war. Even by 1923, the work force had increased only marginally. This employment trend shows up in industry after industry. Those sectors that saw tremendous increases in size as a result of the war saw equally dramatic slippage in the postwar recession. Thus, for example, employment in steel rose from 66 000 in 1910 to a high of 90 000 by 1918. By 1921, it was back to 61 000. The rise and fall of employment in the chemical industries were even more dramatic. The industry expanded from slightly fewer than 11 000 employees in 1910 to a high of 55 000 by 1917. By 1921, it was back down to 12 000. Nor can this be explained easily by technological change. The trend is apparent whether one looks at employees, production levels, or the number of plants.

In the manufacturing sector, the only exception to this trend was in the automobile industry. The war just happened to coincide with the auto's transformation from exotic toy to means of transport. In 1913, only 50 558 vehicles had been registered. By 1918, the figure was 275 746. As a result, employment rose dramatically through the war but did

Figure 14.4 Value of Canadian Manufacturing, 1910–1925

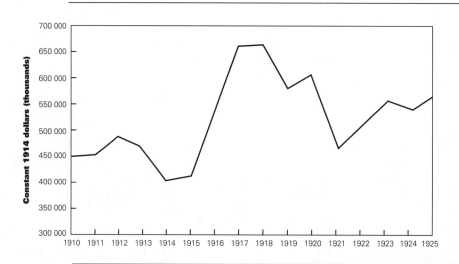

Source: M.C. Urquhart, "New Estimates of Gross National Product, Canada, 1870–1926: Some Implications for Canadian Development," in Stanley L. Engerman and Robert E. Gallman, eds., *Long-Term Factors in American Economic Growth*, National Bureau of Economic Research, Studies in Income and Wealth, vol. 51 (Chicago: University of Chicago Press, 1986), tables 2.1, 2.9.

not slide back in the postwar recession. It is likely, however, that this overall growth would have taken place with or without the war, though the precise timing of it might have been altered. The automobile was a revolutionary new technology and a natural growth sector. This does not alter the basic fact that, in general, whatever increases in employment were brought about by the war were lost in the postwar recession. It would be 1928 before employment in manufacturing surpassed the wartime figure.

If the work force in manufacturing was not growing, it was changing. As Table 14.2 indicates, there was a decline in the number of "production workers" between 1910 and 1923, which occurred even before the postwar recession. Conversely, the number of supervisory and office employees increased by a phenomenal 70 percent in the same period. By 1923, this group accounted for one in six manufacturing employees, compared with one in twelve in 1910. Finally, and perhaps, in part, because of this structural shift, real wages increased significantly between 1910 and the early 1920s, though the increases varied tremendously from sector to sector and region to region.

Overall, then, the war did increase the importance of manufacturing in Canada, but it actually decreased the opportunities for a "blue-collar" worker. Conversely, the white-collar component was growing, though there are indications that this development was the result of trends in the business world that predated the war.

The growth, stresses, and structural changes of manufacturing had significant consequences for the Canadian economic and social makeup. The war, and the boom economy it engendered, especially in manufacturing, also raised serious questions concerning the regional distribution of economic growth. Thus, any discussion of the impact of manufacturing must look at both the social and the regional consequences.

In social terms, the economics and politics of the war did much to change the role of women. To a large degree, this change was occasioned by the longer-term rise of the non-production sectors mentioned above. In 1901, only one in twentywomen in the paid labour force worked as a clerk or secretary. By 1911 it was one in ten, and by 1921 one in six. The new clerical and secretarial jobs developing in the office very quickly became female-dominated.[22] Even in more traditional areas of manufacturing, however, women found at least temporary opportunities as a result of the war. The rapid development of manufacturing in the war years, coupled with the labour shortage discussed earlier, expanded the role of women in industry beyond the traditional needle trades, though not as extensively as would be the case during World War II.

The effect of the war must be distinguished from the effect of the war years, for there is no doubt that the percentage of women in the paid labour force increased on a permanent

Table 14.2 Manufacturing Employment, Canada, 1914–1923

Year	No. of Production Workers	No. of Supervisory and Office Employees	Ratio
1910	465 029	42 948	0.092
1917	523 491	62 454	0.119
1920	499 063	75 558	0.151
1923	437 259	73 849	0.169

Source: Statistics Canada, *Historical Statistics of Canada*, 2nd ed., cat. no. 11-516E (Ottawa: Supply and Services, 1983), series R1–22. Reproduced by authority of the Minister of Industry, 1995.

basis. As well, women were pursuing different professions. Domestic service, which had accounted for nearly half of women in the paid labour force in 1900, was down to a quarter by 1921. Conversely, the clerical–secretarial area had increased from 5.3 percent to 18.7 percent in just twenty years. While the war may have accelerated some of these trends, it seems likely that they were due to more basic structural changes in the nature of Canadian society and economy.

Perhaps most importantly, the war brought an increasing number of women into the public sphere as organizers and operators of the numerous volunteer agencies that sought to assist in the war effort. Such bodies as the Patriotic Fund, the YWCA, and the Imperial Order Daughters of the Empire operated on both the local and the national levels and were organizations of considerable size and scope. This was important for the services the organizations provided, which filled a crucial gap in an era when government did not fully comprehend or accept the social burdens imposed by war. It was also important because the success of women, both in industry and in patriotic activities, did much to undermine Victorian stereotypes of women as weak and frail creatures.

None of this is to say that World War I revolutionized the role of women. At war's end, most industrial jobs would once again be reserved for men. Yet, change was occurring. The structural revolution in head offices meant that an increasing number of relatively well-educated women would be a growing presence in the world of paid work. Second, the activities of women in the war, in wartime politics, and in longer-standing reform movements had won women the right to vote in national elections by 1918. The twentieth century was already eroding the rigid stereotypes that placed men in the "public sphere" and women in the "private" one.

The war also had significant effects on labour. In the early years of the war, workers, glad for a job and imbued with patriotic fervour, had put aside longstanding grievances. By 1916–17, however, rising inflation as well as the obvious wealth being acquired by some employers, brought considerable tension to labour–management relations. The government, determined to maintain production, showed little sympathy for workers' demands, while intemperate rhetoric on both sides inflamed matters.

This growing tension was most dramatic in the West. Western unionism had traditionally been more militant than its eastern counterpart, and by the end of World War I it was considerably more so. Radical union leaders and social reformers saw the war as a critical juncture in history. Would the rhetoric of freedom and democracy apply to the home front or not? Such beliefs led to new experiments in unionism, including such syndicalist notions as the One Big Union that flourished briefly in the West in the postwar years. In a series of escalating clashes, unions across the region, and in the nation as a whole, confronted management. In 1919, in a number of general strikes, of which the one in Winnipeg was the most famous, unions sought to demonstrate that they had the power to change the direction of Canadian society. As it turned out, they did not have that power, and most of the strikes were lost at great cost to the workers involved. In the wake of these events, the national mood of militancy declined, though individual pockets of unrest remained.

Related to this debate about the impact of war on class and sex roles is one about the impact of wartime manufacturing on regional economic activity in Canada. One school of thought argues that the government deliberately favoured the development of industrialization in the central provinces, especially at the expense of the West, which was supposed to grow wheat.[23] This view requires qualification. The vast war contracts of such bodies as the Imperial Munitions Board did go largely to Ontario and Quebec. Such firms as the Steel Company of Canada in Hamilton, the T.A. Russell Automobile Company of Toronto, the Dominion Bridge Company of Montreal, and branch plants such as Canadian

Westinghouse received the lion's share of contracts.[24] There is, however, no evidence of any deliberate intent here. Cost-effective war production, not regional equity, was the goal of policy-makers in this period. Thus, production tended to go to existing industries, and, since nearly eight out of ten prewar jobs in Canadian manufacturing were located in Ontario and Quebec, it is not surprising that these provinces got the great majority of the contracts. Indeed, there were times when deliberate searches were undertaken, on political grounds, for a western firm with which to do business.

Moreover, while the period 1910–21 did increase central Canada's share of total national manufacturing, it is hard to pinpoint the exact cause. It is impossible to say with any certainty that this was the result of the war itself, and even more difficult to claim that it was the result of IMB war orders. Just as important was Ontario's ability to weather the postwar Depression. Moreover, the West saw an increase in manufacturing, as did central Canada. While not a great number of war contracts went to the West, manufacturing centres such as Winnipeg gained tremendously from the prosperous agricultural sector. Winnipeg was the third-largest city in the nation, and its population grew by more than 40 000 between 1911 and 1921. Overall, therefore, Manitoba in particular, and the West in general, saw its share of Canadian manufacturing employment grow in spite of the failure of the IMB to give the region what it felt to be its fair share of contracts.

The gains of the West and central Canada were not shared by the Maritime provinces. Though the Maritimes saw an increase in the absolute gross value of production during the war, the growth was slight and did not prevent the further erosion of the relative position of the region.[25] It is revealing, for example, that the Maritimes' share of national manufacturing employment dropped from 11 percent in 1910 to just over 6 percent by 1921. The number of employees in this sector of the economy dropped by approximately 45 percent in ten years! This is especially important because the Maritime resource industries were mature, and significant new growth was not to be expected from them. Only manufacturing could provide the necessary growth, and it was not doing so.

Even this dramatic decline, however, cannot be attributed to the war with any certainty. As has already been discussed, the problems of Maritime manufacturing had already begun to show up during the previous boom. From 1880 to 1910, the real output of Maritime manufacturing had grown at only about 60 percent of the national rate.[26] Moreover, the worst was yet to come. Indeed, wartime activity may have slowed the decline, at least in some parts of the region. It is most likely that the deindustrialization of the Maritimes that was taking place was part of a longer-term trend and not specifically as a result of the war.

This leaves one other question: Was agriculture in the West led into destructive practices as a result of the temptations of the war? Specifically, three charges have been laid. The first is that wartime demands led the farmer to a dangerous reliance on wheat. The second is that the rise in debt that accompanied the farmers' search for short-term gains hurt them in the long run. The third is that the high prices in the later part of the decade meant that farmsteads were extended onto marginal lands that should never have been opened.

Of these, the first charge seems the least relevant. Western farmers had always been grain growers and, in spite of pleas from agricultural officials that they should turn to mixed farming, would have remained grain farmers, with or without the war. The increase in wheat during the war was, therefore, not a major step and could easily be reversed. Given that, the increase in wheat production was a rational response to high prices. The second point is true, but not directly attributable to the war. Farmers were, indeed, heavily in debt at the end of the war, but, as argued above, this response on their part would likely have taken place in any boom, given the experience of recent years.

282

The third point does have some merit, though it, too, is only partly attributable to the war. Western farms continued to increase in number through the war, and many farmers moved to areas that were marginal at best. Thousands of new homesteads were established, for example, in parts of the infamous Palliser's Triangle stretching through southeastern Alberta and southwestern Saskatchewan. The results were disastrous. From 1918 to 1921, the region experienced drought. Poor crops in the last year of the war only foreshadowed the disasters that were to come. In 1919, many areas in this region saw the entire crop wiped out. Through the early 1920s, farm abandonment replaced homesteading, foreshadowing the population exodus that would come in the Great Depression of the 1930s. In all of this, the war was to blame, but only in part. So, too, was the Canadian government, which, even before the war, had encouraged settlement of a region that should never have been settled.[27] With this important exception, however, the evidence indicates that many long-standing assumptions about the impact of the war are, at best, only partly correct and often quite wrong.

Conclusion

The war brought important changes in the Canadian economy, changes that would last long beyond the war itself. The size and role of government had changed. Agriculture and manufacturing were both profoundly affected by the war and by postwar recessions. Regional shifts were taking place, and the long-term movement of the economy toward urbanization and industrialization continued. Yet, all this was but a small part of the effect of the war. The conflict killed 60 000 Canadians, and millions of combatants overall. It also left the international financial and economic structure in a state of chaos. The question for the future was whether the international community would have the resiliency and the wisdom to reassert some long-term stability. As some at the time recognized, the war had unravelled the old economic system, but there was, as of 1920, no certainty as to what was being built on its ruins. What emerged would determine the economic future of Canada, as it would that of other nations.

NOTES

1. Dudley, Leonard. *The Word and the Sword: How Techniques of Information and Violence Have Shaped Our World.* Cambridge: Blackwell, 1991.
2. Keegan, John. *The First World War.* New York: Vintage Canada, 2000.
3. M.C. Urquhart, "New Estimates of Gross National Product, Canada, 1870–1926: Some Implications for Canadian Development," in Stanley L. Engerman and Robert E. Gallman, eds., *Long-Term Factors in American Economic Growth*, National Bureau of Economic Research, Studies in Income and Wealth, vol. 51 (Chicago and London: University of Chicago Press, 1986), table 2.4.
4. Robert Craig Brown and Ramsay Cook, *Canada, 1896–1921: A Nation Transformed* (Toronto: McClelland & Stewart, 1974), 230.
5. The provinces and municipalities were accumulating greater debt loads, however. See Royal Commission on Dominion–Provincial Relations, *Report*, Book 1: *Canada, 1867–1939*, 81–82.
6. J. Deutsch, "War Finance and the Canadian Economy," *Canadian Journal of Economics and Political Science* 6(4) (1940): 527.
7. Brown and Cook, *Canada, 1896–1921*, 231.
8. See C.A. Curtis, "The Canadian Banks and War Finance," in E.P. Neufeld, ed., *Money and Banking in Canada*, Carleton Library Series no. 17 (Toronto: McClelland & Stewart, 1964), 206–17.
9. Cited in Brown and Cook, *Canada, 1896–1921*, 234.

10. The following paragraphs on the IMB are drawn from Michael Bliss, *The Life and Times of Sir Joseph Flavelle* (Toronto: Macmillan, 1979).
11. Ian Drummond, *Progress Without Planning: The Economic History of Ontario from Confederation to the Second World War* (Toronto: University of Toronto Press, 1987), appendix, table 9.1.
12. Brown and Cook, *Canada, 1896–1921*, 240.

13. David J. Bercuson, *Confrontation at Winnipeg* (Montreal and Kingston: McGill–Queen's University Press, 1974), 26.
14. Urquhart, "New Estimates," table 21.
15. John Thompson, *The Harvests of War: The Prairie West, 1914–1918* (Toronto: McClelland & Stewart, 1978), 61.
16. P. Voisey, *Vulcan: The Making of a Prairie Community* (Toronto: University of Toronto Press, 1988), 40.
17. Drummond, *Progress Without Planning*, 291.
18. These figures are from Drummond, *Progress Without Planning*, 41.
19. Johnathan Vance, *Death So Noble: Memory, Meaning, and the First World War* (Vancouver: UBC Press, 1997).
20. Desmond Morton, *When Your Number's Up: The Canadian Soldier in the First World War* (Toronto: Random House, 1993), 277.
21. Donald Creighton, *Canada's First Century* (Toronto: Macmillan, 1970), 136.
22. Graham Lowe, *Women in the Administrative Revolution* (Toronto: University of Toronto Press, 1987).
23. Thompson, *Harvests of War*, 59–72.
24. Bliss, *Sir Joseph Flavelle*, 259–83.
25. David Alexander, "Economic Growth in the Atlantic Region, 1880–1940," in P.A. Buckner and David Frank, eds., *Atlantic Canada After Confederation*, The Acadiensis Reader, vol. 2 (Fredericton: Acadiensis Press, 1985), 146–75.
26. David Alexander, "Economic Growth in the Atlantic Region," tables 6 and 7.
27. See David Jones, *Empire of Dust: Settling and Abandoning the Prairie Dry Belt* (Edmonton: University of Alberta Press, 1987).

FURTHER READING

Alexander, David. "Economic Growth in the Atlantic Region, 1880–1940." In P.A. Buckner and David Frank, eds., *Atlantic Canada After Confederation*, The Acadiensis Reader, vol. 2. Fredericton: Acadiensis Press, 1985.

Bliss, Michael. *A Canadian Millionaire: The Life and Business Times of Sir Joseph Flavelle Bart, 1858–1939.* Toronto: University of Toronto Press, 1992.

Brown, Robert Craig, and G. Ramsay Cook. *Canada, 1896–1921: A Nation Transformed.* Toronto: McClelland & Stewart, 1974.

Deutsch, J. "War Finance and the Canadian Economy." *Canadian Journal of Economics and Political Science* 6(4) (1940): 525–42.

Drummond, Ian. *Progress Without Planning: The Economic History of Ontario from Confederation to the Second World War.* Toronto: University of Toronto Press, 1987.

Edelstein, Michael. "Imperialism: Cost and Benefit." In Roderick Floud and Deirdre McCloskey, eds., *The Economic History of Britain Since 1700, Volume 2: 1860–1939.* Cambridge: Cambridge University Press, 1994.

Lowe, Graham. *Women in the Administrative Revolution.* Toronto: University of Toronto Press, 1987.

Morton, Desmond. *When Your Number's Up: The Canadian Soldier in the First World War.* Toronto: Random House, 1993.

Thompson, J. *The Harvests of War: The Prairie West, 1914–1918.* Toronto: McClelland & Stewart, 1978.

Vance, Johnathan F. *Death So Noble: Memory, Meaning, and the First World War.* Vancouver: UBC Press, 1997.

Chapter Fifteen

Uneven Growth, 1919–1929

THE DECADE of the 1920s has always posed a problem to those seeking to describe it historically. Until recently, there had been no clear overall picture of these years.

The 1920s were a fragmented decade, confusing in its complexity and denying easy categorization. For one thing, it was sharply divided chronologically. Canada began these years with a sharp recession, and growth remained low throughout much of the country until mid-decade. Then, all seemed to change, as Canadians embarked on an investment and consumption spree. The boom came faster to some areas than to others; in some parts of the country, it never came at all. Some industries, such as coal mining, were in trouble throughout the period, wherever they were located, while others, such as automobile manufacturing, grew at an amazing rate. Some, such as the steel industry, seemed divided within themselves; Stelco recovered well from the 1921 recession, while such firms as the British Empire Steel Company (Besco) and Algoma struggled.

Agriculture, and the related theme of western settlement, had shaped economic thinking and political argument for a generation. In absolute terms, agriculture would continue to be important in the 1920s, but the great infilling of the Prairies was largely complete. As a result, the agricultural sector never regained the leading role it had enjoyed before the war.

The question was what would become the new "engine of growth," and there were various possible answers. Other primary resources and primary-resource industries grew rapidly in the decade. So, too, did manufacturing, which continued the rise to the prominence that had been a feature of previous decades. Finally, there was the growing importance of the tertiary sector. Related to this development was continued urbanization. In this decade, Canada became more urban than rural; it was also a time when the larger urban centres took a more prominent role than ever in the economy.

These economic shifts meant that the nineteenth-century strategy that had emphasized an east–west flow of manufactures from the centre to a resource-based hinterland seemed, to the degree it had ever been fully accepted, increasingly outmoded. Provincial government functions grew in relative importance, and national political parties were increasingly challenged by regionally based movements.

Sectoral, regional, and chronological fragmentation thus marked the decade and explains much of the confused imagery that surrounds it. Yet, it is possible to delineate certain crucial elements that shaped these events and give at least a modicum of unity to any discussion of the decade. In particular, this was an era of American economic power and new technologies, particularly in consumer goods. These three forces, in turn, provide a means by which this complex decade can be comprehended.

Overview

The immediate postwar period was one of great uncertainty. Wartime orders ended, but the fall in demand was buffered to some extent by increases in raw-material exports, by the relatively slow decline in government expenditures, and by consumer spending fuelled by a drawing down of accumulated assets. Still, real GNP fell by nearly 6 percent in 1918 and nearly 7 percent in 1919, before levelling out in 1920 (Figure P5.1). Inflation continued to be a problem; the aggregate price index (1900=100) rose by 13.1 percent in 1918, the last year of the war. Prices increased by a further 10.1 percent in 1919 and by 16 percent in 1920.

There was a sharp recession in 1921 as the slowdown in the Atlantic economy spread to Canada. Real GNP fell by 9.6 percent in that year. Exports led the decline, falling from $1.2 billion in 1920 to $894 million in 1921. Export spending in 1921 was just 28 percent of GNP in 1921, down markedly from its peak of 37 percent in 1917. Investment increased slightly faster than GNP, and Canada became a net capital importer again by 1919 (until 1923, when the trend was reversed once again). Inflationary pressures were eased, however. Prices fell by 11 percent in 1921 and by a further 9.3 percent in 1922.

Unlike the downturn a decade later, this recession was very brief. Real GNP increased by 14.5 percent in 1922 and rose every year thereafter until the end of the decade. The stimulus to growth was quite evenly spread across the main components of aggregate demand. Government spending was still nearly 14 percent of GNP in 1921, but thereafter it fell back to prewar levels. Exports equalled 28 percent of GNP in 1921, rose to over 31 percent in 1925 and 1926, and ended the decade at 26 percent. Investment spending rose more slowly than GNP until mid-decade, and then increased to 22 percent by 1929. Canada exported capital on a net basis from 1923 to 1927, and then became a borrower again until well into the Great Depression.

Banking and Monetary Policy

Canada remained off the gold standard at the end of the war. In its place, the Finance Act of 1914, as amended in 1923, continued to prevail. There was no central bank (the Bank of Canada was formed in 1935), although all the functions of a central bank were undertaken by the private banks or by the government directly.[1] The Canadian Bankers' Association maintained a clearing house that controlled and supervised bank activities. Branch-banking meant fewer problems with seasonal liquidity crises such as the ones that affected the United States, with the result that there was less need for a lender of last resort. The practice of holding reserves as call loans in New York, and calling on them as necessary, added to the public's confidence. As it had for decades, the Bank of Montreal continued to operate as the government's bank where needed.

The system provided for an elastic and responsive money supply. The banks could receive unbacked Dominion notes from the government by pledging collateral, widely defined. With these as reserves, they could then expand their loans and note issues as required. In effect, by providing this rediscount facility, the government acted as lender of last resort. The overissue of notes and deposits by individual banks was generally precluded by the operation of the clearing mechanism and by the expectation that the gold standard would eventually be resumed at rates close to what they had been at suspension in 1914.

Canada returned to the gold standard in 1926, when Britain did. The gold standard was suspended, in effect, two years later, although the banks were still required to convert their notes into Dominion notes on demand. The gold standard was formally and permanently abandoned in 1931 when the government placed a formal embargo on gold exports.

The shocks of the war and postwar years revealed some weaknesses in the banking system, however. Some of Canada's financial institutions, it turned out, were not as sound as had been thought. Most serious was the 1923 failure of the Home Bank. Unexpectedly, 71 branches closed their doors and announced to shocked customers that they would not be able to get their money out. In addition, the Bank of Hamilton, the Bank of Ottawa, and the Merchants Bank, among others, sought mergers to avoid collapse or were taken over by larger institutions. In 1900, there were 36 active chartered banks in Canada; by 1929, this number had fallen to 11.[2] The public became increasingly nervous with each merger, revelation, and news story. More and more, deposits concentrated in the hands of the largest banks —the ones thought safest. By 1928, as Michael Bliss noted, the "Montreal, the Commerce, and the Royal [banks] controlled 70 percent of the banking assets" in Canada.[3]

The Wheat Economy

The prairie wheat economy continued to prosper in the immediate postwar period. Demand was strong, and prices remained high as the war-torn nations of Europe struggled to rebuild their agricultural capacities. This situation changed in the second half of 1920, however. Farm prices overall fell by nearly one-half between 1920 and 1923; wheat prices fell by nearly 60 percent. Coupled with a succession of relatively poor crop years, this deterioration in the terms of trade meant great hardship for prairie farmers. Debts, built up during the war and immediate postwar years, became onerous. Abandoned farms became a common sight in the Palliser's Triangle area of southwestern Saskatchewan and southeastern Alberta.

The situation changed again around the middle of the decade, as prices recovered somewhat and yields improved. With rising incomes came the first major mechanical revolution in prairie agriculture. The adoption of gasoline tractors on Prairie farms during and immediately following World War I was in response to labour scarcity and rising grain prices.[4] While the use of and rates of adoption of tractors varied by location on the Prairies, the percentage of farms with tractors rose from as low as 10 percent in 1920 to almost 30 percent in 1931.[5] There were no combines reported in the 1926 census, but nearly 9000 were reported in 1931. Farm trucks became common in the same period.

The expansive phase of prairie settlement was, however, over. The number of farms in the prairie provinces fell from the 256 000 reported in the 1921 census to 248 000 in 1926, before rising again to 288 000 in 1931. Most of the additional output came as farmers added to the amount of land under cultivation. The area of improved land increased by over 33 percent between 1921 and 1931, and the area under field crops rose by 24 percent. Average farm size in Manitoba increased only slightly in the same period, and more significantly in Saskatchewan and Alberta.

As noted earlier, the wheat boom induced a frenzy of railway construction. By midwar, the long-emerging crisis with the new railways came to a head and forced both a restructuring of much of Canada's railway system and a new commitment by government. Underlying this was the imminent collapse of the sprawling, debt-ridden Canadian Northern Railway system and the increasing difficulties of its rival, the Grand Trunk Pacific Railway. In their bid for transcontinental status, both companies had spent recklessly and then had looked to governments, federal and provincial, to bail them out. The war only made matters worse as private money markets dried up. By 1916, the government grants, given with increasing reluctance, were the only things that prevented the railways from collapsing. In that same year, a royal commission was appointed to investigate the problem. Before long, the government was moving toward ownership of the railways.

Between the initial move and the final result, there was much agonized political discussion and much expenditure of money. How much should be paid in compensation to shareholders? Should the relatively healthy parent company of the Grand Trunk Pacific, the Grand Trunk, be taken over? (It was.) Were alternatives to outright government ownership possible? (They weren't.) In the end, there was no choice. The government simply could not allow these private companies to beg endlessly for more handouts. However, neither could the government allow them to collapse. Nationalization was the only answer and, in 1922, the new Canadian National Railways system was created.

The absence of any real freedom of choice is apparent in the basic numbers involved. For example, the Canadian Northern had, by 1916, amassed an amazing $104 million in loan guarantees from the Dominion government. Had it collapsed, the Dominion would have had to make good on that amount. Even more seriously, Ontario and the western provinces had also given guarantees. The largest amounts were from Manitoba and British Columbia, which had guaranteed $25.5 million and $40 million, respectively.[6] To put these numbers in perspective, each figure represented three to four years' current revenue for the province in question. To have let the Canadian Northern collapse would have endangered the solvency of at least two, and perhaps more, Canadian provinces; would have seriously hurt the finances of the Canadian government; and would likely have taken a national bank along for good measure.

The federal and provincial governments were to some extent the architects of the railway crisis. The loan guarantees that they provided to Canadian Northern Railway induced the railway's promoters to undertake a project with a high probability of failure and built almost exclusively with debt rather than their own equity. Essentially the governments created a situation where the promoters were gambling with "house money" on a transcontinental railway that Frank Lewis and Mary MacKinnon estimate had a 70 percent *ex ante* probability of going bankrupt.[7] Thus, by the time the dust had settled, the Canadian government found itself the reluctant owner of more than 32 000 km of railway lines.

The New Resources and the American Market

Of all the international circumstances that affected Canada in the 1920s, perhaps the most important was the economic power of the United States. For Canadian businessmen and investors, this was the overriding reality of the decade. The vast, prosperous, and growing American market was essential to any country that depended on exports; it was especially crucial to Canada, which had long depended on trade with the international community. Moreover, given the relative decline in British capital flows, Canadian development would need alternate sources of foreign capital. The Americans had the vast savings; thus American inflows of capital would shape Canadian economic development. American markets and American investment would have a significant effect in determining what sectors of the Canadian economy prospered over the coming years.

The importance of the United States to Canadian economic development can be seen even in the most general figures. Britain's declining role in the Canadian economy is equally apparent with imports of British goods in decline for some time. The war accelerated that decline, and imports from Britain dropped to 15 percent of the Canadian total by 1919. That figure was artificially low, and Britain did regain some of the market. Never again, however, would it account for even 20 percent of Canadian imports. In contrast, by the 1920s, approximately two-thirds of all imports came from south of the border (see Figure 15.1).

Canada's orientation toward American imports had always been balanced by its orientation toward Britain as an export market. By the 1920s, however, the Americans were also becoming Canada's most important destination for exports. In 1923, for the first time in history, Canada exported more to the United States than to Great Britain. The two would alternate positions as export receivers over the next few years, but the trend was clear. After declining to a low of $292.6 million in 1922, Canadian exports to the United States rose until, by 1928, they reached $478 million and accounted for nearly 40 percent of all Canadian exports (see Figure 15.2). The United States was by far Canada's most important trading partner by the end of the decade.

Patterns of international investment in Canada are even more revealing. As Table 15.1 indicates, as late as 1914 British investment accounted for more than 70 percent of total foreign funds coming into the country. The war changed that. Britain fell into debt, while the United States found its international financial position strengthened. In just nine years, British investment fell to 46 percent of the total, while American capital imports rose to 52 percent. Never again would the mother country come close to the United States in its investment in Canada.

Figure 15.1 Canadian Imports from the United States and Britain, 1881–1931, as a Percentage of Total Imports

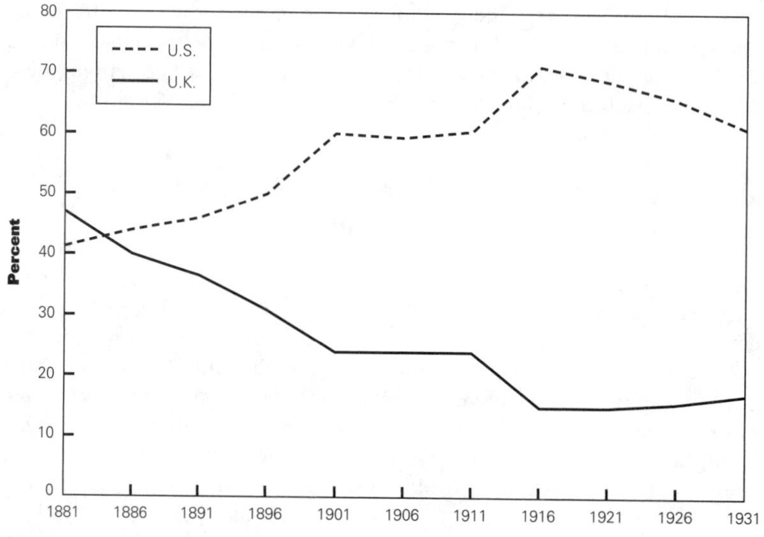

Source: Derived from Statistics Canada, *Historical Statistics of Canada*, 2nd ed., cat. no. 11-516E (Ottawa: Supply and Services, 1983), series F342–47. Reproduced by authority of the Minister of Industry, 1995.

Figure 15.2 Canadian Exports to the United States and Britain, 1886–1931, as a Percentage of Total Exports

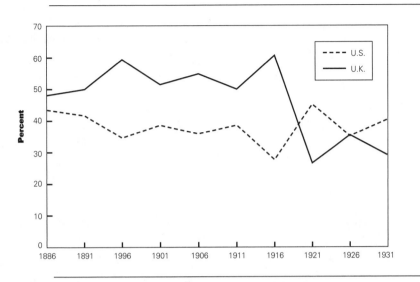

Source: Derived from Statistics Canada, *Historical Statistics of Canada,* 2nd ed., cat. no. 11-516E (Ottawa: Supply and Services, 1983), series F334–41. Reproduced by authority of the Minister of Industry, 1995.

This American investment was different in character than that from Britain. The British had favoured bonds that gave them a relatively stable rate of return but conferred no direct control of the company. American investors were interested in equity investment — that is, in common shares — and with American money, therefore, often came American control. Indeed, much of the American investment in the years after the war was involved in the setting up of branch plants. The Canadian tariff made it attractive for American companies to establish in Canada in order to avoid the tariff.

Over the longer term, the branch-plant phenomenon would become a contentious political issue in Canada. There is a danger, however, of projecting post–World War II concerns with American investments into this earlier era. All American investment, whether in bonds or shares or in the establishment of new branch plants, was considered desirable. Canada's primary concern was to create jobs in Canada rather than in the United States for the processing of Canada's exports. Moreover, given the inability of British capital to continue its role as Canada's main banker, the American funds were a much-needed replacement. Without them, Canada's rate of growth would have been much slower in the postwar decade.

Certain sectors of the Canadian economy were more favoured than others by American customers and capitalists who found goods or opportunities in Canada that could not be matched south of the border. By examining those areas that did or did not appeal to Americans in these years, it becomes easier to comprehend the mixed pattern of growth and stagnation that characterized the 1920s.

What Americans seemed to want from Canada more than anything else in this period was pulp and paper. As was shown in Part Four, the increase in the size and readership of newspapers helped expand the demand for pulp and paper. Canada, it was also shown,

Table 15.1 British and American Investment in Canada, 1910–1930

	Amount		Proportion	
	U.S.	U.K.	U.S.	U.K.
Year	*($ millions)*		*(% of total investment)*	
1910	487	1958	19	77
1911	563	2203	20	77
1912	645	2417	20	76
1913	780	2793	21	75
1914	881	2778	23	72
1915	1070	2772	27	69
1916	1307	2840	30	66
1917	1577	2739	35	61
1918	1630	2729	36	60
1919	1818	2645	39	57
1920	2128	2577	44	53
1921	2260	2494	46	51
1922	2593	2464	50	47
1923	2794	2471	52	46
1924	3094	2372	55	42
1925	3219	2346	56	41
1926	3465	2355	58	40
1930	4660	2637	61	36

Source: Statistics Canada, *Historical Statistics of Canada*, 2nd ed., cat. no. 11-516E (Ottawa: Supply and Services, 1983), series G188–202. Reproduced by authority of the Minister of Industry, 1995.

was well situated to take advantage of the demand because of its large supply and because the American Underwood tariff lowered duties on Canadian paper exports to the United States. The results were dramatic. American newsprint production remained more or less constant between 1913 and 1919, while Canadian production more than doubled, to more than 840 million tons (764 million t).

The recession of 1921 slowed growth only temporarily, for the American demand for newsprint seemed insatiable. By 1929, the 61 million newspapers read at the end of the war had increased to 93 million.[8] Canada supplied the demand. Through the 1920s, some $356 million was invested in the industry — the largest investment in any of the primary-resource industries. Jobs increased to more than 30 000, and Canadian output of newsprint tripled between 1920 and 1929. That was a sixfold increase from 1914. Canada produced more than twice as much newsprint as the United States and was the world's largest papermaker (see Table 15.2). The importance of the American market can be seen in the fact that 80 percent of this massive production went south of the border.

Not surprisingly, an industry of this much interest to the United States was, to a significant degree, developed with the aid of American capital. Entrepreneurs south of the border were quick to recognize the rising demand for newsprint in their own country and the possibilities of Canadian stands of timber. Thus, for example, the Brooks-Scanlon Company, based in Minnesota, established the first successful paper mill in British

Table 15.2 Newsprint Production, Canada and the United States, 1913–1930

Year	Canada (millions of tonnes)	United States
1913	402	1305
1914	470	1313
1915	549	1239
1916	662	1315
1917	726	1359
1918	770	1260
1919	841	1324
1920	938	1512
1921	849	1225
1922	1142	1448
1923	1315	1485
1924	1453	1481
1925	1633	1530
1926	2075	1684
1927	2286	1485
1928	2645	1417
1929	2981	1392
1930	2985	1282

Source: Trevor Dick, "Canadian Newsprint, 1913–1930: National Policies and the North American Economy," *Journal of Economic History* 42(3) (1982): 678. Reprinted with permission of Cambridge University Press.

Columbia. In Ontario, Quebec, and New Brunswick, Canadian mills already existed, but American funds flowed north into the expansion or reorganization of existing ventures or in the creation of new ones.

Another area dependent on American demand and American investment was mining, especially of such non-ferrous products as gold, nickel, asbestos, and copper. New consumer products, such as the automobile, and new technologies, such as electricity, were all growth industries, as were their components and accessories. In this way, asbestos in brake linings, nickel and zinc in automobiles, and copper wiring in the new electrical devices on the market fuelled the mining industry.

As was the case for pulp and paper, the major part of this growth was the result of international demand, especially from the United States. In some cases, such as asbestos, practically all the product went south. In others, there was a greater demand in Canada; in all cases where strong growth occurred, the international market was crucial. In some cases, this growth was spectacular. Thus, for example, the value of zinc exports more than quintupled. Those of nickel also quintupled, in spite of the absence of armament production. Gypsum exports tripled between 1918 and 1929 and were practically unaffected by the recession of the early 1920s. Of course, not all minerals exhibited such dramatic increases, but the overall impact was a sharp increase in the exports of a crucial sector of the economy.

At the same time, the growth of the 1920s, whatever its peculiar characteristics, was part of a longer cycle in mining. The boom had begun in 1900 and continued until 1930.

Before that time, only gold and coal had been of importance in Canadian mineral production. By the end of the 1920s, things had changed. Coal was still important, but it was not growing in value. Gold was experiencing considerable growth, however, and had been joined, in descending order of importance, by copper, nickel, lead, silver, asbestos, and zinc. The mining industry, which had been centred in the Yukon and British Columbia, was now important in several provinces, foremost in Ontario. A total mineral production of $64.4 million in 1900 had grown to $307.1 million by 1929.

Domestic Demand: Consumers and the New Technologies

In some instances, dramatic growth was fuelled by domestic demand. The 1920s were an era in which technologies developed in the prewar years became more practical in design and more widespread in use. This application, both in industry and in consumer durables, revolutionized the way of life of Canadians and provided the decade with some of its most important growth.

Looking back at the postwar period, Canada's senior political economist, Harold Innis, would characterize this era as one in which, above all else, new sources of power replaced old. Specifically, it was during this period, he argued, that coal and steam, which had powered the first industrial revolution, were being replaced by electricity. Certainly, if one is looking at the new technologies of the postwar period, electricity is the place to begin.

In the 1920s, electricity had been around for some time. By World War I, considerable progress had been made in the development of practical applications of electricity in street lighting and industry. Important though the prewar period was in terms of the application of electricity, in the 1920s electricity became a common source of power, both in the home and in the factory. For the more affluent urban consumer, electricity provided new comforts, ranging from reliable evening light to refrigerators, radios, and electric stoves. These comforts spawned new industries, some sizable and some quite small. The important point, however, is that all of them were new technologies, and therefore their development represented the growth of new opportunities. The shipment of radios, for example, grew from 48 531 in 1925 (the first year for which statistics are available) to more than 170 000 by 1930.

Moreover, the production of electricity was itself a major source of capital development. The prewar period brought about a significant rationalization of the earlier combinations of private and municipal generating companies. The growth in demand that had permitted those steps, however, was nothing compared with that in the twelve years after World War I. Between 1919 and 1930, the amount of electricity generated by Canadian utilities rose from 5.5 million to 19.5 million kilowatt hours. Such growth required a tremendous increase in generating capacity and, thus, the construction of electricity-generation facilities became a major source of economic growth in the decade. The development of electric-power stations created capital investment of some $690 million, an amount greater than that invested in the entire primary sector during the same period.[9]

For all its importance, electricity and its products were overshadowed by another technology — the automobile. By the 1920s, the automobile too had been around for some time. The first automobile plant in Canada dated from the late nineteenth century. Within a few years, there were enough cars on the road for the provinces to implement a system of licences. In 1903, the first year that it had licences, Ontario registered 220 vehicles. Obviously, the automobile was still very much an experimental technology.

Even in these early years, however, two interesting patterns existed. First, automobiles provide a clear example of user fees. The new technology required improved roads, for the car travelled at much higher speeds and was much more destructive to existing road surfaces than was the horse. In response, the provinces borrowed from American practice and implemented a series of gasoline taxes to defray the cost of improved roads. Over the years, gasoline taxes and licence fees became a major new source of revenue and a practical means to cope with the burden imposed by a new form of transportation.

Second, the industry was shaped by the tariff structure of the country. At first, this meant that a large number of companies moved into the market, protected from the larger and more efficient American operation by a 35 percent tariff. As time passed, however, the American corporations also established plants in Ontario, absorbing or out-competing their smaller Canadian counterparts.

It was in the 1920s that the automobile became a standard feature of Canadian transportation. Before that time it had remained a toy, for the enthusiast and the well-off. In 1911, for example, there was one automobile in Canada for every 335 people. In the 1920s, however, increasingly efficient production systems and basic designs pioneered by such firms as Ford began to make the automobile affordable to larger segments of the public. The Canadian public responded with enthusiasm. In a large nation with a thinly spread population and a cold climate, efficient transportation had always been in demand. The automobile was the latest in a line of advances that went back to canals, steamboats, and primitive pioneer roads. In 1918, some 275 000 automobiles were registered in Canada. By 1923, that number had more than doubled, in spite of recession; by 1929, it had risen to nearly 1.9 million (see Table 15.3).[10]

Table 15.3 Automobile Production and Registrations, Canada, 1917–1929

Year	No. of Cars Produced	No. of Cars Registered
1917	93 810	197 799
1918	82 408	275 746
1919	87 835	341 316
1920	94 144	407 064
1921	66 246	465 378
1922	101 007	513 821
1923	147 202	585 050
1924	132 580	652 121
1925	161 970	728 005
1926	204 727	836 794
1927	179 054	945 672
1928	242 054	1 010 664
1929	262 625	1 888 929

Source: T. Traves, *The State and Enterprise: Canadian Manufacturers and the Federal Government, 1917–1931* (Toronto: University of Toronto Press, 1979), p. 102.

294

This growth made automobile manufacturing one of Canada's major growth industries through the 1920s. Although some automobiles were imported, generally the Canadian automotive business was competitive internationally, with 30 percent of production going overseas by 1928.[11] To meet domestic and foreign demand, more than a quarter-million automobiles a year were made in Canada by the latter part of the decade. Automobile assembly was only a part of the story. Auto parts and services, gas stations, and the improvement of roads to accommodate the automobiles provided jobs. Road expenditures, largely financed by taxes on gasoline and vehicle registrations, were also important. The capital expenditure on highways alone was greater than that in mining. Nearly 15 000 men and women were employed by auto or auto-parts producers by the end of the decade. As one business magazine said at the time, "If the production value of the plants producing automobile supplies, tires and refined petroleum be added to that of the automobile industry proper, the total considerably exceeds that of any other industry."[12]

The automobile revolutionized individual travel and living habits. It provided people with a new, convenient, and rapid form of transportation from door to door. Though its effects were not fully apparent until after World War II, the automobile would forever change the layout of cities, separating homes from work to a greater degree than the street railway ever could. It would allow the farmer to by-pass the local corner store for the larger centre and give the salesman from the city quicker access to the byways of the country. Already, in the 1920s, commercial trucks were becoming important to deliveries and transport, challenging both the horse-drawn carriage and the railway. By 1928, there were more than 130 000 commercial vehicles registered in Canada.[13] Like the railway in the nineteenth century, the automobile would eventually become an essential part of the lives of Canadians. Even in the 1920s, the love affair was apparent. Canada had a greater number of passenger cars per capita than any country in the world, except the United States.

The impact of the automobile was, however, uneven. Regional inequities existed as a result of income disparities, need, and the availability of roads. Ontario was, by far, the most motorized province by the end of the decade, with nearly 47 percent of all automobile registrations. It was also the province with the greatest hard-surface road mileage, outside of major cities. The first intercity concrete highway had been completed between Toronto and Hamilton in 1915; by 1928, there were 8600 km of concrete or macadamized roads in the province. Of the other provinces, only Quebec, with 2900 km, and British Columbia, with 555 km, had any significant hard-surface roads at all. Cars and trucks were popular on the Prairies, however. Level terrain made gravel or dirt roads relatively easy to build and maintain, and the vast distances made efficient transportation essential.

Traffic jam, 1923. In the 1920s the automobile became a part of Canadian life, necessitating many changes in the traffic laws. In 1918 some 275 000 automobiles were registered in Canada; by 1923 that number had more than doubled, in spite of recession; by 1929 it had risen to nearly 1.9 million.

Toronto Transit Commission.

Motorized vehicles were also quickly incorporated into farming to make transportation more efficient. Saskatchewan had as many motor vehicles per capita as Ontario and 50 percent more than the Canadian average.

The automobile industry grew as a result of domestic demand, which would seem to make it distinct from those resource industries that depended on the United States. Yet, even in this industry, the United States was important. The automobile first became a mass-market phenomenon in the United States. That combination of technology and marketing was, to a large degree, what shaped the automobile industry in Canada after World War I. During that decade, the independent Canadian automobile industry disappeared, to be replaced by branch plants of the giant American corporations.

As with many other new technologies, the automobile was initially made by a variety of small firms in both Canada and the United States. New businesses, former carriage-makers, and others got involved in turning out this new transportation novelty in the prewar years. Not-so-famous lines such as the Fossmobile, the London Six, the Redpath, the Russell, and the Everitt were all produced in Canada by Canadian manufacturers in the early years. As the automobile moved from novelty to mass market, however, low

Mechanized assembly line, 1914. The Ford Motor Company was the first to adapt the assembly line to the auto industry. Ford of Canada was started by Gordon McGregor in the Walkerville Wagon Works on August 17, 1904, under an agreement with the Ford Motor Company. In 1913 the company was turning out more cars than any other factory in the British empire, and all parts of the vehicles were 100 percent Canadian. The Brooks Automobile Company produced the last distinctively Canadian automobile in the mid-1920s, but in July 1927 it ceased production.

Courtesy of Ford of Canada Archives.

production costs were essential. That could be accomplished only with a good design and with a large-scale plant. Mass advertising by larger companies ensured that people gravitated toward better-known names at the sake of the lesser-known ones.

By the end of World War I, the process of consolidation was well under way. Smaller firms fell by the wayside or were taken over by larger ones. This was a process common both to Canada and to the United States, but the harsh reality in Canada was that the smaller firms tended to be Canadian, the larger ones American. Successful U.S. firms such as Ford had both the money and the technology to outperform smaller Canadian firms. Ford took over the McGregor Company and was, by 1913, producing more cars than any other factory in the British empire.[14] General Motors took over McLaughlin of Oshawa, while other companies folded. By the mid-1920s, the Brooks Automobile Company produced the last distinctive Canadian automobile. Both its method of locomotion — it was steam-powered — and its price— nearly eight times the price of a Model T — indicated its limited future. It ceased production in 1927 and, henceforth, the Canadian automobile industry would be a branch-plant operation.

Urbanization

The economic developments of the 1920s helped reshape the urban centres of the nation. Those that could take advantage of the sectors of growth increased their own prosperity and importance, while others sank in standing. In part, this was a continuation of general, longer-term trends toward urbanization. Indeed, the 1920s can be seen as the first decade in which urban concerns and urban life were as important to the economy as were rural ones. By the end of the decade, census data show that more Canadians were classified as urban than rural. More significant than this was what was happening among "urban centres." The smallest towns and villages were not growing nearly as quickly as were the larger ones. As transportation facilities improved and as manufacturing was concentrated, local services and small-scale business disappeared. Larger metropolitan centres took over. The trend toward urbanization suggested by census data is, if anything, understated. Anyone who moved from an incorporated village of 1500 people to a city of 100 000 was not judged by the census to have contributed to the rural–urban shift. Yet, there is no doubt that, in terms of the nature of employment, consuming habits, and leisure activities, the person who had made the move had become urbanized.

There were winners and losers, even among the larger centres, during the decade. The most spectacular winner was Vancouver, which more than doubled in population between 1911 and 1931, becoming Canada's third-largest city. Vancouver had had the potential for rapid growth from the time that the Canadian Pacific Railway decided to make that city its western terminus. Until World War I, however, it had never really been able to extend its hinterland eastward, over the Rocky Mountains. The growing timber and pulp-and-paper industries in British Columbia and the increased importance of shipments to the Far East contributed to the city's growth before and during the war. With the opening of the Panama Canal in 1914, Vancouver became a major port for goods headed across the Pacific and to the eastern United States and Europe. Moreover, goods flowing in from those points could now come via Vancouver rather than Winnipeg. Even grain bound for Europe from the Prairies became more economical to ship west rather than east for Alberta grain farmers. By 1928, some 79 million bushels were exported via Vancouver. By the end of the decade, Vancouver had more than 6 million tons (5.5 million t) of shipping clearing through its harbour, by far the largest amount in Canada.

Vancouver, B.C., 1897 and 1931. Vancouver had had the potential for rapid growth from the time that the Canadian Pacific Railway decided to make the city its western terminus. But it was not until 1911 that its dramatic development began: it more than doubled in population between 1911 and 1931, and became Canada's third-largest city.

City of Vancouver Archives/STR.P.1 N.22/AIR.P.53 N.28.

298

The other major gains, made from the early 1900s to 1930, were Toronto's. From the mid-nineteenth century onward, Toronto had been contending with Montreal for dominance in Canada. It had always been contending from a position of second place, however, and had never really threatened Montreal's dominance as the population and business centre of Canada. It would be a while yet before Montreal's position was surpassed, but it is plausible to argue that Toronto became sufficiently powerful in this period that it could seriously challenge Montreal for economic supremacy in Canada, though the challenge would not be resolved until well after World War II.

There were several reasons for this. Perhaps most importantly, Toronto's immediate hinterland continued to see rapid growth and the Oshawa–Toronto–Hamilton "golden horseshoe" was the most industrialized area of Canada. By 1929, nearly 40 percent of all of Ontario's manufactures came from Toronto and Hamilton alone.[15] Crucial new industries, such as automobile manufacturing, were centred in this area. Toronto's aspirations were also nicely matched by those of the provincial government located in that city. Also important to Toronto's economy was the role played, after 1900, by the Ontario government and Toronto-based financiers in the mining activities on the Canadian Shield. In the 1920s, as the mining boom continued, Toronto financial operations dominated Canadian-owned activities, and Toronto financial intermediaries handled American investments in the Shield or American mergers with Canadian firms. Toronto had become the mining

Toronto railyards, 1926. The extent and bustle of the railyards demonstrate Toronto's rapid growth into a major city, centre of the Oshawa–Toronto–Hamilton "golden horseshoe"—the most industrialized area of Canada. By 1929, nearly 40 percent of Ontario's manufactures came from Toronto and Hamilton alone.

National Archives of Canada/PA-161576.

centre of Canada; when operations expanded into northern Quebec and Manitoba, they continued to be centred in Toronto rather than in Montreal or Winnipeg.

The result of all this was dramatic growth for the city. Its population increased from 381 000 in 1911 to 631 000 by 1931, and the figures would be much larger if surrounding communities were taken into account. Towns such as Mimico, Forest Hill, Eastview, Thornhill, and Oshawa had, among them, a population greater than that of Halifax or Edmonton, yet all were satellite communities to Toronto. By the latter part of the decade, building permits in Toronto alone were greater than those issued in Montreal, Quebec City, and Trois-Rivieres put together, or — to use another comparison — greater than all the building permits of the three Prairie provinces.[16]

In contrast, Winnipeg underwent a relative decline. It was still the most important prairie city, but its aspirations to become the "Chicago of the North" faded rapidly. Vancouver cut into its hinterland from the west, while other western centres, such as Edmonton, Calgary, Regina, and Saskatoon, grew larger and more able to handle local distributing and wholesaling functions. The removal of wheat trading from the activities of the Winnipeg Grain Exchange with the creation of the Canadian Wheat Board lessened that city's hold over the Prairies' major crop. Population growth in Manitoba was slower than in the more westerly (and increasingly Vancouver-oriented) areas of Alberta.

Though some cities gained more than others, all the major cities of Canada increased in population during the decade (see Table 15.4). The population of the nation was growing, and a larger and larger percentage of it was living in the cities. Further, for those employed in manufacturing, real wages increased during the decade.[14] The combination of people flowing into the cities and of rising incomes in many areas of the country created a considerable boom in housing construction once the recession of 1921 had passed. Streetcars

Table 15.4 Urban Populations of Major Centres, Canada, 1901–1931

City	1901	1911	1921	1931	1931 as % of 1901
Montreal	328 172	490 504	618 506	818 577	249
Toronto	209 892	381 833	521 893	631 207	301
Vancouver	29 432	120 847	163 220	246 593	838
Winnipeg	42 340	136 035	179 087	218 785	517
Hamilton	52 634	81 969	114 151	155 547	296
Quebec	68 840	78 710	95 193	130 594	190
Ottawa	59 928	87 062	107 843	126 872	212
Calgary	4 392	43 704	63 305	83 761	1907
Edmonton	4 176	31 064	58 821	79 197	1896
London	37 796	46 300	60 959	71 148	188
Windsor	12 153	17 829	38 591	63 108	519
Verdun	1 898	11 629	25 001	60 745	3200
Halifax	40 832	46 619	58 372	59 275	145
Saint John	40 711	42 511	47 166	47 154	116

Source: Derived from *Canada Year Book*, 1932, cat. no. 11-402E (Ottawa: King's Printer, 1933). Reproduced by authority of the Minister of Industry, 1995.

and automobiles made the separation of home and work more and more possible. In all but the smallest cities, new residential neighbourhoods began to spread outward from industrial areas, as the "respectable working class" and the white-collar "middle class" sought to escape the social and physical ills that they associated with the heterogenous mix of the inner city.

By the late 1920s, the contribution of this residential construction to capital formation was considerable. Between 1924 (a year of relatively slow construction) and 1929, building construction of all types more than doubled, to $572 million; residential construction accounted for about $230 million of that. The process of urbanization was not only a response to economic conditions but a significant economic force in its own right.

All of this domestic capital expenditure, in housing and elsewhere, raises a question about the nature of the prosperity of the latter half of the decade. This chapter has argued that the relationship with the United States was central to Canadian prosperity in the 1920s, whether in terms of sales or investment. Yet, the building-construction boom, as well as the amounts spent on, for example, road construction and the expansion of paper mills, has led to the argument that, after 1925, "it was domestic capital formation, not export growth, which was propelling Canada's economy upward."[18]

The point about the importance of domestic capital formation is relevant, as Figure 15.3 indicates. In the latter part of the decade, the ratio of gross capital formation to GNP did increase significantly, even approaching something akin to the heady days of the prewar wheat boom. Yet, it would seem impossible to separate capital formation from external relationships, in terms of both exports of merchandise and the inflow of investment. Canada was a small economy, very much dependent on exports. Exports such as wheat, pulp and paper, and minerals were crucial to the Canadian economy. Moreover, export/GNP ratios remained high in the latter part of the decade — higher than comparable figures in the prewar years.[19] Capital formation, whether in industry or housing, occurred in good measure simply because Canadians and foreign investors continued to be optimistic about Canadian prospects and because increased exports, among other things,

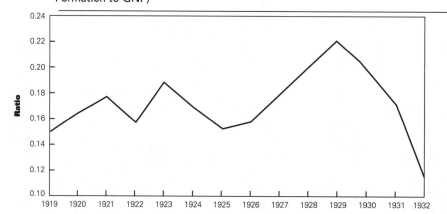

Figure 15.3 Domestic Capital Formation, Canada, 1919–1932 (Ratio: Gross Capital Formation to GNP)

Source: M.C. Urquhart, "Canadian Economic Growth, 1870–1980," Department of Economics, Queen's University, discussion paper no. 734, 1988, table 4.

had allowed the Canadian standard of living to rise, at least in some regions of the country. When the prospects for external trade fell, as they were about to, domestic capital formation would also fall.

Government

These economic changes brought about important political changes. The most obvious one was the relative decline in the importance of the federal government and the relative rise of provincial governments. The federal government owed its earlier prominent position to its efforts to promote a transcontinental economy. With the end of the expansive phase of the prairie wheat economy, this role was over. In the 1920s, Ottawa established commissions to set the terms for the transfer of ownership of land and natural resources to the three Prairie provinces. The transfers were completed in 1930, bringing these provinces into line with the others in this respect.

The growth of public demand for government services that fell under provincial and municipal government jurisdiction continued in this decade. Along with increasing their spending on education, roads, sewers, and the like, the provinces also began to implement new welfare measures. Ontario introduced a Workmen's Compensation Act in 1914, the first formal piece of social legislation in Canada. In 1920, British Columbia introduced a Mothers' Pension Act, providing a small, assured monthly income for female-headed households. The three Prairie provinces and Ontario followed suit almost immediately, but the easternmost provinces were still without such programs in 1929.

The 1920s were the era of classical federalism, or, in another famous phrase, of watertight compartments. The federal and provincial governments carried out their respective taxing, spending, and regulatory roles largely independent of each other. In 1930, federal transfers to the provinces amounted to only 9 percent of the latter's total revenues, the lowest figure until then or since.[20]

There was some overlap between the federal and provincial governments, however. In 1900, the federal government offered grants to cover 50 percent of the costs of provincially sponsored 4-H clubs, the first federal–provincial shared-cost program in Canada's history. A second shared-cost program, covering the construction of railway crossings, was introduced in 1909; and a third one, for agricultural instruction, was implemented in 1913. The postwar period saw a number of further shared-cost programs: in 1918, for part of the cost of co-ordinating provincial employment offices; in 1919, for approved technical-education programs, highway construction, and venereal-disease control.

The most significant shared-cost initiative, however, came in 1927. Pressured by Progressive and Labour members in a minority Parliament, Prime Minister Mackenzie King in 1927 introduced an old-age-pension scheme. British subjects aged 70 years and over, living in Canada at least twenty years and in the current province of residence for at least five years, were awarded an annual pension of $240, as long as they passed a "means test" where their total annual income did not exceed $365. Ottawa paid 50 percent of the costs of the scheme, and the provinces paid the other 50 percent. British Columbia joined the plan immediately, Manitoba and Saskatchewan did in 1928, and Ontario and Alberta did in 1930.

The 1927 old-age-pension scheme did not represent a radical departure from earlier arrangements for public assistance for the "needy." First, setting the age of eligibility at age 70 when life expectancy at birth was only 60 years, meant that the government was insuring Canadians against the unfortunate circumstance of out-living one's human resources. Second, in addition to means testing on the basis of income, income values were attributed to a pensioner's assets as a percentage of the asset values. To prevent the elderly from transferring real property to qualify for the government pension, applicants for the pension had to disclose all sales and gifts of real property made in the five years prior to the application. Further, the application for the government pension in Ontario required a list of the applicant's living children and the details of their contribution towards their parent's maintenance. This interest in the pensioner's children and support stemmed from Ontario's 1927 Parents Maintenance Act that made adult children liable for the support of their aged and dependent parents.[21]

302

Conclusion

What can be said about the 1920s as a whole? First, Canada was a very different nation economically than it had been even twenty years before. World War I and the subsequent decade had changed many things. Of these, perhaps two general themes stand out. First, manufacturing — whether primary or secondary — was now an important part of the Canadian economy, accounting for a greater percentage of total Canadian production than did agriculture by 1927. By the same year, manufacturing and construction, together,

General office, Canadian Aeroplanes Ltd., Toronto, 1918. The "white-collar revolution," which began around the turn of the century and was still under way at the end of the 1920s, brought with it a revolution in office procedures that created the secretarial and clerical role, as it is known in the modern world. In creating a whole new range of occupations, it provided an entry point (and a ghetto) for women in the work force.

National Archives of Canada/PA-25186.

made up an absolute majority of that production. Agriculture was still very valuable, of course, and primary production (which included some processing) was greater than secondary. Still, the trends were apparent. The rural–agricultural nation of the late nineteenth century was now becoming an urban and industrial one.

The second, and obviously related, structural change came in the composition of the work force. Two things were happening. First, as might be expected, a smaller and smaller percentage of people worked in agriculture. Whereas, in 1901, more than 40 percent of Canadians were classified as following "agricultural pursuits," by 1931, that figure had fallen to less than 29 percent. Even more interesting was the rapid growth of new areas in the non-agricultural sector. The first half of the twentieth century was the great era for the rise of the white-collar occupations: first, as front-office staff for corporations, then in "white-collar" corporations and activities such as finance, and finally (and still largely in the future in 1929) in government. For example, employment in finance, insurance, and real estate was among the fastest-growing of any type of employment in Canada between 1911 and 1931, rising from just under 37 000 to more than 92 000.

Along with the white-collar revolution, which, it must be emphasized, was still under way at the end of the 1920s, a revolution in office procedures occurred. It created the clerical and secretarial role, as it is known in the modern world; it also provided an entry point (and a ghetto) for women in a whole new range of occupations. To continue the example of finance: female employment went from 3500 in 1911 to nearly 25 000 by 1931. Contemporaries in both world wars paid a great deal of attention to the women who left the home to work in industry as a part of the war effort. This emphasis, though useful for war morale, tended to underplay the longer-term forces of industrialization and bureaucratization that were changing and increasing women's role in the work force in more fundamental ways. It is not surprising to say that many women did not work outside the home in the 1920s. That is generally known. What is surprising, perhaps, is the number who did. When these new clerical and secretarial employees are added to such "traditional" female occupations as teaching (71 000 women by 1931), health (nearly 53 000), and the harsher working-class world of textiles (61 737), it becomes clear that women's role in the economy was of much greater importance than was acknowledged at the time, or for a long time afterward. By 1931, some 750 000 women worked, accounting for one job in five in the country.[22]

What, then, of the material position of Canadians, whether male or female, in the years after World War I? Overall, the standard of living in Canada appears to have gone up significantly. Only the period 1900–10 saw a greater growth in real GNP per capita. It is difficult to translate this statement on overall wealth to one that gives some estimate of the distribution of that wealth. Recent estimates, however, have concluded that real wages did increase for the period 1913–26 and that, on average, the employed worker was in better economic circumstances by the later 1920s than he or she had been at the end of the war.[23]

It is also clear, however, that not all people experienced this rise in the standard of living or enhanced opportunities for work. For those living through the decade, the nature of the 1920s depended on the region in which one lived and the sector of the economy in which one worked. In the larger cities, especially in central Canada and on the West Coast, job opportunities expanded, at least after 1921. New areas opened up, and many more people worked in either manufacturing or the burgeoning tertiary sector. Employment as clerks, truck drivers, nurses, and teachers was much more common by the end of the decade than before, as were factory workers. In the Prairie west, and in parts of central Canada, that prosperity was felt only toward the end of the decade. The first half of the 1920s was spent simply recovering from the postwar recession. In contrast, those in the Maritimes or in marginal agricultural areas did not have a good decade. Unemployment and management–union confrontations in depressed areas, such as Cape Breton, revealed dramatically that prosperity was far from universal.

304

Uneven though this prosperity was, it would soon be looked back upon with nostalgia. By the end of the decade, the entire international trading and monetary systems were on the verge of collapse. Canada, as a small nation that depended on massive exports for prosperity, was to be affected more than most. The nation was on the eve of the Great Depression.

NOTES

1. See Michael D. Bordo and Angela Redish, "Why Did the Bank of Canada Emerge in 1935?" *Journal of Economic History* 47 (June 1987): 405–18.
2. E.P. Neufeld, *The Financial System of Canada: Its Growth and Development* (Toronto: Macmillan, 1972), table 4:1, 77–80.
3. Michael Bliss, *Northern Enterprise: Five Centuries of Canadian Business* (Toronto: McClelland & Stewart, 1987), 387. On banking reorganization in the 1920s generally see pages 385–88 of that book.
4. Byron Lew, "The Diffusion of Tractors on the Canadian Prairies: The Threshold Model and the Problem of Uncertainty," *Explorations in Economic History* 37, 2000, 189–216.
5. See Byron Lew; also, see Paul Voisey, Chapter 2 "Farm Size" in *Vulcan: The Making of a Prairie Community* (Toronto: University of Toronto Press, 1988).
6. These figures are taken from John Eagle, "Sir Robert Borden and the Railway Problem 1911–1920," Ph.D. thesis, University of Toronto, 1972, 9.
7. Frank Lewis and Mary MacKinnon, "Government Loan Guarantees and the Failure of the Canadian Northern Railway," *Journal of Economic History* 47(1) (March 1987): 175–96.
8. John Thompson and A. Seager, *Canada, 1922–1939: Decades of Discord* (Toronto: McClelland & Stewart, 1985), 79.
9. Royal Commission on Dominion–Provincial Relations, *Report*, book 1: *Canada, 1867–1939*, 116.
10. T. Traves, *The State and Enterprise: Canadian Manufacturers and the Federal Government, 1917–1931* (Toronto: University of Toronto Press, 1979), 102.
11. Ian Drummond, *Progress Without Planning: The Economic History of Ontario from Confederation to the Second World War* (Toronto: University of Toronto Press, 1987), 152.
12. Cited in Traves, *The State and Enterprise*, 103.
13. *Canada Year Book*, 1930 (Ottawa: King's Printer, 1931), 653.
14. Bliss, *Northern Enterprise*, 396–97.
15. Drummond, *Progress Without Planning*, 182.
16. *Canada Year Book*, 1930 (Ottawa: King's Printer, 1931), 451–52.
17. Gordon W. Bertram and Michael B. Percy, "Real Wage Trends in Canada, 1900–1926: Some Provisional Estimates," *Canadian Journal of Economics* 12(2) (May 1979): 299–311.
18. R. Bothwell, I. Drummond, and J. English, *Canada, 1900–1945* (Toronto: University of Toronto Press, 1987), 219.
19. M.C. Urquhart, "Canadian Economic Growth, 1870–1980," Department of Economics, Queen's University, Discussion Paper 734, table 4a.
20. A. Milton Moore, J. Harvey Perry, and Donald I. Beach, *The Financing of Canadian Federation: The First Hundred Years* (Toronto: Canadian Tax Foundation, 1966), table 29, 119–20.
21. Guy St-Denis, "Passing the Means Test: The Old-Age Pension Applications of Norfolk County, Ontario, 1929–1948," *Archivaria* 37 (Spring, 1994): 75–95. For an overview of public pensions in Canada, see Kenneth Bryden, *Old Age Pensions and Policy-Making in Canada* (Montreal and London: McGill-Queen's University Press, 1974).

22. Statistics Canada, *Historical Statistics of Canada*, 2nd ed. (Ottawa: Supply and Services, 1983), 107–23. These figures probably underestimate the female labour force because they likely miss many temporary and part-time workers who drifted in and out of the labour force as family and economic circumstances demanded.

23. Royal Commission on Dominion–Provincial Relations, *Report*, Book 1: *Canada, 1867–1939*, 116; Bertram and Percy, "Real Wage Trends"; Elizabeth Bartlett, "Real Wages and the Standard of Living in Vancouver, 1901–1929," *B.C. Studies* 51 (Autumn 1981): 3–62.

FURTHER READING

Bothwell, R., I. Drummond, and J. English. *Canada, 1900–1945*. Toronto: University of Toronto Press, 1987.

Dick, Trevor J.O. "Canadian Newsprint, 1913–1930: National Policies and the North American Economy." In Douglas McCalla, ed., *Perspectives on Canadian Economic History*. Toronto: Copp Clark, 1987.

Drummond, I. *Progress Without Planning: The Economic History of Ontario from Confederation to the Second World War*. Toronto: University of Toronto Press, 1987.

Thompson, J., and A. Seager. *Canada, 1922–1939: Decades of Discord*. Toronto: McClelland & Stewart, 1985.

Traves, T. *The State and Enterprise: Canadian Manufacturers and the Federal Government, 1917–1931*. Toronto: University of Toronto Press, 1979.

Chapter Sixteen

Regional Growth and Welfare

THE REGIONAL DIMENSION always figures prominently in discussions of Canadian economic growth and welfare. As we have seen, Canadian economic history before 1867 consists of the separate stories of several distinct territories that had relatively little to do with each other until political union brought them together. It is natural, then, to want to follow the subsequent progress of these individual entities.

The interest runs deeper than mere historical curiosity, however. Canada was established as a federation in 1867. This action acknowledged the provincial loyalties of the time, but it also ensured that regionalism would remain a part of the Canadian political and economic scene. We need only recall that the preamble to the BNA Act promises that "Union would conduce to the Welfare of the *Provinces*" (emphasis added). It was inevitable, then, that Confederation would be judged not just by how well the new national economy performed, but also by how individual provinces fared within it.[1]

The end of the 1920s is a good time to take stock of the regional economies in Canada. The great prairie settlement era was over, the nation was on the eve of a major depression and, after that, a new era of state intervention. As well, the years after World War I had brought regionalism to the fore. New political movements, such as the Progressive Party in the West, or the Maritimes Rights Movement in the East, challenged the political balance. Many of the major fiscal issues of the day, from the Crow Rates through the tariff, had regional dimensions. This regionalism and the progress of regional economies was thus an active issue at the time. What had happened after more than half a century to keep the issue so alive? How had Confederation affected both the political economy and the economic growth of regionalism in Canada?

Overview of Regional Economic Growth

Population is often used as a summary measure of economic performance on the grounds that migration flows are broadly responsive to relative economic incentives. By this measure, as Table 16.1 shows, there was a significant shift of economic activity in the 60 years following Confederation. The most notable change, understandably, is the rise in the importance of the western provinces. There were just under 110 000 people living west of the Ontario–Manitoba border in 1871 — only slightly more, in other words, than the population of Prince Edward Island at the time. By 1891, this figure had jumped to 350 000, pushing the region past New Brunswick but not yet Nova Scotia. By 1911, population was over 1.7 million, nearly double that of the three Maritime provinces together and only just

Table 16.1 Share of Population by Province, Canada, Census Years 1871–1931

Region	1871	1881	1891	1901	1911	1921	1931
				(% of total)			
Maritimes	20.7	20.1	18.2	16.7	13.0	11.4	9.6
Prince Edward Island	2.5	2.5	2.3	1.9	1.3	1.0	0.8
Nova Scotia	10.5	10.2	9.3	8.6	6.8	6.0	4.9
New Brunswick	7.7	7.4	6.6	6.2	4.9	4.4	3.9
Quebec	32.3	31.4	30.8	30.7	27.8	26.8	27.7
Ontario	43.9	44.6	43.7	40.6	35.1	33.4	33.1
Prairie provinces	0.7	1.4	3.2	7.9	18.4	22.2	22.7
Manitoba	0.7	1.4	3.2	4.8	6.4	6.9	6.7
Saskatchewan	—	—	—*	1.7	6.8	8.6	8.9
Alberta	—	—	—*	1.4	5.2	6.7	7.1
British Columbia	1.0	1.1	2.0	3.3	5.4	6.0	6.7
Yukon	—	—	—	0.5	0.1	—	—
North-West Territories	1.3	1.3	2.0	0.4	0.1	0.1	0.1

*INCLUDED WITH NORTH-WEST TERRITORIES.

Source: Calculated from M.C. Urquhart and K.A.H. Buckley, eds., *Historical Statistics of Canada* (Toronto: Macmillan, 1965), series A2–14.

short of that of Quebec. By 1931, the population of the western provinces and the territories was nearly 3.1 million.

Put differently, at Confederation, the western region accounted for just 3 percent of Canadian population, one-third of which was in British Columbia. By 1911, its share had risen to nearly a quarter (24 percent), and by 1931 to nearly 30 percent. Within the region, Manitoba's share rose every decade until 1921, and then fell slightly in 1931. The shares of the other three western provinces rose throughout the period. Saskatchewan was the largest of the four western provinces by 1911 and retained this position through to 1931.

The West's relative gain must obviously be reflected in a relative loss somewhere. Interestingly, the largest drop in share of population between 1871 and 1931 was Ontario's decline of over 10 percentage points, from 43.9 to 33.1 percent of the total. Quebec's share fell by 4.6 percentage points in the same period, to below 28 percent, and that of the three Maritime provinces by 11.1 percentage points, or from 20.7 percent of the Canadian total in 1871 to 9.6 percent of it by 1911. Prince Edward Island actually lost population in every decade after 1891; in all other provinces losing relative share, natural increase was larger than net migration.

The westward shift is evident in the regional distribution of output as well. Table 16.2 presents Alan Green's estimates of gross value added (GVA) by province for 1890, 1910, and 1929. The three Prairie provinces accounted for only 5 percent of national output in 1890, but more than 17 percent in 1910 and nearly 20 percent in 1929. British Columbia's share rose from 3.3 to nearly 9 percent over the same period, meaning that the western provinces, together, produced over 28 percent of national GVA in 1929, compared with

Table 16.2 Gross Value Added by Province, Canada, 1890, 1910, and 1929

Province	1890		1910		1929	
	$ millions	*% of Canada*	*$ millions*	*% of Canada*	*$ millions*	*% of Canada*
Prince Edward Island	14.1	1.8	16.0	0.8	25.6	0.4
Nova Scotia	64.1	8.1	114.2	5.6	215.0	3.5
New Brunswick	49.1	6.2	75.7	3.7	140.0	2.3
Quebec	208.7	26.3	474.8	23.2	1603.0	26.0
Ontario	391.2	49.3	845.5	41.4	2423.0	39.3
Manitoba	30.3	3.8	133.1	6.5	382.0	6.2
Saskatchewan	9.7	1.2	121.4	5.9	415.0	6.7
Alberta	*	*	98.7	4.8	411.0	6.7
British Columbia	26.1	3.3	165.6	8.1	547.0	8.9
Canada	793.3	100.0	2045.0	100.0	6161.0	100.0

*INCLUDED WITH SASKATCHEWAN.

Source: Alan Green, *Regional Aspects of Canada's Economic Growth* (Toronto: University of Toronto Press, 1971), tables B-1, B-2, B-3, pp. 85–87.

only 8 percent in 1890. Again the relative loss is spread over all other provinces, and again the largest relative drop is in Ontario — from nearly 50 percent of national output in 1890 to 39.3 percent in 1929.Quebec's share remained nearly constant, and the Maritimes' share fell from 16 to 6 percent.

The relative sizes of provincial economies, as measured by population or gross value added, provide one perspective on the regional make-up of the nation. Another, in many respects a more interesting one, is relative economic well-being. How well off was the average Maritimer in 1890, compared with his or her central Canadian counterpart? What effect did the ensuing decades of technological changes, the opening of the West, new resource industries, industrialization, and urbanization have on this statistic?

Table 16.3 shows the values of gross value added per capita for each province, relative to the national average, for the three years 1890, 1910, and 1929. Two impressions emerge from the table. The first is the large gap between the richest and the poorest province in each of these years. In 1890, per capita GVA in British Columbia was 2.75 times larger than in Saskatchewan. This gap remained virtually unchanged in 1910 (compare B.C. to P.E.I.), and rose to over three times in 1929 (compare B.C. to P.E.I.). Even ignoring these extremes, there was a substantial gap between the richer provinces and the poorer ones in each year represented in the table.

The other impression is the persistence of the pattern of regional disparities. British Columbia ranked first by a large margin in all three years, although its relative position fell consistently from 165 percent of the national average in 1890 to 135 percent by 1929. Ontario was the only other province with a per capita GVA consistently above the national average, ranging from 113 percent in 1890 to 118 percent in the other two years. Quebec was consistently below the national average, but less so in 1929 than in the previous two years.

Table 16.3 Gross Value Added per Capita for Provinces Relative to National Average in 1890, 1910, and 1929

Province	1890	1910	1929
Prince Edward Island	0.78	0.62	0.44
Nova Scotia	0.87	0.81	0.69
New Brunswick	0.94	0.76	0.58
Quebec	0.85	0.83	0.94
Ontario	1.13	1.18	1.18
Manitoba	1.19	1.02	0.91
Saskatchewan	0.60	0.87	0.76
Alberta	—*	0.92	0.99
British Columbia	1.65	1.50	1.35

*INCLUDED WITH SASKATCHEWAN.

Source: Calculated from Alan Green, *Regional Aspects of Canada's Economic Growth* (Toronto, University of Toronto Press, 1971), tables II-4 and II-5.

The Prairie provinces display a quite disparate pattern. Manitoba's per capita GVA was second only to British Columbia's in 1890, at 119 percent of the national average. It fell to the national average in 1910 and to nine percentage points below it in 1929. Saskatchewan's relative position fluctuated greatly, but never reached 90 percent of the national average. Alberta gained in relative well-being between 1910 and 1929, falling just short of the national average in the latter year.

The Maritimes are consistently the poorest provinces in the Dominion by this measure. Prince Edward Island produced 78 percent of the national average per capita GVA in 1890, and by 1929 this figure had fallen to just 44 percent. Nova Scotia and New Brunswick were close to the national average in 1890, at 87 percent and 94 percent respectively. But these relative positions deteriorated over the decades as well, falling to 69 percent and 58 percent of the national average by 1929.

Green's estimates of regional GVA are now nearly 25 years old. A recent contribution, however, demonstrates that this pattern of income disparities was present as early as 1870 for the provinces that were in Confederation at that time.[2] Inwood and Irwin begin with the Urquhart national income data discussed above and break it down into provincial and subprovincial measures of commodity income per capita. Table 16.4 summarizes their findings. As long ago as 1870, Ontario's per capita commodity income was nearly 20 percent above the national average. Nova Scotia was the poorest province at this time, with per capita income equal to only 75 percent of the Canadian average. New Brunswick, at 83 percent, and Quebec, at 86 percent, were between these two extremes.

Table 16.4 also illustrates that economic disparities existed within each province as well as among them. In Nova Scotia's case, the indices run from a low of 65 percent of the national average to 85 percent. In New Brunswick, the range is even greater; from 65 percent to 89 percent. The poorest region in Quebec had a per capita commodity income equal to 68 percent of the national average, while one region — southeastern Quebec — exceeded that average slightly. One region in Ontario fell slightly below the national average, while the most prosperous region — the Golden Horseshoe — exceeded the average by 45 percent.

Explaining Regional Disparities

The information in Tables 16.3 and 16.4 raises two questions: what accounts for the disparities in regional economic well-being, and why do these disparities persist? What is there about the British Columbia economy, for example, that apparently allowed it to produce from two to three times as much output per capita as the poorest province in each of the three years represented in the table? Or, to consider the matter from a slightly different perspective, why did one central Canadian economy, that of Ontario, consistently produce more output per capita than the other, Quebec, in these years?

It is not surprising to find differences in regional output per capita in any given year. Market economies are subject to a great number of different shocks, and, since endowments vary, these shocks will have quite different impacts on regional economies. Over

Table 16.4 Sectoral Distribution of Income, Canada, 1870

Region	Income per Capita
Canada	100
Nova Scotia	75
New Brunswick	83
Quebec	86
Ontario	120
Eastern Nova Scotia	65
Central Nova Scotia	85
Western Nova Scotia	71
Southern New Brunswick	89
Northern New Brunswick	65
Gulf of St. Lawrence	68
Lower St. Lawrence	74
Northern Quebec	82
Southeastern Quebec	102
Montreal area	91
Eastern Ontario	100
Huronia	117
Golden Horseshoe	145
Western Ontario	133
Northern Ontario	97

Source: Derived from Kris Inwood and James R. Irwin, "Canadian Regional Commodity Income Differences at Confederation," in Kris Inwood, ed., *Farm, Factory and Fortune: New Studies in the Economic History of the Maritime Provinces* (Fredericton: Acadiensis Press, 1993), table 2, p. 102.

time, however, these differences would be expected to disappear. Immigrants will be drawn disproportionately to the relatively more prosperous areas of the country, and internally, workers have an incentive to migrate from low-wage to high-wage regions. These migration flows act to reduce wages in the destination region and to raise them in the region of origin. Migration will continue until the wage differential, net of any migration costs, is removed. Similar reasoning applies to capital flows and the rates of return to investment in each region.

These types of factor reallocations seem to have occurred in Canada. Work by Alan and David Green suggests that international migration responded to interregional differences in per capita income.[3] Quigley et al. show that the Canadian branch-banking system was adept at transferring savings from regions where they were in excess supply to regions where there was an excess demand for loans.[4] The question that remains, therefore, is why these flows were apparently insufficient to remove regional income differences.

In a purely statistical sense, aggregate output per capita can be different among provinces for one of two reasons. Output per person will be lower in a region, all else being equal, if the ratio of those working to the total population is lower — that is, if the dependency rate is higher. This circumstance arises when age structures (more very young or very old), labour-force participation rates (less participation by women, for example), or unemployment rates are different.

Second, per capita output will vary if output per worker does, even if employment rates are constant. There are two reasons why output per worker might be different across regions. The first is what is termed an industry-mix effect. If output per worker is higher in some sectors than in others (manufacturing compared with fishing, for example), and if industrial structures differ across regions (fishing is more pertinent in one region, and manufacturing in the other), measured aggregate output per worker will differ. For example, the Maritimes will be poorer, on average, if there are more fishers in the labour force and if fishers are poorer than other workers. The other possible explanation is a productivity effect. Industrial structures may be similar, but output per worker in any given sector is higher in one region than in another. Fishers and factory workers may both earn more in Ontario than in the Maritimes, for example, because both are more productive in the former province. Both situations can be true, in which case disparities are even greater. Or they can be offsetting, in which case measured disparities will be less.

Alan Green's regional GVA data can be used to examine each of these explanations of the pattern of regional disparities. The picture that emerges from their analysis can be summarized as follows. First, differences in employment rates explain some of the overall disparity in output per capita, though they do not do so in a way that reveals much about underlying mechanisms. Computing output per member of the labour force rather than per person brings most provinces closer to the national average, but it moves some further away (Nova Scotia and New Brunswick in 1890; Saskatchewan and Alberta in 1910; Alberta in 1929).

The second conclusion is that industrial structure accounts for part of the disparity as well. Output per employed worker did vary significantly across sectors, being highest in forestry and manufacturing, and lowest in agriculture. Likewise, there was some diversity in industrial structure across provinces. Prince Edward Island and the Prairie provinces were disproportionately agricultural, the Maritimes and British Columbia were more heavily dependent on fishing, and Ontario and Quebec were the most industrialized. Still, there was less variation as a result of industrial structure than a contemporary observer might expect. The share of manufacturing in provincial output in Nova Scotia, New Brunswick, and British Columbia was only slightly below the proportions of Ontario and

Quebec, and Ontario was the most agriculturally dependent economy in 1890 after Prince Edward Island, Manitoba, and Saskatchewan.

If participation rates and industrial structure do not explain much of the regional variation in GVA per capita, productivity per worker within given activities must. This factor is both significant and consistent, as it turns out. Per capita output in Ontario is consistently among the highest in the country in all sectors, for example, while the corresponding figures for the Maritimes are consistently among the lowest. Part of the variation might still be an industry-mix effect, as the industry categories used are still quite broad. But the impression remains that the main cause of regional income disparities, even at this early stage of Canadian economic history, was differences in labour productivity. For whatever reasons— differences in scale of output, in capital per employee, in education and skills, in access to technology— the value of output per worker apparently varied systematically and significantly. As will be shown below, this finding can be duplicated using data for the post–World War II period, which makes the conclusion more plausible, but also more depressing.

These conclusions about industrial structure and productivity within sectors are consistent with Inwood and Irwin's data for 1870.[5] They find an inverse relationship between commodity income differences and population density, contradicting any simple Malthusian explanation for low-income provinces. They also find no connection between per capita income differences and the degree of industrialization. The richest province, Ontario, had the second-smallest share of manufacturing in total commodity income, surpassing only Nova Scotia. Fully 59 percent of Ontario's commodity income originated in agriculture in 1870, the largest share of any province by far. Ontario was relatively prosperous, they argue, at least partly because its farms were larger and more productive than those in the other three provinces.

Regional Equity Concerns

Canada has a long tradition of attention to regional equity. When Confederation was established, various concerns were raised about the fairness of the arrangement. The Maritimes feared that they were being swamped by Upper Canadian greed and Upper Canadian tariffs. The Métis, under Louis Riel, protested against eastern annexationists assuming control of their land. British Columbia demanded a railway and threatened secession when it was slow in coming. Moreover, the Dominion government gave explicit recognition of the principles of regional equity (though the term was not used until long after) when it provided a series of provincial subsidies, railway guarantees, and promises of special consideration.

THE MARITIMES

Maritime economic difficulties were linked to Confederation early on. The region prospered in the 1850s and 1860s, the account would have it, but began to lag thereafter. In part, the view was based on the apparent coincidence: the Maritimes' relative economic decline began about the time of Confederation. Connections between these two events were made, however, particularly to tariffs and railway policies. Tariffs allegedly diverted the region's attention from its traditional trading partners to the central Canadian provinces; the completion of the transcontinental rail system brought Canadian manufactured goods into the region rather than taking Maritime goods west, as had been hoped;

and the expectation that Atlantic cities would serve as ice-free ports for exports to Europe never materialized. Thus were born the legacy of Maritime dissatisfaction with Confederation that fuelled secessionist movements at the time, the Maritimes Rights Movement in the 1920s, and the resentment that has lingered to today.

This view was challenged in an influential study prepared for the Rowell–Sirois Commission by Maritime economic historian S.A. Saunders.[6] He linked the problems of the region to the unfortunate fates of its staples products, and to its natural disadvantages with respect to the new industries. The region's relative decline set in when demand for its main exports fell off. The British market for timber and ships fell off completely in the 1880s. The West Indies trade slowed as well, and, with it, the profitable carrying trade. Finally, the appearance of steam and steel ships on world trade routes spelled the end of the successful North Atlantic carrying trade.

The decline persisted because of an inability to compete in new ventures. The failure of the region to switch from wood and sails to steel and steam doomed shipbuilding and shipping. Geography and a relatively poor resource endowment put the region at a disadvantage with respect to manufacturing development. As the natural barriers of transportation costs fell away, it was inevitable that central Canadian concerns would dominate the national market. Distance meant, as well, that hopes for being the eastern terminus for the trade of the continent were unrealistic. Boston and New York in the United States and Montreal in Canada were much better positioned for that role.

A new and more sophisticated view of Maritime economic decline began to develop in the 1970s. Labelled by Kris Inwood as the "structuralist" view,[7] this approach puts considerable emphasis on the loss by Maritimers of control over private and public life. In the public sphere, the argument is that the Confederation arrangements transferred important powers to the federal government, and that Ottawa used these powers to pursue economic growth based on western expansion and central Canadian industrialism. National economic policies, particularly tariffs and railway freight rates, were not set with due regard to Maritime economic needs.

With respect to freight rates, the argument is not so much that the arrangements of 1867 worked *against* the interests of the region as that they did not work actively enough *for* it. Why, it is asked, did the Dominion government not choose to subsidize its Maritime transport the way it did its inland rail lines, and thereby ensure that Atlantic ports would serve the transcontinental trade? Why were even more favourable freight rates (the rate structure was biased in favour of shipments west from the Maritimes already) not extended on the Intercolonial Railway, to allow Maritime coal and manufactured goods to compete in central Canadian markets?

The link to private-sector control is developed by T.W. Acheson in an influential essay on Maritime industrialization between 1880 and 1910.[8] He finds that Maritime entrepreneurs responded initially to the opportunities offered by the national policy tariffs of 1879–87. Iron and steel and textiles were the main focuses, with attention given as well to sugar-refining and a range of miscellaneous manufacturing. For a time, progress was marked: Nova Scotia's industrial growth rate in the 1880s was the highest in Canada, for example. The ventures were indigenous, put in place by individuals or groups of individuals with long-time attachments to the region, and were scattered throughout the region rather than being concentrated in one or two larger centres.

These enterprises were unable to weather the long depression of the 1880s and 1890s, however, and eventually went out of business or were taken over by outside interests. Valiant efforts at adapting to change notwithstanding, the adjustment was simply too momentous. The problem was that the age of wood and sail had not created the proper conditions for a transition to industrial development. The new transportation routes and the new industrialism required a regional metropolis, a concept that was entirely foreign to the region. The early industrialization attempts failed because they had taken place in scattered communities that, however natural they were for Atlantic markets, were unsuited for continental ones. Communities that might have assumed this leadership role — Halifax, for example — failed the region because their merchants preferred to invest in banks and stocks rather than in industry.

The challenge in this interpretation to Saunder's position (outlined above) is important. For Saunders, there never could have been much diversification in the region beyond the original staples base. Natural disadvantages were just too great. No amount of tinkering with tariff or freight rates would have made much difference, and no group of merchants, however astute, could have held off the inevitable decline for long. For Acheson, there could have been sustained industrial growth, and there very nearly was. The essentials were there; the failure was human. The blame, if there is to be any, lies with regional merchants, who did not, or could not, make the transition to the new age.

Inwood provides a wide-ranging critique of the structuralist view. His most telling point perhaps is one already noted: the pattern of regional income disparities extends back to at least 1870, only three years into Confederation. The Maritimes were no less industrialized than central Canada at this time, but their manufacturers apparently were less efficient. Compared with establishments in central Canada, particularly Ontario, "Maritime factories were small, unproductive in their use of capital and labour, paid low wages and, at least in Nova Scotia, relatively unprofitable."[9]

Inwood is equally critical of the specific claims of the structuralist view. Since the federal government spent heavily on construction of the Intercolonial Railway in the years after Confederation, it is difficult to argue that there was a spending bias. Intercolonial tariffs were relatively low in 1867, so it is unlikely that the creation of an internal customs union disrupted Maritime manufacturing significantly. The 1879 national policy tariffs may have speeded up the rate of industrialization in Canada, but, if so, this policy itself is unlikely to have favoured one region over another. To the extent that Maritime savings flowed to other regions, this fact likely illustrated the relative lack of good investment opportunities in the region.[10] Freight-rate increases cannot have been a factor since the rate increases came in 1912 and 1917, long after the region's manufacturing disadvantage was apparent.[11] Even in the case of steel and coal, often cited by structuralists as an industry that suffered from the loss of local control, its difficulties are more likely explained by a small scale of operations, diminishing resources, and distance to markets.

In place of the structuralist interpretation of Maritime industrial decline, Inwood suggests a return to an older interpretation focusing on resource characteristics and technological developments.[12] Thin soil, a poor climate, and limited urban markets deterred agriculture. Technological change in ocean shipping undercut traditional wooden shipbuilding and shipping activities. Limited water power and hydro-electric potential hindered the development of new manufacturing industries. Diminished stocks reduced profitability in fishing, just as declining resources made coal mining a high-cost endeavour.

THE PRAIRIES

The Prairie provinces are the other region with a long tradition of economic grievances against Canada's national economic-development policies. Very briefly, the claims are that tariffs and railway freight rates reduced farm incomes and worked against the region's industrial development, and that Dominion land policies distorted the pattern of settlement and deprived provincial governments of an adequate source of revenue.

When examined more closely, however, these claims are less certain.[13] Already by 1895, Canadian rail rates for hauling grain to lakehead ports compared favourably with those for lines in the northern United States, the next-most-likely alternative to the Canadian system for prairie farmers. The Crow's Nest Pass Agreement and the Manitoba Agreement increased the Canadian advantage further. The same pattern was true for rail rates on incoming manufactured products. Since prairie farmers faced fixed prices for both what they produced and what they purchased, these favourable rates would have acted to increase farm incomes above what they would have been otherwise.

Although tariffs on manufactured products did cut into annual farm incomes, the tariffs were in place before settlement occurred, and thus this effect would be reflected in lower sale prices for land. If the tariffs had not been present, annual farm incomes would have been higher, and thus land prices— the entry fee, in effect — would have been higher too. Indeed, the fact that tariffs came down over time, albeit relatively little and only very slowly, would have increased the price of agricultural land and given its owners an unanticipated capital gain on this asset.

The evidence on the effects of Dominion land policy is less clear. The major problem lies in deciding what land-disposition policies the provincial governments would have put in place had the land been transferred to them at the time of their entrance into Confederation, as it had for all other provinces. It is not evident, for example, that provincial policies necessarily would have been any less distorting of the pattern of settlement than the Dominion ones. On the question of revenue, however, there is considerable evidence that the provincial governments were reasonably compensated for the fact they did not control their public lands until 1930.

These points notwithstanding, it was certainly not irrational for prairie farmers and other groups to lobby for lower freight rates and tariffs. This action was an obvious way to improve farm incomes, and was especially appealing when grain prices and yields were relatively low. The long tradition of prairie farm protest is certainly understandable in economic terms.

Conclusion

Three conclusions emerge from this brief look at the regional dimensions of Canada's economic growth to 1929. First, the regional economies grew at quite different rates in an aggregate sense, which is not surprising given their very different basic endowments. Second, there was little apparent convergence of per capita incomes over the period, which is more surprising given the apparent opportunities for interregional trade and for capital and labour to move internally. Third, there is a long tradition, not always well supported, of seeing national policies as being at the root of the disparities. All three points are as relevant today as they were in 1929, as subsequent chapters will demonstrate.

NOTES

1. There is some concern that the traditional Canadian focus on the regional perspective crowds out attention to questions of class, occupation, gender, and so forth.
2. Kris Inwood and James Irwin, "Canadian Regional Commodity Income Differences at Confederation," in Kris Inwood, ed., *Farm, Factory and Fortune: New Studies in the Economic History of the Maritime Provinces* (Fredericton: Acadiensis Press, 1993), 93–120.
3. Alan G. Green and David A. Green, "Balanced Growth and the Geographical Distribution of European Immigrant Arrivals to Canada, 1900–1912," *Explorations in Economic History* 30 (1993): 31–59.

4. Neil C. Quigley, Ian M. Drummond, and Lewis T. Evans, "Regional Transfer of Funds through the Canadian Banking System and Maritime Economic Development, 1895–1935," in Inwood, ed., *Farm, Factory and Fortune*, 219–50.

5. Inwood and Irwin, "Canadian Regional Commodity Income Differences at Confederation."

6. S.A. Saunders, *The Economic History of the Maritime Provinces*, edited and with an introduction by T.W. Acheson (Fredericton: Acadiensis Press, 1984).

7. Kris Inwood, "Maritime Industrialization from 1870 to 1910: A Review of the Evidence and Its Interpretation," in Inwood, ed., *Farm, Factory and Fortune*, 149–70.

8. T.W. Acheson, "The National Policy and the Industrialization of the Maritimes, 1880–1910," in P.A. Buckner and David Frank, eds., *Atlantic Canada After Confederation*, The Acadiensis Reader, vol. 2, 176–201.

9. Inwood, "Maritime Industrialization from 1870 to 1910," 156.

10. See also Quigley, Drummond, and Evans, "Regional Transfers of Funds."

11. See also Ken Cruikshank, "The Intercolonial Railway, Freight Rates and the Maritime Economy," in Inwood, ed., *Farm, Factory and Fortune*, 171–96.

12. Inwood, "Maritime Industrialization from 1870 to 1910," 164–70.

13. See Kenneth H. Norrie, "The National Policy and Prairie Economic Discrimination, 1870–1930," *Canadian Papers in Rural History* 1 (1978): 13–32.

FURTHER READING

Acheson, T.W., David Frank, and James D. Frost, eds. *Industrialization and Underdevelopment in the Maritimes, 1880–1930.* Toronto: Garamond Press, 1985.

Buckner, P.A., and David Frank, eds. *Atlantic Canada After Confederation.* The Acadiensis Reader, vol. 2. Fredericton: Acadiensis Press, 1985.

Green, Alan. *Regional Aspects of Canada's Economic Growth.* Toronto: University of Toronto Press, 1971.

Hiller, James, and Peter Neary, eds. *Newfoundland in the Nineteenth and Twentieth Centuries.* Toronto: University of Toronto Press, 1980.

Inwood, Kris, ed. *Farm, Factory and Fortune: New Studies in the Economic History of the Maritime Provinces.* Fredericton: Acadiensis Press, 1993.

Chapter Seventeen

The Great Depression, 1929–1939

IN 1929, the Canadian business cycle turned downward. This event in itself was not unusual; the economy was often characterized by short, sharp fluctuations in economic activity. This time, however, the pattern was different. What initially appeared to be a regionally based agricultural slump proved to be a major economic collapse. Its effects were soon felt across the nation, and, over the next months and years, the economy not only failed to recover but slid inexorably downward in what seemed an endless decline. By the time the bottom was reached, in 1933, more than one in four Canadians was out of work, many municipalities and even some provinces hovered on the edge of bankruptcy, and thousands of individuals had been forced to shut down their businesses or farms.

Haltingly, the economy did begin to recover. First one sector and then another would show modest improvement, and newspapers and politicians would trumpet the beginning of good times. Yet the good times proved to be elusive, and promising recoveries were checked by renewed problems. Thus, in 1937, after the best year of the decade, a recession occurred, wiping out much of the gain that had been made. Even a decade after the slide began, more than one in ten Canadians was out of work, and farm income was still less than half of what it had been at its peak, in 1928. Only in 1939 did GNP in constant dollars finally surpass that of 1929.

This was the decade of the Great Depression. No other industrial downturn in history was so massive or so persistent. Tremendous psychological, social, and political tensions resulted. New attitudes were born, as were new political parties. Regional balances and regional outlooks shifted. The beliefs held about the industrial system also shifted, as did the demands for action by the state. Years, even decades, after the Depression ended, people would point back to it and its lessons as a dire warning against smug comfort in the midst of prosperity. It is no exaggeration to say that this economic cataclysm altered some of the most basic assumptions of Canadians and shaped much of the following political, social, and economic history in Canada, as it did elsewhere.

Economic Collapse

The Great Depression was not peculiar to Canada, though there were aspects unique to this country. Rather, Canada was caught up in a vast international collapse, over which it had little control. The Canadian economy had weaknesses of its own, of course, but economic collapse was unavoidable, given events elsewhere in the Atlantic economy.

What were the causes of the Great Depression? For Canada, developments in the international economy are the most likely sources of the downturn. As Pierre Siklos notes, Canadian and U.S. recessions up to and including the Depression were remarkably similar suggesting that Canadian recessions, and the Depression, originated in the U.S. and were quickly transmitted to Canada.[1] The close economic ties between the two countries and the adherence of both countries to the gold standard monetary regime would be the mechanisms by which the American downturn that became the Great Depression was transmitted to Canada. Thus, an understanding of the economic collapse in Canada after 1929 requires an understanding of two issues. First, why did the U.S. economy experience its downturn in the late 1920s, and second, how were recessions transmitted internationally under the gold standard monetary regime.

While there is no consensus as to the causes of the Depression, a popular account comes from Christina Romer who argues that the American Depression was distinct from that of other economies that experienced Depressions at about the same time.[2] Economic decline and subsequent recovery were more extreme in the U.S. than in any other economy. Unlike other economies, the U.S. Depression began with a decline in consumption and ended with an increase in investment. In 1928, the U.S. monetary authority contracted the money supply, thereby increasing interest rates (to encourage people to hold bonds rather than money, and to invest in bonds rather than equities) to cool off a booming stock market. Rising interest rates slowed down interest rate sensitive activities like construction and consumer spending on durable goods like automobiles or appliances. Thus, tight monetary policy in 1928 and early 1929 drew the U.S. economy into a mild recession. According to Romer, the Great Depression began in earnest with the U.S. stock market crash in October 1929. While the loss of wealth experienced by a minority of Americans in the crash likely reduced consumption, the bigger effect of the stock market crash was creation of uncertainty in the minds of consumers and owners of firms over future incomes. Thus, consumers stopped spending on consumer durables and firms delayed making investments. Also, following the stock market crash, things got worse in the U.S. economy as banking panics and other financial crises led to further contractions in the money supply. In response to financial crises, lending practices by banks were more restrictive which was yet another channel by which the money supply contracted.

Peter Temin argues that there is a short and straightforward explanation for how the Great Depression spread quickly from country to country: fixed exchange rates under the gold standard monetary regime that had been in place before World War I and restored in the 1920s.[3] Barry Eichengreen argues that by tying the economic policies of different nations together, the gold standard made the destabilizing force of the restrictive U.S. monetary policies in 1928 extremely powerful because it made the U.S. policy a global policy.[4]

Under the gold standard the values of national currencies were fixed in terms of quantities of gold, and hence against other national currencies. Once the value of a national currency is set, the size of the nation's money supply is set by the quantity of gold reserves held by that nation. If the value of a currency is to be maintained, then the money supply in the nation rises if gold flows into the country's reserves and contracts if gold outflows. Flows of gold between countries reflect a nation's balance of payments position. A country with a balance of payments deficit (if the value of imports exceeds the value of exports and/or if the country is a net exporter of capital) exports gold and the money supply contracts. Analogously, a country with a balance of payments surplus imports gold and can increase its money supply. To consistently run a balance of payments deficit, a country faces the threat of running out of gold reserves and hence, being unable to maintain the value of its currency. The deficit position might require that the country devalue its currency; that is, exchange a unit of currency for a smaller amount of gold. Devaluation can be beneficial for a nation by reducing imports (since imported goods cost more for domestic residents) and by increasing exports (since the prices of them are lower for foreign consumers). Under the rules of the gold standard, however, defaulting on the commitment to maintain the fixed value of the currency also has its costs. Foreign loans may cease in response since repayment of the loans denominated in the nation's own currency become riskier to make from the perspective of foreign lenders. Thus, if the value of a currency is to remain fixed, then the mechanism of adjustment for addressing a balance of payments deficit is deflation; domestic prices fall instead of the exchange rate. Ideally, lowering domestic prices reduces imports and stimulates exports, improving the balance of trade and attracting gold into the domestic economy.

Barry Eichengreen describes how the U.S. economy continued to expand after 1928 despite the tight monetary policies that were used to cool off the New York stock market. At the same time, the U.S. monetary policy was slowing the economies of other nations. As the U.S. money supply shrank, interest rates in the U.S. rose and, as a consequence, U.S. foreign lending fell. Under the gold standard, these events resulted in gold flowing from the rest of the world into the United States. For countries like Canada to maintain their exchange rates as required under the gold standard, these nations had to follow the U.S.'s lead and raise interest rates and restrict credit. Thus, money supplies in countries like Canada contracted as a consequence of U.S. monetary policy.[5]

Eichengreen notes that many exporters of primary products (like Canada's wheat exports) attempted to boost their exports and limit their imports to attract gold back into their reserves. This response resulted in an even more rapid deterioration of commodity prices that was already occurring prior to the U.S. monetary contraction in 1928. If it was only one primary-producing nation expanding productive capacity, then that country's export revenues and national income could have been expected to increase. When all countries attempted to do this at the same time, the glut of primary products depressed commodity prices causing economic conditions of primary-producers to deteriorate further. Thus, increasing commodity exports provided little relief. A second option for indebted commodity exporting countries like Canada was to suspend debt service payments to foreign lenders and use what foreign exchange they had to import essential items. While many debtor countries chose this default option after 1931, once American foreign lending collapsed in 1928 and 1929, this option was avoided as much as possible since the debtor countries could not afford to disrupt their access to foreign capital markets. Default on existing debts posed a serious threat to a country's reputation as a good borrower.

Ultimately, Eichengreen argues that countries dependent on U.S. capital for their external (exchange rate) stability faced the situation that "a draconian compression of domestic spending was the only option consistent with the continued maintenance of the gold standard." Peter Temin argues that the choice of deflation over devaluation under the rigid adherence to the gold standard by most of the nations in Europe and North America after World War I was the impetus that transmitted the Great Depression internationally. Temin views that an abandonment of the gold standard was the only way for economic decline to be halted as "going off of gold" severed the connection between price levels and the balance of payments. Temin argues that the single best predictor of the severity of a country's Depression is how long they "stayed on gold." According to Peter Temin, the gold standard need not have been so devastating to economies in 1929. What was lacking was international coordination on monetary policy, something that was extremely difficult in the aftermath of World War I. Temin argues that a universal devaluation would have increased the value of world gold reserves and increased the world money supply, and allowed for worldwide economic expansion.

Given the international scope of the Great Depression, several features of the Canadian economy left Canada particularly vulnerable to the deflationary pressures emanating from the U.S. and the rest of the Atlantic economy in 1929. For Canada, the effect of the United States and Britain reducing imports (hence Canadian exports) would have been enormous. In addition, the U.S. and Britain were reducing capital exports that were vitally important for investments in the Canadian economy.

While going off of the gold standard was the best prescription for recovery, abandoning the commitment to the gold standard proved difficult for Canada because of her reliance on U.S. capital. According to Barry Eichengreen, Canada lost one quarter of her gold in 1928 and as the gold outflows continued, the Department of Finance stopped redeeming Dominion notes for gold in late 1929. In addition, the government of Canada, with the cooperation of Canada's banks, imposed an informal embargo on gold exports. Thus, while Dominion notes continued to be valued in terms of a fixed domestic currency price of gold, in 1929 Canada was for all intents and purposes off of the gold standard.[6] Despite its abandonment of the gold standard for its currency, however, the Canadian government managed the money supply and maintained a stable exchange rate from 1929 to 1931. Michael Bordo and Angela Redish attribute the rigid adherence to the formerly fixed rate to the government's commitment to the gold standard to which it expected to return at some point in the future. Canada also feared the punitive costs of potentially large devaluations given the size of her U.S. dollar-denominated debt. Thus, Canada did not take advantage of exchange rate flexibility until Britain abandoned the gold standard in 1931, and the threat of punishment was reduced.[7]

Canada was especially dependent on exports, with some 22 percent of gross national expenditure attributable to merchandise exports in 1929, compared with less than 5 percent in the United States. In some sectors, the export market was the only meaningful market. Some 80 percent of Canadian produce from forests, farms, and mines was exported. The nation's largest export, wheat, accounted for an incredible 40 percent of all world exports and thus, if that international market collapsed, Canada would be harder hit than most.[8]

Moreover, Canada's huge dependence on exports rested on relatively few products. As Table 17.1 indicates, wheat and wheat flour together accounted for more than 36 percent of all exports. When forest products, such as paper and boards, were added, the figure amounted to more than half. Automobiles provided the only exception among leading exports to Canada's reliance on primary resources or their direct manufactured products. To state the figures in a slightly different way, exports from farm products, animal products, and forest products in total accounted for nearly 80 percent of all Canadian exports. The lack of diversification in Canadian export goods therefore made the nation vulnerable. A decrease in demand for relatively few goods could cripple Canadian foreign trade.

This vulnerability was made worse because such a large percentage of Canadian exports depended on just one market — the United States. In 1929, well over one-third of all Canadian exports went to the United States, and products headed south of the border were concentrated in a few key areas. Wood and paper, animal products, and non-ferrous metals (for example, copper, nickel, and gold) accounted for more than three-quarters of all Canadian exports to the United States. Two of the largest growth areas of the 1920s, mining and pulp and paper, had grown in response to the demands of the American market. Further, in a general sense, trade with the United States had been one of the most important factors in shaping Can-ada's development in the decade after the war.

Table 17.1 Major Canadian Exports, 1929

Product	Value ($ millions)	% of Total Exports
Wheat	428.5	31.5
Paper	142.3	10.5
Flour	65.1	4.8
Boards	47.7	3.5
Autos	43.1	3.2
Fish	34.9	2.6
Copper	26.9	2.0
Barley	25.7	1.9

Source: Derived from Statistics Canada, *Canada Year Book*, 1930, cat. no. 11-402E (Ottawa: King's Printer, 1931), p. 477. Reproduced by authority of the Minister of Industry.

Just how dependent Canada was on the United States quickly became apparent with the economic collapse in 1929. The U.S. economy fell farther than that of any other industrialized nation in the world (see Table 17.2). American domestic investment and output rapidly declined through 1930 and 1931 and, with them, American purchases abroad. To make matters worse, the U.S. government reacted to the sliding economy by retreating even further behind tariff barriers. The Hawley–Smoot tariff of 1930 raised tariffs on both agricultural and manufactured goods, which had a devastating effect on Canadian trade. By 1932, Canadian exports to the United States in such important areas as meats and agricultural products were worth less than they had been at the beginning of World War I. Metals were not much better off. The combination of the decline in U.S. activity and the protectionism that it wrought meant that by 1932 the total level of Canadian exports to the United States was less than half of what it had been in 1929. Indeed, that 1932 total of just over $235 million was less than exports in wood and paper alone had been just three years earlier.

The decline of exports to the United States is not the whole story. Canada's largest single export, after all, was wheat, and that was marketed not in the United States but in Europe, especially in the United Kingdom. Nearly $277 million in Canadian wheat and wheat flour was sent to the United Kingdom in 1929— a figure of greater value than that of any single item exported to the United States. Agricultural produce of all sorts accounted for more than $325 million of the total of $433.9 million. In other words, the British were only slightly less important than the Americans as a market for Canadian exports, and the British dependence on Canadian wheat meant that Canadian exports to Britain were even more concentrated on a single commodity than were exports to the United States.

Britain's economy did not decline as severely as that of the United States and might have served, therefore, to restrain the fall in Canadian exports. Unfortunately for Canada, however, the worldwide glut of agricultural goods forced prices rapidly downward. By 1932, the value of Canadian agricultural exports to Britain had been reduced by two-thirds. The impact of this drastic decline of exports was reflected in a disastrous domestic situation. The Depression was hardest on those who farmed or depended on the farmer for a livelihood. The Depression in Canada began on the Prairies, and it was there that its effects were felt most fully.

Table 17.2 International Impact of the Great Depression — 1932 as a Percentage of 1929

Nation	Industrial Production	National Income
Austria	61	83
Canada	58	55
France	77	84
Germany	58	59
Japan	98	84
United Kingdom	83	85
United States	53	48

Source: A.E. Safarian, *The Canadian Economy in the Great Depression* (Toronto: University of Toronto Press, 1970), p. 98.

For some time, international wheat prices had been weakening, but for Canada, this had been masked by two things. First, the wheat pools and the government had been increasing the amounts of wheat held rather than selling in poor international markets. Second, Canadians had been growing more wheat. In 1928, for example, the Canadian wheat crop was a record 566 million bushels, which meant that the total value of wheat production was only a little lower than the previous year, in spite of a sharp decline in prices.

A boom crop that allowed farmers merely to maintain their standard of living was an ominous sign; the next year, things began to fall apart. Average yield on the Prairies declined almost 40 percent, and the crop was cut by nearly 100 million bushels. National income in agriculture declined from $856 million in 1928 to $608 million in 1929.[9] Farmers could no longer compensate for falling prices with increased volume, and the entire economy of the Prairies headed into a decline that began to undermine the whole wheat-marketing system and, soon after, the political and economic infrastructure of the Prairie provinces.

The declining prices that set in toward the end of 1929 created havoc in the wheat pools. It was pool practice to give out an initial (and conservative) payment to farmers when they brought their grain to the elevators in the fall or winter. Once the grain was sold and the yearly returns had been determined, "bonus" payments would be made. The better the price, the larger the bonus. In the fall and winter of 1928–29, the wheat pools gave out an initial payment of $1 a bushel. This was, as usual, below the current price. Before long, however, wheat prices had declined below the $1 prepayment. In response, the pools held back wheat, hoping that the decline was a temporary one. As a result, Canadian wheat exports declined by more than 160 million bushels in 1929 (see Table 17.3).

The collapse in wheat prices created an immediate crisis for farmers. Many had expanded their land under production after the bumper crop of 1928, and had accumulated additional debt to do so. Now, not only were there to be no bonus payments, but the full elevators indicated that prices next year were to be low. Further, the pools were in serious financial trouble because of their failure to foresee the collapse of wheat prices, and only loans from the provinces allowed them to continue. Even so, the existing debts would have to be recovered out of next year's profits. The best a farmer could hope for was a mediocre year in 1930, and that would happen only if crops were good and prices remained more or less steady.

Table 17.3 Wheat Prices and Production, Canada, 1927–1933

Year	Price (cents per bushel)	Production (000 bushels)
1927	146.3	479 665
1928	124.0	566 726
1929	124.2	302 192
1930	64.2	420 672
1931	59.8	321 325
1932	54.3	443 061
1933	68.1	281 892

Source: Statistics Canada, *Historical Statistics of Canada,* 2nd ed., cat. no. 11-516E (Ottawa: Supply and Services, 1983), series M228–238 and M249–257. Reproduced by authority of the Minister of Industry, 1995.

Instead, what farmers got was an average harvest and a continued decline in prices. Yield was up somewhat, but it was apparent, even before the crops were harvested, that the international wheat market was becoming a major disaster. Wholesale prices were barely half what they had been the previous year, and the total value of the wheat crop was only 45 percent of what it had been in 1928. The next year was worse, and the year after that worse still, as the vast unused stocks of wheat were dumped on the world market and prices continued downward. By 1932, the total value of Canadian wheat was less than one-third of the 1928 figure. The wheat pools were collapsing under the debt they had assumed, and prairie farmers were being forced out of operation by the thousands. Net farm income for the three Prairie provinces together in 1932 was *minus* $3.1 million. Only four years before, it had been $363 million![10]

Although the disaster on the Prairies had many profound effects throughout the 1930s, the collapse in wheat alone would have created serious economic problems for Canada. Since the 1890s, grain farming had been central to Canadian economic welfare in general, including Canadian exports. Even had there not been a general collapse, Canada would have had to cope with significant adjustments in its trade prospects and with a region that was plunging into greater poverty than the country had ever known.

The collapse of Canadian exports explains, to a large degree, why Canada's economy suffered so much more than many others. Its American markets failed because the United States was devastated, and Canada's largest single export, wheat, was devastated by a general fall in the international value of that product. This collapse in prices was exacerbated over the next few years by bad weather and irregular crops throughout much of the Prairies. As a result, overall Canadian merchandise exports declined from a high of $1.27 billion in 1929 to $396 million by 1932.[11]

The lagging of overall economic recovery behind the recovery in exports was due to the nature of investment in Canada. In the later 1920s, there was a tremendous amount of investment in Canada. Capital formation provided a major engine of growth in these years. There were new hydro-electric plants, new automobile factories, and new pulp-and-paper mills. The problem, as A.E. Safarian concluded, was not only that good investment opportunities were used up, but that such investment could continue only if there was ongoing expansion in the Canadian economy. Canada, in sum, went on a building binge reminiscent of that undertaken by railways before World War I. The fastest-growing part of national income was investment in durable assets.

Such levels of investment were exceedingly optimistic, even for the heady days of the later 1920s. The newsprint industry, for example, had been such a growth area that investors began to pour money into new facilities to satisfy the seemingly insatiable appetite of American newspapers. Nearly $200 million was invested in pulp and paper from 1926 to 1929. By the end of the decade, Canadians had made investments that could be recouped only if the market expanded at a very healthy rate. The declining price of newsprint, and the fact that market growth was not increasing as fast as Canadian capacity, indicated, even before the crash, that such growth was unlikely. With the Depression, of course, newsprint markets collapsed, and Canada was burdened with a great deal of excess capacity. By 1932, according to one industry estimate, only 51 percent of newsprint capacity was being utilized.[12]

The automobile industry, like that of pulp and paper, had seen heavy capital investment in the latter part of the decade, and automobiles too were vulnerable to the Depression. For one thing, nearly one-third of automobiles manufactured were exported. For another, many people saw automobiles as a relative luxury and would quickly postpone the decision to purchase one (or replace an old one) in hard times. By 1932, the number of automobiles registered in Canada actually declined. At the low point, automobile production was employing only about one-tenth of existing capacity.

One could go on to cite equally dramatic incidents of decline in other industries. In the years 1929 to 1933, no sector of the economy showed any meaningful growth, and most showed tremendous decline.[13] Even at the industry level, the exceptions are so few as to illustrate in a stark way the widespread nature of the Depression. Only electric refrigerators and gold, two rather different products, resisted the tendency to decline.

The heavy investment of the 1920s and the resultant excess supply of the 1930s caused an almost total collapse in domestic investment. Exports may have fallen to less than half of what they had been, but gross domestic investment fell to an incredible 11 percent of what it had been in the heady days of the later 1920s. From being 22.1 percent of GNP in 1929, it declined by 1933 to 8.6 percent,[14] and this at a time when overall GNP was falling. Construction workers were, with farmers, the hardest hit of all groups of workers in Canada. Some 60 percent of carpenters and 55 percent of labourers were unemployed in the relatively prosperous city of Toronto.[15]

Further, the simple recovery of production to 1929 levels would not guarantee renewed investment. Even before the Depression, most sectors had adequate plant and machinery to meet demand. Recovery would soak up excess capacity rather than generate new investment. Only significant new growth or the longer-term effects of obsolescence would generate domestic investment, and, even then, only if business saw improved prospects for the future. Lack of domestic investment would thus prove a crucial factor retarding the recovery of the economy once the bottom of the Depression was reached in 1932–33. It would be 1945 before business investment recovered to the absolute level of the 1920s, and 1949 before it reached the same percentage of GNP![16]

Perhaps one of the greatest limitations on investment was the effect of the Depression on the international capital market. Without work and a paycheque, many Canadians were forced to spend from their accumulated savings in the 1930s, causing the pool of domestic savings available for investment to decrease from the 1920s. As the Depression was international in scope, foreign sources of capital, particularly from the United States, were also much more limited than they had been in the 1920s.

Related to the heavy capital investment of the 1920s was the growth of debt. Businesses, farmers, and governments took on increased liabilities to meet the opportunities and demands that faced them, especially in the years after 1925. Those new paper mills, houses, apartment buildings, roads, and auto-parts factories had been built on the assumption that debts would be retired easily over a few years. Thus, not only was there excess capacity in the system because of past expansion but that useless capacity also drained wealth to meet interest payments. High fixed debts, largely owed to foreign borrowers, thus exacerbated the burdens of declining revenue. Further, the Depression meant that debt levels were, in real terms, not only fixed but increasing. As prices declined from 1929 through 1932, the real value of debt increased accordingly. The real value of a debt contracted in 1929 would increase almost 30 percent by 1933.

Nowhere were past expansion and high debt to haunt Canadians more than in the case of railways. The drive to establish new transcontinentals in the years after 1900 had led Canadian railways to a point where they were overexpanded by 1915. The result had been both the creation of the new nationally owned Canadian National Railways (CN) and the end of massive railway construction. In the 1920s, for example, railway construction increased the length of track from 61 000 km to only 66 000 km.

This lack of growth does not mean that the railways were putting their houses in order and building up surpluses against a rainy day. Both CN and the Canadian Pacific Railway indulged in considerable expansion through the 1920s in such areas as hotels and steamships. The debt of both companies increased, even during this prosperous decade.[17] To make matters worse, CN was saddled with a large debt left over from the earlier consolidation process. The charges on this debt, as well as the new debt acquired through the decade, meant that, even in the good times of the later 1920s, CN was unable to cover operating expenses and debt charges. Losses between 1923 and 1931 were a staggering $546 million, and, even during the bumper crop year of 1928, annual losses for the government system were nearly $48 million.[18] It was a burden on the public accounts in the best of times. The worst of times were about to come.

As the Rowell–Sirois Commission would note a few years later, the collapse of western agriculture that came about in the Depression "struck at the heart of the Canadian railway structure."[19] The Canadian railways had been developed in the image of the national policy's vision of an east–west exchange of primary resources and manufactured goods. Hauling the millions of bushels of wheat off the Prairies and carrying the consumer goods, the farm implements, and the immigrants to the West had dictated railway construction in Canada during the previous half-century. Suddenly, there was less grain to be hauled, and the people in the West could not afford all of those manufactured goods from the East. In addition, the huge quantities of logs and newsprint that had been brought by rail out of Ontario, New Brunswick, and British Columbia were less in demand. Between 1928 and 1931, the annual total tonnage of forest products hauled by Canadian railways had decreased by half. Total railway freight in Canada declined from a record 141 million tons (128 million t) in 1928 to 75 million tons (68 million t) by 1936. The annual number of passengers carried declined from a 1926 figure of more than 40 million to fewer than 20 million by 1933.

Such a decline in traffic meant disaster for the debt-laden railways. Even the formerly profitable Canadian Pacific went into the red and suspended dividend payments for several years. It looked healthy compared with Canadian National, however. Annual losses on that line rose to an incredible $112 million a year, an amount equivalent to more than one-third of the annual revenue of the Dominion government! By 1935, the funded debt level of the railway system had climbed to more than $3 billion, in spite of severe cost-cutting measures.

The debts of the railways were so massive that they affected the public accounts, but the problems of rigid and high debts applied to many factories, farms, and governments in the country. Indeed, many farmers faced a parallel circumstance, albeit on a smaller scale, to those of the railways. Mortgages of $5000 or $10 000, which seemed a reasonable investment back in 1925 or 1926, became a crushing burden when wheat prices collapsed. In many cases, debt levels exceeded the newly depressed total values of the whole farming operation. The payment of interest often exceeded the annual income in farming operations. And banks were much less willing to wait upon a farmer's future than they were a railway's.

Each of the circumstances described above was harmful enough individually; however, their total effect and the relationship among them created the sequence leading to the Great Depression. To recapitulate: by the later 1920s, international commodity gluts posed a serious problem for world trade. Canada, as a nation dependent on that trade, was bound to suffer from the increasingly inevitable adjustments that would be needed to rid the world of excess inventories. Already by 1929 the Prairie west was feeling the effects of such adjustments. Such adjustments had occurred before, but this time it was different. The international trading and currency systems were unstable, and the beginning of recession, exacerbated by the collapse of the New York markets, led to protectionism and the progressive shrinkage of world trade. For the next three or four years, the world lurched from crisis to crisis, as the international economy continued to shrink and as international financial and monetary systems proved incapable of handling the drastic downturn.

All of this was bad enough, but Canada was also hampered by two additional circumstances. First, the massive capital investment of the later 1920s meant that the economic recovery would have to be considerable before there was a significant demand for new investment. Second, and worst of all, since Canada's was an export-dependent economy with only a small domestic market, there was little that could be done. Exports would recover only when the international community decided it needed Canadian products again. Domestic investment and, eventually, expansion, would come only some time after that.

Economic Recovery

Recovery, like the Depression itself, began with international events. Peter Temin submits that the abandonment of the gold standard regime kick-started Canada's economic recovery. As Bordo and Redish argue, for Canada to benefit from this policy option, she had to wait for England to go off of gold in 1931 and the U.S. to go off of gold in 1933. Only then was it possible for Canada to ease its commitment to maintaining the Canadian currency's exchange rate against the British and U.S. currencies.[20]

Perhaps the biggest contributing factor to Canada's economic recovery was the recovery of the U.S. economy, though as Pierre Siklos notes, recovery in Canada was not as complete as in the U.S.[21] There are several explanations put forward for the timing of the U.S. economic recovery. Milton Friedman and Anna Schwartz argue that the introduction of Deposit Insurance in 1934 restored financial stability to the U.S. economy that, in turn, encouraged the recovery by increasing the money supply. Wigmore identifies the U.S. going off of gold in 1933 as the turning point that facilitated a larger money supply. Recent work by Patrick Coe suggests that Deposit Insurance, not going off of gold, was probably the turning point of the Depression in the United States.[22] While Christina Romer identifies large increases in the money supply, following Roosevelt's use of emergency powers to depreciate the value of the American dollar, as the turning point in the Depression. Romer also suggests that political unrest in Europe arising from Hitler's activities in the 1930s resulted in Europeans investing in American assets with U.S. dollars in gold, which further stimulated the U.S. expansion of the money supply.[23]

Canadian trade with Britain increased considerably between 1932 and 1937, reaching 90 percent of the 1928 figure. This helped Canada's overall level of exports, which began their long climb back toward the levels of the 1920s. For the next three years, recovery continued. Central to this recovery was the slow recovery of exports to the United States. Between 1932 and 1937, total exports more than doubled and were once again approaching the levels of the later 1920s.

Though led by exports, this recovery was reflected as well in a gradual increase in consumer purchases and in employment. Current-account balances remained strong, largely because Canadians were purchasing much less abroad than they had been in the 1920s. The one area that lagged was domestic investment because the improvement that was taking place had not yet removed the depression psychology that made businesses hesitant to invest, nor had it utilized the excess capacity still existing in many industries.[24]

There was one final setback. In 1937, the United States economy slumped badly, wiping out many of the gains made in the previous few years. Canada was directly affected, as American purchases of Canadian goods decreased by almost one-quarter between 1937 and 1938. In Canada, this decrease directly affected numerous jobs and indirectly affected the psychology of recovery. Practically all major indicators slumped.[25] By the end of 1938, the slump was over, and there was modest improvement once again in the overall Canadian economy.

Still, the 1937–38 recession showed the fragile nature of the recovery that had been taking place and, most importantly, reinforced the psychology of depression. Only the most extreme external events could overcome such a psychology and bring the international economy fully out of the Depression within the foreseeable future. Unfortunately, those events did indeed come, as Europe moved toward war. Modern industrial warfare, as World War I had clearly shown, placed tremendous demands on both agricultural and industrial economies. As war neared, the psychology of depression began to lift and, with war itself, the greatest economic depression in history was over. The world traded in one catastrophe for another, more horrendous, one.

Government Responses to the Depression

The response of government to the Depression was shaped, above all, by one basic fact. The responsibilities and demands on the government had changed dramatically in recent years, but constitutional rigidities under the BNA Act and other factors had prevented a smooth adjustment of financial resources to respond to these new demands. Specifically, the twentieth century had made certain responsibilities of the province much more important and, consequently, much more expensive. Children were staying in school much longer. Thus, education costs rose dramatically. With the development of the automobile, roads and bridges became a much more expensive proposition as well. Finally, the demands of new technologies, such as electricity and telephones, often fell to the municipalities or provinces. As a result, provincial expenditures soared in the years after World

War I. In 1913, total current expenditures for all provinces had been only $48.9 million. By 1929, the total was $163 million.

Such a rapid rise in expenditures meant increased debt. While the Dominion government was actually reducing its debt level through the 1920s (and trying, therefore, to repay some of the costs of the war), the provinces and municipalities found debt a convenient way to defray some of the immediate burdens imposed by public demand. Total provincial and municipal debt charges increased from just over $51 million in 1921 to more than $85 million by 1930. Like the farmer's mortgage or the business's bank loan, there were fixed charges that would become an increasing problem as revenues declined and relief burdens mounted.

Clearly, most of the provinces were in no shape to undertake major new initiatives during the Depression. The majority were scrambling simply to survive, and realized very quickly that they would be able to do so only if the Dominion government assumed some of their financial burden. As for the Dominion government, it ultimately had no choice. If the provinces began to go bankrupt, the responsibilities would inevitably fall to the Dominion anyway, and there was, with each passing year, an ever-better chance that some bankruptcies would, indeed, occur. By 1935, the outgoing prime minister, R.B. Bennett, warned his successor, Mackenzie King, that several provinces, especially in the West, were effectively bankrupt.[26]

Initially, the Dominion government took an active if somewhat unimaginative role in facing the Depression. Mackenzie King's Liberals were unceremoniously tossed out by the electorate in 1930, and R.B. Bennett's Conservatives came into office pledged to quick action. This they took by raising the tariff and by initiating a series of public-work programs to provide employment in hard-hit spots of the nation. Also, they undertook a series of ad hoc grants to the provinces to assist in relief payments and brought in such measures as the Unemployment and Farm Relief Act of 1931. Dominion welfare payments alone rose from a negligible $2 million in 1929 to $48 million by 1932. Overall, Dominion expenditures increased by $132 million between 1929 and 1932. In the meantime, revenues had decreased by $140 million, as tax revenues dried up. The net effect of this was that government expenditures did work in a countercyclical fashion during the initial years of the Depression. The Dominion actually increased expenditures but, even if the struggling provinces and municipalities are included, the expenditures were the component of national income most resistant to decreases.[27]

This situation did not last. The tremendous rise in costs necessitated by municipal and provincial relief and by Dominion assistance programs caused deficits to rise inexorably. By 1933, provincial debt levels had risen to more than $1.5 billion, and the Dominion balance changed from a budgetary surplus of $68 million on the 1928 year, to a deficit of $160 million on that of 1935. Accumulated federal government debt increased from $3.2 billion in 1929 to $4.1 billion by 1933 and to $4.5 billion by 1935.

The rising deficits soon paralyzed government. In 1931, with international financial collapse well underway, Bennett became nervous about the level of Dominion expenditures. "We must now talk in thousands where we previously spoke in millions," he wrote, "or we will be bankrupt."[28] Saving dollars became the major theme of government administration. Thousands of civil servants were let go, while those who retained their jobs in government service had their salaries cut. Public-works expenditures were slashed, as building construction and even repairs were postponed. Contracts for new construction were lower than at any time since the early 1890s. Thus, even the most standard and traditional of government unemployment measures — public works — was abandoned by 1932–33 as a means of dealing with the Great Depression. The collapse was thought too massive and the government deficit too large.

As Figure 17.1 shows, cutbacks after 1933 meant that the government no longer acted as a countercyclical force (albeit an ineffective one) and may actually have slowed potential recovery in the subsequent years. For this it has received much criticism. If only the Dominion government had accepted the new currents of Keynesianism, the argument runs, it would have seen the advantage of massive deficits and have undertaken greater initiatives. Yet such criticism is really beside the point, for several reasons. First, the deficit was a real problem. Annual debt charges had before World War I amounted to less than 9 percent of annual revenue. The war had changed all that, and the debt carried out of the war drained 26 percent of current revenue by 1928. By 1935, it would consume 43 percent of annual revenues. Almost one dollar in two in the Dominion budget was going just to handle the national debt. Both the level of the debt and the dramatic change in that level were bound to affect politicians. In a post-Keynesian world, it would have taken considerable faith in economic theory to have maintained spending in such a fiscal position.

Even if the Canadian government had maintained the desire to continue deficit financing of its spending, the sources of domestic savings and of foreign loans necessary to finance spending on a scale to have the desired economic impact were in all likelihood not available in the early 1930s. Barry Eichengreen notes that no country was able to borrow on a significant scale in the 1930s. American lending collapsed in 1929 and after a temporary revival in 1930, collapsed permanently in 1931.[29] Canada was one of the last major countries to borrow from the United States before international lending completely dried up. This status was in all likelihood the result of Canada's commitment to preserving a reputation as a good

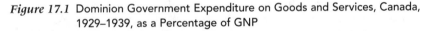

Figure 17.1 Dominion Government Expenditure on Goods and Services, Canada, 1929–1939, as a Percentage of GNP

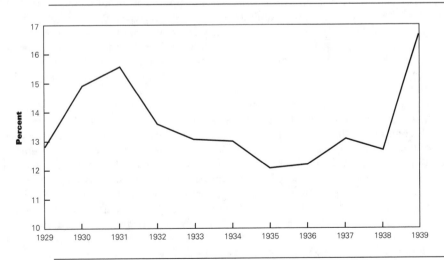

Source: Derived from Statistics Canada, *Historical Statistics of Canada*, 2nd ed., cat. no. 11-516E (Ottawa: Supply and Services, 1983), series H1–51, F1–152. Reproduced by authority of the Minister of Industry, 1995.

329

debtor by not depreciating its currency or defaulting on its debt service payments owing to foreign lenders.[30]

Second, the government was not yet a large enough institution to be able to affect the direction of the whole economy. Public works and such measures might provide short-term relief, but the fiscal power of government was not as great as it would be in the post-1945 period. In 1929, for example, Dominion government expenditure was 6.3 percent of GNP. In 1975, it was more than 21 percent.[31] For the government to have had an effect on the Canadian economy, it would have had to adopt a level of spending and a deficit completely out of accord with Canadian history and existing wisdom. It is hardly surprising that such a course was not followed.

The third problem was constitutional. Under the British North America Act and subsequent court decisions, the powers of the Dominion government were severely limited in areas that became crucial during the Depression. In particular, section 92 gave responsibility for welfare and unemployment to the provinces. As has been discussed, the provincial control of welfare created difficulties for recipients in terms of residency and equity, both in the capacity of the provinces and in the treatment of Canadians. From the governmental point of view, however, the most serious problem was one of divided jurisdiction. Those that had the constitutional jurisdiction (the provinces) could not, with a couple of exceptions, pay for it. However, the only body in the nation that might be able to co-ordinate some sort of national response to the Depression, and had the fiscal power to develop necessary welfare schemes, was seriously hampered by constitutional barriers — barriers it often used to avoid responsibility.

The result was an unsatisfactory series of compromises and ad hoc programs. Once R.B. Bennett gave up on his initial public-works schemes, he increasingly funnelled funds to the provinces to handle the growing relief problems. By 1934, with provincial and municipal credit exhausted throughout much of the nation, the Dominion was funding more than 30 percent of all relief expenditures. On the Prairies, the Dominion government had, by this time, assumed the vast proportion of relief costs. At the same time, constitutional rigidities meant that the government paying the funds had little or no say as to where much of the money was going. Dominion politicians and civil servants mumbled darkly of inefficient and corrupt provincial governments. More imaginative proposals for Dominion action (on the occasions when they did come) always faced the constitutional barrier, and as a result the most unimaginative expenditure of all — relief, or the dole, as it was known — became, almost by default, the only serious fiscal outlay of the government in the face of the Depression.

As Figure 17.1 indicates, this was true of both the Bennett administration, which lasted until 1935, and the revived King administration, which was returned in that year. The funds continued to flow outward to the provinces because there was practically no way to stem the tide. In other areas, both the Liberals and the Conservatives were much more cautious. Budgetary expenditure by the Dominion actually decreased relative to gross national expenditure in the latter half of the Depression. This shift was intentional, as the Liberals, seeing an opportunity in the modest recovery that was taking place by 1935, moved to try to balance the budget. "I believe," said Liberal finance minister Charles Dunning, "that no country can go on indefinitely with heavily unbalanced budgets."[32] Thus, while government expenditures may have been a positive force in slowing the decline from 1929 to 1933, they were, if anything, a force working as a modest brake on growth during the period of recovery. Only in 1939, as defence expenditures began in preparation for war, did Dominion expenditures as a percentage of GNE recover to 1935 levels.

Such restricted expenditures meant, of course, that it was practically impossible for government to undertake meaningful new social or economic programs. It was very difficult, for example, to create a systematic "safety net" for those caught in the downturns of modern economic cycles. It was simply too expensive. A decade of economic depression, therefore, failed to bring about any significant improvements in social security; those would come later.

There was one exception to this tendency, but it, too, proved how unprepared the Canadian governmental structure was for a crisis such as the Great Depression. This exception came in 1935, when R.B. Bennett announced a wide-ranging series of reforms patterned on the American New Deal. Speeches urging a minimum wage, unemployment insurance, and other far-reaching measures were, after some delay, brought to Parliament. There was a great deal of debate at the time about Bennett's motivation and whether this was a sincere effort to reform capitalism or a cynical election ploy. In terms of results, however, the debate is largely irrelevant, for two things occurred that prevented Bennett's New Deal from being implemented. First, Bennett was defeated by King's Liberals, and, second, the New Deal ran into a constitutional problem. In 1937, the Judicial Committee of the Privy Council of the United Kingdom, then the final court of appeal for the Commonwealth, declared key elements of Bennett's program *ultra vires*. Even when the will did exist, the federal structures of Canada imposed serious barriers to economic reform.

By and large, therefore, constitutional and economic restraints meant that government policy under Bennett and King concentrated on less far-reaching (and less expensive) reforms. In general, these reforms took two directions. One was toward regulation in the marketplace in the name of economic order. Excess production, fierce competition, and unregulated capitalism were seen by the pundits of the day as central to the Depression. It is not surprising, therefore, that this tendency toward regulation emerged. Many of the agricultural quota systems that exist today have their roots in such Depression legislation as the Natural Products Marketing Act (1934). The Bank of Canada was established the same year, in response to internal demands for an end to the deflation for which many blamed Canada's concentrated banking system, and to external pressures for increased international monetary cooperation.[33] These were Conservative measures, and Mackenzie King was more reluctant to enter into the regulation of economic activity. Even he found, however, that many of the measures he inherited, including the Canada Wheat Board, were sufficiently popular to justify his expanding their activities.[34]

The other major direction of government policy during the Depression was the manipulation of trade with the outside world through tariffs and negotiated agreements. Initially, as has been shown, the tendency was toward massive protectionism. Bennett's first action on assuming office was to raise tariffs on a number of goods. In so doing, he was following the general international tendency and retaliating, in particular, against the extreme protectionism of the United States. It was conventional wisdom and completely standard policy; however, it was of dubious benefit.

The problem for Canada in such a measure was twofold. First, it only exacerbated the international trend toward restrictions on international trade, when such trade was vitally important for Canada. Second, in Canada, protectionism had significant regional implications. Domestic manufacturing and a few specialty crops were protected — largely in Quebec and southern Ontario. Resource production, dependent on exports and largely free from serious import competition, gained nothing. Those who worked in those sectors thus bore the burden that the tariff imposed in terms of higher costs. In regional terms this meant, in effect, that southern Ontario and the industrial portions of Quebec gained, while the vast hinterland — in both the East and West — suffered.[35] Much of the effect of Dominion money funnelled into the devastated West in the Depression was probably offset by the high tariff policy pursued, at least in the early years of the Depression.

Yet high tariffs were never, in themselves, a primary goal of Canadian trade policy. Bennett came into office promising to "blast" his way into the markets of the world. That is, with high tariffs in place, he could approach Canadian trading partners for specific arrangements. For reasons of patriotism and because the Americans showed no inclination to deal, Bennett's first approach was to the British. Ottawa convinced the Commonwealth that Canada should host a 1932 imperial economic conference to discuss ways and means of combating the Depression. After much rhetoric and some hard negotiating, that conference gave Canada preference in the British market for such key products as wheat, apples, and lumber. In return, Britain got concessions in the Canadian market, largely at the expense of the United States. Over the next months and years, Canada and Britain negotiated further arrangements within the Commonwealth so that a freer, though hardly free, trade zone did emerge within the Commonwealth.

King and the Liberals pursued this policy of bilateral trade arrangements with enthusiasm when they were elected in 1935. Liberals traditionally believed in free trade, but it was also an inexpensive policy. Following a failed Bennett initiative, King moved, soon after his election, to negotiate a trade deal with the United States. In 1938, his government further reduced duties in a trilateral arrangement with Britain and the United States.

These agreements did not end the Depression in Canada. The reality was that international protectionism might have impeded recovery but the forces underlying the Depression were so deep that trade agreements by themselves could not have a significant effect on the general course of the Canadian economy. The agreements undoubtedly did help certain sectors, at least to a degree. More dramatic, perhaps, was the fact that they rechannelled existing trade. By the end of the 1930s, more trading was done in economic blocs such as the Commonwealth,[36] and in the wake of the 1932 agreement Canadian exports to Britain surpassed those to the United States. Conversely, by 1939, with subsequent agreements in place, the Americans had again become Canada's primary export market (see Table 17.4), though long-term trends as well as specific agreements accounted for this fact.

Overall, then, government response to the Depression was a mixture of the old and new. There were significant new interventions in the marketplace through the regulatory bodies that were established, and there was the potential inherent in such bodies as the Bank of Canada for a much more interventionist approach than was taken during the 1930s. Yet these innovations were limited in scope, and their full potential would often not be realized until later. The most important government instrument for manipulating the economy was the same one it had always been —the tariff structure — and fiscal practices, though evolving, remained fundamentally the same as before.

While governments stumbled along — trying what they could and what they dared — new parties promised recovery through nationalism and central planning, through unorthodox monetary measures, and a host of other schemes. At the provincial level, the public turned increasingly to varying degrees of economic and political unorthodoxy. Premiers Duff Pattullo in British Columbia, Mitch Hepburn in Ontario, Maurice Duplessis in Quebec, and, most unorthodox of them all, William Aberhart, who was elected in Alberta in 1935, promised solutions to the Depression. Whatever else they may or may not have accomplished, however, none of them ended the Depression. The fact was that government, as it was known in Canada, could have, at best, a marginal effect on the course of the Depression.

Table 17.4 Destination of Canadian Merchandise Exports, 1929–1939

Year	United States ($ millions)	United Kingdom ($ millions)	Total (Excluding Gold) ($ millions)
1929	488	290	1146
1930	369	235	868
1931	237	170	583
1932	157	178	487
1933	166	210	526
1934	217	270	646
1935	260	303	722
1936	333	395	935
1937	359	402	994
1938	270	339	835
1939	380	328	922

Source: Statistics Canada, *Historical Statistics of Canada,* 2nd ed., cat. no. 11-516E (Ottawa: Supply and Services, 1983), series G389–400. Reproduced by authority of the Minister of Industry, 1995.

Social Cost and Social Response

There is a danger in presenting all these trends and numbers: while they illuminate the causes of the Great Depression, they tend to understate its effects. The Depression was more than an economic curiosity; it was an event that engulfed the lives of most Canadians. It is at the level of the individual and the family that the bloodless figures of economics turn into a very human story of hardship. Beginning in 1929, with the farmers and those small-town tradespeople dependent on farmers, people began to see their livelihoods slip away. The local hardware or feed store that had prospered during the 1920s suddenly found its clients delinquent in their accounts, or simply absent altogether. From the farms and the local suppliers, it spread to the larger western centres and to companies dependent on farmers — implement firms, railways, and others. Then, by the fall and winter of 1929–30, industrial centres began to be affected. Layoffs occurred, and then plant closings. Declining auto sales meant that the industrial heartland of Ontario began to experience serious unemployment. In three years, the number of employees in manufacturing decreased by nearly 200 000; more than half of this decline was in Ontario.[37] With each layoff, of course, local stores suffered a loss in business. There was no unemployment insurance to cushion the blow, and labour unions rarely had the strength to prevent wages from being lowered or benefits trimmed in those companies that still operated.

Shrinking markets and declining expectations meant that businesses avoided new investment. New machinery was not ordered, the new factory was not built, and production was cut to allow time to get rid of the suddenly stagnant inventory. More factory workers, more construction workers, and more suppliers found themselves without work. Thus, the interdependent nature of the Canadian economy became apparent, as the troubled economy of 1929 turned into the recession-laden one of 1930 and the collapsing one of 1931 and 1932.

By the time the census of 1931 was taken, overall unemployment in Canada stood at more than 20 percent, and it was much worse in parts of the West. Many prairie cities had more than one in four unemployed, and in Vancouver the ratio was one in three. Nor were there any clear alternatives. As one study concluded, "Once a person was jobless, in whatever occupation or city, chances of finding a long-term job were slim.'[38] As well, these figures, harsh though they may be, understate the real degree of hardship. Reduced hours and smaller pay packets were the norm. Worst of all, every indication is that, though there are no firm numbers, unemployment got even worse through 1932 and 1933.

Initially, Canadians reacted by doing two things. First, they postponed the purchase of "consumer durables," or what might, in modern parlance, be termed the "big-ticket items." This was why automobile consumption fell so sharply, as did the price of housing. However, Canadians tried to maintain their standard of living in other ways. Consumer spending decreased by only 4 percent in 1930, as people dipped into their savings in the desperate hope that better times would return before the funds ran out.[39] Such expenditures helped to slow the onslaught of the Depression but were far from sufficient to stem the tide and, of course, savings did not last forever. By 1932 and 1933, as unemployment brought more and more families into poverty, people were avoiding not only the major expenditures but also the minor and normal ones. People were driving not only older cars but fewer of them. In 1932, for the first time since the invention of the automobile, the number of automobiles registered in Canada decreased.[40] Clothes that had been patched in 1930 became shabby and threadbare by 1932. Children often went without shoes in summer, especially in the hard-hit Prairies, and the housing stock began to deteriorate, as little new construction was undertaken and as renovations went undone for lack of funds. Health deteriorated, as people avoided trips to doctors and dentists. Each year, the Depression exacted a little more from the people.

All of this took a severe psychological toll as well. The rhythms of the seasons and the boom-and-bust cycle inherent in many primary-resource industries had the result that Canadians were used to periodic unemployment. The 1930s were different, however, for two reasons. First, unemployment now had a longer duration: people were out of work not for a month, or for six months, but often for years. For those graduating from school, the prospects of getting a job, any job, were daunting at best. For employees who lost their jobs after years with a company, for farm families who lost years of work, or for the young person unable to find work, the most discouraging thing was the sheer length of time before prospects eventually improved.

Unemployment hit unevenly. Westerners were more likely to be unemployed than those in the East; blue-collar or primary-resource workers were more likely than white-collar workers; men more likely than women; those over 45 more than those in their thirties. Nevertheless, the Depression was different in part because even the more favoured groups were seriously affected. Unemployment struck whole groups of occupations and classes of citizens that had previously been assumed to be free of such cyclical variations. The middle classes, who had previously looked with a certain disdain and suspicion upon those out of work, now found themselves just as vulnerable to unemployment as the working classes. A good many prejudices had to be discarded as the newly unemployed learned what it was like to be without work for prolonged periods.

What they found out was that it was not very pleasant. The support systems that existed for those who were out of work were minimal. Much of the reason behind this was historical. The unemployed and indigent are in a different position in an urban–industrial society than in a rural and agriculturally based one. In the latter, lack of mobility preserves family networks, which can be turned to in times of difficulty. Further, the line between "employment" and "unemployment" is less well-defined in a system based on agriculture.

The mobility that came from urbanization and the dependence on wage employment that went with industrialization, however, made for a very different world and demanded a different series of support systems. In Canada, however, industrialization and urbanization were very recent phenomena. Only in the fifteen years or so before the Depression had Canadians even begun to grapple with the implications of industrial unemployment.[41] Some measures had been introduced, such as Workmen's Compensation and Dominion-sponsored labour-referral services. Overall, however, progress had been limited.

There was no unemployment-insurance system, no health care for the poor (except charity wards), no family allowance, and only the most rudimentary of old-age pensions. There were systems in place to prevent starvation for the indigent. Aside from private charities and churches, there was a complex and uneven public-relief system to provide for those with no other means of support. The character of this relief system was shaped by constitutional law and by public prejudice. Constitutionally, under the British North America Act, welfare was a provincial responsibility and, in fact, relief had always been seen as a local responsibility, rooted in the municipality or county and usually dependent on the local property-tax base. Second, there was a widespread feeling that relief systems would only encourage indigence unless they were made as basic and rudimentary as possible. Under what was known as the doctrine of "less eligibility," this was often translated into the maxim that relief should always guarantee a standard of living lower than that attainable through the worst job available, lest people be tempted out of the productive work force.[42]

When the Depression hit, two problems quickly became apparent. First, the demeaning aspects that had been built into the system made it all that much harder for those faced for the first time in their lives with the need to ask for assistance. Regulations varied from community to community (in itself, a problem of inequity) but the doctrine of "less eligibility" meant that, with few exceptions, for people on relief, life was encumbered by rules that made little sense. Rules against drinking and against the possession of a telephone, for example, were often argued to be measures to ensure the public charge did not become too extravagant. They were also, however, often indications of petty bureaucratic suspicion that the person on welfare was prone to dishonesty and lazy indulgence. What, for example, can one make of the Saskatchewan regulation that a person on relief not only not own a car (which might make some sense) but not possess a driver's licence? Likewise, it is possible to understand the concept of "make-work projects" if the work being done provided a useful service to the community supporting those on relief. When, as James Gray relates of his own experience in Winnipeg, that project involved digging a hole,

Soup kitchen, Edmonton, 1933. During the Great Depression, many homeless and unemployed people depended on soup kitchens for their one meal of the day. Private charities and churches often sponsored soup kitchens, depending on volunteers (sometimes matrons from the most wealthy areas of town) to staff them.

Western Canada Pictorial Index/48-1458.

putting rocks into it, and refilling it, then the only purpose seemed to be to punish the unemployed. Those dependent on this sort of system knew exactly what such rules and activities implied about them, and they often found it one of the most humiliating things about being out of work.

Aside from being inhumane and inequitable, the system was financially fragile. The municipally based relief system could function only so long as a small minority of citizens depended on relief at any given time. With the deepening of the Depression, more and more people flooded on to relief rolls and stayed there longer than had previously been the case. As a result, as Table 17.5 shows, the relief burden increased enormously. By 1931, three provinces were each spending more than all together had the year before. The relief burden had increased sixfold in one year and, by 1934, it would be up eightfold. And 1930 had been a bad year by previous standards![43]

The problems in the relief system increased because of the tendency of many people to leave their homes and set out for new areas. Single males were especially transient, using some of Canada's underutilized freight capacity to move around the country. It was not just single males, however; whole families moved as well. On the Prairies, people moved from the drought-ridden south, northward to the relatively favoured parkland. In Ontario and Quebec, people drifted from the lumber communities to the larger cities. The long-term depopulation of the Maritimes continued, though there were few prospects anywhere else. In some cases, the moves were rational attempts at material betterment. In many instances, however, the very process of movement was sufficient rationale in an age that was otherwise so confining.

Such movement made the already overburdened relief system even more ineffective. Municipalities were not prepared for the influx of thousands of new unemployed into their already hard-hit centres. Cities such as Vancouver, which attracted so many of the unemployed, would quickly have gone bankrupt had they tried to support them all. Other cities, less affected by unemployment, nevertheless wanted to keep tax rolls down, and, finally, many citizens just wanted to keep these "undesirables" away. The result was a series of residency requirements for relief that prevented new arrivals from getting assistance locally. In this way, too, the local nature of relief systems did not reflect the reality of Canada.

Table 17.5 also indicates how unevenly the burden of relief in Canada was distributed. The western provinces in general, and Saskatchewan in particular, were hit much harder

Table 17.5 Canadian Relief Burden, by Province, 1930–1937

Province	1930	1931	1932	1933 *($ millions)*	1934	1935	1936	1937
Prince Edward Island	0.03	0.32	0.24	0.06	0.41	0.94	0.62	0.58
Nova Scotia	0.10	2.60	3.80	3.20	2.40	3.00	2.70	2.60
New Brunswick	0.30	2.60	0.50	1.90	1.30	2.40	2.50	1.50
Quebec	2.00	17.30	18.80	22.20	31.80	26.50	35.40	30.80
Ontario	2.40	21.30	33.40	32.40	60.70	54.50	38.50	28.20
Manitoba	1.60	8.60	7.40	7.10	7.50	9.80	12.20	9.80
Saskatchewan	5.90	24.00	13.20	10.30	21.10	18.60	22.70	62.30
Alberta	2.40	6.70	5.90	4.90	6.00	7.00	9.20	7.60
British Columbia	2.20	8.40	8.90	8.10	9.90	11.30	10.00	9.00
Total	16.93	91.80	92.10	90.20	141.10	134.00	133.80	152.40

Source: Canada, Privy Council Office, Royal Commission on Dominion–Provincial Relations, *Report*, book 1, tables 59–68. Reproduced with permission of the Minister of Supply and Services Canada, 1995.

The transient hitches a ride on a freight train, c. 1934. During the Depression, single males were especially transient, hopping freight trains ("riding the rods") to move around the country. Sometimes whole families moved: on the Prairies, from the drought-ridden south to the north; in Ontario and Quebec, from the lumber communities to the larger cities.

337

Glenbow Archives/NC6-12955B.

than were eastern provinces. Relief costs rose more quickly and remained higher for longer periods of time. Overall relief expenditures in the 1930–37 period stood at an average of 3.6 percent of provincial incomes. The burden ranged tremendously, however: Ontario had an average burden of 2.7 percent, and New Brunswick, 2.4 percent; in contrast, Saskatchewan's was a staggering 13.3 percent. At the local level, the burdens could often become even more dramatic. Small rural municipalities in southern Saskatchewan might have 50 percent of their population on relief, with the other 50 percent behind in their taxes! Obviously, the municipal-based system of funding could not survive under such circumstances. Equally obvious, however, was the fact that with burdens like these, several provinces were bound to prove as incapable of bearing this burden as were the municipalities.

In sum, then, the impact of the Depression was made worse by the absence of any meaningful social-security system. The system that did exist was rudimentary both in the services it was intended to deliver and in the tax base upon which it rested. Municipalities, and then provinces, were driven to the edge of bankruptcy as relief costs spiralled. The whole system would have collapsed had it been left unaided. Necessity made it very quickly apparent, therefore, that unemployment, and the human misery that went with it, were a national rather than a local crisis.

Fragile Citizenship

The discussion of the impotence, or indifference, of government to provide true relief or assistance to those suffering from the hardship brought on by the Depression glosses over some of the darker details of how the Canadian government chose to deal with social challenges. For example, some unemployed men in the 1930s were "repatriated," deported to their country of origin, particularly if they appeared to be individuals who may have been agitators, or "Communists." After the Winnipeg General Strike, the Immigration Act had been amended so that in cases where men were "known to be dangerous," they could be arrested and deported without trial. Tim Buck notes that until that amendment, a person from the British Isles could not be deported.[44] Vagrancy laws provided communities with a tool to jail "drifters" or at least encourage the unemployed to move on to the next town. The unemployed were defined as out of the community and often, not even welcome as a visitor.

In line with the out of sight, out of mind approach to dealing with the unemployed, in 1932 the federal government created the "Unemployment Relief Scheme," a nationwide system of relief camps for single, homeless and unemployed men. Most of the camps were located far away from Canada's urban centres — often bush camps in northern Ontario or mountain camps in British Columbia. The men lived in bunkhouses and were provided with meals, clothing, and soap. They were expected to work 44 hours per week on projects devised by the Corps of Royal Canadian Engineers in return for twenty cents a day. Men who qualified for living at the camps were not entitled to collect relief if they left. To qualify to live in a relief camp, a man had to be single, transient, physically fit, unemployed, free of communicable disease, and not known to be a political agitator.[45]

While good intentions may have created the relief camps, the actual purpose of them appears to have been to placate the ever-growing army of restless, unemployed, and hungry young men. By isolating these men and removing them from the cities, they would be easier to manage, and it was hoped, disorder on the scale seen in Winnipeg in 1919 could be avoided. While some projects like the construction of the Trans-Canada Highway may have been meaningful, many of the make-work projects run from the camps were designed solely to keep the men busy and amounted to moving dirt for the sake of moving dirt. For Prime Minister Bennett, the remote camps effectively disenfranchised unemployed men who in all likelihood were hostile towards his government. It is of note that to vote in the 1935 election, the men could only vote in their home constituencies.[46] The dissatisfaction of men in the camps grew over time and the camps were closed but only after a bloody clash between the unemployed and the government.

In April 1935, 1500 relief camp workers in British Columbia left their camps for Vancouver to gain an audience with representatives of the federal government to voice their complaints over conditions in the camps and to call for a government-funded work and wages program. On June 3, with nothing resolved, the striking relief camp workers boarded freight trains with the intention of travelling to Ottawa to confront Prime Minister Benett with their demands. This action became known as the "On To Ottawa Trek" and by the time the trekkers reached Regina in late June 1935 their numbers had grown to around 2000. As publicity for the trek grew, Prime Minister Bennett decided that the trekkers should not be allowed to reach Ottawa. They were stopped in Regina with the arrest of the leaders of the movement under section 98 of the Criminal Code. Section 98 was created in response to the Winnipeg General Strike of 1919 and stated that any association that advocated political or economic change by violence could be declared unlawful. Because of the nature of the "crime," the burden of proof was on the accused since he could be found guilty, not only by action, but also by "look or intent." In turn, his guilt could be proved by concrete action, or by other actions in which the intent would be implicit.[47]

On July 1, 1935, the "On To Ottawa Trekkers" held a rally in downtown Regina. When the RCMP attempted to arrest the leaders at the rally, a bloody battle known as the Regina Riot ensued. The police fired shots into the crowd and many trekkers and bystanders were wounded in the chaos. The trekkers boarded trains and returned west, never having reached Ottawa. At the same time, as a consequence of the publicity from the trek and the reaction of the public to the Regina Riot, the relief camps were closed.

One of the more extreme examples of a civil liberties violation was the arrest and imprisonment of Tim Buck and several other officers of the Communist Party of Canada under section 98 of the Criminal Code. In 1931, Tim Buck was an organizer and leader of the Communist Party of Canada. Like their American counterparts who passed laws that made the Communist Party an illegal and underground party in that country, the Canadian establishment considered Communists and their ideology to be a serious threat to Canadian society, particularly given the agitation role attributed to Communists in the 1919 Winnipeg General Strike. By 1931, the Communist Party in Canada was publicly active and advocating alternatives to market capitalism as a solution to the existing economic problems. In 1931, there were probably no more than 1300 Communist Party members in Canada but to appear more important, the Party claimed a membership of 4000 members. To bolster its image as a defender of Canadian society through its harassment and containment of Communists, the RCMP estimated the Communist Party of Canada's membership to be 5000. For the threat that Communism posed to Canadian society, Tim Buck and several other Party members were arrested under section 98 of the Criminal Code. A conviction meant not only a jail term (of no less than two years and no more than twenty years) for Buck, but the Party would be declared illegal and the property of any member of an illegal association was liable to seizure and forfeiture.[48]

The Crown prosecutor for the case accused the Communists of taking advantage of the economic crisis to spread false rumours and to arouse people with false promises that serious problems could be solved overnight with the "mass actions" advocated by the Communists. The Communists were accused of encouraging lawlessness in Canada by encouraging resistance of layoffs, of property foreclosures and sheriff's sales, by force if necessary. The case also linked Tim Buck and the other officers to strikes where violence had occurred between the RCMP and strikers, thus meeting section 98's requirement of demonstrating seditious intent to encourage violence through previous actions. The ultimate threat of Communism was its advocacy of resisting the laws of the land. In later years, Tim Buck characterized the activities of the Communists somewhat differently: the Party was trying to raise awareness amongst Canadians that the growth of Canada had rendered the BNA Act obsolete and that the problems of recurring economic crises could not be dealt with under the terms of the Act.

For their "seditious" views about the BNA Act, Buck and seven other officers of the Communist Party were found guilty and sentenced to concurrent five-year terms of imprisonment to be served in the Kingston Penitentiary. Buck was shot during a prison riot. He believed that the shooting and possibly even the riot, were the machinations of the Canadian government to assassinate him. Public pressure led to the release of Buck and the other imprisoned Communists before their full terms had been served in 1935. Mackenzie King repealed section 98 of the Criminal Code in 1936, restoring the Communist Party to legal status as he promised in the 1935 election, and well after economic recovery was underway.

Conclusion

The Great Depression was in many ways an economic anomaly. This was a cycle that was more persistent, deeper, and more widespread than had been seen in the history of the western world. In North America, the effects were especially severe. The self-correcting mechanisms of the past failed to work, at least in the short run. Currency instability, shrinkage of trade, and mass unemployment left governments seeking new remedies. The cycle would do much to topple traditional views and to install a new economic orthodoxy — Keynesianism — among much economic writing and, eventually, policy formation.

340

Yet the anomaly of the Depression must be set against the broad disruptions of the first 40 years of the twentieth century. Massive international migration, economic boom, and new technologies marked one part of that rapid change. So, too, did the unravelling of the gold standard and the failure to establish a stable system of international exchange. Another factor was World War I, by far the largest-scale and most destructive war in human history. Nor did the instability end with the Depression. Another war loomed on the horizon, even more destructive than the previous one. This war, however, would break the patterns of the first 40 years and usher in a new, long-term economic pattern.

NOTES

1. See Pierre Siklos, "Understanding the Great Depression in the United States Versus Canada," prepared for Theo Balderston, ed., *World Economy and National Economies in the Interwar Slump* (Basingstoke: The MacMillan Press, 2001).

2. Christina D. Romer, "The Nation in Depression," *Journal of Economic Perspectives* 7(2) (1993): 19–39. See Pierre Siklos "Understanding the Great Depression in the United States Versus Canada," prepared for Theo Balderston, ed., *World Economy and National Economies in the Interwar Slump* (Basingstoke: The MacMillan Press, 2001) for a sceptic's view of Romer's explanation. Siklos suggests that slumping commodity prices in the late 1920s may be a better candidate for explaining the downturn.

3. Peter Temin, "Transmission of the Great Depression," *Journal of Economic Perspectives* 7(2) (1993): 87–102.

4. Barry Eichengreen, *Golden Fetters: The Gold Standard and the Great Depression 1919–1939* (New York: Oxford University Press, 1992).

5. Barry Eichengreen, *Golden Fetters*.

6. Barry Eichengreen, *Golden Fetters*, 240.

7. Michael D. Bordo and Angela Redish, "Credible Commitment and Exchange Rate Stability: Canada's Interwar Experience," Canadian *Journal of Economics* XXIII (2) (1990): 357–380.

8. J.H. Thompson and A. Seager, *Canada, 1922–1939: Decades of Discord* (Toronto: McClelland & Stewart, 1985), 195; and A.E. Safarian, *The Canadian Economy in the Great Depression* (Toronto: McClelland & Stewart, 1970), 42.

9. Safarian, *The Canadian Economy*, table 50.

10. The figures in the previous few paragraphs generally come from the *Canada Year Book* for 1930 and 1933. The net-income figures come from Statistics Canada, *Historical Statistics of Canada*, 2nd ed. (Ottawa: Supply and Services, 1983).

11. Statistics Canada, *Historical Statistics*, G57–83.

12. Safarian, *The Canadian Economy*, 131.

13. Edward J. Chambers, "Canadian Business Cycles and Merchandise Exports," *Canadian Journal of Economics and Political Science* 24 (1958): 166–89.

14. M.C. Urquhart, "Canadian Economic Growth, 1870–1980," Queen's University, Department of Economics, discussion paper no. 734, 1988, table 4a.

15. Alan Green and Mary MacKinnon, "Interwar Unemployment and Relief in Canada," in B. Eichengreen and T.J. Hatton, eds., *Interwar Unemployment in International Perspective* (Kluwer Academic Publishers, 1988), 353–96, table 3. Reprinted in Douglas McCalla and Michael Huberman, eds., *Perspectives on Canadian Economic History* (Toronto: Copp Clark Longman, 1994), 224–62.

16. Statistics Canada, *Historical Statistics*, F14–32, column under "Business Gross Fixed Capital Formation"; Urquhart, "Canadian Economic Growth 1870–1980," table 4a.

17. Thompson and Seager, *Canada, 1922–1939*, 94.

18. Figures are drawn from Safarian, *The Canadian Economy*, 50; and Royal Commission on Dominion–Provincial Relations (hereinafter cited as R–S), *Report*, Book 1: *Canada, 1867–1939*, 161.

19. R–S, *Report*, Book 1, 161.

20. Michael D. Bordo and Angela Redish, "Credible Commitment and Exchange Rate Stability: Canada's Interwar Experience," *Canadian Journal of Economics* XXIII (2) (1990): 357–380.

21. Pierre Siklos, "Understanding the Great Depression in the United States versus Canada," prepared for Theo Balderston, ed., *World Economy and National Economies in the Interwar Slump* (Basingstoke: The MacMillan Press, 2001).

22. Milton Friedman and Anna J. Schwartz, *A Monetary History of the United States* (Princeton: Princeton University Press, 1963). B.A. Wigmore, "Was the Bank Holiday of 1933 Caused by a Run on the Dollar?" *Journal of Economic History* 97 (1987): 739–55. Patrick J. Coe, "Financial Crisis and the Great Depression: A Regime Switching Approach," *Journal of Money, Credit and Banking.*

23. Christina Romer, "The Nation in Depression," *Journal of Economic Perspectives* 7(2) (1993).

24. Edward J. Chambers, "The 1937–38 Recession in Canada," *Canadian Journal of Economics and Political Science* 21 (1955): 293–308.

25. Chambers, "The 1937–38 Recession."

26. D. Owram, *The Government Generation: Canadian Intellectuals and the State, 1900–1945* (Toronto: University of Toronto Press, 1986), 228.

27. Safarian, *The Canadian Economy*, 77.

28. Cited in James Struthers, *No Fault of Their Own: Unemployment and the Canadian Welfare State, 1914–1941* (Toronto: University of Toronto Press, 1983), 57.

29. Barry Eichengreen, *Golden Fetters: The Gold Standard and the Great Depression 1919–1939* (New York: Oxford University Press, 1992), 231.

30. Michael D. Bordo and Angela Redish, "Credible Commitment," *Canadian Journal of Economics* XXIII (2) (1990): 372.

31. W. Irwin Gillespie, *Tax, Borrow and Spend: Financing Federal Spending in Canada, 1867–1990* (Ottawa: Carleton University Press, 1991), table C-3.

32. Cited in J.H. Perry, *Taxes, Tariffs and Subsidies*, vol. 1 (Toronto: University of Toronto Press, 1955), 294.

33. See Michael D. Bordo and Angela Redish, "Why Did the Bank of Canada Emerge in 1935?" *Journal of Economic History* 47 (June 1987), 405–18.

34. On King and the wheat board see H.B. Neatby, *William Lyon Mackenzie King*, vol. 3: *1932–1939: The Prism of Unity* (Toronto: University of Toronto Press, 1976), 305–308.

35. See W.A. Mackintosh, *The Economic Background of Dominion–Provincial Relations* (Toronto: McClelland & Stewart, 1964), chapter 7.

36. Safarian, *The Canadian Economy*, 140.

37. Statistics Canada, *Historical Statistics*, R1–22.

38. Green and MacKinnon, "Interwar Unemployment and Relief in Canada," 238. The unemployment figures cited in this paragraph come from table 2 in this article.

39. The 4 percent figure comes from Safarian, *The Canadian Economy*, 76.

40. *Canada Year Book*, 1933 (Ottawa: King's Printer, 1934), 686.

41. See, for example, Province of Ontario, "Report of the Commission on Unemployment," Ontario sessional paper no. 55, 1916. See also D. Owram, *The Government Generation*, 23, 50–79.

42. Struthers, *No Fault of Their Own*, 57.

43. R–S, *Report*, Book 1, 163.

44. William Beeching and Phyllis Clarke, eds., *Yours in the Struggle: Reminiscences of Tim Buck* (Toronto: NC Press Limited, 1977): 82.

45. Ronald Liversedge, *Recollections of the On To Ottawa Trek* (Toronto: McClelland and Stewart Limited, 1973).

46. Pierre Berton, *The Great Depression: 1929–1939* (Toronto: Penguin Books, 1990).

47. William Beeching and Phyllis Clarke, eds., *Yours in the Struggle*, 82.

48. William Beeching and Phyllis Clarke, eds., *Yours in the Struggle*, 163.

FURTHER READING

Green, A.G., and G.R. Sparks. "A Macroeconomic Interpretation of Economic Recovery from the Great Depression: Australia – U.S. – Canada." Discussion paper no. 615. Kingston: Queen's University, 1987.

Inwood, Kris, and Stengos, Thomas. "Discontinuities in Canadian Economic Growth, 1870–1985," in *Explorations in Entrepreneurial History* (1991).

Kindleberger, Charles P. *The World in Depression, 1929–1939*. Los Angeles: University of California Press, 1975.

Mackinnon, M. "Relief Not Insurance: Canadian Unemployment Relief in the 1930s." *Explorations in Economic History* 27 (January 1990): 46–83.

Owram, Doug. "Economic Thought in the 1930s: The Prelude to Keynesianism," *Canadian Historical Review* 66(3) (September 1985): 344–77.

Safarian, A.E. *The Canadian Economy in the Great Depression*. Toronto: McClelland & Stewart, 1970.

Struthers, James. *No Fault of Their Own: Unemployment and the Canadian Welfare State, 1914–1941*. Toronto: University of Toronto Press, 1983.

Thompson, J.H., and A. Seager. *Canada, 1922–1939: Decades of Discord*. Toronto: McClelland & Stewart, 1985.

Chapter Eighteen

World War II, 1939–1945

WHEN WORLD WAR II BEGAN in September 1939, it marked the final of the three great external cataclysms (along with World War I and the Great Depression) that rocked the Canadian economy in the first half of the twentieth century. It also helped bring the Depression to an end. For that reason, the war can be seen as a part of the turbulent era that began in 1914, and it is so treated in this book. Yet, it should be noted that the postwar world is understandable only in the light of what happened during the war.

First, the war saw the beginning of a long-term cycle of prosperity, marked by only short interruptions. By the time that cycle drew to a close in the early 1970s, the Canadian standard of living had increased to a level unimaginable during the pessimistic years of the 1930s. Second, the war and postwar years brought dramatic sectoral shifts within the economy. For much of the twentieth century, industry had been challenging agriculture's dominance. During and immediately after World War II, however, this shift from farm to factory was most pronounced. The war gave a tremendous impetus to large-scale industry and heavy manufacturing. Hundreds of thousands of new jobs were created during the war, and most of these were maintained afterward. In contrast, though farming prospered considerably from the war, it would not be a source of new jobs. Technological changes on the farm and the lure of the manufacturing sector meant that people would continue to leave the farm in significant numbers. The tertiary sector of the economy had grown fairly rapidly in the interwar years, but between 1939 and 1971 it became the fastest-growing area of the economy and would transform the social and economic structure of the nation.

Finally, there was government. Until World War II it occasionally played an active, developmental role in Canadian history. The canals of the 1840s, the transcontinental railways, and other ventures revealed that Canada always had a government willing to participate in economic matters. Yet, the slump of 1919, and especially the Great Depression, also indicated just how limited governments were in the face of major economic forces.

Part of the problem was the size of the Canadian governments, which, in the nineteenth and early twentieth centuries, were puny affairs. World War I aside, governments had neither the revenues nor the willingness to take on the management of a whole economy. In 1939, Dominion government revenue amounted to only $562 million, or $49.73 for every man, woman, and child in the nation. Even had the modern theories of interventionism been accepted in Ottawa, such paltry revenues meant that governments could have had little effect on the nation's economic direction. For such reasons, government policy has, thus far in this book, emerged into the foreground only rarely. That will change in the next several chapters, however, as the role and power of government expanded dramatically after 1939.

The Early Period

Only twenty years after the "war to end all wars" had ended, Europe was again plunging toward conflict. By spring of 1939, both Britain and France had ended their policy of appeasement toward Germany. Further aggression by Hitler and the Nazis would mean resistance. Thus, when Hitler invaded Poland at the beginning of September, war became inevitable. Canadians knew, moreover, that they would be participants. The pull of empire and the sense of concern for Britain were still strong. When Britain and France declared war on Germany, Canada soon followed suit.

Though Canadians went to war, they did so without the optimism of 1914. The memories of World War I were too fresh in their minds. The human slaughter seemed about to be repeated. Moreover, the fear of national disunity hung over the people and the government. Finally, the mentality of the Depression was very much present as well, as people wondered how the fragile recovery of the last few years would be affected by war. Revenues remained sluggish, and deficit reduction, so long a goal of governments, seemed unlikely with the tremendous new demands of war.

For all these reasons, the first months of war were characterized, not by total effort, but by concerns about overcommitment and by a strong interest in ensuring that the war benefited the Canadian economy. The cynical might even argue that the domestic economy was paramount in government thinking. In fact, UnderSecretary of State for External Affairs O.D. Skelton argued in a 1939 brief to the prime minister, "It is in the economic field that we can give aid that will be most effective to our allies and most consistent with Canadian interests."[1]

This policy of what one historian has called the "reign of the dollar" came to an end in the disastrous spring and summer of 1940.[2] With German military victory in Denmark, the Netherlands, Belgium, and France, Canadian policy-makers finally realized that any doctrine of limited war made no sense. Henceforth, the Canadian economy moved toward total war. Peacetime calculations of budget-balancing or appropriate taxation levels disappeared, to be replaced by the much grander concept of the nation's total economic capacity.

Even before this policy of total effort had completely taken hold, the war brought about immediate changes. War orders flowed to manufacturers, who began to gear up idle capacity for the work that was beginning to come their way. Not all would immediately get what they wanted, but the effect overall was dramatic. The number of employees in manufacturing increased by 300 000, or some 50 percent, between 1939 and 1941. In the meantime, ever-larger numbers of men and women were being taken into the armed forces. The persistent unemployment of the Great Depression was but a memory by 1941. The problem was now shortages of labour, especially skilled labour, which brought the difficulties of supplying the tremendous demands of a modern industrial war to the fore. From the economics of overcapacity, Canada quickly came to experience the complex changes of rapid growth and structural transformation.

The same rapid transformation affected the international economy, on which Canada was so dependent. Trade patterns shifted dramatically as Britain ceased to export goods, while looking to Canada to supply both the traditional primary resources and, before long, manufactured materials. Exports to the United Kingdom increased 50 percent from 1939 to 1940, and, by 1944, had increased 300 percent, to $1.194 billion.[3] Such rapid shifts would, before long, create serious concerns over the balance-of-payments situation and long-term currency relationships. In other words: who was going to pay for the British orders?

Domestic or international, however, the situation was complicated by the necessity of ensuring maximum effectiveness for the war machine. The economy could not be left to work out its future through some sort of invisible hand. The demands of government, not the open marketplace, would determine the direction in which production, employment, export trade, and many other things moved. In understanding the complex patterns of World War II, it is thus with government that one must begin, for government, more than ever before, was truly central to the direction of the Canadian economy.

Constructing a Wartime Economy

As in World War I, the government faced two basic economic challenges in constructing a wartime economy. First, it had to lay claim to the goods and services that it needed to support a major military commitment. As long as the economy was operating at less than full employment, as it still was at the end of the 1930s, these needs could be met without having to reduce private-sector spending. As excess capacity disappeared, however, the government had to find ways to increase its share of aggregate output at the expense of private uses, particularly private consumption spending.

The second challenge was related to the first. The government needed not only to increase its share of aggregate output, but also to shift the composition of this output from civilian to military ends. Market incentives would bring about some reallocation, but much of it would have to come from government direction and regulation.

THE SETTING

On the surface, the Canadian government seemed little prepared for war. A decade of economic depression had taken its toll in Canada, as elsewhere. In spite of the cutbacks, debt had continued to climb for all levels of government. By 1939, it was more than $5 billion for the Dominion government alone, and politicians maintained their steady warnings of disaster if this burden was not diminished. Moreover, though more diverse than in 1914, the sources of revenues (see Figure 18.1) still rested mainly on customs duties (23 percent), excise tax (15 percent), and sales taxes (27 percent). All of these depended, to a degree, on the consumption of goods and, as Prime Minister Robert Borden found in 1914, wartime stringency demanded a reduction in such consumption.

The financial limitations were compounded by the relatively restricted role of the Dominion government. The civil service consisted of only 45 000 people, of whom nearly 12 000 were involved in delivering the mail. Aside from the obvious need for growth in the armed forces (they had fewer than 10 000 permanent members in 1939, even after four years of modest rearmament), the government would need to increase its capacity tremendously if it was to oversee a modern industrial war.

In spite of these problems, the government managed the transition from peace to war, and the subsequent management of the war, extremely well. In the process, government expenditures would increase some 800 percent; the armed forces would reach 4.3 million; and the civil service would mushroom into dozens of new agencies, employing 115 000 men and women. The national debt, which seemed so horrific at a little over $5 billion in 1939, would be more than $18 billion by the end of the war. There were numerous crises and many mistakes along the way, but the amazing thing was that, relatively speaking, it went as well as it did.

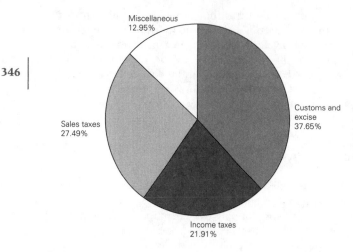

Miscellaneous
12.95%

Customs and
excise
37.65%

Sales taxes
27.49%

Income taxes
21.91%

Figure 18.1
Sources of Federal
Government Revenue,
Canada, 1937

Source: Derived from Statistics Canada,
Historical Statistics of Canada, 2nd ed., cat.
no. 11-516E (Ottawa: Supply and
Services, 1983), series G1–25.
Reproduced by authority of the Minister
of Industry, 1995.

As such success implies, the government was better prepared for the crisis than its size in 1939 would indicate. Many individuals inside and outside the government had, in the interwar years, been discussing the role of government planning and intervention in the modern state. The shocks of World War I, and of the postwar slump, had created severe criticisms of laissez-faire economics. More and more government officials, politicians, and members of the public concerned with government called for an interventionist state that would help regulate, or at least ameliorate, the swings of the economic cycle. This new attitude was paralleled, and reinforced, by the growing presence in the civil service of a coterie of individuals trained in modern social-science theory. The old generalist was being replaced by the new expert. Such people as former Queen's University professors O.D. Skelton and Clifford Clark, under-secretary of state in the Department of External Affairs (appointed 1925) and deputy minister of the Department of Finance (appointed 1932), were creating an activist civil service that believed in the possibilities of economic and social planning.

In the 1920s, such changes had been slow. Public desire for a more efficient response to an urban–industrial society was muted by memories of the huge interventionist government of World War I and by fear of high taxation. In the 1930s, the Depression had provided a powerful impetus for discussions of change. The new experts had gained an influence, and such key interventionist measures as the Bank of Canada Act were passed. Economic theory also encouraged an activist government. The famous British economist John Maynard Keynes was, by the middle 1930s, advocating the use of massive counter-cyclical fiscal and monetary measures to help dampen the effects of economic cycles. Moreover, an increasing number of Canadian economists, and even a few politicians, were beginning to listen to what he said.

At the same time, the Depression limited what could be done. Concern with deficits was ever-present and limited any expensive new measures. Constitutional barriers also blocked interventionist action in the key areas of welfare and social security. Moreover, the whole debate over intervention became highly charged ideologically. Advocates of socialism or of regulated capitalism mixed with social-welfare measures had not gained sufficient support to allow any drastic departure from existing structures and practices.

The war changed that. For one thing, it gave the government an authority it had not had during the crises of the Depression years. The War Measures Act, passed in 1914, was still on the books and was proclaimed even before the war began. This act allowed for a central direction of the economy in a way not possible in peacetime situations. The normal legislative processes could be set aside and orders-in-council used for a series of sweeping measures that would not have even been dared in peacetime. In effect, a command economy became possible, in theory, and was utilized, to at least a limited degree. Before long, wages and prices, essential industries, strikes, employment, and a host of other things usually mediated by the marketplace were brought under strict government control.

One of the most important assertions of Dominion power came at the expense of the provinces. As we have seen, constitutional divisions had limited the abilities of governments to respond to the Depression. The Dominion government had even set up a royal commission in 1937 (the Rowell–Sirois Commission) to look at the problem of such divided jurisdictions. In its 1940 report, the commission recommended that the federal government collect all personal and corporate income taxes and succession duties. In return, Ottawa would make unconditional transfers to the provinces. These grants, furthermore, would be designed so as to be explicitly equalizing. Each province would be guaranteed sufficient revenue to allow it to provide services equal to the average Canadian standard without having to resort to taxes of greater than average severity.

When several provinces failed to accept the provisions of the Rowell–Sirois report at a federal–provincial conference in 1941, Mackenzie King moved to take over the major tax sources for the duration of the war. The April 1941 budget introduced what came to be known as tax rental agreements. Under this arrangement, Ottawa collected all personal and corporate income taxes. As compensation for abstaining from taxing corporations and personal incomes, the provinces received unconditional transfers. The same budget announced large increases in existing taxes and introduced a federal inheritance tax. Given the wartime circumstances, all provinces agreed to the arrangement.

Revenue was another area where things had changed drastically after the Depression. Now that the Dominion had control of fiscal planning, it was able to introduce a series of new measures. Those measures, moreover, were possible and successful because the economy was buoyant. A nation of full employment and production was able to generate taxes for government activity in a way that the depression-ridden 1930s could not. Finally, war made high taxation acceptable. Canadians who normally would have balked at rapid increases in taxation accepted increase after increase in the name of the war.

FINANCING GOVERNMENT WARTIME EXPENDITURE

The federal government had three means by which it could increase its share of aggregate output at the expense of private spending: borrowing, taxing, and printing money.

On the borrowing front, war-bond drives began almost immediately and continued for the duration of the war. Eventually, $9 billion would be raised from the Canadian public.[4]

Much more than in World War I, however, the government recognized from the outset the necessity of increased taxation. The minister of finance said in 1939, "We shall follow as far as may be practicable a pay-as-you-go policy."[5] There was a desire to keep long-term debt down, and a recognition, moreover, that taxation, by forcing a reduction in private consumer demands, would lessen inflationary pressures. As a contemporary economist noted, inflation, "uncertain in its course and uneven in its effects, makes impossible the equitable allocation of the burden of war."[6]

The results were crucial to the government's war effort. Revenue from personal income taxes rose from $45.8 million in 1939 to more than $683 million in 1945.[7] These changes also made it a tax that affected the average Canadian and not just the wealthy. In 1938–39, a little more than 250 000 Canadians, just over 2 percent of the population, paid income tax. By 1941, the figure had risen to 871 000 and, by 1945, to 2.25 million, or between 18 and 19 percent of the population.[8]

Revenue from the corporate income tax rose from $79.7 million in 1939 to more $320 million in 1943, before falling back to $232 million in 1945. The other major innovation in taxation was excess-profits taxes (something argued about for a long time during World War I). These were introduced in 1941 and yielded more than $400 million by the middle of the war. Succession duties, adjustments to sales taxes, and other less significant changes also brought increased revenue. Even the post office saw its revenue increase by some $15 million during the conflict.[9]

The results of such increases in taxation in a healthy economy were dramatic. As Figure 18.2 indicates, revenue rose dramatically each year, from just over $500 million in 1939 to a peak nearly six times as great by the end of the war. Expenditures were, naturally, much greater, increasing eightfold, from $632 million in 1939 to more than $5 billion in 1945. In 1939, total federal government expenditure had amounted to less than 11 percent of gross national expenditure. This figure peaked in 1943, at nearly 45 percent, and stood at 42.5 percent in 1945. Even in World War I, when GNP was much smaller, federal government spending never reached 16 percent of GNP.[10] It was really only in the 1940s that Canadians experienced Big Government for the first time.

Not only did the revenue-gathering capabilities of government change, but so, too, did the sources of that revenue. Indeed, World War II marked the culmination of a long-term shift in Canadian taxation policy. Until World War I, as was shown earlier, government revenue depended almost completely on customs and excise duties. In 1914, these two

Figure 18.2 Federal Government Revenue and Expenditures, Canada, 1938–1945

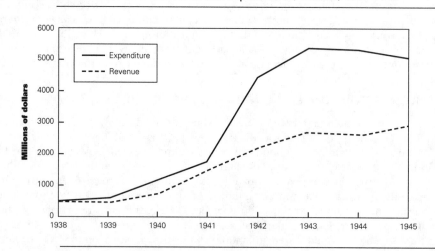

Source: Statistics Canada, *Historical Statistics of Canada*, 2nd ed., cat. no. 11-516E (Ottawa: Supply and Services, 1983), series G1–25. Reproduced by authority of the Minister of Industry, 1995.

categories accounted for more than 77 percent of all government revenues. World War I introduced the new income and corporate taxes that began the shift from indirect to direct taxation. Even in 1937, however, as Figure 18.1 indicates, these sources were central to government financing.

World War II completed the process begun by the Great War. The new taxes supplanted the old as the primary source of government revenue and, therefore, as the central features of any fiscal management of the economy. By 1947 (allowing for the winding down of the war), customs and excise taxes accounted for only 14.5 percent of total revenue, while income taxes had risen to almost a third. When excess-profits taxes are added to the income taxes figure, the result is 45 percent (see Figure 18.3).

The third means open to the government to finance its wartime expenditures was the age-old expedient of printing money. The governor of the Bank of Canada (formed only in 1935), Graham Towers, resisted this option, citing as a better model the monetary practices of Nazi Germany![11] The result was that the federal government managed to cover nearly 57 percent of its expenditures between 1940 and 1946 out of current revenue. Of the accumulated debt of more than $10 billion in these years, $8 billion was covered by borrowing and only $2.7 billion by money creation.

DIVERTING PRODUCTION TO WARTIME NEEDS

The revolution in fiscal matters alone would have marked a major change in the nature and scope of government in Canada. Taxation and borrowing, however, were only the most basic parts of the complex government system that evolved to fight the war. Getting the money was only the first step, for, as has already been stated, modern total warfare demanded a sweeping series of innovations to allow the government to use its new revenues and powers with maximum efficiency.

What developed in World War II was a complex series of arrangements between various government circles and between government and the private sector. In order to make the chaotic structures of these years comprehensible, it is worth dividing the situation into two categories: macroeconomic measures (of which the fiscal measures discussed earlier were a component) and microeconomic measures to alter the structure of industrial production.

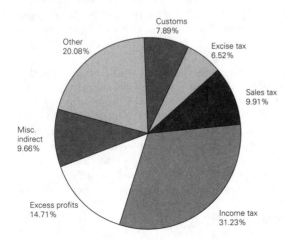

Figure 18.3
Sources of Federal Government Revenue, Canada, 1947

Source: Derived from Statistics Canada, *Historical Statistics of Canada,* 2nd ed., cat. no. 11-516E (Ottawa: Supply and Services, 1983), series G1–25. Reproduced by authority of the Minister of Industry, 1995.

Macroeconomic Measures

Though many early steps had been taken in the prewar years, in 1939 the government was groping its way toward some sort of comprehensive approach to macroeconomic management. Keynesian theory, with its concept of managing aggregate demand, contained within it the potential for a wide-ranging approach to economic planning. It is a long way from theory to practice, however, and, though Keynesian theory was known to many civil servants in 1939, they had not had the time, the mandate, or the knowledge to institute some sort of grand master plan. Rather, much of what they did in the first years of the war would be defined in modern terminology as "crisis management." Hundreds of issues pressed upon an overworked civil service, and they responded as best they could.

While no master plan was instituted at the beginning, there did evolve, over time, a fairly comprehensive economic system. The planners at the Bank of Canada, the finance department, and the Privy Council knew that economic stability was crucial to the successful prosecution of the war. Whereas in World War I the government had hoped to run "business as usual," no such illusions existed in World War II. Crises led to responses. Key goods were rationed to ensure supplies for the army and for war industry. Taxation policy, as we have already noted, ensured that consumer demands were restrained. Credit arrangements with Britain ensured a continual flow of production for the sake of the war effort. Two examples, however, indicate the structure and range of government economic intervention during the war years.

The first of these, and the most important for the average Canadian, was the institution, in 1941, of strict wage and price controls. By that time, the slack in the economy had been absorbed, and prices were beginning to rise. Government officials recognized that inflation could lead to labour instability and production uncertainties. Thus, in spite of the concerns of Prime Minister Mackenzie King that the marketplace could not be ignored, finance officials persuaded the government to institute a tremendously complex bureaucracy known as the Wartime Prices and Trade Board to control prices across the nation. In spite of occasional problems, both with workers and with manufacturers, the system worked. Inflation remained modest, averaging between 5 and 6 percent per annum over the whole period, compared with more than 20 percent in World War I.

The second example is in the area of international trade. With the war, demand for Canadian goods — both agricultural and manufactured — increased dramatically as the United Kingdom and other Allies equipped themselves with Canadian agricultural produce. Canadian exports to the United Kingdom doubled between 1939 and 1942 and almost doubled again between 1942 and 1944. At the same time, imports — these from the United States — also increased, at almost as great a rate.

Such growth created problems, however, due to the unusual wartime situation. Serious imbalances soon developed because Britain had turned its productive capacity inward. It was thus no longer exporting and, therefore, was unable to earn foreign currency. Until about 1941, Britain was able to pay Canada by depleting its reserves. Even then, however, there were problems caused by British restrictions on the pound's convertibility. By 1941, the British supply of foreign-currency reserves was seriously depleted. In terms of international currency flows, the nation was broke. Canada, of course, had no intention of cutting off a war ally from valuable supplies and, thus, undertook a series of credit arrangements and outright gifts to ensure the continued flow of supplies across the Atlantic.

This situation meant that the traditional balance between British surpluses and American deficits was disrupted. Purchases from the neutral United States between 1939 and 1941 had to be paid for in American dollars. Canadian reserves of American dollars and gold were, thus, under pressure from Canada's mounting trade deficit with the United States. In 1940, that deficit was $269 million; in 1941, $313 million.

The government recognized the potential of currency problems from the beginning of the war and, in response, had established a body known as the Foreign Exchange Control Board. Over the first two years, it progressively stepped up measures to discourage the expenditure of American dollars for non-war purposes. Regulators met on a weekly basis in Ottawa to use the vast powers that existed in wartime to reshape Canadian consumption. Certain imports were restricted or abolished. Tourist travel was curtailed, and a number of imported goods rationed.

In this case, though, even the most ardent efforts of the civil service seemed insufficient. The outflow of currency and gold increased and was stemmed, not because of Canadian regulations but because the United States acted. In spring 1941, in what is known as the Hyde Park Agreement, the Americans agreed to undertake a series of defence-related purchases in Canada. Thereafter, the pressures eased, though controls were maintained by Ottawa for the duration to ensure that the war effort, not the Canadian consumer, benefited by this agreement.

These two measures indicate something of the degree to which the normal marketplace system of the Canadian economy was altered by government intervention during the war. The war was being fought as much on the home front as it was on the battlefield. Moreover, unlike what had occurred during World War I, politicians, the public, and especially the civil service saw control of the economy, in the broad sense, as an inherent part of that war effort. Issues that had been the subject of hot debate for decades were suddenly resolved as the government moved to intervene directly in managing the economy. By the end of the war, thousands of orders-in-council and approximately 115 000 civil servants testified to the changes that had been wrought. Emergency powers would eventually lapse and the budgets would be trimmed, but there was no returning to the prewar concept of government. Economic management was now seen by the public, by enthusiastic civil servants, and by many politicians as the responsibility of government. For better or worse, the efforts to succeed at this enormous task have shaped much of Canadian government history since the war.

War Production Measures

The other and closely related aspect of the war effort was the production of resources for military use, not only by Canadian forces but by the British and the other Allies. The term "resources," rather than "equipment," is used to indicate just how sweeping the production effort for the war was. There were military items, such as tanks, airplanes, ammunition, mechanical parts, uniforms, boots, shelter, and on and on. There were also the components and materials required to manufacture such items, such as steel, lumber, and mine output. Energy was also necessary, and, thus, oil and electric production were items of concern throughout the war. Food had to be delivered to feed the troops, the workers who supplied the troops, and the population generally. Finally, efficient transportation, especially across the Atlantic, demanded a rapid increase in merchant-marine capacity and in escort vessels. In other words, just as the financial planning of modern warfare encompassed the whole economy, so, too, did the supply of modern warfare draw in most sectors of production.

At the centre of Canadian war production was the newly created (April 1940) Department of Munitions and Supply and its energetic minister, C.D. Howe.[12] Howe was extremely competent and willing to assume command. Indeed, given the powers of the War Measures Act, Howe was, through much of the war, effectively a dictator of Canadian war production. At his command, key resources could be allocated, plants taken over for war production, vast orders let without tender, and new lines of production ceased or begun.

352

Much of the success of the operation rested on Howe's decision to use what became known as the "dollar-a-year" men. These were senior businessmen who were willing to work for Howe for the famous "dollar-a-year" retainer in order to help war production. Because they were experienced in production and because they often already knew the particular sector they were assigned to, they could take up their tasks relatively quickly and pursue them effectively. Howe also trusted them to make decisions and gave them considerable power. There were problems and scandals, but by and large the crisis atmosphere of the war led to co-operation, while the tremendous power of these men made them able to do things that would never have been possible (or desirable) in peacetime.

One of the most striking legacies of Howe's munitions and supply department was the crown corporation. These government-owned businesses became a favourite technique of Howe and his officials for filling gaps within the private sector. To coax a new company into life (even with promises of government contracts) would take time — too much time. However, a stroke of the pen could create a crown corporation, and necessity caused Howe to use his pen often. During the war the government created 28 crown corporations, including such major presences on the postwar scene as Eldorado Mining, Polymer Corporation, and much of the Canadian aircraft industry.[13] Overall, the government built 98 war plants and had acquired, by the end of the conflict, hundreds of millions of dollars in assets. As with the changing patterns of taxation and economic management, the presence of the crown corporations and these assets helped transform the nature of Canadian government, not just during the war but after.

By the time Munitions and Supply was fully in operation at midwar, it was a vast government agency that was rivalled only by the defence department itself in terms of importance. More than 5000 people were employed by it directly, and as many as 25 000 worked for crown corporations set up to handle war production. More than 800 000 worked in war production overall, and, in one way or another, most of their jobs were connected to the activities of Munitions and Supply.[14] Overall, it produced some $9.5 billion worth of war materiel for the Canadian and Allied armed forces. Through this department flowed the great bulk of wartime contracts from the government, an amount reaching $797 million by the peak of the war.[15] It alone was spending considerably more than the entire prewar budget and did so, historians have generally concluded, with a fair degree of efficiency.

Within a short period of time, Munitions and Supply greatly expanded the capacity and expertise of new industries and, indeed, whole sectors of the economy. Thus, for example, such a high-technology industry as aircraft production started from practically nothing in 1939–40 but increased dramatically so that, by midwar, Canada was producing more than 4000 aircraft a year. Likewise, Canada was able to develop both the large merchant marine and the necessary naval-escort vessels, even though, after years of economic depression, shipbuilding had been practically extinct. Finally, in this list of examples, the excess-steel capacity that had plagued that industry during the 1930s was suddenly insufficient, and Munitions and Supply moved forcefully to expand the industry to meet the needs of war production.

The activities of the Department of Munitions and Supply provide the link between the war-related activities of the government and the broader question of the impact of the war on the economic activity of Canada as a whole. They also give us an idea of the different aspects of that impact. On the one side, there was the actual effect of the war on day-to-day activity — in business, labour, and other areas. As the legacy of the crown corporations reveals, however, the war also had a longer-term impact. Considerable structural change was wrought by such a massive infusion of war-related activity. The following discussion considers the impact of the war on the broader economy, and then the structural legacy of the war itself.

The Economic Impact of the War

When the war began in autumn 1939, the Canadian economy, though far improved from the dark days of 1932–33, was still mired in depression. The net value of production for industry was still below 1929 levels, as was GNP.

The story was the same when it came to investment. The excess capacity that had plagued industries at the beginning of the Depression had effectively halted capital investment. Even after a decade, this had not been reversed. Gross capital formation at the end of the 1930s was only half what it had been in 1929.[16] By 1939, however, a new problem had developed. Much of Canada's machinery and plant was aging. Many factories, mills, and mines desperately needed an infusion of capital in order to make them efficient producers. Yet, a depression psychology still plagued many businessmen, and without some guarantee of increased business, they were unlikely to take the necessary risks.

All of this showed up in unemployment and the general standard of living across the country. The stock of residential housing was run down, and building permits remained well below 1920s levels. Instead, many, especially young people, remained at home or resided in boarding houses. Marriages were postponed, as were families. Marriage ages were higher, and overall fertility rates lower, in 1939 than they had been in the 1920s. The most persistent reminder that the economy had not recovered was the continuing unemployment. A survey in June 1939 indicated that more than 11 percent of unionized employees in Canada were without work.[17]

The war finally ended the Depression, and did so very quickly. The twin demands of the army and war production quickly soaked up unemployment: by 1941, the 11 percent figure had dropped to 4 percent. Similarly, the war provided the incentive for businesses to overcome their reservations about the economy and invest in new plant and equipment. Those who continued to have reservations would be cajoled by Howe and his officials; failing that, the investment would be made directly by the government. The result was an investment upswing that took capital formation over $1 billion in 1941 for the first time since the boom days of the later 1920s.

More revealing, however, is the quadrupling of capital investment in manufacturing between 1939 and 1941. Over the first four years of the war, manufacturing investment accounted for nearly one-third of all capital formation in the country. The dominance of the manufacturing sector was also shown in other areas. Thus, while the overall labour force increased by 14 percent, manufacturing employment increased from 627 000 in 1939 to more than 1.25 million by 1943, or by 100 percent. Gross value of production in manufacturing more than doubled during the war, while total wages paid more than tripled.[18]

Thus, while practically all sectors were affected by the war, it was manufacturing that changed the most. In effect, the war was leading — much more than World War I had done — to a restructuring of the Canadian economy. World War II ushered in the age of heavy manufacturing in Canada. Steelmaking, transportation manufacturing, the refining of minerals, aircraft production, and a dozen other areas received such a boost from the war that they became newly important and vibrant industries for the postwar world. By 1943, when the Dominion Bureau of Statistics analyzed Canadian production by sectors, "manufactures" accounted for more than 70 percent of the total. In contrast, during the 1920s, the comparable figure had been 57 percent.[19] Once-mighty agriculture had slipped from 29 to 12 percent in the same years.

Such differences in growth between sectors raised all sorts of questions at the time, and afterward. First, and most importantly, if manufacturing was the key to economic growth in this new era, would that growth be distributed evenly across the country? Ontario and Quebec had always dominated manufacturing in Canada, and therefore, as occurred in World War I as well, the fear was expressed that the rapid growth of the war would primarily benefit those provinces. Politicians from the West and the Maritimes called loudly on Howe and others to ensure that they got their "fair share" of the new production bonanza.

This happened but only to a degree. The government and Howe made occasional efforts to look for regional contracts but they did not see the primary role of the Department of Munitions and Supply as one of redistributor of wealth. War production was the primary concern and speed was of the essence. Existing capacity (whether in terms of plant or work force) made it easier to get an operation going and, thus, the great bulk of Munitions and Supply activity was centred in Ontario and Quebec. More than half of all wartime industrial employment was located in Toronto and Montreal.[20]

Yet the western provinces did gain ground. British Columbia boomed through a combination of industrial activity and important primary resources. Alberta also grew in both absolute and relative terms. Indeed, in these two provinces, it might be argued that the foundations of the new west were laid by the war. In other provinces the effect was less dramatic. It is true that Manitoba and Saskatchewan saw growth. However, given the miserable state of their economies in the later 1930s this is not surprising. The problem is that the growth rates were not sustained and the post-war years saw both provinces fall back relative to British Columbia and Alberta or to the economy as a whole.

It is important to keep these events in perspective. The focus of the government was on the war rather than on regional issues. All regions did well by the war. Agriculture rebounded in the west. In the Maritimes both the lumber industry and the large naval presence brought new jobs. Indeed, while Ontario had a large absolute growth it actually saw less relative growth than some of the smaller provinces. In terms of per capita income, though, Ontario and British Columbia were the only two provinces above the national average.[21]

That said, the continued concentration of manufacturing in central Canada had important implications. Some of the best-paying and steadiest employment was in the manufacturing sector, and that sector was less susceptible to the boom-and-bust syndrome of natural-resource economies — partly because it was more easily protected by tariff barriers. Also, though this was not known at the time, certain key industries centred in Ontario and Quebec would experience considerable growth in the postwar years. Finally, one of the most dramatic areas of postwar growth would not be manufacturing but related financial services. These would tend to cluster in the largest cities of the nation — Toronto, Montreal, and Vancouver — where the manufacturing capacity was already centred.

Because that manufacturing capacity was concentrated in central Canada, with new plant, machinery, and expertise, the war had a long-term regional effect. Coupled with the decline of agriculture and with the disastrous regional implications of the Depression, the dynamics of growth for the Canadian economy would rest for some years in a narrow corridor running from Windsor to Montreal. In contrast, the Maritimes and the Prairies, though better off than during the Depression, lagged behind central Canada in terms of economic growth after the war. Only the discovery of large oil fields in Alberta in 1947 and 1948 prevented the Prairies, as a whole, from returning to long-term relative decline in terms of value of production, population, and personal wealth. To sum up, in regional terms the war reinforced the existing wealth and economic power of the industrial centre of Canada, though the whole nation benefited from overall rapid growth.

Changes in labour reflected both the structural changes that were taking place and the rising level of wealth in the country. The dramatic nature of the doubling in the number of manufacturing workers is apparent compared with the case in other sectors. Mining decreased in numbers, transportation remained steady, and trade increased by 20 percent. Farming also seemed to be a declining source of employment, with the farm population decreasing. Thus, the profile of the Canadian work force was changing. By 1945, more than half of the non-farm portion of it was employed in some form of manufacturing, and that manufacturing activity was both more likely to be secondary and increasingly located in or around a few major urban centres. Nearly 85 percent of manufacturing employment was in the provinces of Ontario, Quebec, and British Columbia.

The prosperity of the war years and the rise of urban manufacturing also encouraged the growth of labour unionism. These unions were now largely, but not completely, within the internationalist framework of pragmatic, or "bread and butter," unionism and were represented by the two competing national labour organizations, the Trades and Labor Congress and the Canadian Congress of Labour. There were, in addition, the Canadian and Catholic Confederation of Labour, as well as smaller umbrella organizations. Unionism, though not united, thus entered the war with a series of national organizations and with much greater clout than it had had on the eve of World War I.

Organized unions found the war a contradictory period. In one sense, the war years were frustrating ones. Wage and price controls, the Defence of Canada regulations, and public opinion hemmed in union activity and restricted meaningful collective bargaining. Yet, the war also gave organized labour unions tremendous benefits. The King government, determined to avoid the mistakes of World War I, carefully sought out union opinion and acted sympathetically to union organizers, at least the moderate variety. Thus, between 1939 and 1944, union membership in the country more than doubled, to some 750 000 workers.

Another, and potentially even more significant, result of the war was the tremendous increase in the numbers of women in the work force and the range of occupations in which they were active.[22] Behind this, of course, was economic necessity. The military recruitment of males and the general demand for workers made the recruitment of labour from new sources essential. Women, traditionally excluded from most areas of industrial work, suddenly found themselves able to gain entry. Two further factors were present that attracted women into the workplace. First, there was economic need. Many families were still recovering from the Depression, and the opportunity to gain income was not to be passed over lightly, especially when the husband was often in a low-paying armed-forces position. Second, the social stigma attached to middle-class women entering the work force was reversed. To work in, say, an aircraft plant or a truck factory was suddenly a patriotic duty. By 1942, the need was so great that the Women's Division of the Selective Service Agency was established to register women between the ages of 20 and 24. The intention was to recruit them into war work.

The changes were dramatic. Tens of thousands of women who would never otherwise have considered work headed off to the factories. By the middle of 1943, more than 200 000 women were engaged in war work directly, and more than a million were in the

356

Women factory workers, World War II. During the wartime labour shortage, many women who otherwise would not have been working took jobs in plants and factories as a patriotic duty. By the middle of 1943, more than 200 000 women were engaged in war work directly, and more than a million were in the labour force.

National Archives of Canada/C-467.

labour force. Some 50 000 served in the armed forces. By this time, as well, the government was actively recruiting married women into the war industry, in spite of the strong social belief that women with children should remain in the home. Indeed, so great was the demand for female labour that the government even made provisions for Dominion–provincial day-care funding.

At the end of the war, the forces that brought women into the labour market were reversed. Previously it was their patriotic duty to go to work; now it was considered their motherly or wifely duty to leave the workplace and free up jobs for men. Women, it was argued in endless fashion as the end of war approached, should return to their nurturing roles within the family and allow men to return to their areas of expertise. Thousands of women did leave the work force, as marriage and birth rates soared. For most of these women, and for society as a whole, the idea of working and raising a family at the same time was unacceptable. Personal choice, social pressure, and economic circumstance thus meant that female participation rates dropped from a high of 33 percent to a postwar level of 25 percent. Still, the effect of women in war and their success at their jobs were one more blow struck at sex-role stereotypes. Since many women, moreover, enjoyed the taste of independence that a job and a paycheque created, the participation rate remained higher after the war than before. By 1956, the *number* of women working had surpassed the high point of the war (see Table 18.1). It was not until 1967, though, that the *percentage* of adult women in the work force surpassed that of World War II.

Looking to Reconstruction, 1943–1945

By 1943, with rearmament accomplished and with the war beginning to turn in the Allies' favour, citizens and officials increasingly looked beyond the immediate pressures of the war to the sort of life that would face them once the conflict ceased. The memories of the

Table 18.1 Number of Women with Jobs, Canada, 1937–1956

Year	Total (000s)	Year	Total (000s)
1937	688	1947	898
1938	677	1948	914
1939	686	1949	967
1940	733	1950	1019
1941	800	1951	1063
1942	874	1952	1094
1943	1184	1953	1124
1944	1199	1954	1146
1945	1193	1955	1191
1946	889	1956	1259

Source: Statistics Canada, *Historical Statistics of Canada*, 2nd ed., cat. no. 11-516E (Ottawa: Supply and Services, 1983), table D-261. Reproduced by authority of the Minister of Industry, 1995.

Depression were vivid, and many expressed the concern that the prosperity of the war was an exception that would fade away once peace returned. Such thoughts were reinforced by the experience of World War I, which had ended in victory only to see mass unemployment and economic instability. The public, recorded one government agency, faced the postwar world with a "feeling akin to dread." This was reflected in the polls, where the social-democratic Cooperative Commonwealth Federation (CCF) was, by 1943, at its highest standing ever. The message was clear. The war effort was all very fine, but those who could provide some economic security — some plan to hold on to what had been gained — would receive a favourable hearing from the electorate.

By this time, however, the government was seriously beginning to turn its attention to plans for the postwar period. The officials of the Bank of Canada and the Departments of Finance and Munitions and Supply were increasingly concerned with how the eventual transition from war to peace could be managed without severe shock to the economy. As a result, the last half of the war saw an increasing number of committees, task forces, and parliamentary hearings called to address what became known as the period of "reconstruction." Though there were differing ideas of what reconstruction should emphasize, it had two general elements. First, it involved the idea that a considerable degree of planning and of intervention by government would be necessary to ensure that the demobilization of military and of war industry went smoothly. It also had broader connotations, involving the idea of a reshaping of social and economic structures to usher Canada into a new era and thereby prevent it from slipping into the malaise that had characterized the Depression years.

Reconstruction had different emphases, depending on the part of the government from which the plans emanated. Some of the most enthusiastic and far-reaching schemes came from those who felt that the war had to be used as an opportunity to restructure the capitalist system. Memories of the Depression, as well as inspiration drawn from social-planning documents in Britain and the United States, led them to advocate a widespread system of social security. Giving the public a sense of security, they argued, was crucial to preventing the return of a depression psychology. Further, it was a matter of social justice to ensure that the new-found prosperity of the war led to a redistribution of wealth among the population.

Such themes had been a general part of political and intellectual discussion in Canada for some years. They became a serious part of discussion for reconstruction when the Report on Social Security was released by Leonard Marsh in 1943. Marsh was director of research for a committee formed by Ian Mackenzie, the minister of labour; and Marsh's report ranged freely across the whole panoply of social-security measures. A comprehensive rather than piecemeal approach must be devised, he warned, and accordingly he advocated an immediate move toward such measures as public health care, children's allowances, improved old-age pensions, and unemployment benefits. Even funeral benefits were advocated.

Marsh's report received a great deal of publicity. Ultimately, however, reconstruction did not take the path advocated in that report, or by Ian Mackenzie. Others in government, though also concerned with reconstruction, felt that much of Marsh's work was hasty and ill-conceived. They, too, had memories of the Depression, but those memories centred on the large budget deficits, the constriction in trade, and other factors that had prevented recovery. To them, social security, though worth considering, would be idle dreaming unless the economy was healthy enough to support such expensive measures. The business cycle, not the welfare state, was their primary focus.

The military and C.D. Howe's people were especially concerned with the short-term impact that the end of war would bring. Close to two million troops and war-industry workers would have to find new occupations once the war ended. This vast movement would be happening at the time that government production was winding down and thus, presumably, in a climate of economic downturn. In order to prevent the sharp economic dislocation that had characterized the end of World War I, a complex series of plans and programs was developed. A new department, Veterans' Affairs, implemented a wide range of benefits for returning soldiers, including subsidized mortgages, health- and hospital-care benefits, job training, and education allowances. For industry, Howe's department, which would formally change roles in 1944 when it became the Department of Reconstruction, introduced a number of programs designed to ensure that industry continued a high level of production once war contracts ended. Typical were a series of beneficial depreciation allowances brought in for industries buying new equipment to shift from wartime to peacetime production. Quick writeoffs of new equipment against current high profit levels made the new investment attractive to companies. To the government, the immediate cost in tax revenues was worthwhile because the writeoffs encouraged companies' continued investment at war's end.

In the Department of Finance and the Bank of Canada, the concern was to take the Howe plans, Veterans' Affairs measures, Marsh proposals, and the myriad other schemes floating around and try to package them so that they made sense in terms of macroeconomic planning. Indeed, the belief that macroeconomic planning was possible and that government could influence the direction of the economy was perhaps one of the most significant factors influencing the planning for the postwar world. By the 1940s, experience and theory were coming together. The theory was that of Keynes, and the experience was the success of the civil service in harnessing the economy of the nation, particularly in such measures as wage and price controls. Now, the civil service felt the time had come to take what they had learned and put it to use in the postwar era. Only such confidence allowed a government white paper on reconstruction to commit itself in 1945 to "a high and stable level of employment."

The belief in economic planning and the theory behind it are complex and cannot be described fully here. Some dominant themes, however, typify the changes that were taking place. The first was the belief in the importance of maintaining aggregate demand. If people and businesses could be kept purchasing, then their demands would create the jobs and profits to allow continued consumption. Success, in other words, was self-ful-filling. The trick was to provide consumers with the incentive, material and psychological, to go out and spend. Once again, various measures were eventually put in place. Taxes were lowered, war bonds were cashed, and compulsory savings plans (used by government during the war) were ended. Most dramatically, the planners borrowed from the social-security side of things by supporting the implementation of the family allowance in 1945. This scheme was unique because it handed out government money, not on the basis of direct need but on the basis of the presence of children in a family. This vast giveaway of $250 million a year was calculated to put spending dollars in the hands of Canadians so that they would consume. It was also designed to assist in the re-election of the hard-pressed Liberal government. It succeeded on both counts.

The other thing the planners had learned from the prewar period was the essential reality that Canada could not succeed without international prosperity. Given the nation's orientation to exports, all those schemes to encourage Canadian business and consumers would eventually crumble if international customers weren't found for Canadian products once the war ended. W.A. Mackintosh of the Department of Finance summed it up very well: "The kind of world which will emerge after the war, will have more effect on Canada's destiny than any changes which are taking place in Canada during the war."[23] As a result, Canadian politicians and civil servants were generally very internationalist at the end of the war. They were as active as possible in supporting the establishment of international monetary relations at such conferences as the one held at Bretton Woods in 1944, which founded the International Monetary Fund.[24] They were enthusiastic in their support for the lessening or removal of barriers to international trade, and in their support of United Nations agencies seeking to rationalize trade.

At the end of World War II, the Americans moved aggressively onto the world stage. It was, by 1945, by far the most powerful nation in the world. Had its tremendous wealth not been circulated widely in the world, the same instabilities that had marked the 1920s and had ultimately so hurt the United States would have all too probably recurred. The Americans recognized this danger; thus, they, too, came down in favour of an international monetary order (now resting largely on their dollar) and, through such schemes as the Marshall Plan, moved to rebuild Europe as far as possible. As the largest trading partner of the United States, Canada could only benefit from such openness and vast wealth.

Conclusion

Both domestically and internationally, Canada moved into the postwar world with relative ease economically. GNP did drop a little in 1945 and 1946, but had rebounded by 1947, and would increase consistently through the postwar years. Likewise, unemployment increased only temporarily and, even at that, never approached the levels of the 1930s. Indeed, levels of less than 4 percent were standard throughout the postwar years. Finally, real gross national expenditure dropped only marginally at the end of the war, and then moved upward again. There was no significant drop, even in per capita GNE, in spite of the end of war production (see Figure 18.4). Given the shift from war materiel to consumer goods, this meant that the standard of living of Canadians improved substantially in the immediate postwar years.

International trade was also a success story for Canada. Although there was a drop of more than a quarter in exports from 1945 to 1946, this was hardly surprising, given the end of the vast industrial war machine. Thereafter, however, exports recovered, with the United States (39 percent) and the United Kingdom (25 percent) as, by far, Canada's most important customers. Conversely, the United States was, for at least a while after the war, practically Canada's only source of foreign goods, accounting for more than 70 percent of all imports to Canada through the rest of the 1940s.

Prosperity and the ever-greater importance of the United States were two legacies of the war. A third was the much larger government that has been the subject of so much discussion in this chapter. The size of budgets and civil servants also declined only temporarily at the end of the war. New taxes, coupled with postwar prosperity, gave governments the opportunity to continue the sort of wide-ranging planning that had characterized the war years. Often, the plans were more grandiose than the practice, and the ability to control the economy was often overstated, but the reality was that World War II brought Canada into an era when government had a much more profound impact on the economy than it had had in the past.

Yet, there is a danger in placing too much emphasis on the successes. The postwar prosperity had not ended regional disparity and regional tension. One of the major failures of bureaucratic planning at the end of the war came at the hands of provinces insistent on retaining or regaining their rights. In the postwar years, federal–provincial relations would grow increasingly acerbic, and the concern for regional equity would become a major issue in politics. Likewise, whatever social-security measures were brought in by 1945, a whole host of them had been set aside for want of money, jurisdiction, or will. The next twenty years would see an ongoing debate as to how much social welfare was possible and desirable. Finally, the great prosperity of the United States and Canada's dependence on that

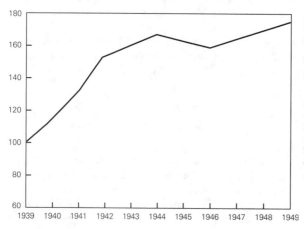

Figure 18.4
Index of Gross
National Expenditure,
Canada, 1939–1949
(1939 = 100)

Source: Derived from Statistics Canada, *Historical Statistics of Canada*, 2nd ed., cat. no. 11-516E (Ottawa: Supply and Services, 1983), series H1–151. Reproduced by authority of the Minister of Industry, 1995.

prosperity would create new concerns in the postwar decades. American trade and American investment would be central to Canadian hopes and fears in the postwar world.

NOTES

1. Cited in C.P. Stacey, *Arms, Men and Governments: The War Policies of Canada, 1939–1945* (Ottawa: Supply and Services, 1970), 9.
2. Stacey, *Arms, Men and Governments*, 6.
3. Statistics Canada, *Historical Statistics of Canada*, 2nd ed. (Ottawa: Supply and Services, 1983), G389.
4. Robert Bothwell, Ian Drummond, and John English, *Canada, 1900–1945* (Toronto: University of Toronto Press, 1987), 363.
5. Cited in J.H. Perry, *Taxes, Tariffs and Subsidies*, vol. 2 (Toronto: University of Toronto Press, 1955), 335.
6. A.F.W. Plumptre, *Mobilizing Canada's Resources for War* (Toronto: Macmillan, 1941), 113.
7. W. Irwin Gillespie, *Tax, Borrow and Spend: Financing Federal Spending in Canada, 1867–1990* (Ottawa: Carleton University Press, 1991), table C-2.
8. Perry, *Taxes, Tariffs and Subsidies*, 697.
9. This summary of changing taxation is from Perry, *Taxes, Tariffs and Subsidies*.
10. These figures are from Gillespie, *Tax, Borrow and Spend*, tables C-2 and C-3. 11. See Thomas J. Courchene, "The Interaction Between Economic Theory and the Bank of Canada Policy," in David C. Smith, ed., *Economic Policy Advising in Canada: Essays in Honour of John Deutsch* (Montreal and Kingston: McGill–Queen's University Press, 1981), 163.
12. The following paragraphs rely on R. Bothwell and W. Kilbourn, *C.D. Howe: A Biography* (Toronto: McClelland & Stewart, 1979).
13. On crown corporations see J. de N. Kennedy, *A History of the Department of Munitions and Supply*, 2 vols. (Ottawa: King's Printer, 1950).
14. Kennedy, *History of the Department of Munitions and Supply*, vol. 2, viii.
15. Kennedy, *History of the Department of Munitions and Supply*, vol. 2, 298. This includes only the "Canadian account." If amounts handled through the department for British and other purchasers were included, the figure would be much higher.
16. Statistics Canada, *Historical Statistics of Canada*, 2nd ed. (Ottawa: Supply and Services, 1983), F135–52.
17. This is from *Canada Year Book*, 1946 (Ottawa: King's Printer, 1947), 751.
18. Statistics Canada, *Historical Statistics of Canada*, D318–28; D124–33. M.C. Urquhart, "Canadian Economic Growth 1870–1980," Queen's University, Department of Economics, discussion paper no. 734, table 6.
19. These figures are from *Canada Year Book*, 1946, 191; and 1930, 185. They may not be directly comparable with other figures, and that is why they are introduced as they are. Also note that these figures include primary manufacturing.
20. R. Bothwell, "'Who's Paying for Anything These Days?': War Production in Canada, 1939–1945," in N.F. Dreizeger, ed., *Mobilization for Total War* (Waterloo: Wilfrid Laurier University Press, 1981); on employment figures see Kennedy, *History of the Department of Munitions and Supply*, vol. 2, 503.
21. Robert Bothwell, Ian Drummond, and John English, *Canada Since 1945* (Toronto: University of Toronto Press, 1981), 24.
22. For a detailed study of women in World War II see Ruth Roach Pierson, *They're Still Women After All: The Second World War and Canadian Womanhood* (Toronto: University of Toronto Press, 1986).
23. Cited in Doug Owram, *The Government Generation: Canadian Intellectuals and the State, 1900–1945* (Toronto: University of Toronto Press, 1986), 301.

24. One of the nicest summaries of these events is in A.F.W. Plumptre, *Three Decades of Decision: Canada and the World Monetary System, 1944–1975* (Toronto: McClelland & Stewart, 1977), chapters 1 and 2.

FURTHER READING

Bothwell, R. "Who's Paying for Anything These Days?': War Production in Canada, 1939–1945." In N.F. Dreizeger, ed., *Mobilization for Total War*. Waterloo: Wilfrid Laurier University Press, 1981.

Bothwell, R., Ian Drummond, and John English. *Canada, 1900–1945*. Toronto: University of Toronto Press, 1987.

Bothwell, R., and W. Kilbourn. *C.D. Howe: A Biography*. Toronto: McClelland & Stewart, 1979.

Granatstein, J.L. *Canada's War: The Politics of the Mackenzie King Government*. Toronto: Oxford University Press, 1975.

Pierson, Ruth Roach. *They're Still Women After All: The Second World War and Canadian Womanhood*. Toronto: University of Toronto Press, 1986.

Plumptre, A.F.W. *Three Decades of Decision: Canada and the World Monetary System, 1944–1975*. Toronto: McClelland & Stewart, 1977.

Stacey, C.P. *Arms, Men and Governments: The War Policies of Canada, 1939–1945*. Ottawa: Supply and Services, 1970.

Part Six

The Modern Era: Since 1945

A cargo ship docks at Vancouver's international seaport to load

lumber. Lumber is among many of Canada's important export

commodities. Nik Wheeler/Corbis/MAGMA/NW007537.

364   **THE DECADES** after World War II are among the most difficult in Canada's economic history to summarize, partly because the economy was more complex and partly because more is known about it. Data are more plentiful; records are more complete; and, for some readers more than others, as well as for some events more than others, memories are still relatively fresh. Nonetheless, recognizing the considerable risk of oversimplification, four features stand out when looking back on these years.

The first impression is that of significant growth. The economy in the mid-1990s was larger, richer, and much altered compared to that of 1945. In current dollar terms, GDP increased from $13.9 billion in 1947 to $776.3 billion in 1995 or by nearly 55 times. Much of this increase is simply price inflation, however. In real terms (1986 dollars), GDP rose from $91.7 billion in 1947 to $608.8 billion in 1995, or by more than 6.6 times. Canada's population more than doubled over the same period, from 12.6 million to 29.6 million, meaning that real GDP per capital nearly tripled. By this measure, the average Canadian in 1995 was nearly three times as well off as his or her counterpart at the end of World War II.[1] We will treat the years since the mid-1990s separately in the final chapter.

The second impression is that of ongoing structural change. The most notable features in this respect are the steady decline in the proportion of Canadian workers employed in agriculture and the steady increase in the proportion of those employed in service industries. As Figure P6.1 illustrates, both trends have been underway since at least 1881. Manufacturing's share of total employment peaked in the mid-1950s and has been declining slowly ever since. In 1993, this sector's share was only slightly above what it was at the beginning of the Great Depression. Resource industries other than agriculture have maintained their small share of total employment over more than a century.

The third observation is that, in terms of overall macroeconomic performance, the postwar era divides naturally into two subperiods, or possibly three considering the last five or six years. The first runs from the end of the war to the early 1970s (1973, for convenience), while the second runs from 1973 to the mid-1990s. The dominant characteristic of the first subperiod was growth and prosperity, while that of the second was economic challenge. To illustrate, real GDP grew at an average annual compound rate of 5 percent between 1947 and 1973, but at only 2.9 percent between 1973 and 1992. In per capita terms, real GDP grew at an average 2.8 percent in the earlier period, compared with 1.7 percent in the later one. As noted already, we will refer to the most recent years in Chapter 22.

This structural break in the early to mid-1970s shows up in other ways. Figure P6.2 shows that unemployment rates fluctuated from year to year in the 1950s and 1960s, but around a near-constant average of 4.5–5 percent. Thereafter, however, unemployment displays a clear upward trend. The average annual unemployment rate for the 1970s is well above that for the 1960s; that for the 1980s is above that for the 1970s; and that for the 1990s is above that for the 1980s. Prime Minister John Diefenbaker was in political trouble in the early 1960s for unemployment rates that prime ministers in the 1990s would have been delighted with.

As if rising unemployment rates were not problem enough in the 1970s and 1980s, Figure P6.3 shows that they were accompanied by relatively high rates of inflation. Prices rose dramatically during the Korean War, before falling to an annual rate of increase in the 1–2 percent range to the mid-1960s. They began to rise thereafter, reaching an annual rate

Figure P6.1 Composition of Canadian Employment, 1881–1993

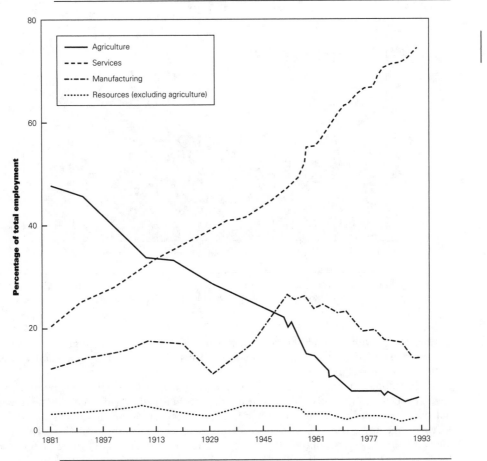

Source: Statistics Canada, *Agenda: Jobs and Growth, Canada Year Book* and Department of Finance, cat. no. 11-402E (Ottawa, 1994), chart 18, p. 32. Reproduced by authority of the Minister of Industry, 1995.

of nearly 5 percent by decade's end, and then dropping slightly in 1970 and again in 1971. The inflation rate began to rise the following year, approaching 8 percent in 1973 and 11 percent in 1974 and 1975. The rate fell to 7.5 percent in 1976, but began to rise again the year thereafter, reaching double-digit levels once more in 1980–82. Inflation then dropped sharply to about 4 percent by 1984 and to near zero in 1994. The coincidence of rising inflation and unemployment rates that characterized much of the 1970s and 1980s became known as stagflation and provided a major challenge to policy authorities in Canada as elsewhere.

The fourth observation on the postwar period is that this turnaround in economic performance in the 1970s was accompanied by a distinct shift in attitudes to economic management. Much had been expected of government in 1946. The success in restructuring the economy to meet wartime needs seemed to indicate that it could be similarly engineered to meet peacetime challenges. New Keynesian techniques promised to even out

Figure P6.2 Unemployment Rate, Canada, 1953–1993

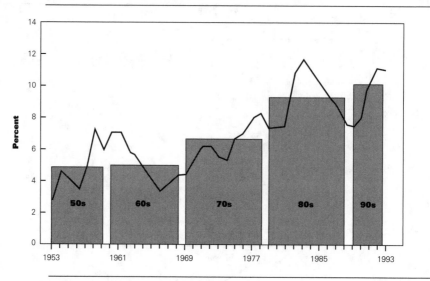

Source: Statistics Canada, *Agenda: Jobs and Growth, Canada Year Book* and Department of Finance, cat. no. 11-402E (Ottawa, 1994), chart 11, p. 19. Reproduced by authority of the Minister of Industry, 1995.

business fluctuations. Ambitious plans for health, education, and income-security measures were planned to ensure that some of the fruits of the growth and prosperity flowed to the less fortunate in society.

The economic difficulties after 1973 seriously challenged this faith in economic management. Economic theorists had to rethink notions of inflation and unemployment, while policy-makers sought remedies for them in everything from monetary and fiscal measures to wage and price controls. Attempts to direct and regulate the economy came to be viewed increasingly as policies that acted instead to distort it. Fine-tuning at the micro level went the way of the stabilization-policy counterpart. No major social programs were introduced after the late 1960s. Instead, efforts turned to cutting back existing ones to make them fit tighter government budgets, and to reforming them to remove what were considered to be their perverse incentives.

Canada shared many of these developments with other western industrial nations. The technology that raised Canadian living standards and that moved workers off farms and out of the mines and forests and into the cities did so in other nations as well. Women are more active in labour markets everywhere now, and increasing numbers of ethnic minorities can be found in many western countries, tempted by economic opportunity. Even new social values such as feminism and ecological awareness reflect broader international trends. Thus, much as we like to take the credit for our accomplishments, or to focus the blame, as the case may be, in many respects Canada remains what it has always been, a small part of a very large world.

Some developments were specific to Canada, however. Although technology and trade liberalization proceeded worldwide after 1945, the particular impact these developments had on Canada was a function of the nation's resource endowments, its human skills, and even its policies. No other nation quite mixed economic and constitutional issues the way

Figure P6.3 Inflation Rate: Consumer Price Index, Canada, 1950–1994

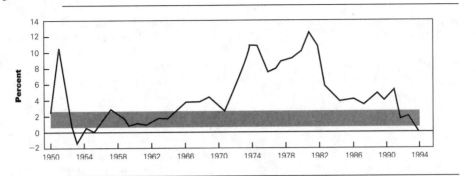

Source: Statistics Canada, *Agenda: Jobs and Growth, Canada Year Book* and Department of Finance, cat. no. 11-402E (Ottawa, 1994), chart 7, p. 13. Reproduced by authority of the Minister of Industry, 1995.

Canada did, whether with respect to the implementation of the welfare state, energy policy, the sovereignty-association referendum in Quebec, or the debate over the internal economic union. In at least a few respects, then, in the postwar period, as in earlier times, the story is uniquely Canadian.

International Background

The immediate economic concern in North America in 1945 was the prospect of stagnation. Those responsible for economic policy remembered that it had taken a world war to wrench the economies out of their decade-long slump of the 1930s, and they wondered whether the end of hostilities meant a return to Depression conditions. All countries had significant numbers of men and women in their armed forces who would somehow have to be reabsorbed into the civilian labour force. Machinery and equipment diverted earlier to wartime use likewise would have to be reconverted to peacetime employment. With governments cutting back on spending, concern arose in each nation as to where the demand would come from to absorb the peacetime output of goods and services.

For the nations of Europe, the problem was exactly the reverse. Their economies were too badly damaged to meet even the immediate needs for food and shelter, much less the longer-term one of reconstruction. North America had the capacity to meet these needs, but Europe did not have the dollars, earned from export sales, to pay for them. Even without this "dollar gap," as it came to be called, resurrecting international exchange would be no easy task. Depression and war had left in their wake a great number of restrictions on the international flow of goods, services, capital, and labour. Nearly every country had imposed high tariffs and quotas on imports, and had made it difficult or impossible for immigrants to enter. Most, as well, had instituted exchange controls during the war, and had left them in place in the uncertainties of the immediate postwar period.

As it turned out, the problems in North America never emerged, and the European ones were quickly solved. Aggregate demand was unexpectedly high in North America in the postwar years. Consumers drew upon assets accumulated during the war to make postponed purchases, and businesses responded by investing in plant and equipment to turn out these products. The dollar shortage was solved by a series of loans and export credits. The first was the Anglo–American Loan of 1946, but the most famous were those under the Marshall Plan. Between 1947 and 1950, a total of $9.4 billion went from the United States to the neediest countries of Europe. The Organization for European Economic Co-operation (OEEC), formed in 1948 as a framework for this aid, eventually became known as the Organization for Economic Co-operation and Development (OECD).

More important for the longer term was the manner in which the world's leaders turned to the task of resurrecting international exchange. A meeting at Bretton Woods, New Hampshire, in 1944 set out the basis of the postwar international system of exchange. Signatories agreed to remove, in stages, all exchange controls. They further committed themselves to a system of fixed exchange rates. In effect, currencies henceforth were to be fixed relative to the U.S. dollar, which, in turn, was tied to gold. Exchange-rate adjustments were allowed if balance-of-payments conditions warranted, but only within a small range, without prior consultation and approval. Credit was available to countries experiencing temporary difficulties. A permanent agency, the International Monetary Fund (IMF), was established to police the Bretton Woods Agreement and to provide loans to members. IMF membership was 44 in 1947, but grew to 107 twenty years later.

The main progress in liberalizing trade in goods and services came under the General Agreement on Tariffs and Trade (GATT). The GATT came into existence at a conference held in Geneva in 1947. Originally, it was intended to be an interim arrangement until the Havana Charter of the International Trade Organization (ITO) was ratified. The ITO died in 1950, but GATT survived to play a leading role in postwar trade liberalization. It set out a code of conduct that member nations were expected to follow with respect to their exports and imports, and it provided a forum for ongoing negotiations aimed at reducing trade barriers. The 1947 session managed to reduce or bind more than 45 000 tariff rates. A subsequent session in France, in 1949, continued this process and set the stage for the more significant liberalizations to come.

The results of these initiatives on the trade and monetary fronts were impressive. There were some initial economic difficulties in the immediate postwar period as the new institutions and arrangements were introduced and as reconstruction began. Conditions in Europe improved in 1945 and 1946, before suffering a setback in 1947. But, by 1948, the level of production in this region exceeded that of 1939, and growth continued thereafter. Trade increased faster than production, a result of the liberalization and a foreshadowing of a trend that was to continue well into the future. Most of this trade was among the industrial nations, and most of it was in manufactured goods.

The formation of the OEEC was but a start to economic integration in Europe. The European Payments Union was established in 1950 to facilitate capital movements within Europe, to be replaced by the European Monetary Agreement of 1958. Most importantly, an initiative for a French–German coal-and-steel pool led, in 1953, to the establishment of the six-nation Common Coal and Steel Market. The success of this venture helped to overcome opposition on the continent to further economic integration, and, on June 1, 1958, the Treaty of Rome was signed, establishing the European Economic Community (EEC).

International trade continued to benefit from liberalization measures initiated under the IMF and GATT. Negotiating sessions were held in England in 1951, in Geneva in 1956, at the Dillon Round in 1960, and at the Kennedy Round between 1964 and 1967. Significant tariff reductions were achieved at these sessions, and progress was made on regulating the use of non-tariff barriers (NTBs). The Kennedy Round was particularly successful. Duties on 60 000 tradeable industrial products were reduced an average of 35 percent. Major industrial nations went even further. Sectoral arrangements were initiated for certain products, and less-developed countries participated on a less than fully reciprocal basis.

Partly as a consequence of these initiatives, world trade grew sixfold between the years 1948 and 1973, or at an annual rate of about 7 percent. This increase was faster than that for production, meaning that the ratio of trade to output grew in all OECD nations. Most of the trade was among western nations, and it was concentrated in manufactured products. Between 1963 and 1973, for example, total world trade grew by 6 percent per year, while that in manufactured goods rose by nearly double that, at 11 percent.[2] The phenomenon came to be known as "intra-industry trade," with products from the same broad industrial grouping appearing as both exports and imports in each country's balance-of-payments accounts.

Complementing this growth in trade was one in capital movements. Portfolio investments were common prior to the Great Depression, and they continued as restrictions were removed and exchange convertibility was re-established. The major development, though, was the dramatic increase in direct investment, mainly by multinational corporations (MNCs). These took all kinds of forms. Some MNCs integrated vertically backward to raw-material sources or transportation and distribution facilities, or forward to processing facilities. Others set up subsidiary operations in other nations, to duplicate parent-company operations in some cases, and as part of intra-industry specialization in others. Direct investment was a way of transferring technology and managerial expertise in addition to capital, so the contribution to world economic growth was accentuated. American MNCs were the most prominent by far, but companies based in Japan, Britain, the Netherlands, Germany, and even Canada were important.

Sometime in the early 1970s (1973, for convenience), circumstances changed markedly. The next ten years were marked by serious, widespread, and sustained deterioration in the macroeconomic performance of the western industrial nations. Prices had been gradually increasing in the late 1960s, but this phenomenon seemed easily explainable as classic demand–pull inflation. The surprise came after 1972, as economic growth slowed and unemployment rates began to climb. Inflation did not recede as the (then) orthodox Phillips Curve analysis predicted, but remained steady or rose even further.

Table P6.1 shows the extent of the change in the economic performances of the main western industrial nations at this time. Real GDP per capita rose an average of 2.6 percent in the United States between 1962 and 1973, but only 0.6 percent between 1973 and 1982. Prices increased by 3 percent on average over the earlier period, and 8 percent in the later. The average unemployment rate changed from 4.9 to 7 percent. The deterioration was not as marked in Europe or Japan, but it was significant nonetheless. Real growth rates fell by a factor of 3.6 in the United Kingdom between the two periods, by nearly three times in Japan, and by more than twice on the Continent. Unemployment and inflation rates climbed commensurately.

This mixed economic record after 1973 left observers searching for an explanation. Inflation received a major push in 1971 and 1972 in the face of the robust and widespread economic boom of those years. The magnitude and breadth of the expansion were largely unanticipated, which meant that producers of a broad range of primary products were caught unawares as demand grew faster than available supplies. Crude-oil prices had been creeping up gradually under these pressures, but jumped precipitately in 1973 with the outbreak of the Arab–Israeli War and the consequent embargo on international oil shipments. The failure of the Peruvian anchovy harvest and of crops around the world added to the upward pressure on commodity prices.

These were the supply-side implications, but there were aggregate-demand ones as well. The rise in raw-material prices meant a terms-of-trade movement in favour of

Table P6.1 Measures of Stagflation in Major OECD Countries, 1962–1982

Country	Average Growth of Real GDP per Capita (%)	Average Growth of Value-Added Price (%)	Average Unemployment Rate (%)
United States			
1962–73	2.64	3.18	4.90
1973–82	0.55	8.13	6.99
Japan			
1962–73	7.31	5.13	1.13
1973–82	2.64	6.34	1.94
Germany			
1962–73	3.31	3.30	0.74
1973–82	1.66	4.66	3.65
France			
1962–73	4.11	3.93	1.51
1973–82	1.94	11.09	4.50
United Kingdom			
1962–73	2.43	4.72	1.98
1973–82	0.68	14.93	5.61
Italy			
1962–73	3.59	4.35	4.73
1973–82	1.74	17.72	7.07
Canada			
1962–73	3.80	3.27	4.44
1973–82	0.84	10.24	7.48

Source: John F. Helliwell, "Comparative Macro-Economics of Stagflation," *Journal of Economic Literature* 26(1) (March 1988): 2.

primary-product producers and against those nations importing them on a net basis. Since the OECD countries are mainly in the latter category, the commodity-prices boom meant a reduction in aggregate real incomes and a consequent fall in spending, adding to the economic slowdown. Some western governments resisted the cuts in real incomes, initially by attempting to maintain aggregate demand through expansionary monetary and fiscal policies. These moves postponed the eventual adjustment, but added to the inflationary impetus, so the record was not much improved.

　　Real incomes did eventually fall everywhere, as adjustment to the terms of trade effect set in. Unemployment rates rose as expected, but so did inflation rates. The notion of a stable trade-off between these two variables (the Phillips Curve) that had dominated economic thinking for a decade or more had to be abandoned as economic theorists sought explanations for the stagflation phenomenon. Now, as a result of this experience, macro-economics distinguishes between long- and short-run trade-offs, emphasizes the role of expectations in decision making, and concentrates on wage and price flexibility over the business cycle.

Any hope that the slowdown of the 1970s might be a cyclical phenomenon vanished in the next decade and a half. Figure P6.4 shows that average annual growth rates of real GDP for Canada and the other G-7 nations were lower in the 1980s than in the 1970s, and lower thus far in the 1990s than in the 1980s. Increasingly, analysts began to speak of a productivity slowdown. Aggregate economic growth was lower, they argued, not because capital and labour inputs were growing more slowly, but because the effectiveness with which they were being combined was declining. Figure P6.5 shows how well this explanation fits the Canadian record. Virtually all of the decline in the average rate of real GDP growth since 1963 can be attributed to lower productivity growth.

Many explanations were offered for this apparent decline in productivity.[3] The rise in oil prices in the 1970s and early 1980s induced a shift away from energy and capital and toward labour in many production processes. The gradual shift of the economy from high-productivity primary and manufacturing pursuits to lower-productivity services dragged down aggregate-growth rates. The greater participation of women and youths in the job market reduced the average experience of the work force. The greater emphasis on environmental control resulted in lower measured output increases, as did the growth of the underground economy. Infrastructure attracted considerable attention with the discovery of an apparent decline in spending on roads, education facilities, sewers, and so on in the late 1960s.

Attention eventually turned to even more fundamental explanations. In the words of an OECD report,

[There is a] contradiction between the apparently rapid acceleration in technical progress since the end of the 1970s and the absence of any significant measurable impact on the growth of total factor productivity. The analysis here suggests that the causes of the observed contradiction lie in a mismatch between earlier forms of corporate organization, as well as

Figure P6.4 Growth of Real GDP, Canada and Other G-7 Nations, 1960s–1993

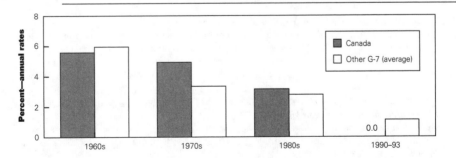

NOTE: REAL GDP IS IN CONSTANT 1985 U.S. DOLLARS, AT PURCHASING POWER PARITY EXCHANGE RATES. THE DEFINITION OF THE DECADES WAS DETERMINED BY DATA AVAILABILITY. CANADA'S GROWTH RATE IS THE ANNUAL AVERAGE COMPOUND RATE. OTHER G-7 GROWTH IS THE SIMPLE AVERAGE OF THE INDIVIDUAL COUNTRIES' COMPOUND RATES.

Source: Statistics Canada, *Agenda: Jobs and Growth, Canada Year Book* and Department of Finance, cat. no. 11-402E (Ottawa, 1994), chart 3, p. 11. Reproduced by authority of the Minister of Industry, 1995.

Figure P6.5 Sources of Growth: Commerical Sector Real Potential GDP, Canada, 1963–1993

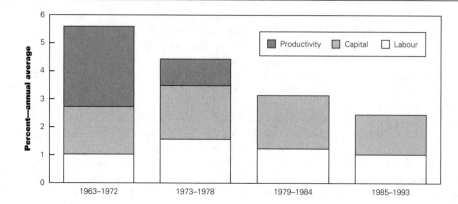

NOTE: PRODUCTIVITY IS TOTAL FACTOR PRODUCTIVITY. SUB-PERIODS CHOSEN TO HIGHLIGHT CHANGES IN THE TRENDS OF THE COMPONENTS OF GDP.

Source: Statistics Canada, *Agenda: Jobs and Growth, Canada Year Book* and Department of Finance, cat. no. 11-402E (Ottawa, 1994), chart 17, p. 29. Reproduced by authority of the Minister of Industry, 1995.

those of the public sector, and the characteristics of the new technologies, notably information technology. The slow rate of productivity growth could also be due to deficiencies of countries and firms in the training and management of human resources.[4]

This final part of the text looks at Canada's experiences since 1945. It first considers the period of growth and prosperity to 1973, and then the series of policy innovations generated by that period. It then examines the period of economic challenge and policy frustration between 1973 and 1982, and concludes by examining the record since 1982.

NOTES

1. These data are from CANSIM (d11000, d14442, d31248).
2. Jock A. Finlayson, "Canadian International Economic Policy: Context, Issues and a Review of Some Recent Literature," in Denis Stairs and Gilbert R. Winham, eds., *Canada and the International Political/Economic Environment*, Royal Commission on the Economic Union and Development Prospects for Canada, Research Study no. 28 (Ottawa: Supply and Services, 1985), 13.
3. See, for example, the symposium "The Slowdown in Productivity Growth," in *The Journal of Economic Perspectives* 2(4) (Fall 1988): 3–97.
4. Quoted in Government of Canada, *Agenda: Jobs and Growth*, (Ottawa, 1994), 29. See also Richard Lipsey, "Globalization, Technological Change and Economic Growth," *Canadian Business Economics* 2(1) (Fall 1993), 3–9.

FURTHER READING

Bothwell, Robert, John English, and Ian Drummond. *Canada Since 1945: Power, Politics, and Provincialism*. Rev. ed. Toronto: University of Toronto Press, 1989.
Canada. Royal Commission on the Economic Union and Development Prospects for Canada. *Report*, vols. 1–3. Ottawa: Supply and Services, 1985. The commission also published 72 volumes of

research grouped into four areas: economics, political science, law, and the interdisciplinary area of federalism and the economic union. These studies are an obvious starting point for anyone interested in postwar Canadian economic, political, and constitutional development.

Government of Canada. *Agenda: Jobs and Growth* (Ottawa, 1994).

Lipsey, Richard. "Globalization, Technological Change and Economic Growth." *Canadian Business Economics* 2(1) (Fall 1993): 3–9.

Symposium. "The Slowdown in Productivity Growth." *Journal of Economic Perspectives* 2(4) (Fall 1988): 3–97.

Chapter Nineteen

Growth and Prosperity, 1946–1973

THE PERIOD from the end of the war to the early 1970s ranks as one of the most prosperous in Canada's economic history. The nation was well placed to benefit from the economic changes sweeping the world. The liberalization of trade opened markets for Canadian goods and services and provided lower-cost imports. The resumption of international capital and labour flows expanded the capacity of the Canadian economy to meet the demands for the products. Added to these stimuli were other more internal factors, such as growing population and income, rising labour-force participation rates, new infrastructure developments, more education and training, the reallocation of activity from slow-growth to rapid-growth sectors, and new resource discoveries.

The period was not without its problems and setbacks, of course. Postwar stagnation was feared in Canada as much as anywhere else. Inflation was a problem in the early 1950s, and sluggish growth was in the latter half of the decade, when politicians clashed with the central bank over the appropriate policy stance. Already in the late 1960s there were signs of the stagflation that was to preoccupy policy-makers in the next decade. Concern was growing about the capacity of the economy to continue absorbing immigrants at the same rate, and discussion of the costs of relying on foreign investment were becoming common. But these items were minor compared with what Canadians had just been through and, still unbeknownst to them, what they were about to encounter.

Conversion to a Peacetime Economy, 1945–1950

The transition to a peacetime economy took a different turn than expected. Economic growth in the immediate postwar period was far more robust than most had dared predict. Real GNP declined in 1946 but rose consistently thereafter (Figure 19.1). Increases in aggregate demand were strong and widely based. Ottawa cut back its expenditures on military supplies in 1946–48, but these reductions were partially offset by new projects, such as the Trans-Canada Highway cost-sharing venture, signed with the provinces in 1948. Difficulties reaching international markets were reflected in early postwar export figures, but, again, not as badly as feared. Beginning in 1948, European nations could use American credit under the Marshall Plan to buy Canadian goods, and that provision, together with Canada's own export credits, meant that sales abroad fell less than might otherwise have been the case.

Other components of aggregate demand picked up the early slack left by the government's demilitarization. Consumer spending had been curtailed during the war by

Figure 19.1 Percentage Change in Real GDP, Canada, 1947–1973

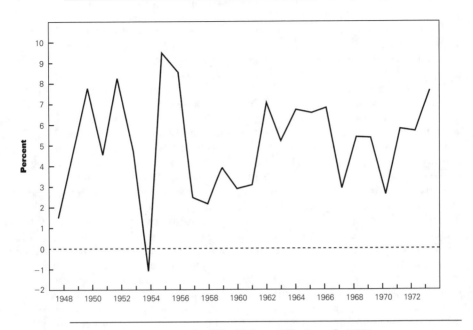

Source: Canada, Department of Finance, *Economic and Fiscal Reference Tables*, September 1994.

rationing and the absence of key goods such as new automobiles, so there was considerable pent-up demand and a large stock of liquid assets in the hands of the public to finance it. Consumption rose by over 11 percent in real terms in 1946, and by 7 percent in 1947; it fell off in 1948, and then rose by over 6 percent in 1949 and 1950. Business investment was particularly strong, as firms set about retooling to meet peacetime demands, stimulated, at least in part, by federal tax provisions. Spending on new plant and equipment rose by over 30 percent in 1946 and nearly the same amount in 1947, and remained strong for the next three years.[1]

Much of the growth in investment spending represents the switch of manufacturing capacity from military to civilian use. But the numbers also reflect a significant recovery of the major resource industries from the lull they found themselves in in the latter stages of the war. Pulp and paper, lumber, asbestos, gypsum, primary aluminum, and other minerals were able to expand production, in part in response to U.S. demands, until by 1948 they had regained their prewar position in Canada's export trade.

One notable example of this early resource development was the discovery of significant oil and gas reserves in western Canada, Alberta in particular. Leduc #1 came in on February 1947, followed in quick order by a number of other large discoveries. Regional demand for petroleum was quickly met, and surplus supplies became available. The Interprovincial Pipeline Corporation was incorporated under federal legislation to take oil eastward. The line reached Regina by June 1949 and the Manitoba–North Dakota border by the fall of that year. From there, it proceeded through U.S. territory to a terminus at

Superior, Wisconsin, where lake tankers picked up supplies for Sarnia. Plans were under way at this time to take crude oil west and to transport natural gas, but approval had not yet been given.

Joy Parr presents an overlooked feature of the rising aggregate demand after the war. While there was strong growth, unlike the United States, the Canadian economy faced important materials shortages and such shortages forced choices.[2] Thus, Canadians went shopping not to purchase a new appliance, but often to negotiate with retailers for a spot on a buyer's waiting list. The Canadian government's commitment to post-war Keynesian planning reflected the concern that to leave the allocation of scarce materials to the market and price signals was a threat to economic stability. Besides the risk of inflation, consumption of luxury items would divert resources and materials away from longer-term capital investment needed to revitalize and expand Canada's productive capacity. For these reasons, government planners, like C.D. Howe (Canada's "Minister of Everything"), circumvented the price system and turned to direct intervention in the economy.

Canadian policy for the short run after the war was designed to encourage rebuilding of the capital goods sector and to discourage the expansion of the consumer goods sector. Encouraging investment by raising real interest rates (by contracting the money supply) could choke off the economic recovery, thus, the government chose to encourage firms to invest by offering accelerated depreciation allowances to lower and defer their tax burdens. The majority of approved special depreciation allowances were for industries producing materials for construction and capital expansion, and industries producing for export. To stem the destabilizing influences of consumer spending the Canadian government used policy instruments to defer consumer spending. These policy instruments included direct and indirect taxes and credit, and exchange and import controls. Thus, for Canada, the post-War recovery was not necessarily raising high material standards of living for householders. For many Canadians, their demands would remain pent-up beyond the end of World War II and into the 1950s.

Stabilization Policy, 1945–1950

With the unexpected strong aggregate demand, inflation rather than stagnation was the main policy problem in the immediate postwar period. The consumer price index, which had moved very little during the war, leapt up in 1947 and 1948, as wartime controls were removed. Little use was made of active stabilization measures, however, bows to the new Keynesian demand management theory notwithstanding. Budgets were consistently set, not to regulate aggregate demand but to reduce the share of government in the economy. Taxes were reduced in every budget from 1945 to 1949, and they remained unchanged in 1950. Monetary policy was concerned mainly with supporting government bond prices, meaning that interest rates were kept low, so there was little restraint on inflation from this quarter.

Exchange-rate policy in the immediate postwar years was erratic, to say the least. As a signatory to Bretton Woods, Canada was committed to maintaining a fixed exchange rate and to removing restrictions on exchange convertibility. There was considerable difficulty finding the correct price for the dollar. It was appreciated to par with the U.S. dollar in 1946, largely as an anti-inflationary measure. The jump was too large, as it turned out, contributing to a balance-of-payments crisis in 1947 that was countered by increasing the severity of exchange controls. The British pound was devalued in 1949, and Canada

Imperial Oil's Leduc #1 "blows in." The first Leduc (Alberta) oil discovery was made in February 1947 and was followed by a number of other large discoveries of oil and gas reserves in western Canada. A pipeline was built to take oil eastward, reaching Regina by June 1949 and the Manitoba–North Dakota border soon after. From there, it crossed U.S. territory to a terminus at Superior, Wisconsin, and thence was transported by steamer to Sarnia, Ontario.

Imperial Oil Limited.

responded with a 10 percent cut of its own. Now, the rate was too low, resulting in a speculative capital inflow. Thus, in 1950, international commitments notwithstanding, a decision was made to float the dollar. One year later, the last of the wartime exchange restrictions was removed.

The net impact of reconstruction in Europe and rapid growth in the United States was to alter Canadian trading patterns in a fundamental and, as it turned out, permanent fashion. Canada had, for a very long time, imported more from the United States than it exported, and it exported more to Europe than it imported. A trade deficit with America was offset by a surplus with Europe. The pattern of imports changed little after the war, but that for exports shifted dramatically. The United States took 38 percent of Canada's exports in 1946, and Britain and western Europe took 47 percent. These proportions had shifted to 50 percent and 33 percent, respectively, just two years later and to 65 percent and 21 percent by 1950. Henceforth, the United States was to be Canada's dominant market, as well as supplier, meaning that their economic fortunes would be intertwined to an even greater extent than before.

War and the Resource Boom, 1951–1956

Economic growth was very rapid between 1951 and 1956 (see Figure 19.1). Except in 1954, when output actually declined, growth rates were above 4.5 percent in two years, above 8 percent in two others, and at a postwar high of 9.5 percent in 1955. Unemployment, which had been at 3.6 percent in 1950, dropped to 2.4 percent the next year and rested at the 3 percent level until 1953. The recession in 1954 drove the rate up to 4.6 percent, but it fell below 4 percent again by 1956. The boom was also reflected in inflation rates. The consumer price index jumped nearly 11 percent in 1951, before dropping to 2.5 percent in 1952, then below 1 percent until 1956.

The origins of this growth were war, resource development, and demographic change. The outbreak of the Korean War in June 1950 provided an immediate stimulus to the economy. Government expenditures increased by over 30 percent in real terms in 1951, and 23 percent in 1952, as Canada rebuilt the military apparatus it had demobilized after World War II. The ongoing Cold War would keep military expenditure high through much of the decade. Exports boomed, as the war created a demand for Canadian resource products, in particular. Both components of spending fell off in 1953, accounting for the lower growth rates of that year, and both declined in real terms in 1954, contributing to the fall in real GNP. Spending on consumer and investment goods was weak in 1954 as well. The upswing in 1955 and 1956 was centred in resource exports and the investment needed to bring these projects into being. Strong consumer spending added fuel to the boom.

Several high-profile resource and investment projects dominated the headlines. Sometimes these were aimed at serving the growing Canadian market, but more often they had a continental component. Indeed, the resource development of Canada in the 1950s depended to a large degree upon the fact that Canada was next door to the richest, most robust economy in the world. For two decades after the war, the American economy was unrivalled in the world. Looking for raw materials to feed both military preparedness and growing consumer demand, American businesses looked northward. In a pattern that resembled the 1920s, large Canadian projects depended on American dollars or the expectation of American markets.[3]

The petroleum industry expanded greatly in these years. As demand in Ontario markets grew, the interprovincial pipeline was extended to Sarnia, reaching that city in 1953. Transmountain's plans to take oil west, through the Yellowhead Pass to Vancouver and Seattle, received considerable impetus from the Korean War emergency. Crude-oil production rose significantly, from 47.6 million barrels in 1951 to 181 million in 1956, at the height of the Suez crisis. Exports increased even more dramatically, going from a mere 342 000 barrels in 1951 to 55.7 million in 1957.

Natural-gas projects had a tougher time with regulatory authorities. Already in 1949, Alberta had moved to control the export of gas from the province and had created Alberta Gas Trunk Lines (AGTL) to prevent the outside control of gas collection. Federal authorities were concerned with ensuring that any gas exports were surplus to domestic needs, and thus the authorities were insistent that pipelines to eastern and western markets pass through Canadian territory. This stance contrasted sharply with that adopted for crude oil, where there had been virtually no debate over the ownership of the pipeline companies or routing of the lines.

Permission was given in 1951, in the midst of the Korean War, to build a line from southeastern Alberta to Montana, to fuel the Anaconda Copper smelter. Another permit was given to Westcoast Transmission to ship gas from its northern fields to Vancouver and to the U.S. Pacific Northwest. Exports were approved, in this instance, because Vancouver demand was insufficient to support a pipeline by itself and because the northern supplies were judged to be surplus to Canadian needs.

The most controversial project, by far, concerned transporting natural gas to markets in Ontario and Quebec. Unlike oil pipelines that had taken the most direct route to eastern markets, natural-gas pipelines, it was generally agreed, should run entirely through Canadian territory. There was also concern over foreign ownership of this utility, so much so that Minister of Munitions and Supply C.D. Howe merged one American company with a Canadian one to form Trans-Canada PipeLines Limited before a permit was issued to begin construction. A bill to provide government financial assistance to the project required closure before it was passed by Parliament in 1956, a move that is widely cited as being the issue John Diefenbaker used to bring down the Liberals the following year. Assistance was given, the line was constructed on Canadian territory, the loan was repaid, natural gas flowed to Toronto and Montreal in 1958, and the company ended up Canadian-controlled. Natural-gas production, which had been 67.8 million cubic feet in 1950, jumped to 320 million by 1957.

Other projects were equally high-profile. The idea of improving the St. Lawrence Seaway to allow ocean-going vessels to sail into the heart of the continent goes far back in Canadian history, as the earlier discussion of the nineteenth-century canal system indicated. The St. Lawrence Seaway Authority was established in 1951 as a crown corporation, authorized to construct a deep waterway between Montreal and Lake Erie, in conjunction with the United States if possible, but otherwise alone. American interest in the project had never been great, but it was stimulated at this time by the hydro-electric potential of the system and by a growing demand for iron ore from Quebec and Labrador.

A treaty was signed in 1954, providing for joint construction and ownership of the works. The Seaway was opened in 1959, and various initial operating difficulties overcome by 1962. The completion of the Seaway had important benefits for Canada. It lowered the cost of shipping prairie grain to export markets, thereby raising farm incomes. By allowing Quebec–Labrador iron ore to reach steel centres in central Canada and the United States, it opened up a new and important staple. These two products dominated Seaway shipping from the beginning. Finally, it added to the hydro-electric capacity of the two central provinces.

As noted, U.S. interest in the Seaway stemmed, in part, from the access this route gave the Great Lakes steel towns to Labrador iron-ore resources. By 1947, it had become clear that the Mesabi range in Minnesota would not be able to meet U.S. requirements for much longer. The Iron Ore Company of Canada, formed as a consortium of Canadian and American firms in 1949, began a massive development of the Schefferville deposits the following year. U.S. Steel began development at Lac Jeannine a few years later, with the first rail shipment coming in 1961. Other, smaller developments followed, with some sales being made in Japan and Europe in addition to the United States. The result was that Canadian iron-ore production, which had been about 2 million gross tons in 1945, jumped to 14.5 million by 1955 and over 21 million before the decade ended. One-third of production was exported to the United States in 1945, and over 60 percent by 1959.

The uranium industry grew dramatically for a time as well. The U.S. and the U.K. governments were the main buyers of the ore in the immediate postwar period. The U.S. government subsidized production via the Atomic Energy Commission through an elaborate system of contracts and price supports. The Atoms for Peace initiative by President Dwight Eisenhower in 1953 opened up civilian access to uranium, giving spur to the nuclear-power industry. The combination of military and civilian demand in the United States generated an export boom in Canada, with sales jumping from $1.6 billion in 1956 to $13.5 billion by 1959. Canada set up the Atomic Energy Control Board in 1946 to conduct research and to regulate all aspects of the nuclear industry. Atomic Energy of Canada Limited (AECL) was created as a crown corporation in 1952 to develop a capacity in nuclear power. AECL had the first CANDU reactor in operation by 1962.

The other resource industries also benefited from growing international demand. The U.S. government used stockpiling practices to increase world nickel production and to reduce Inco's monopoly of the metal. Falconbridge was the main Canadian beneficiary of this practice. Inco expanded into northern Manitoba toward the end of the decade, opening a mine at Thompson in 1960. Quebec's asbestos industry grew, although it is probably most famous for its 1949 strike and the catapulting into politics of Pierre Trudeau and other Quebec intellectuals. Canada's cheap hydro resources continued to draw metal-refining activities, the Canadian Reynolds smelter at Baie-Comeau, built in 1955, being one of the more notable projects.

380

Economic growth in these years also rested on high levels of investment and personal consumption. Canada, along with the United States and Australia, underwent a major demographic shift in the period after World War II. This was the famous baby boom, which, as Figure 19.2 shows, involved a reversal in a long-term decline in the birth rate at a time when infant-mortality rates were declining sharply as a result of improvements in nutrition and medical techniques. Through the 1950s, the marriage rate soared, family formation followed, and with it came a lifestyle that dictated high consumption.

Houses had to be bought to accommodate all these new families. As the houses were often suburban, automobiles had to be bought to take the breadwinner to work and to move the rest of the family to school and to shopping and recreation areas. Radios, and then television sets, were bought in record numbers to entertain the young families. Likewise, in an era of affluence, business soon learned that children themselves were a consumer market. New products were spawned, from Davey Crockett hats to hula-hoops. Unprecedented affluence marked the rise of this new and large generation of children. Materialism became a deeply imbued social ethic that was tied to the provision of security. This was, after all, only fifteen years after the Great Depression.

Public expenditures to accommodate the baby boom were sometimes as massive as any great resource development. Education is a good example. Beginning in about 1950, the baby boom hit the school system. From then until the late 1960s, governments scrambled to expand the system sufficiently to handle the new students. By 1961 alone, the number of students in primary and secondary systems had doubled in Canada. As early as the mid-1950s, school construction costs alone averaged more than $200 million a year. To put this number in perspective, even a relatively small province like Nova Scotia was opening a new school every five days. Quebec was opening schools at a rate of one every 24 hours.[4]

Figure 19.2 Crude Birthrate per Thousand of Population, Canada, 1926–1970

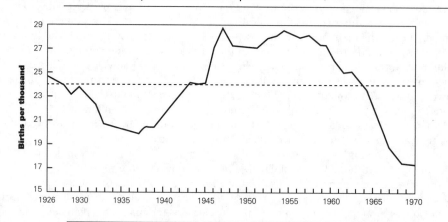

Source: Statistics Canada, *Historical Statistics of Canada*, 2nd ed., cat. no. 11-516E (Ottawa: Supply and Services, 1983), table B4. Reproduced by authority of the Minister of Industry, 1995.

Stabilization Policy, 1951–1956

Fiscal policy continued to be neglected in favour of other government-spending and taxation objectives, as it had been in the immediate postwar period. Financing the Korean War effort obviously dominated objectives in 1951 and 1952, and cutting back on the government sector did in 1953. There was little change in either spending or taxation in 1954, even as the economy slipped into recession. The 1955 budget has been described as the first truly "Keynesian" one in the postwar period, aimed, as it was, at stimulating the economy in the face of the slack evident in the 1954 data. It is widely acknowledged to have come too late, however, as the economy was already into the 1955–56 resource and investment boom by then.

Monetary policy was used more actively beginning in 1950. The first increase in the bank rate in the postwar period took place in October of that year as an anti-inflationary measure. Under the then governor of the Bank of Canada, Graham Towers, monetary policy relied less on controlling the overall growth of the money supply and more on restricting credit through selective controls and moral suasion directed at the banking sector. James Coyne replaced Towers as governor in 1954, and monetary policy was eased as the Korean War pressures ended. It was tightened again in 1955, and more so in 1956, in the face of the boom of those years. A notable parallel development was the steps taken in 1953 and 1954 to broaden the Canadian financial market by introducing government Treasury Bills and by giving dealers in them access to Bank of Canada credit lines.

The Canadian dollar was floated in October 1950, as noted above; all restrictions on foreign-exchange transactions were removed the following year. The dollar appreciated, gradually reaching par with the U.S. dollar, and then traded at a premium from 1952 on. This appreciation served as an effective anti-inflationary tool, as the rise in the dollar reduced the demand for Canadian exports and increased the demand for, and reduced the price of, imports.

Recession, 1957–1961

As Figure 19.1 illustrates, economic growth slowed appreciably toward the end of 1956 and remained at relatively low levels for the next five years. Consumption spending grew at half the rate in 1957 and 1958, as it had done in 1956, rose slightly in 1959, and then slowed again for two more years. Investment was especially weak, dropping, in real terms, to a 6 percent increase in 1957 from 18 percent the previous year, and then declining in three of the next four years. Exports stagnated in 1957 and 1958, and rose at only a fraction of their mid-1950s rate through to 1961. The consequence of this weak growth in aggregate demand was that unemployment rates rose from 3.4 percent in 1956 to over 7 percent in 1960 and 1961. As if this development were not perplexing enough, inflation jumped in 1957, and was higher in 1958–60 than it had been in 1955, at the height of the boom.

In part, the Canadian economy was following the American one into this downturn. Another factor accounting for the severity of the recession in Canada is that the major investments associated with resource exploitation were nearly completed. With no new major projects in the wings, investment spending would naturally fall off. Further, many of the market opportunities for Canadian products had been the consequence of unusual circumstances — the Korean War, the Suez crisis — and these would inevitably reverse as normal conditions returned. The U.S. government had announced, in 1956, the end of the price supports and subsidies for uranium production to take effect in 1962, for example, and Canadian sales fell dramatically from 1959 on.

The performance of the petroleum sector provides a good example of the difficulties facing the economy in these years. High-cost oil from Saskatchewan and Alberta had been unable to penetrate markets east of the Ottawa River. Refiners in Quebec and the Atlantic provinces were supplied, instead, by imports from the Middle East and Venezuela. The U.S. market had not grown as much as had been hoped, either, as a result of these same cheap offshore supplies. The American government instituted a system of voluntary import limitations in 1957, and made them mandatory two years later. Canada was exempted from the quotas on security grounds, but sales of western crude oil and natural gas in the United States rose slowly, and, except during the Suez-crisis years, the industry operated well below capacity.

Western provincial governments and the smaller independent producers lobbied hard for guaranteed access to the large Montreal market in the face of this excess capacity. The response of the Diefenbaker government was to appoint the Royal Commission on Energy (the Borden Commission) in 1957 to look at petroleum production and marketing. The report resulted in the creation of the National Energy Board in 1959 and what became known as the National Oil Policy (NOP) in 1961. Known as the deal with something for everyone, the NOP essentially ratified the continental marketing pattern that had operated since 1947. The Atlantic provinces and Quebec continued to import cheaper offshore oil. Ontario and the western provinces received western Canadian crude. Ontario paid slightly more for its oil as a result, but a prohibition on refinery shipments from Montreal allowed it to develop its own petrochemical industry. The United States agreed to import more Canadian crude, thereby providing compensation to the independents for their "loss" of Quebec. Guaranteed access to Ontario and expanded markets in the United States provided increased employment and economic activity for the western provinces. It also reinforced the notion that oil and natural gas were not just ordinary resources, but valuable national interests that had to be regulated. Politics and economics would continue to mix in this sensitive sector.

The Diefenbaker government did try to develop new areas of production in the economy in this period. It came into office in 1957, trumpeting the idea of a northern vision, including a "Roads to Resources" proposal. This idea essentially involved overseeing the construction of expensive infrastructure to open up the supposed vast economic potential of the Canadian North. Some facilities were built, and some new resource projects were begun, but, generally, the scheme came to little, given the economic realities of the time. There were other projects, such as the South Saskatchewan River Dam, price supports for agricultural products, winter-works grants, and an attempt to develop European and Commonwealth trade. One of the most promising areas, especially for the Prairies, was the successful sale of wheat to China, the Cold War notwithstanding.

Stabilization Policy, 1957–1961

The period from 1957 to 1961 ranks as one of the most interesting in the postwar period in terms of stabilization policy. It was the first evidence of what was to become known later as stagflation — a simultaneous rise in both inflation and unemployment. The government, and some economists, interpreted this phenomenon as implying that the problems were structural rather than cyclical. Labour demand and labour supply were becoming increasingly mismatched, as a result of technical change and related factors. The solution, accordingly, was seen to lie in labour policies, such as those for winter works mentioned above, and in retraining and education. Partly as a result of this view, fiscal policy was not used expressly in a counter-cyclical fashion. Finance minister Donald Fleming attempted consistently to run a balanced budget, although the poor economic conditions meant this goal was never achieved. Only in 1961 and 1962 did he propose to use spending and taxation to create jobs and reduce unemployment, but by that time both the recession and the Progressive Conservatives' political time were coming to an end.

Monetary policy dominated professional and even public discussion. Monetary policy was restrictive for the first three-quarters of 1957, before becoming appropriately expansionary for the last quarter and for most of 1958. Difficulties soon arose, however. A massive amount of wartime debt was coming due in 1958. The government opted to refinance the entire amount through the issuing of new debt — the so-called conversion loan of 1958. The refinancing was carried out, but only by increasing the average maturity of the debt significantly, driving up interest rates and offsetting attempts to expand the economy.

This problem was compounded in the next two years by the decision by James Coyne, governor of the Bank of Canada, to adopt an extremely restrictive monetary stance. Money-supply growth virtually ceased, and interest rates rose from 1959 through to mid-1961. High interest rates, in turn, attracted short-term capital inflows, driving up the Canadian dollar and further dampening economic growth. A very public dispute arose between the governor and the government over the appropriateness of this policy and over who had ultimate responsibility for the conduct of monetary policy. The confrontation ended with Coyne's forced resignation in July 1961, but only after considerable uncertainty in Canadian financial markets and untold political embarrassment to the government.

An Extended Boom, 1962–1973

The economy took a significant turn for the better after 1961 (Figure 19.1). Real GNP grew at 7.1 percent in 1962, compared with the average of 2.9 percent from 1957 to 1961. Except in 1967 and 1970, when growth slowed momentarily, GNP expanded by between 5.2 and 7.7 percent every year until 1973, creating the longest sustained boom in modern times. Unemployment, which had been over 7 percent in 1961, fell to below 4 percent in 1966, before creeping up to over 6 percent by the early 1970s. The move to full employment was reflected in the inflation rate. Consumer prices were rising at less than 1 percent in 1961, but increased to over 4 percent by the end of the 1960s, and were at 7.7 percent in 1973, after slowing somewhat in 1970 and 1971.

All components of aggregate demand contributed to this boom. Consumption demand was strong in every year except 1970, and then rose again until 1973. Exports were especially robust, compared with earlier years. After a slow start in 1962, they rose by over 9 percent in real terms in 1963, and by over 13 percent the next year. A slight weakening in 1965 was followed by five buoyant years, a slackening in 1971, and two expansions thereafter.

Mild bouts of inflation notwithstanding, the 1960s and early 1970s were prosperous years, and this prosperity was reflected in the rising levels of consumption. Between 1963 and 1973, retail sales increased more than $20 billion, and automobile registrations by 40 percent. Dwelling starts went from an already healthy 150 000 in 1962 to an amazing 268 000 a decade later. Even that figure understates the change, for houses were steadily increasing in size and amenities.[5] Affluence and a changing job market also meant that more Canadians could proceed to higher education than ever before. Undergraduate enrolment at universities more than doubled, to nearly 285 000 students — more than quadruple the number at the beginning of the 1950s. Very real poverty still existed, but Canadians, as a group, were enjoying a level of prosperity that was unparalleled in their history.

Several factors contributed to the strength and duration of this economic expansion. Some of the economic prosperity evident in Europe spilled over into Canada. The most obvious explanation, though, is the vigorous, sustained, and broadly based boom that was under way in the United States, aided in the early years by tax cuts and other stimulative policies, and in later ones by spending on the Vietnam War. The devaluation of the Canadian dollar to 92.5 cents (U.S.) in 1962 and its pegging at that level gave Canadian products, manufactured ones in particular, a competitive edge in U.S. markets. Large wheat sales to China and the Soviet Union brought the agricultural sector out of the generally flat state it had been in since 1952. Large public-sector spending on educational facilities to deal with the children of the baby boom continued, much of it now targeted at universities.

Another new staple developed at this time as well. Saskatchewan potash reserves had been known for some time, but technical difficulties had interfered with all attempts to exploit them. A solution to the flooding problem allowed the first mine to open at Esterhazy in 1962. Nine others followed, the last being completed in 1970. Production rose from nothing in 1961 to 3.6 million tons in 1970. Output was mainly (about 95 percent) for export to the United States for use in fertilizer production, although there were some sales to Ontario and Quebec and to Pacific Rim nations. Production capacity increased much faster than demand, and the industry operated well below its potential throughout the decade.

The petroleum sector grew steadily in these years, buoyed by the generally prosperous times and the support of the NOP. Output of crude oil rose from 189.5 million barrels in 1960, to 350 million in 1967, and to 654.3 million in 1973. Exports rose consistently as well, from only 42.2 million barrels in 1960 to 414.4 million in 1973. Natural-gas production and exports grew apace. Permission had been granted in 1962 to build a 31 500-barrel-per-day oilsands plant in Fort McMurray, Alberta. It began operation in 1967 as the world's first "oil mine," but was plagued by a host of technical problems and showed continued losses until 1974, when oil prices improved.

The most notable development in the manufacturing sector in this period undoubtedly was the Auto Pact. In the early 1960s, the Canadian auto industry was a high-cost miniature replica of its U.S. counterpart. Branch plants of the Big Three American companies assembled the full range of automobiles in Canada behind a tariff wall of 17.5 percent. Auto-parts imports faced a duty of the same level as well unless certain Canadian-content rules were met, in which case the parts came in duty-free. The American duty was lower, at 6.5–8.5 percent, but was still high enough to shut out assembly in Canada for export. Prices for automobiles were about 10 percent higher in Canada than in the United States, and Canadian wages were around 30 percent lower.

A royal commission (the Bladen Commission), charged in 1961 with looking into the industry, recommended an extension of the Canadian-content definition as a means of promoting production for export. The government opted, instead, for an extended-duty remission plan, whereby duties paid by the firms were returned according to the increase in parts exports reported. U.S. authorities responded by initiating a countervail hearing, charging unfair export subsidies. A frenzy of political negotiations followed, resulting in an agreement signed by Prime Minister Lester Pearson and President Lyndon Johnson in January 1965.

The agreement brought about duty-free trade in new vehicles and parts between Canada and the United States, but, at Canadian insistence, only for vehicle manufacturers. There was a 50 percent North American content provision in the agreement, and some safeguards to Canadian parts producers. More significant, though, were letters of agreement that the Canadian government managed to obtained from the Big Three auto producers, guaranteeing minimum levels of production in Canada.

The agreement had an immediate and dramatic impact on automobile and parts production in Canada. In 1965, motor vehicles and parts surpassed pulp and paper, in terms of value of shipments, to become Canada's most important industry. The increase took the form of an integration of the North American market. Imports of vehicles from the United States accounted for 40 percent of the Canadian market in 1968, compared with just 3 percent in 1964. Of vehicles produced in Canada in 1968, 60 percent were exported to the United States, compared with 7 percent four years earlier. The number of lines produced in Canada decreased, but the production of retained lines jumped sharply to take advantage of scale economies. Automobiles and parts became the leading item in Canada's trade accounts and made up most of the increase in finished manufactured products. Auto prices became more nearly even between the two countries, and the wages of Canadian auto workers rose to equal those of their American counterparts.

Stabilization Policy, 1961–1973

Fiscal and monetary policies operated more consistently after James Coyne was replaced as governor by Louis Rasminsky. The first Liberal budget in June 1963, by finance minister Walter Gordon, aimed at reducing the deficit, and was, thus, mildly contractionary. It is better known, though, for its attempts to limit the flow of foreign capital into Canada by imposing special taxes on foreign takeovers and on foreign firms operating here. The measures were so widely condemned that they were withdrawn shortly afterward. The next three budgets were neutral, or slightly expansionary, reflecting the buoyant economic times. Inflation was a problem by 1966 (the government had already asked the Economic Council of Canada to look at inflation in the economy, in 1965), so the budget of that year was mildly contractionary. A brief slowdown in 1967 prompted a more expansionary budget, but this was quickly corrected as the temporary nature of the slowdown was recognized.

Inflation was the explicit concern of the budgets of 1968 and 1969. A ceiling was placed on expenditure increases, civil-service hiring was frozen, and a tax surcharge was imposed. Further measures were adopted in 1969, as the government announced that it "really meant business." The stance was eased slightly in March 1970 in the face of the apparent slowdown in economic activity, and was reversed in December of that year, as concern shifted to rising unemployment. Additional funds were poured into high-unemployment areas, unemployment-insurance benefits were increased, and incentives were offered to encourage business investment.

Concern with unemployment continued in the next three budgets, as the government interpreted record levels of unemployment as indicating substantial excess capacity in the economy. The 1971 budget was substantially more expansionary than that of the preceding year, the most notable provision being the substantial extension and broadening of unemployment-insurance benefits. Job creation was recognized as the most urgent priority in May 1972, as additional tax and expenditure measures were introduced. This period ends with a budget in February 1973 that was described by finance minister John Turner as "strongly expansionary." Taxes were cut, expenditures were increased, and a number of tariff and excise taxes were reduced to ease inflationary pressures.

386

Monetary policy was expansionary in the early years of the expansion as well. This stance was changing by the spring of 1965, as inflationary pressures became evident. Policy became restrictive for the remainder of the decade, except during a brief period from mid-1966 to early 1967, and again in mid-1968, as the economy softened temporarily.

Two factors prevented the bank from exercising the degree of restraint it wished in these years, however. As is well understood now, but was only imperfectly so at the time, a small open economy such as Canada's cannot maintain both a fixed exchange rate and an inflation rate different from that of its major trading partners. To understand this dilemma, consider the situation facing the bank as it attempted to deal with inflationary pressures in the late 1960s. Tighter credit conditions led to higher interest rates, which meant short-term foreign capital was attracted to Canada. As the demand for Canadian dollars grew, the central bank had to intervene to keep the dollar fixed, which meant that the initial attempt to restrict the growth of the money supply was offset.

To exacerbate this problem, Canada had agreed, in 1962, to a ceiling on its holding of foreign-exchange reserves in return for exemption from the U.S. Interest Equalization Tax. This provision meant that Canadian interest rates could not rise above those in the United States since the bank was constrained in the volume of U.S. dollars it could purchase to keep the dollar pegged. The result of these two factors was that the money supply grew much faster in the late 1960s than was warranted by the inflationary pressures, and in spite of the declared intentions of the bank to restrain inflation.

Pressure built up on the Canadian dollar to the point that the authorities decided to unpeg it in May 1970. It appreciated immediately, reaching par with the U.S. dollar in 1971, and rising to a premium for the next few years. This decision was anti-inflationary in two respects. Appreciation reduces pressures of aggregate demand on supply, and it lowers the price of imported goods and services that figure prominently in the Canadian consumer price index. It also makes monetary policy an especially effective policy tool. The capital flows induced by monetary tightening put further pressure on the dollar, which complements the anti-inflationary effects of the higher interest rates.

Unfortunately, Canadian authorities did not avail themselves of this opportunity to reduce inflationary pressures. Inflation did come down in 1970, a direct reflection of the appreciation. But the money supply grew very rapidly, from the float through to 1975, in the range of 10–15 percent. There are two explanations for this seemingly perverse behaviour. Like the fiscal authorities, the bank was misled into thinking that the unemployment statistics indicated excess slack in the economy when they really were showing a change in the nature of declared unemployment. There is also some indication that the bank was under pressure to prevent too much appreciation of the dollar, meaning that interest rates could not be allowed to rise as much as purely anti-inflationary objectives demanded. Whatever the reason, most analysts now believe that this excessive growth in the money supply fuelled the inflationary pressures that mark the beginning of the next period of our chronology.

Conclusion

Overall, Canada was by the beginning of the 1970s a much richer nation with a much-altered economy. It is important not to forget what this means in human terms. The standard of living, as measured by real per capita income, had more than doubled in a generation, and this was reflected in the vast array of consumer goods that the middle-class family of 1970 owned. As late as 1941, many standard conveniences, long available technologically, were not common properties for Canadians. Most Canadians (four out of five) still had ice boxes, and the vast majority (nine out of ten) used coal or wood as a heating source. A bare majority (six out of ten) had piped water in their houses, but fewer than half had a bath or shower. Even the flush toilet was far from universal; just over half of Canadian dwellings possessed one.[6] There were about a million automobile registrations, or one for every eight Canadians.

By 1970, central heating, electric appliances, and hot and cold running water were available to all but the very poor or most remote locales in society. Automobile registration quadrupled from war's end to 1965, and the car was now, like the home conveniences mentioned above, available to all but the very poor. Two-and even three-automobile families were no longer a rarity.

An indirect measure of the economic growth of Canada is also important. Between 1945 and 1976, average life expectancy increased by 5.5 years for men and 9.5 years for women. Part of this increase was due to medical discoveries such as the polio vaccine, but medical technology was only part of the story. Growth meant that there were more and better-trained medical personnel, better-equipped hospitals, and, after the mid-1960s, a universal and government-supported health-care system. These social benefits of wealth accumulation were the other side of the two-car garages and television sets that dotted the nation.

Still, there were problems. The very prosperity of the 1960s made poverty all the more stark by contrast. Social reforms (like medicare) sought to spread the prosperity outward, but critics pointed out that income disparity remained as great as it had been two decades earlier. Some groups, such as the Native population, seemed to have benefited little if at all from the prosperity of recent years. Such concerns put pressure on governments to find more effective means of using accumulated wealth to resolve disparities within society. Moreover, advances in the field of economic planning increased expectations that the government should have the expertise to find solutions to such problems. Thus the issue of what governments should do and how they should do it forms a significant part of the history of the Canadian economy after World War II. It is to these issues that we now turn.

NOTES

1. The data are from Canada, Department of Finance, *Economic and Fiscal Reference Tables*, various issues.
2. Chapter 3, "Gender, Keynes and Reconstruction," in Joy Parr, *Domestic Goods: The Material, the Moral and the Economic in the Postwar Years* (Toronto: University of Toronto Press, 1999).
3. Canada, *Report of the Royal Commission on Canada's Economic Prospects* (Ottawa, 1957). See also Lawrence Aronsen, "An Open Door to the North: The Liberal Government and the Expansion of American Foreign Investment, 1945–1953," *American Review of Canadian Studies* (Summer 1992): 167–97.
4. "The Huge Demand for New Schools," *Financial Post*, February 18, 1956, 52.
5. John R. Miron, *Housing in Postwar Canada* (Montreal and Kingston: McGill–Queen's University Press, 1988), 175.
6. John R. Miron, *Housing in Postwar Canada: Demographic Change, Household Formation, and Housing Demand* (Montreal and Kingston: McGill–Queen's University Press, 1988), 183–87.

FURTHER READING

Bothwell, Robert, Ian Drummond, and John English. *Canada Since 1945: Power, Politics, and Provincialism*, 2nd ed. Toronto: University of Toronto Press, 1989.

Campbell, Robert M. *Grand Illusions: The Politics of the Keynesian Experience in Canada, 1945–1975*. Peterborough: Broadview Press, 1987.

Canada. Royal Commission on the Economic Union and Development Prospects for Canada. *Report*, vols. 1–3. Ottawa: Supply and Services, 1985. See also the 72 research volumes published in conjunction with the commission's report.

Economic Council of Canada. *Annual Review* (annual issues beginning in 1964).

McDougall, John M. *Fuels and the National Policy*. Toronto: Butterworths, 1982.

Simeon, Richard, and Ian Robinson. *State, Society, and the Development of Canadian Federalism*. Toronto: University of Toronto Press, 1990.

Chapter Twenty

Policy Innovation, 1946–1973

Canadians responded well to the opportunities available in the 25 years after World War II. They were able to marshal the requisite supplies of capital, labour, and technology and to allocate them to meet the growing demand for their goods and services. For the most part, this supply response was market-driven. In some instances, however, government policies facilitated the growth or shaped it in particular ways. Some measures, such as immigration and foreign-investment policies, were aimed at increasing the supply of factors, with a view to promoting extensive growth. Others, for example commercial and transportation policies, were aimed more at increasing the efficiency with which capital and labour, domestic or foreign, were allocated within the economy.

Still other policies introduced after 1946 were less attempts to promote economic growth than they were moves to take advantage of it. There was a determination to use the apparatus of the state to provide for the health, education, and income-security needs of individual Canadians, coming out of the experiences of the Great Depression and World War II. Regional economic disparities, long a feature of the federation and occasionally the target of isolated and ad hoc policy responses, became a major policy concern. This new, or at least intensified, commitment to seeking equity reflected the prosperity of the time and the growing fiscal resources of the state. Redistribution is more palatable politically in an expanding economy than in a stagnant or shrinking one, as experience after 1973 would show.

Aggregate Supply Policies

Canada was a net exporter of capital from the outbreak of World War I until the end of World War II. This trend was reversed after 1950. Canadian savings grew, as population and incomes did, but they were not sufficient to finance the high rates of investment taking place. Net capital inflow was highest during the 1950s. It fell off, in relative terms, thereafter, even becoming negative (Canada was again a net capital exporter for a couple of years in the early 1970s, and again in 1982). Even at its highest point, though, foreign capital's relative position fell far short of the levels it reached in the first fifteen years of the twentieth century.

This foreign investment was different from that received earlier in Canada's history in two important senses. First, it was predominantly American in origin. Second, and related to the first observation, it was predominantly direct (equity) as opposed to portfolio (bonds and other financial instruments), with the result that control usually resided with the foreign investor. The great surge in investment came in the 1950s; by 1960, the basic patterns were set — 80 percent of the capital was held by Americans; 60 percent of Canadian manufacturing was foreign-controlled, including 75 percent of oil and gas and 60 percent of mining, but a minuscule amount of railways and utilities. Within manufacturing, foreign control ranged from almost none in some sectors to nearly all the assets in others. Investment continued after 1960, but it was more or less in step with the growth in the economy. Canadians invested abroad at the same time as foreign savings were entering the country; the capital flow was not all one way.

Foreign capital entered Canada to take advantage of the earnings opportunities available, but that entry was facilitated by a relatively liberal policy. With a few notable exceptions, such as financial institutions and utilities, foreign capital was welcomed in the 1950s; indeed, it was eagerly sought. This open stance came under considerable scrutiny in the late 1960s and early 1970s. The Watkins Report in 1968 and the Gray Report in 1972 focused on what they saw as the costs (economic and political–cultural) of reliance on foreign investment. These concerns, and the political support they generated, led to the creation of the Canada Development Corporation (CDC) in 1971 and the Foreign Investment Review Agency (FIRA) in 1973. The CDC was intended to promote investments by Canadians in Canadian companies. FIRA's mandate was to screen new foreign investments to determine whether they were of significant benefit to the Canadian economy. "Benefit" was defined by five specific criteria. FIRA was criticized from the outset, both by those who saw it as unnecessarily constraining necessary foreign investment and by those who saw it as an ineffective guardian of Canadian interests.

The supply of labour to the economy grew over time in three separate ways — in domestic population, in immigration, and in increases in participation rates. As mentioned earlier, Canada experienced a baby boom in the immediate postwar years, with births running at 27 to 28 per 1000 population (see Figure 19.2). These began to decline by the late 1950s, falling to 15.6 per 1000 by 1973. Death rates declined slowly but continuously throughout. These trends in birth and death rates altered the age structure of the population notably. The proportion of the population aged 0–14 grew rapidly between 1941 and 1961, but fell off thereafter and, in 1981, was below its 1941 level. Not surprisingly, those aged 15–24 increased in relative importance after 1961, and those aged 25–64 after 1971. Persons aged 65 and over rose in relative importance throughout.

The second source of the requisite labour skills was immigration. Mainly, immigrants respond to economic incentives in the receiving country relative to those in their home country. Canada was growing rapidly in these years, creating both high and rising wages and employment opportunities, and was thus an attractive destination. Its political stability and generally high quality of life merely added to its attractive powers.

Canada's policy facilitated this immigration, but only after it adjusted to take account of changing conditions in the world supply of immigrants. As seen earlier, the policy to 1930 was aimed at populating the farms, mines, and woods of the nation with workers that were as white and as British as possible. Restrictions on immigration had been tightened in the Great Depression and in wartime, but these were gradually loosened after 1946, as the demand for labour grew faster than did internal supplies. Sponsorship privileges were widened, preference was extended to unskilled and general labourers (though ethnic-group restrictions still applied), and most-preferred status was accorded to citizens of France in 1948 and to those of Germany and Italy in 1950.

Regulations were further loosened in the early 1950s. The inflow of displaced persons had largely ceased in 1953, although an estimated 32 000 Hungarians were admitted in 1957, following an unsuccessful attempt at revolution in their country. The overall immigration stance was definitely expansionary in the mid-1950s, reflecting the economic boom that was under way. An interesting debate went on at this time over the correct posture to take with respect to immigration. One view, associated since with the Department of Labour, was that flows should be tuned to reflect the short-term requirements of the labour market. The other perspective, held by the Department of Citizenship and Immigration, was that the policy must be longer-term and structural in nature, ignoring temporary shortages or surpluses of labour.

A major shift in the orientation of Canadian immigration policy came after 1956. The expansionary stance began to change as unemployment rates crept up. Now there was an abundance of unskilled workers but a continuing shortage of skilled ones, professionals, and entrepreneurs with capital. Numbers needed to be regulated, and the skill composition changed. The ethnic composition had to change as well. Whatever genuine embarrassment there was with Canada's overtly racist policy at this time, there was also a practical consideration. Supplies from traditional sending areas were drying up, as economic expansion in Europe continued. There was no choice but to move to other areas of the world for the type of immigrant needed.

The new policy came by order-in-council in 1962. Emphasis was put on immigration of professionals and other highly skilled immigrants. Unskilled ones were discouraged. National preferences were also abolished; entrance, in principle at least, was open to anyone meeting the skill qualifications. A new department was created in 1965, and a formal credits system introduced in 1967. Candidates could earn points up to some maximum in each of several categories. The criteria were a blend of the two perspectives mentioned above. Some were identifiably short-term in outlook, intended to adjust supplies to current labour-market conditions. Others were longer-term in nature, with the emphasis on skills.

The third component of the increase in labour supply was a rise in the overall participation rate, almost entirely the result of the entrance of large numbers of women and youths into the labour force. Figure 20.1 shows the trends. The participation rate for men aged 25–54 remained roughly constant, at around 95 percent. Those for youths aged 15–24 and for women 25–54 rose dramatically, from 55 percent to nearly 70 percent for the former and from less than 40 percent to nearly 70 percent for the latter. Put differently: males held more than three-quarters of the jobs in the economy in 1956, about two-thirds of them in 1973, and fewer than 60 percent in 1983.[1]

These shifts in participation rates were partly an economic phenomenon, as women and youths responded to the new types of jobs available and to the higher wages they offered. Nearly half the jobs held by females in 1983 were in personal and business services, and another 18 percent were in wholesale and retail trade. Only in finance, insurance, and real estate and in personal and business services were women the majority of workers. The changes in female participation rates were partly social in origin as well, reflecting changing attitudes of women toward the home and the workplace. By increasing the total labour supply and by altering its age and skill mix, these changes in participation rates are as much a contributor to the postwar economic record as a reflection of it.

The efficiency of the economy was enhanced to an uncertain extent by a series of policy initiatives designed to affect the allocation of resources in the economy. Commercial policy is a prime example. Canada was well situated to prosper from the liberalization of the international economic environment taking place after 1945, which explains, in part, why this nation was so active and visible in the reconstruction efforts. The last of the wartime foreign-exchange restrictions were gone by the early 1950s, as noted above. That left tariffs and other trade barriers, and here the process was both slower and more complicated than for exchange restrictions.

Figure 20.1 Participation Rates among Certain Demographic Groups, Canada, 1966–1983

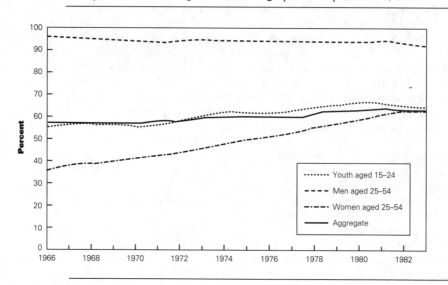

Source: Canada, Privy Council Office Royal Commission on the Economic Union and Development Prospects for Canada, *Report*, vol. 2 (Ottawa: Supply and Services, 1985), p. 16, Reproduced with the permission of the Minister of Supply and Services Canada, 1995.

Canada signed the GATT agreement in October 1947. Interestingly, however, the first substantive move to liberalize trade came not in a multilateral but rather a bilateral framework. In one of the lesser-known stories of the immediate postwar period, Canadian negotiators, with the explicit blessing of Prime Minister Mackenzie King and his important advisers, obtained a general trade agreement with their American counterparts. All duties between the two countries were to be removed immediately, quantitative restrictions on imports were to disappear over a five-year period (with important exceptions on both sides), and there was to be joint consultation on agricultural marketing. But, at the last moment, the prime minister, fearing a political backlash on the political implications of turning to the Americans and away from the British, vetoed the proposal. Forty years later it would be taken up again, and this time it would go through.

Canada participated in the early GATT rounds, although not much progress was made. The Kennedy Round, beginning in Geneva in 1964, was more successful. Canada objected to the concept of linear tariff reductions (50 percent across the board) introduced at that time, on the grounds that the system worked against countries dependent on raw-material exports and manufactured imports. Canada preferred to negotiate, instead, on a product-by-product basis, a position reluctantly agreed to by the other participants. The end result was that Canada made concessions on some $2.5 billion of imports, about $2 billion of which were from the United States, in exchange for concessions of a similar amount by the Americans.[2]

As a result of Canada's participation in these GATT rounds, its tariff levels came down significantly. The ratio of duty collected to total imports stood at 11.1 percent in 1945, at 9.7 percent in 1960, and at 6.4 percent in 1970. This large drop in average protection came

Officials of the Canadian Embassy process visa applications from Hungarian refugees after the Hungarian Revolution. In 1957, an estimated 32 000 Hungarians were admitted to Canada, reflecting the expansionary immigration policy of the mid-1950s—a result of the economic boom that was then under way. However, this policy began to change after 1956, when unemployment rates crept up.

National Archives of Canada/C-7108.

about, in part, from a reduction in tariff levels on dutiable imports and, in part, from an extension of the range of items admitted duty free. Duty collected as a percentage of dutiable imports was 21.1 percent in 1945, 17.7 percent in 1960, and 15.2 percent in 1970. At war's end, 40 percent of imports entered duty free. In 1960, 44 percent did and, in 1970, nearly 60 percent.[3]

Transportation issues have always loomed large in Canadian policy debates, and the postwar period was no exception. A major change in policy toward the railways came in 1967 with the passage of the National Transportation Act. Believing that developments in trucking had introduced competition where there had been little or none before, the government gave the railways considerably more freedom to set rates according to market considerations. There were exceptions, the most notable of which were the retention of the statutory grain rates and the controls on the abandonment of prairie branch lines. All provinces but Alberta regulated the entry and operation of trucking within their jurisdictions, and Ottawa set out the terms for interprovincial hauls. Airlines were tightly regulated, through control over fare schedules and routes.

Two policy areas of much smoke but no fire were tax reform and competition policy. The Royal Commission on Taxation (the Carter Commission) recommended a fundamental restructuring of the Canadian tax system in its report, published in 1967. The reforms did not survive the lobbying pressures they encountered, though, and little change was made. Similarly, studies of competition policy and proposals for reform met stiff opposition and were abandoned, with little or no legislative changes.

Provinces were active in promoting economic development as well. Like the national government, they intervened with tax incentives, subsidies, and regulations to increase the amount of economic activity within the province. Some, notably the smaller ones, were as intent on affecting the mix of activity, to diversify away from what they saw as excessive dependence on a few cyclically unstable resource industries. These efforts attracted little attention in the 1960s and early 1970s, but became the focus of a major policy debate a decade later.

Seeking Equity

The period from 1945 to 1973 was exceptional in one way, if in no other. Most of the social policies and regional-development commitments now taken for granted as an essential part of the Canadian fabric had their beginnings in these years. Federal and provincial governments played a relatively small role in these areas before the Great Depression. Welfare was a private responsibility, assisted by churches and other charitable institutions, and, as a last resort, by municipalities. Attitudes changed significantly during the Great Depression, however; the state was forced to take a more active role in managing the economy and in providing relief to the unfortunate. These tasks increasingly fell to the federal government.

There were some joint federal–provincial education and retraining programs after World War I, a variety of workers' compensation schemes, and mothers' pensions in some of the provinces. The most notable achievement, perhaps, was the introduction of old-age pensions in 1927; Ottawa and the provinces shared the costs of providing pensions to those over age 70 who met certain residence requirements and income restrictions. The federal share of old-age pensions was raised to 75 percent in 1931 as an inducement to provinces not yet in the scheme, and assistance was extended to blind persons in 1939. Further progress was stalled by constitutional challenges, and then by the emergencies of war, but was not completely halted. A constitutional amendment was secured in 1940 to allow the federal government to implement contributory unemployment insurance, and a national scheme was introduced the following year. Family-allowance payments were begun in 1944, introducing the country's first universal welfare-payment program.

Enthusiasm for social-policy reform was high coming out of the war, but political and constitutional realities soon resurfaced. The Veterans' Rehabilitation Act was passed in 1945 to provide educational benefits to returning veterans. Federal civil servants had drawn up a blueprint for a postwar social-policy system in a document known as the Green Book proposals, and the Conference on Reconstruction was convened in Ottawa in 1945 to discuss them. The provinces, or at least the larger and wealthier ones, immediately rejected these proposals, as they did those put forward in 1946 at a reconvened session. Hopes for any type of comprehensive national social policy were emphatically quashed. Henceforth, social-policy formation was to be as much an exercise in federal–provincial relations as it was in program design.

The next 25 years or so saw a bewildering series of proposals, negotiations, counterproposals, more negotiations, program implementations, and program redesigns. To make some sense of the sequence, it helps to keep a few general points in mind. It is useful to know, first, that, while there are a great many programs, each with its own acronym, they fall broadly into three types: education and occupational training, health and hospitalization insurance, and income security. The "income security" category can be further subdivided into four types of policies, each with its own objectives.[4] Some programs (demogrants) apply to all Canadians who fall into certain classes, such as those based on age, irrespective of income or anything else. Family allowances and old-age security are examples. Another type, such as guaranteed income supplements, provide income assistance to those meeting means tests. A third type of program is aimed at particular groups in society, such as the blind and disabled. The final type is social insurance, which provides benefits in times of need, based on contributions during working years. The Canada and Quebec pension plans and unemployment insurance are examples.

The second essential point is to understand the challenge policy-makers faced. Everyone's objective was to provide health, education, and income security to individual Canadians. The only question was how to do it. Secondary motives, such as political and bureaucratic rivalry — which were certainly present — aside, both Ottawa and at least some provincial governments felt they should have the paramount role. Ottawa was interested in national standards and transferability among provinces. The provinces claimed the constitutional right that was certainly theirs, but also wanted the freedom to tailor policies to meet their own particular needs. Manitoba Premier Stuart Garson commented in 1946, "A very substantial part of this increase [in expenditure] must come under provincial jurisdiction, namely in education, health and public welfare, natural resource development, road building, provincial public works."[5] Such a shopping list made provincial claims on the public purse a central part of postwar development of social programs.

The need to compromise brings up the third, and final, point. Social-policy formation in Canada was inextricably bound up with federal–provincial fiscal arrangements. To understand the sequence of development, then, one must have some notion of developments in this most complex and arcane area.

The federal government took over exclusive authority for personal and corporate income taxes and succession duties during World War II, providing compensation to the provinces in the form of unconditional transfers. The first postwar arrangements, in 1947, continued this format. Ottawa offered to "rent" exclusive access to personal and corporate income taxes and succession duties. Provincial governments that agreed not to exercise their constitutional rights to tax in these areas received transfers from Ottawa. Provinces could remain outside the scheme, in which case the federal government offered tax credits to their residents. Seven provinces signed up for the scheme in 1947, while Ontario and Quebec opted to impose their own corporate tax. The same basic system was implemented again in 1952, with Ontario joining in for personal income tax this time but Quebec remaining entirely outside.

Tax rentals were replaced in 1957 by tax sharing. Ottawa still collected all the personal and corporate income taxes and succession duties for provinces participating in the scheme. The new feature was that payments to each province in lieu of levying their own taxes were geared to the revenue Ottawa actually collected in that province. Transfers were set at 10 percent of the personal income tax collected in the province, 9 percent of the taxable income of corporations, and 50 percent of the succession duties collected. As before, provinces not agreeing to the scheme received tax abatements of the same amount, providing them with the room to levy their own charges. Eight provinces took up the complete offer; Ontario agreed to the guidelines for personal income taxes, but levied its own corporate income tax and succession duties; Quebec levied all three taxes itself.

This change in the basis of the tax-rental payment opened up a new issue in federal–provincial fiscal relations — that of differential tax-revenue capacities among provincial governments. As long as rental payments were made on a per capita basis, the fact that some provinces were wealthier than others, and thus had richer tax bases than

396

others, made little difference. Once payments were expressed as a share of revenue actually collected in the province, though, the rough equity disappeared; for example, 10 percent of personal income tax collected in British Columbia was worth more on a per capita basis than 10 percent of it collected in Newfoundland. The British Columbia government would be in a better position to provide public services to its residents than would Newfoundland, and the principle of general equity among Canadians, regardless of where they lived, would be compromised. Since provinces played a key role in funding social programs, the problem was potentially serious.

The solution was to introduce a formal system of equalization payments, modelled along the lines of the National Adjustment Grants proposed by the Rowell–Sirois Commission nearly twenty years earlier. Briefly, the formula worked as follows: officials first calculated the per capita transfers due to the two wealthiest provinces (Ontario and British Columbia, at this time) under the tax-sharing formula, and then took a weighted average of the two. Each province was then entitled to receive an unconditional transfer in an amount necessary to bring its payment, calculated on its own base over these three tax sources, up to that weighted average. Nine provinces received transfers (only Ontario did not). In this way, the principle that each province should be able to provide services equal to the average Canadian standard without having to resort to taxes of greater-than-average severity was preserved.

A major change in federal–provincial fiscal arrangements came in 1962, when tax-sharing was replaced by tax-collection agreements, instituting the system still in place today. Provinces were required to pass legislation setting their own personal and corporate income-tax rates. In return, Ottawa lowered its rates to give the provinces the "tax room" they needed. The federal government agreed to collect the provincial taxes free of charge if certain conditions were met, the most important being that provincial rates were expressed as a percentage of basic federal tax. Eight provinces agreed to the system for both personal and corporate taxes. Ontario agreed for personal income taxes, but levied and collected its own corporate income tax. Quebec stayed out of the system entirely. Much the same arrangements were set in 1967 and again in 1972.

The basis of equalization was changed in 1962 from that of the two wealthiest provinces to the average of all provinces, and 50 percent of provincial natural-resource revenues were included as part of the tax base. These changes had the effect of removing the two westernmost provinces from the recipient category. The system was further extended in 1967, when equalization entitlements were calculated on the basis of sixteen separate provincial tax sources. A further four categories were added in 1972, and one more in 1973, for a total of 21. Fiscal capacities were calculated for each province for each tax source, and a payment was made only if the sum over all sources was negative. Since the base was intended to be broadly representative of taxes open to provinces, the principle of equalization was more securely met.

With these backgrounds in mind, the sequence of social-policy innovation can be briefly outlined. The first, and perhaps most important, area to be discussed is that of health care. For constitutional reasons, the early efforts came from the provinces. For reasons that are less apparent, but no less fascinating, these were almost entirely in the West.

The first major government initiative came in 1947, when Saskatchewan introduced its Hospital Services Plan. Residents paid a compulsory monthly premium and received, in return, free hospital care. British Columbia followed with a similar scheme in 1948, although it was financed by an increase in the provincial sales tax. The federal government became involved the same year. National health grants were introduced to provide funds to the provinces for health surveys, hospital construction, tuberculosis control, professional training, mental health, cancer control, medical rehabilitation, and children with physical disabilities. All grants were closed-ended. Some required matching contributions by the provinces; others did not. This program is of special note in that the federal–provincial cost-sharing aspect serves as an early indication of the form that social policies were to take over the next two decades. The national health grants were extended in 1953 to cover child- and maternal-health programs.

A major advance in health care came in 1957, with the Hospital Insurance and Diagnostics Services Act. Provinces making in-patient hospital services available upon specified terms and conditions were eligible to receive federal transfers of approximately 50 percent of total outlays. Only five provinces entered the program as it began, although by 1961 all were participating.

Progress toward a comprehensive national health-insurance scheme continued in the 1960s. Once more, Saskatchewan was the pioneer. The CCF government of that province introduced a comprehensive medical-insurance scheme, to come into effect in July 1961. Financing came from increases in provincial sales taxes, personal and corporate income taxes, and from annual premiums. It is, unfortunately, equally famous for the political furor it caused, including a virtually unheard-of event, a doctors' strike. As fondly as the move is now looked upon in the history of Canadian social policy, it is sometimes forgotten that the CCF lost the next election, largely because of the fallout from the medicare issue.

The next step was the appointment of the justly famous Royal Commission on Health Services (the Hall Commission, after Justice Emmett Hall). Its report, issued in 1964, called for a full-scale government-sponsored health-insurance program. The Medical Care Act was passed in 1966, establishing a health-insurance system to come into effect in 1968. It, too, was a shared-cost program. Provinces had to tailor medical-insurance plans to meet federal definitions of universality of coverage, portability of benefits, accessibility without user fees, and administration by a non-profit agency. In return, they were entitled to claim approximately 50 percent of their total expenditures on medical care over the year (the formula was devised in such a way that an individual province could get slightly more or slightly less than 50 percent, depending on its costs relative to the national average).

The net result of these changes was a revolution in government expenditures. Medical care was taken on as a social responsibility, rather than as an individual one. A generation or more of Canadians have since grown up assuming they have a right to free, accessible health care. At the same time, the costs to the public purse have been enormous. Health is now the largest single item in provincial-government expenditures, and fears have been expressed as to whether current levels of health care will be affordable in the face of an aging population.

Education was the next category to receive attention. In 1951, Ottawa began to pay a grant of $0.50 per capita to universities and colleges. Quebec did not allow its institutions to accept the grants, although eventually (in 1960) it did receive a tax abatement as compensation. The net initiative was the Technical and Vocational Training Assistance Act of 1960, which committed federal funds to capital construction and to a wide variety of educational programs. The Canada Student Loans Act was passed in 1964. Under this legislation, the federal government agreed to guarantee loans taken out by students and to pay interest on them while the student was attending school. Quebec did not participate in the plan, but received grants instead.

One other change came as a provision of the 1967 Fiscal Arrangements Act and, in retrospect, can be seen as a forerunner to an important restructuring of the system a decade later. Ottawa ended its system of per capita grants to colleges and universities. In its place, it agreed to pay 50 percent of eligible operating costs of postsecondary institutions, financed in part by a further transfer of tax room to the provinces and in part by cash grants.

398

There were some important changes in the area of income security. Since the British North America Act excluded the federal government from participating in contributory pension schemes, the 1927 legislation was designed as a shared-cost, non-contributory plan. The constraint was removed by a constitutional amendment in 1950; in 1951, the Old Age Security Act was passed. Under this legislation, Ottawa took over sole responsibility for pensions for persons over age 70. The next year, the Old Age Assistance Act was passed, wherein the federal government agreed to pay 50 percent old-age assistance for those aged 65–69, with a means test. A companion act extended pensions to blind persons, continuing a feature of the former Old Age Pension Act. The eligibility age was reduced to 65 years in 1965, to be fully in effect by 1970. Finally, the Guaranteed Income Supplement was introduced in 1967, to add to the incomes of low-income pensioners.

These pensions were all non-contributory. Moves to establish a national contributory plan began with a proposal by Prime Minister Diefenbaker to the provinces in 1962. Negotiations were continued the following year by the new Liberal government, running into opposition from Quebec, which had its own scheme in mind, and Ontario, which favoured reform of private schemes. A series of compromises and modifications followed that overcame Quebec plans. The Canada and Quebec pension plans came into effect in January 1967. Pensions were to be paid from a fund supported by contributions from employers and employees. The fund was to be self-supporting, with early surpluses lent to the provinces (a factor in their decisions to go along with the scheme, no doubt).

There were numerous federal–provincial shared-cost programs based on tests of needs or means in existence by the 1960s. The Canada Assistance Plan was introduced in 1966 to bring separate programs for old-age assistance, blind persons' allowances, allowances to the disabled, and unemployment assistance into one comprehensive package. Ottawa shared the cost of these programs equally, subject only to a few conditions on terms and operations. Analysts ever since have pointed to this plan as one of the more successful of the co-operative social-policy efforts.

The final item to be discussed is that of unemployment insurance. The 1940 plan remained in existence after 1945, and coverage was gradually broadened to include more occupations. A major, and as it turned out, controversial, reform was introduced in 1971: coverage was extended to nearly every worker in the labour force, and the plan was made significantly more generous. The qualifying period for benefits was reduced, benefits were raised, regional and extended benefits were recognized, and sickness and pregnancy were included. The intent was to ease the plight of the unemployed. It did this, but at the cost, subsequent analysis seemed to show, of raising the average unemployment rate.

As this period of Canada's history ended, Canada had in place a comprehensive social-security system. Hospital and medical costs were covered, postsecondary and technical education were being funded, contributory and non-contributory pension plans were in place, special benefits were available to particular groups, and a fairly generous unemployment-insurance scheme was in place. All had been introduced in a uniquely Canadian fashion, through what one influential text termed "federal–provincial diplomacy."[6]

Regional Development and Policy

Social policy is aimed at individuals grouped by categories, such as age or particular need, irrespective of where they may live. It took on a federal–provincial perspective in Canada only for constitutional reasons. Regional-development policy has precisely the opposite perspective: it is aimed at disadvantaged regions, as defined by measures such as average income or unemployment rates, irrespective of the individual incomes within them. As is the case for social policy, though, serious interest in it is a postwar phenomenon.

Figure 20.2 shows GDP per capita by province relative to the Canadian average in 1973. Two observations are obvious. First, there is a considerable difference between the average income of the richest province and that of the poorest. Personal income per capita in Newfoundland in 1973 was 52 percent of the national average, while in Ontario it was 116 percent, more than twice as great. Second, these disparities have not changed much from what they were in 1929 or, for that matter, 1870.

These figures raise two interesting questions: How can the disparity at any time be explained? How can one explain the pattern over time, particularly the remarkable constancy of relative positions? Unfortunately, there are no clear answers to either of these questions. The factors associated with disparities are well known. Low-income regions tend to have a smaller proportion of their population in the 16–64 age category, lower labour-force participation rates, higher unemployment rates, lower wages for given occupations, lower capital–labour ratios, and a slower rate of adopting technical change. However, these are as much symptoms as they are causes of underdevelopment, and, to date, analysts have not made much progress in explaining the spread of earnings disparities.

The constancy in relative positions in the postwar period is surprising, given the type and magnitude of economic change that has taken place. The resource boom of the early 1950s, the stubborn recession that followed, and the boom of the 1960s altered the trend lines only a little, and only temporarily. Aggregate growth rates did differ markedly among provinces. But interregional trade and capital and labour flows were sufficiently responsive to offset

Figure 20.2 GDP per Capita by Province, Relative to Canada, 1973

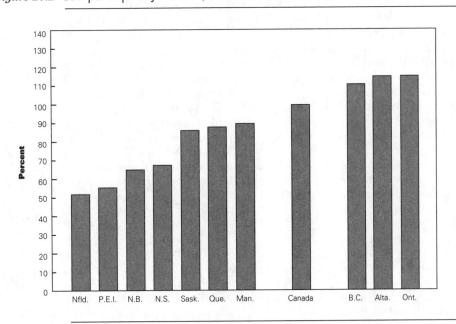

Source: Adapted from Canada, Department of Finance, *Economic and Fiscal Reference Tables* (Ottawa, September 1994), table 8.2, p. 16.

these differences in economic opportunity. Ontario, Alberta, and British Columbia grew faster in these years, but they did not noticeably get relatively richer. Atlantic Canada grew more slowly, but managed to retain its relative living standard.

While concern over the economic fate of lagging regions is as old as Confederation, recognition of the issue reached a new stage with the publication of the Gordon Commission report in 1957. At first, the policy emphasis was on rural poverty. The Agriculture Rehabilitation and Development Act of 1961, which dealt mainly with the utilization of marginal farmland, was superseded in 1964 by the Agriculture and Rural Development Act, which was more explicitly developmental in nature. The Fund for Rural Economic Development carried this orientation even farther, designing economic-development strategies for areas deemed to be "promising" and providing for adjustment assistance for those not so designated.

The scope of regional-development policy soon expanded to focus on particular regions and to include industrial development. The Atlantic region, comprising Canada's poorest provinces, first received explicit attention in 1962 with the establishment of the Atlantic Development Board. It was converted, the next year, from a research and advisory body to one with some program responsibilities and funds to disburse, most of which went to social-infrastructure projects. The Area Development Agency was established in 1963 to promote industrial development in poorer regions. Firms locating in specified areas were eligible for tax benefits and, after the introduction of the Area Development Incentives Act in 1965, for cash grants.

Regional development was given a more focused orientation and a higher profile with the formation of the Department of Regional Economic Expansion (DREE) in 1969 and the appointment of a powerful minister. Certain urban areas in poorer provinces were designated as special areas, qualifying for funds to support the provision of social infrastructure and intended to act as nodes or growth poles around which other developments would cluster. The earlier industrial-subsidy practice was continued under the Regional Development Incentives Act (RDIA), again providing grants and other concessions to firms willing to locate in designated areas of the country.

DREE did not live up to its early expectations, however. It gained a reputation for spending vast sums of money with little appreciable effect on regional disparities. RDIA grants were particularly suspect. Critics claimed that only rarely did they actually influence a location decision; that, when they did, it was to draw a firm from one poor region to another; and that they seriously distorted the allocation of resources. There were also criticisms of its administrative procedures. The provinces found it too centralized and inflexible. Other federal departments with sectoral responsibilities resented DREE's economic-development mandate. What seemed to be good regional-development policy was not always good transportation or agriculture or industrial policy. A change of direction was imminent as the 1970s began.

Conclusion

The period 1946 to 1973 was remarkable for its policy innovation. Governments of the time had two broad aims. First, they wished to facilitate the growth of the Canadian economy, or to shape it in particular ways. To this end, they worked to increase the supplies of capital and labour to the economy, and to increase the efficiency with which these factors were employed. Second, they wished to ensure that the fruits of economic growth were spread as widely as possible. To this end, they introduced a broad range of policy measures to provide for the health, education, and income security needs of Canadians, and to reduce regional economic disparities. By and large, Canadian federalism proved sufficiently flexible to accommodate this policy innovation in the face of inevitable concerns about jurisdiction.

There was considerable controversy surrounding each of these policy initiatives, of course. Likewise, it is always difficult to know to what extent policies affected actual events. Still, this period was one where bureaucrats and citizens alike were generally confident in the abilities of governments to bring about positive changes in the economy and in society. The dramatic events of the next decade, however, were to challenge this optimistic view.

NOTES

1. Royal Commission on the Economic Union and Development Prospects for Canada, *Report*, vol. 2 (Ottawa: Supply and Services, 1985), table 7-10, 20.
2. J.L. Granatstein, "Free Trade Between Canada and the United States: The Issue That Will Not Go Away," in Denis Stairs and Gilbert R. Winham, eds., *The Politics of Canada's Economic Relationship with the United States*, Royal Commission on the Economic Union and Development Prospects for Canada, Research Study no. 29 (Ottawa: Supply and Services, 1985), 45.
3. J. Harvey Perry, *A Fiscal History of Canada: The Postwar Years* (Toronto: Canadian Tax Foundation, 1989), 837.
4. See Keith G. Banting, *The Welfare State and Canadian Federation* (Montreal and Kingston: McGill–Queen's University Press, 1982).
5. Douglas Owram, *The Government Generation: Canadian Intellectuals and the State, 1900–1945* (Toronto: University of Toronto Press, 1986), 324.
6. Richard Simeon, *Federal–Provincial Diplomacy* (Toronto: University of Toronto Press, 1972).

FURTHER READING

Banting, Keith G. *The Welfare State and Canadian Federation*. Montreal and Kingston: McGill–Queen's University Press, 1982.

Courchene, Thomas J. *Equalization Payments: Past, Present and Future*. Toronto: Ontario Economic Council, 1984.

Guest, Dennis. *The Emergence of Social Security in Canada*. Vancouver: University of British Columbia Press, 1980.

Norrie, Kenneth. "Intergovernmental Transfers in Canada: An Historical Perspective on Some Current Policy Choices." In Peter M. Leslie, Kenneth Norrie, and Irene K. Ip, eds., *A Partnership in Trouble: Renegotiating Fiscal Federalism*, Policy Study 18. (Toronto: C.D. Howe Institute, 1993): 87–129.

Owram, Douglas. *Government Generation: Canadian Intellectuals and the State, 1900–1945*. Toronto: University of Toronto Press, 1986.

Perry, J. Harvey. *A Fiscal History of Canada: The Postwar Years*. Toronto: Canadian Tax Foundation, 1989.

Savoie, Donald. *Regional Economic Development: Canada's Search for Solutions*. Toronto: University of Toronto Press, 1986.

Simeon, Richard. *Federal–Provincial Diplomacy*. Toronto: University of Toronto Press, 1972.

Chapter Twenty-One

Economic Challenge and Policy Frustration, 1973–1982

THE DECADE AFTER 1973 was one of the most challenging in Canada's political and economic history. Macroeconomic performance deteriorated markedly and in ways that seemed to contradict current theory about the operation of a modern industrial economy. Growth slowed, leading some to look beyond cyclical factors to fundamental weaknesses in the economy. Policies that were once thought to promote growth or equity were now often thought to do just the opposite. The federal–provincial consensus, which had seemed (more to some than others, admittedly) to facilitate innovative policy formation, disintegrated into regional strife.

Many of Canada's difficulties in this period stemmed from the international economy. As a trading nation, and a small one at that, Canada could not avoid dealing with the growth slowdown and stagflation that were gripping the industrial world. But, as always in its economic history, some developments in this challenging time can be traced to purely domestic factors.

Economic Performance

The macroeconomic record in this period illustrates the extent of the difficulties. Figure 21.1 shows the annual percentage changes in real GDP for these years, with those for the period 1948–73 included for comparison purposes. Real GDP growth fell to 4.4 percent in 1974, from 7.7 percent the year earlier, and to 2.6 percent in 1975. It rose to a respectable 6.2 percent in 1976, but declined thereafter, before actually falling for only the second time since the war, in 1982.

The slow growth was reflected in unemployment rates (Figure P6.2). The unemployed proportion of the labour force jumped from 5.3 percent in 1974 to 6.9 percent the next year, then rose to over 8 percent and finally to 11 percent in 1982. The genesis of the term "stagflation" grew from the fact that consumer prices did not fall, even in the face of this great slack in the economy. The inflation rate jumped to over 10 percent in 1974 and 1975, came down a couple of percentage points to 1979, and then rose again to double-digit levels through to 1982 (Figure P6.3).

Rethinking Stabilization Policy

Canadian policy-makers were as uncertain of how to deal with these new macroeconomic challenges as were their counterparts elsewhere. Allowing the exchange rate to float in

Figure 21.1 Percentage Change in Real GDP, Canada, 1948–1982

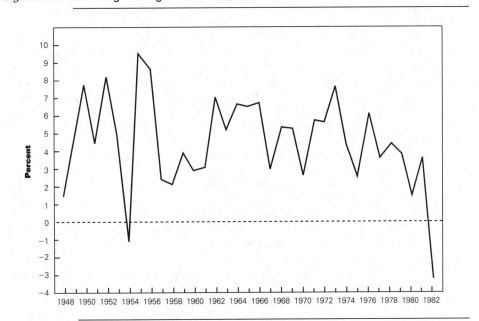

Source: Adapted from Canada, Department of Finance, *Economic and Fiscal Reference Tables* (Ottawa, September 1994), table 4.1, p. 8.

1970 created the opportunity to isolate Canadian price increases from those abroad, which did happen in the first year, as the currency jumped to par with the U.S. dollar. The money supply grew very rapidly for a period thereafter, though, as officials were concerned with preventing a further appreciation of the exchange rate. This fact, combined with generally expansionary fiscal policy, meant that Canadian inflation rates hit double-digit figures by 1975.

Stabilization efforts in this period faced not just slower economic growth but also changes in the underlying structure of the labour market. The natural rate of unemployment (or, in more modern terminology, NAIRU — nonaccelerating inflation rate of unemployment) had risen significantly, although this shift was not recognized at first. Changes in the composition of industry and, hence, in required labour skills, the entrance of women and younger workers into the labour force, and more generous unemployment-insurance benefits added to the numbers of workers reporting spells of unemployment in any period. Attempts to reduce unemployment below this new higher NAIRU through expansionary monetary and fiscal policy in 1973 and 1974 merely exacerbated the inflation rate.

Stabilization policy took two dramatic turns in 1975. The Bank of Canada abandoned its practice of monitoring credit conditions and adopted, in its place, an avowed monetarist approach to monetary policy. In a speech that had been dubbed the "Saskatoon Monetary Manifesto," Bank of Canada Governor Gerald Bouey acknowledged that control of inflation required control of the money supply and, in particular, that the rate of growth of money had to be slowed if inflation were to be lowered. Applying the monetary brakes too rapidly would be disruptive, however, so a policy of monetary gradualism was introduced. Money-supply growth-rate targets were announced, initially in the range of 10–15 percent, to fall to 8–12 percent in 1976 and eventually to 4–8 percent.

A few weeks after the governor's speech, the government announced a comprehensive system of wage and price controls and established the Anti-Inflation Board (AIB) as a monitoring and research agency. Ceilings were imposed on prices and wages for larger firms and in the government sector. The AIB had the power to review wage settlements in larger companies and to roll them back if they were deemed excessive. The board could also monitor price increases and profit margins of the companies and roll these back if warranted. There was a large number of exceptions to this latter provision, however, notably food products and imports.

These anti-inflation policies were only partially successful. The money-supply targets proved notoriously difficult to achieve, partly because the bank continued to pay attention to the value of the exchange rate and partly because of the instability of demand for the money-supply variable (M1) chosen. High interest rates encouraged financial innovation by the banks to the point where the traditional correlation between interest rates and the demand for money, as represented in M1, broke down completely. Subsequent research has shown that the AIB likely had some success in bringing down the rate of increase of money wages and, thus, of inflation. It created considerable social tension in the process, however. It was opposed throughout by the labour movement and eventually ended up being challenged in the Supreme Court of Canada.

It took an international slowdown and the drastic monetary stringency of 1981 to bring inflation really under control. In mid-1981, the Bank of Canada applied the monetary brakes. The nominal stock of money actually fell in the last half of the year, at an annual rate of 14 percent. Interest rates shot up as a direct consequence. The 90-day Treasury bill rate reached 21 percent, creating a large wedge between Canadian and U.S. rates. The depreciation of the dollar was reversed as a result, but at the expense of a significant decline in real economic activity. Inflation declined, and unemployment rose about 12 percent. The Canadian economy entered into what has since been dubbed "the Great Recession."

Another prominent and closely related feature of this period was the secular deterioration of government-budget balances, that of the federal government in particular. Before 1974, as Figure 21.2 illustrates, Ottawa's revenues and expenditures were in approximate balance. After that date, however, rising expenditures coupled with the introduction of de-indexation and tax credits turned the balance consistently negative. The deficit on a national accounts basis was $3.8 billion in 1975, $7.4 billion in 1977, $10.7 billion in 1980, and a whopping $20.3 billion in 1982. Economic views of government deficits slowly altered as a result. Where once it was common to teach that debts governments owed to their own citizens did not matter, now it became fashionable to worry about the distortionary implications of large public-sector borrowing requirements.

Rethinking Framework Policies

As stagflation continued, Canadians, too, began to debate whether the difficulties went beyond a macroeconomic slowdown to reflect a more fundamental productivity decline. To some observers at least, Canada's long-term economic prospects were particularly unfavourable. At issue was the nation's ability to compete successfully in what was widely acknowledged to be an increasingly difficult international economic environment. Those

Figure 21.2 Federal Government Budget Balance (National Accounts Basis), Canada, 1950–1992

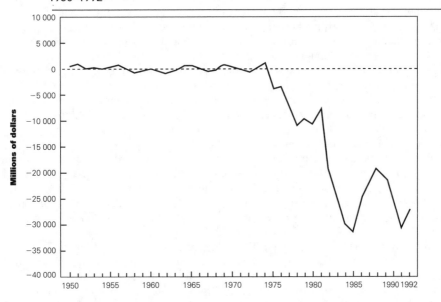

Source: Adapted from Canada, Department of Finance, *Economic and Fiscal Reference Tables* (Ottawa, September 1994), tables 54, 55, pp. 102, 103.

expressing concern saw the difficulties as partly external and partly internal. The obvious external factor was the dramatic success of Japan in making inroads into western markets and, even more ominously perhaps, the appearance of a whole set of Japan imitators known as newly industrializing countries. Japan appeared to have cornered the high-technology end of the market, while the other countries had taken over the production of standard-technology items. Canada was able to secure contracts for some resource products with these nations, but those sales fell far short of the mounting import bill for manufactured products.

The internal factors were related to perceived difficulties with the structure of the Canadian economy. Many felt that Canada's historical advantage in natural-resource industries was ending as it cut the last of the virgin timber, mined the last of the high-quality ore, moved to the Arctic and offshore for its petroleum, and witnessed the salinization of its soils. Other analysts continued to point out that Canada's secondary manufacturing was less efficient than that of its trading partners as a result (depending on the writer) of its tariff policies and those of its trading partners, of government sponsorship, of foreign ownership, or even of the conservatism and myopia of the Canadian business class.

The Canadian manufacturing sector is perceived as weak and problem-plagued, yet that perception is not consistent with reality. Recent work by Ian Keay examines relative productivity of Canadian and American manufacturers at the industry and firm level for much of the twentieth century. Keay finds that while Canadian manufacturing has lower labour productivity than its American counterpart, when measured by total factor productivity there is no evidence of consistent and substantial relative technical inefficiency of Canadian producers.[1] In other work, Keay addresses whether the perceived weaknesses and failures of the Canadian manufacturing sector may be why Canadian per capita incomes have fallen behind American incomes. Once again, Keay's evidence does not support the claims that there are problems with Canadian manufacturers. He finds that for the period 1907 to 1990 Canadian manufacturing firms responded to changes in their input prices in a manner consistent with cost minimization and theories of induced innovation.

Another class of perceived problems with the Canadian economy involves Canadian policy decisions of the past. Some observers see Canada's problems as rooted in the rigidity and inflexibility that decades of well-intentioned but misguided policy interventions had imparted to the economy. Unemployment insurance was the most-often cited of these examples. The increase in benefits and the liberalization in terms introduced in 1971 were held by many to have added one to two points to the unemployment rate by encouraging longer job searches and less interregional and intersectoral mobility. Inappropriately high minimum wages, rent controls, regional-development incentive grants, bailouts of troubled firms, agricultural price supports, trucking regulations, and so forth — all were cited at one time or another as examples of the factors behind the increased rigidity of the economy.

There was considerable debate at this time about the need for a coherent strategy for economic development to overcome these internal and external obstacles. Two main views developed, with the contrast between them marked by the fact that each was associated with a federal government research agency. The Economic Council of Canada considered trade liberalization the best way to bring about the necessary reorganization of industry, with a bilateral Canada–United States free-trade arrangement as the most promising vehicle. Access to the large U.S. market would allow industries in which Canada had a comparative advantage to exploit economies of scale in production and distribution. Those that could not compete after a suitable adjustment period would be phased out of existence.

The Science Council of Canada advocated trade liberalization too, although not of the bilateral variety. Unlike the Economic Council, it wished to develop Canadian industrial expertise through some sort of industrial strategy before entering into such arrangements, rather than relying on the liberalization to achieve it. A wide variety of industrial strategies were proposed, although most contained some element of selecting particular sectors for promotion ("picking winners"), based on assumed comparative advantage, degree of Canadian ownership, or level of technological sophistication. Promotion was to take the form of relaxing anti-combines regulations to allow larger operations, research and development grants, special tax incentives for modernization or Canadianization, and occasionally even public-sector equity and management participation.

Neither proposal attracted Ottawa at this time, or rather both did. Trade liberalization proceeded with Canada's participation in the Tokyo Round of GATT. Negotiations began in 1973, but stalled soon thereafter as a result of political difficulties in the United States and the European Economic Community. When meetings finally resumed, they proceeded quickly, resulting in significant tariff concessions and some progress on non-tariff issues. Reductions commenced in 1980, to be spread over eight years. Once these concessions were in place, a Canadian government study estimated that tariffs on most manufactured goods in Europe and Japan would be around 5–7 percent and those for the United States about 4 percent, and that about 90 percent of current Canadian exports would be entering their markets duty free.[2] The world had come a long way from the prohibitive protection of the 1930s.

The Tokyo Round also paid considerable attention to non-tariff barriers. There was concern that progress made in eliminating duties could be more than offset by nations protecting domestic industries through technical regulations, quotas, customs procedures, and the like. A list prepared by the GATT staff at the time listed 600 separate measures. Progress was sought, and some was achieved, on ways to adjudicate disputes as they arose, so as to avoid retaliatory action. Considerable problems remained, however.

Industrial strategies proved more elusive. The minister of industry, trade and commerce announced intentions of developing a coherent policy in 1972, but nothing specific emerged from this initiative. The Foreign Investment Review Agency (FIRA) was established in 1974 in response to a recommendation of the reports on foreign investment mentioned above. It was empowered to screen takeover proposals above a certain size and to recommend rejection if it felt there were not sufficient demonstrable benefits for Canada. It was also to negotiate to increase these benefits whenever possible. A related initiative was the Canada Development Corporation, established in 1971 to provide a mixed public–private presence in key sectors of the economy.

Pursuit of a comprehensive industrial strategy continued later in the decade with the establishment of 23 sectoral task forces, charged with making recommendations for 21 manufacturing industries, plus construction and tourism. These tier-1 committees were followed by tier-2 ones that concentrated on more broadly based economic strategies rather than on specific sectoral issues. Both measures fell victim to government austerity before they could have any significant legislative impact.

An interesting initiative came at the very end of this period, in November 1981, with the economic statement released as part of the budget of that year. It was based on the view that Canada's economic future lay in its rich natural-resource base. These sectors would be the leading ones around which manufacturing and services would evolve to serve them. Numerous resource megaprojects such as oil-sands plants, offshore exploration and development, pipelines, and hydro-electric developments were envisioned. Soon, however, energy prices began to fall and, with them, the notion that resources could be a permanent leading edge to growth.

Immigration policy underwent a fundamental review in the 1970s as well. A green paper issued in 1975 led, after public debate, to the new Immigration Act in 1978. Compared with previous Canadian immigration policies, this one was relatively restrictive, reflecting, among other things, the much higher unemployment levels of the period. Canadian officials were required, for the first time, to announce target levels, or quotas, for total immigration. The act also linked the volume and composition of the flow of independent or "economic" immigrants to narrowly defined labour-market conditions. Separate provisions applied to family reunification and refugee flows. The point system was retained, and the goal of removing the racial and other discrimination that had dominated early Canadian policies was reaffirmed. With fine-tuning, this system prevails today.

Rethinking Equity

Framework policies were not the only ones to come under scrutiny in the 1970s. Just as a buoyant economy and growing government revenues had facilitated the introduction of a broad range of social and regional-development measures, so too did a slowly growing economy and mounting government deficits lead to pressure for reform and retrenchment. The oil crisis, the Quebec sovereignty-association debate, and other developments so poisoned federal–provincial relations that whatever reform was needed was doubly difficult to achieve.

SOCIAL POLICY

408

With fiscal dividends replaced by large and growing budget deficits, it is not surprising that one of the distinguishing features of the period after 1973 was a retrenchment on the social-policy front. A sweeping social-security review early in the decade proposed the introduction of a guaranteed annual income, for example, but the idea was never acted upon. Family allowances were made more generous in 1973, and the provinces were given more control over the structure of benefits. Refundable child tax credits were introduced in 1979, providing welcome relief to low-income Canadians. Generally, though, it was no longer possible in the climate of the 1970s to attack a problem by throwing public-sector money at it.

The focus in the social-policy area shifted from providing new programs to deciding how existing ones should be funded. The main concern lay with the federal–provincial shared-cost formulae. While, arguably, it had been necessary to circumvent the constitutional roadblock that existed in 1946, neither level of government was happy with this technique in the 1970s. Without the extra revenue from robust economic growth, Ottawa became concerned with the open-ended commitment it had for funding provincially administered programs. Federal officials began to speak of the programs as "established," meaning that more direct responsibility for them could be turned over to the provinces. The provinces, for their part, long had had difficulty with conditional grants, arguing that they forced the federal social-policy agenda upon them and restricted their administrative freedom, once in place.

Ottawa had proposed several times in the 1960s to pull back in the social-policy field, and had even done so, in part, for postsecondary education in 1967. It made good on these proposals in a major way in the 1977 Federal–Provincial Fiscal Arrangements and Established Programs Financing Act. The federal share of the costs of postsecondary education, hospital insurance, and medicare was now to be paid half by cash grants and half by a transfer of tax points to the provinces. This technique made the federal grant a lump-sum one, with the provinces free to allocate these funds among those programs or any others as they wished. The grants were still broadly conditional, but much less so than they had been in their original formulation.

As it turned out, however, it was far from clear what the federal government had in mind in 1977. They continued to keep track of established program transfers by major category, even though the grant was lump-sum. As provinces began to reallocate monies among programs, as the terms of the arrangements seemed to allow, they opened themselves up to charges that they were diverting funds to uses for which they were not intended. The extra-billing dispute is another example of this confusion. The Canada Health Act (1984) punished provinces that allowed doctors to bill patients beyond medicare rates by reducing transfers dollar for dollar. Provinces eventually had to comply with the act, given the stakes involved, but not without considerable resentment over what they saw as federal government interference in the operation of the plans.

REGIONAL-DEVELOPMENT POLICY

Regional-development policy received a change of emphasis in the 1970s in much the same direction as did social policy. The centralized system established under the

Department of Regional Economic Expansion (DREE) was discarded in favour of one that placed more emphasis on provincial government participation. Beginning in 1974, each province signed a General Development Agreement (GDA) with the federal government. The agreements established the goals of regional development in that jurisdiction and broad guidelines as to how the programs were to be implemented. Specific projects were then drawn up by a committee of officials from the two governments, and administered by the province. Ottawa contributed 50 percent of the project costs in the wealthier jurisdictions and up to 90 percent in the poorest ones.

409

Predictably, GDAs soon came under fire. Federal officials felt they were losing control over regional-development projects, and politicians saw all the credit going to their provincial counterparts. The GDA was abandoned in 1982. Responsibility for regional development was spread more widely throughout the federal bureaucracy. DREE, and Industry, Trade and Commerce, were combined into one department — Regional and Industrial Expansion. Economic and Regional Development Agreements were signed with each province, and the federal role in planning and administration was made more explicit. The cycle of regional-development policies was complete. In fifteen years, a highly centralized system (DREE) had given way to the highly decentralized one (GDAs), which had, in turn, been abandoned for something in between.

Efficiency and Equity in the Economic Union

A related set of regional issues in this period stemmed from the regional make-up of the economy and the political system. There was a growing perception that the Canadian economy was becoming increasingly fragmented along regional lines and that this development, together with frequent and serious federal–provincial disputes, was reducing the efficiency of the national economy and compromising Canada's ability to manage its economic and social policy effectively. Just as the need to be competitive and to plan effectively was greater than ever, it seemed to many, the domestic market was becoming increasingly fragmented and the institutional ability to carry them out was diminishing.

The debate on regional fragmentation and policy co-ordination came to be expressed in a language developed for the European Economic Community. Canada was viewed as an economic union, with ten (or more, if the North was included) members. Analysts looking at the national economy from this perspective found numerous examples of barriers to the interprovincial flow of goods, services, capital, and labour. Agriculture marketing boards were organized along provincial lines, liquor regulations protected local suppliers, provincial government procurement policies discriminated against non-residents, professional associations restricted out-of-province firms, the trucking industry faced ten sets of regulations, and so forth. Tax harmonization, or rather the lack of it, became an issue, and provinces increasingly used this tool to achieve their own economic and social goals. Further, the fact that the equalization scheme did not fully offset the fiscal disadvantages of the poorer provinces in the federation was held to cause socially inefficient interprovincial migration. Early work on each of these topics seemed to indicate that the efficiency losses were small — about 1 percent of GNP at most — but there was always the nagging doubt that these findings were a product of the methodology used and that the true costs were understated.

The concern with economic management stemmed from the recognition that provinces had considerable economic powers under the Constitution, and that they would be led to use them in ways that were consistent with their own economic objectives, even if these conflicted with central government objectives. Any number of examples were cited. Federal government counter-cyclical stabilization efforts could be thwarted by pro-cyclical provincial ones, especially given the increase in the share of spending and taxation accounted for by the provinces by this date. Federal trade negotiators constantly had to worry whether provinces would implement provisions of international treaties that came under section 92 responsibilities. Environmental regulations often stopped at provincial borders, even if the water or ducks or polluted air did not.

Perhaps the most dramatic issue to arise was that of regional fairness, long a salient factor in Canada. Notions that the federation operated consistently to the advantage of some regions and to the disadvantage of others were rife in the 1970s. Interestingly, all regions felt aggrieved at some time or other and to varying degrees. Atlantic Canadians chafed at the failure of national economic growth and decades of regional-development policy to pull their region out of its long-term relative economic decline. Federal policies on fisheries, energy, tariffs, and transportation were cited as factors contributing to this decline.

The development of an Ontario view on national-policy issues was a relatively new phenomenon. Ontario's interests had always been equated, fairly or not, with those of the national government. Energy issues, in particular, altered this perception somewhat, as the province began to press more openly for policies that reflected its status as the major consuming province. The design of the equalization scheme meant that firms and persons resident in Ontario were carrying the major tax burden for the payments that western resource-revenue windfalls were generating, so there was pressure to alter the scheme.

The most dramatic developments took place in Quebec and the West, though. Quebec nationalists have long argued that the Canadian federation is biased against that province's long-term economic and social development. This debate took on an urgent form after 1976 with the election of the separatist Parti Québécois government and the ensuing debate about its plans for sovereignty-association with Canada. This was the time of the famous "battle of the balance sheets," with the Quebec government publishing one set of accounts showing that Confederation was a net financial drain to Quebec and the federal government publishing figures that showed exactly the opposite. The defeat of the referendum in 1980 somewhat reduced the fervour of this dispute. The promise of a renewed federalism made during the debate set the stage for the patriation of the Constitution and the Canadian Charter of Rights and Freedoms in 1982 and, given Quebec's refusal to sign at that time, ultimately the Meech Lake Accord.

Economic alienation in the West in this era found its most formal expression at the Western Economic Opportunities Conference in 1973. Convened by the federal government, it gave vent to a series of grievances on the alleged adverse effects on the West of federal policies on freight rates and transportation generally, government purchasing practices, banking and monetary policy, and tariffs. It was energy, though, that gave the sentiment its most dramatic expression. The Organization of Petroleum Exporting Countries (OPEC) price increases of 1973–74 and 1979–80 put the federal government in the position of having to reconcile the directly competing interests of the producing and consuming regions. While Ontario, at times, may have thought its interests were being sacrificed, as noted above, western governments had no doubts that theirs certainly were.

The first steps taken by Ottawa, in September 1973, in response to rising world oil prices were to freeze the domestic price and to impose an export tax on shipments to the United States. The producing provinces responded by increasing their royalty charges for the use of crown reserves; Ottawa retaliated by declaring royalty payments not eligible as deductions for purposes of calculating federal corporate income tax. Western premiers expressed a sense of outrage at federal policy, the like of which had not been seen in decades. There followed a long series of federal–provincial negotiations in which tax loads were shifted and oil and gas prices brought more into line with those prevailing internationally.

This relatively harmonious state of affairs was shattered by the doubling of oil prices in 1979–80, following the outbreak of the Iran–Iraq War. The federal government reacted to this development with the National Energy Policy (NEP). Among its various measures were ones to maintain Canadian oil and natural-gas prices well below projected international values, to tax a significant portion of the economic rent through a variety of measures, to redirect exploration and development to the north and east coasts, and to increase the degree of Canadian ownership in the sector. The producing provinces reacted very bitterly to this announcement, resorting in the end to reducing shipments of oil to the East, withholding permission to begin construction of a proposed oil-sands plant, and launching a court challenge to some features of the act.

A truce of sorts was reached in 1981, as the producing provinces agreed to a revised set of pricing and taxation arrangements. Unfortunately for the planners, agreement was reached just as international oil prices began to decline. Now the policy problem was reversed. At issue was how to back out of the taxation imposed on the industry so as to keep it viable. The producing provinces cut back on royalty charges, and the federal government suspended some NEP taxes and reduced the incidence of others. Difficulties remained, however, and demands came from both the industry and the producing provinces that all remaining petroleum taxes and all regulations on pricing and sales be removed.

The equalization scheme came under great pressure after 1973 as a result of these energy developments. The problem lay in the fact that the resource revenues were concentrated in a few small western provinces. The mechanics of the equalization formula meant that Ottawa had to compensate all other provinces, including populous Ontario and Quebec, for their lack of such revenues. To make matters even worse, Ontario eventually became a "have not" province under the formula, entitled to receive equalization payments.

411

René Lévesque, premier-elect of Quebec, speaking to supporters on November 15, 1976. Quebec nationalists have long argued that the Canadian federation is biased against Quebec's long-term economic and social development. This debate grew dramatically in urgency after the 1976 election of the separatist Parti Québécois government.

Bettmann/CORBIS/MAGMA.

The solution was sought, first, in a series of ad hoc adjustments to the existing formula (including a provision that effectively excluded Ontario) and then in a change in the formula itself. Beginning in 1982, the base on which entitlements were calculated was changed from an average of all provinces to an average of five only. Alberta and the four Atlantic provinces were excluded. By omitting Alberta's revenues from the calculation, the problem of equalizing oil and gas revenues was avoided. Leaving the Atlantic provinces out as well, with their lower average tax bases, was a way of reducing the impact of the loss of energy revenues.

Conclusion

Canada faced some considerable challenges in 1982. Inflation had just been brought down from its recent near-record levels, but at a huge cost in terms of unemployment. Federal deficits were large and growing, reducing the government's ability to react to economic challenges, as well as creating problems of its own. The international economic environment appeared to threaten in ways it had not since the Great Depression. Talk of renewed protectionism, especially in the United States, was common. The success of the "new Japans" in capturing market shares for everything from textiles to automobiles was evident. The Canadian economy seemed poorly equipped to deal with these challenges, given the continued poor record in the high-technology areas and renewed fears about the long-run viability of many of its major resource sectors. The impacts that the brand-new Charter of Rights would have on Canada's political and economic life were unknown. The economic union was still fragmented, and memories of separatism and of acrimonious disputes over energy pricing and taxation were still fresh.

As if the number and seriousness of the threats were not enough, there was also a sense that Canadians' ability to deal with them was eroding. At times, the problems seemed to elude conventional understanding and analysis. Stagflation and persistent regional disparities are good examples of these types of problems. In other instances, the solution seemed clear, but Canada's institutions did not seem up to the challenge. Governments, federal and provincial, seemed unable or unwilling to undertake fundamental reform. They appeared at times to be paralyzed by the complexity of the issues: mounting debt, jurisdictional disputes, and regional alienation. Policies had swung from centralizing to decentralizing, and then back to centralizing, in less than a decade. They embraced elements of reliance on the market (multilateral trade liberalization) and elements of interventionism (the NEP). Policies were primarily traditional (tight monetary and fiscal policy) and partly experimental (wage and price controls). This sense of uncertainty and indecision, of being genuinely stumped as to how to proceed, was particularly evident in the early 1980s.

NOTES

1. Ian Keay, "Canadian Manufacturers' Relative Productivity Performance, 1907–1990," *Canadian Journal of Economics* 33(4) (November 2000): 1049–68. Ian Keay, "Scapegoats or Responsive Entrepreneurs: Canadian Manufacturers, 1907–1990," *Explorations in Economic History* 37(3) (July 2000): 217–40.
2. J. Harvey Perry, *A Fiscal History of Canada: The Postwar Years* (Toronto: Canadian Tax Foundation, 1989), 835.

FURTHER READING

Courchene, Thomas J. *Money, Inflation and the Bank of Canada*, 2 vols. Toronto: C.D. Howe Institute, 1981.

Norrie, Kenneth, Richard Simeon, and Mark Krasnick. *Federalism and the Economic Union in Canada*. Royal Commission on the Economic Union and Development Prospects for Canada, Research Study no. 59. Ottawa: Supply and Services, 1985.

Perry, J. Harvey. *A Fiscal History of Canada: The Postwar Years*. Toronto: Canadian Tax Foundation, 1989.

Royal Commission on the Economic Union and Development Prospects for Canada. *Report*, 3 vols. Ottawa: Supply and Services, 1985. See also the 72 research volumes published by the Commission.

Trebilcock, M.J., J.R.S. Prichard, T.J. Courchene, and J. Whalley, eds. *Federalism and the Canadian Economic Union*. Toronto: Ontario Economic Council, 1983.

413

Chapter Twenty-Two

Conclusion: 1982 to the Present

It is now possible to discern another significant shift in the Canadian and, to a lesser extent, world economic history in the late twentieth century. This shift is marked by two distinct occurrences. First, however, it is important to remember that the backdrop for the post-war years had definite patterns. As we have seen, the exceptionally prosperous years from the late forties until the late sixties gave way to slower growth and higher inflation rates through the 1970s. Government policy reflected a certain unity that spanned the entire period from 1945 to the early 1980s. Governments and voters believed that a modern urban-industrial society required a strong social safety net for all and specific efforts to redistribute by income and region. New programs and expanding real expenditures occurred at both provincial and federal levels.

From the early 1980s until the turn of the twenty-first century saw this depression-rooted set of assumptions come under challenge. The "stagflation" of the 1970s raised doubts about the ability of nations to manage their economies. Deficits began to mount in many countries. In the United States and Great Britain the conservative regimes of Ronald Reagan and Margaret Thatcher were elected just as electorates began to doubt the viability or desirability of continuing to expand expenditure. In Canada the turn would be less strident and careful but there was a turn nonetheless.

In the fall of 1982 the Trudeau government recognized similar concerns when it appointed the Macdonald Commission to investigate "the long term economic potential, prospects and challenges facing the Canadian federation, as well as the implications that such prospects and challenges have for Canada's economic and governmental institutions and for the management of Canada's affairs." Further, the commission was to recommend "the appropriate institutional and constitutional arrangements to promote the liberty and well-being of individual Canadians and the maintenance of a strong competitive economy."

In 1984, the federal government changed from Liberal to Progressive Conservative and with the change came an apparent new logic or underlying unity to their agenda. The key features of this new government's agenda were a hesitant and partial, but nonetheless clear, tendency to reject economic planning in favour of market solutions, and an effort to take the regional character of the country more into account when formulating economic and social strategies. This orientation reflected, in about equal measure, the legacies of the sequence of economic and social policies followed before 1984, and the underlying global challenges of the 1980s.

The Progressive Conservative government of Brian Mulroney served two terms, 1984–88 and 1988–93. Over this period, it did manage to bring about a number of signif-

icant reforms to the Canadian economy, from free trade through tax reform to deregulation. Mulroney's Conservatives left office, however, more remembered for its failure on
two major policy fronts: bringing the fiscal situation under control and establishing har-
mony in the Canadian federation.

Yet the tide had shifted both under the later years of Trudeau and under the
Conservatives. Concerns about deficits had grown. This prompted the new Liberal government to take a bold step in the 1995 budget. That budget set out a plan which allowed
for a transition from two decades of mounting deficits to small but mounting surpluses. At
the provincial level, deficits forced most provinces to turn their attention to the balance
sheet. In Alberta and Ontario aggressive budget cutting with an ideological underpinning
won voter support. Most provinces, however, spent the 1990s moving to reduce or eliminate deficits. Throughout Canada the emphasis on the "market" and the "entrepreneur"
gained ground. Critics condemned this "turn to the right" and voters still insisted that
health care be preserved untouched. Much of the language and outlook of the post-war
years, however, seemed to have come undone.

The language of markets and entrepreneurship solidified government commitment to
the North American Free Trade Agreement. The Liberal Party under Jean Chrétien had
criticized NAFTA while it sat as the Official Opposition Party but altered its position once
it came to power. Canada's economic future now seemed fully linked with the policies of
a North American market. There are questions, however, that still must be resolved. Free
trade was designed in part to force economic competitiveness upon participants. Yet, for
reasons that are still unclear, aggregate productivity growth in Canada has fallen behind
that of the United States, meaning that Canadian living standards have not kept pace with
those south of the border. The other question involves the future of Canada's social programs, health care in particular. The tension between a cautious attitude toward deficits
and a market driven tax regime on the one side and the demand for programs on the
other, especially health care, remains present and may well grow as the population ages.

Economic Performance

After the economic disaster of 1981, real GDP grew at quite respectable rates for the next
six years. The unemployment rate rose to 11.8 percent in 1983, before beginning to
decline. It stood at 7.5 percent by 1989, a marked improvement over the 1983 figure but
still well above its long-term average. The inflation rate fell to 5.7 percent in 1983, from
10.9 percent the year before. It then remained fairly constant for three years before beginning to turn up again in 1987.

This resurgence of inflation led to one of the most interesting and controversial episodes
in Canada's monetary-policy history. In January 1988, Bank of Canada Governor John
Crow delivered the Eric J. Hanson Memorial Lecture at the University of Alberta.[1] In it, he
argued that the proper goal of monetary policy must be price stability, by which he meant
a zero rate of inflation. This objective, which Crow restated on other public occasions in
the following months, came to be dubbed ZIT — zero inflation target.

By mid-1989, if not earlier, it was clear that the Bank meant business. Monetary policy
was tightened, interest rates shot up, and the Canadian dollar appreciated relative to the
American one. As a result, real GDP rose by only 2.4 percent in 1989 compared with 5 percent in 1988, declined in both 1990 and 1991 for only the third and fourth time in the
postwar period, and rose by less than 1 percent in 1992. Unemployment increased

significantly, from 7.5 percent of the work force in 1989 to 8.1 percent in 1990, to 10.3 percent in 1991, and to 11.3 percent in 1992. The Canadian economy entered into its second recession in a decade, this one the worst since the Great Depression.

The bank's policies and the recession did wring inflation out of the economy. The consumer price index rose by 5.6 percent in 1991, but by only 1.5 percent in 1992. Allowing for the various biases in the consumer price index, the Canadian inflation rate had effectively dropped to zero. Governor Crow made good on his promise, but at the cost of a serious recession. To this day, analysts remain divided on the merits of this policy.[2]

Economic growth strengthened after 1993. Real GDP grew at an annual average rate of 3.7 percent between 1994 and 2000, compared to 2.7 percent between 1983 and 1993. Unemployment rates fell in response to below 7 percent for the first time in a long while. Inflation has remained within the 1 to 3 percent target set jointly by the government and the Bank of Canada. Much of this growth was the result of an extraordinary economic expansion in the United States after 1995, dubbed the economic miracle because of the combination of unexpectedly low unemployment and inflation rates. The U.S. economy slowed appreciably in the winter of 2001 and, predictably, the Canadian economy is following suit.

Framework Policies

The framework policies undertaken by the Mulroney government after its election in September 1984 fit a general pattern. Similar to initiatives elsewhere in the industrial world, Reagan's United States and Margaret Thatcher's United Kingdom in particular, there was renewed emphasis on resource allocation through markets rather than government directive, which, in practical terms, meant trade liberalization and deregulation.

The energy sector received almost immediate attention from the new government. Accords were signed with the western and Atlantic provinces after extensive negotiations. The main objectives were to deregulate the petroleum sector and to remove the special taxes that had been imposed on the industry in the previous decade. Henceforth, oil prices were to be established in the international marketplace. Natural-gas prices were to follow, but more slowly, since deregulating this product was more difficult. Most of the taxes were removed at this time, as well. The Petroleum and Gas Revenue Tax (PGRT) was to be phased out gradually, but was ended prematurely in October 1986, in response to worsening economic conditions in the industry.

Deregulation was not limited to the energy industry, however. Beginning in 1979 and extending through to the present, the nation's major telephone companies faced increasing competition in the provision, first of data communication services, and then of long-distance telephone services. Railway companies were given increased flexibility to allow them to compete more effectively with trucking services. Even the venerable statutory grain rates were affected, as railways in 1983 were allowed to raise their rates on export grain for the first time since 1926 (they were still at 1897 levels in 1983). Airline deregulation in the United States forced the Canadian government to respond by increasing competition in this country. Banking and financial industries underwent significant deregulation as the federal and provincial governments alike responded to the challenges posed by new technologies and emerging global financial markets.

One of the most dramatic developments came on the international trade front. For the first time in more than 130 years, Canada and the United States entered into a bilateral free-trade arrangement. As we have seen throughout this text, few other policy issues have as long a pedigree. We noted how Canadian politicians and business leaders clung to the idea of a reciprocal trading arrangement in natural resource products with the United States for several decades after the cancellation of reciprocity in 1866. We saw the fate of the Laurier government in 1911 when just such an agreement was put to an electoral test. We saw Prime Minister Mackenzie King's last-minute change of heart immediately after World War II.

The genesis of this effort lies in the so-called Shamrock Summit, held in Quebec City on March 17–18, 1985. Prime Minister Mulroney and President Reagan agreed on that occasion to give the highest priority to finding ways to reduce trade barriers between the two countries. Six months later, letters were exchanged between the two leaders, pledging to negotiate a bilateral trade agreement. Negotiating teams were established and immediately began a long and intensive series of negotiations. Talks threatened to collapse on several occasions, including literally in the very last hour. An accord was signed on October 4, 1987, containing the elements of a comprehensive bilateral free-trade arrangement. After some legal drafting, it was tabled in the House of Commons in December and signed by the two leaders in January 1988.

The agreement still needed formal approval by both parties. The Americans ratified the agreement after only perfunctory debate. The Canadians, however, did so only after an election that concentrated almost entirely on the free-trade issue and reached levels of passion and emotion that had rarely been seen. In a delicious historical reversal of the situation in 1911, the Conservatives were the party of free trade, and the Liberals the guardians of Canadian identity and independence. The free-traders won: the agreement was passed by the House of Commons, and Canada–United States free trade came into effect January 1, 1989.

The agreement committed the two countries to remove nearly all existing barriers to the free exchange of goods and services over a ten-year period. There were exceptions to this provision, notably in agriculture and in cultural industries. True to the definition of a free-trade area, each country was free to impose whatever barriers it wished on trade with non-members. The agreement went beyond trade in goods to include provisions for liberalizing trade in services. Again, there were exceptions: transportation, basic telecommunications, medical, legal, child care, and government-provided social services. The agreement also featured special provisions relating to energy products, automotive products, agricultural products, and capital flows. Finally, a resolution mechanism was established to cover disputes emanating from the treaty or from future countervailing decisions of either country.

This pact was barely in place when the Mexican government requested free-trade negotiations with the United States. In early 1991, Canada asked to join these talks. The idea of a hemispheric free-trade area evoked considerable debate and discussion in the United States and Mexico, but surprisingly little in Canada. The three nations reached agreement in principle in August 1992 and signed a treaty in December of that year. On January 1, 1994, the North American Free Trade Agreement (NAFTA) came into effect.

The main provisions of NAFTA can be summarized briefly.[3] Like the Canada–U.S. pact that preceded it, NAFTA creates a free-trade area; economic exchange among the partners is to be liberalized, but each nation is free to establish its own trade policies with respect to non-member countries. All tariffs on trade in goods among the three countries are to be removed within ten years. Trade in services is to be greatly liberalized, as is access to government-procurement contracts. The agreement also provides protection for investors against discriminatory practices, and for intellectual property. It establishes a set of

Les Grands Ballets Canadiens performs Carl Orff's *Carmina Burana*, choreographed by Fernand Nault. Such "cultural industries" as the ballet are notable and controversial exceptions to the North American Free Trade Agreement (NAFTA), which has removed nearly all barriers to the free exchange of goods and services among Canada, the United States, and Mexico.

Andrew Oxenham/Les Grand Ballets Canadiens de Montreal.

institutions to resolve disputes arising from trade and investment activities. There are also a great number of specific provisions dealing with the environment, energy, agriculture, telecommunications, financial services, and health and safety standards.

The Canada–U.S. Free Trade Agreement and NAFTA appear to have had the predicted economic effects. International trade has grown significantly relative to interprovincial trade, making Canada even more integrated with the U.S. Economic ties with Mexico are more limited yet are still growing. As expected, Canadian manufacturing went through a stressful adjustment period with large reductions in output and employment. The situation turned around after 1993, as manufacturing industries experienced substantial growth in both output and employment. The evidence now seems clear that the FTA in particular brought about significant productivity gains for Canadian manufacturing.[4]

NAFTA continues to enjoy broad acceptance among Canadians, despite disputes with the U.S. over specific products, in particular, softwood lumber exports. Indeed, the sentiment in the Liberal government is for expanded trade and economic liberalization. Canada has since signed free trade arrangements with Chile (1997) and Costa Rica (2001). Prime Minister Chrétien is among the most active and vocal leaders supporting a Free Trade Association of the Americas. Most recently, however, growing numbers of Canadian activists have joined their counterparts from around the world in increasingly violent protests against economic liberalization, the "battle of Seattle" and the Quebec City

Summit being the most notable examples. One thing is certain: international trade issues will continue to dominate the Canadian policy agenda as they have throughout history.

Tax reform was another fact of the Progressive Conservative economic program. Specific plans were announced after much study and consultation. Reform was to proceed in two distinct steps. The first dealt with personal and corporate income taxes. The objects were to enhance horizontal equity (treatment across equals); modify vertical equity by increasing the degree of progressivity, particularly toward low-income groups; and enhance neutrality vis-à-vis the tax systems of other countries, particularly the United States.[5]

The second step was to replace the Federal Sales Tax (FST), which dated back to 1924. The FST was widely condemned for damaging Canadian competitiveness, favouring imports over domestic production, distorting production decisions, and being narrow and exceedingly complex.[6] In its place, the government introduced a new federal sales tax, the goods and services tax, or GST, which came into effect on January 1, 1991. The GST imposes a single rate (7 percent, rather than the 9 percent originally proposed) on the vast majority of goods and services sold in Canada. The main tax-free items are basic groceries, prescription drugs, medical devices, health and dental care, educational services, residential rents, and financial services. The tax is collected at the retail level, and merchants remit the sales tax they collect less the tax paid on purchases. Low-income individuals and families are eligible to receive a GST rebate, administered through the personal income tax system. There have been no significant tax reforms under the current government.

Aggregate productivity growth is the new concern of policy analysts. The purchasing power of total real national income per adult (the best measure of the standard of living) rose in Canada relative to the U.S. throughout the 1970s, from about 72 percent at the beginning of the decade to nearly 84 percent by the end. This trend flattened in the 1980s, however, and then declined precipitously in the 1990s. By 1998, the Canadian figure had fallen below 74 percent of the U.S. figure, putting Canadians back where they were in a relative sense three decades earlier.[7] Since Canadians have always judged their economic progress against that of their powerful neighbour to the south, this trend has caught the attention of policy analysts.

The explanations for the relative real income decline are many, but productivity growth appears to be a significant factor. It now seems clear that aggregate productivity grew significantly faster in the U.S. than it did in Canada in the last three decades.[8] The reasons for the differences are less clear, however. One intriguing possibility of particular interest to economic history students is that we are experiencing the very early stages of a third industrial revolution, this one based on information/communications technology and biotechnology. The U.S., as the world's undisputed leader in research and development in these areas, will naturally experience the first surge in productivity growth as the discoveries become part of the economy. The Canadian government appears to accept this view as, at the time of writing it is making significant investments in Canada's research and development capacity.

Debts and Deficits

An early priority of the Conservative government was to reduce the size of the federal deficit. Finance minister Michael Wilson released an economic and financial statement in November 1984, just two months after assuming office. That document outlined the

419

government's concern about the size of the deficit and the mounting debt, and outlined plans for bringing it down to a more appropriate level. The stance was supply-side oriented and geared to restoring confidence in the economy. There was no talk of using taxes and expenditures to stimulate demand in the traditional Keynesian sense, even though the economy was obviously seriously underemployed.

Deficit reduction remained a major concern of the Mulroney government throughout its tenure, although success proved elusive. On a national accounts basis, the federal government deficit stood at over $31 billion in 1985, fell to just over $19 billion in 1988, but climbed back to more than $30 billion in 1991 and over $26 billion in 1992 (Figure 21.2). Figure 22.1 shows net federal government debt as a percentage of GDP for the postwar period. From a high of over 100 percent in 1946, net debt fell more or less continuously to reach a low of less than 20 percent of GDP in 1974. Thereafter, as a result of the continuous string of deficits, this ratio climbed continuously to reach just under 80 percent in the early 1990s.

The long string of large deficits after 1974 put the federal government in a difficult fiscal situation. To understand this challenge, it is useful to distinguish between the overall budget balance and the operating balance. The latter is the difference between total revenues and total expenditures on all items other than interest on the debt (pensions, unemployment insurance payments, transfers to provinces and municipalities, the cost of the civil service, capital expenditures, and the like). If the operating balance is negative in any given period, as it was throughout most of the 1970s and 1980s, and there are interest payments owing on the public debt, as there have been throughout the postwar period, net federal debt will clearly rise. But the net debt will also rise even if the operating balance is positive, whenever this balance is smaller than the interest owing on the accumulated debt. This was the case in the late 1980s and explains why deficit reduction became such a salient policy issue. The government was having to borrow money to pay the interest on the accumulated debt, thereby pushing the debt up further, thereby increasing the interest obligations, and thereby making next year's budget challenge even greater.

Debts and deficits dominated the early agenda of the new Chrétien government. The 1994 budget disappointed those hoping for fiscal reform, but the 1995 budget was a bold

Figure 22.1 Net Federal Debt as a Percentage of GDP, Canada, 1946–1993

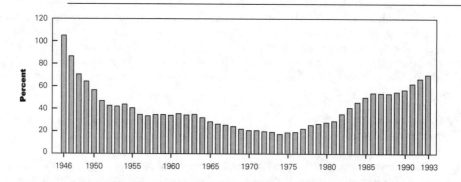

Source: Statistics Canada, *Agenda: Jobs and Growth, Canada Year Book* and Department of Finance, cat. no. 11-402E (Ottawa, 1994), chart 35, p. 80. Reproduced by authority of the Minister of Industry, 1995.

420

step towards correcting two decades of deficits and mounting government debt. A combination of spending cuts, lower carrying charges on the public debt due to lower interest rates, and increased tax revenues from a growing economy turned a $42 billion deficit into a $3.5 billion surplus in fiscal year 1997–98 and into surpluses ever since. The government has split the surplus between debt reduction and increased spending. The debt to GDP ration has declined every year since 1995–96, from a high of nearly 72 percent to a current level of about 53 percent.

Equity

Federal government social policies were an inevitable target for deficit-reduction measures.[9] Throughout the 1980s, the government took a series of ad hoc steps to limit fiscal transfers to the provinces for health care and postsecondary education under the 1977 Established Programs Financing (EPF) arrangements. Finally, in the 1990 budget, the per capita entitlements were frozen for two years, and in the 1991 budget the freeze was extended to 1994–95. The effect of this move was to reduce the amount of cash transferred to the provinces each year. The implication was that federal contributions to health care and postsecondary education would eventually (sometime after the year 2000, earlier for Quebec) be funded entirely out of tax points transferred to the provinces in 1977. Some observers welcomed this prospect, feeling that it would finally remove the federal government from what were purely provincial concerns. Others, however, were worried that the end of federal cash transfers meant the end of any kind of national standards.

The Canada Assistance Plan (CAP) came in for special consideration as well. In its 1990 budget, Ottawa announced a ceiling of 5 percent growth on the total amount it would transfer under the CAP in the next two fiscal years to those provinces not receiving equalization payments — British Columbia, Alberta, and Ontario. In the 1991 budget, this provision was extended to 1994–95. British Columbia challenged the action in the courts, but in August 1991 the Supreme Court of Canada ruled in favour of the federal government. This "cap on CAP," as it has been dubbed, hit Ontario especially hard, given that province's welfare case load and relatively generous benefit schedule.

The 1995 federal budget altered the social policy framework significantly. The federal government replaced EPF and CAP programs with the Canada Health and Social Transfer (CHST). The CHST is a block fund arrangement whereby the federal government makes specified payments to provinces for purposes of health, post-secondary education, and social assistance. The original 1995 version has been altered several times to increase total payments and to move the scheme to equal per capita payments among provinces. The CHST continues to be a controversial issue in Canadian fiscal federalism. The provinces view the federal government transfers as too little and too constraining. The federal government in turn argues that it does not get sufficient credit for major contributions to Canadian social programs.

Federalism and the Economic Union

The federation and the economic union were major preoccupations of the Mulroney government in both terms. The Constitution Act, 1982, had been signed over the bitter objections of Quebec. The Progressive Conservatives came to power in 1982 promising to find a way to bring that province into the fold. In May 1986, the Quebec government released the five conditions that had to be met to secure its signature on the 1982 act: constitutional recognition of Quebec as a distinct society, a guaranteed role in immigration, a guaranteed role in Supreme Court of Canada appointments, limitations on the federal government's spending power, and a veto over future constitutional amendments.

A series of dramatic federal–provincial meetings followed and produced the terms of a proposed constitutional amendment, dubbed the Meech Lake Accord. The accord met Quebec's conditions, and that province quickly ratified it. The federal government and seven other provinces ratified it as well, but in the end Manitoba and Newfoundland did not, and in June 1989 the Meech Lake Accord died. There followed another complex round of constitutional debate, featuring much public discussion and debate along with the usual set of federal–provincial negotiations. The result was yet another agreement reached late in the summer of 1991, this one dubbed the Charlottetown Accord. The terms of this accord were put to a national referendum in the fall of 1991 and were soundly defeated. The Mulroney government left office in 1993 having failed to achieve one of its principal goals.

Things were to get much more dramatic very quickly. The Quebec government held a referendum on sovereignty in 1995. The "Yes" vote failed by the narrowest of margins, prompting a visibly shaken Prime Minister Chrétien to promise reforms to the federal system. Whether because of these efforts or other factors, the national unity question is on the backburner at the time of writing, although it would be foolhardy to expect it to remain there.

Conclusion

If the 1980s brought significant changes in policy directions, they also brought failures and retreats. As mentioned above, the government's efforts at deficit reduction were halting and ineffective. By 1994, when the Liberals replaced the Progressive Conservatives in Ottawa, the federal debt had surpassed 60 percent of GDP and the demand to cut government costs had become a major political issue. The Reform Party gained more than 50 seats — the largest number of any third party since the Progressives in the 1920s — based to a large degree on concern about government spending. The 1995 federal budget indicated that government itself had moved deficit cutting to the top of its agenda. Deficits have turned to surpluses, and the debate has turned to how to spend the new revenue. Government debt remains high, however, so it would be naïve to suggest that this issue is gone from the policy agenda.

The other major failure of the 1980s was constitutional reform. The impetus to the Meech Lake and Charlottetown initiatives lay in the arena of federal–provincial relations, especially those involving Quebec. A part of each package, though, had involved significant change in the social and economic arenas. Provinces would have been able to opt out of federal social programs, and the federal government's ability to shape the economic climate would have been weakened. In this sense, the constitutional proposals were consistent with the market-oriented tendencies of recent years in other areas. After a near major disruption in 1995, national unity is on the backburner at the time of writing, but it would be foolish to suggest this situation will last for long.

The policy changes and policy failures of the last decade or so can, in retrospect, be seen as part of a larger pattern. The mixed directions through the 1980s were not merely the result of government vacillation or ineptness. Like the 1970s, many of the problems of the decade reflect frustration and uncertainty about the changes taking place in the economy. Basic structural changes were transforming Canada and, as with other eras, policy often lagged behind. So too did public perception, which often looked to old panaceas for new and different problems.

Now it seems fairly clear that the 1970s mark the beginning of a new era in Canadian economic history. The postwar years, 1945 to 1973, were characterized by certain key tendencies. Prosperity in the industrial heartland and in most resource sectors, albeit with considerably more volatility, was one feature. A second feature was the expansion of the welfare state, based on prosperity and a popular definition of Keynesian economics that emphasized macroeconomic policy. If one were looking for symbols of the economy in these years it would probably be the Auto Pact and medicare, for between them they represent the twin pillars of growth and expansion in the postwar years.

The symbols for the 1970s through to the present would be different. Basic structural changes have occurred. The manufacturing sector has become much more volatile. Old smokestack industries have stagnated or died, while new "high-tech" firms have appeared. Faith in government has faded, often within government itself. Interventionist policy no longer seems to bring the desired results. Deficits made it next to impossible to expand social programs and budgets continued to constrain actions. Thus the period since the 1970s must be seen as one of transition. Old policies were no longer appropriate, but new approaches were neither fully accepted nor fully understood.

At the end of nearly five centuries of Canadian economic history, however, one thing should be obvious. Talk of volatility, government debt, policy failure, global markets, and rapid technical change should be viewed in context. All of these issues have a long and persistent history. It is the nature of a small, open economy.

NOTES

1. John W. Crow, "The Work of Canadian Monetary Policy," Eric J. Hanson Memorial Lecture, University of Alberta, January 1988.
2. David Laidler and William Robson outline the pros and cons of price stability in chapter 2 of their monograph, *The Great Canadian Disinflation: The Economics and Politics of Monetary Policy in Canada, 1988–93*, Policy Study 19 (Toronto: C.D. Howe Institute, 1993). For a more sceptical view see Pierre Fortin, "The Unbearable Lightness of Zero-Inflation Optimism," *Canadian Business Economics* 1(3) (Spring 1993): 3–18.
3. See Richard G. Lipsey, Daniel Schwanen, and Ronald J. Wonnacott, *The NAFTA: What's In, What's Out, What's Next*, Policy Study 21 (Toronto: C.D. Howe Institute, 1994).
4. See Daniel Trefler, *The Long and Short of the Canada–US Free Trade Agreement* (Paper Number 6 in the Industry Canada Research Publications Program "Perspectives on North American Free Trade," Ottawa, September, 1999).
5. Thomas J. Courchene, "Tax Reform: The Impact on Individuals," in Edward A. Carmichael, ed., *Tax Reform: Perspectives on the White Paper* (Toronto: C.D. Howe Institute, 1988).
6. The Honourable Michael H. Wilson, *Goods and Service Tax: An Overview* (Ottawa: Government of Canada, Department of Finance, 1988).
7. See Pierre Fortin, *The Canadian Standard of Living: Is There a Way Up?* (C.D. Howe Benefactors Lecture, 1999).
8. Industry Canada's website contains a useful bibliograpghy of work on the productivity issue.
9. See Kenneth Norrie, "Intergovernmental Transfers in Canada: An Historical Perspective on Some Current Policy Choices," in Peter M. Leslie, Kenneth Norrie, and Irene K. Ip, *A Partnership in Trouble: Renegotiating Fiscal Federalism*, Policy Study 18 (Toronto: C.D. Howe Institute, 1993), 87–129.

FURTHER READINGS

Banting, Keith G., Douglas M. Brown, and Thomas J. Courchene, eds. *The Future of Fiscal Federalism.* Kingston: School of Policy Studies, Queen's University, 1994.

Courchene, Thomas J. *Social Canada in the Millennium: Reform Imperatives and Restructuring Principles.* Toronto: C.D. Howe Institute, 1994.

Government of Canada. *Agenda: Jobs and Growth*: "Creating a Healthy Fiscal Climate." Ottawa, 1994.

Government of Canada. *Agenda: Jobs and Growth*: "A New Framework for Economic Policy." Ottawa, 1994.

Laidler, David E.W., and William B.P. Robson. *The Great Canadian Disinflation: The Economics and Politics of Monetary Policy in Canada, 1988–93.* Policy Study 19. Toronto: C.D. Howe Institute, 1993.

Leslie, Peter M., Kenneth Norrie, and Irene K. Ip. *A Partnership in Trouble: Renegotiating Fiscal Federalism.* Policy Study 18. Toronto: C.D. Howe Institute, 1993.

Lipsey, Richard G. "Globalization, Technological Change and Economic Growth." *Canadian Business Economics* (Fall 1993): 3–17.

Lipsey, Richard G., Daniel Schwanen, and Ronald J. Wonnacott. *The NAFTA: What's In, What's Out, What's Next.* Policy Study 21. Toronto: C.D. Howe Institute, 1994.

Young, Robert A. *The Secession of Quebec and the Future of Canada.* Montreal and Kingston: McGill-Queen's University Press, 1995.

424

Index

428